NOTED GUERRILLAS,

OR THE

WARFARE OF THE BORDER.

BEING A HISTORY OF THE LIVES AND ADVENTURES OF

QUANTRELL, BILL ANDERSON, GEORGE TODD, DAVE POOLE,
FLETCHER TAYLOR, PEYTON LONG, OLL SHEPHERD,
ARCH CLEMENTS, JOHN MAUPIN, TUCK AND
WOOT HILL, WM. GREGG, THOMAS MAU-
PIN, THE JAMES BROTHERS, THE
YOUNGER BROTHERS,
ARTHUR McCOY,

AND NUMEROUS OTHER WELL KNOWN

GUERRILLAS OF THE WEST.

BY

JOHN N. EDWARDS,

Author of "Shelby and His Men," "Shelby's Expedition to Mexico," Etc.

ILLUSTRATED.

Press of

Morningside Bookshop

1976

FACSIMILE
34

ISBN - O-89029-034-X

Original Printing by
Bryan, Brand & Company
St. Louis, Mo. 1877

CHARLES WILLIAM QUANTRELL.

FOREWORD TO THE MORNINGSIDE EDITION

To appreciate this book we must know something about its author. John Newman Edwards was born January 4, 1839 at Front Royal in the Shenandoah Valley of Virginia. As a boy he fell in love with words — and perhaps they remained his greatest love. Although he had little formal education, he read omnivorously. Sir Walter Scott, Victor Hugo, and Alexander Dumas were his favorite writers, the life and times of Napoleon his favorite subject. At fourteen he wrote a story which gained him "wide celebrity" — presumably around Front Royal.

He also learned the printer's trade, and in 1854 or 1855 moved to Missouri where he worked for the **Lexington Expositor,** eventually becoming its editor. A fervent secessionist, he joined, after the Civil War came to Missouri, the Confederate cavalry of his friend Colonel, later Brigadier General, Jo Shelby. By 1863 he had risen to major and was Shelby's adjutant and de facto chief of staff. In that capacity he wrote Shelby's reports for him. Undoubtedly they are the most remarkable documents of their kind ever produced. Purple prose interspersed with quotations from English ballads describes deeds of derring do. Shelby's commanding general, on reading one of these reports, exclaimed, "Why, Shelby is a poet as well as a fighter!"

"No," replied the courier who had delivered the report, "but his adjutant is a born poet."

Edwards, however, was more than just a desk soldier. "It was a grand sight," a comrade recalled, "to see him in battle. He was always where the fight was the thickest. He was absolutely devoid of fear." The only thing that exceeded his bravery was his modesty. Not once in the reports or in his lengthy history of Shelby's operations did he mention himself.

When the Confederacy collapsed Shelby — probably at Edwards' urging — led 500 of his troops into Mexico and offered their services to Maximilian. The doomed emperor declined the offer but did give Shelby and a number of other high ranking Confederates land on which they founded a colony named Carlota in honor of Maximilian's beautiful consort. Edwards, however, remained in Mexico City where he and ex-Governor Henry W. Allen of Louisiana published **The Mexican Times,** an English language paper subsidized by Maximilian. He also wrote **Shelby and His Men: or, The War in the West.** Despite much exaggeration and even fabrication, this book is an invaluable record of the Civil War in the Trans-Mississippi. Someday, hopefully, it too will be reprinted, for extant copies are as rare as they are expensive.

In 1867 Maximilian's empire toppled and Edwards, along with most of the other Southern exiles, fled Mexico, refugees from another lost cause. Returning to Missouri, he published **Shelby and His Men,** wrote a sequel entitled **Shelby's Expedition to Mexico: An Unwritten Leaf of the War** which appeared in 1872, and embarked on a stormy career as editor of various newspapers in Kansas City, St. Louis, Sedalia, and St. Joseph. In the words of a fellow editor, "life for him was indeed a warfare," as he lived "over and over again in journalism and politics the days of wild dash when he rode by the side of General J. O. Shelby. . . ." Once he fought a duel (bloodless) with a rival editor, and more than once he issued challenges to others who aroused his ire.

He also publicly championed Frank and Jesse James, whom he had known during the war and whom he believed had been driven into outlawry by Unionist persecution. His 1881 editorial denouncing "The Killing of Jesse James" by "highwaymen and prostitutes" was reprinted nationally and remains a classic of vituperative journalism. That same year he escorted Frank James to the Missouri governor's office, where the famous bandit surrendered.

Professionally successful ("He was the best known newspaperman west of the Mississippi"), personally popular despite his outspokeness ("Every time he met a man he made a friend"), and a happily married father of three children, Edwards nevertheless sought in the bottle something which eluded him in life, with the tragic consequence that he sank into the "living hell" of alcoholism. "Why do I drink?" he asked a friend. "Omniscience knows." He struggled desperately to "break with the monster of drink, famishing days and horrible midnights." In 1887 and again the following year he went to sanitariums. Each time he pronounced himself cured, each time he relapsed. On May 4, 1889 he died in a Jefferson City hotel room of what a doctor officially diagnosed as "inanition of the cardiac nerves." But perhaps in a deeper sense an obituary in a St. Louis paper came closer to the truth when it stated that "his high spirit simply fretted itself out against the bars of a utilitarian civilization."

Edwards wrote **Noted Guerrillas, or The Warfare of the Border** in 1875 while "between jobs" and living with his wife's family in Dover, Missouri. Like **Shelby and His Men** and **Shelby's Expedition** it is done in the style of Hugo and in the spirit of Dumas. Like them too it is a mixture of fact and fancy. The fact he obtained mainly from the surviving guerrillas, most of whom were natives of West Missouri who had served occasionally with Shelby. The fancy he supplied himself. For his object in this book, as in the earlier ones, was less to produce a history than it was to create a legend.

In this he succeeded. To this day for many Missourians Quantrill and his men are heroes (see Merle Miller, **Plain Speaking: An Oral Biography of Harry S. Truman,** pp. 73-7), and **Noted Guerrillas** is in large part responsible for their attitude. Furthermore, it probably did more than any other book to establish and perpetuate the fame of the James Boys. Shortly before it was published they had made the sensational Northfield, Minnesota Raid in which the Younger Brothers had been captured. Edwards, who was leading a campaign to have Frank and Jesse pardoned, depicted them in the book in a highly sympathetic and romantic fashion, all the while magnifying or falsifying their Civil War exploits (e. g., Jesse James, far from playing a conspicuous role in the Lawrence Raid, had not even joined the guerrillas at that time!).

Therefore, given its origin and purpose, it is not surprising that **Noted Guerrillas** is filled with errors of both commission and omission: The real name of its hero was William Clarke Quantrill, not Charles William Quantrell. He was born July 31, 1837 in Canal Dover, Ohio, not July 20, 1836 in Hagerstown, Maryland. He and his older brother were not attacked by Jayhawkers in 1855 while crossing Kansas en route to California; he had no such brother and he came to Kansas in 1857 with a group of settlers from Ohio. Needless to say, he did not proceed to slay over one hundred Jayhawkers; instead he tried farming, accompanied an army expedition to Utah as a teamster, prospected for gold in Colorado, and taught school in Kansas before turning bandit. Not only did he commit a number of crimes in Kansas, he stole livestock and kidnapped Negroes from Missouri. When the Kansas law authorities made it too hot for him there, he decided to switch to the Missouri side. In order to gain the confidence of the Missourians he led three (not seven) Jayhawkers into the trap at the Morgan Walker farm and also concocted the story about his Maryland birth, the murder of his brother, and his subsequent campaign of vengeance.

Edwards may have been honestly ignorant of the facts of Quantrill's pre-war career, but he had ample opportunity to learn about such things as Quantrill's arrest by a Confederate general in Texas, the gun fight between Todd's and Anderson's guerrillas, and Quantrill's overthrow as leader by Todd in the spring of 1864 — happenings at which he just vaguely hints. Nor does he mention the sordid aspects of the guerrillas' existence — the quarrels over plunder, the drunken sprees, the robberies of Southern as well as Northern civilians, the torture of prisoners and the obscene mutilation of Union dead, the brothels, and Quantrill's thirteen year old mistress. And although the guerrillas were brave men and good shots, they did not constantly slaughter huge hordes of Federals at little or no loss to themselves. With regard to Edwards' battle accounts, a good rule of thumb to follow is to reduce the size of Union forces by one half. For example, General Blunt's escort at Baxter Springs consisted of less than 100, not the 210 soldiers reported by Edwards. Similarly, instead of 300 troops, Major Johnston (not Johnson) had at Centralia only 147.

Yet, in spite of the exaggeration, fiction, and rampant bias, **Noted Guerrillas** is a valuable historical work. After all Edwards did ride, live, and talk with the men about whom he writes. The story he tells is in broad outline accurate enough — other and reliable sources confirm it. Moreover, he does not deny that the guerrillas committed terrible deeds. He merely insists that they did so in response to equally heinous acts performed by their enemies — and here he is not without justification. Above all, he presents information — information which has an inherent ring of authenticity — that is available nowhere else. Any modern day historian dealing with the guerrilla war in the West will go to Edwards often — although with caution.

Last, but far from least, the book is great reading. Edwards may have borrowed his literary style from Hugo but he borrowed it well. So, Reader, if you like the past served up highly seasoned with blood and thunder, turn a few pages and enjoy a feast.

Albert Castel
Kalamazoo, Michigan

Bibliographical Notes: Although the author is as biased on the Northern side as Edwards is on the Southern, the best source of data on the Missouri guerrillas is William E. Connelley, **Quantrill and the Border Wars** (Cedar Rapids, Iowa, 1910). Modern scholarly accounts of the guerrilla war in the West are offered by Richard S. Brownlee, **Gray Ghosts of the Confederacy** (Baton Rouge: Louisiana State University Press, 1958) and Albert Castel, **William Clarke Quantrill: His Life and Times** (New York: Frederick Fell, Inc., 1962). The best study of the James Boys is William A. Settle, Jr., **Jesse James Was His Name** (Columbia: University of Missouri Press, 1966). For Edwards himself, the best and practically only source is **John N. Edwards: Life, Writings, and Tributes,** compiled by his wife, Jennie Edwards, and published by her in Kansas City, Missouri in 1889. This work, which is quite rare and difficult to obtain, contains Edwards' **Shelby's Expedition to Mexico.**

ILLUSTRATIONS.

Copyright, 1877, by
N. M. Bryan.

Becktold & Co., Binders,
St. Louis, Mo.

"The standing side by side till death,
  The dying for some wounded friend,
  The faith that failed not to the end,
  The strong endurance till the breath
  And body took their ways apart,
  I only know. I keep my trust,
  Their vices! earth has them by heart.
  Their virtues! they are with their dust."

CONTENTS.

CHAPTER I.

INTRODUCTION.

CHAPTER II.

THE CAUSES THAT PRODUCED THE GUERRILLA.

CHAPTER III.

AMERICAN GUERRILLAS COMPARED WITH THOSE OF OTHER COUNTRIES.

CHAPTER IV.

QUANTRELL.

CHAPTER V.

QUANTRELL AND THE KANSAS JAYHAWKERS.

CHAPTER VI.

QUANTRELL'S FIRST BATTLES OF THE CIVIL WAR.

CHAPTER VII.

BATTLES AND SURPRISES.

CHAPTER VIII.

INDEPENDENCE.

CHAPTER IX.
LONE JACK.

CHAPTER X.
THE MARCH SOUTH.

CHAPTER XI.
QUANTRELL VISITS RICHMOND.

CHAPTER XII.
LAWRENCE.

CHAPTER XIII.
A COUNTER-BLOW.

CHAPTER I.

INTRODUCTION.

I WRITE of an organization whose history might well have massacre put over against it as an epitome. I do not say epitaph, because only the equable, perhaps, are entitled to epitaphs. He who wore the blue or the gray—if starred, or barred, or epauletted—needed simply the recognition of a monument to become a martyr. But the Guerrilla had no graveyard. What mutilation spared, the potter's field finished. No *cortege* followed the corpse; beneath the folds of the black flag there was no funeral. Neither prayer, nor plaint of priest, nor penitential pleading went up for the wild beast dead by his lair, hard hunted yet splendid at last in the hopeless equanimity of accepted death. But the wild beast was human. The sky was just as blue for him; in the east the dawn was just as strange for him; the tenderness of woman was just as soft for him; the trysting by the gate was just as dear to him; the cottage hearth was just as warm for him, and the fields beyond the swelling flood were just as green for him, as though upon the crest of the blithe battle he had ridden down to the guns as Cardigan did, impatient bugles blowing all about him—or, scarfed and plumed, he had died as Pelham died, the boy cannonier—

> "Just as the spring came laughing through the strife
> With all its gorgeous cheer."

Some of the offspring of civil war are monstrous. The priest who slays, the church which becomes a fortress, the fusillade that finishes a capitulation, the father who fires at his son, the child who denies sepulchre to its parent, the tiger instinct that slays the unresisting, the forgetfulness of age, and the cruel blindness that cannot see the pitifulness of woman—these sprang

from the loins of civil war, as did also the Guerrilla—full-armed,
full-statured, terrible! His mission was not to kill, alone, but
to terrify.   At times he mingled with the purr of the tiger the
silkiness of the kitten.   Hilarity was a stage in the march he
made his victim take to the scaffold.   Now and then before a
fusillade there was a frolic. Harsh words were heard only when
from the midst of some savage *melee* a timid comrade broke
away or bent to the bullet blast. The softer the caress the
surer the punishment. The science of killing seemed to bring
a solace with it, and to purr also meant to be amiable. Sharing
his blanket like Rhoderick Dhu shared his plaid, on the morrow
his Coliantogle Ford was the contents of his revolver.

It is not easy to analyze this species of murder, all the more
certain because of its calculation. The time to refuse quarter
is in actual conflict. Conscience then—a sleepy thing in civil
war at best—is rarely aroused in time to become aggressive.
Through the smoke and the dust it is difficult to see the white,
set face and the haunting eyes of the early doomed. In
the rain of the rifle-balls, what matters the patter of a
prayer or two? Discrimination and desperation are not apt to
ride in the same squadrons together, and yet the Guerrilla, with
a full revolver, has been known to take possession of his victim
and spare him afterwards. Something, no matter what—some
memory of other days, some wayward freak, some passing
fancy, some gentle mood, some tender influence in earth, or air,
or sky—made him merciful when he meant to be a murderer.

The warfare of the Guerrilla was the warfare of the fox joined
to that of the lion. He crept from the rear, and he dashed from
the front. If the ambuscade hid him, as at Lone Jack, the
noonday sun shone down full upon the open prairie slaughter of
Centralia. In either extreme there was extermination. Death,
made familiar by association, merged its constraint into comradeship, and hid at the bivouac at night the sword-blade that
was to be so fatal in the morning. Hence all the roystering in
the face of the inevitable—all that recklessness and boisterousness which came often to its last horse, saddle and bridle, but
never to its last gallop or stratagem.

There are things and men one recognizes without ever having
seen them. The Guerrilla in ambush is one of these. Before a
battle a Guerrilla takes every portion of his revolver apart and

lays it upon a white shirt, if he has one, as carefully as a surgeon places his instruments on a white towel. In addition, he touches each piece as a man might touch the thing that he loves. The words of command are given in low tones, as if in the silence there might be found something in mitigation of the assassination. Again, he is noisy or indifferent to his purposes. He acts then upon the belief that doomed men, whose sense of hearing is generally developed to the greatest acuteness, lose effect in this advance upon the unknown.

And how patient they were—these Guerrillas. One day, two, three—a couple of weeks at a stretch—they have been known to watch a road—cold it may be, hungry most generally, inexorable, alert as the red deer and crouching as the panther. At last a sudden ring of rifles, a sudden uprearing of helpless steeds with dead men down under their feet, and the long vigil was over, the long ambuscade broken by a holocaust.

Much horse-craft was also theirs. Born as it were to the bare-back, the saddle only made it the more difficult to unseat them. Create a Centaur out of a Bucephalus, and the idea is fixed of their swiftness and prowess. Something also of Rarey's system must have been theirs, as a matter of course, for the Guerrilla was always good to his horse. He would often go unfed himself that his horse might have corn, and frequently take all the chances of being shot himself that his horse might come out of a close place unhurt. In situations where a neigh would amount almost to annihilation, even so much as a whinny was absolutely unknown. Danger blended the instinct of the one with the intelligence of the other. For each there was the same intuition. Well authenticated instances are on record of a Guerrilla's horse standing guard for his master, and on more than one occasion, when cut off from his steed and forced to take shelter from pursuit in fastnesses well nigh inaccessible, the Guerrilla has been surprised at the sudden appearance of his horse, no more desirous than himself of unconditional captivity. Much, therefore, of humanity must have entered into the relationship of the rider with his steed. He had to blanket him of nights when the frost was falling and the north wind cut as a knife; he had to talk low to him, rest him when he was tired, feed him when he was hungry, spare the spur when there was no need for it, slacken the girth when the column was at rest, cast aside as inhuman the accursed Spanish bit, and do generally unto him as the Guerrilla would have been done by had nature reversed the order of the animals and put a crupper in lieu of a coat. Kindness makes cavalry. Murat said once that the best among the cuirassiers were those who embraced their horses before they did their mistresses. He found a trooper walking, one day, who was leading a horse. Both were wounded, the dragoon a little the worst. " Why do you not ride?" asked the Prince. The soldier saluted and answered: "Because my horse has been shot." " And you?" " I have been shot, too, but I can talk and my horse cannot. If he could, maybe he would say that he is harder hit than I am." Murat made the cuirassier a captain.

The Guerrilla also had a dialect. In challenging an advancing enemy the cry of the regular was: " *Who goes there?*" That of the Guerrilla: " *Who are you?*" The regular repeated the question thrice before firing; the Guerrilla only once. No higher appreciation had ever desperate courage, or devoted comradeship, or swift work in pitiless conflict, or furious gallop, or marvelous endurance, than the Guerrilla's favorite summing up: "Good boy to the last." If upon a monument he had leave to write a folio, not a word more would be added to the epitaph. Sometimes the Guerrilla's dialect was picturesque; at other times monosyllabic. After Lawrence, and when Lane was pressing hard in pursuit, a courier from the rear rode hurriedly up to Quantrell and reported the situation. "How do they look?" enquired the chief. "Like thirsty buffaloes making for a water course." "Can't the rear guard check them?" "Can a grasshopper throw a locomotive off the track, Captain Quantrell?"

"Once," relates a Lieutenant of a Kansas regiment, "I was shot down by a Guerrilla and captured. I knew it was touch and go with me, and so I said what prayers I remembered and made what Masonic signs I was master of. The fellow who rode up to me first was stalwart and swarthy, cool, devilish-looking and evil-eyed. Our dialogue was probably one of the briefest on record, and certainly to me one of the most satisfactory. 'Are you a Mason?' he asked. 'Yes.' 'Are you a Kansas man?' 'Yes.' 'G—d d—n you!' This did not require an answer, it appeared to me, and so I neither said one thing nor another.

He took hold of his pistol and I shut my eyes. Something began to burn my throat. Presently he said again, as if he had been debating the question of life and death rapidly in his own mind: 'You are young, ain't you?' 'About twenty-five.' 'Married?' 'Yes.' 'Hate to die, I reckon?' 'Yes.' 'You are free!' I tried to thank him, although I did not at first realize his actions or understand his words. He got mad in a moment, and his wicked eyes fairly blazed. 'You are free, I told you! D—n your thanks and d—n you!'" "From that day to this," the Lieutenant continued, "I am at a loss to know whether my wife saved me or the Masons."

Neither; and yet the Guerrilla himself might not have been able to tell. Perhaps it was fate, or a passing tenderness, or something in the prisoner's face that recalled a near one or a dear one. Some few among them, but only a few, believed that retaliation should be a punishment, not a vengeance; and these, when an execution was unavoidable, gave to it the solemnity of the law and the condonement of civilization. The majority, however, killed always and without ado. They had passwords that only the initiated understood, and signals which meant everything or nothing. A night bird was a messenger; a day bird a courier. To their dialect they had added woodscraft, and to the caution of the proscribed men the cunning of the Indian. They knew the names or the numbers of the pursuing regiments from the shoes of their horses, and told the nationality of troops by the manner in which twigs were broken along the line of march. They could see in the night like other beasts of prey, and hunted most when it was darkest. No matter for a road so only there was a trail, and no matter for a trail so only there was a direction. When there was no wind, and when the clouds hid the sun or the stars, they traveled by the moss on the trees. In the day time they looked for this moss with their eyes, in the night time with their hands. Living much in fastnesses, they were rarely surprised, while solitude developed and made more acute every instinct of self-preservation. By degrees a caste began to be established. Men stood forth as leaders by the unmistakable right of superior address and undaunted courage. There was a kind of an aristocracy of daring wherein the humblest might win a crown or establish a dynasty. Respect for personal prowess begat discipline, and

2

discipline—strengthened by the terrible pressure of outside circumstances—kept peace in the midst of an organization ostensibly without a government and without a flag. Internal feuds came rarely to blows, and individual quarrels went scarcely ever beyond the interests of the contending principals. Free to come and go; bound by no enlistment and dependent upon no bounty; hunted by one nation and apologized for by the other; prodigal of life and property; foremost in every foray and last in every rout; content to die savagely and at bay when from under the dead steed the wounded rider could not extricate himself; merciful rarely and merciless often; loving liberty in a blind, idolatrous fashion, half reality and half superstition; holding no crime as bad as that of cowardice; courteous to women amid all the wild license of pillage and slaughter; steadfast as faith to comradeship or friend; too serious for boastfulness and too near the unknown to deceive themselves with vanity; eminently practical because constantly environed; starved to-day and feasted to-morrow; victorious in this combat or decimated in that; receiving no quarter and giving none; astonishing pursuers by the swiftness of a retreat, or shocking humanity by the completeness of a massacre; a sable fringe on the blood-red garments of civil war, or a perpetual cut-throat in ambush in the midst of contending Christians, is it any wonder that in time the Guerrilla organization came to have captains, and leaders, and discipline, and a language, and fastnesses, and hiding places, and a terrible banner unknown to the winds, and a terrible name that still lives as a wrathful and accusing thing from the Iowa line to the Pacific Ocean?

CHAPTER II.

IT IS the province of history to deal with results, not to condemn the phenomena which produce them. Nor has it the right to decry the instruments Providence always raises up in the midst of great catastrophes to restore the equilibrium of eternal justice. Civil war might well have made the Guerrilla, but only the excesses of civil war could have made him the untamable and unmerciful creature that history finds him. When he first went into the war he was somehow imbued with the old-fashioned belief that soldiering meant fighting and that fighting meant killing. He had his own ideas of soldiering, however, and desired nothing so much as to remain at home and meet its despoilers upon his own premises. Not naturally cruel, and averse to invading the territory of any other people, he could not understand the patriotism of those who invaded his own territory. Patriotism, such as he was required to profess, could not spring up in the market-place at the bidding of Red Leg or Jayhawker. He believed, indeed, that the patriotism of Jim Lane and Jennison was merely a highway robbery transferred from the darkness to the dawn, and he believed the truth. Neither did the Guerrilla become merciless all of a sudden. Pastoral in many cases by profession, and reared among the bashful and timid surroundings of agricultural life, he knew nothing of the tiger that was in him until death had been dashed against his eyes in numberless and brutal ways, and until the blood of his own kith and kin had been sprinkled plentifully upon things that his hands touched, and things that entered into his daily existence. And that fury of ideas also came to him slowly which is more implacable than the fury of men, for men have heart, and opinion has none. It took him likewise some time to learn that the Jayhawker's system of saving the Union was a system of brutal force, which bewailed not even that which it crushed; that it belied its doctrine by its tyranny; stained its arrogated right by its violence, and dishonored its vaunted struggles by its executions. But blood is as contagious as air. The fever of civil war has its delirium. When the Guerrilla awoke he was a giant! He took in, as it were, and at a single glance, all the immensity of the struggle. He saw that he was hunted and proscribed; that he had neither a flag nor a government; that the rights and the amenities of civilized warfare were not to be his; that a dog's death was certain if he surrendered even in the extremest agony of battle; that the house which sheltered him had to be burnt; the father who succored him had to be butchered; the mother who prayed for him had to be insulted; the sister who carried food to him had to be imprisoned; the neighborhood which witnessed his combats had to be laid waste; the comrade shot down by his side had to be put to death as a wild beast—and he lifted up the black flag in self-defence and fought as became a free man and a hero.

Much obloquy has been cast upon the Guerrilla organization because in its name bad men plundered the helpless, pillaged friend and foe alike, assaulted non-combatants and murdered the unresisting and the innocent. Such devil's work was not Guerrilla work. It fitted all too well the hands of those cowards crouching in the rear of either army and courageous only where women defended what remained to themselves and their children. Desperate and remorseless as he undoubtedly was, the Guerrilla saw shining down upon his pathway a luminious patriotism, and he followed it eagerly that he might kill in the name of God and his country. The nature of his warfare made him responsible of course for many monstrous things he had no personal share in bringing about. Denied a hearing at the bar of public opinion, the *bete noir* of all the loyal journalists, painted blacker than ten devils, and given a countenance that was made to retain some shadow of all the death agonies he had seen, is it strange in the least that his fiendishness became omnipresent as well as omnipotent? To justify one crime on the part of a Federal soldier, five crimes more cruel still were laid at the door of the Guerrilla. His long gallop not only tired but infuriated his hunters. That savage standing at bay and dying always as a

wolf dies when barked at by hounds and bludgeoned by coun-
trymen, made his enemies fear him and hate him. Hence from
all their bomb-proofs his slanderers fired silly lies at long range,
and put afloat unnatural stories that hurt him only as it deepened the savage intensity of an already savage strife. Save in
rare and memorable instances, the Guerrilla murdered only
when fortune in open and honorable battle gave into his hands
some victims who were denied that death in combat which they
afterward found by ditch or lonesome roadside. Man for man,
he put his life fairly on the cast of the war dice, and died when
the need came as the red Indian dies, stoical and grim as
a stone.

As strange as it may seem the perilous fascination of fighting
under a black flag—where the wounded could have neither surgeon nor hospital, and where all that remained to the prisoners
was the absolute certainty of speedy death—attracted a number
of young men to the various Guerrilla bands, gently nurtured,
born to higher destinies, capable of sustained exertion in any
scheme or enterprise, and fit for callings high up in the scale of
science or philosophy. Others came who had deadly wrongs to
avenge, and these gave to all their combats that sanguinary hue
which still remains a part of the Guerrilla's legacy. Almost
from the first a large majority of Quantrell's original command
had over them the shadow of some terrible crime. This one
recalled a father murdered, this one a brother waylaid and shot,
this one a house pillaged and burnt, this one a relative assassinated, this one a grievous insult while at peace at home, this
one a robbery of all his earthly possessions, this one the force
which compelled him to witness the brutal treatment of a mother
or sister, this one was driven away from his own like a thief in
the night, this one was threatened with death for opinion's
sake, this one was proscribed at the instance of some designing
neighbor, this one was arrested wantonly and forced to do the
degrading work of a menial; while all had more or less of wrath
laid up against the day when they were to meet face to face and
hand to hand those whom they had good cause to regard as the living embodiment of unnumbered wrongs. Honorable soldiers in
the Confederate army—amenable to every generous impulse and
exact in the performance of every manly duty—deserted even
the ranks which they had adorned and became desperate Guer-

rillas because the home they had left had been given to the
flames, or a gray-haired father shot upon his own hearth-stone.
They wanted to avoid the uncertainty of regular battle and
know by actual results how many died as a propitiation or a
sacrifice. Every other passion became subsidiary to that of
revenge. They sought personal encounters that their own
handiwork might become unmistakably manifest. Those who
died by other agencies than their own were not counted in the
general summing up of a fight, nor were the solacements of any
victory sweet to them unless they had the knowledge of being
important factors in its achievment. As this class of Guerrillas
increased, the warfare of the border became necessarily more
cruel and unsparing. Where at first there was only killing in
ordinary battle, there became to be no quarter shown. The
wounded of the enemy next felt the might of this individual
vengeance—acting through a community of bitter memories—
and from every stricken field there began, by and by, to come
up the substance of this awful bulletin: Dead such and such a
number—*wounded none*. The war had then passed into its fever
heat, and thereafter the gentle and the merciful, equally with
the harsh and the revengeful, spared nothing clad in blue that
could be captured.

CHAPTER III.

THERE have been Guerrillas in other countries, notably in France, Spain, Italy and Mexico. Before the days of breech-loaders and revolvers, and in fields of operation almost wholly unfit for cavalry, it was easy warfare for irregular bands to lie along mountainous roads, or hide themselves from ordinary pursuit in tangled thickets and stretches of larger timber. They fought when they felt like it, and were more formidable in reputation than in prowess. The American's capacity for war can be estimated in a great degree by the enterprising nature of his individual efforts. If, as a Guerrilla, he can guard defiles, surprise cantonments, capture convoys, disappear in the mountains, make at times and before superior numbers the difficulty not so much in fighting him as in finding him, discover and hold his own passes, learn the secrets of nature so that the rain or the snow storm will be his ally and the fog his friend—be sure the seeds are there for a harvest of armed men—no matter whether regular or irregular—that need only the cultivation of sensible discipline to become the most remarkable on earth. Essentially a nation of shop-keepers, trades-people and farmers before the great civil struggle began, the rapidity with which armies were mobilized and made into veterans, was marvelous. Nothing like a Guerrilla organization had ever before existed in the history of the country, and yet the strife was scarcely two months old before prominent in the field were leaders of Guerrilla bands more desperate than those of La Vendee, and organizers and fighters more to be relied upon and more blood-thirsty than the Fra Diavolas of Italy, or the El Empecinados of Spain.

La Vendee, among other things, was the war of a republic

upon a religion; of Marat, which meant pandemonium, upon
the Pope, who meant Christ. The cities fought the country,
the forests were attacked by the plains. In the gloom of the
fastnesses giants were developed. Beneath the mask of the
executioner was the cowl of the monk, and behind the judge of
a court martial sat the implacable embodiment of Jacobin sur-
veillance. On one side cynicism, on the other ferocity; on one
side blind fury buttressed upon fanaticism, on the other the air-
iness of a skepticism which denied the priesthood that it might
succeed to its possessions. From amid this chaos of contending devils—preying alike upon the province which held to the
crown, or the city which had adoration for the Directory, La
Rochejacquelin was born. He was an inferior Quantrell wearing a short sword instead of a six-shooter. He went often to
mass, and on the eve of every battle he took the sacrament.
Sometimes he fought well and sometimes badly. A word unknown to border warfare belonged to his vocabulary, and history has repeated it often when writing of Hoche and Houchard.
It was *Panic.* Victory was near to La Rochejacquelin often,
but just as his hands opened wide as it were to lay hold thereon
and close again in exultation, Panic dashed them aside as
though smitten by a sudden sword-blade. It was so at Mar-
tigne Briant, and Vihiers, at Vue and at Bonquenay. These
desperate Guerrillas of La Vendee—these monks in harness
and high priests in uniform—made *bonnets rouge* out of buck-
ram, and fled from imaginary grenadiers who were only shocks
of wheat. It was also a war of proclamations. In the charges
and counter-charges, the appeals on the one side to the good
God and on the other to the omnipotent Committee of Public
Safety, many a forlorn Frenchman, given over to contemplated
death, slipped through everybody's fingers; another evidence
of palpable weakness which was as foreign to the Missourian's
executive economy as the word panic to his vocabulary.

Michael Pezza, surnamed Fra Diavolo, from his diabolic cunning in escaping all pursuit, was an Italian, half patriot and
half brigand. Much of his reputation is legendary, but for all
that it has inspired one or two operas and a dozen romances.
He was to Italy what El Empecinado was to Spain, Canaris to
Greece, and Abd-el-Kader to Africa. Born amid the mountains, he knew the crags by their sinister faces, and the precipi-

ces from the roar of their cataracts. Before he fought Napoleon he had stopped travelers upon the highway. When he had
use for the robber, however, Ferdinand IV. made him a colonel
and a duke and set him to guard the passes of the Apennines.
A dozen audacious deeds will cover the space of his whole
career—one which was unquestionably bold but scarcely enterprising. All who spoke his language were his friends. He had
eyries like the eagle, and fought fights where, when he was shot
at, it was declared to be like shooting at the sky. Beyond a
convoy or two made to lose their property, and a straggling
band or two cut to pieces, he did no devil's work in a twelve-
month of splendid opportunity for all who hated the invaders
and saw from their mountain fastnesses the very blackness of
darkness overshadow a land that wore perpetually the garments
of Paradise. Finally a French detachment—especially charged
to look after the much dreaded Guerrilla—struck his trail and
followed it to the end. The French numbered eight hundred,
the Italians fifteen. Take Quantrell, or Todd, or Anderson,
or Pool, or Coleman Younger, or Jesse James, or Haller, or
Frank James, with fifteen hundred men, and put to catch them
eight hundred Federals! What analyst now, in the light of past
history, will say that out of the eight hundred six might safely
return alive to tell the story of the slaughter.

The hunt went on, the hunted having every advantage over
the hunters. They saw him, touched him, had him; suddenly
nobody was there. He did not fight; he only hid himself and
ran away. Nothing stopped the pursuit, however. Neither
mountain torrent, nor full-fed river, nor perpendicular rock, nor
tempests by night, nor hurricanes by day. When brought to
bay at last, Fra Diavola did what never Guerrilla did yet of
Anglo Saxon birth or raising, he disguised himself as a charcoal
dealer, mounted an ass, deserted his followers, and sought to
creep out of the environment as best he could. He did not succeed, but the effort exhibited the standard of the man.

The list is a long one to choose from, but apposite selections
are difficult to handle. At every step taken towards a contrast
between a Missouri Guerrilla and a Guerrilla of foreign reputation, there is an obstacle. Nowhere exists the same civilization.
In no single instance are the surroundings and the institutions
the same. One common bond, however, is the fiery crucible of

civil war, and by this and from out this must they come to judgment, standing or falling.

There was El Empecinado, the Spaniard. He did in the Pyrenees what Fra Diavolo did in the Apennines. Each system was the same—perpetual skirmishes, mostly unimportant, and sudden disappearance. Both fought the French. The nobility were for Napoleon, the peasants against him, and this added intensity to the strife. But to beat El Empecinado was to accomplish nothing. His band scattered on all sides into fastnesses where it was impossible to find them, and reorganized at some place in the mountains which they had intrenched, provisioned, and made inaccessible. He was the creature of the Junta, and the Junta was the hunted mother of liberty in Spain. Hurled from village to village, threatened hourly, attacked at all times, having the chief seat of its administration in some ruined chapel, some hovel in the shrubbery, or some hole in the ground, it decreed, notwithstanding it all, the independence of Spain. But in fight after fight El Empecinado was so badly worsted that he began to be accused of treason by his own men and suspected by the Junta. Finally, and after many races, and chases, and ambuscades, he was brought to his last assurance and stratagem at Cifuentes. The war of the thickets and the ravines was over. Having in his favor the enormous advantage of four men to his adversary's one, he stood forth in battle against General Hugo, of the French grenadiers, and was destroyed. At Centralia, and with the odds reversed and largely on the other side, George Todd rode over and shot down a superior column of Federal infantry massed upon open ground and standing in line, shoulder to shoulder, with fixed bayonets and loaded muskets.

There were the bands of Mina and El Pastor, who instead of being Guerrillas were barbarians. By these neither age nor sex was spared. Not content with killing women and children, they tortured them; they burned them alive. The elder Mina had carried before him in battle a flag bearing the device of *vae victis*. As he was more formidable and unsparing than either El Empecinado or Fra Diavolo, he was to the same extent more popular. Success, however unsatisfactory, made him dangerous in more ways than one to the invaders. Germans, English, Italians, and even French, deserted to him. In the course of five days fifteen hussars, twenty artillerymen, a company of British sappers, and fourteen French foot soldiers came over to his banner. Of course none of these could ever surrender, and became in time the most ferocious of this ferocious band. Underneath all the terrible vengeance taken by these Guerrillas there was the undying consciousness of terrible wrongs. Fra Diavola had been tied up in a public market place and scourged brutally by the public executioner; El Empecinado had had his ears slit; the younger Mina's mistress had been outraged before his eyes, her piercing cries haunting his sleep for months thereafter; El Pastor's old father, in returning late from a country town, had been first robbed and then beaten to death; and Xavier, the youngest of the Junta's bloody instruments and the most chivalrous, knew scarcely anything of the war until he had barely escaped assassination with his life. Does not history repeat itself? From the brooding vision of Quantrell there was never absent the white, set face of a murdered brother. To make tense the nerves and steel the heart of Coleman Younger, there, wet with his life's blood, were the white hairs of a loved father slain upon the highway. Anderson remembered to his dying day one beautiful sister buried beneath the falling walls of her prison house, and another so disfigured that when those dearest to her dug her out from the wreck they did not know her.

Of the Minas there were two—uncle and nephew. It was the strange destiny of the elder to have to encounter in his own field of operations a woman. Unnatural as it may appear the most ferocious band which infested Biscay was commanded by a woman named Martina. So indiscriminating and unrelenting was this female monster in her murder of friends and foes alike, that Mina felt himself compelled to resort to extermination. Surprised with the greater part of her following, not a soul escaped to tell the story of the massacre. One wild beast had devoured another, and that was all!

Treachery of comrades is a somewhat prominent feature in all these records of Spanish Guerrilla warfare, but in Missouri it was absolutely unknown. Mina himself had a sergeant named Malcarado who attempted to betray him to the enemy. He succeeded so far as to lead a French patrol to the room in which his chief was still sleeping in bed. But suddenly aroused, Mina defended himself desperately with the bar of the door and kept the attacking party at bay until Gustra, his chosen comrade, assisted him to escape. Taking Malcarado afterwards he shot him instantly, together with the village cure and three alcaldes implicated in the effort at kidnapping.

In Mexico, under Maximilian, the French had, an organization known to the army of occupation as the Contre Guerrillas, that is to say Imperial Guerrillas, who fought when they could and exterminated where they could the Republican Mexican Guerrillas. Colonel Dupin, who commanded them, more nearly assimilated Quantrell in his manner of fighting than any other leader of Guerrillas history has yet passed in review. He was desperately cruel, but he fought fast and hard. Distance was nothing to him, nor fatigue, nor odds, nor the difficulties of a position necessary to assault, nor any *terra incognita* the tropics could array to ride into. He had the flexibility of the panther and the grip of the bull-dog. Nothing uniformed and allied to Juarez ever lived after he once laid hold upon it. Past sixty, bronzed brown as a bag of leather, a school girl's face, covered with decorations, straight as Tecumseh, he led his squadrons through ambuscades sixty miles long, and made the court martial bring up eternally the rear of the combat. Any weapon fitted his hand, just as any weapon fitted the hand of Quantrell. Ruse, stratagem, disguise, ambushment, sudden attack, furious charge, unquestioned prowess, desperate resolve in extremity, unerring rapidity of thought—all these elements belonged to him by the inexorable right of his profession, and he used them all to terrify and to exterminate.

With Dupin also in Mexico was Captain Ney, Duke of Elchingen, and grandson of that other Ney who, when thrones were tumbling and fugitive kings flitting through the smoke of Waterloo, cried out to D'Erlon: "Come and see how a Marshal of France dies on the field of battle."

Ney had under him an American squadron, swart, stalwart fellows, scarred in many a border battle and bronzed by many a day of sunshiny and stormy weather. Names went for naught there. Hiding themselves in the unknown beyond the Rio Grande, those cool, calm men asked one of another no question of the past. Nothing of retrospect remained. Content to march and fight and be prodigal of everything save brag or boast, they carried no black flag and they often gave quarter.

And how they fought! Dupin—taking note of many other things besides—took note also of this. Once when a day of battles opened ominously, and when from the far front the story came back of repulses savoring strongly of disaster, he chose this little band alone for a desperate charge and patched with it swiftly the riven ranks of his routed soldiery. When the hot work was over and done, and when not anywhere in street, or town, or chapparal beyond the town, an enemy struggled save in the last sure agonies of death, he bade the balance of the regiment defile past their guidon and salute it with sloping standards and victorious music. In that day's fierce *melee* rode some of Quantrell's best and bravest. Their comrades knew them not, for they made no sign; and yet thrice was the sword of Captain Ney put out to wave the foremost back—it being a point of honor with a French cavalry officer to permit no subaltern to pass him in a charge—and thrice did he cry aloud and warn the boldest that if they went by him they went by at their peril. One of these pressing thus hard behind the gallant Ney was John C. Moore, once a member of Marmaduke's staff, and later a trained *athlete* in the arena where Shelby's giants struggled only for renown and glory. War found him an enthusiast and left him a philosopher. He drifted into Mexico a little behind the tide which bore his chieftain out, and for want of other things to do joined the Contre Guerrillas. He was always merciful in combat, and fought in the reckless old style just because it was fashionable to fight so, and because he gave so little thought to-day whether the morrow would be peaceful in bivouacs or stormy with sudden ambuscades. He was the centre of a group of dauntless spirits who dreamed of empire in the land of the Aztecs, and who never for a moment lost faith in the future or saw need for despair in the present until imbecility rose upon and mastered resolution and forced Maximilian from a throne to a dead-wall.

There were no Guerrillas in the days of the revolution, for in no sense of the word could General Marion and his men be considered as such. Strictly partisan in some respects, and fighting here, there, and everywhere as occasion or opportunity permitted, he never for a moment severed communication with the goverment his patriotism defended, nor relied for a day upon other resources than those of the departments regularly

organized for military supremacy.   As part of the national
army, he entered as an important factor in the plans of every
contiguous campaign.   His swamp warfare made him formidable but never ferocious.   He rarely killed save in open battle,
and being seldom retaliated upon, he had nothing to retaliate
for in the way of an equilibrium.   It required, indeed, all the
excesses of the civil war of 1861–5 to produce the genuine
American Guerrilla—more enterprising by far, more deadly,
more capable of immense physical endurance, more fitted by
nature for deeds of reckless hardihood, and given over to less
of penitence or pleading when face to face with the final end,
than any French or Spanish, Italian or Mexican Guerrilla
notorious in song or story.   He simply lived the life that was in
him, and took the worst or best as it came and as fate decreed
it.   Circumstances made him unsparing, and not any predis-
position in race or rearing.   Fought first with fire, he fought
back with the torch; and branded as an outlaw first in
despite of all reason, he made of the infamous badge a birth-
right and boasted of it as a blood-red inheritance while
flaunting it in the face of a civilization which denounced the
criminals while condoning the crimes that made them such.

CHAPTER IV.

QUANTRELL.

ONE-HALF the country believes Quantrell to have been a highway robber crossed upon the tiger; the other half that he was the gallant defender of his native South. One-half believes him to have been an avenging Nemesis of the right; the other a forbidding monster of assassination. History cannot hesitate over him, however, nor abandon him to the imagination of the romancers—those cosmopolitan people who personify him as the type of a race which reappears in every country that is a prey to the foreigner—the legitimate bandit in conflict with conquest. He was a living, breathing, aggressive, all-powerful reality—riding through the midnight, laying ambuscades by lonesome roadsides, catching marching columns by the throat, breaking in upon the flanks and tearing a suddenly surprised rear to pieces; vigilant, merciless, a terror by day and a superhuman if not a supernatural thing when there was upon the earth blackness and darkness.

Charles William Quantrell was to the Guerrillas their voice in tumult, their beacon in a crisis, and their hand in action. From him sprang all the other Guerrilla leaders and bands which belong largely to Missouri and the part Missouri took in the civil war. Todd owed primary allegiance to him, and so did Scott, Haller, Anderson, Blunt, Poole, Younger, Maddox, Jarrette, the two James brothers—Jesse and Frank—Shepherd, Yager, Hulse, Gregg—all in fact who became noted aftewards as enterprising soldiers and fighters. His was the central figure, and it towered aloft amid all the wreck and overthrow and massacre that went on continually around and about him until it fell at last as the pine falls, uprooted by Omnipotence or shivered by its thunderbolt.

The early life of Quantrell was obscure and uneventful.
Born in Hagerstown, Maryland, July 20, 1836, and raised there
until he was sixteen years of age, he remained always an obedient and an affectionate son.   His mother had been left a
widow when he was only a few years old, and had struggled
bravely and with true maternal devotion to keep a home for her
children and her children in it.   Inheriting self-reliance in an
eminent degree, and something of that sadness which is the
rightful offspring of early poverty, the boy Quantrell was taken
in his sixteenth year to Cleveland, Ohio, by an old friend of
his family, a Colonel Toler, and there given an excellent English
education.   He never saw his mother again.   His first separation was his final one.

As early as 1855 Missouri and Kansas had been at war.
Seward's Irrepressible Conflict began then—passed from its
quiescent to its aggressive stage then, and opened the *crevasse*
in the embankment then which was to let through all the floods
of sectional bitterness and strife and deluge the whole land with
the horors of civil war.   Men were baptized then who were to
become later notorious apostles of plunder and invasion.   Old
John Brown was a creature of that abolition madness which
began at Osawatomie Creek and ended at Harper's Ferry.
Jim Lane killed his first man in that war; Montgomery came
first to the front after the adoption of the Lecompton Constitution, and learned so well the uses of the torch that later he
burned Rome, Georgia, wantonly, and hung a dozen or so of its
non-combatants; Jennison gave something of the robber promise that was in him; General John W. Reid added greener
laurels to his Mexican wreath; Jo. Shelby, that eagle of the
foray, first changed his down for his feathers; there were fierce
sectional fires lit all along the border; the two States hated
each other and harried each other's accessible lands; from
Leavenworth south to Fort Scott dragon's teeth were sown
broadcast as wheat is sown in the fall, and so when the first
drum beat was heard in 1861, and when the first bugle note was
sounded, the throat-cutting had already begun.

For some time preceding 1855, Quantrell's only brother had
been living in Kansas.   He was older by several years than
Charles, had been more of a father to him than a playmate, and
was then the mainstay of the struggling widow, still fighting

the uncertain battles of life heroically and alone. The strife
along the border had somewhat subsided, and something of
comparative peace had succeeded to the armed irruption, when
the elder Quantrell wrote to the younger and urged him to come
at once to his home in the disputed Territory. A trip to
Cal·fornia was contemplated, and the one in Kansas would not
go without the one in Ohio.

About the middle of the summer of 1856 both brothers began
their overland journey, each having a wagon loaded with
provisions, four good mules each, and more or less money
between them. One negro man was also carried along—a sort
of general utility person—part hostler and part cook. In
addition he was also free. The three were together when that
unprovoked tragedy occurred which was to darken and blacken
the whole subsequent current of the younger brother's life, and
link his name forever with some of the savagest episodes of
some of the most savage Guerrilla history ever recorded.

Although there was comparative peace at that time, armed
bands still maintained their organization throughout the entire
State. Some were legitimate and some illegitimate. A few
lived by patriotism, such as it was, and a good many by plunder. Here and there worse things than stealing were done, and
more than one belated traveler saw the sun set never to rise
again, and more than one suspected or obnoxious settler disappeared so quietly as scarcely to cause a ripple of comment upon
the placid surface of neighborhood events. Especially implacable were one or two companies owing allegiance to Lane. In
the name of Abolitionism they took to the highway, and for the
sake of freedom in Kansas great freedom was taken with other
people's lives and property. Camped one night on the Little
Cottonwood River, *en route* to California, thirty armed men
rode deliberately up to the wagons where the Quantrells were
and opened fire at point-blank range upon the occupants. The
elder Quantrell was killed instantly, while the younger—
wounded badly in the left leg and right breast—was left upon
the bank of the stream to die. The negro was not harmed.
Scared so dreadfully at first as to be unable to articulate, he yet
found his speech when the robbers began to hitch up the teams
and drive off the wagons, and pleaded eloquently that food and
shelter might be left for the wounded man. "Of what use?"

3

the leader of the Jayhawkers sneered, "he will die at best, and
if we did not think that he would die, we would be sure to
finish him." And so they drove away, taking not only the
wagons and teams, but the tent and the negro, leaving Quantrell alone with his murdered brother, the wide wilderness of
prairie and sky above and about him everywhere and death's
door so close to his own hands that for the stretching out he
might have laid hold thereon and entered in. Not content,
however, with being robbers and cut-throats, they added petty
thieving to cowardly asssasination. The pockets of both were
rifled, every dollar was taken from each, a ring from a finger
of the living and a watch from the person of the dead.

It was two days before the wounded brother was found—two
days of agony, retrospects, and dreams it may be of a stormy
future. Something of the man's wonderful fortitude abode
with him to the end. He heard the clangor of ominous pinions
and the flapping of mysterious wings that splotched the prairie
grass with hateful splotches of beak and claw. He dragged
himself to the inanimate heap lying there festering in the summer's sun, and fought a desperate double fight against the
talons that would mutilate and the torments of fever and thirst
that were burning him up alive. And in the darkness came
other sounds than the rising of the night wind. A long, low
howl at first that had the subdued defiance of hunger in it, and
then the shuffling of creeping feet and the mingling of gray and
darkness in the nearest cover. The wolves were abroad—
coming ever closer and closer, and crouching there in the
prairie grass, knowing scarcely aught of any difference between
the living and the dead. He did not cry out, neither did he
make moan. All night long by the corpse he watched and
defended—seeing on the morrow the sun rise red out of a sea
of verdure, and hearing again on the morrow the clangor of
ominous pinions and the flapping of mysterious wings.

From the road to the stream it was fifty good steps, and between the two an abundance of luxuriant grass. The descent
to the water was very steep, and broken here and there by gul-
lies the rains had cut. Until an intolerable thirst drove him to
quit his watch by his brother's corpse, and quit his uncomplaining fight against buzzard and prairie wolf, he never moved from
the dead man's side. In the two nights and days of this mourn-

ful vigil he did not sleep. He could not walk, and yet he rolled himself down to the river and back again to the road—dragging his crippled body over the broken places and staunching his wounds with the rankest grass. He would live! He had never thought how necessary life could become to him. There was much to do. The dead had to be buried, the murder had to be avenged, and that demand—fixed as fate and as inexorable— had to be made which required sooner or later an eye for an eye and a tooth for a tooth. What he suffered during the two days and nights, when the mutilated brother watched by the murdered one, he would never tell. Indeed, he rarely referred to his past, and spoke so little of himself that those who knew him longest knew the least of his history, and those who questioned him the most assiduously got less satisfaction than those who questioned him not at all.

Early in the morning of the third day, and just after Quantrell had dragged himself back from the river to the road, suffering more and more of agony from his already swollen and inflamed wounds, an old Shawnee Indian, Golightly Spiebuck, happened to pass along, and became at once the rough but kindly Samaritan of the Plains. The dead man was buried, and the wounded one placed gently in the Indian's wagon and carried by easy stages to his home, a few miles south of Leavenworth. Spiebuck died in 1868, but he often told the story of the rescue. It took him four hours to dig the grave deep enough for the dead man. There was neither coffin, nor shroud, nor funeral rite. Dry-eyed and so ghastly white that he looked to Spiebuck like the ghost of the departed come back to claim the due of decent sepulchre, Quantrell watched the corpse until the earth covered it, and then he hobbled to his knees and turned his dry eyes up to where he believed a God to be. Did he pray? Yes, like Caligula, perhaps, and that the whole Jayhawking fraternity had but a single neck, capable of being severed by a single blow.

CHAPTER V.

QUANTRELL recovered slowly. He had youth, a fine physique, great energy and determination of character; but his mind appeared to dominate over and hold his body in subjection. He would lay for hours at a time with his hands over his eyes—his pale cheeks lit up with a kind of hectic flush, and his respiration so noiseless and imperceptible that Spiebuck's old Indian wife and nurse more than once declared him dying. But he was not dying; he was thinking. Afterwards there came weary weeks of the stick and crutch. Summer was dead on the hills, and autumn had already begun to frighten the timid leaves with the white ghost of the snow. The cripple had become to be a convalescent, the convalescent had become to be a man—a little pale, it may be, but cured of his wounds and his reveries. If any knew of the murder and the robbery upon the Cottonwood, they had forgotten both. Either was so familiar and so matter of fact that the law regarded the thief complacently, and public opinion took sides with the murderer—thus making for each an equal justification. One man remembered, however— one calm, grave man—something of a set sadness always about his features, and now and then an eager, questioning look that seemed to appeal to the future while recalling and re-establishing the past.

Quantrell was very patient. Sometimes tigers lick the crucifix; sometimes sheep become wolves. He took a school; taught the balance of the year 1856; got into his possession all the money he needed; paid Mr. and Mrs. Spiebuck liberally for every care and attention; shook hands cordially with the good old Indians on the 15th day of August, 1857, and went to Leavenworth. As he had never permitted confidences, he had no need of a disguise. The simple Charley Quantrell had become to be the simple Charley Hart, and that was all. The Nemesis was about to put on the national uniform. The lone grave by the Cottonwood river had begun to have grass upon it, and there was need that it should be watered.

Leavenworth City belonged at that time to the Jayhawkers, and the Jayhawkers to all intents and purposes belonged to Jim Lane. The original Jayhawker was a growth indigenous to the soil of Kansas. There belonged to him as things of course a pre-emption, a chronic case of chills and fever, one starved cow and seven dogs, a longing for his neighbor's goods and chattels, a Sharpe's rifle, when he could get it, and something of a Bible for hypocrisy's sake—something that savored of the real presence of the book to give backbone to his canting and snuffling. In some respects a mountebank, in others a scoundrel, and in all a thief—he was a character eminently adapted for civil war which produces more adventurers than heroes. His hands were large, hairy and red—proof of inherited laziness—and a slouching gait added to the ungainliness of his figure when he walked. The type was all of a kind. The mouth generally wore a calculating smile—the only distinguishable gift remaining of a Puritan ancestry—but when he felt that he was looked at the calculating smile became sanctimonious. Slavery concerned him only as the slave-holder was supposed to be rich; and just so long as Beecher presided over emigration aid societies, preached highway robbery, defended political murder, and sent something to the Jayhawkers in the way of real fruits and funds, there surely was a God in Israel and Beecher was his great high priest. Otherwise they all might go to the devil together. The Jayhawker was not brave. He would fight when he had to fight, but he would not stand in the last ditch and shoot away his last cartridge. Born to nothing, and eternally out at elbows, what else could he do but laugh and be glad when chance kicked a country into war and gave purple and fine linen to a whole lot of bummers and beggars? In the saddle he rode like a sand bag or a sack of meal. The eternal "ager cake" made a trotting horse his abomination, and he had no use for a thoroughbred, save to steal him. When he abandoned John Brown and rallied to the standard of Jim Lane —when he gave up the fanatic and clove unto the thief—he simply changed his leader without changing his principles.

General James H. Lane, for some time previous to the breaking out of the war and for sometime afterwards, was omnipotent in Kansas. Immense *bonhommie*, joined to immense vitality, made him a political giant. Of infinite humor, rarely skilled in the arts of judging human nature, passably brave, though always from selfish impulses, brilliant in speech, exaggerated in sentiment, vivid in expresson, and full of that intangible yet all-mastering pathos which has ever and will ever find in the West its most profitable employment, he soon became the Melchisedec of the Kansas militia and the founder of a line of Jayhawkers. Blood had already stained his hands. The civilization to which his principles owned origin permitted him the wives of other people if he could win them, and he went about with the quest of a procuress and the encompassment of Solomon. Reversing the alphabet in the spelling out of his morals, he made v the first letter of the new dispensation, because it stood for virility. The mantle of John Brown had fallen upon his shoulders, and yet it did not fit him. John Brown was the inflexible partisan; Jim Lane the ambitious man of talent. One would have given everything to the cause which he espoused—did give his life; the other stipulated for commissions, senatorial robes, and political power. John Brown could never have passed from the character of destructive to that of statesman; but Jim Lane, equal to either extreme, put readily aside with one hand the business of making raids, and took up with the other the less difficult though more complicated business of making laws.

Jennison was of inferior breed and mettle. None of his ideas ever rose above a corral of rebel cattle, and he made war like a brigand, and with a cold brutality which he imagined gave to his unsoldierly greed the mask of patriotism.

Montgomery, dying by inches of consumption, and feeling a craving for military fame without having received from society or nature the means of acquiring it, was content to become infamous in order to become notorious. He was the patron of the assassin and the incendiary.

These three embryotic embodiments of all that was to be forbidding and implacable in border warfare came in and out of Leavenworth a great deal in those brief yet momentous months

preceding that mighty drama which from a small Kansas pro-
logue was to overshadow and envelop a continent. Quantrell,
known now as Charles Hart, became intimate with Lane, and
ostensibly attached himself to the fortunes of the anti-slavery
party. If, in order to advance an object or to get a step nearer
to the goal of his ambition, it became necessary to speak of John
Brown, he always spoke of him as of one for whom he had great
admiration. General Lane, at that time a Colonel, was in command of a regiment whose headquarters were at Lawrence.
Thither from Leavenworth went Quantrell, and soon became
enrolled in a company to which belonged all but two of the men
who did the deadly work at the Cottonwood river. If the whole
Quantrell episode had not been forgotten, however, certainly
there was nothing to recall it in the sad face, slender figure,
drooping blue eyes and courteous behavior of the new recruit.
He talked little and communed with himself a great deal.
While others amused themselves with cards, or women, or wine,
Quantrell rode over the country in every direction, and made
himself thoroughly acquainted with its geography and topography. Who knows but what even then the coming events of
that terrible sack and pillage were beginning to cast their shadows before.

First a private and then an orderly sergeant, Quantrell soon
won the esteem of his officers and the confidence of his men.
It was getting along pretty well through 1858, and what with
brushes with the Border Ruffians, as the Missourians were
called, and scouting after depredating Indians, Lane's command
was kept comparatively active. It was required also to furnish
covering parties for trains running on the Underground Railroad, and scouts along the whole line of the border from Kaw
River to the Boston Mountains. One day Quantrell and three
men were sent down to the neighborhood of Wyandotte to meet
a wagon load of negroes coming out of Missouri under the
pilotage of Jack Winn, a somewhat noted horse-thief and
abolitionist. One of the three men failed to return when
Quantrell and his comrade did, nor could any account be given
of his absence until a body was found near a creek several days
afterward. In the centre of the forehead was the round,
smooth hole of a navy revolver bullet. Those who looked for
Jack Winn's safe arrival were also disappointed. He had been

shot just inside the fence of a cornfield, and in falling had fallen face foremost in some rank weeds and briars which completely covered him. People traveling the road passed and repassed the corpse almost hourly, but the buzzards found it first and afterwards the curious. There was the same round hole in the forehead, and the same sure mark of the navy revolver bullet.

Somebody's hand-writing was becoming to be legible!

Next, four companies received marching orders for service down about Fort Scott, and Quantrell's was among the four. The Missourians of late had been swarming over the border thick in that direction, and Lane wanted to know more of what they were doing. Some skirmishing ensued, and now and then there was a sudden combat. Quantrell was the first in every adventurous enterprise and the last to leave upon every skirmish line. Of the four companies detailed to do duty in the vicinity of Fort Scott, all the members of each returned except sixty. The death of forty-two of these was attributed to the enemy, of the other eighteen to the manifold calamities of war. Two of the eighteen bodies were recovered, however, and there was the same round, smooth hole in the middle of the forehead. Evidently the Border Ruffians had navy revolvers and knew just where to shoot a man when it was intended to shoot him only once.

Things went on thus for several months. Scarcely a week passed that some sentinel was not found dead at his post, some advanced picquet surprised and shot at the outermost watch station. The men began to whisper one to another and to cast about for the cavalry Jonah who was in the midst of them. One company alone, that of Captain Pickens—the company to which Quantrell belonged—had lost thirteen men between October, 1857, and March, 1858. Another company had lost two, and three one each. A second Underground Railroad conductor named Rogers had been shot through the forehead, and two scouts from Montgomery's command named Stephens and Tarwater.

From the privates this talk about a Jonah went to the Captains, and from the Captains to the Colonel. Just as Lane began to busy himself with this story of an epidemic whose single symptom was a puncture in the forehead the size of a navy revolver bullet, Quantrell was made a Lieutenant in

Pickens' company. Therefore if this Jonah was in the line of promotion, it certainly was not in contemplation to cast him overboard to the fishes.

Quantrell and Pickens became intimate—as a Captain and Lieutenant of the same company should—and confided many things to each other. One night the story of the Cottonwood River was told, and Pickens dwelt with just a little of relish upon the long ride made to strike the camp of the unsuspecting emigrants, and the artistic execution of the raid which left neither the dead man a shroud nor the wounded man a blanket. The Lieutenant turned his face away from the light of the bivouac fire and essayed to ask a question or two. Could Pickens just then have seen his eyes—scintillant, and dilated about the pupils as the eyes of a lion in the night—he might have been tempted to try over again the argument of the Cottonwood crossing-place. He did not see them, however, and so he told all—how the plunder was divided, the mules sold, the money put all together in one pile and gambled for, the kind of report made to headquarters, and the general drunk which succeeded the return and ushered in forgetfulness.

Three days thereafter Pickens and two of his most reliable men were found dead on Bull Creek, shot like the balance in the middle of the forehead.

This time there was a genuine panic. Equally with the rest, Quantrell exercised himself actively over the mysterious murders, and left no conjecture unexpressed that might suggest a solution of the implacable fatality. Who was safe? What protection had Colonel Lane in his tent, or Lieutenant-Colonel Jennison in his cabin? The regiment must trap and slay this hidden monster perpetually in ambush in the midst of its operations, or the regiment would be decimated. It could not fight the unkown and the superhuman.

For a time after Pickens' death there was a lull in the constant conscription demanded by the Nemesis. Mutterings of the coming storm were beginning to be heard in every direction, while all over the political sky there were portents and perturbations. Those who believed that the nation's life was at hazard had no time to think of men. The new Lieutenant bought himself a splendid uniform, owned the best horse in the Territory, and instead of one navy revolver now had two.

It is not believed that at this time Quantrell was suspected, for in a long conversation held with him by Lane, the full particulars of the plan adopted to discover and arrest the mysterious murderer were discussed in every detail. He waited several weeks to see what would become of the exertions made to trace the handwriting on the foreheads of the victims, and then apparently dismissed the subject from his mind. At all events he no longer referred to it in conversation, or expressed an opinion upon it one way or the other. He had his duties to perform as an officer of cavalry, and he had no inclination to help on the work of the detectives. Probably two months after his conversation with Lane, Quantrell was ordered to take his own company and details from three others—amounting in the aggregate to one hundred and fourteen men—and make a scout out towards the extreme western border of the Territory. Although the expedition saw neither a hostile Indian nor a Missourian, thirteen of the Jayhawkers never again answered at roll-call. The old clamor broke out again in all its fury, and the old suspicions were extravagantly aroused. Quantrell was called upon to explain the absence of his men, and reported calmly all that he knew in the premises. Detached from the main body and ordered out on special duty, they had not returned when their comrades did. The bodies of three of them had been found shot through the forehead, and although he had tried every art known to his ingenuity to learn more of the causes which produced this mysterious fatality, he was no nearer the truth than his commanding officer. Not long after this report two men from another company were missing, and then an orderly attached to the immediate person of Colonel Lane. This orderly had been killed under peculiar circumstances. The citizens of Lawrence gave a supper one night to some distinguished Eastern people, and Colonel Lane presided at the table. His orderly was with him, and as the night deepened he drank freely and boasted a great deal. Among the things which he described with particular minuteness was an attack upon a couple of emigrants nearly two years before and the confiscation of their property. Quantrell was not at the banquet, but somehow he heard of the orderly's boast and questioned him fully concerning the whole circumstance. After this dialogue there was a dead man!

There came also from the East about this time some sort of a disease known as the club mania. Those afflicted with it—and it attacked well nigh the entire population—had a hot fever described as the enrollment fever. Organizations of all sorts sprang up—Free Soil Clubs, Avengers, Men of Equal Rights, Sons of Liberty, John Brown's Body Guard, Destroying Angels, Lane's Loyal Leaguers, and what not—and every one made haste to get his name signed to both constitution and by-laws. Lawrence especially affected the Liberator Club, whose undivided mission was to find freedom for all the slaves in Missouri. Quantrell took its latitude and longitude with the calm, cold eyes of a political philosopher and joined it among the first. As it well might have been, he soon became its vitalizing influence and its master. The immense energy of the man—making fertile with resources a mind bent to the accomplishment of a certain fixed purpose—suggested at once to the Club the necessity of practical work if it meant to make any negroes free or punish any slaveholders. He knew how an entire family of negroes might be rescued. The risk was not much. The distance was not great. The time was opportune. How many would volunteer for the enterprise? At first the Club argued indirectly that it was a Club sentimental—not a Club militant. It would pray devoutly for the liberation of all the slaves in all the world, but it would not fight for them. What profit would the individual members receive if, after gaining all Africa, they lost their own scalps? Quantrell persevered, however, and finally induced seven of the Liberators to co-operate with him. His plan was to enter Jackson county, Missouri, with three days' cooked rations, and ride the first night to within striking distance of the premises it was intended to plunder. There—hidden completely in the brush and vigilant without being seen or heard—wait again for the darkness of the second night. This delay of a day would also enable the horses to get a good rest and the negroes to prepare for their hurried journey. Afterwards a bold push and a steady gallop must bring them all back safe to the harbor of Lawrence. Perhaps the plan really was a daring one, and the execution extremely dangerous; but seven Liberators out of eighty-four volunteered to accompany Quantrell, and in a week everything was ready for the enterprise.

Morgan Walker was an old citizen of Jackson county—a veritable pioneer. He had settled there when buffalo grazed on the prairies beyond Westport, and when in the soft sands along the inland streams there were wolf and moccasin tracks. Stalwart, hospitable, broad across the back, old-fashioned in his courtesies and his hospitalities, he fed the poor, helped the needy, prayed regularly to the good God, did right by his neighbors and his friends, and only swore occasionally at the Jayhawkers and the Abolitionists. His hands might have been rough and sun-browned, but they were always open. None were ever turned away from his door hungry. Under the old roof of the homestead—no matter what the pressure was nor how large the demand had been—the last wayfarer got the same comfort as the first—and altogether they got the best. This man Morgan Walker was the man Quantrell had proposed to rob. Living some five or six miles from Independence, and owning about twenty negroes of various ages and sizes, the probabilities were that a skillfully conducted raid might leave him without a servant.

Between the time the Liberators had made every preparation for the foray and the time the eight men actually started for Morgan Walker's house, there was the space of a week. Afterwards those most interested remembered that Quantrell had not been seen during all that period either in Lawrence or at the headquarters of his regiment.

Everything opened auspiciously. Well mounted and armed, the little detachment left Lawrence quietly, rode two by two and far apart until the point of the first rendezvous was reached—a clump of timber at a ford on Indian Creek. It was the evening of the second day when they arrived, and they tarried long enough to rest their horses and eat a hearty supper. Before daylight the next morning the entire party were hidden in some heavy timber two miles to the west of Walker's house. From this safe retreat none of them stirred except Quantrell. Several times during the day, however, he went backwards and forwards ostensibly to the fields where the negroes were at work, and whenever he returned he always brought something either for the horses or the men to eat.

Morgan Walker had two sons—true scions of the same stock —and before it was yet night these two boys and also the father might have been seen cleaning up and putting in excellent order their double-barrel shot-guns. A little later three neighbors, likewise carrying double-barrel shot-guns, rode up to the house, dismounted, and entered in. Quantrell, who brought note of many other things to his comrades, brought no note of this. If he saw it he made no sign.

The night was dark. It had rained a little during the day, and the most of the light of the stars had been put out by the clouds, when Quantrell arranged his men for the dangerous venture. They were to proceed first to the house, gain possession of it, capture the male members of the family, put them under guard, assemble the negroes, bid them hitch up all the wagons and teams possible, and then make a rapid gallop for Kansas.

Fifty yards from the main gate the eight men dismounted and fastened their horses. Arms were looked to, and the stealthy march to the house began. Quantrell led. He was very cool, and seemed to see everything. The balance of the marauders had their revolvers in their hands; his were in his belt. Not a dog barked. If any there had been aught save city bred, this, together with the ominous silence, would have demanded a reconnoissance. None heeded the surroundings, however, and Quantrell knocked loudly and boldly at the oaken panels of Morgan Walker's door. No answer. He knocked again and stood perceptibly to one side. Suddenly, and as though it had neither bolts nor bars, locks nor hinges, the door flared open and Quantrell leaped into the hall with a bound like a red deer. 'Twas best so. A livid sheet of flame burst out from the darkness where he had disappeared—as though an explosion had happened there—followed by another as the second barrels of the guns were discharged, and the tragedy was over. Six fell where they stood, riddled with buckshot. One staggared to the garden, bleeding fearfully, and died there. The seventh, hard hit and unable to mount his horse, dragged his crippled limbs to a patch of timber and waited for the dawn. They tracked him by his blood upon the leaves and found him early. Would he surrender? No! Another volley, and the last Liberator was liberated. Walker and his two sons, assisted by three of his stalwart and obliging neighbors, had done a clean night's work and a righteous one. Those who had taken the sword had perished by it.

Events traveled rapidly those fiery and impatient days, and soon all the county was up and exercised over the attack made upon Morgan Walker's house, and the deadly work which followed it. Crowds congregated to look upon the seven dead men, laid one alongside of another, and to see what manner of a man remained a prisoner. Thus was Quantrell first introduced to the citizens of Jackson county, but little could any tell then of what iron nerve that young stripling had, what grim endurance, what inexorable purpose to make war practical and unforgiving.

Morgan Walker kept his own counsel. Quantrell was arraigned before a grand jury summoned especially for the occasion of his trial, and honorably acquitted. The dead were buried, the living was let go free, and the night attack soon became to be a nine days' wonder. Men had their suspicions and that was all. Some asked why seven should be taken and the eighth one spared, but as no answer came in reply, the question was not repeated. Little by little public interest in the event died out, and Quantrell went back to Lawrence. There, however, the hunt was up, and he saw at a glance and instinctively that the desperate game he had been playing had to be played, if played any longer, on the edge of a precipice. Salvation depended alone upon something speedy and sure. His intention at this time was undoubtedly to have killed Lane before he abandoned Lawrence forever, and he went deliberately to his quarters for that purpose. Called away in the forenoon to some point thirty miles distant, Lane had not returned when Quantrell's blood-thirsty preparations had all been finished. Time pressed, and he could not wait. Associating with himself two desperate frontiersmen from Colorado, and openly defying the Jayhawkers and the Abolitionists, Quantrell simply changed the mode of his warfare without mitigating aught of its affectiveness. Infuriated at the intrepid actions of the man, and learning more and more of that terrible disease whose single symptom has already been described, Lane offered heavy rewards for the Guerrilla's head. Quantrell laughed at these and fought on in his own avenging fashion all through the balance of the year 1860 and up to within a few months of the fall of Fort Sumpter in 1861. He probably told but twice in his career the true story of his life in Kansas—once to George

Todd, and once to Jesse and Frank James. Each time he dwelt upon the fact that out of the thirty-two men who killed his brother and wounded him, two only escaped the final punishment, and these because they left the Jayhawkers and moved to California. Every Jayhawker shot in the forehead had been shot by his own hand, and every sentinel killed at his post, and every picquet left dead at the outtermost station, was but another victim offered up as a sacrifice to appease the unquiet spirit of the elder Quantrell. The younger never made an official estimate of the number slain in this manner, but the evidence is almost indisputable that a few over a hundred fell by his hand and the hands of the two Colorado trappers who joined him about nine months before the war commenced. The raid upon Morgan Walker was the work of Quantrell's contriving. Understanding in a moment that only through their fanaticism could three of the original thirty-two who murdered his brother and who belonged to the Liberator Club—be made to get far enough away from Lawrence for an ambuscade, he set the Jackson county trap for them, baited it with the rescue of a negro family, and they fell into it. His week's absence preceding the attack was spent in arranging its preliminaries. Neither Walker nor his friends were to fire until he had abandoned the balance of the party to their fate, and each time that he had left the camp in the woods the day that was to usher in the bloody night, he had been to Walker's house and gone through with him, as it were, and carefully a rehearsal of all the more important parts of the sanguinary play.

No consuming passion for revenge—no matter how constantly fed and persistently kept alive—was adequate to the part Quantrell played in Kansas from 1857 to 1861. Something his character had—some elements of nerve, cunning, and intellect belonging to it by the inherent right of training and development—that carried him successfully through the terrible work and left his head without a single gray hair, his face without a single altered feature. The attitude must have been superb, the daily equanimity royal. The march was towards ruin or deification, and yet day after day he anointed himself, made awry things smooth before a mirror, put perfume upon his person, and a rose in his button-hole. Under waning moons of nights, by lonesome roadsides and haunted hollows, he took kid gloves from his hands as he writ legibly the writing of the revolver. Women turned back upon him as he passed them on the streets, and felt to stir within their hearts—as the blue eyes lit up in courtly recognition and the pale face flushed a little in glad surprise—the girls' romantic hunger for the men. He never boasted. So young, and yet he was a Sphinx. Eternally on guard. when he was not in ambush, he no more mispronounced a word than he permitted rust to appear upon his revolver barrels. If it could be said that he ever put on a mask, the name for it was gravity. He never endeavored to make death ridiculous, for he knew that in the final summing up death had never been known to laugh. He ate with those doomed by his vengeance, touched them, knee to knee, as they rode in column, talked with them of love, and war, and politics, lifted his hand to his hat in salute as he bade the stationed guards of the night be vigilant, and returned in an hour to shoot them through the forehead. Dead men were brought in, slain undoubtedly by the unerring hand of that awful yet impalpable Nemesis, and he turned them nonchalantly over in the sunlight, recognized them by name, spoke something of eulogy or comradeship by the wet blankets whereon they lay, and wrote in his dairy, as the summing up of a day's labor: "Let not him that girdeth on his harness boast himself as 'he that putteth it off." If any—thinking strange things of the plausible, reticent, elegant man going his way and keeping his peace—shot some swift, furtive glance at him as he stood by the dead of his own handicraft, the marble face moved not under the scrutiny. He had mastered all human emotion, and sat superbly waiting the *denouement* as though he felt to the uttermost that

"The play was the tragedy Man,
And its hero the Conqueror Worm."

There are those who will denounce him for his treachery and seek to blacken his name because of the merciless manner in which he fought. He recks not now of either extreme—the comradeship that would build him a monument durable as patriotism—or the condemnation which falsified his motives in order to lessen his heroism. For Quantrell the war commenced in 1856. Fate ordered it so, and transformed the ambitious yet innocent boy into a Guerrilla without a rival and without a peer. It was the work of Providence—that halt by the river, that murderous onslaught, that two days' battle with things which mutilated, those hours given for the revenge of a lifetime to be concentrated within a single span of suffering—and Providence might well cause this for epitaph to be written over against the tomb of Quantrell:

> "The standing side by side till death,
> The dying for some wounded friend,
> The faith that failed not to the end,
> The strong endurance till the breath
> And body took their ways apart
> I only know. I keep my trust.
> Their vices! earth has them by heart;
> Their virtues! they are with their dust."

4

CHAPTER V.

THE war drums were being beaten all over the land. Prone amid the ruins of Fort Sumpter the United States flag—symbolical of an indivisible nation—was down amid its *debris*, the Palmetto, in lieu of it, waving high over the ramparts. It was as though a mighty torch had been cast in the midst of the hatreds and the passions of two desperate sections, and that the thing called Civil War was its conflagration. Armies began to muster. People with picking and stealing fingers had already commenced to count the chances of the strife and take sides with the strongest. In the womb of the future the typical American Guerrilla quickened preternaturally. Politicians became soldiers, and statesmen took to the field. Battle was about to kill men; posterity to judge them. A few peace ravens—notably in Kentucky, Maryland, and Missouri—croaked out something about armed neutrality with a fiery energy of words which cost nothing to weaponless hands. Here and there compromise—with the beautiful mask of patriotism hiding its Medusa head—seduced from the standards of the right some noble and generous spirits. Imbecility crept into corners, and hypocrisy admitted at last that war cut through everything. The hour of those adventurous souls had struck who believed it a necessary diversion to the universal ferment. They hoped to change the fanaticism of secession into the fanaticism of glory, and to satisfy the conscience of the border States by intoxicating it with victory. A few conservatives—sporadic rather than epidemical—threw themselves helplessly across the path of the Revolution, and betwixt weeping and lamentation entreated a hearing. It was accorded by both sections, but like people of half parties and half talents, they excited neither hatred nor anger. Events stepped across their prostrate bodies and marched on towards results that were utterly absolute.

Quantrell did not enquire which side he should defend; brave, the weaker; Southerner, the Confederacy; sincere, the right. His position made his creed. From Marion to him the appreciation of duty was not wide apart, the one understanding it as a Christian who never had to wear sackcloth because he was out of money to buy absolution, the other as a helpless waif blown westward by restless emigration winds and wrecked upon the pittiless lee-shore of Kansas hospitality. If for both there had been the same auspices, one would have cut off the left ear while the other cut off the right.

In May, 1861, Quantrell enlisted in Captain Stewart's company of cavalry, an organization composed of hardy settlers from what was then known as the Kansas Neutral Lands. As a private he served with conspicuous daring in the battles of Carthage, Wilson's Creek, and Lexington, but especially at the latter place did his operations in presence of the enemy attract attention. Mounted there on a splendid horse, armed with a Sharpe's carbine and four navy revolvers, for uniform a red shirt, and for oriflamme a sweeping black plume, he advanced with the farthest, fell back with the last, and was always cool, deadly, and omnipresent. General Price—himself notorious for being superbly indifferent under fire—remarked his bearing and caused mention to be made of it most favorably.

Quantrell marched with the army retreating from Lexington as far southward as the Osage River. Winter was approaching, active operations could not go on in the nature of things for some time, and the old yearning for Guerrilla service came over him again with an influence that would not be resisted. Stewart, the captain, knew of his aspirations for several days, and so did General Rains, the commander of the division to which his company was attached as an independent company. Neither objected and Quantrell turned back alone from the Osage River, skirted rapidly the flanks of the detached cavalry columns pursuing General Price, and arrived in Jackson county late in the autumn of 1861. At first his exploits were confined to but eight men—a little band that knew nothing of war save how to fight and to shoot—who lived along the border and who had already some scores to settle with the Jayhawkers. The original eight—the nucleus of a Guerrilla organization which was to astonish the whole country twice—once by its ferocity and once by its prowess—were William Haller, James and John Little, Edward Coger, Andrew Walker—the son of that Morgan Walker Quantrell had known under sterner auspices — John Hampton, James Kelly, and Solomon Basham.   Haller — a young and dauntless spirit—was one of those men who are themselves ignorant of their own powers until a crisis comes in their experience and circumstances give them a duty to perform. Just of age, impetuous as Murat, of an old and wealthy family, handsome, to the grace of a cavalier adding the stern political conviction of an Ironside, he rode through his fitful military life at a gallop and drank the wine of battle to its dregs before they brought him back from his last combat—

> "The life upon his yellow hair,
> But not within his eyes."

These eight men, or rather nine, for Quantrell commanded— encountered first their hereditary enemies, the Jayhawkers. Lane entered Missouri only upon grand occasions; Jennison every once and awhile and as a frolic.   One was a colossal thief; the other a picayune one.   Lane dealt in mules by herds, horses by droves, wagons by parks, negroes by neighborhoods, household effects by the ton, and miscellaneous plunder by the city full; Jennison contented himself with the pocket-books of his prisoners, the pin money of the women, and the wearing apparel of the children.   Lane was a real prophet of demagogueism, with insanity latent in his blood; Jennison a *sans culotte* who, looking upon himself as a bastard, sought to become legitimate by becoming brutal.

It was again in the vicinity of Morgan Walker's that Quantrell with his little command ambushed a portion of Jennison's regiment and killed five of his thieves, getting some good horses, saddles, bridles, and revolvers.   The next fight occurred upon the premises of Volney Ryan, a citizen of Jackson county, and with Company A., of Burris' regiment—a regiment of Missouri militia, notorious for three things—robbing hen-roosts, stealing horses, and running away from the enemy.   The eight Guerrillas struck Company A. just at daylight, charged it home, charged through it, and charged back again, and when they

GEORGE TODD.

returned from the pursuit they counted fifteen dead, the fruits of a running battle.

Chaos had now pretty well come again. In the wake of a civil war which permitted always the impossible to the strongest, beggars got upon horseback and began driving every decent thing before them to the devil. In the universal upheaval lean people saw how they might become fat, and paupers how they might become kings. To the surface of the cauldron—because of the tremendous heat beneath it—there came things mean, cowardly, parasitical, crouching, contemptible, bad. Beasts of prey became numerous, and birds of ill-omen flew hither and thither. The law—it was the sword; the process—it was the bayonet; the constitution — it was hung upon a gibbet; the right—the

> "Good old rule, the simple plan,
> That he can get who has the power,
> And he can keep who can."

One Searcy, claiming to be a Southern man, was stealing all over Jackson county and using violence here and there when he could not succeed through persuasion. Quantrell swooped down upon him one afternoon, tried him that night, and hung him the next morning. Before they pulled him up, he essayed to say something. He commenced: "Not so fast, gentlemen! It's awful to die until red hands have had a chance to wash themselves." Here his voice was strangled like the voice of a man who has no saliva in his mouth. Four Guerrillas dragged on the rope. There seemed to be—as his body rested at last from its contortions—the noise as of the waving of wings. Could it be that Searcy's soul was taking its flight? Seventy-five head of horses were found in the dead man's possession, all belonging to citizens of the county, and any number of title deeds to lands, notes, mortgages, and private accounts. All were returned. The execution acted as a thunder-storm, it restored the equilibrium of the moral atmosphere. The border warfare had found a chief.

The eight Guerrillas had now grown to be thirty. Among the new recruits were David Pool, John Jarrette, William Gregg, John Coger, Richard Burns, George Todd, George Shepherd, Coleman Younger, and several others of like enterprise and daring. An organization was at once effected, and

Quantrell was made Captain; William Haller, 1st Lieutenant; William Gregg, 2d; George Todd. 3d; and John Jarrette, Orderly Sergeant. The eagles were beginning to congregate; the lions to hunt *en masse.*

Pool, an unschooled Aristophanes of the civil war, laughed at calamity and mocked when any man's fear came. But for its picturesqueness, his speech would have been comedy personified. He laughed loudest when he was deadliest, and treated fortune with no more dignity in one extreme than another. Gregg—a grim Saul among the Guerrillas—made of the Confederacy a mistress, and, like the Douglass of old, was ever tender and true to her. Jarrette, the man who never knew fear, added to an immense activity an indomitable will. Events bent to him as distance disappeared before his gallops. He was, *par excellence,* a soldier of the saddle. John Coger never missed a battle nor a bullet. Wounded twenty-two times, he lived as an exemplification of what a Guerrilla could endure—the amount of lead he could comfortably get along with and keep fat. Steadfastness was his test of merit—comradeship his point of honor. He who had John Coger at his back had a mountain. Todd was the incarnate devil of battle. He thought of fighting awake, dreamed of it when asleep, mingled talk of it with topics of the day, studied campaigns as a relaxation, and went hungry many a day and shelterless many a night that he might find an enemy and have his fill of battle. Quantrell had always to hold him back, and yet he was his thunderbolt. He discussed nothing in the shape of orders. A soldier who discusses is like a hand which would think. He only charged. Were he attacked in front—a charge; in the rear—a charge; on either flank—a charge. Finally, in a desperate charge, and doing a hero's work upon the stricken rear of the 2d Colorado, he was killed. This was George Todd. Shepherd—a patient, cool, vigilant, plotting leader—he knew all the roads and streams, all the fords and passes, all modes of egress and ingress; all safe and dangerous places; all the treacherous non-combatants and the trustworthy ones—everything, indeed, that the few needed to know who were fighting the many. Burns fought. Others might have ambition and seek to sport the official attributes of rank; he fought. In addition there were among the Guerrillas few better pistol shots. It used to do Quantrell good to see him on the skirmish line. Coleman

Younger—a boy having about his neck still the purple track a rope ploughed the night the Jayhawkers shot down his old father and strung him up to a black jack—spoke rarely, and was away a great deal in the woods. What was he doing, his comrades began to enquire, one of another. He had a mission to perform—he was pistol practicing. Soon he was perfect, and then it was noticed that he laughed often and talked a great deal. There had come to him now that intrepid gaiety which plays with death. He changed devotion to his family into devotion to his country, and he fought and killed with the conscience of a hero.

The new organization was about to be baptized. Burris, raiding generally along the Missouri border, had a detachment foraging in the neighborhood of Charles Younger's farm. This Charles Younger was an uncle of Coleman, and he lived within three miles of Independence, the county-seat of Jackson county. The militia detachment numbered eighty-four and the Guerrillas thirty-two. At sunset Quantrell struck their camp. Forewarned of his coming, they were already in line. One volley settled them. Five fell at the first fire and seven more were killed in the chase. The shelter of Independence alone, where the balance of the regiment was as a breakwater, saved the detachment from utter extinction. This day—the 10th of November, 1861, Cole Younger killed a militiaman seventy-one measured yards. The pistol practice was bearing fruit.

Independence was essentially a city of fruits and flowers. About every house there was a *parterre* and contiguous to every *parterre* there was an orchard. Built where the woods and the prairies met, when it was most desirable there was sunlight, and when it was most needed there was shade. The war found it rich, prosperous and contented, and it left it as an orange that had been devoured. Lane hated it because it was a hive of secession, and Jennison preyed upon it because Guerrilla bees flew in and out. On one side the devil, on the other the deep sea, patriotism, that it might not be tempted, ran the risk very often of being drowned. Something also of Spanish intercourse and connection belonged to it. Its square was a plaza; its streets centered there; its court house was a citadel. Truer people never occupied a town; braver fathers never sent their sons to war; grander matrons never prayed to God for right, and purer women never waited through it all—the siege, the sack, the pillage and the battle—for the light to break in the east at last, the end to come in fate's own good and appointed time.

Quantrell had great admiration for Independence; his men adored it. Burris' regiment was still there—fortified in the court house—and one day in February, 1862, the Guerillas charged the town. It was a desperate assault. Quantrell and Pool dashed down one street, Cole Younger and Todd down another, Gregg and Shepherd down the third, Haller, Coger, Burns, Walker and others down the balance of the approaches to the square. Behind heavy brick walls the militia of course fought, and fought besides at a great advantage. Save seven surprised in the first moments of the rapid onset and shot down, none others were killed, and Quantrell was forced to retire from the town after taking some necessary ordnance, quartermaster and commissary supplies from the stores under the very guns of the court house. None of his men were killed, though as many as eleven were wounded. This was the initiation of Independence into the mysteries as well as the miseries of border warfare, and thereafter and without a month of cessation, it was to get darker and darker for the beautiful town.

Swinging back past Independence from the east the day after it had been charged, Quantrell moved up in the neighborhood of Westport and put scouts upon the roads leading into Kansas City. Two officers belonging to Jennison's regiment were picked up—a Lieutenant, who was young, and a Captain, who was of middle-age. They had only time to pray. Quantrell always gave time for this, and had always performed to the letter the last commissions left by those who were doomed. The Lieutenant did not want to pray. "It could do no good," he said. "God knew about as much concerning the disposition it was intended to be made of his soul as he could suggest to him." The Captain took a quarter of an hour to make his peace. Both were shot. Men commonly die at God's appointed time; beset by Guerrillas, suddenly and unawares. Another of the horrible surprises of civil war.

At first, and because of Quantrell's presence, Kansas City swarmed like an ant-hill during a rain-storm; afterwards, and when the dead officers were carried in, like a firebrand had been cast thereon. A regiment came out after the Guerillas, but

Quantrell fell back through Westport, killed nine straggling
Federals there, and made his camp, after a rapid march, at
David George's place on the Sni, a large stream of water in
Jackson county, abounding in fastnesses and skirted by almost
inaccessible precipices and thickets. From the Sni to the Blue
—another Jackson county stream historic in Guerrilla annals—
Quantrell returned the third day. While at the house of Charles
Cowherd a courier came up with the information that Independence, which had not been garrisoned for some little time, was
again in possession of a company of militia. Another attack was
resolved upon. On the night of February 20th, 1862, Quantrell
marched to the vicinity of the town and waited for the daylight.
The first few faint streaks in the east constituted the signal.
There was a dash altogether down South Main street, a storm
of cheers and bullets, a roar of iron feet on the rocks of the
roadway, and the surprise was left to work itself out. It did,
and reversely. Instead of the one company reported in possession of the town, four were found, numbering three hundred
men. They manned the court house in a moment, made of its
doors an eruption and of its windows a tempest, killed a noble
Guerrilla, Young George, shot Quantrell's horse from under him,
held their own everywhere and held the fort. As before, all
who were killed among the Federals, and they lost seventeen,
were those killed in the first few moments of the charge. Those
who hurried alive into the court house were safe. Young
George, dead in his first battle, had all the promise of a bright
career. None rode further nor faster in the charge, and when
he fell he fell so close to the fence about the fortified building
that it was with difficulty his comrades took his body out from
under a point-blank fire and bore it off in safety.

It was a part of Quantrell's tactics to disband every now and
then. "Scattered soldiers," he argued, "make a scattered
trail. The regiment that has but one man to hunt can never
find him." The men needed heavier clothing and better horses,
and the winter, more than ordinarily severe, was beginning to
tell. A heavy Federal force was also concentrating in Kansas
City, ostensibly to do service along the Mississippi River, really
to drive out of Jackson county a Guerrilla band that under no
circumstances possible at that time could have numbered over
fifty. Quantrell, therefore, for an accumulation of reasons,

ordered a brief disbandment. It had hardly been accomplished before Independence swapped a witch for a devil. Burris evacuated the town; Jennison occupied it. In his regiment were trappers who trapped for dry goods, fishermen who fished for groceries. At night passers-by were robbed of their pocketbooks; in the morning market women of their meat baskets. Neither wiser, perhaps, nor better than the Egyptians, the patient and all-suffering citizens had got rid of the lean kine in order to make room for the lice.

Alert always, and keeping a vigilant eye ever upon the military horizon, Quantrell ordered a rally of his disbanded Guerrillas. As it was in the days of the raiding Highlanders, so in the times that tried men's souls along the border. If Rhoderick Dhu had his Malise, Captain Quantrell had his splendid rider. From house to house the summons flew. The farmer left his plow to speed it, the maiden forgot her trysting to help on the messenger, settlement spoke to settlement through a smoke in a hollow or a fire on a hill, patriotism had a language unknown to the invaders, and the mustering-place rarely ever missed a man.

At the appointed time, and at the place of David George, the reassembling was as it should be. Quantrell meant to attack Jennison in Independence and destroy him if possible, and so moved in that direction as far as the Little Blue Church. Here he met Allen Parmer, a regular red Indian of a scout, who never forgot to count a column or know the line of march of an enemy, and Parmer reported that instead of three hundred Jayhawkers being in Independence there were six hundred. Too many for thirty-two men to grapple, and fortified at that, they all said. It would be murder in the first degree and unnecessary murder in addition. Quantrell, foregoing with a struggle the chance to get at his old acquaintance of Kansas, flanked Independence and stopped for the night at the residence of Zan. Harris, a true Southern man and a keen observer of passing events. Early the next morning he crossed the Big Blue at the bridge on the main road to Kansas City, surprised and shot down a detachment of thirteen Federals watching it, burned the structure to the water, and marched rapidly in a south-west direction, leaving Westport to the right. At noon the command was at the residence of Alexander Majors, a partner in that celebrated freighting firm of Russell, Majors & Waddell, the pioneers of the West as well as its victims. Russell was a giant in a civilization which produced big men. The plains were immense and so was his intellect. He planned business as generals planned campaigns, and took in the whole territory from Philadelphia to Santa Fe at a glance. Waddell was his cabinet man, Majors his man for the field. Altogether they established an empire and created a dynasty which took the unscrupulous power of a venal government to uproot and destroy. It was the empire of business sense and the dynasty of executive ability. When the war came they were looked upon as disloyal in order that they might be robbed, and Congress finished what the government had begun. In revolutions there is no repentance, there is only expiation; but who in the end is to make good this plunder of its citizens by a power constituted solely to protect them?

After the meal at Majors', Quantrell resumed his march, sending Haller and Todd ahead with an advance guard and bringing up the rear himself with the main body of twenty-two men. Night overtook him at the Tate House, three miles east of Little Santa Fe, a small town in Jackson county close to the Kansas line, and he camped there. Haller and Todd were still further along, no communication being established between these two parts of a common whole. The day had been cold and the darkness was bitter. That weariness which comes with a hard ride, a rousing fire, and a hearty supper, fell early upon the Guerrillas. One sentinel at the gate kept drowsy watch, and the night began to deepen. In various attitudes and in various places, twenty-one of twenty-two men were sound asleep, the twenty-second keeping watch and ward at the gate in the freezing weather. It was just twelve o'clock, and the fire in the capacious fire-place was burning low. Suddenly a shout was heard. The well-known challenge of "Who are you?" arose on the night air, followed by a pistol shot, and then a volley. Quantrell, sleeping always like a cat, shook himself loose from his blankets and stood erect in the glare of the firelight. Three hundred Federals, following all day on his trail, had marked him take cover at night and went to bag him boots and breeches. They had hitched their horses back in the brush and stole upon the dwelling afoot. So noiseless had been their advance, and so close were they upon the sentinel before they were discovered, that he had only time to cry out, fire, and rush for the timber. He could not get back to his comrades, for some Federals were between him and the door. As he ran he received a volley, but in the darkness he escaped.

The house was surrounded! To the men within-side this meant, unless they could get out, death by fire and sword. Quantrell was trapped, he who had been accorded the fox's cunning and the panther's activity. He glided to the window and looked out cautiously. The cold stars shone, and the blue figures under them and on every hand seemed colossal. The fist of a heavy man struck the door hard, and a deep voice commanded: "Make a light." There had been no firing as yet save the shot of the sentinel and its answering volley. Quantrell went quietly to all who were still asleep and bade them get up and get ready. It was the moment when death had to be looked in the face. Not a word was spoken. The heavy fist was still hammering at the door. Quantrell crept to it on tip-toe, listened a second at the sounds outside, and fired. "Oh!" and a stalwart Federal fell prone across the porch, dying. "You asked for a light, and you've got it, d—n you," Quantrell ejaculated, cooler than his pistol barrel. Afterwards there was no more bravado. "Bar the doors and barricade the windows!" he shouted; "quick, men!" Beds were freely used and applicable furniture. Little and Shepherd stood by one door; Jarrette, Younger, Toler, and Hoy barricaded the other and made the windows bullet-proof. Outside the Federal fusilade was incessant. Mistaking Tate's house for a frame house when it was built of brick, the commander of the enemy could be heard encouraging his men to shoot low and riddle the dwelling. Presently there was a lull. Neither party fired for the space of several minutes, and Quantrell spoke to his people: "Boys, we are in a tight place. We can't stay here, and I do not mean to surrender. All who want to follow me out can say so; all who prefer to give up without a rush can also say so. I will do the best I can for them." Four concluded to appeal to the Federals for protection; seventeen to follow Quantrell to the death. He called a parley, and informed the Federal commander that four of his followers wanted to surrender. "Let them come out," was the order. Out they went and the fight began again. Too eager to see what manner of men their prisoners were, the Federals holding the west front of the house huddled about them eagerly. Ten Guerrillas from the upper story fired at the crowd and brought down six. A roar followed this, and a rush back again to cover at the double quick. It was hot work now. Quantrell, supported by James Little, Cole Younger, Hoy, and Stephen Shores, held the upper story, while Jarrette, Toler, George Shepherd, and others held the lower. Every shot told. The proprietor of the house, Major Tate, was a Southern hero, gray-headed but Roman. He went about laughing. "Help me to get my family out, boys," he said, "and I will help you to hold the house. It's about as good a time for me to die, I reckon, as any other, if so be that God wills it. But the old woman is only a woman." Another parley. Would the Federal commander let the women and children out? Yes, gladly, and the old man too. There was eagerness for this, and much of veritable cunning. The family occupied an ell of the mansion with which there was no communication from the main building where Quantrell and his men were save by way of a door which opened upon a porch, and this porch was under the concentrated fire of the assailants. After the family moved out the attacking party would throw skirmishers in, and then—the torch. Quantrell understood it in a moment, and spoke up to the father of the family: "Go out, Major. It is your duty to be with your wife and children." The old man went, protesting. Perhaps for forty years the blood had not coursed so pleasantly and so rapidly through his veins. Giving ample time for the family to get safely beyond the range of the fire of the besieged, Quantrell went back to his post and looked out. He saw two Federals standing together beyond revolver range. "Is there a shot-gun here?" he asked. Cole Younger brought him one loaded with buck-shot. Thrusting half his body out the nearest window, and receiving as many volleys as there were sentinels, he fired the two barrels of his gun so near together that they sounded as one barrel. Both Federals fell, one dead, the other mortally wounded. There followed this daring and conspicuous feat a yell so piercing and exultant that even the horses. hitched in the timber fifty yards away, reared in their fright and snorted with terror. Black columns of smoke blew past the windows where the

Guerrillas were, and a bright red flame leaped up toward the sky on the wings of the wind. The ell of the house had been fired, and was burning fiercely. Quantrell's face—just a little paler than usual—had a set look that was not good to see. The tiger was at bay. Many of the men's revolvers were empty, and in order to gain time to load them, another parley was had. The talk was of surrender. The Federal commander demanded immediate submission, and Shepherd, with a voice heard above the rage and the roar of the flames, pleaded for twenty minutes. No. Ten? No. Five? No. Then the commander cried out in a voice not a whit inferior to Shepherd's in compass: "You have one minute. If, at its expiration, you have not surrendered, not a single man among you shall escape alive." "Thank you," said Cole Younger, *sotto voce*, "catching comes before hanging." "Count sixty then, and be d—d to you," Shepherd shouted as a parting volley, and then a strange silence fell upon all these desperate men face to face with imminent death. When every man was ready, Quantrell said briefly: "Shot guns to the front.' Six, loaded heavily with buck-shot, were borne there, and he put himself at the head of the six men who carried them. Behind these were those having only revolvers. In single file, the charging column was formed in the main room of the building. The glare of the burning ell lit it up as though the sun was shining there. Some tightened their pistol belts. One fell upon his knees and prayed. Nobody scoffed at him, for God was in that room. He is everywhere when heroes confess. There were seventeen who were about to receive the fire of three hundred.

Ready! Quantrell flung the door wide open and leaped out. The shot-gun men—Jarrette, Younger, Shepherd, Toler, Little and Hoy were hard behind him. Right and left from the thin short column a fierce fire beat into the very faces of the Federals, who recoiled in some confusion, shooting, however, from every side. There was a yell, and a grand rush, and when the end had come and all the fixed realities figured up, the enemy had eighteen killed, twenty-nine badly wounded, and five prisoners, and the captured horses of the Guerrillas. Not a man of Quantrell's command was touched, as it broke through the cordon on the south of the house and gained the sheltering timber beyond. Hoy, as he rushed out the third from Quantrell and fired both barrels of his gun, was so near to a stalwart Federal that he was struck over the head with a musket and knocked senseless. To capture him afterwards was like capturing a dead man. But little pursuit was attempted. Quantrell halted at the timber, built a fire, reloaded every gun and pistol, and took a philosophical view of the situation. Enemies were all about him. He had lost five men—four of whom, however, he was glad to get rid of—and the balance were afoot. Patience! He had just escaped from an environment sterner than any yet spread for him, and fortune was not apt to offset one splendid action by another exactly opposite. Choosing, therefore, a rendezvous upon the head-waters of the Little Blue, another historic stream of Jackson county, he reached the residence of David Wilson late the next morning, after a forced march of great exhaustion. The balance of the night, however, had still to be one of surprises and counter-surprises not alone to the Federals, but to the other portion of Quantrell's command under Haller and Todd. Encamped four miles south of the Tate House, the battle there had aroused them instantly. Getting to saddle quickly, they were galloping back to the help of their comrades when a Federal force, one hundred strong, met them full in the road. Some minutes of savage fighting ensued, but Haller could not hold his own with thirteen men, and retreated, firing, to the brush. Afterwards everything was made plain. The four men who surrendered so abjectly at the Tate House imagined it would bring help to their condition if they told all they knew, and they told without solicitation the story of Haller's advance and the whereabouts of his camp. An hundred men were instantly despatched to surprise it or storm it, but the firing had aroused the isolated Guerrillas, and they got out in safety, after a rattling fight of some twenty minutes.

Moving up from David Wilson's to John Flannery's, Quantrell waited until Haller joined him, and then disbanded for the second time, fixing his rendezvous—when all the men were well mounted again—at a designated point on the Sni.

In April, 1862, Quantrell, with seventeen men, was camped at the residence of Samuel C. Clark, situated three miles southeast of Stony Point, in Jackson county. He had spent the night there and was waiting for breakfast the next morning, when

Captain Peabody, at the head of one hundred Federal cavalry, surprised the Guerrillas and came on at the charge, shooting and yelling. Instantly dividing the detachment in order that the position might be effectively held, Quantrell, with nine men, took the dwelling, and Gregg, with eight, occupied the smoke-house. For a while the fight was at long range, Peabody holding tenaciously to the timber in front of Clark's, distant about one hundred yards, and refusing to come out. Presently, however, he did an unsoldierly thing—or, rather, an unskillful thing—he mounted his men and forced them to charge the dwelling on horseback. Quantrell's detachment reserved their fire until the foremost horsemen were within thirty feet, and Gregg permitted those operating against his position to come even closer. Then a quick, sure volley and twenty-seven men and horses went down together. Badly demoralized, but in no manner defeated, Peabody rallied again in the timber, while Quantrell, breaking out from the dwelling-house and gathering up Gregg as he went, charged the Federals fiercely in return and with something of success. The impetus of the rush carried him past a portion of the Federal line, where some of their horses were hitched, and the return of the wave brought with it nine valuable animals. It was over the horses that Andrew Blunt had a hand-to-hand fight with a splendid Federal trooper. Both were very brave. Blunt had just joined. No one knew his history. He asked no questions and he answered none. Some said he had once belonged to the cavalry of the regular army; others, that behind the terrible record of the Guerrillas he wished to find isolation. Singling out a fine sorrel horse from among the number fastened in his front, Blunt was just about to unhitch him when a Federal trooper, superbly mounted, dashed down to the line and fired. Blunt left his position by the side of the horse and strode out in the open, accepting the challenge defiantly and closing with his antagonist. The first time he fired he missed, although many of the men believed him a better pistol shot than Quantrell. The Federal calmly sat his horse, fired the second shot deliberately and again missed. Blunt went four paces towards him, took a quick aim and fired very much as a man would at something running. Out of the Federal's blue overcoat a little jet of dust spurted up and he reeled in his seat. The man, hard hit in the right breast, did not fall, however.. He gripped his saddle with his knees, cavalry fashion, steadied himself in his stirrups, and fired three times at Blunt in quick succession. They were now but twenty paces apart, and the Guerrilla was shortening the distance. When at ten he fired his third shot, the heavy dragoon ball struck the gallant Federal fair in the forehead and knocked him dead from his horse. While the duel was in progress, brief as it was, Blunt had not watched his rear, to gain which a dozen Federals had started from the extreme right. He saw them, but he did not hurry. Going back to the coveted steed, he mounted him deliberately and dashed back through the lines closed up behind him, getting a fierce hurrah of encouragement from his own comrades and a wicked volley from the enemy.

It was time. A second company of Federals in the neighborhood, attracted by the firing, had made a junction with Peabody and were already closing in upon the houses from the south. Surrounded now by one hundred and sixty men, Quantrell was almost in the same desperate strait as at the Tate House. His horses were in the hands of the Federals, it was some little distance to the timber, and the environment was complete. Captain Peabody, himself a Kansas man, knew who led the forces opposed to him and burned with the desire to make a finish of this Quantrell and his reckless band at one clean sweep. Not content with the one hundred and sixty men already in positions about the house, he sent off post haste to Pink Hill for additional reinforcements. Emboldened also by their numbers, the Federals had approached so close to the positions held by the Guerrillas that it was possible for them to utilize the shelter the fences gave. Behind these they ensconced themselves while pouring a merciless fusillade upon the dwelling-house and smoke-house in comparative immunity. This annoyed Quantrell, distressed Gregg and made Cole Younger—one of the coolest heads in council ever consulted—look a little anxious. Finally a solution was found. Quantrell would draw the fire of this ambuscade; he would make the concealed enemy show himself. Ordering all to be ready and to fire the very moment the opportunity for execution was best, he dashed out from the dwelling-house to the smoke-house, and from the smoke-house back again to the dwelling. Eager to kill the daring man, and excited somewhat
5

by their own efforts made to do it, the Federals exposed themselves recklessly. Then, owing to the short range, the revolvers of the Guerrillas began to tell with deadly effect. Twenty at least were shot down along the fences, and as many more wounded and disabled. It was thirty steps from one house to the other, yet Quantrell made the venture eight distinct and separate times, not less than one hundred men firing at him as he came and went. On his garments there was not even the smell of fire. His life seemed to be charmed—his person protected by some superior presence. When at last even this artifice would no longer enable his men to fight with any degree of equality, Quantrell determined to abandon the houses and the horses and make a dash as of old to the nearest timber. "I had rather lose a thousand horses," he said, when some one remonstrated with him, "than a single man like those who have fought with me this day. Heroes are scarce; horses are everywhere."

In the swift rush that came now, fortune again favored him. Almost every revolver belonging to the Federals was empty. They had been relying altogether upon their carbines in the fight. After the first onset on horseback—one in which the revolvers were principally used—they had failed to reload, and had nothing but empty guns in their hands after Quantrell for the last time drew their fire and dashed away on the heels of it to the timber. Pursuit was not attempted. Enraged at the escape of the Guerrillas, and burdened with a number of dead and wounded altogether out of proportion to the forces engaged, Captain Peabody caused to be burned everything upon the premises which had a plank or a shingle about it.

Something else yet was also to be done. Getting out afoot as best he could, Quantrell saw a company of cavalry making haste from towards the direction of Pink Hill. It was but a short distance to where the road he was skirting crossed a creek, and commanding this crossing was a perpendicular bluff inaccessible to horsemen. Thither he hurried. The work of ambushment was the work only of a moment. George Todd, alone of all the Guerrillas, had brought with him from the house a shot-gun. In running for life, the most of them were unincumbered. The approaching Federals were the reinforcements Peabody had ordered up from Pink Hill, and as Quantrell's defence had lasted one hour and a half, they were well on their way. As they came to the creek the foremost riders halted that their horses might drink. Soon others crowded in, until all the ford was thick with animals. Just then from the bluff above a leaden rain fell as hail might from a cloudless sky. Rearing steeds trampled upon wounded riders. The dead dyed the clear water red. Wild panic laid hold of the helpless mass cut into gaps, and flight beyond the range of the deadly revolvers came first to all and uppermost. There was a rally, however. Once out from under fire the Lieutenant commanding the detachment called a halt. He was full of dash, and meant to see more of the unknown on the top of the hill. Dismounting his men and putting himself at their head, he turned back for a fight, marching resolutely forward to the bluff. Quantrell waited for the the attack to develop itself. The Lieutenant moved right onward. When within fifty paces of the position, George Todd rose up from behind a rock and covered the young Federal with his unerring shot-gun. It seemed a pity to kill him, he was so brave and collected, and yet he fell riddled just as he had drawn his sword and shouted "Forward!" to his lagging men. To Todd's signal there succeeded a fierce revolver volley, and again were the Federals driven from the hill and back towards their horses. Satisfied with the results of this fight—made solely as a matter of revenge for burning Clark's building— Quantrell fell away from the ford and continued his retreat on towards his rendezvous upon the waters of the Sni. Peabody, however, had not yet had his say. Coming on himself in the direction of Pink Hill, and mistaking these reinforcements for Guerrillas, he had quite a lively fight with them, each detachment getting in several vollies and killing and wounding a goodly number before either discovered the mistake.

CHAPTER VII.

QUANTRELL and his command were all on foot again, and Jackson county was filled with troops. At Kansas City there was a large garrison, with smaller ones at Independence, Pink Hill, Lone Jack, Stoney Point, and Sibley. Peabody caused the report to be circulated that a majority of Quantrell's men were wounded, and that if the brush was scoured thoroughly they might be picked up here and there and summarily disposed of. Raiding bands therefore began the hunt. Old men were imprisoned because they could give no information of a concealed enemy; young men were murdered outright; women were insulted and abused. The uneasiness that had heretofore rested upon the county gave place now to a feeling of positive fear. The Jayhawkers on one side and the militia on the other made matters hot. All travelling was dangerous. People at night closed their eyes in dread lest the morrow should usher in a terrible awakening. One incident of the hunt is a bloody memory yet with many of the older settlers of Jackson county. An aged man by the name of Blythe, believing his own house to be his own, fed those whom he pleased to feed, and sheltered all whom it suited him to shelter. Among his many warm personal friends was Coleman Younger. The Colonel commanding the fort at Independence sent a scout one day to find Younger, and to make the country people tell where he might be found. Old man Blythe was not at home, but his son was—a fearless lad of twelve years. He was taken to the barn and ordered to confess everything he knew of Quantrell, Younger, and their whereabouts. If he failed to speak truly he was to be killed. The boy, in no manner frightened, kept them some moments in conversation, waiting for an opportunity to escape. Seeing at last what he imagined to be a chance, he dashed away from his captors and entered the house under a perfect shower of balls. There, seizing a pistol and rushing through the back door towards some timber, a ball struck him in the spine just as he reached the garden fence and he fell back dying but spendid in his boyish courage to the last. Turning over on his face as the Jayhawkers rushed up to finish him, he shot one dead, mortally wounded another, and severely wounded the third. Before he could shoot the fourth time, seventeen bullets were put into his body. It seemed as if God's vengeance was especially exercised in the righting of this terrible wrong. An old negro man who happened to be at Blythe's house at the time, was a witness of the bloody deed, and, afraid of his own life, ran hurriedly into the brush. There he came unawares upon Younger, Quantrell, Haller, Todd, and eleven of their men. Noticing the great excitement under which the negro labored, they forced him to tell them the whole story. It was yet time for an ambuscade. On the road back to Independence was a pass between two embankments known as "The Blue Cut." In width it was about fifty yards, and the height of each embankment was about thirty feet. Quantrell dismounted his men, stationing some at each end of the passage-way, and some at the top and on either side. Not a shot was to be fired until the returning Federals had entered in, front and rear. From the Blue Cut this fatal spot was afterward known as the Slaughter Pen. Of the thirty-eight Federals sent out after Cole Younger, and who, because they could not find him, had brutally murdered an innocent boy, seventeen were killed, while five—not too badly shot to be able to ride—barely managed to escape into Independence, the avenging Guerrillas hard upon their heels.

The next rendezvous was at Reuben Harris', ten miles south of Independence, and thither all the command went, splendidly mounted again and eager for employment. Some days of preparation were necessary. Richard Hall, a fighting black-smith who shot as well as he shoed, and knew a trail as thoroughly as a piece of steel, had need to exercise much of his handiwork in order to make the horses good for cavalry. Then there were many rounds of cartridges to make. A Guerrilla knew nothing of an ordnance-master. His laboratory was in his luck. If a capture did not gain him caps, he had to fall back on ruse, or stratagem, or blockade-running square out. Powder and lead in the raw were enough, for if with these he could not make himself presentable at inspection he had no calling as a fighter in the brush.

It was Quantrell's intention at this time to attack Harrisonville, the county-seat of Cass county, and capture it if possible. With this object in view, and after having made every preparation available for a vigorous campaign, he moved eight miles east of Independence, camping near the Little Blue, in the vicinity of Job Crabtree's. He camped always near or in a house. For this he had two reasons. First, that its occupants might gather up for him all the news possible; and, second, that in the event of a surprise a sure rallying point would always be at hand. He had a theory that after a Guerrilla was given time to get over the first effects of a sudden charge or ambushment, the very nature of his military *status* made him invincible; that after an opportunity was afforded him to think, a surrender was next to an impossibility.

Before there was time to attack Harrisonville, however, a scout reported Peabody again on the war-path, this time bent on an utter extermination of the Guerrillas. And he well nigh kept his word. From Job Crabtree's Quantrell had moved to an unoccupied building known as the Low House, and then again from this house he had gone to some contiguous timber to bivouac for the night. About 10 o'clock the sky suddenly became overcast, a fresh wind blew up from the east, and rain fell in torrents. Again the house was occupied, the horses being hitched along the fence in the rear of it, the door on the south, and the only door, having a bar put across it in lieu of a sentinel. Such soldiering was perfectly inexcusable, and it taught Quantrell a lesson he remembered to the day of his death. In the morning preceding the night of the attack Lieutenant Nash, of Peabody's regiment, commanding two hundred men, had struck Quantrell's trail, lost it later on, and then found it again just about sun-set. He was advised of his having gone from the Low House to the brush, and of his having come back to it when the rain began to fall heavily. To a certain extent this seeking shelter was a necessity on the part of Quantrell. The men had no cartridge boxes, and not all of them overcoats. If once their ammunition was permitted to become damaged, it would be as though sheep should attack wolves. Nash, supplied with everything needed in any weather, waited patiently for the Guerrillas to become snugly ensconced under shelter, and then surrounded the house. Before a gun was fired, the Federals had every horse belonging to the Guerrillas, and were bringing to bear upon the only door every available carbine in the command. At first all was confusion. Across the logs which once had supported an upper floor, some boards had been laid, and sleeping upon them were Todd, Blunt, and William Carr. Favored by the almost impenetrable darkness, Quantrell determined upon an immediate abandonment of the house. He called loudly twice for all to follow him and dashed through the door under a galling fire. Those in the loft did not hear him, and maintained in reply to the Federal vollies a lively fusillade. Then Cole Younger, James Little, Joseph Gilchrist, and a young Irish boy—a brave new recruit—turned back to help their comrades. The house became a furnace. At each of the two corners on the south these four men fought, Younger calling on Todd in the interval of every volley to come out of the loft and come to the brush. They started at last. It was four hundred yards to the nearest shelter, and the ground was very muddy. Gilchrist was shot down, the Irish boy was killed, Blunt was wounded and captured, Carr surrendered, Younger had his hat shot away, Little was unhurt, and Todd, scratched in four places, finally got safely to the timber. But it was a miracle. Twenty Federals singled him out as well as they could in the darkness and kept close at his heels, firing whenever a gun was loaded. Todd had a musket which, when it seemed as if they were all upon him at once, he would point at the nearest and make pretense that he was going to shoot. When they halted and dodged about to get out of range, he would dash away again, gaining what space he could until he had to turn and re-enact the same unpleasant pantomime. Reaching the woods at last, he fired point blank and in reality now, killing with a single discharge one pursuer and wounding four. Part of Nash's command were still on the track of Quantrell, but after losing five killed and a number wounded, they returned again to the house but returned too late for the continued battle. The dead and the two prisoners were all that were left to them.

Little Blue was bankfull, and the country was swarming with militia. For the third time Quantrell was afoot with unrelenting pursuers upon his trail in every direction. At daylight Nash would be after him again, river or no river. He must get over or fare worse. The rain still poured down; muddy, forlorn, well-nigh worn out, yet in no manner demoralized, just as Quantrell reached the Little Blue he saw on the other bank Toler, one of his own soldiers, sitting in a canoe. Thenceforward the work of crossing was easy, and Nash, coming on an hour afterwards, received a volley at the ford where he expected to find a lot of helpless and unresisting men.

This fight at the Low House occurred the first week in May, 1862, and caused the expedition against Harrisonville to be abandoned. Three times surprised, and three times losing all horses, saddles, and bridles, it became again necessary to disband the Guerrillas in this instance as in the two preceding it. The men were dismissed for thirty days with orders to remount themselves, while Quantrell—taking Todd into his confidence and acquainting him fully with his plans—started in his company for Hannibal. It had become urgently necessary to replenish the supply of revolver caps. The usual trade with Kansas City had been cut off. Of late the captures had not been as plentiful as formerly. Recruits were coming in, and the season for larger operations and enterprises was at hand. In exploits where peril and excitement were about evenly divided, Quantrell took great delight. He was so cool, so calm; he had played before such a deadly game; he knew so well how to smile when a smile would win, and to frown when a frown was a better card to play, that something in this expedition appealed to everything quixotic in his intrepidity. Todd was all iron; Quantrell all guile. Todd would go at a circular-saw; Quantrell would sharpen its teeth and grease it where the friction was. One purred and killed; the other roared and killed. What mattered the mode, however, so only the end was the same.

Clad in the full uniform of Federal Majors—supplies of which Quantrell kept constantly on hand even at a day so early in the war as this—they rode to Hamilton, a little town on the Hannibal and St. Joseph Railroad, and remained for the night at the principal hotel. A Federal garrison was there—two companies of Iowa infantry—and the Captain commanding took a great fancy to Todd, insisting that he should leave the hotel for his quarters and share his blankets with him.

Two days were spent in Hannibal, where an entire Federal regiment was stationed. Here Quantrell was more circumspect. When asked to give an account of himself and his companion, he replied promptly that Todd was the Major of the Sixth Missouri Cavalry and himself the Major of the Ninth. Unacquainted with either organization, the commander at Hannibal had no reason to believe otherwise. Then he asked about that special cut-throat Quantrell. Was it true that he fought under a black flag? Had he really ever belonged to the Jayhawkers? How much truth was in the stories the newspapers told of his operations and his prowess? Quantrell became voluble. In rapid yet picturesque language he painted a perfect picture of the war along the border. He told of Todd, Jarrette, Blunt, Younger, Haller, Poole, Shepherd, Gregg, Little, the Cogers, and all of his best men just as they were, and himself also just as he was, and closed the conversation emphatically by remarking: "If you were here, Colonel, surrounded as you are by a thousand soldiers, and they wanted you, they would come here and get you."

From Hannibal—after buying quietly and at various times and in various places fifty thousand revolver caps—Quantrell and Todd went boldly into St. Joseph. This city was full of soldiers. Colonel Harrison B. Branch was there in command of a regiment of militia—a brave, conservative, right-thinking soldier—and Quantrell introduced himself to Branch as Major Henderson, of the Sixth Missouri. Todd, by this time, had put on in lieu of a Major's epaulettes, with its distinguishing leaf, the barred ones of a Captain. "Too many Majors traveling together," quaintly remarked Todd, "are like too many roses in a bouquet: the other flowers don't have a chance. Let me be a Captain for the balance of the trip."

Colonel Branch made himself very agreeable to Major Henderson and Captain Gordon, and asked Todd if he was any relation to the somewhat notorious Si. Gordon, of Platte, relating at the same time an interesting adventure he once had with him. *En route* from St. Louis, in 1861, to the headquarters of his regiment, Colonel Branch, with one hundred and thirty thousand dollars on his person, found that he would have to remain over night in Weston and the better part of the next day. Before he got out of the town Gordon took it, and with it he took Colonel Branch. Many of Gordon's men were known to him, and it was eminently to his interest just then to renew old acquaintanceship and be extremely complaisant to the new. Wherever he could find the largest number of the Guerrillas, there he was among them, calling for whisky, every now and then, and telling incessantly some agreeable story or amusing anecdote. Thus he got through with what seemed to him an interminably long day. Not a dollar of his money was touched, Gordon releasing him unconditionally when the town was abandoned and bidding him make haste to get out lest the next lot of raiders made it the worse for him.

For three days, off and on, Quantrell was either with Branch at his quarters, or in company with him about town. Todd elsewhere and indefatigable was rapidly buying caps and revolvers. Branch introduced Quantrell to General Ben. Loan, discussed Penick with him and Penick's regiment — a St. Joseph officer destined to give Quantrell in the near future some stubborn fighting—passed in review the military situation, incidentally referred to the Guerrillas of Jackson county and the savage nature of the warfare going on there, predicted the absolute destruction of African slavery, and assisted Quantrell in many ways in making his mission thoroughly successful. For the first and the last time in his life Colonel Branch was disloyal to the government and its flag—he gave undoubted aid and encouragement during those three days to about as uncompromising an enemy as either ever had.

From St. Joseph Quantrell and Todd came to Kansas City in a hired hack, first sending into Jackson county by a man unquestionably devoted to the South the whole amount of the purchases made in both Hannibal and St. Joseph.

Within three miles of Kansas City a Federal sentinel on outpost duty rudely halted the driver of the hack, an Irishman as belligerant as a game cock, and wanted to know who *he* was, what sort of people his passengers were, and what business decent hackmen had traveling at such an unseemly hour of the night. The driver answered curtly, assuring the soldier that his passengers were two Illinois gentlemen, and that they were going about their own business and into Kansas City. During the dialogue Todd quietly opened the hack door opposite to the sentinel and stepped out. Quantrell followed him. It was quite dark, but they knew the direction from the course of the river and followed it down to the farm of William Bledsoe, a staunch Southerner and a man of immense assistance to the Guerrillas in many ways. The poor driver, however, fared badly. In order to verify the truth of his report, the sentinel examined the hack for himself, only to find it empty. Neither his vociferations, nor the look of genuine surprise upon his face at the trick his passengers had played him, saved him from the guard house that night, and from a good long term in prison afterwards.

Blunt, entirely recovered from his wound, was at Bledsoe's. Three nights after his capture he had escaped from Peabody, taking with him a captain's horse, saddle and bridle, and killing two of the guards who tried to halt him. With Blunt were six others of the command, who joined Quantrell and came on with him to Jackson county. At David George's, Gregg, with another detachment, was ready for work, and at John More's Jarrette and Younger—having in charge another detachment— were waiting for the sounding of the tocsin. Soon a veritable hornet's nest was stirred up, the swarming, buzzing, and sting- ing of the next few days being desperately wicked. Quantrell had not yet succeeded in getting all of his men together when a scout of twenty-five Federals struck four of his men at John Shepherd's, killed Theodore Blythe, and burned a couple of houses belonging to two friends of the Guerrillas. An eye for an eye was the edict, and a tooth for a tooth. Quantrell, resting a little from his recent trip, was at Toler's when the news of the raid was brought to him. Taking eight men instantly and selecting a spot on the Independence and Harri- sonville road eight miles south of Independence, as the place of ambuscade, he stationed eight as deadly men to do his deadly work as ever mounted a horse or fired a pistol. Quantrell and George Shepherd occupied what might be called the centre of the line, Jarrette, Oll. Shepherd, and Mart. Shepherd, the rear or left, and Todd, Blunt, Little, and Younger the front or right. As a signal—when the rear files of the Federal column had passed well beyond John Jarrette and his two comrades—Jar-

rette was to fire, and then the entire squad was to charge.
Every order was obeyed to the letter.   Never a bloodier overthrow followed a b i :fer fight.   Three minutes—five at the very
furthest—ended all.   Only one out of twenty-five escaped.
Furious before, this savage episode made Peabody ferocious.
He swarmed out of Independence with two hundred men and
spread himself over the country, shooting at every male thing
he saw.   Quantrell, Jarrette, and Todd were together and were
pressed by twenty Federals for seventeen miles.   It was a stern
chase and a long one, and ended only when the night fell, each
Guerrilla losing his horse, and each receiving a slight wound.
Seven of the twenty pursuers were killed and five wounded.
At John Shepherd's, Younger, Oliver Shepherd and George
Shepherd were surrounded by another detachment of Federals
numbering thirty-two.   Everything fought about the premises.
Indeed it was a day of battles in Jackson county—battles of
twos and threes—battles of squads and parts of companies—
battles by bush and stone—battles here, there, and everywhere.
It was getting hot for the three Guerrillas in John Shepherd's
house, and Cole Younger was just on the eve of sallying out at
the head of the two Shepherds, when Scott, Martin Shepherd,
John Coger, and Little attacked the Federals furiously in the
rear, making a sufficient diversion for all purposes of escape.

It was time to concentrate; the Guerrillas were being
devoured piece-meal.   Quantrell multiplied himself.   Gathering
up Haller at Morgan Walker's, and Gregg at Stony Point, he
galloped down into Johnson county in order to scatter his trail
a little.   In the intervals of picquet fighting he recruited.
Some splendid fellows came to him here—John Brinker, Ogden,
Halley, McBurgess, Thomas Little, Joseph Fickell, William
Davenport, and several others.   In a week he was back again
in Jackson county, and from Jackson county into Kansas,
surprising the town of Aubry, capturing its garrison, consisting
of one company, and putting all but one to the sword who were
not killed in the attack.   This single exception was a young
Lieutenant from Brown county, clever of speech, amiable of
disposition, and artless as a school girl.   He seemed never to
have realized the manner of men who had him.   Not so much a
philosopher as he was free from guile, he became an enigma to
the Guerrillas because they had never made the acquaintance of

his species. Quantrell kept him for purposes of exchange. A good man of his, Hoy, had been knocked senseless the night of the fight at the Low House, and captured, and he wanted to get him released. The Lieutenant was offered in exchange for the private, but not for the Guerrillas were any of the immunities of civilized war; Quantrell's courteous application was thrown back rudely in his face. The lines were being drawn tightly now, and before the summer was over and the harvests were ended, the Black Flag would be raised.

What should be done with the Lieutenant? Many said *death*. To spare a Kansas man was to offend the God of a Guerrilla. To take a prisoner and then not to kill him, was an insult to the inspiration of the ambuscade. These desperate men had laws, however—unwritten but none the less inexorable on account of it. One especially accorded life to any prisoner vouched for or endorsed by any Guerrilla. Quantrell stood for the Lieutenant. Thenceforward those who at first demanded his life, would have defended it to the last cartridge. As Quantrell was in the act of releasing him a few days afterwards, he said in parting: "Go back to your people. I like you very much, but between them and me there can never again be peace." Still as one who seemed incapable of understanding his situation, the Lieutenant thanked him and replied: "As for me, I never hurt any one in my life." Civil war, which leaves nothing but tombs, here left a fountain.

The conflict deepened. The tide of the conflict was at its flood. Many eyes were attracted towards Quantrell, and many journalists were busy with the tale of his exploits. Imagination made of him a monster. No crime was too black for him; no atrocity too brutal; no murder too monstrous; no desperate deed too improbable. Let all the West be harried, and the tiger slain in his lair!

The hunt began. Quantrell passed again through Jackson county and entered Johnson from the west. At Mrs. Davonport's he met first a company of militia and dealt them one of his telling blows, killing eleven, and pushing the balance back into Warrensburg. The taste of such Guerrilla work as this was bitter in the mouth of the Federal commander at Warrensburg, and he spat his dread at Quantrell over the petticoats of a lot of women. Arresting Miss Brinker, the sister of John

Brinker, and one of the most beautiful and accomplished women of the West, he put her at the head of two hundred men, together with four other Southern girls, and rode through the county in this fashion, hunting for Quantrell. Ambushed along the high road, and having in his favor position, prowess, and experience, Quantrell yet saw the whole line pass by him as it were in review, firing not a gun at them, nor charging a single squadron. Unknown to all of them, these angels of the column had saved it from destruction. Baffled thus thrice by the presence of these women, who were held a week as hostages, Quantrell abandoned active operations for the time and went into camp at Captain Perdue's, sending out detachments hither and thither in quest of ammunition and adventure. The supplies sent forward from St. Joseph some time before had not yet arrived. Stinted somewhat in revolver caps, and deficient somewhat in navy revolvers, a well contested fight of an hour or two generally left the command unable to be effective until the next day. Cole Younger and George Shepherd were sent into Jackson county, therefore, to procure ammunition; others were ordered into Cass for horses; while Todd, having a command of twelve men, had made for him the opportunity so ardently desired, of conducting a raid into Kansas. Then the fighting began again—a week of fruitful and extended fighting. Haller, in Cass, the very first day, met twenty militia on an open prairie with five men and cut the whole squad to pieces. He relied always on the charge, and drilled his men constantly in horse-back firing, the faster the horses went the better the shooting. When these twenty Federals came upon him, he halted his squad and asked each man by name what should be done. "A fight or a foot race, eh, boys?" This was Haller. Little said charge, Coger said charge, Poole said the same, Blunt the same, they all said it, and charge it was. A charge on the prairie means death. No trees, no hollows, no stones, no shelter—body to body and hand to hand—this is prairie fighting. Prowess tells. Death helps him who fears him least. He who dodges is in danger. Fortune's great uncertain eye looks down upon the *melee* and brightens when it falls upon the bravest. The quickest is the safest; the coolest the least exposed.

Haller's attack was a hurricane; a little cloud no bigger than a man's hand grappled with the horizon. His pistol practice

was superb. Beyond the killing there was a singular episode.
With the Federals, and in the forward file, was a scout, sun-
browned and huge, who had for uniform a complete suit of
buckskin. Evidently a plainsman and an ugly customer, he
shot swiftly yet without effect. Some about him stood not for
the onset; he awaited it as though it were the coming of
buffalo. Dave Poole singled him out, and as he closed with
him, contrary to his custom, demanded a surrender. Buckskin
laughed a little scornfully, lifted himself up high in his stirrups,
leant over far to the right and grasped with his left hand, as
with a grasp of iron, Poole's long black beard. In his right
hand a bright bowie knife shone. "Gracious!" cried Poole,
always grotesque, "here's your regular Indian fighter; but
scalp or no scalp, he's powerful strong." And he was. He
held Pool so close to him that he could not use his revolver, and
while he held him he was working viciously with his knife. One
slash cut into his right shoulder, another gashed his cheek, a
third scored his left arm deeply, and the fourth might have
gone surer home, when Haller, acquit of all who had come
before him, turned back to the rescue and shot the frontiersman
dead from his saddle. "As he lay," said Poole afterwards,
"he looked in length about eight feet."

Younger and Shepherd worked hard and fast, and got
together a load of ammunition—sufficient for a week of solid
service. While after a wagon to haul it out, seventy-five
Federals surrounded them in a house and demanded a surrender. No! the word was not in their vocabulary. Close to
the house stood an orchard, and growing luxuriantly in this a
heavy crop of rye. Where it was thickest their horses had
been hitched, and beyond the horses was a skirt of timber.
Gaining the first under a shower of balls, they soon gained the
other, but not unhurt. Four buckshot had struck Younger,
three drawing blood, and Shepherd was hit too hard to ride
beyond the nearest shelter.

As Todd came along on the road to Kansas, Younger joined
him near the Blue and struck the enemy about the line. Some
fighting occurred, as the night came, but Todd changed his
position further to the west, crossing into Kansas to the right of
Olathe. Six government wagons loaded with supplies, and
convoyed by parts of two infantry companies, were his first

emoluments. Scattered along the highway in disorder, and drunk, some of them, to incapacity, the poor infantry fellows didn't know a Guerrilla from a gate-post. Todd went through the convoy at a canter, sparing nothing along the line. One huge Dane, very drunk and very noisy, took a couple of minutes to die, seventeen revolver bullets in his body, and four thrusts of his own bayonet.

In one wagon there was whisky, and before Todd knew it, several of his men were boisterous; they demanded more blood. Having turned back with his captures toward Missouri, Todd left with them a small escort and started forward again in order to gratify this demand—one which accorded so well with his own desires. Where Quantrell had burned the bridge over Big Blue upon the road leading from Independence to Kansas City, the Federals had established a ferry. An old *tete du pont* there had been turned into a stockade, garrisoned by half a company. Todd stalked it as a Highlander stalks red deer. When he could no longer walk, he crept; when he could no longer creep, he crawled. Some fog was on the river, and here and there a fire with a smoke, which lay heavy along the undergrowth. Doomed men have no dreams. Armed shadows rose slowly out of the ground, and yet they did not see them. This mirage of the rising of armed men is well known to persons accustomed to frequent ambuscades. This day at the ford nineteen Federals were doing duty, and when Todd reached the river they were in a large flatboat crossing from the Independence to the Kansas City side. Merriment abounded with them, and a sentimental young soldier was heard clearly to sing:

> "The cruel war is over,
>   Once more with her is he:
> 'You've learnt to love since last we met,'
>   He says, but nought says she.
> 'You'll wed the happy Somebody,
>   And me you'll quite forget!
> Would I were he, my darling!'
>   '*You are!*' cried Colinette."

It was of love and a furlough, and something sweet at the last—something that tasted of red lips and of devotion. Poor fellow! He did not wait until the end of the war before his furlough came to him forever. Others talked loudly. Some trailed trickling fingers through the water. A few scanned the western bank, but saw nothing. The boat's bow was on the beach, and a hand had been lifted to the rope to make it fast; but what mattered the boat—death was there. Not a soul escaped. Ten fell dead the first fire, four leaped into the river and were drowned, and five were finished leisurely. Todd's ambushments were parts of the ferocity of a system, and not the ferocity of his nature. The youth of the love song might have been spared had the bullets been any respecter of persons. The boat was sunk, the dead were not even buried, and Todd galloped on to rendezvous at Reuben Harris'. With the blood scarcely washed from his hands, or the powder smoke from his face, he hastened on the next morning to another ambuscade on the Harrisonville and Independence road. South of the residence of John Fristoe there grew a hazel thicket of conspicuous hiding capacity. Up from the midst of it a lone elm reared itself, tall and shapely. Todd remarked it standing like a sentinel, and spoke to Younger: "God put it there for some wise purpose. Let a good climber climb to its top and tell us of the country." This unaffected reliance upon the wisdom of God is heard often where the work to be done is veritable devil's work.

Martin Shepherd, agile as a squirrel of the hills, mounted quickly to the lookout, and reported just as quickly the advance of a Federal column. Fired upon at the distance of twenty feet, and charged simultaneously with the volley, five fell from their horses dead and a number wounded rushed away in retreat, keeping their saddles with difficulty. Only the covering party of a column two hundred strong had been encountered, and while Blunt, Younger, James Von, William Bledsoe, Dick Yager, and Vis. Acres were down in the road gathering up revolvers, ammunition, and such other things of the dead as were needed, the main body came rushing on, firing furiously and bent on revenge. Todd fell back slowly on foot to his horses, mounted in no haste, and skirmishing then and in fine order gained the timber. Each soldier, besides the horse he rode, had three others to protect, thus making the question not so much one of fighting as taking care of the captures. Five scouts—Yager, Blunt, Von, Younger, and Shepherd—were thrown forward to find the enemy, who had not pursued. Five

6

better men never took a hot trail at a gallop—eager, daring, splendidly mounted, and pressing always forward for a closer fight. After a swinging gallop of several miles, a Federal rear guard, seventy-five strong, was struck at the house of Dr. Pleasant Lee. The five fought the seventy-five. At the first fire Von killed an orderly sergeant, and kept closing up. For twenty seconds or so the *melee* was fierce. The first line formed across the road to stop the Guerrillas was rode over or cut to pieces, the second gave way, and the third faltered. Then the whole rear guard formed behind a stone fence, the balance of seventy-five on the defensive against five. At such odds the Guerrillas fought continually. Younger returned to Todd, reported the coast clear, and advised that a push be made rapidly and at once for the camp of Quantrell, the captured Kansas wagons now having come up, and the necessary horses to mount all the new recruits having been secured.

Moving by way of Blue Springs and Pink Hill, and on towards headquarters at Stony Point, Todd was set upon and hard bestead. The prince of ambuscaders fell into an ambuscade. The man of the surprise and the sudden volley, had his own tactics administered to him, none the less unpalatable because of their being familiar. Seventy-five Federals laid a trap for him close to the Sni, and he rode into it snugly. If to the skillfulness of the ambushment there had been added the coolness of the Guerrilla, decidedly the credit side of the killing would have been the Federal side. But just outside the teeth of the trap a tremulous watcher let his gun go off. It signalled a volley of course, but a volley of miscalculation. No charge followed it. Loading where they stood, and forgetting to all appearances every reliance upon the revolver, Todd got time to break out from his bad position. The carbine he carried in his hand was shot in two, and Martin Shepherd, a lion in every combat, mortally wounded. As he reeled he fired both barrels of his shot-gun, killing a Federal at each discharge, and before he fell Cole Younger caught him in his arms and brought him out. Others were wounded, though not mortally. Todd, coolest in danger, like Massena, and deadliest, dashed through the ambushment and on towards the Pink Hill bridge across the Sni, the seventy-five Federals following fast, soon to be reinforced by one hundred and twenty-five more. Skirmishing ensued heavily. The wagons, before encountering the enemy at the ambuscade, had been parked in an out of the way place far from a main road, and only the extra horses now had to be looked to. The bridge was in sight, and beyond it was Quantrell and reinforcements. The trot quickened into a gallop and Todd had struck the west end of it, well ahead of the pursuers in the rear, when from the eastern approach a fierce fire beat into his very face and a blue mass rushed into the road and halted. Hemmed in as he was, and hampered with horses, he rushed at the squadrons blocking up his passage way and strove to cut through. The fire was too severe, the odds too unreasonable. Blunt was wounded, Yager was wounded, Younger had two horses killed under him, Von was wounded, Bledsoe was wounded twice, Todd had his hat shot off and four holes through his coat, and those covering his rear could hold it only a moment or two longer. At the bridge the Sni made a bend, the bulge of the stream pushing towards the east; when he got to the western approach he was in the complete envelopment of a *cul de sac*. Neither able to move backwards nor forwards; on the right hand the Sni, and on the left hand the Sni; two hundred Federals in his rear and an unknown number in his front—this was Todd's predicament. The river was there, it is true, but the banks on the west were ten feet high and perpendicular. He would take to the water below the bridge, and be the first also to take the leap. Twice his horse refused him, but lifting him the third time by a spur stroke, and giving him the rein and a cheering cry, he sprang sheer over the steep into the river, halting there under fire to guide, as it were, and encourage his men. All 'got over in safety, carrying with them the bulk of the extra horses, and at daylight the next morning he was in the camp of Quantrell, near Pallett's on the Sni.

While encamped here, and waiting for the operations of the various detachments sent out to be completed, Quantrell had received the consignment of arms and ammunition forwarded to Quantrell by Quantrell from St. Joseph. In addition to an unusually large number of revolver caps, one hundred and sixty-eight new navy revolvers—worth every one of them its weight in gold —made glad the eyes of the Guerrillas and light their hearts. They would try them also in a forward movement the next day.

Todd's old antagonists were in Pink Hill, easy of access, and thither Quantrell marched. Choosing a position west of the place that was a natural ambuscade, he made ready to execute a manœuvre never before attempted. Behind an embankment that was a perfect shelter, the horses were hitched. To the right and left of the road, and running parallel with it for two hundred yards and more, were ditches for draining purposes, now dry and deep enough to shelter the men; in these fifty soldiers could fight five hundred. Gregg was chosen to command a decoy party consisting of ten men, and sent forward at once to fight the Federals awhile, retreat slowly, fight again, then retreat, then turn once more about, and finally—with nothing of trepidation and with scarcely a show of speed, lead them into the lion's den. The name of Gregg was even then beginning to make the Jayhawkers tremble. He had the nerve of an inflexible will in council, and on the battle-field the impetuosity of youth. Under all circumstances his example was one of intrepidity. He seemed to recognize no other aspiration than the triumph of his cause. He devoted himself to Quantrell—like Todd, Cole Younger, Poole, Blunt, the Shepherds, the Littles, and many others—by a double worship, to his principles as a Guerrilla, to his person as a friend. Honest, modest, silent—without other ambition than that of serving his country as became a hero, he did superbly the hardest thing to do on earth—his whole duty.

Keeping well under cover until within one hundred yards of Pink Hill, Gregg broke out of the timber at a run and dashed furiously into the town. For the first few moments all was dire confusion, no one heeding orders, and none making head against the Guerrillas until they had shot down fifteen in the streets, wounded eleven, and crippled, cut loose, and stampeded not less than sixty horses. Afterwards from dwellings, garden fences, store-houses, corn cribs, from behind chimneys and out of the tops of hay stacks and wheat stacks two hundred Federals took shelter and drove Gregg out. He retreated a short distance and turned about. They would not follow him. Try how he would, not a soldier left his place of security. He tempted them next with bravado. Sending Cole Younger, James Vaughn, and James Tucker back to ride about and around Pink Hill, he calmly waited himself just beyond gunshot until they should get ready to follow. These three skirmished with everything they saw for an hour. Now on one side of Pink Hill and now on another, no one would come out to try a grapple with them. At length, and as if to vary the monotony of so much recklessness on the one side and so much cowardice on the other, a splendid horse broke away from the town and ran some distance in the direction of the three Guerillas. Vaughn rode forward to capture him. If he dashed at the Federal horse he knew he should scare him and lose him, but if he went gently the chances were good for success. Fifty concealed soldiers fired at him incessantly as he rode slowly up to the horse and as slowly back again. Twice he took off his hat and waved it towards the nearest marksmen who shot the closest to him, and twice he dismounted within easy range to adjust his saddle. Fortune deserted him at last, however, and when he had the least reason to expect it. Full five hundred yards from the nearest house, he was struck in the right breast by a heavy ball, which passed through the lung and out at the back, near the spine. In losing him, Quantrell lost a soldier conspicuous for enterprise, and remarkable for the coolness of an intrepidity which was unconscious of its own excess.

Unwilling to follow Gregg, and afraid to move out of Pink Hill, the commander of the two hundred Federals cooped up there sent a Union citizen who knew the country well post-haste to Independence for reinforcements, but Quantrell moved that night into Johnson county, and camped for several days on Walnut creek. They were after him, however. Commanded by a dashing officer, one hundred Federal calvary came up from Clinton, in Henry county, and struck Quantrell afoot at the house of William Asbury. In his front was an open prairie, and in his rear a large orchard in which his horses were hitched. The Federals came right onward at a gallop, fronted into line swiftly, and dashed down to within thirty yards of the house only to meet a withering volley and to fall back in much confusion, leaving behind them all their dead and wounded. Rallying beyond range, the gallant leader of the Federals formed another line, placed himself again at its head, and strove to urge it forward. Instead of men he talked to stocks or stones. Some make-believes of charges fooled him twice or thrice, when drawing off in sheer disgust, he took up a position of masterly observation something over a mile away upon the prairie. Gregg, with three men—Cole Younger, Henry Ogden, and George Maddox—followed him and fought him at every step, driving in his picquets twice, and keeping his cowardly detachment in a constant state of uproar.

While preparing to mount and attack in return, Dave Poole and John Brinker hurried up with the unpleasant information that two hundred Federals, attracted by the firing, were coming up rapidly from the direction of Harrisonville. Quantrell's force numbered exactly sixty-three, capable of whipping easily the one hundred within striking distance, but inadequate to the other task. The Federal wounded, numbering eighteen, he had looked after carefully. Not belonging to any of the commands waging upon him a war of extermination, he had no desire to make them responsible for the cruelties of other organizations. Rapid always, whether in retreat or advance, Quantrell traveled two miles in a southeast direction through some heavy timber, thence across a prairie to Big Creek, over Big Creek to Devil's Ridge, and from Devil's Ridge northeast towards Pleasant Hill. By this time seven hundred Federals were on his track, well mounted and full of fight. It rained all day the first day out from Asbury's, the roads became muddy, and the streams began to rise. During most of the second night Quantrell scattered his trail at suitable places, and used whatever of stratagem was best to retard pursuit. At daylight Pleasant Hill was three miles to the right, and Big Creek within sight on the left. The sky had cleared up, and Quantrell stopped for breakfast six miles west of the town. All night long also had the Federals marched, reaching Pleasant Hill an hour later than Quantrell and breakfasting there. Peabody led their advance with three hundred cavalry, four hundred more marching on in supporting distance behind him. He had some old scores to settle and some ugly old wounds to get ointment for.

Quantrell had halted in Swearingen's barn, and the Guerrillas were drying their saddle-blankets. One picquet, Hicks George —an iron man, who could sleep in the saddle, and eat as he ran, who faced every suspicious thing until he fathomed it, and explored every mysterious thing until he mastered it—watched the rear against attack. Peabody received George's fire—for George would have fired at angel or devil in the line of his duty—and drove him towards Quantrell at a full run. Every preparation possible under the circumstances had been made, and if the reception was not as warm as expected, the Federals could attribute much of it to the long night march and the rainy weather. The horses were hitched in the rear of the barn to protect them as far as possible, and the Guerrillas lined and lay along the fence in front.

Quantrell stood by the open gate calmly, with his hand upon the latch; when George entered in he would close it and fasten it. The crest of the wave of Peabody's onset had reared itself up to within thirty feet of the fence when the Guerrillas delivered a crushing volley, and sixteen Federals, borne on by the impetus of the rush, crashed against the barricade and fell there, some wounded and some dead. Others fell as the ebb came, and more dropped out here and there before the disorganized mass got back again safely from the deadly revolver range. After them hot dashed Quantrell himself, George Maddox, Jarrette, Cole Younger, George Morrow, Gregg, Blunt, Poole and Haller, following them fast to the timber and gathering upon their return all the arms and the ammunition of the killed and wounded. At the timber Peabody rearranged his lines, dismounted his men, and came forward again at a double-quick and yelling. Do what he would, the charge spent itself before it could be called a charge. Never nearer than one hundred yards of the fence, he skirmished at long range for nearly an hour and finally took up a position one mile south of the barn, awaiting reinforcements. Quantrell sent out Cole Younger, Poole, John Brinker and William Haller, to "lay up close to Peabody," as he expressed it, and keep him and his movements steadily in view. The four dare-devils multiplied themselves. They attacked the pickets, rode around the whole camp in bravado, firing upon it from every side, and finally agreed to send a flag of truce in to Peabody with this manner of a challenge:

"We, whose names are hereunto annexed, respectfully ask of Colonel Peabody the privilege of fighting eight of his best men, hand to hand, and that he himself make the selection, and send them out to us immediately." This was signed: Coleman Younger, William Haller, David Poole and John Brinker.

Younger bore it. Tieing a white handkerchief to a stick he

rode boldly up to the nearest picket and asked for a parley. Six started toward him, and he bade four go back. The message was carried to Peabody, but he laughed at it and scanned the prairie in every direction for the coming reinforcements. Meanwhile Quantrell was retreating. His four men cavorting about Peabody were to amuse him as long as possible and then get away as best they could. Such risks are often taken in war; to save one thousand men sometimes one hundred are sacrificed. Death equally with exactness has its mathematics.

The reinforcements came up rapidly. One hundred joined Peabody on the prairie, and two hundred masked themselves by some timber on the north and advanced parallel with Quantrell's line of retreat—a flank movement intended to be final. Haller hurried off to Quantrell to report, and Peabody, vigorous and alert now, threw out after the three remaining Guerrillas a cloud of cavalry skirmishers. The race was one for life. Each started for the barn on a keen run. It was on the eve of harvest, and the wheat, breast high to the horse, flew away from before the feet of the racers as though the wind was driving through it an incarnate scythe blade. As Pool struck the eastern edge of this wheat, a very large jack, belonging to Swearingen, joined in the pursuit, braying loudly at every jump, and leading the Federals by a length. Comedy and tragedy were in the same field together. Carbines rang out, revolvers cracked, the jack brayed, the Federals roared with merriment, and looking back over his shoulder as he ran, Poole heard the laughter and saw the jack, and imagined the devil to be after him leading a lot of crazy people.

The barn was almost gained, and Brinker and Younger were through the gate, into the lot, and away on the track of Quantrell, when the two hundred flanking Federals burst from their cover on the north and cut Poole squarely off from the gap he had to go through to get out of the barn lot. It was a rain of bullets now. His gun was shot out of his hand. His horse was wounded and blown; he was in a trap; and something like a roar went up of "surrender!" "surrender!" "surrender!" But he did not surrender. Turning his horse to the west where it seemed to him there was a panel lower than the rest, he drove on it, or through it, or over it, with a crashing and a splintering that jarred the whole fence and dragged him well nigh from his saddle. Younger and Brinker were not yet out of sight when he was up with them again, the whole three dashing on together upon Quantrell's trail, the pursuing Federals close behind.

In a hollow close to Fred. Farmer's house Quantrell formed his sixty-three men on foot to fight seven hundred. Peabody struck him first and got his fire at ten steps before he knew it. Fifteen saddles were emptied here—James Morris. and young More, son-in-law of David Yeager, performing several acts of conspicuous bravery. In each hand a revolver, and advancing continually, they fired so rapidly and so accurately that it might well have been taken for a company. Peabody, sick of fighting Quantrell on horseback, dismounted beyond range and divided his command—sending one part of it to the west and keeping the other at the south. The flanking detachment, closing up from the north, also divided, keeping one portion there and sending the other to close up the gap on the east. Thus was the environment complete; sixty-three men were surrounded by seven hundered. A series of desperate combats followed in the thick brush; charging those on the south and killing and wounding twenty-two, those on the north were then looked to, and then those on the east and the west. One charge followed another, the combats culminating at every point over desperate rallies for the horses. This hollow held by Quantrell vomitted fire and smoke as the mouth of a volcano. In the gloom Titans struggled. To the long roll of musketry—full, sonorous, resonant—there succeeded the shriller and sharper notes of the revolver vollies. The two lines marked the strife thus: the Federals with the more melodious music, the Guerrillas with the more discordant.

Quantrell was getting anxious. Some of his horses had been killed, and many of his best men were wounded. Gregg, Coger, Poole, Cole Younger, Moore, Maddox, Morris, Brinker, Haller, and a dozen others shot, more or less severely, fought on, yet slowly. Attrition alone would make this conflict only one of time; to fight further, was to waste precious blood unnecessarily.

To the left-front of the hollow—the south-front—there lay wounded probably a dozen Federals, and some of them had dragged their hurt bodies below its crest for such shelter as it afforded from the balls, now coming from every direction. As Quantrell passed hurriedly through them, from the south, to repel a furious attack upon the north—conspicuous alike by his presence and the splendid coolness of his bearing—a Federal soldier raised himself up on his knees and fired at him, point blank. The bullet, intended for the breast, struck Quantrell in the right leg, below the knee, and cut clean through, narrowly missing the bone. Quantrell fell, but leaped so quickly to his feet, that his men imagined he had only stumbled. Gregg's quick eyes, however, fathomed the movement at a glance, and in an instant he had a pistol at the assassin's ear. "Pray!" he said. The wounded Federal only shut his eyes and bowed his head; he had played a desperate game and lost—that game that men sometimes play with death when they know death must win. Gregg blew his brains out.

"Say nothing of my wound," Quantrell said to Gregg, so low that none heard him, "and tell the men to mount rapidly and at once."

Yelling, and charging upon the hollow from all sides, the jubilant enemy now had everything their own way. To get out was touch and go; to stay there was absolute death. At the mounting time, Jarrette found his horse dead, and so did Gregg, George Shepherd, Toler, Tucker, Henry Ogden, Dick Maddox, James Morris, and Dick Burnes. These men had been doing splendid work on the east, and had had no time to look to their horses. They now broke through this line again on foot, and fought slowly north, gaining a little at every step, and getting little by little all their enemies behind them. To the combat of the squad, the individual combat succeeded. Quantrell and John Coger went out together, each losing his horse a mile from the battle-field. Will Haller and Gregg led a furious charge to the north, broke through Peabody's lines in that direction, dashed back by the barn of the morning's conflict, on past Swearingen's house, and then east again. As they struck the line under a steady fire, Kit Chiles, who was riding side by side with Cole Younger, felt his horse sink beneath him. "I'm gone," he said to Younger." "No; courage Kit," and Cole dismounted there, helped him out from under his dead horse, and up behind him on his own. Thus they rode away, and to his dying hour Kit Chiles bore testimony with gratitude, that he owed his life to his intrepid comrade. This standing side by side with one another was Guerrilla tactics; they never abandoned their wounded if one could ride or walk, or even crawl. Sometimes three on one horse have been carried out from some disastrous melee; not unfrequently back to back two have stood—one unhurt the other hurt too grievously to escape—and died together. Quantrell taught such comradeship; in his bivouacs and about his camp-fires he pictured to them what a blessed thing was devotion. Frank Ogden carried out Jarrette, Blunt carried out Hart, Poole carried out Haller. Those who rode the strongest horses picked up the heaviest among the dismounted men, and so on down this way in gradation, until not even so much as a wounded horse, not too badly hurt to travel, was left to the seven hundred Federals, still scouting through the brush, firing into the hollow, and wondering what had become of the encompassed Guerrillas.

Safely through the toils, and used up quite seriously in men and horses, Haller rode rapidly for the Harrisonville and Independence road, and reached it, after heavy skirmishing, at James Wilson's. Thence marching north to Dupre's, and concentrating finally at Major J. F. Stonestreet's, the command was disbanded until the following night, with the rendezvous agreed upon—the house of Fleming Harris. Quantrell himself was one of the first to arrive, mounted on an old blind mare, saddleless and bridleless, John Coger leading her into camp with a rope. Within a mile from the place of the fight, twenty cavalrymen overtook them, killed their horses, wounded Coger and drove each afoot into the timber, Quantrell walking with great pain. After night, Coger stumbled upon a blind mare by accident, and as it was the best that could be done, Quantrell rode her bare-back, while he walked and led her—the blind emphatically leading the blind—for Coger had an old wound not entirely healed, and a new one, that though comparatively slight, gave him some trouble.

CHAPTER VIII.

INDEPENDENCE.

QUANTRELL recovered slowly. His wound was more serious than he at first admitted, and to neglect there had succeeded erysipelas. Forced to change his positions in the brush often, and cut off frequently from needful medical attention, several weeks elapsed before his men could be got together again. Not idle, however, in the interval nor indifferent to events, they had worked faithfully for Col. Upton Hays, who was recruiting a regiment for the Confederate service.

Colonel Buell, of soldierly character, honor and courage, held Independence with six hundred men. The citizens respected him because he was just; the Guerrillas because he was merciful; his soldiers because he was firm. Order and stability are the two necessities of a garrison. Buell was the same one day as another. A patriot without being a proscriptionist; a stern fighter who was not a hangman; a rigid executive officer without being an executioner—he sometimes was twice successful: once by his manhood and once through his magnanimity.

In pursuance of superior orders issued through his head-quarters, every male citizen of Jackson county between the ages of eighteen and forty-five was required to take up arms and fight against the South. They did take up arms, but they did not fight against the South. Providence sent to their especial deliverance a giant by the name of UPTON B. HAYS—a military Moses indeed, who, raised up for a certain glorious work, died before reaching the promised land. Death smote him in the harness, and he fell where it was an honor to die.

Hays was of a family famous for great physical vigor and courage. A plains' man before he was a soldier, immensity had taught him self-reliance, and isolation that searching communion which decides and hardens character. Treachery was abhorrent to him, and baseness of heart aroused his indignation. Of enormous energy, commanding presence, sonorous voice, splendid horsemanship, he won men to him by the magnetism of a magnificent manhood, and held them there through the gentler gifts of appreciation and generosity. He understood the war, for he had summed it up early. He disputed nothing; he sang no good man's song by the cradle of a young Confederacy who had suspended the *habeas corpus* and was muttering of conscription; he only stipulated that every blow should be decisive. He believed that the people possessed no other conviction than that of their emotion; that in revolution temerity was prudence; and that on desperate occasions there was no hope save in that despairing patriotism which risked everything with the idea of saving it.

Indefatigable in recruiting as in other things, Colonel Hays soon had organized for active service the materials of as fine a regiment as ever followed a competent leader to war. It had need to be baptized; through baptism—that sort of baptism which picks out the bravest and the best and puts them in the fore front of the regiment to die—came the touching of elbow to elbow in battle, the winnowing that forever estopped a rout; tenacity, endurance, fatalism—that something of insanity which made them charge like Murat and die like Leonidas.

Well up from his ugly wound, and anxious for battle air and exercise, Quantrell had sped the mustering cry from Guerrilla to Guerrilla until at the Flannery rendezvous not six of his trusty veterans were absent. Hays came also and talked of taking Independence. Between the two the plan was arranged, and ten days given to gather the forces and mould the bullets. Recruiting officers from the South were entering Missouri in every direction—Col. Gideon W. Thompson, Col. John T. Coffee, Col. Vard Cockrell, Capt. Jo. O. Shelby, Col. John T. Hughes, Col. S. D. Jackman—and it was necessary to strike a blow. The more resounding it was made the better. After a serious hurt, or when a bold dash left behind it a trail of clean fighting and killing, the Federals always concentrated. The little posts ran into the big ones. Scouting parties staid at home for several days; on the arms of the heavier headquarter people there was crape. Fasting and prayer, of course, never

came by way of propitiation, but cattle-stealing was less luxuriantly indulged in, and bedeviling citizens not so much of a
frolic. But then the wind that ruffled so rudely the blue uniforms blew benedictions to the recruiting folk. Borrowing
three of Quantrell's old men—Cole Younger, Dick Yager and
Boon Muir—and taking two of his own—William Young and
Virgil Miller—Col. Hays concluded to make a tour of his cantonments. Buell's order had put into the brush well nigh the
entire arms-bearing population of Jackson county. On all the
streams there were camps. Men drilled on the prairie edges
nearest to the timber, and where the undergrowth was thickest
there generally were silent ambuscades. The woods were inhabited. Women sewed in the shade of the trees; children
sported among the leaves. Uniformed as Federal soldiers, Col.
Hays and his little party rode into Westport where there was a
garrison fifty strong. Simulating a loyalty totally unfelt, the
citizens had just given to the breeze a magnificent flag worth a
hundred dollars. It flew high and free as he rode in; as he
rode out it was trampled and torn. The fifty soldiers garrison-
ing Westport were part of Jennison's regiment, especially obnoxious to the citizens, and given up, more or less, to predatory
excursions in the country round about. It was the same old
story of splendid personal recklessness and prowess. As Hays
trotted leisurely in at the head of his squad, an orderly at a corner saluted him, supposing him to be a Federal officer; the salute
was returned. As Dick Yager followed on behind, the orderly,
looking upon him only as a private, did not salute. "Why
do you refuse?" asked Dick. "You are a fool," said the
orderly. "But I am a fine shot," replied Yager, and he was, for
he put a dragoon pistol ball fair through the man's forehead.
The Jayhawkers swarmed. Seizing upon houses, fifty men
under cover fought five. Hays separated his soldiers and kept
up an incessant fusillade. A German living in the place had
boasted a few days before of a desire to lead a company of extermination against rebel women and children; it was an effective way to end the war, he said. Younger treed the Dahomey
man in a house, which was barricaded, and swept the street in
front of it, while Yager was battering down the door to get in.
The doomed man fought like a wolf, but they killed him in his
den and flung his body out of a window. Then they ran fight-

COLEMAN YOUNGER.

ing and separated. Hays cut the flag ropes and dragged the loyal banner after him as he gallopped south, followed by Muir, Young and Miller; Younger and Yager took the Kansas City pike, ran north a mile and into one hundred cavalry coming up to understand the battle. Jayhawkers front and rear, and a blind lane running square to the right like a *cul de sac*. They turned into it; at the far end and across it a heavy fence had just been built. Their pursuers yelled once in exultation—they knew the barrier at the finish—and poured into the lane's mouth a flood of steeds and steel. But the heavy new rails were as pasteboard. Both horses—held hard together and massed, as it were, for the shock—launched themselves forward like a bolt from a catapulet, and Younger and Yager stretched away and beyond in a free, full gallop.

The capture of Independence having been agreed upon, Hays asked of Quantrell some accurate information touching the strongest and best fortified points about the town. It was three days to the attack; the day before it was begun the information should be forthcoming. "Leave it to me," said Cole Younger, when the promise made to Hays had been repeated by Quantrell, "and when you report, you can report the facts. A soldier wants nothing else." The two men then separated. It was the 7th day of August, 1862.

On the 8th, about 10 o'clock in the morning, an old woman with gray hair and wearing spectacles, rode up to the public square from the south. Independence was alive with soldiers; several market wagons were about the streets; the trade in vegetables and the traffic in fruits was lively. This old woman was one of the ancient time. A faded sun-bonnet, long and antique, hid almost all the face. The riding-skirt, which once had been black, was now bleached; some tatters also abounded, and here and there an unsightly patch. On the horse was a blind bridle, the left rein leather and the right one rope. Neither did it have a throat-latch. The saddle was a man's saddle, strong in the stirrups and fit for any service. Women resorted often to such saddles then; civil war had made many a hard thing easy. On the old lady's arm was a huge market basket, covered by a white cloth. Under the cloth were beets, garden beans and some summer apples. As she passed the first picket he jibed at her: "Good morning, grand-mother," he

said. "Does the rebel crop need any rain out in your country?"
Where the reserve post was, the sergeant on duty took her
horse by the bridle, and peered up under her bonnet and into
her face. "Were you younger and prettier I might kiss you,"
he said. "Were I younger and prettier," the old lady replied,
"I might box your ears for your impudence." "Oh! ho! you
old she-wolf, what claws you have for scratching!" and the
rude soldier took her hand with an oath and looked at it sneer-
ingly. She drew it away with such a quick motion and started
her horse so rapidly ahead that he did not have time to examine
it. In a moment he was probably ashamed of himself, and
so let her ride on uninterrupted.

Once well in town no one noticed her any more. At the
camp she was seen to stop and give three soldiers some apples out
of her basket. The sentinel in front of Buell's headquarters
was overheard to say to a comrade: "There's the making of
four good bushwacking horses yet in that old woman's horse;"
and two hours later, as she rode back past the reserve picket
post, the sergeant, still on duty, did not halt her himself, but
caused one of his guards to do it; he was anxious to know what
the basket contained, for in many ways of late arms and ammunition had been smuggled out to the enemy.

At first the old lady did not heed the summons to halt—that
short, dry, rasping, ominous call which in all tongues appears
to have the same sound; she did, however, shift the basket
from the right arm to the left and straighten up in the saddle
just the least appreciable bit. Another cry, and the old lady
looked back innocently over one shoulder and snapped out:
"Do you mean me?" By this time a mounted picket had
galloped up to her, ranged along side and seized the bridle of
the horse. It was thirty steps back to the post, maybe, where
the sergeant and eight men were down from their horses and
the horses hitched. To the out-post it was a hundred yards,
and a single picket stood there. The old lady said to the
soldier, as he was turning her horse about and doing it roughly:
"What will you have? I'm but a poor lone woman going peace-
ably to my home." "Didn't you hear the sergeant call for
you, d—n you? Do you want to be carried back?" the
sentinel made answer.

The face under the sun-bonnet transformed itself; the de-

mure eyes behind their glasses grew scintillant. From beneath
the riding-skirt a heavy boot emerged ; the old horse in the blind
bridle seemed to undergo an electric impulse ; there was the
gliding of the old hand which the sergeant had inspected into the
basket, and a cocked pistol came out and was fired almost before
it got straight. With his grasp still upon the reins of the old
woman's bridle, the Federal picket fell dead under the feet of
her horse. Then, stupefied, the impotent reserve saw a weird
figure dash away down the road, its huge bonnet flapping in the
wind, and the trail of an antique riding-skirt, split to the shoulders, streaming back as the smoke that follows a furnace. Coleman Younger had accomplished his mission. Beneath the bonnet and the bombazine was the Guerrilla, and beneath the
white cloth of the basket and its apples and beets and beans,
the unerring revolvers. The furthest picket heard the firing,
saw the apparition, bethought himself of the devil, and took to
the brush. That night Quantrell made his report to Hays, and
the next night the mustering took place at Charles Coward's.

Col. John T. Hughes was there, a Christian who had turned
soldier, and who fought as he prayed. As the author of Doni-
phan's Expedition to Mexico, he had planted some fruits in the
fields of literature, and added some green things to the chaplets
of war. The soldiers knew him as a hero. Constitutionally
brave in the presence of men whom he wished to recruit, he
added to intrepidity, recklessness.

At daylight, on the morning of the 11th, Hays, leading three
hundred and fifty men, saw the spires of Independence loom
up indistinctly through the morning mist. An attack was in
process of consummation ; some brave men were about to die.
Quantrell led the advance ; the Guerrillas, jauntily dressed,
looked lithe and lean and tawny. Thanks to Younger, the leap
had not to be made in the dark ; spectres might be where the
spires were, but not the unknown.

Due west a mile from the town, the garrison had a camp ;
about it were stone fences and broken ways—bad for cavalry.
Buell had his headquarters in some strong houses, southwest of
the square ; guards were on duty about the town. Cole Younger led the advance. The east was yet dim and uncertain ; the
grasses and the earth smelt sweet ; it was a blessing to live.
The first picket—a quarter of a mile from the square—fired and

7

ran, the pursuit thundering at his heels. Buell's guard at his
headquarters fired on the advance, and Kit Chiles fell. "First
his horse, then the rider; poor Kit," and Quantrell left the dead
body to lie until the battle was decided.

The camp was in the midst of the long roll when Quantrell
struck it; Haller shot down a drummer with uplifted stick.
John Jarrette was first over a stone fence, running along in front
of a line of tents, and as he alighted, he killed a big corporal at
his tent door. The Federals rallied manfully and fought from
the fences about their flanks, and from the broken ways and the
hollows. Hays' men dismounted, and rushing up afoot, surrounded the encampment. Rock walls now replied to rock
walls, and cover answered cover. Buell, pent up in the houses
of his headquarters, fought stubbornly there with such forces as
were left to him; the guards upon the streets had mostly been
killed. When the people of the place awoke, in many directions dead men were visible.

When once fairly joined, the issue thereafter, at no moment,
was in doubt. The line of fire contracted about the doomed
camp; the enterprise of the sappers was making way fast
towards the doomed commander. Not a point in the hazardous
game of attack had been lost. As Younger had traced upon a
piece of paper, so were found the route, the streets, the guards,
the camp, the defences, the strong places and the weak places,
the Colonel's commodious dwelling house, and the sentinels'
approachable barracks.

Hays relieved Quantrell at the stone walls, and Quantrell
threw himself upon Buell. Buell fought from every door and
window of his domicile. A hundred men in houses are terrible.
If they fight, and if there is no artillery, they are murderous.
Buell fought, and there was no artillery. Hays kept creeping
slower and slower; the rifles of the woodsmen kept telling and
telling. Quantrell could not advance—there were the houses
that were no longer houses—those fortresses of the besieged.
Yager was for smoking them out; Poole suggested a keg of
gunpowder; George Maddox, fire; Haller, fire; Jarrette, fire—
the majority said fire—a wagon loaded with hay was brought
and volunteers ran with it to the rear of an out-building and
fired it speedily. The out-house caught; the roof of the fortress
caught; the red heat eat its way downward; the ashes as they

fell scorched and blistered, and then the calm, grave face of Buell blanched a little. He grappled with his fate, however, and fought the flames. Revolver vollies drove his men from the roof. He put himself at the head of a forlorn hope, and went at the double danger like a hero. Some wind blew. George Shepherd lifted his hat from his hot brow and felt it blow cool there: "God is here," he said reverently. "Hush," replied Poole, "God is everywhere." At that moment Colonel Hughes fell.

A great cheer from the camp now—a full, passionate, exultant cheer, and then not a gunshot more. All was over. Colonel Buell, no longer in command of a force, surrendered unconditionally. As he had done unto others, so in a greater degree did others do unto him. Black flag men were about him in great numbers, but not so much as a single upbraiding was ever heard from a Guerrilla's lips. If Quantrell's men could have been decorated for that day's fight, and if at review some typical thing that stood for glory could have passed along the ranks, calling the roll of the brave, there would have answered modestly, yet righteously: Haller, Gregg, Todd, Jarrette, Morris, Poole, Younger, James Tucker, Blunt, George Shepherd, Yager, Hicks George, Sim. Whitsett, Fletch. Taylor, John Ross, Dick Burns, Kit Chiles, Dick Maddox, Fernando Scott, Sam. Clifton, George Maddox, Sam. Hamilton, Press. Webb, John Coger, Dan. Vaughn, and twenty others, dead now, but dead in vain for their country. There were no decorations, however, but there was a deliverance. Crammed in the county jail, and sweltering in the midsummer's heat were old men who had been pioneers in the land, and young men who had been sentenced to die. The first preached the Confederacy and it triumphant; the last to make it so enlisted for the war. These jail-birds, either as missionaries or militants, had work to do.

CHAPTER IX.

AFTER Independence there was a lull of a few brief days. Kansas City drew in all of its outposts and showed a naked front to whoever would attack. The swoop of the eagles outside of it had alarmed the border; Kansas prairies might next resound with the iron feet of the marching squadrons.

Recruiting officers were riding up from the South through all the summer days—some to tarry awhile in Jackson county, and some to borrow guides from Quantrell and strike unguarded fords along the river. Enthusiasm—that virile breeder of volunteers—was abroad in Missouri. Even in her remotest extremities the Confederacy's life blood was in vigorous circulation; ossification at the heart commenced only when a factious Congress began to put on crape at the mention of martial law.

En route to regions where battalions grew, Col. John T. Coffee had entered the Southwest from Arkansas. He had been the stern nurse of hardy men. The war found him a politician and made him a patriot. He had great popularity through much patience with the people. Men of the scythe-blade and the plow, men who mowed in the lowlands and reaped on the hillsides were not damned on the drill ground and badgered at the inspection because Hardee and heathen with all too many were synonymous terms. Round-shouldered riflemen shot none the worse for dressing up badly in parade with square-shouldered giants, and the stammerer—who to keep some tryst or to receive some blessing begged for a furlough—got no aloes at least in the little wine of human nature the service let be doled out to him. Coffee recruited a regiment.

Col. Vard Cockrell, preceding Coffee a day's march or two, awaited a junction at the Osage River. Cockrell was a Christian who sometimes preached. His revolutionary ideas were but a form of his evangelical faith. He believed the devil the author of all evil in a spiritual point of view, the Abolitionists the cause of all the trouble in a political. To fight both was superlative orthodoxy. In battle it is believed that he prayed— notably short prayers like Lord Astley made at Edgehill, which battle was fought between Charles I. and the Puritans: "Oh! Lord, thou knowest how busy I must be this day. If I forget Thee, do not Thou forget me. March on, boys!" Like Coffee, Cockrell also recruited a regiment.

Captain J. O. Shelby—only a captain then, leading Cockrell's advance—had marched from Tupuelo, Mississippi, on foot, through Arkansas on foot, into Missouri on foot, and still north- ward and northward on foot until he struck the horse line. The most of those who followed him had no beards. He found them ruddy country lads with here and there a city's eager, sallow face, and he left them Indians. Shelby understood war both as an instinct and a religion. He did not play the great man; he was one. Some soldiers understood the movement solely of the revolution; Shelby both its movement and its direction. Some had its intoxication; he both its intoxication and its love. Its energy, agitation, generosity, intrepidity—all were his; but nothing of its ferocity. His genius was his audacity; but it was more. He saw God in men and he used them; a fatalist, and yet he left nothing to chance; ardent, he made his enthu- siasm subsidiary to his thought; feeling the passions, he yet represented the superiorities of the epoch; young, older officers trusted their interests and ambitions to his keeping; a giant, he lifted his soldiers up to him; after caressing popularity, he braved it as a wild beast which he dared to devour him; a gen- eral, beyond the mechanism of a division he grasped the ideal; courageous, his intrepidity had soul; he had passions, but he was generous; crushing incapacity, he also plucked favoritism up by the roots and out of his own breast; he entered Missouri a captain, and he left it a brigadier general, carrying his brigade with him.

Col. S. D. Jackman, part Guerrilla and part regular, carried over to the line the circumspection of the ambuscade. He fought to kill, and to kill without paying the price that ostenta- tious fighting invariably costs. Patient, abiding as a rock in the tide of battle; satisfied with small gains, but not carried away by large ones; serene under any sky, and indomitable to the end of the play, he also recruited a regiment which afterwards grew into a brigade.

Col. Charles Tracy—lying along the southern border of the State for several months, waiting for a dash—hurried up with the crowd and threw himself in the van of the recruiting service. Indefatigable; once an Indian fighter; on a trail like a Comanche, and in the darkness like a night hawk; winning with young men and enterprising with brave ones; a cavalryman by education and a leader through great vitality and perception, he gathered up a regiment in the midst of his enemies, and had it baptized before it was armed.

Col. D. C. Hunter came also from his lair, as a grizzly might, where the winter had been hard and the deep snows frozen. In gaps in the Boston Mountains he had held on to roads until their names grew evil, and on to passes until Federal detachments swore the devil was there. He was a still hunter. No pomp, nor circumstance, nor rattling scabbards made women turn and curiosity preak out its neck when Hunter marched down to a fight. Everything was matter of fact; so many rounds so many killed. To-morrow was to take care of itself; to-day belonged to clean guns and dry powder. Eat—certainly, when there was anything to eat; sleep—most assuredly, when sleep could be had. If neither was possible, then patience and another round or two at the enemy. Such a man of course had no difficulty in getting a regiment.

Coffee, Cockrell, Tracy, Hunter and Jackman, therefore—having communicated with Hays—commenced recruiting. Neither of these men desired a battle. The brush of Western Missouri was full of Southern men, driven from their homes by the militia. Little camps in the counties of Jackson, Clay, Platte, Lafayette, Johnson, Cass, Bates and Ray, sent their squads daily to either officer—sent fours, twos, single volunteers, bent only upon getting to the regular army and getting arms after they reached there. Certainly, therefore, it was not tactics for the Confederates to hunt for a fight, much less to take the chances of a doubtful one.

Even the Guerrillas, as desperate as the nature of their services had become, saw a single company swelled nearly to a regiment. Establishing a rendezvous first in the neighborhood of Blue Springs, and next at the residence of Luther Mason, three hundred splendid young fellows came trooping in to Quantrell. Jarrette commanded one company, Gregg one, Scott one, and Haller the old original organization. For the time Quantrell had a battalion. Todd was lieutenant under Haller, Coleman Younger under Jarrette, Hendrix under Gregg, and Gilkey under Scott. Of the above, Quantrell is dead, Gilkey dead, Haller dead, Hendrix dead, Todd dead—all slain in desperate battle.

The fall of Fort Sumter, like a huge mine, had exploded the passions of a continent. Missouri, hearing the deep and portentous reverberations, listened with her hand upon her sword. She had politicians but no statesmen; determination but no unanimity. Her Governor, reared in the facile and compromising school of American Democracy, showed a gloved hand to those who kept perilous ward in the St. Louis Arsenal. Beneath all its velvet, however, there was no iron. Three days after Lyon took command he laughed; as he looked city-ward he was bland. In a week he was sullen and dangerous, and began to show his teeth. In a month he was vicious and shed the blood of women in the streets of St. Louis. It may have been necessary. Trades-people and farmers need death dashed against their eyes in some terrible way to understand revolution.

Far west in the State some hastily gathered volunteers met the United States dragoons under Sturgis. Retreating sullenly, the dragoons turned once fairly to bay and Halloway and McClannahan fell. Another necessity in this that it taught younger officers how to die. The issue was made; blood had been spilt in the East and in the West; Governor Jackson was a fugitive; his young men were mustering; the din of preparation resounded throughout the State, and Lexington was named as a mustering place.

Hither came a young man leading a cavalry company. His uniform was attractive and differed only from that of the men in the single point of a feather. Women lifted their eyes as he passed and said: "How handsome he is." Men gazed after him and his uniform and said complacently: "He dresses like' a soldier." Quite a difference, truly, in the opinion expressed. One reasoned from the head, and the other from the heart.

This uniformed company had something of drill, something

of discipline, more of stalwart vigor and bearing. Its commander was Jo. O. Shelby, swarthy as an Arab, brown-eyed, loved of the conflict, and having over him, as an invisible aureole, the halo of an hundred battles.

The weeks and the war grew old together. Through Carthage, through Oak Hills, through Sugar Creek, through Elk Horn, this man led his followers, and those who fought him best will bear witness that only at long intervals did any enemy see Jo. Shelby's back.

Shiloh lit all the Southern cotton-fields with fire, and Johnston fell with the beautiful corpse of victory dead upon his dead, cold heart. When the burial bugles sounded, mistress and lover were buried together. And Farmington followed, and a great retreat, and in the rear marched Shelby, the jaunty uniforms stained with mud of Corinth trenches—the flowing feather drooping in the rain of Corinth bivouacs. The sunshine was alone upon their bayonets and in their faces. The first glistened all along the route to Tupuelo, the last lit up with a great joy when by the camp fires it was told how their captain had been ordered to march two thousand miles into Missouri—march to the river—to the Missouri river—to halt there, fight there, recruit there, and return from there a Colonel commanding.

From a Captain to a Colonel is a rugged way upwards at times. Every step that Shelby took ran over in blood. He had little faith in battles where nobody was killed, and he valued his fields by the number of the dead upon them. The richest acres were those where the wreck lay thickest, and where, on either flank, "men's lives fell off like snow."

Past the Mississippi, fretted with iron islands; past White River, black with the sombre fate of the Mound City; past Little Rock, listening to a siren's song, and dreaming of an early peace; past the Arkansas, sickly with conscripts; up upon the borders of Missouri, the promised land, he came, this leader Shelby, having in his hands a last commission from Earl Van Dorn, that peerless Launcelot, over whom the famous funeral oration might have been pronounced when they carried him away and buried him in Joyeuse Guard, the truest, noblest, simplest ever uttered:

"Ah! Sir Launcelot, there thou liest that never wert matched of earthly hands. Thou wert the fairest person, and the good-

liest of any that rode in the press of Knights; thou wert the
truest to thy sworn brother of any that buckled on the spur;
and thou wert the faithfulest of any that have loved women;
most courteous wert thou, and gentle of all that sat in hall
among dames; and thou wert the sternest Knight to thy mortal
foe that ever laid spear in the rest.''

Patience! It is of the Lone Jack battle I write, but all things
must have a beginning. Had there been no Shelby, there would
have been no Lone Jack battle. With this commission, therefore, of Gen. Earl Van Dorn in his hands, Shelby waited two
brief days on the Missouri border, next door to Arkansas.

With his brown eyes fixed on the buff sash of a Brigadier,
Shelby led Cockrell's advance with a speed that annihilated
distance, and gave no time for fatigue. If he slept at all, he
slept in the saddle. For food, the men drew as rations ten
roasting-ears a day. There was no time to kill or to cook what
might be eaten.

Preceding this march by a dozen summer days, Col. John T.
Coffee had come with his irregular cavalry, and news drifted
back of broken skirmishes wherein he was worsted. Shooting
at long range and not of necessity always, Coffee's scant ammunition had grown scantier, and hemmed in upon the Osage
river, he had sent a bold borderer forward praying for help and
succor in extremity. Cockrell was in Johnson county when
the messenger came. Coffee was southward still some thirty
miles. "The horses are tired, the men are tired, we have little
time. Shall we countermarch, Shelby?" "Yes, if it takes the
last soldier, and the last horse, and the last cartridge. Fall in!
Trot—march!" And the black plume galloped back thirty
miles, and the brown eyes had found a battle-light, and the
bronzed face smiled only at intervals now. Coffee was not a
prudent man always, and whether knee deep or breast deep in
danger, Shelby meant to cut him out or die there.

The rescue, however, cost no gunpowder. The stream,
which was at first merely a rivulet, had become to be a river.
The tide set strongly in towards the west again, and divided
only upon the line of Jackson county—Coffee and Cockrell
going to Independence, Shelby to Waverly, where a massed
regiment of Confederates awaited him.

And now the work of Shelby in the Lone Jack battle: Cock-

rell, left to himself and his own resources, would not have
countermarched. Coffee, without succor and a swift column to
help him, might have perished. There would, consequently,
have been no commingling of forces, no aggressive movements
on the part of Cockrell's weak detachment, no attack anywhere,
and in the end a distant bow to the resolute Federals keeping
grim watch and ward upon the Sni hills, and holding Lone Jack
and all the country roundabout.

It was an August day, hot but with some wind. God had
blessed the earth; the harvests were abundant. On the afternoon of the 13th some clouds began to gather about Lone Jack,
a small village in the eastern portion of Jackson county. Once
a lone black jack tree stood there—taller than its companions
and larger than any near to it; from this tree the town took its
name. The clouds that were seen gathering there were cavalrymen. Succoring recruits in every manner possible, and
helping them on to rendezvous by roads, or lanes, or water-
courses, horsemen acquainted with the country kept riding
continually up and down. A company of these, on the evening
of the 15th, were in the village of Lone Jack. Cockrell was
also in the neighborhood, but not visible. Coffee was there
also, and Tracy, Jackman, Hunter and Hays—that is to say,
within striking distance.

Major Emory L. Foster, doing active scouting duty in the
region round about Lexington, had his headquarters in the
town. The capture of Independence had been like a blow
upon the cheek; he would avenge it. He knew how to fight.
There was dash about him; he had enterprise; he believed in
esprit du corps; prairie life had enlarged his vision and he did
not see the war like a martinet; he felt within him the glow of
generous ambition; he loved his uniform for the honor it had;
he would see about that Independence business—about that
Quantrell living between the two Blues and raiding the west—
about those gray recruiting folks riding up from the South—
about the tales of ambuscades that were told eternally of
Jackson county, and of the toils spread for unwary Jayhawkers. He had heard, too, of the company which halted a
moment in Lone Jack as it passed through, and of course it was
Quantrell.

It was six o'clock—the hour when the Confederates were

there—and 8 o'clock when Col. Foster marched in, leading nine hundred and eighty-five cavalry, with two pieces of Rabb's Indiana battery—a battery much celebrated for tenacious gunners and accurate firing. Cockrell knew Foster well; the other Confederates knew nothing about him. He was there, however, and that was positive proof enough that he wanted a fight.

Cockrell, Hays, Hunter, Tracy, Coffee and Jackman had between them about nine hundred men. Coffee with two hundred men did not arrive in time to participate in the fight, and this *contretemps* simplified the situation thus: Seven hundred Confederates—armed with shot guns, horse pistols, squirrel rifles, regulation guns, and what not—attacked nine hundred and eighty-five Federals in a town for a position, and armed with Spencer rifles and Colt's revolvers, dragoon size. There was also the artillery. Lone Jack sat quietly in the green of its emerald prairies, its orchards in fruit and its harvests goodly. On the west was timber, and in this timber a stream ran musically and peacefully along. To the east the prairies undulated, their grass waves crested with sunshine. On the north there were groves in which birds abounded. In some even the murmuring of doves was heard, and an infinite tremor ran over all the leaves as the winds stirred the languid pulse of summer into fervor.

In the center of the town a large hotel made a strong fortification. The house, from being a tavern, had become to be a redoubt. From the top the stars and stripes floated proudly— a tri-color that had upon it then more of sunshine than of blood. Later the three colors had become four.

On the verge of the prairie nearest the town a hedgerow stood as a line of infantry dressed for battle. It was plumed on the sides with tawny grass. The morning broke upon it and upon armed men crouching there, with a strange barred banner and with guns at a trail. Here Bohannon waited, his calm eyes fixed on the stark redoubt of the Cave House and eager for the signal.

On the north and northwest there were cornfields as well as groves. In the cornfields Hays held his men in the hollow of his two hands—that is to say, perfectly under his control. The dew upon his beard glistened. It was not yet five o'clock. In the east the sleepy soul of the sunshine had not yet clothed itself with the sweet, gracious wings of warmth and moisture. The great face of the dawn was unveiled and looked down upon the earth tenderly. It was that sacred hour when the faint, universal stir of awakening life ·gives glory to God and grandeur to nature. No white dimple stirred among the corn, Hays' men were so still. The low ripple of the leaves had a tremor and a shiver that were ominous. By and by in the east a sunrise-city was open-gated and all unfastened flashed a golden door. The sun would be up in an hour.

Joining Hays on the left was Cockrell, and the detachments of Cockrell, Hays, Rathburn and Bohannon. Their arms were as varied as their uniforms. It was a duel they were going into and each man had the gun he could handle best. From the hedge-row, from the green-growing corn, from the orchards and the groves the soldiers could not see much, save the flag flying skyward on the redoubt of the Cave House.

At five o'clock a solitary gunshot alarmed camp and garrison, and outlying videttes, and all the soldiers face to face with imminent death. No one knew thereafter how the fight commenced. It was Missourian against Missourian—neighbor against neighbor—the rival flags waved over each, and the killing went on. This battle has about it a strange fascination. The combatants were not numerous, yet they fought as men seldom fight in detached bodies. The same fury extended to an army would have ended in annihilation. A tree was a fortification. A hillock was an ambush. The corn fields from being green became to be lurid. Dead men were in the groves. The cries of the wounded came up from the apple orchards. All the houses in the town were garrisoned. It was daylight upon the prairies, yet there were lights in the windows—the light of musket flashes. The grim redoubt of the Cave House grew hotter and hotter until it flared out in a great gust of fire. There was a woman there —Mrs. Cave—young, beautiful, a mother. She tried to escape, but muskets hemmed her in. Corpses lay in her path upon the right hand and upon the left. There was blood upon her feet, and a great terror in her soft, feminine eyes. She did not even cry out. In one sublime moment the tender young matron had caught a heroism not of this earth. In the next she was dead upon her own doorstep, a bullet through her maternal breast. Oh War! War!

There is not much to say about the fight in the way of description. The Federals were in Lone Jack; the Confederates had to get them out. House fighting and street fighting are always desperate. Cool men allied to walls defy everything except fire. The bullet rain that in an open field would scarcely penetrate, in the angles and protuberances of a street is a tempest. Where once were curtains, white or damask—transfigured faces, powder-scorched; where once were latch-strings—gaping muzzles; among the roses—dead men; where lovers lingered late and trystings were sweet or stolen—pitiful pale faces, wan in the light that never was on sea or shore. Smoke came from chimneys—marksmen were there; at the garden gates skirmishers crouched; upon the street corners companies concentrated; the hotel was a hospital, later a holocaust; the cannoniers stood by their guns and died there; and over all rose and shone a blessed summer sun, while the airy fingers of the breeze ruffled the oak leaves and tuned the swaying branches to the sound of a psalm.

The gray coats crept nearer. On the east, west, north or south Hays, Cockrell, Tracy, Jackman, Rathburn, or Hunter gained ground. Farmer lads in their first battle began gawky and ended grenadiers. Old plug hats rose and fell as the red fight ebbed and flowed; the shotgun's heavy boom made clearer still the rifle's sharper crack; under the powder-pall boyish faces shone in the glare with the bearded ones. An hour passed; the struggle had lasted since daylight.

Foster fought his men splendidly. Wounded once, he did not make complaint; wounded again, he kept his place; wounded the third time, he stood with his men until courage and endurance only prolonged a sacrifice. Once Haller, commanding thirty of Quantrell's old men, swept up to the guns and over them, the play of their revolvers being as the play of the lightning in a summer cloud. He could not hold them, brave as he was. Then Jackman rushed at them again and bore them backward twenty paces or more. Counter-charged, they hammered his grip loose and drove him down the hill. Then Hays and Hunter—with the old plug hats and the wheezy old rifles—finished the throttling; the lions were done roaring.

Tracy had been wounded, Hunter wounded, Hays wounded, Captains Bryant and Bradley killed, among the Confederates, together with thirty-six others, and one hundred and thirty-four wounded; among the Federals, Foster, the commander, was nigh unto death; his brother, Captain Foster, shot mortally died afterwards; one hundred and thirty-six dead lay about the streets and houses of the town, and five hundred and fifty wounded made up the aggregate of a fight, numbers considered, as desperate and bloody as any that ever crimsoned the annals of a civil war. A few over two hundred breaking through the Confederate lines on the south, where they were weakest, rushed furiously into Lexington, Haller in pursuit as some beast of prey, leaping upon everything which attempted to make a stand between Lone Jack and Wellington.

Dies iræ! The moan that went up through Poictiers and Aquitaine when at Lussac bridge the lance head of a Breton squire found the life of John Chandos, had counterpart at Kansas City and all the country round about. Again did the little posts run into the big ones. Commanders turned pale. A mighty blow seemed impending, and lest this head or that head felt the trip-hammer, all the heads kept wagging and dodging. Burris got out of Cass county; Jennison hurried into Kansas; the Guerrillas kept a sort of open house, and the recruits—drove after drove and mostly unarmed, hastened southward. Then the Federal wave—which had at first receded beyond all former boundaries, flowed back again and inundated Western Missouri. Quantrell's nominal battalion—yielding to the pressure of the exodus—left him only the old guard as a rallying point. It was necessary again to reorganize. Gregg was made First Lieutenant; Todd, Second; Scott, Third; Blunt, Orderly Sergeant; James Tucker, First Duty Sergeant; Younger, Second; Hendrix, Third; Poole, Fourth; James Little, First Corporal; Dick Burnes, Second; Hicks George, Third, and Hi. George, Fourth. After this re-organization, the Guerrillas stripped themselves for steady fighting. Incidents and personages suited the epoch. Federal troops were everywhere; infantry at the posts, cavalry on the war paths. The sombre defiance mingled with despair did not come until 1864; in 1862 the Guerrillas laughed as they fought. And they fought by streams and bridges, where roads crossed and forked and where trees or hollows were. They fought from houses and hay-stacks; on foot and on horseback; at night, when the

THE WARFARE OF THE BORDER

weird laughter of the owls could be heard in the thickets; in daylight, when the birds sang as they found sweet seed. The black flag was being woven, but it had not yet been unfurled.

Breaking suddenly out of Jackson county, Quantrell raided Shawneetown, Kansas, and captured its garrison of fifty militia. Then at Olathe, Kansas, the next day, the right hand did what the left one finished so well at Shawneetown; seventy-five Federals surrendered here. Each garrison was paroled and set free —each garrison save seven from Shawneetown; these were Jennison's Jayhawkers and they had to die. A military execution is where one man kills another; it is horrible. In battle one does not see death. He is there surely—he is in that battery's smoke, on the crest of that hill fringed with the fringe of pallid faces, under the hoofs of the horses, yonder where the blue or the gray line creeps onward trailing ominous guns—but his cold, calm eyes look at no single victim. He kills there— yes but he does not discriminate. Harold, the dauntless, or Robin, the hunchback—what matters a crown or a crutch to the immortal reaper?

The seven men rode into Missouri from Shawneetown puzzled; when the heavy timber along the Big Blue was reached and a halt had, they were praying. Quantrell sat upon his horse looking at the Kansans. His voice was unmoved, his countenance perfectly indifferent as he ordered: "Bring ropes; four on one tree—three on another." All of a sudden death stood in the midst of them, and was recognized. One poor fellow gave a cry as piercing as the neigh of a frightened horse. Two trembled, and trembling is the first step towards kneeling. They had not talked any save among themselves up to this time, but when they saw Blunt busy with some ropes, one spoke up to Quantrell: "Captain, just a word: the pistol before the rope; a soldier's before a dog's death. As for me, I'm ready." Of all the seven this was the youngest—how brave he was!

The prisoners were arranged in a line, the Guerrillas opposite to them. They had confessed to belonging to Jennison, but denied the charge of killing and burning. Quantrell hesitated a moment. His blue eyes searched each face from left to right and back again, and then he ordered: "Take six men, Blunt, and do the work. Shoot the young man and hang the balance."

Hurry away! The oldest man there—some white hairs were

in his beard—prayed audibly. Some embraced. Silence and twilight, as twin ghosts, crept up the river bank together. Blunt made haste, and before Quantrell had ridden far he heard a pistol shot. He did not even look up; it affected him no more than the tapping of a woodpecker. At daylight the next morning a wood-chopper going early to work, saw six stark figures swaying in the river breeze. At the foot of another tree was a dead man and in his forehead a bullet-hole—the old mark.

When in every hour in every day a man holds his life out in his open hands, he becomes at last to be a fatalist; and fatalism is granite. It stands like a rock. It abides the worst without a tremor. Fernando Scott was one of those men whom revolutions cast up, sometimes to be Titans and sometimes monsters. Todd said that he did not know the meaning of the word fear, and of all the men Todd led or rode with, he wept for Scott alone the night they buried him.

There came one day to Quantrell an old man, probably sixty years of age, who was tremulous and garrulous. He had a boy, he said, just turned of eighteen, who was his main stay and his sole reliance. Trouble had been heavy upon him of late. His wife had died, a daughter had died, the Jayhawkers had driven off his stock, and now the militia had arrested his boy. Would Quantrell help him to get his son back? He was in jail in Independence; they were cruel to him; his old heart was desolate and his old home was without a prop. Quantrell listened coldly. He had no prisoners to exchange for his son, and even if he had, he was not giving soldiers for citizens. Why was not his son in the army?

It was pitiful to watch the look of hopeless despair which came to the old man's face when Quantrell's practical reply pierced his fond illusions like some sharp thing that froze as it cut. He slid down from a sitting posture to a crouching one and began to moan helplessly, tears forcing themselves through his withered fingers as he tried in vain to cover his eyes with his hands. Some of the Guerrillas turned away their heads; others of them jeered at him. Scott did neither. He went to the old man kindly and lifted him up. "Do not despair," he said, almost as gently as a saint might have pleaded with a sinner, "and you shall have your boy. Silence, men! Do you not see

that the old man is crying?'' Quantrell humored his Lieutenant. He controlled his desperadoes by seeming not to control them. His discipline was rigid, but iron as it was, it never
clanked, or corroded, or hurt one's self-respect.

Independence was strongly garrisoned again, and a picquet
station on the Blue Springs road had at the outpost four men,
and at the reserve sixteen—twenty in all. Five horsemen in the
dusk of a summer evening, were riding up from towards the
east—very quiet for comrades and very watchful for people who
seemed to have business there. If a moon had been in the sky,
by the light of it one could have recognized the faces of Scott,
Will Haller, Cole Younger, Sim Whitsett and David Poole—
volunteers all in Scott's endeavor to solace the last days of an
old man whom he did not even know. Upon the left flank of
the road on which were the picquets, they were manœuvering
to get between the reserves and the outpost. One thing alone
favored them—they knew the country. It was a gentle night,
all starlight and summer odor. The men might not have to
fight—no matter, they were there just the same. A little halt
was called, and Scott spoke low to the group: ''I thank you,
men, for coming here. If you asked me why the old man's tale
stirred me so, and why the yearning was so strong to do a good
act, in perhaps a bad way, I could not tell you for my life. May
be it is fate. Do any of you understand what fate is? The
other day at Lone Jack, you know, we charged the cannon,
under Haller there. About the guns it was hell, wasn't it, Bill?
I had four revolvers, and never a shot left. A Federal at the
corner of a house, not twenty yards away, fired at me six times
and missed me every time, though I did not dodge. That was
fate.'' But the Guerrillas were in no mood to moralize. Poole
broke in grimly: ''That was d—d bad shooting.'' The poor
fellow's consoling castle fell as walnut leaves before a frost, and
he added but this: ''They won't give the boy up for less than
two, perhaps for less than four. Their militia are not set much
store by, even among the commanders of them; but the prisoner is a citizen and not a Guerrilla; a Guerrilla is not for exchange at any price. We must have the outpost intact, if possible.'' ''Hush!'' said Younger, in a whisper, his head turned
to one side as a stag's head, ''I hear horses.'' Behind them
from toward the reserves, the steady tramp of regular feet were
  8

audible, the gait being a walk. "It is the relief," spoke up
Whitsett, in a moment; and "follow me," was heard from
Scott, as he hurried from the road into the brush and drew up
again in its heavy shadow, every man peering forward and waiting eagerly.

One file, eight, twenty, fifty, a hundred—instead of a relief
picquet going forward to the outpost, it was a marching column
of Federal cavalry moving the Guerillas did not know where.
What a noisy column! Some sang from the rear, and others
from the front. Jest, and joke, and badinage flew along from
squadron to squadron. Quantrell was everything—a horse-
thief, murderer, scoundrel, villain, man-eater, cannibal, devil-
fish. They would roast him, draw him, quarter him, boil him
in oil, flay him alive—they only wanted to find him and get one
fair chance at him. Scott's little band heard all this militia
ebullition and laughed in their throats a leather-stocking laugh.
Let once a mare whinney, however, or a horse neigh, and then
those who laughed best would have to laugh last.

The rear guard of the marching column was barely out of
sight when Scott fell in behind it. As he neared the Independence outpost it did not even halt him; luck certainly was his
to-night. "One each for all of you, none for me," Scott said,
a little regretfully, as he was upon the four militia sitting
quietly in their saddles, "and now to work, kill only in extremity." There was no need to kill. In an instant Haller had a
pistol to one head, Whitsett to another, Younger to a third, and
Poole to the fourth; the excitement of the capture was scarcely
enough to add to it interest. The Federals, confident to the
end that the Guerrillas were but a portion of the command which
had just passed, did not so much as even imagine an enemy
until they were powerless. It was best so. Flight could not
have saved them, and resistance such as their's must have been,
meant simply sheep against the shearers. When disarmed and
dismounted, the Federals stood amazed in the presence of their
captors. Scott asked who of the five would carry them to Quantrell. At that name a great fear fell upon the prisoners. One
whispered to another, but his excitement made him audible:
"My God, Joe, has it come to this at last? Quantrell! Quantrell!
Why Quantrell is but another name for death." The leaven was
at work. The two trees by the Big Blue had begun to bear other

fruit than the six men the wood-chopper found of a summer morning as he went singing to his work.

No one would go back; they had tasted the strange thing of a capture without a fight, and it was bitter to the mouth. "Draw lots," said Scott, "and if it falls upon me, I will go back." Whitselt held the hat, Haller put the paper in. They all drew, and Poole drew the slip with the word *guard* on it. "Fall in, milish!" he cried out contentedly, as he saw his luck, and away they all marched through the night. He knew what Scott intended to do, but he had drawn. Scott's quick soldier eye saw that with the silent capture of the out-post the reserve was uncovered, and he would beat it up a little. Not satisfied with doing thoroughly what he had but small hopes of doing at all, he must needs go further if he fared worse. Luck still abode with him, he said, and he would press it. Soldiers also have this term in common with gamblers—the only difference in the dice being the difference between lead and ivory.

It was scant five hundred yards between the reserve and the furthest post, and yet between the two a stream ran which had very steep banks but no bridge. In an enemy's country, also, no intermediate sentinels divided up the distance. The out-post—if it was not actually cut off from its reserve—was almost wholly inaccessible to its succor. Scott saw all this as he rode down and spoke of it: "These militia do nothing right; they do not even know how to kill a gentleman." But they knew how to be on guard. As the four Guerrillas emerged from the darkness into the light, a sergeant with the reserve halted them. "Say nothing," whispered Scott, "do as I do, and when I draw my pistol, charge." Then speaking up to the sergeant, though still advancing, he replied roughly: "Why do you question us? We have just passed through your lines and have been sent back with special dispatches to the Colonel at the post. Give way." He was upon them as he finished and his pistol was out. So close indeed was he that when he shot the sergeant in the middle of the forehead the powder singed his eyebrows. It looked mightily afterwards like a massacre. But ten of the sixteen pickets were mounted, while those on horseback had scarcely time to fire a gun. No one led. When the sergeant fell there was a stampede—a wild, helpless, sudden rending away, no two taking the same direction, and on the

east the town of Independence was absolutely uncovered.
Scott's men were not scratched. Seven dead lay about the
bivouac fires, and several wounded hid themselves in the brush.
By noon the next day the old man's boy was back again at the
homestead, Scott's four militia buying him out after a lengthy
parley.

Those late summer and early autumn days were busy battle
days. Men fought more than they plowed; there were more
forays than furrows. Todd took thirty men and went down
along the Harrisonville and Kansas City road and built him an
ambuscade. Getting together forty or fifty picks and forty or
fifty shovels he dug a series of trenches along the highway deep
enough to shelter a hundred men. From the first one to the
last one it was a hundred yards—a line of fire that would eat its
way furiously through any column. Back of these trenches was
the dry bed of a stream—a natural bomb proof for the horses.
Todd did things in this way generally; he had Scipio's eye and
the brawn of Spartacus.

Working at night and lying by in the day, the birds even
knew nothing of the traps and dead-falls this indefatigable
hunter was setting and digging for larger game than any that
had ever abounded since on Big Creek the buffalo grazed.

Two hundred cavalry with ten wagons were marching up
from Henry county to Leavenworth. New at the business,
Quantrell's name had only came to them as the name of
Jonathan Wild or John A. Murrell. Todd let them pass along
until their line lay against his line, and then the rifle-pits became
a tornado. All that portion of the column in front of them was
torn out as a fierce wind tears a track through the trees, the
two bleeding ends striving helplessly to unite, the wagon train
being the ligature. But while Todd was still keeping his holes
in the ground a veritable furnace, Scott put torches to the
wagons and added to the terrors of the ambuscade the demoralization of a conflagration. Less the vehicles and seventy
wounded and dead men, the stricken remnant of a once dashing
column gained the friendly shelter of Kansas City.

The rifle pits remained. For days and days it was silent
there, and from the torn earth some grass began to grow.
Gregg would see what sort of a footing these gave a Guerrilla
who had some scruples about fighting at odds greater

than twenty to two. He came one evening late, with Haller
and Scott, and prepared to keep a single vigil at least upon the
lonesome water-course. There was a young moon. The night,
jubilant with singing things, seemed to dwell upon peace in
every chirp, or breeze, or song, or monotone. Nature was
glad; its harmonies filled all space and its narcotism all the
senses. Even the Guerrillas felt the Katydid's droning opiate,
and the water's running lullaby. Some stretched themselves at
ease where the shadows were heaviest, and some—yielding to
the witcheries of the hour—let memory re-establish the past
and re-people it with faces, and vows, and pieces of rings.
All were silent.

Suddenly a pistol-shot from the south, a scattering volley,
and then the loud clatter of resounding hoofs transfigured the
dreamers; the lotos leaves had become laurel.

Gregg had sent George Shepherd south along the road before
dismounting, and everything must be safe there. It was Shepherd's pistol shot that he had heard, and the galloping of
Shepherd's horse. Watching with all the eyes he had, and
especially alert and vigilant, this choice scout had not seen an
infantry line approaching him through the brush, however, nor
did he know that beyond a turn in the road three hundred
cavalrymen had ridden up, had dismounted, and were even now
marching forward to surprise the surprisers; that the hunted
were hunting the hunters. But that he was a man of extraordinary coolness and quickness, Shepherd must have fallen without
alarming his comrades. Infantry were all around and about him.
It looked to him strange afterwards, but he had not even heard
the fall of a footstep in the bushes or the breaking of a twig
among the undergrowth. All he understood then was the rising
up of a tall form close to his right stirrup, the leveling of a
gun barrel, and the short, sententious word "Surrender!" As
still as the creeping had been, it was yet no match for
Shepherd's splendid presence of mind. He threw himself
forward on his horse, shot the dismounted trooper in the breast
as he turned, took the fire of all who saw that the game was up,
and then at a long, swinging gallop rushed away to alarm his
comrades. That night saw a fight the whole war failed to
surpass with any stubborn combat. Especially to take a hand
against Quantrell and help drive him to the wall, Major

Hubbard, of the Sixth Missouri Federal Cavalry, came up from Clinton county. He was one of the best fighters the militia produced. He was not afraid to charge; he could stand up square and take and give, man for man; he saw only the soldier in the Guerrilla; he meant to get on Quantrell's track and keep on it until he found him.

As he rode up gaily from the south some one met him north of Harrisonville—some one who knew of the rifle pits—and described accurately the whole lay of the land. Cavalry could not operate against them, the spy said, but infantry might. They were now held by about fifty Guerrillas. This was the substance of the report Hubbard heard some few miles from the ambuscade, and he began to make ready at once to carry it by assault. Failing to silence the single picquet on guard in front of him, he dashed ahead, firing fiercely when he reached the range. Gregg did not return it until he was completely enveloped. Ignorant of the enemy's number, he cared not for further enlightenment. It was first fight, and fight, and fight. When the moon went down the fight was still raging. There could be no manœuvering. Inside the rifle-pits were the Guerillas; outside the militia. All were bent on killing. Gregg's men spoke very little; the Federals scarcely any more. Now and then a fierce yell would usher in a savage rush, and once or twice a bugle sounded. Gregg held on. One charge reached even to his parapets, if such the earth could be called piled in front of the trenches, but it found no lodgment. The beating of a furious revolver rain full in their faces drove the militia back. They seemed not to care for the horses; if they knew anything about them they did not molest them. Hubbard was also a tenacious fighter, as well as a dashing one. He held on to that wild night's work for three mortal hours, charging every twenty minutes and encouraging his men by voice and example. At last he hauled off and mounted, made a detour around that vengeful spot hidden as a sinister thing in mid highway, and hurried onward to Kansas City, leaving his dead, fifty-two in all, to be buried by the citizens, and his wounded in every house for a dozen miles. Gregg's wounded were only eight, thanks to the excellent cover Todd had provided, and killed, none at all.

These two blows, together with a sharp skirmish Quantrell

had with Burris further down in Cass county massed the detached commands in pursuit of him and united them as a single column for his destruction. Calling in every outlying scout or squad in return and getting well together, Quantrell fell back first to Big Blue, fighting. The chase was a long and a stern one. Giving Todd ten men, Haller ten, Gregg ten, Scott ten, and keeping ten himself, he made the hunt for him one long ambuscade of two hundred miles. Tortuous, but terrible; at every ford a fight; in every hollow a barricade; on every hilltop a volley. From Big Blue to Little Blue they chased this lank, bronzed fox of the foray, bugles blowing all about him, and the wild hallooing of the huntsmen coming ever on and on. Away again from the Little Blue to King's, from King's to Dr. Noland's the five detachments fighting and falling back as the pendulum used to swing to and fro in the ancient clocks. Tired, but still determined, Hubbard spoke up at last to Peabody: "Who is this Quantrell you hunt so hard? man or devil, he fights like a wild beast." "And he is; you found one of his lairs, it seems."

Doubling back on the Little Blue lower down, and leading the pursuing column only by an hour, Quantrell—hungry from much fasting and weary at that—found twenty-three militia at Crenshaw's bridge to dispute it. Twenty-three! It was as though a butcher's hand opened all of its bloody fingers at once, fan-fashion, to brush from a slaughtered bullock a bunch of buzzing blue flies. Sim Whitsett and Cole Younger led the advance when the bridge was reached, and they stopped not to count any numbers or any costs. On one side the river was flight and fight; on the other rations and rest. "Altogether, boys," the great voice of Younger roared out, and the bridge shook, and the white splinters flew up from the planks and the timbers there. It is not believed the militia knew their men. The citizens said they seemed appalled at a rush that did not even look up when their volley was fired, and broke for shelter in every direction without reloading. Two escaped, and singularly. One, a mere youth, had done Whitsett a good turn once, and Whitsett saved him. The other, known to Cole Younger in past days as a clever neighbor, reminded him of a favor conferred—the curing of a valuable horse and charging nothing—and Younger put upon him the sign of the Passover.

Down went the bridge after Quantrell was east of the Blue, and up came that long Federal gallop that would not tire. Food and rest came to hunted and hunters alike, but the race was done. Quantrell left for the Lake Hills slowly the next morning, and the Federals on a raft got over during the day and followed on. The carbines rang—the revolvers answered; they were at it again, fifty against a thousand. From the Lake Hills to Johnson county the drive grew rapid. Now Quantrell, now Haller, now Scott, now Gregg, now Todd—if any man fell out of the ranks he was shot out. No rest in Johnson county; none in Lafayette county. Halted at Warren's for a bit or two of bread and corn, Quantrell was driven away; at Graves' it was worse; at Wellington they gave him no rest; down towards Lexington he hadn't even time to water; out south from Lexington six miles it took all five of the chosen fighters to keep the chase a stern one; and back again to Wellington and west by a forced night march, he gained some hours for a needed bivouac.

Day had just broken over a brief bivouac and the men were astir when some friendly citizen brought news to Quantrell of a reconnoitering party occupying Wellington. They were militia but not connected in any manner with the column in pursuit. They might be cut to pieces. To this hour it is not clearly known what business they had in Wellington. Numbering seventy-five, unacquainted with the country, ostensibly aimless and objectless, they poked about the town professing to be after Quantrell, and they found him. He tried to get between them and Lexington, but they were too quick for that. As he reached the main road the rear guard was just disappearing; then came the charge and the rout. One volley only and a great rush. Blood and bottom told in that furious three mile race. Quantrell's own shooting was superb; six saddles were emptied by him, five by Blunt, four by Haller, four by Younger, three by Poole, three by Fletch Taylor, three by George Shepherd, and two each by Todd, Gregg, Whitsett, Coger, Hicks George, Scott, and six or eight others who were riding swift, fresh horses. Of the seventy-five ten alone got back unhurt. It was a blow that carried terror and horror with it. People talked of it as they talked of something sent by God—some pestilence, or drouth, or famine. Dead men along the road were gathered up for a week, and for years belated travelers have told how, when the night turns, there might be heard again the shots, the shrieks, the infernal din and the swift rush of insatiate horsemen that stopped for no prayer and touched no bridle rein until for the want of fuel the fire had burned itself out.

Too late either to pity or save the slaughtered Wellington detachment, the pursuing Federal column might avenge them perhaps and put to the credit side a propitiation or two worthy the comradeship of soldiers. The dust was still heavy upon the garments of the Guerrillas and the foam white upon their horses, when Peabody's pursuit began to thunder again in the rear of Quantrell. It pushed him back again through Wellington; back across the Sni, whose bridge he burned; back through all the open country beyond, and still backward and backward. For five days and five nights Quantrell had been running and fighting. Out of fifty men, twenty-two had been hurt—some badly and some not so badly. They *staid*, however; they reeled in the saddle every now and then, but they fought. Heroic Scott, with a minie ball through his thigh, from the Wellington rout, kept his squad of ten intact and led them to the end.

At Pink Hill it was no better. In his front, near the Blackwater ford of the Sni, Burris was waiting for Quantrell. Todd dashed at the left flank of this not over-bold command and made it huddle, and then away again southwest for Big Creek, Dave Poole leading the rear and Cole Younger the advance. On the divide, between Big Creek and the Sni, the Guerrillas were hemmed at last. Quick work had to be done. If the two millstones were permitted to come together, they would be ground to powder. Quantrell massed his men behind the divide—a bold ridge that rose up abruptly from an otherwise comparatively level country, and made them a little speech: "Men," he said, "you see how it is as plainly as I do. It is my business to get you out of this, and I will get you out. Just over the ridge yonder—you can see them from the summit—five hundred Federals, your old friends under Burris, are coming up to hold you in check until Peabody's column arrives. Then, instead of ten to one, there will be thirty to one. We shall strike Burris first, and trust to luck."

A man of very few words and very few figures of speech, Quantrell arrayed the Guerrillas just as he wanted them, and waited behind the ridge. He kept Todd near to him, and in the rear he stationed Haller and Scott. Gregg was to watch the centre of the line, for he meant to charge in line with double intervals, thus giving free play to the revolvers.

Burris was probably two hundred yards below the summit of the divide when Quantrell crowned its crest at a walk and broke at sight of him into a gallop. The gallop, in an instant, was a fierce run, the whole front of the charging line wrapping itself in a powder cloud from its incessant pistol vollies. Abreast of one another, yet preserving perfect intervals, Quantrell, Gregg, Todd, Younger, Tom Talley, Poole, Hicks George, Sim Whitsett, Haller, Ki Harrison, and John Coger, struck the Federal line about the same time, and such an onset meant the riving of its ranks as a hurricane rives the timber. Then the strange spectacle was presented of a regiment cut half in two, both ends bloody, and between them something that looked like a lurid wedge driven there by a power the dense smoke made invisible.

But Quantrell did not tarry. Harrison was badly wounded in the charge, Hicks George was wounded, George Shepherd was shot, Quantrell himself was wounded again, Todd had blood drawn from him twice, Poole was shot and Scriviner was killed. To the rear the nearest prairie was black with pursuing Federals. Night came on, and Burris followed after, but far behind. Reaching the heavy timber of Big Creek with scarcely an unwounded man in his command, Quantrell disbanded for a little rest and medical attention. By twos and threes, in squads, singly, the Guerrillas went their way as phantoms. There—alert, stalwart, armed, soldierly in every movement—they seemed under the trees and in the uncertain light a host. Look again! The trees are there, the dark waters flow rapidly under them and away, the watch fires burn low, no forms flit there, the silence is supreme, were they ever real? Had they ever flesh and blood and bone and sinew? Spectres, did they not go back into the unknown? Illusions, why trouble the imagination with a mirage that may never come again?

A great roaring laugh awoke the echoes of Big Creek the morning after the night of the disbandment, and Hubbard bantered Peabody: "Here we are, Colonel, without a trail or a track. Has this man Quantrell of yours gone into the earth

or into the water?   Where is his hole; and has he pulled his
hole in after him?   Our work, it appears to me, is pretty well
over.''   "His old trick," replied Peabody, curtly, "he has disbanded.''   "And so should we," rejoined Hubbard, in evident
disgust at the result of the whole campaign.   "Any one
thousand men that can't take fifty ain't worth the pipe clay that
rubs up their sabre-belts.   Your Quantrell is either a myth or
a devil—which?''   "He is both," and Peabody and 'Hubbard
shook hands and parted.

Ostensibly unorganized, the Guerrillas notwithstanding failed
to be quiet.   Indeed the wild life they had deliberately
chosen made successive days of peace absolutely impossible.
In the old fashion—hammer and tongs—they were at it again
in less than forty-eight hours.   Todd struck an isolated scout
on the main Harrisonville and Warrensburg road and charged
it as he always charged.   It was a running fight of eight miles,
wherein no quarter was given and not much asked.   Twenty-
two Federals fell along the roadside and the balance of the
detachment, eighteen, reached Harrisonville through sheer hard
running.

Charley or Ki Harrison, a tall, swarthy, extremely silent,
uncommunicative man lived in Denver City when the war commenced, and went South early.   Colorado bred a set of grave,
inflexible borderers, who—whether Federal or Confederate—
left their hand writing pretty legibly written whenever or
wherever they stood in battle.   Harrison practiced that kind of
revolver shooting which consisted of instantaneous execution.
Between the act of drawing and the act of firing, if it took
longer than two seconds, he argued that no man excelled another as an expert.   For hours and hours he worked at the theory.
Erecting at twenty paces the outlines of a human figure, and
indicating by smaller divisions the eyes, the mouth, the forehead, the heart, the bowels, and the lungs, he would labor with
something of a monomania to excel all in the rapidity of the
process by which he got his revolver from its scabbard, and
the accuracy of its fire afterwards.   Carroll Wood came into
Missouri with Harrison.   He too had been both a mountaineer
and a plainsman.   So, also, did Captain William West, that
man called by Richardson, of the mournful McFarland memory,
"the swarthy Adonis of the Plains."   Each of these men had

either a stern or tragical beginning. Wood, standing at the back of some friends fighting in the streets of Denver, had reflected upon him many of the more sombre lights of the quarrel, and felt to lay hands upon him that most monstrous of all organizations of brutality and cowardice, a western Vigilance Committee. It was ten against two hundred. Word went instantly to John C. Moore, then editor, ex-mayor and lawyer, that the toils had closed over Carroll. He neither asked the right nor the wrong of the arrest—he simply saw the danger; he did not discuss the philosophy or the morality of the proceeding —he only informed himself that they had his friend. As he hurried he buckled on a revolver. Wood's ten comrades were about him and nearest to him, but the peril was imminent. He was known to be a rebel, "dead game," not over given to take a slight or a taunt, and the Vigilantes hated him; the hour had come to cast up and count the score and to settle it. "Hang him!" two hundred bass throats roared out—that volumned, ferocious roar which has in it the malignity of the faction and the selfishness of the born coward on top through circumstances and numbers. Moore was not a second too soon. The rope was being knotted and noosed. Wood, just a little pale from the swift blood that flowed so fiercely, lifted up his undaunted eyes to all the hungry faces in front of him and gazed thereon, steadily but superciliously. Splendid scorn might be all that death intended to leave to him at the finish. Moore put himself before the prisoner and the wild beasts showing their teeth and licking their lips, and spoke to them. That he spoke nobly and eloquently it is not necessary to assert. That he spoke practically and adroitly the sequel made more than manifest. Best of all, however, it was the peroration which exhibited the man. "I have now done," he said quietly in conclusion, "what the duty of the advocate required of me; it is the duty of the friend which I do next." As he finished he came down from the stand and placed himself alongside of Wood, his revolver in readiness and his resolution taken. It is enough to know that there was no hanging. Wood lives to-day, a factor in the great peaceful body of thriving citizens, the past a memory that cannot die, and his acts therein fashioned of soldierly episodes from Lexington, 1861, to Newtonia, 1864.

West came to Gen. Jeff. Thompson scarred from a bowie-knife

duel that had left him little better than dead. On the plains with
a gentleman named Tutt, from St. Louis, a dispute commenced
between them which ended in a challenge from West. Tutt accepted, choosing bowie-knives. The arena was a circle with a
diameter of twenty feet, the combatants stripping to the waist.
Each man was an *athlete*. Tutt cut his antagonist seventeen
times, the last one being the worst one, getting in return only a
few slashes that did not go to the hollow. Die, repeated the
doctors in indignation at a question so clearly out of order—of
course West would die. But he didn't. Nay, more, the man
got better, and better, and finally rode away southward toward
where Jeff. Thompson was writing impossible proclamations and
paddling improbable canoes. Swarthy, splendidly formed, a
horseman who rode like a swan swims, long-haired like Absalom,
and just as fated, the end came speedily. Tarrying late one
afternoon beyond the picquets, and riding homeward under the
moon, the soldier who halted him was furiously charged. West
went at him in sheer wantonness no doubt, but the sentinal gave
him his death wound. As the tide turned, and the night had
fallen, a perfect peace came upon the pallid man, lying just this
side the wonderful river. Not a white dimple stirred among the
corn; not a low ripple shivered through the leaves; flooded with
the moonlight, even the cattle slept; the very air seemed as if
it had no breath of earth to stain it. "West!" something
called. Moore, who sat beside the dying man, heard no word;
McDowell, who held the weak hand, knew no whisper in the
room. "West!" "Here," and the pallid face lit up like a sun-
beam had touched it, and the perfect form lifted itself just a little: "Who called? Here, Colonel, and ready for duty!" Hush!
An angel might have been by the dead soldier. In this world
there are touching illusions that perhaps in the other are sublime realities, and following the angel call he had gone where
the snowy blossoms never wither on the everlasting hills, and
the autumn never braids its scarlet fringing through the green of
eternal summers.

Harrison, on a larger scale, meant to try that rigid revolver
practice of his. Having forty men of his own, and being reinforced by twenty men more under Lieutenant William Haller,
he rode down in the neighborhood of Sibley, nearly on the line
between Jackson and Lafayette counties. Richard Chiles joined

him with ten men more, brother of that Kit Chiles who had fallen in the front of Quantrell's splendid charge at Independence, and who in surviving his brother had received fate's simple lease to fight a little longer. Either in combat was a lion. Chiles led the assault and was shot down. Two hundred Federals in the houses of the town held their own and more, for they repulsed five separate and distinct attacks, and forced Harrison at last to forego the ugly job of getting them out. As he fell back he counted the costs. Six men were dead and thirty-seven wounded—a forbidding aggregate. Revolver practice against brick walls amounted to naught. It was the old lesson, bought by Harrison for a good round price, that hard fighting is not always hard sense. As a Guerrilla, he figured no more in the history of the border, but over his last days there is even yet, as they are recalled, something of the savage light of a massacre.

Shelby was the great banyan-tree, metaphorically speaking, of the Guerrillas. They sat under the protecting shade of his constantly expanding reputation, and were content. No evil after-things followed them there. No sleuth-hound conscription put its nose upon the track that led to the camp of the Iron Brigade. No department officials, or district officials examined into the bloody annals of these migratory people, going South in winter and North when the spring came. In addition, Shelby was their great high priest. They prayed to him, confessed to him, remembered him often in wills and testaments, furnished him spies on the eve of operations and scouts in their consummations, helped his flanks in the raiding season, made Missouri familiar to him as Arkansas, and piloted the way to many a crushing overthrow as the pilot-fishes pilot the sharks to many a stricken squadron.

Captain Harrison believed he could do some excellent service for the Confederacy in Colorado. He believed that he could recruit at least a regiment of Colorado Guerrillas who would inhabit the plains, live like the Indians, destroy supply trains, make the overland routes to California impracticable, eliminate from the military economy of western occupation the frontier post system, enlist the savages to fight against the United States, and break the only link that bound California and the Union together. This was Harrison's plan. It was bold but not feas-

ible, and Shelby told him so. He pleaded just the same, however, to be permitted to try, and Shelby finally prevailed upon
Hindman to grant him the authority. That Colorado *carte
blanche* was his death warrant. Harrison reached the territory
of the Osage Indians with forty-five men and entered it
at a rush. His object was to waste no useless time in fighting
there, nor anywhere until the hour of opportunity. Assailed in
front and rear, hemmed in, overwhelmed, hunted on all sides,
driven from position to position, forty-four of the forty-six men
died at bay, selling dearly all that was left to each—his life.
Two alone escaped. One of these, Colonel Warner Lewis, lives
to day in Fulton, Callaway county, and the other—Clark Hockensmith—fell fighting like the hero he was over Quantrell's
wounded body in Kentucky. Lewis left Harrison dying as the
Indian always dies—killing to the last. Behind his dead horse,
both legs broken, a jaw shattered, and four fingers of his left hand
gone, he shot while a load was left in a single pistol. There
came finally a rush and a volley—then a great stillness. Harrison had been the last to go, and it had taken him three-quarters
of an hour to die. This side the judgment day no one will ever
know what heroic things were done on that last march through
fire and savages—a border Calvary of fifteen hours. Perhaps
some touching talk was had. Husbands were there who were
never to see their wives any more. Fathers were there who in
the dreams of the past night's bivouac had heard the prattle of
blue-eyed children. It was terrible to die so, but they died.
Six months later, as a strong Confederate column marched
through where they fell, more than twenty bodies, shriveled by
wind and weather, claimed even then the last sad rites of comradeship.

CHAPTER X.

THE MARCH SOUTH.

WINTER had come and some snow had fallen. There were no longer any more leaves; nature had nothing more to do with the ambuscades. Some bitter nights, as a foretaste of bitterer nights to follow, reminded Quantrell that it was time to migrate. Most of the wounded men were well again. All of the dismounted had found serviceable horses. On the twenty-second of October, 1862, a quiet muster on the banks of the Little Blue revealed at inspection nearly all of the old faces and forms, with a sprinkling here and there of new ones. Some few, too hard hit in that pitiless pursuit to ride so early, were still awaiting the balm of a much bedeviled Gilead. Quantrell counted them two by two as the Guerrillas dressed up in line, and front rank and rear rank there were just seventy-eight. On the morrow they were moving southward. That old road running between Harrisonville and Warrensburg was always to the Guerrillas a road of fire, and here again on their march toward Arkansas, and eight miles east of Harrisonville, did Todd in the advance strike a Federal scout of thirty militia cavalrymen. They were Missourians and led by a Lieutenant Satterlee. To say Todd is to say charge. To associate him with something that will illustrate him, is to put torch and powder magazine together. It was the old, old story. On one side a furious rush, on the other panic and imbecile flight. Emphatically a four mile race, it ended with this for a score: Todd, killed, six; Boon Schull, five; Fletch. Taylor, three; George Shepherd, two; John Coger, one; Sim. Whitsett, one; James Little, one; George Maddox, one—total, twenty; wounded, *none*. Even in leaving, what sinister farewells these Guerrillas were taking!

The second night out Quantrell stopped over beyond Dayton, in Cass county, and ordered a bivouac for the evening. There came to his camp here a good-looking man, clad like a citizen, who had business to transact, and who knew how to state it. He was not fat, he' was heavy. He laughed a great deal, and when he laughed he showed a perfect set of faultlessly white teeth. If that smile should by any chance become preternaturally fixed, the mouth that before it was winning in repose, would certainly become after it forbidding. He was young. An aged man is a thinking ruin; this one did not appear to think—he felt and enjoyed. He was tired of dodging about in the brush, he said, and he believed he would fight a little. Here, there and everywhere the Federals had hunted him and shot at him, and he was weary of so much persecution. Would Quantrell let him become a Guerrilla? "Your name?" asked the chief. The recruit winced under the abrupt question just the slightest of an almost imperceptible degree, and Quantrell saw the start. Attracted by something of novelty in the whole performance, a crowd collected. Quantrell, without looking at the new comer, appeared yet to be analyzing him. Suddenly he spoke up: "I have seen you before; where?" "Nowhere." "Think again. I have seen you in Lawrence, Kansas." The face was a murderer's face now, softened by a woman's blush. There came to it such a look of mingled fear, indignation, and cruel eagerness that Gregg, standing next to him and nearest to him, laid his hand on his revolver. "Stop," said Quantrell, motioning to Gregg, "do not harm him, but disarm him." Two revolvers were taken from his person, and a pocket pistol —a derringer. While being searched, the white teeth shone in a smile that was almost placid. "You suspicion me," he said, so calmly that his words sounded as if spoken under the vault of some echoing dome, "but I have never been in Lawrence in my life."

Quantrell was lost in thought again, with the strange man— standing up smiling in the midst of all the band—watching him with eyes that were blue at times and grey at times, and always gentle. More wood was put upon the bivouac fire, and the flames grew ruddy. In their vivid light the young man might not be really so young. He had also a thick neck, great broad shoulders, and something of sensuality about the chin.

9

The back of his skull was bulging and prominent. Here and there in his hair were little white streaks. Because there were such bloom and color in his cheeks, one could not remember these. Lacking the consolation of tears, nature had given him perfect health. Quantrell still tried to make out that face, to find a name for that Sphinx in his front, to recall some time or circumstance, or place that made obscure things clear, and at last the past returned to him in the light of a swift revealment. "I have it all now," he said, "and you are a Jayhawker. The name is immaterial. I have seen you at Lawrence; I have seen you at Lane's headquarters; I have been a soldier myself with you; we have done duty together—but I mean to hang you this hour, by g—d!" Unabashed, the threatened man drew his breath hard and strode a step towards Quantrell. Gregg put a pistol to his head: "Keep back. Can't you talk where you are? Do you mean to say anything?"

The old smile again! Could nothing ever drive away that smile—nothing ever keep those white teeth from shining? "You ask me if I want to talk, just as if I had anything to talk about. What can I say? What must I do to prove myself sincere? I tell you that I have been hunted, proscribed, shot at, bedeviled, driven up and down, around and about, until I am tired. I want to kill somebody; I want to know what sleeping a sound night's sleep means." Quantrell's grave voice broke calmly in: "Bring a rope!" Blunt brought it. "Make an end fast, Sergeant." The end was made fast to a low-lying limb; in the firelight the noose expanded. "Up with him, men." Four stalwart hands seized him as a vise. He did not even defend himself. His flesh beneath their grip felt soft and rounded. The face, although all the bloom was there, hardened viciously—like the murderer's face it was. "So you mean to get rid of me in that way? it is like you, Quantrell. I know you, but you do not know me. I have been hunting you for three long years. You killed my brother in Kansas; you killed others there, your comrades. I did not know, till afterwards, what kind of a devil we had around our very messes—a devil who prowled about the camp fires and shot soldiers in the night that broke bread with him in the day. Can you guess what brought me here?"

The shifting phases of this uncommon episode attracted all;

even Quantrell himself was interested. The prisoner—ostensible recruit no longer—threw off all disguise, and defied those who meant to hang him up. "You did well to disarm me," he said, addressing himself to Gregg, "for I intended to kill your Captain. Everything has been against me, however. At the Tate House he escaped; at Clark's it was no better; we had him surrounded at Swearingen's and his men cut him out; we ran him for two hundred miles and he disappeared—devil that he is, or in league with the devil—and now, after playing my last card and staking everything upon it, what is left to me? A dog's death and a brother unavenged. No matter; it's luck. Do your worst." As he finished he folded his arms across his breast and stood stolid as the huge trees overhead. Some pity began visibly to affect the men. Gregg turned away and went out beyond the firelight. Even Quantrell's face softened, but only for a moment. When he spoke again to Blunt, his voice was so changed and harsh that it was scarcely recognized. "He is one of the worst of a band that I failed to make a finish of before the war came, but what escapes to-day is dragged up by the net to-morrow. If I had not recognized him he would have killed me. I do not hang him for that, however. I hang him because the whole race and breed to which he belongs should be exterminated. Sergeant, do your duty." Blunt, by a dexterous movement, slipped the noose about the prisoner's neck, and the four men who had at first disarmed him, tightened it. To the last the bloom abode with his cheeks. He did not pray; neither did he make plaint nor moan. The fitful firelight flared up once and fixed his outline clear against the shadowy background; a sudden breeze made the boughs moan a little; no man spoke a word; something like a huge pendulum oscillated as though spun by a strong hand, quivered once or twice, and then, swinging to and fro and regularly, stopped forever. Just at this moment, three quick, hot vollies and close together, rolled in from the northern picquet post, and the camp was on its feet. If one had looked then at the dead man's face, something like a smile might have been seen there, fixed and sinister, and beneath it the white, sharp teeth. James Williams had accepted his fate like a hero. At mortal feud with Quantrell, and living only that he might meet him face to face in battle, he had joined every regiment, volunteered upon every scout, rode foremost in every raid, and fought hardest in every combat. It was not to be. Quantrell was leaving Missouri. A great gulf was about to separate them. One desperate effort now, and years of toil and peril at a single blow might be well rewarded. He struck it and it cost him his life. To this day the whole tragic episode is sometimes recalled and discussed along the border.

The bivouac was rudely broken up. Three hundred Federal cavalry, crossing Quantrell's trail late in the afternoon, had followed it until the darkness fell, halted an hour for supper, and then again, at a good round trot, rode straight upon Haller holding the rear of the movement southward. He fought at the outpost half an hour. Behind huge trees, he would not fall back until his flanks were in danger. All the balance of the night through he fought them thus, making six splendid charges and holding on to every position until his grasp was broken loose by sheer hammering. At Grand River the pursuit ended, and Quantrell swooped down upon Lamar, in Barton county, where a Federal garrison held the court house and the houses nearest to it. He attacked, but got worsted; he attacked again and lost one of his best men; he attacked the third time and made no better headway. Baffled, finally, and hurt more than was necessary in any aspect of the situation, he abandoned the town and resumed, unmolested, the road to the south. From Jackson county to the Arkansas line the whole country was swarming with militia, and but for the fact that every Guerrilla was clad in Federal clothing, the march would have been an incessant battle. As it was it will never be known how many isolated Federals, mistaking Quantrell's men for comrades of other regiments not on duty with them, fell into traps that never gave up their victims alive. Near Cassville, in Barry county, twenty-two were killed thus. They were coming up from Cassville, and were meeting the Guerrillas, who were going south. The order given by Quantrell was a most simple but a most murderous one. By the side of each Federal in the approaching column a Guerrilla was to range himself, engage him in conversation, and then, at a given signal, blow his brains out. Quantrell gave the signal promptly, shooting the militiaman assigned to him through the middle of the forehead, and where upon their horses twenty-two confident men laughed and talked in comrade fashion a second before,

JAMES YOUNGER.

nothing remained of the unconscious detachment, literally exterminated, save a few who struggled in agony upon the ground and a mass of terrified and plunging horses. Not a Guerrilla missed his mark. It was as though a huge hand had suddenly opened and wiped clean out a column of figures upon a blackboard. This minute instinct with joy and life, the next dead, and their faces in the dust.

Quantrell found Shelby at Cane Hill, Arkansas, and reported to him. Shelby attached the Guerrillas to the regiment commanded by Colonel David Shanks, and busied himself so much with preparations for the great fight that was to come off at Prairie Grove that he saw them rarely until they left him again.

Cole Younger remained in Missouri, and with him a formidable squad of the old Guerrillas, who were not in a condition to ride when Quantrell moved southward. Younger was exceedingly enterprising. He fought almost daily. He did not seem to be affected by the severity of the weather. At night and on a single blanket he slept often in the snow. While it was too bitter cold for Federal scouting-parties to leave their comfortable cantonments or Federal garrisons to poke their noses beyond the snug surroundings of their well furnished barracks, the Guerrillas rode everywhere and waylaid roads, bridges, lines of couriers, and routes of travel. Six mail carriers disappeared in one week between Independence and Kansas City. A load of hay to be safe had to have with it a company of cavalry. A messenger bearing an order required a company as an escort. Quantrell was gone, but Quantrell's mantle had fallen upon one worthy to succeed him.

In a month after Quantrell's arrival in Arkansas, George Todd returned to Jackson county, bringing with him Fletch Taylor, Boon Schull, James Little, Andy Walker and James Reed. Todd and Younger came together by that blood-hound instinct which all men have who hunt or are hunted. Todd had scarcely made himself known to the Guerrillas in Jackson county before he had commenced to kill militia. A foraging party from Independence were gathering corn from a field belonging to Daniel White, a most worthy citizen of the vicinity, when Todd and Younger broke in upon it, shot five down in the field and put the balance to flight. The next day, November 30, Younger—having with him Joshua and Job McCockle, and Thomas Talley, met four of Jennison's regiment face to face in the neighborhood of the County Poor House. Younger, who had a most extraordinary voice, called out loud enough to be heard a mile: "You are four and we are four; stand until we come up." Instead of standing, however, the Jayhawkers turned about and dashed off as rapidly as possible, followed by Younger and his men. Excellently mounted, the race lasted fully three miles before either party won or lost. At last the Guerrillas gained and kept gaining. Three of the four Jayhawkers were finally shot from their saddles, while the fourth escaped by superior riding and superior running.

Younger had now with him George Wigginton, John McCockle, Job McCockle, Tom. Talley, Zach. Traber, Nathan Kerr, John Barker, Dave Hilton, William Hulse, Dr. Hale, Ike Basham, George Clayton, Joseph Hardin and Oath Hinton. Albert Cunningham, another Guerrilla leader of a squad, had a few men—William Runnels, Jasper Rodes, John Hays, Noah Webster, Daniel Williams, Edward Hinks and Sam. Constable. Todd, retaining with him those brought up from Arkansas, kept adding to them all who, either from choice or necessity, were forced to take refuge in the brush. He argued that a man who did not want to fight and was forced to fight, made most generally a desperate fight when he got into it. Whenever he could hear of a citizen being robbed or plundered of property, or insulted in any manner, he always managed to recruit him into his band and make of him in a very short time a most formidable Guerrilla.

Todd, never happy except on the war path, suggested to Younger and Cunningham a raid into Kansas. West of Little Santa Fe, always debatable if not dangerous ground, thirty Guerrillas met sixty-two Jayhawkers. It was a prairie fight, brief, bloody, but finished at a gallop. Todd's tactics—the old yell and the old rush—swept everything. A revolver in each hand, the bridle rein in the teeth, the horses at a full run, the individual rider firing right and left—this is the way the Guerrillas charged. Such was their horsemanship, and such the terrible accuracy of their fire that never in all the history of the war did a Federal line, man for man, withstand an onset. Two to one even did not make it much better, and with the exception of the Colorado troops Quantrell scarcely ever hesitated a moment about attacking an enemy who held against him the enormous odds in battle of three and four to one.

The sixty-two Jayhawkers fought better than most of the militia had been in the habit of fighting, but they would not stand up to the work at revolver range. When Todd charged them furiously as soon as he came in sight of them, they stood a volley at a hundred yards and returned it; but not a closer grapple. Reinforced after an hour of running and fighting by one hundred and fifty additional Jayhawkers, they in turn became the aggressors and drove Todd across a large prairie and into some heavy timber. It was while holding the rear with six men that Cole Younger was attacked by fifty-two and literally run over. Every man among the covering party was wounded but none mortally. In the midst of the *melee*—bullets coming like hailstones in summer weather—John McDowell's horse went down, the rider under him and badly hit. He cried out to Younger for help. Hurt himself, and almost overwhelmed, Younger dismounted, however, under fire, rescued McDowell, and brought him safe back from the furious crush, killing as he ran for succor a Federal soldier whose impetuous horse had carried him beyond Younger and McDowell struggling in the road together. Afterwards Younger was betrayed and by the man to save whose life he had risked his own.

Dividing again, and operating in different localities, Todd, Younger, and Cunningham carried the terror of the Guerrilla name through all the border counties of Kansas and Missouri. Every day and sometimes twice a day from December 3d to December 18th, these three fought some scouting party or attacked some picquet post. At the crossing of the Big Blue, on the road to Kansas City—the place where the former bridge had been burnt by Quantrell—Todd surprised six militia, killed them all, and then hung them up on a long pole, resting at either end upon forks, just as hogs are hung up in the country after slaughtering time. In the morning they were frozen hard as iron. So bold, in fact, did they become, and so unsparing, that as bitter as the weather was the Federals at Kansas City began to get ready to drive them away from their lines of communication. Three heavy columns were sent out to scour the country. Surprising Cunningham in camp on Big Creek, they killed a splendid soldier, Will Freeman, and drove the rest of the Guerrillas back into Jackson county after a running fight of twenty-seven miles.

Todd, joining himself quickly to Younger, ambuscaded the column hunting for him, and in a series of combats between the Little Blue and Kansas City, killed forty-seven of the pursuers and captured five wagons and thirty-three head of horses. There was a lull again in marching and counter-marching, the winter got colder and colder, and some deep snows fell. Christmas had come and the Guerrillas would have a Christmas frolic. Nothing bolder and braver exists to-day upon the records of either side in the civil war, than this so-called Christmas frolic. Col. Henry Younger, father of Coleman Younger, was one of the most respected citizens of Western Missouri. A stalwart pioneer of Jackson county, fourteen children were born to him and his noble wife, a true Christian woman and a veritable and blessed mother in Israel. A politician of the old school; practical and incorruptible; bold in the expression of his opinions and ardent in their support; kind neighbor, liberal citizen, and steadfast friend, Colonel Younger for a number of years was a Judge of the County Court of Jackson county, and for several terms a member of the State Legislature. In 1858, he left Jackson county for Cass, and dealt largely in stock. He was also an extensive farmer, an enterprising merchant, and the keeper of one of the best and most popular livery stables in the West, located in Harrisonville, the county seat of Cass county. His blooded horses were very superior. He had two farms of six hundred acres each, that were in a high state of cultivation, and he generally had on hand for speculating purposes ready money to the amount of from $6,000 to $10,000.

On one of Jennison's periodical raids, in the fall of 1862, he sacked and burned Harrisonville. Col. Younger, although a staunch Union man and known to be such, was made to lose heavily. Jennison and his officers—the officers on all occasions being more rapacious than the privates—took from him $4,000 worth of buggies, carriages and hacks, and forty head of blooded horses, worth at a low average $500 apiece. Then the balance of his property that was perishable and yet not moveable, was burned. The intention also was to kill Col. Younger, upon the principle that dead men could tell no tales, but he escaped with difficulty and made his way into Independence. Spies were on his track. In that reign of hate and frenzy along the border, men were as often murdered for money as for patriotism. Jennison was told that Col. Younger was rich, and that he invariably carried with him large sums of money. A plan was formed immediately to kill him. Twenty cut-throats were organized as a band under a Jayhawker named Whalley, and set to watch his every movement. They dogged him to Independence, from Independence to Kansas City, and from Kansas City down again into Cass county. Coming upon him at last in an isolated place, and within a few miles of Harrisonville, they riddled his body, rifled his pockets, and left the corpse, stark and partially stripped, by the roadside.

The fire and torment of persecution did not end here. The mother and orphan children were driven from Harrisonville. She sought refuge at her farm in Jackson county, but the bloodhounds followed her. There was scarcely a day but what she was robbed of something, until at last there was nothing left. At the muzzles of their pistols, finally, and when all was gone, they forced her to set fire to her own house. She did it for the sake of her children, because she believed that unless it were done her life would be taken, and the homestead to her was nothing in comparison to the comfort that would still be left to her if her life was spared to watch over her little ones. There was a deep snow on the ground when they turned her adrift, penniless, well nigh garmentless, and certainly homeless and shelterless. In a miserable shanty in Lafayette county she took up her abode. Only God and his good angels know how she stood up under it all and suffered. No respite came in any way. She was followed to Lafayette county, her house surrounded, and a younger son, John, shot at and driven to the brush. He was but fourteen years of age and the sole male support of the family. From Lafayette county she was driven to Clay county, suffering privation and want in a Christian-like and uncomplaining manner.

The war closed, and in the last stages of consumption, she dragged her poor emaciated body back to Jackson county to die. Her boys came home, went to work, and tried as best they could to forget the past and look solely to the future. Her cup of misery was not yet full, and one night a mob attacked the house, broke in the doors and windows, and rushed upon the dying woman with drawn revolvers, demanding to know, upon her life, where James and Coleman were. Among the mob she recognized some whose hands had been covered with her husband's blood. Furious at not finding James and Coleman, after having searched for them everywhere and stolen whatever about the scantily furnished house tempted their beggarly greed, they laid hands upon John, the youngest brother, carried him to the barn, put a rope about his neck, threw one end over a joist, and told him to say his prayers, for he had but a little time to live unless he declared instantly where his brothers were. He defied them to do their worst. Three times they strung him up and three times he refused to breathe a word that would reveal the whereabouts of James or Coleman. The fourth time he was left for dead. Respiration had perceptibly ceased. The rope had cut through the skin of the neck and had buried itself in the flesh. It was half an hour and more before he recovered. Not yet done with him, the mob wounded him with sticks, beat him across the shoulders with the butts of their muskets, tormented him as only devils could, and finally released him, half dead, to return to his agonized and brokenhearted mother. Soon afterwards Mrs. Younger died.

But this is a digression that does not belong properly to this history. Over the cold body of his murdered father, Cole Younger registered a vow before God to be revenged upon the cowards who assassinated him, and how sternly he kept to its fulfillment the annals of the border all too well can tell.

Eight hundred Federals held Kansas City, and on every road was a strong picquet post. The streets were patrolled constantly, and ready always for any emergency, horses, saddled and bridled, stood in their stalls. Early on the morning of December 25th, 1862, Todd asked Younger if he wouldn't like to have a little fun. "What kind of fun?" was the enquiry, in reply. "A portion of the command who murdered your father are in Kansas City, and if you say so we will go into the place and kill a few of them. Younger caught eagerly at the proposition and commenced at once to get ready for the enterprise. Six were to compose the adventurous party—Todd, Younger, Ab Cunningham, Fletch Taylor, Zach Traber, and George Clayton. Clothed in the uniform of the Federal cavalry, but

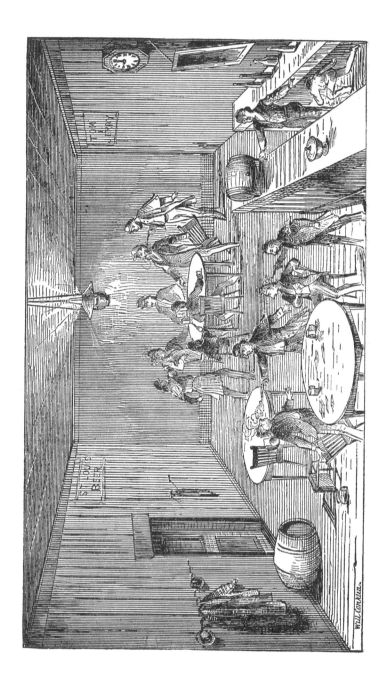

carrying instead of one pistol four, they arrived about dusk at the picquet post on the Westport and Kansas City road. They were not even halted. The uniform was the passport; to get in did not require a countersign. A little south of where the residence of Col. Milt. McGee now stands, the six Guerrillas dismounted and left their horses in charge of Traber, bidding him to do the best he could if the worst came to the worst. The city was royal with revelers. All the saloons were crowded; in many places there was music; the patrols had been doubled and were active and vigilant; comrade clinked glasses with comrade, and Jayhawker drank fortune to Jayhawker.

The five Guerrillas, with their heavy cavalry overcoats buttoned loosely about them, boldly walked down Main street and into the thick of the Christmas revelry. Visiting this saloon and that saloon they sat knee to knee with some of Jennison's most bloodthirsty troopers, and drank confusion over and over again to the cut-throat Quantrell and his bushwhacking crew. Imperceptibly the night had waned. Todd knew several of the gang who had waylaid and slain Col. Henry Younger, but hunt how he would he could not find a single one. Entering near to midnight an ordinary drinking place facing the public square, six soldiers were discovered who sat at two tables playing cards—two at one table and four at another. A man and a boy were behind the bar. Todd, as he entered, spoke low to Younger: "Run to cover at last. Five of the six men before you were in Walley's crowd that murdered your father. How does your pulse beat?" "Like an iron man's. I feel that I could kill the whole six myself." They went up to the bar, called for whisky, and invited the card-players to join them. If it was agreeable the boy might bring them their whisky and the game could go on. "Certainly," said Todd, with the purring of a tiger cat ready for a spring, "that's what the boy is here for."

Over their whisky the Guerrillas whispered. Todd planned the killing as good now as accomplished. Cunningham and Clayton were to saunter carelessly up to the table where the two players sat, and Todd, Younger and Taylor up to the table of the four. The signal to get ready was: "Come, boys, another drink," and the signal to fire was: "Who said drink?" Cole Younger was to give the first signal in his deep, resonant voice, and Todd the last one. After the first each Guerrilla was to draw a pistol and hold it under the cape of his cavalry overcoat, and after the last he was to fire. Younger as a special privilege was accorded the right to shoot the sixth man.

As curious people frequently do in saloons that keep card tables, Cunningham and Clayton walked leisurely along to where the two Jayhawkers were, and took each a position to the right and rear of the players. Todd, Younger and Taylor did the same with three of the other four. In firing they had looked to the danger of hitting one another and in order to avoid it, they had made a right oblique. In the end, however, the fatality would be the same, instead of the back of the head for the muzzle of the pistol it would be the side.

How quiet the room appeared! Every tick of the clock was plainly audible. The bar-keeper leant his head upon his two hands and rested; the boy was asleep. Even the shuffling and dealing of the cards seemed subdued; the necessary conversations of the game were brief and unemphatic.

Cole Younger's deep voice broke suddenly in, filling all the room and sounding so jolly and clear: "*Come, boys, another drink!*" It was an unctuous voice, full of Christmas and brimming glasses. The card players gave heed to it and stayed long enough the tide of the game to assent most graciously.

There was a little pause. Expectant, the bar-keeper lifted up his head; aroused, the sleepy boy forced apart his heavy eyelids. The clock was upon the stroke of twelve. No one had moved. Was the invitation, so evidently *apropos*, to be forgotten? Not if Todd could help it. Neither so loud nor so caressing in intonation as Younger, yet his voice—sharp, distinct and penetrating—prolonged as it were the previous proposition and gave it emphasis: "*Who said drink!*"

A thunder clap, a single pistol shot, and then a total darkness. The bar-keeper, dumb in the presence of death so instantaneous, shivered and stood still. The boy grovelled at his feet. Todd, cool as the winter night without, extinguished every light and stepped upon the street. "Steady!" he said to his men, "and do not make haste." So sudden had been the massacre, and so prompt the movements of the Guerrillas, that the patrols were groping for a clue and stumbling in their eagerness to find it. At every street corner an alarm was beaten. Harsh and high, an ominous of danger imminent, the long roll sent its clangor through the town. Soldiers poured out from every dance house, rushed from every saloon. "Guerrilla!" "Guerrilla!" was the cry; "the Guerrillas are among us in Federal clothing and killing the Kansas men!" Mixing fearlessly with the crowd, and swaying to and fro as it swayed, Todd asked and answered questions as he pressed ever on steadily yet surely towards his horses. None suspected him so far, and the worst was over. Presently a tremendous yell was heard—a yell plaintive yet full of fury, menacing, wrathful, accusing; the bar-keeper had found his voice at last, and had rushed upon the street, shouting, "Murder!" "Murder!" "Murder!" Seized instantly by armed patrols, and shaken into continuity of speech, he understood tolerably well the monosyllable "Where!" "Come with me and see." They went with him, and a great crowd followed. God help them all! Not a man breathed in the mass upon the floor. From the tables to the stove, from the stove to the bar, and from the bar to the door blood had trickled and trickled, and flowed and flowed. One laid upon another. In the hands of two the cards were gripped as in a vice. Another, looking up to the ceiling, seemed to be asleep, his face was so soft and placid. Every bullet had brought sudden death, and in this the Guerrillas were merciful. In and out all night the crowd ebbed and flowed, and still the dead men lay as they fell. Day dawned, and the sun came up, and some beams like a benediction fell upon the upturned faces and the pallid lips. Was it absolution? Who knows? Blessed are the dead who die in their uniforms!

Past the press in the streets, past the glare and the glitter of the thicker lights, past patrol after patrol, Todd had won well his way to his horses when a black bar thrust itself suddenly across his path and changed itself instantly into a line of soldiers. Some paces forward a spokesman advanced and called a halt. "What do you want?" said Todd. "The countersign." "We have no countersign. Out for a lark, it's only a square or two further that we desire to go." "No matter if it's only an inch or two. Orders are orders." "Fire! and charge, men!" and the black line across the streets as a barricade shrivelled up and shrunk away. Four did not move, however, nor would they move ever again until, feet foremost, their comrades bore them to the burial place. But the hunt was hot. Mounted men were abroad, and hurrying feet could be heard in all directions. Rallying beyond range and reinforced, the remnant of the patrol were advancing and opening fire. Born scout and educated Guerrilla, Traber—judging from the shots and the shouts— knew what was best for all and dashed up to his hard pressed comrades with their horses. Thereafter the flight was a frolic. The picquet on the Independence road was ridden over and through, and the brush gained beyond without an effort, and the hospitable house of Reuben Harris, where a roaring fire was blazing and a hearty welcome extended to all.

In a week or less, it began snowing. The hillsides were white with it; the hollows were choked; the briddle-paths obliterated, and the broad highways made smooth as the surface of a frozen stream. After the snow had ceased to fall, there came a rain, and then a furious north wind, which covered the earth with a sheet of ice. Travel stopped, foraging parties staid at home, the bivouacs were pitiless, and the wild beasts—hunting one another along the border—went hungry rather than stir. It really was the first dead calm the West had known since 1856.

Todd established his camp near Red Crenshaw's; Younger eight miles south of Independence, near the farm of Martin O. Jones; and Cunningham near the place of Dr. Thornton, on the east fork of the Little Blue River. Save to get forage for their horses and food for themselves, the Guerrillas made no more exertion than the boughs of the ice-bound trees over their heads; they asked only to hide themselves and to be let alone. John McDowell was in Younger's camp, and once upon a time Cole Younger had saved John McDowell's life at the imminent risk of his own. Certainly he would not make an excuse to see a sick wife, to get into Independence, to talk to Penick long and privately, and to bite hard at the hand which had succored him. John McDowell knew too much of the holy meaning of gratitude for that.

The ice crust, because of successive frosts, got brittle at last and added another misery to the miseries of traveling. In order to get out at all, Younger dug a road out with pick and shovel. The nearest corn to him was on the John Kerr place, where Mrs. Rucker lived, and to this corn the improvised road was made to run. To hide it from the Federals, and to keep the strangest of its features from the too curious eyes of isolated passers by, Mrs. Rucker had her stock fed upon the trail. In twenty-four hours afterwards the rooting of the hogs, the trampling of the cattle, and the pawing of the horses, had made of the Guerrilla road a feeding place.

The nights were long, the days were bitter, and the snow did not melt. On the 10th day of February, 1863, John McDowell reported his wife sick and asked of Younger permission to visit her. It was granted, the proviso attached to it being the order to report again at 3 o'clock. The illness of the man's wife was a sham. Instead of going home, or even in the direction of home, he hastened immediately into Independence and made the commander there, Col. Penick, thoroughly acquainted with Younger's camp and all of its surroundings. Penick was a St. Joseph, Missouri, man, commanding a regiment of militia. The Guerrillas regarded him as an officer who would fight under any and all circumstances, and as one who, operated upon by better fortunes, might have made considerable military reputation. With the men he had, try how he would, the stream never could be made to rise higher than its source. Not homogeneous, possessed of neither *esprit du corps* nor soldierly ambition, nature in forcing them to be born under the contraband flag of inferiority, made it also obligatory that they should join the pirates.

The echoes of the desperate adventure of Younger and Todd in Kansas City, had long ago reached the ears of Col. Penick, and he seconded the traitor's story with an energy worthy the game to be hunted. Eighty cavalrymen, under a resolute officer, was ordered instantly out, and McDowell, suspicioned and closely guarded, was put at their head as a pilot.

Younger had two houses dug in the ground, with a ridge pole to each and rafters. Upon the rafters were boards, and upon the boards straw and earth. At one end was a fire-place, at the other a door. Architecture was nothing; comfort everything.

The Federal officer dismounted his men two hundred yards from Younger's huts and divided them, sending forty to the south and forty to the north; the attack was to be from two directions and simultaneously. No picquets were out; no guards kept watch about the premises. Even the doors were closed; fate at last, it seemed, had cut off the fair locks of this intrepid Sampson and was about to deliver him over, helpless and impotent, into the hands of the Philistines.

The Federals on the south had approached to within twenty yards of Younger's cabins when a horse snorted fiercely, and Younger came to the door of one of them. He saw the approaching column on foot and mistaking it for a friendly column, called out: "Is that you, Todd?" Perceiving in a moment, however, his mistake, he fired and killed the lieutenant in command of the attacking party and then aroused the houses. Out of each the occupants poured, armed, desperate, meaning to fight but never to surrender. It was hot work despite the bitter weather. The Federals on the north were well up to time and fired a deadly volley, killing Ike Basham and Dr. Hale. Younger had four dragoon pistols belted about him, but he husbanded his loads and fired only to do execution. Turning westward as the Federals from the north and south came together, for two hundred yards Penick's men and Younger's men were mixed inextricably, shooting and shouting. Then the Guerrillas began to emerge from the press and to gain a little on their pursuers. Encumbered by heavy cavalry overcoats, heavy boots, spurs and carbines, the militia could not make the speed the Guerrillas did, but they kept pressing forward for all that and shooting incessantly. Younger's devotion that day was simply heroic. In front, guiding his men, because he knew every foot of ground in the neighborhood, he heard Joe Hardin's voice call out to him: "Wait for me, Cole; they have nearly got me." In a moment he was back to his comrade and covering him with his pistol. As he ran down the ranks toward Hardin, he ordered the men to pull off their overcoats and boots, and trust more to running than to fighting. While Hardin was working at his boots and trying to get them off, Younger killed two of the boldest of the pursuers and took the rear himself, the last of all in the desperate race. Twenty yards further Hardin was shot dead, and Oath Hinton needed succor. He was down tugging at his boots and unable to get them off. Younger halted behind a tree and fought fifteen Federals for several moments, killed another who rushed upon him, rescued Hinton and strode away after his comrades, untouched and undaunted. Fifty yards further Tom Talley was in trouble. He had one boot off and one foot in the leg of the other, but try how he would he could neither get it on nor off. He could not run, situated as he was, and he had no knife to cut the leather. He too called out to Younger to wait for him and to stand by him until he could do something to extricate himself. Without hurry, and in the teeth of a rattling fusillade, Younger stooped to Talley's assistance, tearing literally from his foot by the exercise of immense strength the well-nigh fatal boot, and encouraging him to make the best haste he could and hold to his pistols. Braver man than Thomas Talley never lived, nor cooler. As he jumped up in his stocking feet, the Federals were in twenty yards, firing as they advanced, and loading their breech-loading guns as they ran. He took their fire at a range like that and snapped every barrel of his revolver in their faces. Not a cylinder exploded; wet by the snow, he held in his hand a useless pistol. About thirty of the enemy had by this time outrun the balance and were forcing the fighting. Younger called to his men to take to trees and drive them back, or stand and die together. The Guerrillas—barefooted, hatless, some of them, and coatless, rallied instantly and held their own. Younger killed two more of the pursuers here—five since the fight began—and Bud Wigginton, like a lion at bay, fought without cover and with deadly effect. Here Job McCorkle was badly wounded, together with James Morris, John Coger, and five others. George Talley, fighting splendidly, was shot dead, and Younger himself, encouraging his men by voice and example, got a bullet through the left shoulder. The Federal advance fell back to the main body and the main body fell back to their horses. Sick of a pursuit on foot which had cost them seventeen killed and wounded, they desired to mount and try it further on horseback. Instantly ordering a retreat in turn, Younger made a dash for the Harrisonville and Independence road, the men loading their pistols as they ran, and making excellent time at that. The snow, fourteen inches deep, was everywhere. Not four of the Guerrillas had on shoes or boots. The big road, cut into blocks and spears of ice, was like a highway paved with cutting and piercing things. Halting just a moment, Younger said: "Boys, if we can muster up courage enough to run down this road two hundred yards, on our naked feet and over its icicles, worse than Indian arrow-heads, the chances to get away will be splendid. Otherwise, say your prayers." They did dash down the road as though it were carpeted, and kept down it a quarter of a mile to a field in the rear

10

of Mrs. Fristoe's house, where a bridge was, and where to one side of the bridge a hog trail ran. Leaping from this bridge and one at a time into the hog path, the Guerrillas followed it west three hundred yards, and then southwest through the snow a mile, Younger leading and requiring each one of his men to put their feet into the tracks his own feet had made. Baffled, but by no means beaten, the Federals got quickly to horse and dashed on after the retreating Guerrillas. The big road gave no sign, the hog path at the bridge gave no sign, and only a single footstep could be discovered leading off to the southwest from the trail which continued on to the west. Dividing, however, into detachments of ten each, and keeping within due succoring distance, the cavalry began to scour the entire neighborhood. Wherefore? Younger's grim tenacity, woodcraft, and stubborn fighting saved all who had not been killed in open battle. Three miles from the Fristoe house a bluff ran east and west for the distance of several miles, perfectly impracticable for horsemen, and difficult even for footmen who did not know the easy descending places. Thither Younger led his little band, showing them how by the help of trees and bushes they might get down, and leaping himself, wounded as he was, into the top of a contiguous oak by the way of illustration. The sun was sinking in the west, and the night was near when the last wounded Guerrilla, dragging his hurt body along with difficulty, reached the base of the bluff in safety. "Thank God!" cried Younger in exultation, and looking away to the west where some red clouds beamed as with the lurid benediction of the sun, "we'll see to-morrow another sunset." Overhead and firing down upon him some Federal cavalry appeared, as if to prove his boasting vain, but they hit no one and could not descend. There was not time to flank the bluff at either end; the pursuit was ended; the Guerrillas were safe. True to those instincts, however, which make plunderers of battle-fields and robbers of the dead, the returning militia put fire to the houses of Mrs. Rucker and Mrs. Fristoe, and to everything else about their premises that would burn. Mrs. Fristoe was Younger's grandmother, a most intelligent woman of great Christian piety, who had been a widow for twenty years. Her husband had been a lieutenant under Gen. Jackson at the battle of New Orleans, and stood noted in the community

in which he lived for sterling integrity and incorruptible manhood. Vandalism deals generally with such victims; cowardice
is never so happy as when gray heads are made to bow.

With feet torn and lacerated, and their wounded barely able to
hobble along, the Guerrillas reached the house of Old Johnny
Moore, as he was familiarly called by them, and after the darkness set in. Mrs. Josephine Moore, a Southern heroine of
Mary's trust and faith, dressed tenderly all the hurts and
emptied her house of whatever the men could wear. To one
she gave a coat, to one a hat, to one a pair of shoes or boots,
and to all a welcome worth thrice the balance.

The winter of 1862 was a memorable one. The deep snow
stayed deep to the last. Military operations were generally suspended throughout the entire country, and especially did the
spring make haste slowly up the border way. Todd, as terrible
as the roads were, and as pitiless as was the weather, left a comfortable cantoment at the instance of his unfortunate comrades
and found for them rapidly horses, accoutrements, boots and
clothing. Presently the report began to circulate that Younger
was slain. As proof of the fact the Federals exhibited in Independence his coat and hat, and a pair of gloves which had
upon them, "Presented to Lieutenant Coleman Younger by
Miss M. E. Sanders." Above everything else lost by him,
Younger regretted most of all the gloves. Some talismanic
message, perhaps, had made them precious.

Wild as the weather was, and as harsh the aspect of everything, John Jarrette arrived one day from the South, bringing
with him Richard Kenney, Richard Berry, George Shepherd,
and John Jackson. Younger joined these with John McCorkle
and John Coger, and altogether they worked their way down
into Lafayette county, where Poole lived, and where he intended
to recruit a company. Richard Berry, a soldier by intuition,
and a Guerrilla because of the daring life connected with the
service, saw where some choice young spirits might be gathered
up, and he had come to enroll them. Afterwards no more formidable band than his and David Poole's fought in the West.

In Lafayette as in Jackson, the weather was simply impossible. Berry found shelter speedily and disappeared. Others
did the same; and Jarrette, Younger, McCorkle, and Coger
countermarched towards the Sni hills for the same purpose. *En*

route and while on the Georgetown and Lexington road, they surprised and captured Colonel King, Major Biggers, and seven private soldiers. At this time the black flag was generally recognized as the flag under which the militia fought. In no single instance lately had the life of a captured Guerrilla been spared, while step by step and rapidly that period was approaching when all disguise would be thrown off and the combatants, understanding one another thoroughly, would seek only to exterminate. Not one of the nine Federals, however, was hurt. Jarrette was a Free Mason and so were Colonel King and Major Biggers. A vote was taken and much depended upon Younger. McCorkle and Coger had good reason to pronounce for the death penalty. Two men oftener shot at and oftener wounded did not live. Younger bore nothing love that wore the blue, but singular as it seems, in this instance he voted on the side of mercy, and many times thereafter. Acquainted well with a Mrs. Bales, an aunt of King, and regarding her emphatically in the light of a friend, he ranged himself with Jarrette. To break the tie and gain over Coger was not difficult; the Federals were released and paroled. Thus were men's lives played with in those cruel days, and thus upon such slender things did human action depend. Unquestionably, however, it was the influence of Free Masonry working upon Jarrette which first formed the channel for the flowing of the other good impulses, and committed to the cause of mercy two of the most savage men in the ranks of the Guerrillas—Jarrette and Coger.

For a few days towards the latter part of February a south wind blew and some little thawing was observable about the sunny places. Tempted by it, and by the prospect of some further open weather, Colonel Penick sent Captain Johnson out from Independence on a scouting expedition. Not long in finding a fresh Guerrilla trail, he followed it eagerly. Todd, Jarrette and Younger, according to a special agreement, were to dine with Rodney Hines at the Will Howard place, the very day Johnson's expedition got under way. Preceding these three men to Hines' by several hours were William Hulse, Boon Schull and Fletch Taylor. Hulse was a swarthy fighter who had no superior for dead game and bull-dog tenacity. Black eyed, clean limbed, cool always, not much of a sleeper, born to a horse, and skilled in all manly exercises, as he rode he rested, and when he fought he killed.

Boon Schull, destined to give up a dauntless young life early for the cause he loved best, won the respect of all by a generosity unstained of selfishness and the exercise of a courage that in either extreme of victory or disaster remained perfect in attribute and exhibition. None were more gentle than he ; none more courteous, calm and kindly. When he fell, liberty never required upon its altar as a sacrifice a purer victim.

Fletch Taylor was a low, massive Hercules, who, when he had one arm shot off, made the other all the more powerful. Built like a quarter-horse, knowing nature well, seeing equally in darkness and light, rapacious for exercise, having an anatomy like a steam engine, impervious to fatigue like a Cossack, and to hunger like an Apache, he always hunted a fight and always fought for a funeral.

These three men, having passed on carelessly through the snow to the rendezvous at Hines' left a good, broad trail which Johnson—especially commissioned to look after bushwhackers— was not slow in following. Surrounded, but in no manner demoralized, two Federals were already upon the front porch when Hulse, discovering them, fired through a side window and shot down the foremost. The other ran, and Johnson, on foot, began to close up. Hurrying from the front of the house to the rear, and then through an ell and a kitchen, the Guerrillas, gained their horses, hitched to the inner side of an orchard fence, and essayed to mount under a distressing fire. The horses were inexperienced and untried, and struggled so violently to break loose that the men could neither control nor mount them. Fletch Taylor drew a knife and cut the halter of his horse, got into the saddle and opened a furious fire upon the nearest Federals—a pistol in each hand and the bridle rein in his teeth. Somewhat protected by a diversion so gallantly made, Schull and Hulse got mounted finally, joined in the combat with Taylor, and drove to cover the enemy immediately in front of them. Reinforced, the Federals came on with loud cheers as if they were charging a regular line of battle, but the three horsemen—gallantly waving their hats to the ladies of the house where they had expected to dine—cleared the orchard fence at a bound and rode rapidly away. Johnson could not pursue for some time

He had dismounted two companies that *three* Guerrillas might be captured, and when he needed them most he had not at his command even so much as a single mounted trooper. In hearing of the guns, and rushing down to help his comrades, Younger arrived too late to participate; but laying off and on in sailor fashion, he hung about the Howard premises and watched the Independence road for half the night, thinking Johnson might return. Afraid to fire upon him where he was in bivouac, lest in revenge he should kill Hines and burn the house from over the heads of his family, and seeing no indications of a move in any quarter, Younger marched at midnight in the direction of Blue Springs, breakfasting the next morning with Joel Basham. Beyond Basham lived William Hopkins, and there Younger found Todd and his men well mounted and in splendid fighting fix. Fortune also favored Johnson. Jarrette, Gregg and David Hilton, having remained the previous night at the house of Baby Saunders, started for Hilton's early in the morning to meet with Todd, and it was the trail made by them that Johnson found and followed up with considerable energy. As he rode he threatened; wherever he stopped, or whenever he had occasion to question a citizen, he promised invariably in leaving to catch the Guerrillas in front of him and hang them afterwards. Man proposes and God disposes.

Todd, in command of all the united squads by virtue of his rank, and well informed of Johnson's approach, had everything in readiness to receive him. It was going to be a most remarkable fight. Todd, forming the Guerrillas in an open field in the vicinity of the Hopkins house, had on the left of this field a steep bluff, and on the right of it a heavy fence. By this fence a road ran, and through the field to the house, which was upon the bluff, and on past the house and over the bluff into a bottom beyond. An exact count showed thirty Guerrillas and sixty-four militia; on the one side Captain Johnson commanded, on the other, Captain Todd. The prairie wolf was about to encounter the tiger.

Johnson marched up from the bottom to the crest of the bluff, halted his detachment near the Hopkins house, and rode forward himself towards where Todd's line was formed in the field. Todd, Jarrette, and Younger advanced to meet him, and quite a dialogue ensued at the distance of thirty paces:

"Who are you?" asked Johnson. "Kansas troops," replied Todd. "What command?" "Jennison's." "What are you doing here?" "Hunting for Guerrillas." "Excellent employment, but your line looks light; where is the balance of your men?" "What you see are all." "Impossible!" "Come and judge for yourself." Evidently Johnson had discovered enough to convince him of the character of the organization before him, and he wheeled suddenly and put spurs to his horse. As quick as he was, the Guerrillas were quicker. Todd, Jarrette and Younger fired each at him three shots in rapid succession, but splendid shots that they were, they missed him clear. The charge that followed was one of the most furious of all the furious ones of Todd's tempestuous career. Before the Federals could well about face, the Guerrillas were upon them and among them. Coherency was gone in a second. Well dressed ranks fell apart as a house made of cards. The retreat was a panic, the panic insanity. As a tornado the storm of steeds and steel swept to the southwest corner of the field, blue rider and gray side by side and shouting in each other's faces. The road was abandoned. In every direction through the woods the Federals rushed, shooting, each man as he ran, "Hold up!" "Hold up!" but never a halt or a rally.

It had rained lately, some snow had melted, and Little Blue was bankfull. From the corner of the fence on the southwest to the river, it was an hundred yards, and nearer still to the river was a ditch. Into this ditch Johnson, leading his troopers, leaped fearlessly, and from the ditch into the swimming river. Hot upon their track and seeing before them an enemy helpless because paralyzed, the Guerrillas jumped from their horses and lined the east bank of the Blue, attempting to fire upon them with their shotguns. Not a barrel exploded. Wet with the rain of the previous morning, these never to be depended upon weapons failed them utterly. Every revolver had been discharged in the race, the gun barrels would not go off, the Federals at their mercy were struggling and swimming in the river, and yet there was nothing to shoot them with.

Beaten back from the opposite bank by the force of the current, and beaten down some one hundred and fifty to two hundred yards, Johnson landed again on the eastern side of the river and dashed away into Blue Springs, beating the Guerrillas

who had halted long enough to load their revolvers, and who
came into the road some little distance behind them.   Then
there was another charge and another panic.   Side by side, and
leading, Todd and Younger rode together.   Near to the rear,
with pistol in hand and in the act of firing, Todd's horse fell
headlong across the road, and Younger's, swerved aside by its
powerful rider lest his comrade should be hurt, lost his stride
and his pace, and his position at the front.   Close behind them
and thundering on, Boon Schull leaped his horse over Todd and
his crippled steed, followed by James Little, who spoke not nor
touched rein until ranging up along side of the rearmost Federal he shot him from the saddle.   Schull dismounted instantly
over the dead man and appropriated his carbine and his pistols.
Todd mounted his horse and hurried away in pursuit.   The
next victim was the famous Jim Lane.   House-burner, highwayman, spy, something of a scout, theatrical in hair and
toggery, claiming to be brave, notorious for evil deeds, and
known somewhat by his boasts to the Guerrillas, he had taken the
name of Jim Lane as an honor, and swore to set it above the
name of the real one for devilment done to the border ruffians.
Little fired at him and missed; Schull's pistol snapped; but
Younger, dashing by at full speed, shot him square through the
temples.   Jim Lane, junior or inferior, had burnt his last house
and robbed his last Missourian.   To keep to the road in front
of a pursuit as swift and merciless as the pursuit of the Guerrillas, was simple madness, and the road was abandoned by the
larger portion of the Federals as if swayed by some mysterious
yet instantaneous impulse.   Nothing in the semblance of an
array was preserved ; it was every man for himself and God's
mercy for the hindmost.   Taylor, followed by twenty others,
poured through the timber on their trail and killed whenever he
came to one.   Jarrette and George Wigginton were the last to
leave the heels of the flying foe, killing two beyond the bridge
between Blue Springs and Independence, and wounding
another badly under the very range of a sheltering picquet post.
As trooper after trooper galloped into Independence, or limped
in wearily on foot, forlorn, bedraggled, scared well nigh to
speechlessness, Penick, without doubt, developed a clear case
of hydrophobia.   Succeeding every report there was a spasm.
Jerking off his coat in the agony of an uncontrollable paroxysm,

he went about the streets assaulting and knocking down each man encountered who was looked upon as a Southern man or in sympathy with the Guerrillas. One especially, Tobias Owens, should receive a more degrading punishment. Seeking him out and finding him finally, he went into his room with a raw-hide in his hand and locked the door. Owens stood ten, maybe twenty, good, keen cuts, but human nature rose up against and mastered prudence at last, and he in turn became the aggressor. Wrenching the rawhide from Penick's grasp he gave back blow for blow most vigorously, and only ceased from his punishment when the excitement of the assault and the violent exercise completely exhausted him. Before he could be assassinated for an exhibition of manhood justified even in the eyes of a militia garrison, he escaped. Thirty-two Federals per-ished in this ill-starred and wretchedly handled expedition, and nine severely shot, died afterwards. Not so much as a single Guerrilla was wounded. The militia could not or did not fight. They fired more or less, but always with that unsteadiness which comes from a want of nerve. Johnson himself lost his head. The officers had no men, and the men had no officers. If the shot guns of the Guerrillas had gone off on the banks of the Blue, not a soldier due at Independence would ever have returned there. Penick hurried out the next day two hundred cavalry and three pieces of artillery for purposes of display alone, and to hide his regiment's grievous hurt. He shelled the timber on both sides of the road from Independence to Hopkins' house, but the Guerrillas, eating dinner ten miles away, laughed over their plates at the sound of the cannon and told one to another the pleasant story of the Blue Springs races.

A man now by the name of Emmet Goss was beginning to have it whispered of him that he was a tiger. He would fight, the Guerrillas said, and when in those savage days one went upon the war path so endorsed, be sure it meant all that it was intended to mean. Goss lived in Jackson county. He owned a farm near Hickman's Mill, and up to the fall of 1861, had worked it soberly and industriously. When he concluded to quit farming and go to fighting, he joined the Jayhawkers. Jenni-son commanded the 15th Kansas Cavalry, and Goss a company in this regiment. From a peaceful, thrifty citizen, he became

suddenly a terror to the border. He seemed to have a mania
for killing. Twenty old and unoffending citizens probably died
by his hands. When Ewing's famous General Order No. 11
was issued—that order which required the wholesale depopulation of Cass, Bates, Vernon and Jackson counties—Goss went
about as a destroying angel, with a torch in one hand and a
revolver in the other. He boasted of having kindled the flames
in fifty-two houses, of having made fifty-two families homeless
and shelterless, and of having killed, as he declared, until he was
tired of killing. Death was to come to him at last by the hand
of Jesse James, but not yet. He had sworn to capture or kill
Cole Younger, and went to the house of Younger's mother on
Big Creek, for the purpose. She was living in a double-log
cabin built by her husband before his death, for a tenant, and
Cole was at home. It was about eight o'clock, and quite dark.
Cole sat talking with his mother, two little sisters and a boy
brother. No one was on watch. Goss, with forty men, dismounted back from the yard, fastened their horses securely,
moved up quietly and surrounded the house. Between the two
rooms of the cabin there was an open passage way, and the Jayhawkers had occupied this before the alarm was given. Desir-
ing to go from one of the rooms to the other, a Miss Younger
found the porch full of armed men. Instantly springing back
and closing the door, she shouted Cole's name involuntarily.
An old negro woman—a former slave, but more of a confidant
than a slave—with extraordinary presence of mind blew out the
light, snatched a coverlet from a bed, and threw it over her
head and shoulders. "Get behind me, Marse Cole, quick!"
she said in a whisper, and Cole in a second, with a pistol in each
hand, stood up close to the old woman, the bed spread covering
them both. Then throwing wide the door, and receiving in her
face the gaping muzzles of a dozen guns, she queruously cried
out: "Don't shoot a poor old nigger, massa sogers. It's
nobody but me gwine to see what's de matter. Ole Missus is
nearly skeered to death." Slowly then, so slowly that it seemed
an age to Cole, she strode through the crowd of Jayhawkers
blocking up the portico, and out into the darkness and the night.
Swarming about the two rooms and rummaging everywhere, a
portion of the Jayhawkers kept looking for Younger, and swearing brutally at their ill-success, while another portion, watching

the movements of the old negress, saw her throw away the bed spread, clap her hands exultingly and shout: "Run, Marse Cole! run for your life! de debbil can't cotch you this time!" Giving and taking a volley which harmed no one, Cole made his escape without a struggle. As for the old negro woman, Goss debated sometime with himself whether he should shoot her or hang her. Unquestionably a rebel negro, she was persecuted often and often for her opinion's sake, and hung up twice by militia to make her tell of the whereabouts of Guerrillas. True to her people and her cause, she died at last in the odor of devotion.

CHAPTER XI.

QUANTRELL tarried but a little while with the army in Arkansas. Guerrilla, as he was, and hated and proscribed as he was, and savage as he had the reputation of being, the man yet dreamed dreams of empire, and had vivid glimpses or revealments of the future of the war. Taking with him two of his men, Blunt and Higbee, and protected by the necessary passports from department headquarters, Quantrell started directly for Richmond. The old company was left with Gregg until January, 1862, who, turning over the command to Scott, made his way into Missouri with ten Guerrillas. Scott remained until Quantrell returned from Richmond, performing every regular duty with alacrity and giving evidence of the possession of all the inherent qualities of a brilliant soldier. Before the last of the snows had melted, and ere yet the trees had begun to awaken to an idea of verdure and the spring, Quantrell was back again in Jackson county, marshalling his Guerrillas and closing up his ranks.

His interview at Richmond with the Confederate Secretary of War was a memorable one. Gen. Louis T. Wigfall, then a Senator from Texas, was present and described it afterwards in his rapid, vivid, picturesque way. Quantrell asked to be commissioned as a Colonel under the Partisan Ranger Act, and to be so recognized by the Department as to have accorded to him whatever protection the Confederate government might be in a condition to exercise. Never mind the question of men, he would have the complement required in a month after he reached Western Missouri. The warfare was desperate, he knew, the service desperate, everything connected with it was desperate; but the Southern people to succeed had to fight a desperate fight. The Secretary suggested that war had its amenities and its refinements, and that in the nineteenth century it was simple barbarism to talk of a black flag.

"*Barbarism!*" and Quantrell's blue eyes blazed, and his whole manner and attitude underwent a transformation, "barbarism, Mr. Secretary, means war and war means barbarism. Since you have touched upon this subject, let us discuss it a little. Times have their crimes as well as men. For twenty years this cloud has been gathering; for twenty years—inch by inch and little by little those people called the Abolitionists have been on the track of slavery; for twenty years the people of the South have been robbed, here of a negro and there of a negro; for twenty years hates have been engendered and wrathful things laid up against the day of wrath. The cloud has burst. Do not condemn the thunderbolt."

The War Secretary bowed his head. Quantrell, leaving his own seat, and standing over him as it were and above him, went on.

"Who are these people you call Confederates? Rebels, unless they succeed; outcasts, traitors, food for hemp and gunpowder. There were no great statesmen in the South, or this war would have happened ten years ago; no inspired men, or it would have happened fifteen years ago. To-day the odds are desperate. The world hates slavery; the world is fighting you. The ocean belongs to the Union navy. There is a recruiting officer in every foreign port. I have captured and killed many who did not know the English tongue. Mile by mile the cordon is being drawn about the granaries of the South, Missouri will go first, next Kentucky, next Tennessee, by and by Mississippi and Arkansas, and then what? That we must put gloves on our hands, and honey in our mouths, and fight this war as Christ fought the wickedness of the world?"

The War Secretary did not speak. Quantrell, perhaps, did not desire that he should. "You ask an impossible thing, Mr. Secretary. This secession, or revolution, or whatever you call it cannot conquer without violence, nor can those who hate it and hope to stifle it, resist without vindictiveness. Every struggle has its philosophy, but this is not the hour for philosophers. Your young Confederacy wants victory, and champions who are not judges. Men must be killed. To impel the people to passion there must be some slight illusion mingled with the truth; to arouse them to enthusiasm something out of nature must occur. That illusion should be a crusade in the name of conquest, and that something out of nature should be the black flag. Woe be unto all of you if the Federals come with an oath of loyalty in one hand and a torch in the other. I have seen Missouri bound hand and foot by this Christless thing called Conservatism, and where to-day she should have two hundred thousand heroes fighting for liberty, beneath her banners there are scarcely twenty thousand."

"What would *you* do, Captain Quantrell, were your's the power and the opportunity?"

"Do, Mr. Secretary? Why I would wage such a war and have such a war waged by land and sea as to make surrender forever impossible. I would cover the armies of the Confederacy all over with blood. I would invade. I would reward audacity. I would exterminate. I would break up foreign enlistments by indiscriminate massacre. I would win the independence of my people or I would find them graves."

"And our prisoners, what of them?"

"Nothing of them; there would be no prisoners. Do they take any prisoners from me? Surrounded, I do not surrender; surprised, I do not give way to panic; outnumbered, I rely upon common sense and stubborn fighting; proscribed, I answer proclamation with proclamation; outlawed, I feel through it my power; hunted, I hunt my hunters in turn; hated and made blacker than a dozen devils, I add to my hoofs the swiftness of a horse, and to my horns the terrors of a savage following. Kansas should be laid waste at once. Meet the torch with the torch, pillage with pillage, slaughter with slaughter, subjugation with extermination. You have my ideas of war, Mr. Secretary, and I am sorry they do not accord with your own, nor the ideas of the government you have the honor to represent so well." And Quantrell, without his commission as a Partisan Ranger, or without any authorization to raise a regiment of Partisan Rangers, bowed himself away from the presence of the Secretary and away from Richmond.

From Arkansas to the Missouri river the journey in detail would read like a romance. The whole band, numbering thirty, were clad in Federal uniform, Quantrell wearing that of a captain. Whenever questioned the answer was: "A Federal scout on special service.'' Such had been the severity of the winter, and such the almost dead calm in military quarters, that all ordinary vigilance seemed to have disappeared, and even ordinary prudence forgotten. South of Spring river a day's march, ten militia came into Quantrell's camp and invited themselves to supper. They were fed, but they were killed. Quantrell himself was the host. He poured out the coffee, supplied attentively every little want, insisted that those whose appetites were first appeased should eat longer, and then shot at his own table the two nearest to him, and saw the others fall beneath the revolvers of his men with scarcely so much as a change of color.

North of Spring river there was a dramatic episode. Perhaps in those days every county had its tyrant. Most generally revolutions breed monsters, and in the fathomless depths of the unknown horrible things stir and crawl about that otherwise would devour one another and die if the sweep of the war storm did not invade their depths and cast them, clothed with something of the semblance of humanity, into the fields where the red reapers are.

Obadiah Smith, at first a peacable man, and at last a terrible one, operated along Spring river as a base, and ranged at will and when there was game afoot, to the north and the south of it. He would take no chances in open battle. He was not brave. Cunning, of immense energy, having the gift of penetration, and much of the philosophy of individual control, he soon established a local reputation for enterprise, and soon enlisted about him a company of desperate thieves and cut-throats. Terror ensued. Houses were robbed and burnt, some old men killed, much stock was driven off, and outrage and oppression dealt out with no unsparing hand. Quantrell, through the exercise of a little strategy, got Smith into his possession. Passing one afternoon late by a house at which he frequently visited, a message was left to the effect that the commander of a Federal scout, going north on important business, desired to especially confer with him, and that his camp might be found five miles further upon the road. Smith received the message in due time and reported accordingly. He had much talk with Quantrell. He told him of all the devilment he had done, and all he proposed to do. The winter had been hard, and the traveling light, but he thought the spring would soon revive business and give into the nets spread for the unwary many a goodly haul. The next morning, as the Guerrillas broke camp and rode away to the north, one might have seen, if he had been at all curious about such things, an aged oak of many limbs, and on the lowest of these limbs a swaying body.

That day, about ten o'clock, three militia came to the column and were killed. A mile from where dinner was procured, five more. These also were killed. In the dusk of the evening two more — killed; and where they bivouaced, one — killed. The day's work counted eleven as its aggregate, and nothing of an exertion made at that to find a single soldier. Evil tidings were abroad, however—evil tidings that took wings and flew as a bird. Some said from the first that Quantrell's men were not Union men, and some swore that no matter the kind of clothing those inside of said clothing were wolves. Shot evenly—that is to say by experienced hands in the head—the corpses of the first discovered ten awakened from their lethargic sleep the garrisons along Spring river. Smith's executions stirred them to aggression, and the groups of dead militia crossed continually upon the roadside, horrified while it enraged every cantonment or camp. Two hundred cavalrymen got quickly to horse and poured up from the rear after Quantrell. It was not difficult to keep upon his track. Here a corpse and there a corpse, here a heap and there a heap — blue always, and blue continually — what manner of a wild beast had been sent out from the unknown of Arkansas to prey upon the militia?

At the Osage river the Federal pursuit, gathering volume and intensity as it advanced, struck Quantrell hard and brought him to an engagement south of the river. Too much haste, however, cost them dearly. The advance, being the smaller, had out-ridden the main body and was unsupported and isolated when it attacked. Quantrell turned upon it savagely and crushed it at a blow. Out of sixty-six troopers he killed twenty; in those days there were no wounded. Before the main body came up he was over the Osage and away, and riding fast to encompass the immense prairie between the river and Johnstown. Scarcely over it a flanking column made a dash at him coming from the west, killed Blunt's horse, wounded three of the Guerrillas, and drove Quantrell into the timber. Night fell and he rode out of sight and out of hearing. When he drew rein again it was at the farm of Judge Russell Hicks, on the Sni, in Jackson county. The next morning at David George's he disbanded for ten days, sending messengers out in all directions to announce his arrival and make known the rendezvous. Todd went to the Six Mile country to recruit; Scott, to Lee's Summit; Cole Younger, to Big Creek, in Cass county; Poole, to Lafayette county; Gregg and Quantrell remained on the Sni, and Jarrette and Berry ran at large from the Kansas line to Saline county, Missouri. The Federals felt the stir of these rejuvenated Cossacks as the trees the stir of the reawakened sap. They clutched at the Missouri river and held it between Lexington and Waverly as fast as the ice had. Poole, Gregg, Younger, Scott, John Ross, William Greenwood, Jarrette and a few others captured the steamer Sam Gaty, while Jarrette, Reynolds, and three other Guerrillas pounced upon another steamer at Waverly. John Ross and William Greenwood were Guerrillas of splendid dash and intrepidity. In all the war Greenwood was never known to be without a smile upon his face or a load in his revolver. Ross was a boy who grew up in battle and when he became a man he was also a veteran. Either was fit to fight for a crown.

Capt. John G. McCloy commanded the Sam Gaty—a brave, fearless, true-hearted sailor, handy with a pistol himself, and no more afraid of a Guerrilla than a sand-bar. He landed his boat at a wood-yard just below Sibley, but scarcely were the stage planks run out on the shore when Jarrette, Younger, Clifton, Henry Hockensmith, William Greenwood, John Poole, Cole Younger and a dozen others rushed upon the deck. Twenty-two negroes were on board in Federal uniform, together with twelve white soldiers. Capt. McCloy was not on watch at the time, but he hurried from his room half dressed and manfully faced the Guerrillas. Some wanted to kill the negroes. Cole Younger swore they should not be harmed, and Cole Younger's word was law even with the most desperate among the band. Among the white soldiers six belonged to Penick's command and six to McFaren's. Only the six Penick men were killed, and these because Penick had ordered all who belonged to his regiment to never take a bushwacker alive. Capt. McCloy also held out stubbornly against taking human

11

life. His cool courage won the respect of the most cruel among the Guerrillas, and his indomitable firmness saved his boat from being burned. Fifteen hundred sacks of flour were thrown into the river, a large number of government wagons, much harness, and vast quantities of military supplies generally. When this was done the boat was permitted to go on its way.

The ten days allotted by Quantrell for concentration purposes had not yet expired, but many of the reckless spirits, rapacious for air and exercise, could not be kept still. Poole, Ross and Greenwood made a dash into the German settlement of Lafayette county, and left some marks there that are not yet obliterated. Albert Cunningham, glorying in the prowess of a splendid physical manhood, and victor in a dozen combats against desperate odds, fell before the spring came in an insignificant skirmish on the Harrisonville and Pleasant Hill road. Sooner or later the most of them were to fall—these savage Guerrillas, fighting a never ending and hopeless battle; gay, going ever forward with a light on their bronzed faces, and crying out even as the gladiators did: "*Morituri te salutant.*" Cunningham loved the land that he died for. A shade of melancholy covered his features. It may be that it was only the fixed and overcast look of one who was destined to die young. His piercing eyes and the flexibility of his features revealed a temperament impressionable to all beautiful and noble things, and with whom everything is grave, even heroism. If he had a crime it was the pitiless patriotism of his conscience. Fate favored him in this that he was shot dead. When they buried him he had, if beyond the river he knew of it, a priceless funeral service—the Guerrillas wept for him.

In the lull of military movements in Jackson county, Cass was to see the inauguration of the heavy Guerrilla work of 1863. Three miles west of Pleasant Hill, and near the house of Pouncy Smith, Younger and his comrades struck a blow that had the vigor of the old days in it. The garrison at Pleasant Hill numbered three hundred, and from the garrison Lieutenant Jefferson took thirty-two cavalrymen and advanced three miles toward Smith's, on a scouting expedition. Will Hulse and Noah Webster, two Guerrillas who seemed never to sleep, and to be hanging eternally about the flanks of the Federals, discovered Jefferson and reported his movements to the main body encamped at Parson Webster's. Taking with him eight men Joe Lee hurried to cut Jefferson off from Pleasant Hill; Younger, with eight more, was to close up from the west. Lee had with him John Webster, Noah Webster, Sterling Kennedy, David Kennedy, William Hays, Perry Hays, Henry McAninch, James Marshall, Edward Marshall, and Edward Hink. He was to gain the east end of the lane and halt there until Younger came up at its western extremity. Jefferson discovered Lee, however, and formed a line of battle in front of Smith's, throwing some skirmishers forward and getting ready apparently for a fight, although afterwards it was reported that Lee's men were mistaken for a portion of the garrison left behind at Pleasant Hill. Younger had further to go than he at first supposed, but was making all the haste possible when Lee, carried away by the uncontrollable impulse of his men, charged down the lane from the east, at a furious rate. Jefferson held his troopers fair to their line, until the Guerrillas reached a carbine range, but held them no longer. A volley and a stampede, and the wild race was on again. About a length ahead and splendidly mounted, William Hays led the Guerrillas. Shot dead, his horse fell under him and crushed his senses out for half an hour. John Webster and Noah Webster took Hays' place through sheer superiority of horse flesh and forced the fighting, John killing three of the enemy as he ran and Noah four. Noah's pistols were empty, but as he dashed alongside of the rearmost trooper he knocked him from the saddle with the butt of one of them, and seizing another by the collar of his coat, dragged him to the ground. Both were dispatched. Too late to block the western mouth of the lane, Younger joined in the swift pursuit as it passed him to the left, and added much to the certainty of the killing. Of the thirty-two, four alone escaped, and Jefferson was not among them. Hulse shot him running at a distance of fifty yards, and before he got to him he was dead. Pleasant Hill was instantly evacuated. Not a Federal garrison remained in Cass, outside of Harrisonville, and the garrison there was as effectually imprisoned as if surrounded by the walls of a fortress. The Guerrillas rode at ease in every direction. Younger and Lon Railey hung about the town for a week killing its picquets and destroying its foraging parties. Other bands, in other directions, gathered up valuable horses for future service and helped onward to the Southern army troops of recruits who needed only pilots and protection to the Osage river.

Like Cunningham, the man who had fought as a lion in twenty desperate combats, was destined to fall in a sudden and unnoted skirmish. Returning northward in the rear of Quantrell, Lieutenant William Haller was attacked at sunset and fought till dark. He triumphed, but he fell. His comrades buried him, and wept for him, and left him. Impetuous alike in attack or resistance, the resolution that always accompanied his actions gave to his young face that rigid cast which otherwise would only have belonged to maturer age. Romantic in his attachment to the South, and tinged somewhat with the fatalism of a military dreamer, he took no more heed of his life than of the wind which blew out the long locks of his hair—no more thought of the future than if God were liberty, and death but a going to God. As a soldier under fire, his conscience told him that it was his duty to die at any time, and he died. His features when he fell had upon them that strongest expression of his soul—enthusiasm. If he ever thought he was possessed of faults, he would have gone to battle as to a sanctuary to confess them, and to expiate them if need be by the sacrifice of his blood. Just, chivalrous, gentle as a woman yet terrible in combat, staunch to comrade and true to honor's laws, when he fell Quantrell lost an arm and his country a hero.

The battle year of 1863 had commenced; formidable men were coming to the surface in every direction. Here and there sudden Guerrilla fires leaped up from hidden places about the State and burned as if fed by oil until everything in their reach had been consumed. It was a year of savage fighting and killing; it was the year of the torch and the black flag; it was the year when the invisible reaper reaped sorest in the ranks of the Guerrillas and gathered into harvest sheaves the bravest of the brave.

Anderson, newly above the horizon, was flashing across the military heavens as a war comet. Left to himself and permitted to pursue his placid ways in peace, probably the amiable neighbor and working man would never have been developed into a tiger. But see how he was wrought upon. One day late in 1862 a body of Federal soldiers, especially enrolled and

WILLIAM ANDERSON.

uniformed to persecute women and prey upon non-combatants, gathered up in a half day's raid a number of demonstrative Southern girls whose only sin had been extravagant talk and pro-Confederacy cheering. They were taken to Kansas City and imprisoned in a dilapidated tenement close upon a steep place. Food was flung to them at intervals, and brutal guards sang ribald songs and talked indecent talk in their presence. With these women—tenderly nurtured and reared—were two of William Anderson's sisters. Working industriously in Kansas with his father, Anderson knew nothing of the real struggle of the war and nothing of the incarceration of his sisters. A quiet, courteous, fair-minded man, and one who took more delight in a book than in a crowd, he had a most excellant name in Randolph county, Missouri, where he was born, and in Johnson county, Kansas, where he was living in 1862. Destiny had to deal with him, however. The old rickety ramshackled building, within which were the huddled women, did not fall down fast enough for the brutes who bellowed about it. At night and in the darkness it was undermined, and when in the morning a little wind blew upon it and it was shaken, it fell with a crash. Cover up the fair faces disfigured, and the limp, lifeless bodies past all pain! Dead to touch, or kiss, or passionate entreaty Anderson's eldest sister was taken from the wreck a corpse. The younger, injured badly in the spine, with one leg broken, and her face bruised and cut pitifully, lived to tell the terrible story of it all to a gentle, patient brother kneeling at her bedside and looking up above to see if a God were there.

Soon a stir came along the border. A name new to the strife was beginning to pass from band to band and have about the camp fires a respectful hearing. "Anderson?" "Anderson?" "Who is this Anderson?" the Guerrillas asked one of another. "He kills them all. Quantrell spares, now and then, and Poole, and Blunt, and Yager, and Haller, and Jarrette, and Younger, and Gregg, and Todd, and Shepherd, and Cunningham, and all the balance; but Anderson never. Is he a devil in uniform?"

What he was fate made him. Horsemanship and prowess seemed as natural to the Missourian as aristocracy and the sea were to Venice. Dowered thus, Anderson gathered about him a band of Centaurs, and rode at a gallop into terrible notoriety.

Long-haired and lithe as a gray-hound, as he galloped he could swing himself to the earth and pick up a pistol. His forehead was broad, clear, and arched over the eyes as the forehead of a man who can brood and suffer. His nose, slightly aquiline and thin about the nostrils, betokened much of sensitiveness and more of determination. His eyes were variable in their color, gray seemingly in repose, and absolutely black and expanded in battle. The chin, neither square nor massive, was yet a firm chin and hidden with a waving beard. All that was cruel about his face was the mouth—a smiling, handsome, ferocious mouth drawn a little about the corners, and having as cruel attributes lips that were thin, and regular teeth, white and wide apart. Anderson, with his men, was immensely popular. His soldiers adored him. His rigorous discipline was relaxed at the proper moment; under his asperity he concealed genuine *bonhommie.* Possessed of a natural eloquence, and manners at once free and martial, he had only to be firm and his desperadoes were as heated wax in his hands. Such ascendency, unless based upon other qualities than personal accomplishment or individual tact, could never have endured the fierce strains of savage Guerrilla warfare; but wherever danger was blackest, from the midst of it Anderson's cheering voice was heard; and wherever the wreck of ranks and the tearing asunder of battle lines were thickest and deadliest, there, leading the press and raging as a wild beast, Anderson fought as a man possessed of a devil. And he kept a list of his victims. One other Guerrilla alone surpassed him—Archie Clemmens, a boy soldier, blue-eyed and beardless. Each had a silken cord knotted, and every knot stood for a life. What a ghastly memorandum it was! The knots increased. All through the wild war weather of 1863 and 1864 the silken cords came often from their buckskin pouches, and the knots, skillfully tied with deft, deadly fingers, grew and grew. At last on Anderson's there were *fifty-three* and on Clemmens' *fifty-four*—the terrible aggregate *one hundred and seven.* Thereafter Anderson never tied another. In the rear of the raid Price made in 1864—a raid tinged as it were and made splendid with some of the sunset glories of the war in the trans-Mississippi Department—Anderson struck a brigade of Federal infantry across the road he proposed to travel. He was a man who rode over things in preference to riding round them.

He ordered a charge as soon as he struck the skirmishers, and dashed ahead as he always did, the foremost rider in a band that had devils for riders. Hampered by the recruits he was taking to Price, and making no allowance for the timidity of unarmed and undrilled men, he charged, but he charged alone. A minie ball found his heart. Life, thank God, was gone when a rope was put about his neck and his body was dragged as the body of a deer slain in the woods. Many a picture was taken of the dead lion, with his great mane of a beard, and that indescribable pallor of death on his bronzed face.

Jesse and Frank James had emerged now from the awkwardness of youth and become giants in a night. Jesse was scarcely sixteen years of age. Frank a couple of years older. The war made them Guerrillas. Jesse was at home with his step-father, Dr. Reuben Samuels, of Clay county. He knew nothing of the strife save the echoes of it that now and then reached his mother's isolated farm. One day a company of militia visited this farm, hung Dr. Samuels to a tree until he was left for dead, and seized upon Jesse, a mere boy plowing in the field. With a rope about his neck, the soldiers abused him harshly, pricked him with sabres, and finally threatened him with certain death if it was ever reported to them again that he had given aid or information to Guerrillas. The same week his mother and sister were arrested, carried to St. Joseph, and thrown into a filthy prison. The hardships they endured were dreadful. Often without adequate food, insulted by sentinels who neither understood nor cared to learn the first lesson of a soldier—courtesy to women —cut off from all communication with the world, the sister was brought near to death's door from a fever which followed the punishment, and the mother—a high spirited and courageous matron—was released only after suffering and emaciation had made her aged in her prime. Before Mrs. James returned to her home, Jesse had joined Frank in the camp of Quantrell, who had preceded him a few months, and who had already, notwithstanding the briefness of the service, made a name for supreme and conspicuous daring. Jesse James had a face as smooth and as innocent as the face of a school girl. The blue eyes—very clear and penetrating—were never at rest. His form—tall and finely moulded—was capable of great effort and great endurance. On his lips there was always a smile, and for every comrade a pleasant word or a compliment. Looking at the small, white hands with their long, tapering fingers, it was not then written or recorded that they were to become with a revolver among the quickest and deadliest hands in the West. Frank was a little older and taller than Jesse. Jesse's face was something of an oval; Frank's was long, wide about the forehead, square and massive about the jaws and chin, and set always in a look of fixed repose. Jesse laughed at many things; Frank laughed not at all. Jesse was light hearted, reckless, devil-may-care; Frank was sober, sedate, a splendid man always for ambush or scouting parties. Both were undaunted.

Spring had put leaves upon all the trees and birds upon all their branches. The Guerrilla sang as he rode, and blessed in his heart the good God who was also the God of beneficent nature. It was the time for ambushments and obscurations; the time to take hold of roads and strangle the travel upon them; the time to ally with the fastnesses by day and make the night spectral with colossal horsemen; the time to kill in the undergrowth and devour along the highway; the time to put more fuel on the fire beneath the cauldron and stir it until hideous things came to the surface and made parts and parcels of the strife.

Scott, back long from the South and eager for action, crossed the Missouri river at Sibley the 20th day of May, 1863, taking with him twelve men. Frank James and James Little led the advance. Beyond the river thirteen miles and at the house of Moses McCoy, the Guerrillas camped, concocting a plan whereby the Federal garrison at Richfield, numbering thirty, might be got at and worsted. Captain Sessions was in command at Richfield, and his grave was already being dug. Scott found a friendly citizen named Peter Mahoney who volunteered to do the decoy work. He loaded up a wagon with wood, clothed himself in the roughest and raggedest clothes he had, and rumbled away behind as scrawny and fidgety a yoke of oxen as ever felt a north wind in the winter bite their bones or deceptive buckeye in the spring swell their bellies.

"Mr. Mahoney, what is the news?" This was the greeting he got. "No news; I have wood for sale. Yes, but there is some news, too; I like to have forgot. Eight or ten of those Quantrell men are prowling about my way, the infernal

FRANK JAMES.

scoundrels, and I hope they may be hunted out of the county."

Mahoney did well, but Scott did better. He secreted his men three miles from Richfield and near the crossing of a bridge. If an enemy came the bridge was a sentinel; its resounding planks the explosion of a musket. Scott, with eight men, dismounted and lay close along the road. Gregg, with Fletch Taylor, James Little and Joe Hart, mounted and ready to charge, kept still and expectant fifty yards in the rear of the ambush. Presently at the crossing a dull booming was heard, and the Guerrillas knew that Sessions had bit at the bait Mahoney offered. A sudden clicking along the line—the eight were in a hurry. "Be still," said Scott; "you cock too soon. I had rather have two cool men than ten impatient ones." The Federals came right onward; they rode along gaily in front of the ambuscade; they had no skirmishers out; and they were doomed. The leading files were abreast of Scott on the right when he ordered a volley, and Captain Sessions, Lieut. Graffenstien and seven privates fell dead. What was left of the Federal array turned itself into a rout; Gregg, Taylor, Little and Hart thundered down to the charge. Scott mounted again, and altogether and away at a rush, pursuers and pursued dashed into Richfield. Short rally there, and briefer fighting. The remnant of the wreck surrendered, and Scott—more merciful than many among whom he soldiered—spared the prisoners and paroled them.

To Mat. McGinnis' it was twenty miles—a hard ride after a morning's combat—but Scott made it by sunset, and sent Fletch Taylor and Frank James out to scour the country and learn the situation. The situation was exceedingly simple. Startled by the sinister sweep of the Guerrilla pinions, always so dark and threatening, the militia doves about the dove-cotes had begun to mass themselves for protection and to make ready for destroying the intruders. Clay county was not yet used to such riders and raiders; it was part of a border patrimony that had not yet been operated upon by the Guerrillas, and it should not be. Mrs. James gave her son also the further information that the great bulk of the militia from Plattsburg, Clinton county, had been ordered out to hunt for Scott, and that Plattsburg itself and at that very time was at the mercy of any band of heroes. Taylor and James got quick to Scott with the valuable information, and Scott got quick to horse. In the beginning of the second night since the Richfield battle, the march was begun for Plattsburg, Taylor and James leading the advance. Two o'clock in the morning found the Guerrillas on Smith's fork of Grand river, and four miles from the objective point. There was a halt here and a sleep until daylight. Again thrown forward to develop the situation, Taylor, Gregg, Little and James learned speedily that most of the garrison had gone out under Captain Rodgers to capture Scott, and was at least twenty miles from abandoned Plattsburg.

Feeding and resting up to three in the afternoon, Scott at that hour saddled for the attack. In the advance rode Taylor, Gregg, Little and Jackson. They took the main road at a walk; ostensibly they were militia. Three hundred yards from the square the Guerrillas formed fours and dashed ahead. It was hot work. Not by forty-six had the garrison gone on the hunt under Rodgers, and there in the well fortified court house, held their own without a waver. The square was the hot place. All the loopholes of the court house bore upon it; the windows commanded it; the angles were swept by the embrasures cut especially for musketry. Scott dashed into this square, raked and rained upon by minie balls, and so did Taylor, John Jackson, Little, Gregg, and Frank James. Flying swift for succor, and shouting to his men as he ran to open for him, Frank James cut off the Colonel commanding the post from his bomb-proof and turned him over to Scott. "Captain," he said, as he halted under a pitiless fire and delivered over the agitated officer, "kill this man unless he delivers up the court house." "That I will, by g—d," and Scott swore a great oath and put his hand upon his pistol. But the need to kill him never came. The garrison, affected by the appeals of its commanding officer, capitulated without a further fight, forty-six surrendering to twelve. Two hundred muskets were broken to pieces, $10,000 in Missouri defence bonds were appropriated, while the militia were paroled and made to promise better treatment of non-combatants and Southern citizens in the future. Taking supper publicly at the hotel, and having as his guest the commander of the post, Scott played the hospitable soldier courteously, settled his score like a prince, and rode out at dark and rapidly towards the Missouri river. Knowing almost every foot of the country, Scott commissioned Frank James especially to guide the column and conduct it, if that were possible, to a ferry the enemy was not guarding. His mother's house being on the direct line of his march, and knowing how keenly observant and how unusually well informed of military movements she always was, he halted long enough to hear her story. It was not by any means a flattering one. At every point on the river from Kansas City to Lexington where a skiff had ever been, or a boat, or a ferry, or a canoe, Federal soldiers were stationed. Scott had aroused and alarmed four counties, and the determination was either to kill him or to capture him, and the terms were synonymous. Scott would see, however. That night he camped on Fishing river, and the next morning early he sent Taylor, Little and Hart down to the Missouri to beat about the crossings and take a real look at the facts. He would remain in camp himself until they returned or until he was forced to get out of it. He was forced to get out, and that speedily. Captains Younger and Garth struck it about ten o'clock and poured into it a rattling volley. One hundred and fifty strong, what else could the ten Guerrillas do but get up and get away as fast as possible. The pursuit lasted eight miles, Scott fighting every chance he got and holding on to difficult places and crossings until he was either flanked or about to become enveloped. Ahead of pursuit sufficiently at Blue Mills to look to his crossing somewhat, Scott made a rickety raft for the saddles and blankets and for the men who could not swim, and got over safely. On the Jackson side the quicksand laid hold of the horses of Scott, Jackson and James, and inch by inch and struggle by struggle drew them down. It was a pitiful sight. The poor steeds had on their faces a look of human agony. Every effort at rescue only hastened the engulfment. The sand had been fair to look upon; some leaves were upon it as a cover; it reached to the higher ground, smooth as a satin band and springing to the feet of the innocent horses. Take care! First to the fetlock, next to the knees, and the bottom is gone, and the sentient thing, tawny about the muzzle and creeping as a worm, crawls ever and ever and covers as it crawls. When the Guerrillas left their horses the Federals were on the northern side of the river firing futilely across, and the treacherous quicksand—

unflecked by a hoof-mark—spread itself out again under the warm sun and waited, watching. The dismounted men had need to mount themselves rapidly; it was battle everywhere. James Combs especially gave Frank James a horse destined soon to become famous. Wherever he was, there was his rider, and wherever the rider, there tempest and dead men.

Four miles from Independence, and back a little from the road leading to Kansas City, a house stood occupied by several women light of love. Thither regularly went Federal soldiers from the Independence garrison, and the drinking was deep and the orgies shameful. Gregg set a trap to catch a few of the comers and goers. Within the lines of the enemy, much circumspection was required to make an envelopment of the house successful. He chose Jesse James from among a number of volunteers and sent him forward to reconnoitre the premises. Jesse, arrayed in coquettish female apparel, with his smooth face, blue eyes, and blooming cheeks, looked the image of a bashful country girl, not yet acquainted with vice, though half eager and half reluctant to walk a step nearer to the edge of its perilous precipice. As he mounted, woman fashion, upon a fiery horse, the wind blew all about his peach colored face the pink ribbons of a garish bonnet, and lifted the tell-tale riding habit just enough to reveal instead of laced shoes or gaiters, the muddy boots of a born cavalryman. Gregg, taking ten men, followed in the rear of James to within half a mile of the nearest picquet post, and hid himself in the woods until word could be brought from the bagnio ahead. If by a certain hour the disguised Guerrilla did not return to his comrades, the picquets were to be driven in, the house surrounded, and the inmates forced to give such information as they possessed, of his whereabouts. Successful, and Gregg neither by word nor deed, was to alarm the outpost or furnish indication in any manner that Guerrillas were in the neighborhood.

Jesse James, having pointed out to him with tolerable accuracy the direction of the house, left the road, skirted the timber rapidly, leaped several ugly ravines, floundered over a few marshy places, and finally reached his destination without meeting a citizen or encountering an enemy. He would not dismount, but sat upon his horse at the fence and asked that the mistress of the establishment might come out to him. Little by

little, and with many a gawky protest and many a bashful
simper, he told a plausible story of parental *espoinage* and family discipline. He, ostensibly a she, could not have beaux,
could not go with the soldiers, could not sit with them late, nor
ride with them, nor romp with them; she was tired of it all and
wanted a little fun. Would the mistress let her come occasionally to her and bring with her three or four neighbor girls,
who were in the same predicament? The mistress laughed and
was glad. New faces to her were like new coin, and she put
forth a hand and patted the merchantable thing upon the knee,
and ogled her smiling mouth and girlish features gleefully. As
she-wolf and venturesome lamb separated, the assignation was
assured. That night the amorous country girl, accompanied by
three of her young female companions, was to return, and the
mistress—confident in her ability to provide them lovers—was
to make known among the soldiers the attractive acquisition.

It lacked an hour of sunset when Jesse James got back to
Gregg; an hour after sunset the Guerrillas, following hard upon
the track made by the boy spy, rode rapidly on to keep the trysting. The house was gracious with lights, and jubilant with
laughter. Drink abounded, and under cover of the clinking
glasses, the men kissed the women. Anticipating an orgy of
unusual attractions, twelve Federals had been lured out from the
garrison and made to believe that bare-footed maidens ran wild
in the woods, and buxom lasses hid for the hunting. No guards
were out; no sentinels were posted. Jesse James crept close to
a window and peered in. The night was chill and a large wood
fire blazed upon a large hearth. All the company was in one
room, five women and a dozen men. Scattered about yet ready
for the grasping, the cavalry carbines were in easy reach, and
the revolvers handy about the person. Sampson trusting everything to Delilah, might not have trusted so much if under the
old dispensation there had been anything of bushwhacking.

Gregg loved everybody who ever wore the gray, and what exercised him most was the question just now of attack. Should
he demand a surrender? Jesse James, the boy, said no to the
veteran. Twelve men inside of a house, and the house inside
of their own lines where reinforcements might be hurried quickly
to them, would surely hold their own against eleven outside, if
indeed they did not make it worse. The best thing to do was

to fire through the windows and kill what could be killed by a carbine volley, then rush in through the door and finish—under the cover of the smoke, the horror and the panic—what survived the broadside.

Luckily, the women sat in a corner to themselves, and close to a large bed fixed against the wall and to the right of the fireplace. On the side of the house the bed was on, two broad windows opened low upon the ground, and between the windows there was a door, not ajar but not fastened. Gregg, with five men, went to the upper window, and Taylor, with four, took position at the lower. The women were out of immediate range. The house shook; the glass shivered; the door was hurled backward; there was a hot, stifling crash of revolvers; and on the dresses of the women and the white coverlet of the bed great blood splotches. Eight out of the twelve fell dead or wounded the first fire; after the last fire all were dead. It was a spectacle ghastly beyond any ever yet witnessed by the Guerrillas, because so circumscribed. Piled two deep the dead men lay, one with a glass grasped tightly in his stiffened fingers, and one in his shut hand the picture of a woman scarcely clad. How they wept, the poor, painted things, for the slain soldiers, and how they blasphemed; but Gregg tarried not, neither did he make atonement. As they lay heaped where they fell and piled together, so they lay still when he mounted and rode away.

There was riding and mustering in and about the country of the Hudspeths. Every Guerrilla in Missouri knew personally or had heard of the Hudspeths. Owning well nigh a whole neighborhood in the eastern portion of Jackson county, there were four brothers who, when they were not fighting for the Southern Confederacy, were feeding the soldiers. Lane robbed them, Jennison robbed them, Anthony robbed them, militiaman and Jayhawker alike robbed them; they were burnt out and plundered; shot at and waylaid; hunted here, driven there, and persecuted everywhere, but they could not be reduced in either purse or spirit. They still gave and fought. They scouted for Quantrell and killed with Todd; they furnished guides for Anderson and ambuscaded with Gregg. Their land could not be taken from them, that they knew; but if like their other property it had been moveable, the land too would have gone

JESSE W. JAMES.

without a murmur. Patriotism was the standard by which they judged every man, and those who were not patriotic were untrue. No matter the iron emergencies that were sometimes upon the country; no matter what blood-thirsty orders sought to kill comradeship and obliterate sympathy; no matter how all the highways were guarded and all the garrisoned places overgrown with soldiers, the Hudspeths kept the faith and fought the good fight to the end.

It was, therefore, in the Hudspeth neighborhood that a mustering was being had. Todd had sent a message to Scott, and Scott to John Jarrette, and John Jarrette to Gregg, and Gregg to Yager, and Yager to Anderson, and Anderson to Poole, and Poole to Maddox, and so the tidings went from chief to chief until the border was aflame. At the rendezvous each leader hastily arrived bringing in the aggregate about seventy Guerrillas. It was the intention to strike a blow somewhere, but as yet no direction had been agreed upon nor any place designated. A war council fixed upon Kansas City; to such men the impossible was possible. Todd was put in command of the expedition, and made subsidiary to him were Scott, Anderson, Yager, Gregg, Maddox and Jarrette. On the evening of the 16th of June, 1863, Todd formed the Guerrillas in line and laid down the law to them: "It has been settled that we attack Kansas City. The venture is a desperate one; you can only promise yourselves hard fighting and hard riding; the most of us may be killed. If any among you desire to remain behind move two paces to the front." Not a horse stirred; rear rank and front rank the seventy men were as adamant.

It was not to be, however—this attack upon Kansas City. As Todd reached the undulating and expanding prairie close to the residence of Col. Upton Hays, he saw on the road leading from Westport to Little Santa Fe a column of Federals numbering two hundred. They were *en route* from Kansas to Westport, and from Westport of course right on into Kansas City. "These people," Todd said, laconically, "had better be fought outside of brick walls than inside of them, and here we must fight." To cut them off from Westport and bring them to a stand in the open ground, a distance of eight miles had to be traversed while the Federals were marching five. It was done

at a gallop. Todd reached Brush creek in front of the advancing column, formed his men behind an eminence, and rode forward alone to reconnoitre. His signal to advance was the lifting of his hat. If he did this the Guerrillas were to ride slowly
to the crest of the ridge; if he did not do this, they were to file
to the left and let the Kansas column go by. Clear-cut yet
standing massive against the blue sky beyond, Todd silently sat
his horse in front of his line for a few minutes and gazed upon
the advancing enemy. If they saw him, they made no sign. If
he counted them, their numbers did not deter him, for he lifted
his hat once as he turned to his men, and drew from his hips to
his front the pistols of his belt. The combat was certain now.
Boon Schull, Frank James, Geo. Todd and Fletch Taylor led on
the right just a little, while further down the line Anderson, Yager, Gregg, Jarrette, Jesse James, Geo. Maddox and Dick Maddox were slightly in advance of the centre and left. The Federals were a portion of the 9th Kansas Cavalry, and were commanded by Capt. Thatcher. The dust was intolerable. It
arose as a vast cloud and hid the combatants. Friend fired at
friend, and foe rode side by side with foe afraid to shoot. Boon
Schull had killed four of the enemy, and in the gloom was still
ahead and killing when he was shot dead from the saddle by a
Federal trooper. Mistaking him for a comrade and galloping
past in pursuit, the Kansas man fired into his back and finished
one of the chosen ones of a chosen band. Frank James, close
behind him, saw the flash of the Federal's pistol in the yellow
cloud of the dust and killed the Federal as he sat. Another fell
out from the ranks of the Guerrillas in the same manner, Al.
Wyatt, fighting as he always fought, far in the front. Thatcher
could not make headway against men who were ambi-dextered,
whose pistols seemed always to be loaded, who fired and dashed
ahead, and who seemed always to be firing and dashing ahead.
Anderson raged as a tiger unloosed. Todd fought as he always
did—cool, smiling, deadly. Taylor with five loads emptied five
saddles; Jarrette, hemmed in on a flank by three troopers, all
of whom were shooting at him at the same time, killed them all,
and Jesse James — boy that he was — won from Anderson the
remarkable compliment: "Not to have any beard, he is the
keenest and cleanest fighter in the command." Gregg, his
grave face fixed as it was always fixed in absolute repose, added

three to his already long list, and Scott—as if conscious that he was fighting his last battle—multiplied his energy and his prowess. Eighty Federals had already fallen, and the wild rout was already thundering away across the prairies into Kansas, pursued by devils who killed and spared not, when a solid regiment of infantry emerged at the double quick from a line of sheltering timber and formed in front of it for succor. What to the desert-parched and scorched are green things and running water, that to the remnant of the riven Ninth was the sheltering infantry. They ran through it, and behind it, and formed in the lee and the rear of it; but they did not come out again to see the last of the wild beasts retreating, baffled from a barrier they could not break. Todd, knowing in an instant the folly of further fighting, checked his men and rearranged his ranks. At long range—almost a mile—Scott, while calmly watching the enemy, was shot; an Enfield rifle ball had found his heart. It was over this man that Todd wept when they buried him. Perhaps both by nature and temperament no man was better fitted for the life of a Guerrilla than Fernando Scott. Of a highly nervous and sensitive disposition, he slept little; it was not believed that he ever experienced an emotion of physical fear; under fire no soldier could be cooler; he won the love of his men first—later, their adoration; thinking a great deal, he did not talk much; gentle, he scarcely ever spoke harshly; tender-hearted, he very rarely ever killed save in open battle. Above everything else he was true. Nothing deterred him in the line of his duty, and if he had been ordered to blow up a powder-magazine he would have blown it up and himself with it.

Boon Schull was a Missouri Murat, fighting obscurely and under a black flag. If to ride always in the advance, if to fight single-handed or against any odds, if to dash at anything and grapple with anything, if to attract twice—once by his boyishness and once by his desperation—made him in any manner to approximate the great cavalry Frenchman, then was Schull a border Murat, unforgotten of history, but a splendid type of that race of Southern soldiers who, man to man, could have whipped the world.

Todd brought back tenderly the bodies of Scott, Schull and Wyatt, detailing to guard them Richard Berry, Fletch Taylor, James Little, Frank James, John Ross, and Oath Hinton, six

12

comrades who, like the dead ones, knew no fear and shrank from no duty. Schull's body was taken to the house of Mrs. Younger, and his relatives, the Wallaces, informed of h's death. Todd performed the last sad rites for Scott the night of the day of the battle. As his brief lifetime had been stormy, so was his burial. The night was tempestuous. The wrathful wind smote the trees with the wings of a great darkness. All the sky was a void; nothing was there but the unknown. The rain, articulate almost in its beating, fell upon the pallid face of the sleeping man, uncovered for the last time, and murmured, it may be, a benediction. The swirling torches, few and far apart, peopled with spectres the shadows they disturbed. No prayer was said; the good God knew best of all what had been writ in the everlasting book touching the dead Guerrilla, and struck the balance to the side whereon was written courage, manhood, truth.

At the grave of Schull it was not permitted to his comrades to gather about and say any word that would serve to make the long journey shorter or the long sleep lighter in eternity. Federal troops were camped all about the house, and upon all the roads leading to it. At night as the mournful escort bore the young soldier back from the last of his fields, it passed a Federal bivouac twenty paces from the road. The cortege, however, was not halted, and the grave was dug almost within sight of the camp-fires.

The operations of the Guerrillas now became really formidable. Scouting parties of the enemy were cut to pieces, picquet posts exterminated, guards convoying foraging trains slain among their wagons, marching columns ambuscaded, and heavy war bodies fired upon continually and always at a disadvantage. Jesse James headed one squad and lay in wait a whole day long watching for a fishing party. They did not come the first day, nor the second till about noon, but James waited rationless and got a point blank volley into them before he left, killing six out of eight, one of the killed being a Lieutenant.

Frank James, Fletch Taylor, John Ross, Hinton, Little, George Shepherd, Poole, and Cole Younger came suddenly upon a foraging party of eight in a large field in the middle of which there was a barn. Pressed to the girth the Federals took refuge in this and began to make a good fight for their lives.

JOHN JARRETTE.

PEYTON LONG.

ALLEN PARMER.

Taylor and James, covered by the fire of their comrades, made a desperate rush on the building, put a lighted match to some convenient hay, and soon the whole structure was in flames. As the enemy ran out, every one of the eight was killed, two falling back in the barn and being charred there beyond recognition.

Jarrette and Gregg, taking five men apiece, crossed over into Kansas on the west of Westport, and hid themselves until the darkness came. Their operations were confined principally to the main road between Leavenworth and Kansas City, and their first victims were a sergeant and four men carrying dispatches. The whole party were killed, and the dispatches read and destroyed.

The next thing to come along in the way of game was an ambulance containing a Nebraska sutler, the sutler's clerk, two artillerymen from some fort on the plains, and a negro driver. The sutler was drunk, the sutler's clerk was noisy, and the two artillerymen were asleep. Jarrette called to the driver to halt, but the driver, suspecting danger, whipped up his horses. The drunken sutler fired upon Jarrette, with his pistol almost touching him, and the sutler's clerk shouted "Murder!" "Murder!" at the top of his voice. Gregg, galloping ahead and killing the lead horse in the traces, had the ill-assorted ambulance load completely at his mercy. The sutler and the sutler's clerk were killed with scarcely anything of ceremony, and the black driver also for his contrariness, but the artillerymen were regulars and Irish regulars at that, and Jarrette, guarding them until daylight, released them without a pledge.

Scarcely half a mile further upon the road there was a house that in the old-fashioned parlance might be called a tavern. "Entertainment for man and beast," were the words painted upon a board that was nailed to a tree. "Hello!" cried Gregg, in advance with John Ross and Sim Whitsett, "who keeps house?" The landlord came, a rubicund man, all affability and belly. "I keep house, gentlemen," he said, "but you must be light upon me to-night, for I am full." And so he was. Two men remained outside to care for the horses, and ten took a stroll over the premises. In the stable three Federals were dragged out from a lot of straw, in the kitchen the third one was cornered, and in five beds in various parts of the tavern proper, the Guerrillas came upon five more, big with sleep when awakened, and helpless in proportion as they were destitute of clothing. Poor creatures! they were shivering as much from the cold as from their fright when Jarrette shot them all. The landlord went next, killed over a horse he was trying to save, and then the tavern. Burning the tavern, however, was a serious mistake. The flames aroused a cavalry camp three quarters of a mile to the left of the road in some timber, and soon four companies came swarming out to solve the problem of the burning. Jarrette was gone, but the road was alive with soldiers, who hunted all through the night and until late the next morning for something that would tell of the invisible devils who for seventeen miles had strewn it with corpses.

Todd, with ten men, went back to his old intrenchments on the Harrisonville and Kansas City road and hid himself for two days and nights completely. He let couriers go by, scouts go by, detachments of various sizes go by, and here and there a wagon, and once a piece of artillery. He did not fire a single pistol shot. He scarcely allowed a man upon the road. What had come over Todd? this one whispered and that one whispered; didn't he mean to fight? this one asked and that one asked. Somewhere about ten o'clock on the morning of the third day, eighteen Kansas Red Legs, *en route* to Independence to join a battalion there, rode past the trenches singing and swearing. Out of eighteen, three got alive into Independence. Todd, informed before hand of the marching of this detachment, waited thus grimly for its arrival, letting slip through his fingers considerable other game not near so valuable in the estimation of this merciless fighter, *par excellence*, of the border.

Poole also took a turn down towards the Lafayette county line. West of Napoleon three miles there was a spring at which troops marching to and fro along the river road generally stopped to drink. This spring broke out from the bluff's foot, was conveyed through some open box work across the little stretch of level land between the bluff and the road, and made to fall in a huge tank just at the upper verge of the dusty highway. Poole knew it well, a grateful oasis for thirsty cavalrymen. Above the tank was the bluff, and above the bluff exceedingly heavy timber. Ambushed, Poole waited all one night and

DAVE POOLE.

E. P. De HART.

until noon the next day, for what fortune might send to the cooling water. He had thirty good men at his beck and call, and he had the timber. No picquets were out at either end of the road, and none were necessary. It had never happened before that the spring was ambuscaded. Huston's regiment held Lexington, a regiment of regular militia with fair reputation for fighting, and some attainments as soldiers in battle. Eighty-four, commanded by a Captain, stopped at the spring to drink themselves and let their horses drink. From the trees, behind which Poole and his men were hiding to the tank upon the roadside, it was probably fifty paces, the plunging fire the Guerrillas were possessed of, making if anything this distance shorter and deadlier. As the Federals approached the watering-place they broke ranks without an order and hurried forward altogether and crowded. The men were thirsty and the beasts were thirsty. Forty of the eighty horses had their heads together in the tank, while their riders, busy at the trough above, were stooping and drinking leisurely. The woods blazed, the water was bloody, the oasis became a graveyard. After the carbines had commenced the work, the revolvers finished it. Twenty-seven lay dead where they had dismounted, six more perished in the pursuit, and eleven, badly wounded, were spared by Poole because of the regiment's name for fairness and tolerant behavior.

All these blows, coming so thick, and so fast, and so close together, bred something like a cry of wrath along the border. Gen. Thomas Ewing was in command, and he swore a great Democratic oath that until the prairies were made red with the blood of the bushwhackers he would keep daily in the saddle a thousand horsemen. To the threat Quantrell replied by a concentration. Jarrette, Younger, Yager, and Railey were on Big Creek, in Cass county. Todd was in Jackson. Tom Talley, Cole Younger, and Ed Hink were the messengers chosen to speed the time and place of rendezvous. Jarrette, before further operations commenced, reorganized his company. Coleman Younger was elected First Lieutenant; Joseph Lee, Second; Lon Railey, Third, and John Webster, Orderly Sergeant. The roll was called and eighty men answered to their names. Todd, at the house of William Hopkins, on Little Blue, also reorganized. Fletcher Taylor was elected First Lieutenant, James Little, Second; William Anderson, Third, and Isaac Berry, Orderly Sergeant. Anderson, be it remembered, commenced under Todd that career which was to horrify the country. Capt. Richard Yager marshalled his men on Big Blue at the farm of his father, and on the night of July 14th, 1863, Yager, Jarrette and Todd met Quantrell at the Edmond Coward farm, a famous Guerrilla mustering-place. The Cowards were all patriots and all soldiers. They belonged to that indomitable class of citizens in Jackson county whom no terror could affright nor persecution intimidate. Volunteers for the war, the war might take goods, houses, shelter, substance, everything; but never the faith that failed not to the end.

From Coward's Quantrell marched to meet Poole, Blunt and McGrew at David George's, another favorite mustering-place, and then due east for an hour or two. He was hunting for some of Ewing's one thousand horsemen, perhaps for all of them. As he approached the Blue Springs and Pleasant Hill road a long line to the left told him quickly that there was work to be done. Quantrell sent Todd and Little forward at once to uncover the line. Two Federals rode out to meet them promptly and halted at a distance of fifty yards. Quoth Todd: "Who are you?" "It is Major Ransom, with four hundred men and two pieces of artillery." "Your business?" "Looking for that d—d scoundrel Quantrell, and Quantrell's cut-throats and thieves." "Well you can find them, I reckon; but you express yourself too freely. You are not polite." At Todd's order, Little then rode rapidly to Quantrell, reporting the exact condition of affairs and asking for twenty men to skirmish with the enemy. Quantrell sent him the desired number under Lieutenant Coleman Younger, who took with him Jesse and Frank James, George and Richard Maddox, George Wigginton, Sim Whitsett, Tom Talley, and other spirits just as choice and dashing. Todd, seeing at his back so many of those who had followed him in fifty desperate combats, ordered a charge immediately and led it furiously. The Federals advanced, astonished at the unexpected audacity of the rush, were cut to pieces and scattered. Before they could get safely to the shelter of the covering column fifteen had been killed and a dozen wounded. In the race Sim

Whitsett was seen to shoot three, and the two Jameses three each. Todd, being better mounted than any of his company, killed four. Ransom unlimbered his artillery, notwithstanding the heavy odds he held against Quantrell, and opened upon the twenty Guerrillas Todd held in front of him. Quantrell retreated, and Ransom followed slowly. Step by step Quantrell led him on to the Sni, past the old rendezvous-ground at David George's, and past the camp of the day before. Couriers, sent early to Poole, Blunt and Gregg, had ordered them to take position at a crossing upon the Sni, to hide themselves, and hold it. Todd fought and fell back; Quantrell relieved Todd and fought and fell back; Ransom crept on leisurely, feeling his way as he crept and firing his cannon from every hill-top and valley. Finally Ransom halted for dinner, and Quantrell halted in watching distance. The next step was to the ford, and Quantrell passed on through, halting on the ground beyond and forming line of battle. Ransom followed, slow but dogged. The Sni was full, many had crossed over and were waiting for those behind to close up, the thither bank was blue with uniforms when Poole poured out from his ambuscade a terrible fire, and Quantrell charged down upon the demoralized and disorded mass. The fight was brief but bloody. Ransom tried to keep hold upon the timber and rally his men about the artillery, but they broke away from his grasp and forced him to fall back rapidly towards ¦Independence, Todd taking the advance again and driving everything before him. Quantrell pursued until Ransom, under the shelter of his fortified post, saw his roughly handled troops drop from their horses utterly used up and exhausted. His loss he afterwards admitted to be fifty-eight; the Guerrillas figured it up to seventy-three. After this fight Quantrell took position in the neighborhood of Pink Hill and called a council of his officers as to the advisability of attacking Lexington. The vote upon the proposition was a tie —Jarrette, Younger, and Todd voting against the attack, and Anderson, Poole, and Gregg in favor of it. Poole and Anderson especially urged the attack, Poole pledging himself to lead the advance and deliver his first volley in front of the city hotel. He was overruled. Lexington was a fortified place, held by a large garrison, and an assault upon it was a risk that the cooler heads among the Guerrillas were not willing to take; the concentrated command, therefore, separated again, or rather disbanded for fifteen days. Lee went to Saline county, attacked Brownsville, captured its garrison of twenty militia, and operated successfully in its vicinity for nearly a week. Captain Joseph A. Lee, one of the most dashing and successful soldiers the war produced, was a young man as modest as he was brave. He made military honor his guiding star, and fought always as a knight whose lineage was high and whose escutcheon was spotless. Surrounded by desperate circumstances, and called upon oftentimes to do desperate things, he had wisdom allied to valor, and he knew how equally to struggle, to submit, to rise again from prostration refreshed like a giant, and to manifest that species of heroic endurance which, whenever everything else fails, always knows how to die. Poole went to Lafayette county, Jarrette to the Sni Hills, Younger to Big Creek, Todd and Quantrell to Jackson county, Gregg to the Little Blue, Yager to the neighborhood of Westport, and Anderson into Kansas. The old savage work of isolation and ambuscade commenced again. Dead men were everywhere. The militia and the Jayhawkers preyed upon the citizens and the non-combatants, and the Guerrillas preyed upon the militia and the Jayhawkers. To the sword the torch had been added. Two hundred houses in Jackson county had been burnt; Vernon county was a desert; a day's ride in Bates brought no sight of a habitation; Cass was well nigh ruined; a black swathe had been mowed through Lafayette; Butler was in ashes; Harrisonville was in ashes; armed men met in the woods, by the streams, along the highways; there were musket-shots, pistol-shots, cries, the shouts of struggling men, smoke by day and flames by night; the soldiers hated one another; there was no quarter; hogs fed upon human flesh; Ewing's one thousand cavalrymen were in the saddle; the black flag had been lifted; the face of the good God seemed to be turned away from the border; the Lawrence Massacre was making head.

Anderson, taking with him twenty men, made a dash into Kansas, circled Olathe, and came upon a skeleton camp of infantry numbering thirty-eight. He charged the camp and slaughtered every human male thing about it. He fired the tents and the wagons, appropriated the horses, let the loose women go free, and hurried out after a foraging party which had been gone from the camp an hour. It was found in a barn-lot loading six wagons with oats and corn. To each wagon there were four men, who had not even brought their arms with them, and they tried to surrender. No use! Back safe from the jaws of a famishing tiger might rather the stricken deer hope to come than any Kansas·man from the hands of Bill Anderson. He killed the soldiers first, next the teamsters, and then the farmer who owned the corn, and two of his sons who were at home from the army on furlough. The country was up and after him. It was sixty miles to shelter, and upon every mile of that distance Anderson stood and fought, escaping finally after inflicting serious loss upon his pursuers and losing himself in killed seven of his bravest men.

At Blue Mills ferry Captain Parker crossed into Clay county with ten men, rode rapidly to Liberty and charged the town. Captain Henry Hubbard commanded the post, its garrison consisting of twenty-five men. Hubbard was badly wounded, and an old negro by the name of Washington Dale hid him securely under some hay in the loft of a livery stable. With Parker was a young soldier, Harvey Turner, who was surrounded the next day at the house of a Mrs. Carroll by sixty militia, a portion of Penick's regiment. All along the line in those days the watchword was: "No surrender," and Turner rushed from the house to his horse, firing right and left as he ran. Sixty Federals shot at him from every conceivable direction, but he killed one, wounded another, and escaped, joining Parker the next day without even the smell of fire upon his garments. The Liberty militia were not killed, as they had nothing in common with those across the river; but two of them—Wash Huffaker and D. Hubbard—were taken into Jackson county and investigated. Charges touching their behavior towards certain non-combatants had been freely circulated, but not being substantiated upon investigation, Parker paroled them later and released them.

Parker next, in company with Cole Younger, Joe Lee, Joe Hall, Richard Kenney and Charles Sanders, made a dash into Wellington where ten Federals were robbing a store. Parker was killed in the attack upon the town, but his comrades avenged him. Not a man of the ten escaped, and the Guerrillas remained during the day and until late at night, complimented by the citizens and feasted as well.   The road west from Wellington runs between the bluff and the river, and as the Guerrillas rode along under the stars, glad from so much social relaxation and pleasure, five stalwart forms rose up behind them in the road and fired a signal volley.   Instantly the bank next to the river was alive with Federals, and the air thick with bullets.   Seventy men had ambushed five, such at that time was the terror of Quantrell's name, and left at the same time an open space for them to get out at.   Not slow to avail themselves of an opportunity so considerately made, the Guerrillas dashed ahead like the wind, taking the fire of the whole line as they ran past it, and taking it without a scratch. Later, a solitary militiaman rode into their ranks, made himself known, and was shot dead by Kinney for his confidence.

The fifteen days of disbandment were on the eve of expiration. A supply of ammunition ample for all purposes had been procured, and cartridges enough made for a week of constant fighting.   An expedition of an extraordinary character was about to be inaugurated.   The Guerrillas were beginning to concentrate.   The strife in Jackson county had been particularly savage of late.   Many inoffensive citizens had been killed.   Mr. Laws, an old resident, for feeding a squad of Federals disguised as Guerrillas, was shot by the order of Major W. C. Ransom, a Kansas Federal.   Capt. Hoyt, another Kansas officer, rode into Westport one day, took Philip Bucher from his wife and children, marched him out on the commons, made him kneel down and shot him.   Henry Rout, another quiet citizen, was hung. Another Kansas officer, while out on a scouting expedition, wounded and captured an old man who was hunting stock. Lest he should suffer some from his wounds, this considerate officer finished him with a pistol bullet.   A detachment of Kansas soldiers were sent out on the Big Blue to arrest three men.   The men were not at home, but their wives were. These—arrested and forced to walk into Kansas City, a distance of thirteen miles—were put into a brick building with a door which was locked upon the outside.   That night the building, undermined, fell, and the next day the mangled bodies of the innocent women were boxed up and sent back to their homes in an old ox wagon.   Just look at the list: A son of Henry Morris, only fourteen years old, was killed by Penick's troops in Independence. Henry Morris lived five miles north of Lone Jack. Big Jim Cummins was killed, and little Jim Cummins. Little Jim Cummins had been wounded at Lone Jack, but had recovered. John Phillips was hung. James Saunders and Jeptha Crawford were taken from Blue Springs and shot. Their houses were also burned. One of Penick's men, calling himself Jim Lane, killed Dr. Triggs for his money. Kimberlin was arrested, carried to Independence, sent back home under a guard and hung in his barn. Moses Carr was also arrested, carried to Independence, sent back again towards his home, but before reaching it he was tied to a tree in Blue Bottom and shot to pieces. Sam Jones was hung, an old man named Doty was hung, George Tyler was shot, as were Hedrick and Somers of Cass county, Samuels of Bates, Peters, Monroe, Farwell and Lowers, of Vernon, and Givens, Manchester, Bolling, Newton, Beamish, Parker and Ralls, of Jackson. Over two hundred more were killed in the three months preceding the Lawrence Massacre. In mid-winter houses were burned by the hundred and whole neighborhoods devastated and laid waste. Aroused as he never had been before, Quantrell meditated a terrible vengeance.

CHAPTER XII.

LAWRENCE.

ON Blackwater, in Johnson county, and at the house of Captain Purdee, Quantrell called the Guerrillas together for the Lawrence Massacre. Todd, Jarrette, Blunt, Gregg, Anderson, Yager, Younger, Estis and Holt, all were there, and when the roll was called three hundred and ten answered promptly to their names. Up to the mustering hour Quantrell had probably not let his left hand know what his right hand had intended. Secrecy necessarily was to be the salvation of the expedition, if indeed there was any salvation for it. The rendezvous night was an August night—a blessed, balmy, mid-summer night— just such a night as would be chosen to give force to reflections and permit the secrets of the soul to escape. The sultry summer day had lain swarthy in the sun and panting; the sultry summer winds had whispered nothing of the shadowy woods, nothing of the babble of unseen brooks. Birds spoke good-bye to birds in the tree-tops, and the foliage was filled with the twilight. Grouped about him, Quantrell sat grave and calm in the midst of his chieftains. Further away where the shadows were, the men massed themselves in silent companies or spoke low to one another and briefly. Something of a foreboding, occult though it was and indefinable, made itself manifest. The shadow of a great tragedy was impending.

Without in the least degree increasing or decreasing the difficulties of the undertaking, Quantrell laid before his officers his plan for attacking Lawrence. For a week a man of the command—a cool, bold, plausible, desperate man—had been in the city—through it, over it, about it, and around it—and he was here in the midst of them to report. Would they listen to him? "Let him speak," said Todd, sententiously. Lieutenant Fletcher Taylor came out from the shadow, bowed gravely to the group, and with the brevity of a soldier who knew better how to fight than to talk, laid bare the situation. Disguised as a stock trader, or, rather assuming the *role* of a speculating man, he had boldly entered Lawrence. Liberal, bountifully supplied with money, keeping open rooms at the Eldridge House, and agreeable in every way and upon every occasion, he had seen all that it was necessary to see, and learned all that could be of any possible advantage to the Guerrillas. The city proper was but weakly garrisoned; the camp beyond the river was not strong; the idea of a raid by Quantrell was honestly derided; supineness next to unbelief was the most predominant madness of the people; the streets were broad and good for charging horsemen, and the hour for the venture was near at hand.

"You have heard the report," Quantrell's deep voice broke in, "but before you decide it is proper that you should know it all. The march to Lawrence is a long one; in every little town there are soldiers; we leave soldiers behind us; we march through soldiers; we attack the town garrisoned by soldiers; we retreat through soldiers; and when we would rest and refit after the exhaustive expedition, we have to do the best we can in the midst of a multitude of soldiers. Come, speak out, somebody. What is it, Anderson?" "Lawrence or hell, but with one proviso, that we kill every male thing." "Todd?" "Lawrence, if I knew that not a man would get back alive." "Gregg?" "Lawrence; it is the home of Jim Lane; the foster mother of the Red Legs; the nurse of the Jayhawkers." "Shepherd?" "Lawrence; I know it of old; niggers and white people are just the same there; it's a Boston colony and it should be wiped out." "Jarrette?" "Lawrence, by all means. I've had my eye upon it for a year. The head devil of all this killing and burning in Jackson county, I vote to fight it with fire—to burn it before we leave it." "Dick Maddox?" "Lawrence; an eye for an eye and a tooth for a tooth; God understands better than we do the equilibrium of civil war." "Holt?" "Lawrence; and quick about it." "Yager?" "Where my house once stood there is a heap of ashes. I haven't a neighbor that's got a house—Lawrence and the torch." "Blunt?" "Count me in whenever there's killing. Lawrence

first, and then some other Kansas town; the name is nothing."
"Have you all voted?" "All." "Then Lawrence it is; saddle
up, men!" Thus was the Lawrence Massacre inaugurated.

Was it justifiable? Is there much of anything that is justifiable in civil war? Two civilizations struggled for mastery, with
only that imaginary thing, a state line, between them. On
either side the soldiers were not as soldiers who fight for a king,
for a crown, for a country, for an idea, for glory. At the bottom of every combat was an intense hatred. Little by little
there became prominent that feature of savage atrocity which
slew the wounded, slaughtered the prisoners, and sometimes
mutilated the dead. Originally, the Jayhawkers in Kansas had
been very poor. They coveted the goods of their Missouri
neighbors, made wealthy or well-to-do by prosperous years of
peace and African slavery. Before they became soldiers they
had been brigands, and before they destroyed houses in the
name of retaliation they had plundered them at the instance of
individual greed. The first Federal officers operating in Kansas
—that is to say, those who belonged to the State—were land
pirates or pilferers. Lane was a wholesale plunderer; Jennison,
in the scaly gradation, stood next to Lane; Anthony next to
Jennison; Montgomery next to Anthony; Ransom next to
Montgomery; and so on down and down until it reached to the
turn of the captains, lieutenants, sergeants, corporals, and privates. Stock in herds, flocks, droves, and multitudes were
driven from Missouri into Kansas. Houses gave up their furniture; women their jewelry; children their wearing apparel;
store-rooms their contents; the land its crops; the banks their
deposits. To robbery was added murder, to murder arson, and
to arson depopulation. Is it any wonder, then, that the Missourian whose father was killed should kill in return? Whose
house was burnt should burn in return? Whose property was
plundered, should pillage in return? Whose life was made
miserable, should hunt as a wild beast and rend accordingly?
Many such were in Quantrell's command—many whose lives
were blighted; who in a night were made orphans and paupers;
who saw the labor and accumulation of years swept away in an
hour of wanton destruction; who for no reason on earth save
that they were Missourians, were hunted from hiding-place to
hiding-place; who were preyed upon while a single cow remained

or a single shock of grain; who were shot at, outlawed, bedeviled and proscribed, and who, no matter whether Union or Disunion, were permitted to have neither a flag nor a country.

Yes; there was a flag left to them. The Guerrillas, eager to shake off something of a feeling of oppression that had come unaccountably to some of the command, got rapidly to horse and formed as rapidly into column. Then for the first time the black banner was unfurled. In the centre of it, and neatly worked with rêd silk was the single word "Quantrell." As its outlines in the night could be imperfectly seen, and as the men caught the meaning of the sombre banner, waving in the night wind as something spectral and alive, a cheer broke forth impetuously from every Guerrilla. The wish was interpreted, which all felt to be righteous, but which none had ever before uttered even in a whisper. It had voice and utterance now. The border had not only found a chief, but it also had found a banner. Thereafter, if when going into battle Quantrell unfurled this flag, nothing lived that fell into the hands of the Guerrillas; if it were not unfurled, the fight took its chances, and the victims their chances with it.

It was the summer night of August 16th, 1863, that the Guerrilla column, having at its head this ominous banner, marched west from Purdee's place on Blackwater. With it as simple soldiers, or, rather volunteers for the expedition, were Colonels Joseph Holt and Boaz Boberts. Officers of the regular Confederate army, they were in Missouri on recruiting service when the march began, and fell into line as much from habit as from inclination.

The first camp made was upon a stream midway between Pleasant Hill and Lone Jack, where the water was good and the hiding place excellent. All day Quantrell concealed himself here, getting to saddle just at dark and ordering Tood up from the rear to the advance. Passing Pleasant Hill to the north and marching on rapidly fifteen miles, the second camp was at Harrelson's, twenty-five miles from the place of starting. At three o'clock on the afternoon of the second day, the route was resumed and followed due west to the Aubrey, a pleasant Kansas stream, abounding in grass and timber. Here Quantrell halted until the darkness set in, feeding the horses well and permitting the men to cook and eat heartily. At eight o'clock the

march commenced again and continued on throughout the
night, in the direction of Lawrence. Three pilots were pressed
into service, carried with the command as far as they knew
aught of the road or the country, and then shot down remorselessly in the nearest timber.

On the morning of the twenty-first, Lawrence was in sight.
An old man, a short distance upon the right of the road, was
feeding his hogs in the gray dawn, the first person seen to stir
about the doomed place. Quantrell sent Cole Younger over to
the hog-pen to catechize the industrious old farmer and learn
from him what changes had taken place in the situation since
Taylor had so thoroughly accomplished his mission. Younger,
dressed as a Federal Lieutenant, exhausted speedily the old
man's limited stock. Really but little change had taken place.
Across the Kansas river there were probably four hundred soldiers in camp, and on the Lawrence side about seventy-five. As
for the rebels, he didn't suppose there was one nearer than Missouri; certainly none within striking distance of Lawrence.

It was a lovely morning. The green of the fields and the
blue of the sky were glad together. Birds sang everywhere.
The footsteps of autumn had not yet been heard in the land.
Nowhere through the nights had any one seen the creeping of
its stealthy vanguard, stiffening the grass blades, making mute
the melodies of the streams, and putting a pallor as of death
over all the landscape. The dawn of the delicious morning
stirred the blood like wine. Everything was in harmony—the
lowing of the cattle, the crowing of the cocks, the smoke curl-
ing up as incense offered to propitious nature, the haze in the
east, the earth which smelt sweet, the rippling of the South
wind, the placid city asleep in the balm of its verdure and the
blessings of its trees.

"Form fours!" The column agitated itself as though stirred
by an electrical impulse, galloped a little to the right and left,
reined up and dressed up, and looked as though a massive wedge
had fallen there with the blunt point turned towards Lawrence.

Near Mount Orlad, which rises in beauty up from the lower
country at the southwestern edge of the city, a lady and
gentleman rode leisurely along to enjoy the morning breeze
and view the splendors of the rising sun. As they rode they
laughed long and lightsomely. Into the blood of each also

some wine of the morning dawn had gone, and the woman's face was flushed and the man's expectant.   What between the two had been said there, only the blue sky knew overhead and the singing birds singing around.

"Look!" and the bloom had fled from the woman's face and the tenderness from her eyes as she pointed to the southwest, and to the blunt wedge there, and to the black flag waving in the summer wind.   The man looked and saw the wedge transform itself into a column, and the column dash at the town. Then he heard shots, shrieks, the rush of horsemen, the roar of revolver vollies, and then—bidden by the brave young girl to do so—this man dashed away into the open country, pursued by two of Quantrell's worst Guerrillas.   Run out of two corn-fields, across a dozen fences, and from hiding-place to hiding-place, he finally baffled his pursuers and survived the slaughter. His name was John Donnelly, and he lives to-day as an illustration of what trivial circumstances go sometimes to make up the warp and woof of human life.

"The camp first!" was the cry which ran through the ranks, and Todd, leading Quantrell's old company, dashed down upon it yelling and shooting.   Scarcely any resistance was made. Surprised, ridden over, shot in their blankets, paralyzed, some of them, with terror, and running frantically about, what could they do against the quickest and deadliest pistol shots along the border?   Bill Anderson claimed as his share of the killing, and in the count afterwards the number was allowed to him, fourteen soldiers and citizens.   Todd, Jarrette, Anderson, Little, Andy McGuire, Peyton Long, William McGuire, Richard Kinney, Allen Parmer, Jesse James, Frank James, Archie Clements, Shepherd, Oath Hinton, Blunt and the balance of the old men did the most of the killing.   They went for revenge and they took it.   Some plundered—these men killed.   They all burned.   The Federals on the opposite side of the river made scarcely any attempt to cross to the rescue of their butchered comrades; a few skirmishers held them in check.   It was a day of darkness and woe.   Distracted women ran about the streets.   Fathers were killed with infants in their arms.   Husbands in the embrace of their wives were shot down.   One man, shot seven times and not yet dead, raised a little upon one elbow and begged for his life in an

13

agony so piteous that it haunted the after dreams of men; the eighth shot finished him. None who saw that dying expression upon his face ever forgot it. Killing ran riot; the torch was applied to every residence; the air was filled with cries for mercy; on every breeze came the wailing of women and the screams of children. Dead men lay in cellars, upon the streets, in parlors where costly furniture was; on velvet carpets; in hovels, lowly and squalid; by fountains where azure water played; in hidden places everywhere. The sun came up and flooded all the sky with its radiance, and yet the devil's work was not done. Still the smoke ascended, and yet could be heard the shots, the crackling of blazing rafters, and the crash of falling walls.

The true story of the day's terrible work will never be told. Nobody knows it. It is a story of episodes, tragic but isolated; a story full of colossal horrors and unexpected deliverances. Sometimes a pleasant word saved a life, at other times a witticism or a repartee. The heroic devotion of the women shone out amid the black wreck of things—a star. Many a husband was saved by his wife; many a lover by his sweetheart. Something about most of the Guerrillas was human, if the way to reach that something was only hit upon. The girls who were the prettiest had the most influence. Attracted by the boyishness of his face and a look in his blue eyes that seemed so innocent, a young girl came to Jesse James just as he was in the act of shooting a soldier in uniform who had been smoked out of a cellar. His pistol was against the Federal's head when an exceedingly soft and penetrating voice called out to him: "Don't kill him, for *my* sake. He has eight children who have no mother." James looked and saw a beautiful girl, probably just turned of sixteen, blushing at her boldness and trembling before him. In the presence of so much grace and loveliness he was a disarmed man. He remembered his own happy youth, his sister not older than the girl beside him, his mother who had always instilled into his mind lessons of mercy and charity, and he put up his pistol and spoke to the pleader: "Take him, he is yours. I would not harm a hair in his head for the State of Kansas."

In the northwestern portion of the town there was a boarding-house occupied by four young married couples. The men of the party were G. W. Baker, J. C. Trask, editor of the *State Journal*, S. M. Thorp, State Senator, and Dr. Griswold. Trask and Griswold were killed instantly. Thorp and Baker were wounded badly, but lay quiet as if dead. Another squad of Guerrillas passed along in a short time and stopped to examine the bodies. Finding Thorp and Baker still alive, they shot them again. Thorp died, but Baker finally recovered, having been shot through the neck, through one arm and through the lungs.

The lady who in the morning was riding out so early, and who, with her companion, were the first to discover the movements of the Guerrillas, was a Miss Sallie Young, a member of the family of Ex-Governor Wilson Shannon. Separated from her escort, who was riding the best he could to save his life, Miss Young dashed back herself to Lawrence to give the alarm. Frank James politely arrested her and as politely required her to report to Quantrell. During all the long, terrible hours of the burning and killing, this heroic girl—gallantly treated by the worst among the raiders, and exercising over them a mysterious influence—did everything possible to save life and property. Personally interceding for numbers of her friends and acquaintances—sometimes with smiles and sometimes with tears—she was everywhere amid the bullets of infuriated men and the flames of consuming buildings. But succeeding to the fright of the pillage there came a frenzy, and this veritable angel of mercy was arrested by her own people as a Confederate spy and sent to Fort Leavenworth for trial. Innocent of course, her good deeds had only caused in the wildness of the reaction a suspicion of her loyalty. How without collusion she could have influence with any of Quantrell's men was a problem those who had suffered most and were the most bereft did not attempt to solve. Youth, beauty, splendid courage, and admirable self-possession could soften nothing from Missouri, devils that they were, and butchers, but these were all the arts she had and they did their work.

The Mayor of the city, Collamore, took refuge in a well upon his own premises, and perished there. His wife had seen him enter, and close to it and about it all the terrible forenoon she prayed and hovered—afraid to call out to her husband and afraid to go away from the vicinity. At last the Guerrillas were gone, and she rushed wildly to the well's mouth and called aloud for her husband. No answer. Then she called again with a voice pitiful in its agony and its hopelessness. No answer, nor would there ever be answer more this side the river that runs beyond the valley called the Valley of the Shadow of Death. The wretched woman cowered down in her desolate woe and prayed for some one to help her husband. There might be hope yet; life might be lingering yet; silent, perhaps he did not know that the danger was over and the soldiers gone. Melted by her entreaties, a man by the name of Lowe descended into the fatal well. They called *him* also, but he did not answer. Instead of bringing up one corpse from the bottom, there were two.

Judge Carpenter was killed in the yard of H. S. Clarke, and Col. Holt, one of the Confederate officers with the expedition, saved Clarke. Holt saved others there besides Clarke. He had been a Union man doing business in Vernon county, Missouri, as a merchant. Jennison raided the neighborhood in which he lived, plundered him of his goods, burnt his property, insulted his family, and Holt joined the Confederate army. S. A. Riggs was saved by his heroic wife. Peyton Long, one of the best pistol shots in the command, had him covered with a heavy dragoon. Mrs. Riggs seized the horse of the Guerrilla by the bridle and caused him, a high-spirited animal, to rear up suddenly. A woman could do anything with Long, and he relented when Mrs. Riggs explained why, to save her husband, she had caused his horse to disconcert his aim. Cole Younger saved at least a dozen lives this day. Indeed, he killed none save in open and manly battle. At one house he captured five citizens over whom he put a guard, and at another three whom he defended and protected. The notorious General James H. Lane, to get whom Quantrell would gladly have left and sacrificed all the balance of the victims, made his escape through a corn-field, hotly pursued but too splendidly mounted to be captured. Ex-Governor Shannon and Judge George W. Smith, were absent from the city; their houses escaped destruction. Some were saved through the mysteries of the Masonic Order, notably Gen. C. W. Babcock.

There were two camps in Lawrence at the time of the attack, one—the camp of the negro troops—being located at the south-

ern end of Massachusetts street, and the other a camp of white
soldiers, nearer to the heart of the city. In this latter camp
were twenty-one infantry, eighteen of whom were killed in the
first wild charge, and three escaped by running and hiding
themselves. All belonged to the city, and had enlisted from its
offices, stores, and workshops. They were without arms and
fell before the deadly revolvers as unresisting as sheep. The
editor of the *Kansas Tribune*, John Speer, lost two sons, one
shot dead, whose body was found, and the other killed, but
whose body was supposed to have been consumed in a printing
office, together with the body of a young apprentice named
Purington. Mrs. Bromley, from Wisconsin, now Mrs. William Warner, of Kansas City, entertained Bill Anderson and did
it handsomely. George Todd, Coleman Younger, Gregg,
Blunt, Jesse and Frank James, John Coger, and George Maddox, took dinner with William L. Bullene. Quantrell's headquarters were at the City Hotel. Gregg saved the house of
Frederick Reed from destruction, and in saving it saved Reed's
life, for he was concealed in the garret. It would be long to tell
of all the strange, the grotesque, and the horrible sights that
were seen that day; all the puerile, the strong, the generous,
the heroic deeds that were done. Quantrell during the entire
occupation did not fire his pistol. He saw everything, directed
everything, was the one iron man, watchful and vigilant through
everything; but he did not kill. He saved many. He had
lived once in Lawrence, and some people had been kind to him
there. These he spared, for whatever else was said of Quantrell, no one ever said truthfully that he was an ingrate.

Cole Younger had dragged from his hiding place in a closet a
very large man who had the asthma. What with his fright and
what with his hurry, the poor fellow could not articulate.
Younger's pistol was against his heart when his old wife cried
out: "For God's sake do not shoot him; he hasn't slept in a
bed for nine years!" This appeal and the asthma together,
made Younger roar out: "I never intended to harm a hair in
his head." Jarrette, not given overmuch to tenderness or compassion when Kansas men were to be killed, yielded sufficiently
to the requirements of his order to save five prisoners, who gave
him the Masonic sign of recognition, and James Little took a
wounded man away from a Guerrilla, who was proceeding to

dispatch him, because the wounded man, in pleading for his life, had the accent of a Southerner. Blunt, because a young girl gave him a cup of excellent coffee, saved her father, and George Shepherd rescued a wounded man and two children from a burning house because one of the children had given him a rose.

The Eldridge House was on fire, and Todd and Jarrette, while roaming through it in search of adventure, came upon a door that was locked. Todd knocked and cried out to its occupants that the building was in flames; it was time to get away. "Let it burn and be d—d," a deep voice answered, and then the tones of three men were heard in conversation. Jarrette threw his whole weight against the door, bursting it from his fastenings, and as he did so Todd fired, killing one of the three who were hiding there, Jarrette another, and Todd the third. They were soldiers who had escaped from the morning's massacre, and who did not even make an effort to defend themselves. Bewildered by the smoke and almost suffocated, Todd and Jarrette gained the open air with difficulty. Tom Maupin and Pat O'Donnell, operating together throughout the day as two savage comrades in arms, surrounded a house in which six men had taken refuge. Maupin dismounted, entered the house with a pistol in each hand and forced out its occupants one by one. As each one stepped beyond the door-sill O'Donnell shot him dead; where the pile lay when the butchery was done, a blanket might have covered them all.

Perhaps the number killed will never be accurately known. One account puts it at one hundred and forty-three, one at one hundred and eighty-seven, and a third at two hundred and sixteen. It is probable that some were killed and burned and never found. The loss of property was estimated at the enormous sum of $1,500,000, the total aggregate of buildings consumed footing up one hundred and eighty-nine. In the city proper Quantrell had one man killed and two wounded. The man who lost his life was drunk when the fight began, got drunker as it continued, and finally in his helplessness gave his life away. His name was Larkin Skaggs, and his fighting in Lawrence was the first he had ever done as a Guerrilla. After being shot the body was cast in the flames of a partially consumed house and roasted beyond all recognition. Then a rope was put about the neck of the corpse and some negroes dragged it up and down the streets, with yells of infernal exultation; afterwards dry wood was piled upon it until it was entirely consumed.

Fate favored Quantrell from the time he left Missouri until he returned to Missouri. A man from Johnson county, Kansas, started by an Indian trail to inform the people of Lawrence of his coming. He rode too carelessly; his horse fell and so injured him that he died. A full company of soldiers were stationed at Oxford, but they seemed more anxious to keep out of harm's way than to protect the citizens. Colonel Plumb came up in the rear and did not force the fighting. Lane was afraid, as he always was, and Ewing came on just in time to see the rear guard of the Guerrillas entering Missouri at a walk and defiantly. There was some heavy fighting, however, before all was over. Lieut. J. L. Bledsoe was shot while skirmishing with the Federals across the river. The wound was the wound of a minie ball, and he could not ride. Hicks and Hi George, two brothers noted for supreme daring, came to his assistance when the retreat began and took from under the fire of the enemy a comfortable carriage, put Bledsoe into it, and carried him out of Lawrence. These two Georges had never been known to desert a friend in extremity or give up a crippled comrade, no matter what the danger was nor how imminent it pressed upon them. Their father had been murdered, the home of their mother burned three times, each of them had been wounded, a brother had been killed, and they lived solely to fight and to have revenge. It is probable that they will never give in detail the story of each life, nor tell of the unmarked graves they know of between the Blue and the Arkansas. It is not necessary now that they should; the dead past has buried its dead.

Bledsoe's later fate had over it the sombre light of some mediæval tragedy. His Lawrence wound healed slowly. Deep in the recesses of a stretch of heavy timber in Lafayette county, his comrades placed him and left him. At intervals a physician stole to his hiding-place and dressed his hurts. Women also found him out and fed him. He was convalescing just a little when a Federal cavalry scout, numbering twenty-five, came unawares upon the maimed Guerrilla and began to fire. It was a combat *a l'outrance*—one against twenty-five. Bledsoe had kept with him to the end his three dragoon revolvers, and these he laid beside him when he first heard the feet of the approaching horses crashing through the underbrush. He spoke not a word during all the battle; scarcely able to lift up a hand before the final mercy stroke, he did not ask for quarter by a sign. Shot in the right shoulder, he fired with his left hand. Shot in the left arm, he reinforced it with his wounded right and kept up the unequal combat. Two of the enemy were killed, and three wounded. Crippled as he was, and weak from an old hurt, they dared not grapple with him. Dismounted and protected by trees, they took a quarter of an hour to shoot him to death. At last a bullet found his brain, and he fell from his knees to his face, dead. But two chambers remained loaded of his three revolvers; he had literally fought to the death.

As Quantrell retreated from Lawrence he sent upon the right hand William Gregg, with twenty men, and upon the left Bill Anderson with twenty more. Gregg took with him Jesse and Frank James, Arch Clements, Little, Morrow, and others of the most desperate of the command, and Anderson took Henry Hockensmith, Long, McGuire, Parmer, Hicks and Hi George, Doc Campbell, and others equally desperate. Each was ordered to burn a swathe as he marched back parallel with the main body, and to kill in proportion as he burnt. Soon on every hand columns of black smoke began to arise, and there was heard the incessant rattle of firearms as running from their consuming houses the old farmers round about were shot down as a holiday frolic. This unforgiving farewell lasted for twelve miles, or until pressed heavily in the rear Quantrell was forced to recall his detachments and look to the safety of the aggregated column.

Missouriward from Kansas ten miles the Guerrillas halted to rest a little and feed a little. The day's savage work had been exhausting as it had been bloody. Wrought up during all the forenoon to the keenest intensity, the relaxation of the afternoon was beginning to tell upon the men. Before either men or horses had finished eating, the picquets were driven in and the rear pressed to the girth. Todd and Jarrette held it as two lions that had not broken their fast. Step by step, and fighting at every one, they kept pursuit at arm's length for ten miles further. The Federals would not charge. Overwhelming in

numbers and capable of enveloping at any moment everything
of opposition, they contented themselves with firing at long
range and keeping always at about a deadly distance from the
rear. The Guerrillas, relying principally upon dash and the revolver, felt the need of a charge to get rid of the incessant buzzing of the minie balls which now and then stung them grievously.
Todd spoke to Quantrell of the annoyance of the tireless,
tenacious pursuit, and Quantrell halted the whole column for a
charge. The detachments on either flank had sometime since
been gathered up, and the men brought face to face with urgent
need—turned about quick and dressed up in line handsomely.
As Todd came trotting up with the rear guard, he fell in upon
the left and Quantrell gave the word. The Federal pursuit had
barely time to fire a volley before it was rent into shreds and
scattered upon the prairie. The unerring revolver at short
range did its work so well that for several hours thereafter the
pursuit was more respectful by far and considerably less galling
to the Guerrillas. That single volley, however—fired in the
very midst of the gallop—wounded Noah Webster, Geo. Maddox,
Gregg, Peyton Long, Hi George and Allen Parmer, and killed
the horses of Todd, Jarrette, Jesse James and Bill Anderson.
Jarrette laid hold upon a mustang pony some comrade was
leading and tried to saddle it for twenty minutes. Serene
under the fire of quite a regiment, and determined to succeed
in mastering the stubborn animal if he was shot for it, Jarrette
lingered and lingered. In addition, he had in the pockets of
his McClellan saddle over $8,000 in greenbacks, taken from a
Lawrence bank, which he was bringing to Missouri for distribution among the widows and orphans of the war. Try how he
would, however, the mustang was more than a match for the
Guerrilla. He could neither bridle him, saddle him, nor mount
him bareback. The Federals were within pistol-shot and the
bullets were everywhere. Jarrette, until then unconscious of
his danger, or indifferent to it, began to cast his eyes about him
for escape. Across the prairie to Quantrell it was at least a
mile. Arch Clements had carried Jesse James back, Hicks
George had done the same for Todd, and Frank James had
taken up Anderson behind him. Jarrette would not abandon
the pony for anybody's help, and there he was alone and well
nigh succorless. Aware from the reports of those who had

gone forward of Jarrette's desperate extremity, Cole Younger, at the imminent risk of his own life, dashed back to the rescue, took Jarrette up under a distressing fire and regained the column with him, followed by two hundred well mounted cavalry to within pistol range of the rear guard, formed to give him a breathing chance.

From behind every hill top, at the crossing of each creek, from the midst of every belt of timber, Quantrell fought the pursuit, falling back in splendid order and forming again as the country favored, without haste or confusion. At three o'clock in the afternoon Younger and Anderson relieved Todd and Jarrette, fighting equally as well and holding everything in the hands of stubbornness and defiance.

Passing northeast of Paola and halting a short time on Bull Creek unmolested, Quantrell crossed into Missouri near Aubrey, and pushed on at a great pace to Grand River, in Cass county. The morning of his arrival there four hundred Federals were in his front, and before he could find either food or shelter he had to fight again. Wolfish somewhat from long fasting and marching, the Guerrillas went at the enemy in the old fashion—charging as a huge stone shot from a catapult. They drove them eight miles furiously, killing twenty-eight of those who were poorly mounted and clearing out the country for several miles round about. In the pursuit a gallant Federal, pressed to a stand still by Jesse James, who was a light rider and finely mounted, turned at bay and cried out to the young Guerrilla to fight him fair and give him a chance man to man. The spirit of the proposition suited James. It accorded so much with his own adventurous nature, and agreed so thoroughly with what he would himself have done if similarly situated, that he asked Fletch Taylor, close by his side, to halt and let him finish alone with the Jayhawker. Taylor halted and James dashed at the Federal, firing as he rode. The third shot he knocked him dead from the saddle, but not until the undaunted trooper had fired at him four times deliberately and missed him as often. Seeking afterwards something that would serve to identify the dead man, James found upon his person a memorandum book containing only the name of a woman— Isabel Sherman—and a lock of dark brown hair. His own name was not in the book. Among entries of things bought,

GEO. W. MADDOX.

DICK MADDOX.

money received, and scenes and incidents described, there was this single verse of Tennyson's Lady Clara Vere de Vere, writen in a hand-writing different from the balance of the writing in the book:

> "Lady Clara Vere de Vere,
>   You put strange memories in my head,
>   Not thrice your branching limes have blown
>   Since I beheld young Lawrence dead.
>   Oh! your sweet eyes, your low replies;
>   A great enchantress you may be;
>   But there was that across his throat
>   Which you had hardly cared to see."

The dead man was scarcely thirty. His features were refined, very small, and showed some traces of suffering. What his life had been, or what his sins or sorrows, no one knew. It was impossible even to learn his name. The Guerrillas buried him —the first time and probably the last the right of sepulchre was ever extended to a foeman.

Asked afterward to name those who fought bravest and best on the retreat from Lawrence, Quantrell's answer was: "They all fought. No one ever had men to exhibit more coolness and daring." When pressed further to single out a few, he named Tuck Hill, Woot Hill, Will Hulse, James Hinds, Albert Lee, Ben Broomfield, John and Tom Maupin, Allen Parmer, Cave Wyatt, Arch Clements, Gregg, Anderson, Todd, Jarrette, Dick and George Maddox, Dick Yager, Ike and Dick Berry, Payne Jones, Andy Blunt, Peyton Long, Toler, George and Frank Shepherd, Dick Kinney, John Jackson, John Hill, Jesse and Frank James, Oll Johnson, Cole Younger, William and Henry Nolan, Tom Hill, Dick Burnes, Ben Morrow, John Ross, Harrison Trow, Col. John Holt, James Wilkinson, Col. Boaz Roberts, Sid. Creek, William and Andy McGuire, H. and L. Privin, Henry Noland, Richard Hotie, George Webb, Ab. Haller, Wade Morton, William Basham, Dave Hilton, Andy Walker, William Woodward, Mike Parr, William Chiles, Ike Flannery, Fletch Taylor, James Little, John Coger, Sim Whitsett, Wm. Greenwood, Pres Webb, Dan Vaughn, John Poole, and a score of others who formed what might be called the Old Guard. James Hinds was but a boy of seventeen, just a few months younger than Jesse James, and these two sought out as if in boyish wantonness the hottest and most dangerous places it was possible to find, laughing always and always where the killing was.

During the retreat the word also passed from file to file that in case the worst came to the worst the wounded were to be killed by their own comrades. As long as there was a hope or a chance to bring them out safe from the pursuit the detail, especially charged to guard them and help them forward, was to do its whole duty. If neither a hope nor a chance remained in the end, and it was hard riding and running for the best in the band, then was the detail to surrender to the pursuit nothing that was left alive. It was horrible, this alternative, but it was Guerrilla war.

CHAPTER XIII.

A COUNTER-BLOW.

TWO days after his safe arrival in Missouri from the Lawrence Massacre, Quantrell disbanded the Guerrillas. Fully six thousand Federals were on his track. The savageness of the blow struck there had appalled and infuriated the country. The journalistic pulses of the North rose to fever heat and beat as though to their raging fever there had been added raving insanity. In the delirium of the governing powers impossible things were demanded. Quantrell was to be hunted to the death; he was to be hanged, drawn, and quartered; his band was to be annihilated; he was to be fought with fire, proscription, depopulation, and wholesale destruction. At the height of the very worst of these terrible paroxysms, Ewing's famous General Order No. 11 was issued. It required every citizen of Jackson, Cass, Bates, and a portion of Vernon counties to abandon their houses and come either into the lines of designated places that were fortified, or within the jurisdiction of said lines. If neither was done, and said citizens remained outside beyond the time specified for such removal, they were to be regarded as outlaws and punished accordingly. Innocent and guilty alike felt the rigors of this unprecedented proscription. For the Union man there was the same line of demarkation that was drawn for the secessionist. Age had no immunity; sex was not regarded. The rights of property vanished; predatory bands preyed at will; nothing could be sold; everything had to be abandoned; it was the obliteration of prosperity by counties; it was the depopulation of miles upon miles of fertile territory in a night.

General Ewing has been unjustly censured for the promulgation of such an order, and held responsible in many ways for its execution. The genius of a celebrated painter, Capt. George

C. Bingham, of Missouri, has been evoked to give infamy to the
vandalism of the deed and voice to the indignation of history
over its consummation.   Bingham's picture of burning and
plundered houses, of a sky made awful with mingled flame and
smoke, of a long train of helpless fugitives going away they
knew not whither, of appealing women and gray-haired non-
combatants, of skeleton chimneys rising like wrathful and
accusing things from the wreck of pillaged homesteads, of' uniformed things called officers rummaging in trunks and drawers,
of colonels loaded with plunder, and captains gaudy with stolen
jewelry, will live longer than the memories of the strife, and
keep alive after Guerrilla and Jayhawker are well forgotten
manhood's stubborn hatred of the thief and the honest soldier's
righteous horror over battle flags borne aloft to petty larceny or
pitiful picking and stealing.

  Ewing, however, was a soldier.   General Order No. 11 came
from district headquarters at St. Louis where Schofield commanded, and through Schofield from Washington City direct.
Ewing had neither choice nor discretion in the matter.   He was
a brave, conscientious, hard-fighting officer who did his duty as it
came to his hands to do.   He could not have made, if he had
tried, one hair of the head of the infamous Order white or black.
It was a portion of the inexorable order of things, and Ewing
occupied towards it scarcely the attitude of an instrument.   He
promulgated it but he did not originate it; he gave it voice but
he did not give it form and substance; his name has been linked
to it as to something that should justly cause shame and reproach, but history in the end will separate the soldier from the
man and render unto the garb of the civilian what it has failed to
concede to the uniform of the commander.   As a citizen of the
republic he deplored the cruelty of an enactment which he knew
to be monstrous; but as a soldier in the line of his duty the
necessities of the situation could not justify a moment's argument.   He had but to obey and to execute, and he did both
and mercifully.

  For nearly three weeks Jackson county was a Pandemonium,
together with the counties of Cass, Bates, Vernon, Clay, and
Lafayette.   Six thousand Federals were in the saddle, but
Quantrell held his grip upon these counties in despite of everything.   Depopulation was going on in a two-fold sense—once by

emigration or exodus, and once by the killing of perpetual ambushments and lyings-in-wait. In detachments of ten, the Guerrillas divided up and fought everywhere. Scattered, they came
together as if by instinct. Driven away from the flank of one
column, they appeared in the rear of another. They had voices
that were as the voices of night birds. Mysterious horsemen
appeared upon all the roads. Not a single Federal scouting or
exploring party escaped paying toll. Sometimes the aggregate
of the day's dead was simply enormous. Frequently the
assailants were never seen. Of a sudden, and rising, as it were,
out of the ground, they delivered a deadly volley and rode
away into the darkness—invisible. All nature was in league
with them. The trees sheltered them, the leaves hid them, the
blind paths conducted them from danger, the fords over streams
enabled them to check pursuit, the night enveloped them, the
ravines were forts, the country furnished them guides, the
broken ways were watched, they killed always and they kept
at work.

Up to the Lawrence Massacre there had been no scalping
done; after it a good deal. Ab. Haller, brother of Lieutenant
William Haller, and a Guerrilla of great courage and prowess,
was hiding wounded in some timber near Texas Prairie, at the
extreme eastern edge of Jackson county. As did Bledsoe, so
did he, selling his life as dearly as he could. Alone, he faced
seventy-two, killing and wounding five of the attacking party.
When he fell he had been struck eleven times, but he did not
suffer. The last bullet hit him fair in the left breast and penetrated the heart; when they rushed in upon him not a single
load remained in either of his revolvers. Infuriated at a resistance as deadly as it was unexpected, his slayers scalped him
and cut off his ears. In an hour afterwards, probably, Andy
Blunt came upon the body, multilated as it was, and pointed
out the marks of the knife to his companions. "We had something to learn yet, boys," he said, "and we have learned it.
Scalp for scalp hereafter!"

The next day Blunt, Peyton Long, Arch Clements, Bill Anderson and William McGuire captured four militia from a regiment
belonging to North Missouri and shot them after they surrendered. Blunt scalped each of the four, leaving, however, the
ears intact, because, he said, he had no use for the ears.

The killing went on. William Gregg, Fletcher Taylor, James Noland, James Little and Frank James captured between Fire Prairie and Napoleon, six of Penick's militia, and held over them a kind of grotesque court martial. It was on a lazy, lingering summer afternoon that James, as the judge advocate, opened the case for the prosecution, and Gregg, as counsel for the accused, replied to him. Taylor was the president of the court, and when the vote was taken upon the question of life or death, all of the five had voted death. These were not scalped.

The next day Richard Kinney, John Jarrette, Jesse James and Sim Whitsett attacked a picquet post of eight men a mile from Wellington and annihilated it. Cutting them off from the town and running them in a contrary direction, not a man escaped. The last one to be overtaken was an old soldier from Iowa, probably sixty years of age. Jesse James reached him first as he ran and shot him to the left of the spine and high up in the shoulder. He abandoned his horse and took position behind a large tree on the roadside, keeping hold upon his gun and waiting to use it accurately. James dashed up to the tree, pointed his pistol round it and fired down in the top of the old man's head. He sank down all of a heap and murmured once or twice audibly: "My time had come! my time had come!"

Two days afterwards Ben Morrow, Pat O'Donnell and Frank James ambushed an entire Federal company between Salem Church, on the Lexington road, and the Widow Chiles'. These three men, hidden in some dense undergrowth where there were numerous large trees, fought eighty men for nearly an hour, killing seven and wounding thirteen. O'Donnell was wounded three times, and James and Morrow once each and slightly. Todd, gathering together thirty of his old men, and getting a volunteer guide who knew every hog path in the country round about, rode past Kansas City boldly and took position at dusk on the Shawneetown road, looking for a train of wagons bringing infantry into Kansas City. It was midnight before the small cavalry advance in front of the train gave token of its near approach, although the Guerrillas had been waiting for it for several hours. There were twenty wagons with twenty soldiers to the wagon, besides the driver. No order had been preserved in the line of march. Save the cavalry in front, nothing else that betokened watchfulness, existed. Here and there between some of the wagons intervals of fifty yards had been permitted to grow. In others all of the occupants were either asleep or trying to sleep, and worst and strangest of all, lest accidents should occur, the men in taking passage in the morning, had been commanded by the officer at the post from whence they started, not to load their guns. Todd waited until all the wagons of the train except three had passed by the point of his ambushment, when he sprang out upon these and poured into them and upon their jammed and crowded human freight a deadly rain of bullets. Every shot told. The wagons in front left those cut off in the rear to their fate. The cavalry were the first to flee. In front was dire panic, in the rear massacre. Todd in the three wagons butchered sixty, and turned short about from his work of death to pursue the balance. Before he overtook them they had reached the friendly shelter of a regiment of cavalry camped upon the roadside.

Coleman Younger, while Todd was operating in Kansas, gathered about him ten men and hid himself as close to Independence as it was possible to get without getting into the town. His eyes for some time had been fixed upon a large *corral* in the vicinity, and he meant, if the wind blew fair, to beat it up. Sending William Hulse out to reconnoitre the position and bring word of the guard stationed to protect it, he retired deeper into the brush and waited. Hulse, dressed like a Federal, rode boldly about the *corral* for an hour. He talked with several soldiers, but none suspicioned him. At a spring close by he dismounted and drank in the midst of a group of militia. He counted the guards on duty, seventy-two, noted, mentally, the point where the reliefs were stationed, and rejoined his commander between sunset and dark. By nine o'clock Younger was marching. To the *corral*, on the right of the main road several hundred yards, it was about four miles direct, but if the picquets were avoided, six. Younger avoided the picquets and made the distance by eleven, halting at the turning-off place on the main road and giving his horses in charge of two of the detachment. The other eight on foot and led by Hulse, crept close to the reserve post and fired point blank into the sleeping relief guards, some rolled up in their blankets, and some resting at ease and crouched about the fire. Then with a
14

fierce hurrah and a fiercer second volley, the Guerrillas charged furiously into the *corral*—into the midst of the sentinels on duty and the rearing and plunging horses and mules. Keeping together—a small yet solid mass—and firing at everything organized or trying to make head against them—it was not over twenty minutes before the whole force at the enclosure was either killed or scattered, and every animal at the mercy of the Guerrillas. Choosing as well as possible by the uncertain light, Younger escaped unpursued, with three excellent horses to the man, after having killed seventeen Federals in the night attack and wounding as many more.

Capt. Dick Yager, commanding ten men—the usual number the Guerrillas then operated with—engaged twenty Federals under Lieutenant Blackstone, of a Missouri militia regiment, and slew fourteen. Yager had ambushed a ford over the Little Blue, and was behind some large rocks not fifteen feet from the crossing-place. Blackstone, unconscious of danger, rode with his troopers leisurely into the water and halted mid-way the stream that the horses might drink. He had a tin cup tied to his saddle and a bottle of whisky in one of its pockets. After having drank, and while bending down from his stirrups to dip a cup of water, the volley caught him and knocked him dead from his horse, thirteen others falling close to and about him at the same time.

Jarrette and Poole, each commanding ten men, made a dash into Lafayette county and struck some blows to the right and left which resounded throughout the West. In the summer of 1863, Poole, with forty Guerrillas, rendezvoused at Kell. Campbell's in Lafayette county, where Mrs. Campbell and Mrs. William Kirtley made him a splendid Federal flag. In no manner were the women inferior to the men in patriotism, in courage, endurance or devotion. With this flag at the head of the column, Poole dashed into the German settlement and comparatively surprised it. Where Concordia now is there was then a store and a fort. At every alarm the Germans hurried into this fort—strong and well built—and were safe from any ordinary attack. This day, however, Poole came upon them unawares and found many who properly belonged to the militia, feeding stock carelessly and in an exposed position. Ffteen of these he killed, and ten he wounded severely, but not so severely as to prevent them from making their way back to the fort. Poole did not attack the fort. He returned leisurely to the neighborhood of Dover and camped for some time near the residence of Mr. Jo. Hampton, a Union man who was a just, honest, upright man, and one who helped his neighbors and stood by them through all those dark latter days of the desperate border war. None ever went to him in vain for succor or assistance. His hand was always open, and his heart was always in the right place. Equally as sincere in his attachment to the Union as Hampton, and equally as upright and as liberal in his dealings with his old neighbors and friends, was John Ridge, also of Dover. These two men saved many a Southern man's life, many a house from the torch, many a family from penury, and many a lot of valuable property from destruction. They are to-day honored by the community in which they still live popular, trusted and esteemed.

Some savage combats were had generally throughout Lafayette county in the early spring of 1863. James Sullivan was killed this spring. He had lived near Dover for some time and was acquainted with the country thoroughly. Brave, vindictive, cruel to an unusual degree, he was capable of doing an immense amount of harm. Sometimes he was a spy, sometimes a scout, and always an oppressor. Guiding a Federal column one day into the hiding-places of the Guerrillas, William Fell riddled him with buck-shot. Fell, Phil. Gatewood, Lex. James, William Yowell, and Jason James were together in a water-melon patch near James Hicklin's when Sullivan guided the Federals upon them. Fell faced the whole force and fired in their very bosoms. Sullivan and four others were killed, but especially was the death of Sullivan the cause of much rejoicing. If he had lived Dover undoubtedly would have been burnt, and the lives of many valuable citizens sacrificed. About this time O'Hara was killed, and Joe Henning—two Guerrillas of sinister reputation; and about this time another Guerrilla, whose *soubriquet* was Squirrel Tail, had a desperate encounter near Waverly with an Iowa Captain named Hawks. There were twenty men on a side, and the Iowa detachment was cut to pieces, Hawks himself falling desperately wounded. Carried to the hospitable house of George Hall, a prominent citizen of Waverly, he was tenderly nursed, finally cured, and sent home rejoicing. Two miles from

Wellington a squad of militia numbering six were surprised at supper and shot to a man. East of Wellington four miles there was a large house occupied by some lewd women notorious for their favors and their enticements. Poole knew the situation well, and suggested to Jarrette that a sufficient detour should be made to encompass the building. Arriving there about eleven o'clock at night, it appeared from the outside as if some kind of a frolic was going on. Lights shone from many of the windows. Music could be heard occasionally and the sound of dancing feet. Frank James crept to a back door, peered in for a few moments, and counted five women and eleven men. Some of the men were in the laps of the women, and some were so close to them that to risk a volley would be murderous. The Guerrillas waited an hour for a more favorable opportunity to fire, but waited in vain. At no time without hitting a woman could they make sure of shooting more than a single man, but Jarrette solved the problem speedily. He was dressed in Federal uniform, and after placing his men so as to cut off from the house its occupants if they once came outside, he rode boldly up to the fence in front of the premises and cried: "Hello!" A soldier came to the door with a gun in his hand and answered him. Jarrette, authoritatively and positively, continued: "Who are you that come to this place in defiance of every order issued for a month? What business have you here to-night? Who gave you permission to come? Where are your passes? Come out to me that I may read them?" Thinking Jarrette a provost captain scouting for runaways from the Lexington garrison, ten of the eleven militiamen started confidently for the fence, receiving when half way the crushing fire of twenty concealed Guerrillas. In a space four blankets might have covered, the ten fell and died, only one of the lot discharging a weapon or making the least pretence at resistance. Frank James counted them, stooping to do so, and as he arose he remarked, sententiously: "There are but ten here; awhile ago there were eleven." The building was entered, searched from bottom to top, minutely examined in every nook and corner— no soldier. The women were questioned one at a time and separately. They knew only that when the man at the fence called the whole party went out together. Frank James, whose impassive face had from the first expressed neither curiosity nor doubt, spoke up again and briefly. "Awhile ago I counted but five women, now there are six." Save four sentinels on duty at either end of the main road, the Guerrillas had gathered together in the lower large room of the dwelling-house. The fire had burned low, and was fitful and flickering. Where there had been half a dozen candles there were now only two. "Bring more," said Poole, "and we will separate this wolf from the ewes." "Aye, if we have to strip the lot," spoke up a coarse voice in the crowd." "Silence!" cried Jarrette, laying a hand upon a pistol, and turning to his men in the shadow, "not a woman shall be touched. We are wild beasts, yes; but we war on wild beasts.

More lights were brought, and with a candle in each hand Poole went from woman to woman, scanning the face of each long and searchingly, and saying, when he had finished, "I give it up. If one of the six here is a man, let him keep his dress and his scalp." Frank James, just behind Poole, had inspected each countenance also as the candles passed before it, and when Poole had done speaking, he laid a finger upon a woman's shoulder and spoke as one having authority: "This is the man. If I miss my reckoning, shoot me dead." The marvelous nerve, which up to this time had stood with the militiaman as a shield and a defence, deserted him when the extremity came, and he turned ghastly white, trembled to his feet, and fell, sobbing and praying, upon his knees. Horrified by the slaughter of his comrades in the yard, and afraid to rush from the house lest he be shot down also, he hurriedly put on the garments of one of the women, composed his features as best he could, and awaited in agonized suspense the departure of the Guerrillas. Almost a boy, his smooth, innocent face was fresher and fairer than the face of any real woman there. His hair, worn naturally long and inclined to be brown, was thick and fine. The dress hid his feet, or the boots would have betrayed him at the start. Not knowing that an observation had been made before the firing, and the numbers accurately taken of both men and women, he hoped to brave it through and laugh afterwards and tell to his messmates how near death had passed to him and did not stop. The reaction, however, of discovery was pitiful. He was too young to die, he pleaded. He had never harmed a human being in his life. If he was spared he would abandon the army and throw away his gun. As he prayed he wept, but Jarrette prevented instantly a further abasement of his manhood : " He is yours, James," he said, "and fairly yours. When he changed color ever so little under Poole's inspection, you saw it and no other man did, and he belongs to you. Take him!" Property in human flesh was often disposed of in this way. A nod sometimes saved or sacrificed a life. To smile was not always to be merciful ; to look harsh was not always to be cruel.

"Come," said Frank James, lifting the young Federal up from the floor to his feet with his left hand, drawing at the same time his revolver with his right; "come outside. It is not far to go." Scarcely able to stand, yet unresisting, the militiaman followed the Guerrilla—the lamb following the tiger. As they went by the ghastly heap, all ragged and intangible in the uncertain light, the one shuddered and the other was glad. At the fence the prisoner was so weak that he could scarcely climb it. Beyond the fence was the road, and down this road a few hundred yards towards Lexington, Frank James led his victim. Under the shadows of a huge tree he halted. It was quite dark there. Only the good God could see what was done ; the leaves shut the stars out. "Do not kill me, for my mother's sake," came from the pinched lips of the poor penitent, "for I have no one else to pray for me. Spare me, just this once." "You are free," said James, "go!" and as he spoke he pointed in the direction of Lexington. "Free? You do not kill me? You tell me to go? Great God! am I sleeping or awake!" and the man's teeth chattered, and he shook as if in an ague fit. "Yes. Go and go quick! You are past the guards, past all danger ; you belong to me, and I give you your life. Go!" At that moment Frank James lifted his pistol above his head and fired in the air. When he returned to the house, Jarrette, who had heard the pistol shot, rallied him. "Yes," he said, "it was soon over. Boys and babies are not difficult to kill." He had just taken the trouble to save the life of a Federal soldier because he had appealed to him in the name of his mother.

Jarrette continued on upon his raid. South of Lexington six miles he came suddenly upon nine Federals in a school house sheltered against a heavy rain that was falling. After shooting the nine and appropriating the horses, he propped each corpse

up at a desk, put a book before it and wrote upon the blackboard fixed near a wall: "John Jarrette and David Poole
taught this school to-day for one hour. We found its pupils all
loyal and we left them as we found them."

Again in the German settlement a company of militia were
engaged and cut to pieces; near Dover five militiamen from
Carroll county were caught encamped at Tebo bridge and shot;
near Waverly ten men at odd times were picked up and put out
of the way; and on the return march to Jackson county no less
than forty-three straggling Federals, in squads of from three to
nine were either surprised or overtaken and executed without
trial or discussion.

The killing, however, was not all on one side. Two wounded
Guerrillas, Williams and Hamilton, were hid in some brush close
upon Grand river, in Cass county. Clark Hockensmith watched
over them, dressed their wounds and carried them food and
drink. This man Hockensmith was possessed of two natures—
that of the lion in combat and that of the woman in relaxation.
While a battle lasted he did two men's fighting; when the battle
was ended he took just the same chances and ran just the same
or greater risks to succor a wounded comrade or bring away a
dying one. As a scout he was unsurpassed; as a spy Quantrell
trusted him even with his thoughts. Belonging equally to the
Confederates and the Guerrillas, under Shelby he was a cuirassier and under Todd a Cossack. When he was neither he was
a Samaritan. He was watching with these two wounded men
when a Kansas cavalry company came upon their camp in the
woods and fired upon it. Hockensmith leaped behind a tree
and fought for his hurt friends until fighting could do them no
more good forever. Hamilton was riddled at the second volley,
and Williams, standing up splendidly to the last, cried aloud
to Hockensmith, when he got his death wound: "It's all over
with me. Tell the boys how I died, and make haste!" All
the immense intrepidity of the scout and all the extraordinary
coolness and prowess of the man were required to bring him
alive out from the peril of the situation. Hoping against hope,
and striving to keep back a force impossible to resist, his own
life was left to him in the end only by a hand's breadth. Of
the Federals who attacked, four were killed and seven wounded.

Noah Webster, of whom it might be said that he never knew

fear, was surprised on Davis creek, in Lafayette county. Hurriedly surveying the field and seeing from a glance at his surroundings that he could not escape, he chose deliberately to die. Fifty cavalry dashed at him and he faced the fifty and fought them without shelter or protection. A musket ball broke his right arm, but he shifted his pistol to his left hand and killed in his tracks the Federal Lieutenant who commanded the scout. Before they knocked him to his knees he had received eleven wounds, giving and taking with the savage endurance of the bull-dog. On his knees he fought, firing the last chamber of his last revolver and killing a cavalryman who had uplifted his carbine to beat out his brains. Incredible as the story may appear, it is true nevertheless that for his own life he received in selling the lives of seven of his assailants, five killed about him and two wounded so severely that they died in a week. On his own body were fifteen wounds, the last musket fired at him being so close that the powder burnt his forehead black where the ball went in. Thus died a hero—a native born Missourian whose heroic death is yet a precious memory among the few who lived after him.

Near Georgetown, in Johnson county, another hero died as Webster died. Wounded sorely in an isolated fight in St. Clair, and brought by easy stages to the heavy timber of the Blackwater, James Morris was come upon suddenly in his blankets and shot as he lay. Not killed, he turned on his left elbow and fought while life remained to him, killing three of the enemy and wounding two.

Just before the death of Noah Webster, in Lafayette county, he, together with his brother John, William and Perry Hays, Frank and William Beard, and Henry McAninch, were surrounded by eighty Federals in a house near Howard's Mill in Johnson county. The environment was complete, but these desperate Guerrillas resolved to cut through it or die. A pistol in each hand, and firing as they came on, they dashed at the nearest Federals, shoulder to shoulder. At the first volley both of the Beard boys fell dead. Later on Perry Hays was shot through the heart. McAninch, bored through one arm and one leg, killed a Federal and climbed upon his horse with the utmost difficulty. John Webster, as he fled, was literally run over by a Federal Lieutenant and crushed to the earth. He lay on his

back under the belly of the horse, its rider above him reaching
down and shooting at him as he was stretched out prostrate,
and bruised and bleeding from the iron feet of the stallion, as
seemingly ferocious as its master. Webster rallied, however,
almost instantly, and killed the Lieutenant as he sat above him
on his horse. His brother Noah, seeing the desperate extremity
he was in, came back to help him and was shot twice but not
crippled in the effort. John Webster had now to go to Noah's
assistance, which he did speedily on the Lieutenant's own horse,
taking his brother up behind him and escaping without difficulty
from all pursuit. In this savage combat, five Federals were
killed and three Guerrillas, the wounded Federals were eight
and the wounded Guerrillas two. Will Hays was not hurt, and
as he and McAninch came out from the desperate press together,
they ran upon two militiamen hurrying in the direction of
the fight. Hays halted them, shot them, and took from the
body of the youngest a list of the names of certain citizens
whose houses were to be burnt the next day.

September had come while all this fighting was going on, and
some heavy frosts had bitten deeply into the woods and the
hiding-places. Quantrell began to think of getting ready for
the South again. General Order No. 11 had been carried out
to the letter, and from five thousand Federals in August, 1863,
the operating force along the border had been increased by September of the same year to at least ten thousand men. Two
hundred Guerrillas, broken into bands of ten each, were baffling
ten thousand infantry and cavalry, killing picquets, firing upon
marching columns, ambuscading scouting parties, waylaying
roads, interfering with transportation, cutting off foraging convoys, burning wagons, breaking up *corrals*, and killing upon
every by-path and in every direction. But in order to avoid
extermination altogether, Quantrell knew that when nature was
no longer in league with him, he would be compelled to winter
again in the South and recruit himself within the lines of the
protecting Confederacy. Intending, therefore, to do speedily
what had to be done in the end, the old rendezvous at Captain
Purdee's, in Johnson county, was agreed upon, and the men
ordered to assemble there September 10th, 1863. On the evening of the same day the march to the South began. Every Guerrilla had a blue overcoat, blue pants, and a Federal cavalry hat;

they were to re-enact the scenes of the journey up, the spring
before. Attracted by the uniform of the Guerrillas, and assured
by the sight of the Federal flag carried at the head of the column, the first victims to become entangled in the toils were a
Lieutenant and six men with dispatches from Springfield to Kansas City. Quantrell had them all shot by a special detail. At
the crossing of the Osage river there was a large flat-boat
watched over by a homeguard company of thirty men. Of
this number three alone escaped. Beyond the Osage, sixteen
cavalrymen from Fort Scott had been over in Vernon county
hunting beef cattle, and were returning with a drove when
Quantrell came upon them. They were surrounded before they
understood how a government uniform could cover other than a
government soldier, and shot to a man when it was too late for
such information to do them any good.

Baxter Springs, Kansas, held by a substantial garrison, was
more or less scientifically fortified. Quantrell drove in the outlying sentinels covering its approaches, saw by the way it
showed its teeth that it was dangerous, and turned directly to
the west, crossing Spring River in the neighborhood of Fort
Webster. Well across this river a heavy foraging party was
met who were wary and difficult of approach. Neither the
uniform nor the flag imposed upon them a single moment.
They sent two men to investigate the Guerrillas, and these—
halting beyond pistol range—sought to satisfy themselves by
a dialogue. Quantrell got tired of so much by-play, and cut it
rudely short by a dashing gallop. Ten only of the foragers
were killed, the near proximity of the fort saving all the
balance. Defnded by a dry-ditch and having only for entrances
narrow gashes in thick embankments, Quantrell regarded Fort
Webster somewhat attentively, by its bristlings a wild boar,
and from its swarming an ant hill. Many of his men said
charge it. Poole was clamorous for it. Anderson said he must
have a lot of scalps to take into Arkansas. Jarrette voted no,
as did Gregg, Younger and George Todd. Before hesitation
had deepened into either retreat or attack, a compact blue line,
made curious by the firing on the foraging party, came riding
up in warlike guise and wary. Quantrell left to watch each
sally-port of the isolated redoubt a couple of resolute men, and
turned to meet the new comers hastening from the south.

They were great game indeed—General Blunt, General Blunt's band and General Blunt's escort. Blunt was riding carelessly along in a buggy, but behind it a splendid horse, ready bridled and saddled, waited, champing the bit and impatient.

Quantrell formed his line between the Fort and the advancing Federals and halted it. Blunt, imagining it to be friends drawn up to salute him, ordered the band up from the rear and it came playing. Up to this moment he had remained listlessly in his buggy. No braver or better soldier fought upon the border than General James Blunt. All his instincts were honorable. As he understood the meaning of the word war, so he made it. Abrupt, stubborn in battle, difficult to drive, fond of hard knocks, untiring in pursuit, indomitable in action, he had to bear, it is true, many of the sins of his State and his people; but he was never cruel in victory nor unmerciful when fortune gave it into his hands to be autocratic. If Quantrell had known him then as others knew him later, the blood of many a brave though helpless man on the prairies out there would have remained unshed for the autumn rains to wash out and the autumn winds to dry.

Blunt's escort and band numbered altogether two hundred and ten; Quantrell's Guerrillas scant two hundred. As the distance between the two forces had been reduced to a few hundred yards, three Federals rode forward from the main body to reconnoitre more closely. Jarrette, Younger, and Jesse James went from the ranks of the Guerrillas to meet them. This parley, settling nothing and serving only to still further increase the suspicions of the Federals, made Quantrell impatient. He had gained from his disguise about all he had any right to expect; further delay simply meant further preparation. Blunt's actions also hastened the catastrophe. He was still in the rear of his escort probably three hundred yards, but when from each rank the three scouts rode forward to confer, he mounted his hor-e and started for the front. At that instant Quantrell ordered the charge. The Federals, firing only a single volley, broke and fled in every direction. Cut off from the Fort, and pressed on every hand, inevitable death could only be averted by extraordinary speed. Blunt tried thrice heroically to rally his men, but with common prudence, sense, and discretion all gone, they swept past and away from him in the direction of

Fort Scott, halting for neither threat nor command, crazy with panic and he'pless in frenzied terror. The band, in a huge wagon, gaudy but out of place, made haste slowly. The musicians, having revolvers for side-arms, fought a little and died without leaving the vehicle. The pursuit lasted for five miles. Jesse James, singling Blunt out from the press, followed him until distanced in the race, firing at him four times without effect. The speed and vigor of his horse alone saved him. Including foragers, musicians, and body guards, the Federals lost one hundred and thirty. In the charge Jack Bishop was the first to shoot down a Federal, and in the summing up at night, Bishop had put to his account four, Jesse James five, Frank James five, Anderson four, William Greenwood four, Poole four, John Coger four, Dick Yager four, Jarrette five, Todd—riding by odds the fastest horse in the command—ten, George Shepherd four, John Ross four, Fletcher Taylor seven, and others from one to five accordingly as they were well or illy mounted. Peyton Long shot Adjutant General Curtis, nephew of the general of that name. He had upon his person an order signed by his uncle commanding the soldiers of his division to take no prisoners among the Guerrillas, especially among the Guerrillas commanded by Quantrell. This order was attested by the younger Curtis as acting adjutant general, and Long asked him if he wrote it. "Yes, by the orders of my superior officer." "Would you have obeyed it?" "Most certainly." Long shot him at this with scarcely more compunction than he would have shot a cat. With Blunt also was one of Frank Leslie's artists, a young man named O'Neill. He had among his sketches a half finished picture of some hypothetical battle, in which, as was usual for Leslie, there were to be seen rebels in flight — panic-stricken and overwhelmed — with valiant boys in blue slashing about heroically and spitting the laggards with the bayonet as a French cook spits an ortolan. Todd killed the artist, and some of Todd's men appropriated the pictures. Blunt lost his batle-flag, a magnificent silk standard given to him by the ladies of Leavenworth, and a splendid sword. Both sword and banner were presented by Quantrell to General Price, and Anderson, suffering no longer from a dearth of scalps, carried with him into Arkansas what number suited him best.

After the combat at Fort Webster, which after all was more

of a massacre than a combat, Quantrell passed rapidly through the Indian Nation, reaching Red river at Colbert's ferry and crossing there. Beyond the ferry, but contiguous to it, Todd and Anderson, joining companies, went into winter quarters. Jarrette and Poole, reporting later to Shelby, were sent into Louisiana with a company each, while Quantrell keeping well in hand the old company, took position on a small stream fifteen miles northwest of Sherman.

Active Guerrilla operations, except with Jarrette and Pool, ceased until the next spring; but these two enterprising officers, while making arrangements for a campaign in Louisiana, left their company in command of Lieutenant Coleman Younger, who reported at once to General Henry E. McCulloch, having his headquarters at Bonham, Texas. McCulloch commanded the western district of the State, and formed an especial attachment for Younger, who scouted a great deal for him, and brilliantly. Colonel Ricord, the quartermaster of the district, together with the commissary, made themselves thoroughly acquainted with the circumstances under which the Guerrillas operated, and informed themselves intelligently of the condition of those Missourians who were driven penniless from their homes at the commencement of a rigorous winter. As a consequence, they furnished them bountifully with supplies and provided comfortable shelter for the wives and the children of the refugees.

Lieutenant Younger, introduced to General E. Kirby Smith through a most flattering letter from General McCulloch, reported to him at Shreveport, Louisiana, the headquarters of the Trans-Mississippi Department. Jarrette and Poole rejoined him at Shreveport, and received from General Smith minute orders for an especial campaign. Along the Mississippi river, and for a score of miles inland, cotton thieves and speculators were swarming thick about the Louisiana plantations. They dealt with the planters and demoralized the troops. Federal officers were in league with them, and government gun boats helped to make all their operations successful. They had cavalry escorts to accompany distant journeys, and infantry succors as a shelter for the booty secured. They brought into the Confederacy quinine, opium, whisky, gun caps, clothing, many necessaries, and a few luxuries, but with the speculators came such

an army of spies that Smith could neither issue a secret order
in safety nor make an important military movement unreported
to the headquarters of the Federals.   He had heard of the
savage fighting of the Guerrillas along the western border of
Missouri, and he determined to try the efficacy of a crushing
blow or two along the Louisiana border of the Mississippi river.   Jarrette and Poole were ordered there with two
companies, Poole commanding one, Younger one, and Jarrette
the united forces.   Halting a sufficient length of time at Bastrop to recruit the horses and refit the men, Jarrette crossed
Bayou Bœuf at Wallace's Ferry, and pushed on to Floyd, in
Carroll parish.   From the camp at Bonaparte Wade's he went
across Bayou Mason the next morning at Tester's ferry, and
was then clearly within the Federal lines.   Hot work was at
hand.   A cotton train, composed of fourteen six-mule teams
and convoyed by fifty cavalrymen, were met five miles from the
ferry and charged at sight.   So unexpected was the apparition,
and so little idea of opposition had been entertained by the
enemy, that their carbines remained slung and their column
stretched out for a quarter of a mile.   The convoy, cut to
pieces, saved probably ten troopers from the wreck, and the
train—every driver shot from every team—was in absolute possession of the Guerrillas.   Behind the rear wagon was an ambulance, and in this ambulance were four cotton buyers.   One
was from Springfield, Illinois, one from Cincinnati, and two from
Chicago.   Between them all there were counted out to
their captors one hundred and eighty thousand dollars.   In
that country trees were scarce, and hanging places few and far
between.   Jarrette, noting to the left a large cotton gin, found
withinside speedily a comfortable beam, and had a rope noosed
at once, then another, and another, until there were four.   The
scene that followed was one of human nature in its abasement.
The doomed men grovelled.   They offered everything for life;
they promised everything; they knelt in agony and prayed so
pitifully that the least hardened among the Guerrillas turned
away and felt something about the heart that they had never felt
before.   Later, four stark corpses swung from the huge beam
overhead, and four graves at nightfall received them without
coffin or shroud.   The warfare of the Missouri prairies had been
transferred to the Louisiana cotton-fields.

The mules, the wagons, the ambulance and the money were all sent back to Bastrop in charge of Lieutenant Greenwood, while Jarrette—elated at the vigor of his first blow—pushed on towards the river. Well across Bayou Tensas, and well up on the higher lands, Lieut. Younger saw, while he was bringing up the rear, a large plantation upon his left. The field nearest to him was dotted with blue specks and white with wagons, cotton-laden. He did not stop to count the cost of a charge, nor to ascertain how clear the coast was. A small bayou, Monticello, was between him and the enemy, but he called upon his men to follow, and plunged in. Down he went, head and ears. As he arose he spluttered, and floundered, and swam, and finally reached the thither shore without looking back. Younger's men, however, seeing how deep the water of the little stream was, galloped to a ford higher up and left him alone to hold his own among the Federals. He did it desperately, galloping about in every direction and firing here at one squad and there at another, until he had killed three and wounded two others. By this time the rear guard came to his support and finished the fight. Eighteen wagons and teams were captured here, and fifty-two negro soldiers killed in a vain effort to protect them.

Five miles from Goodrich's ferry on the Mississippi river, Lieut. Little, leading the advance, met the head of a Federal column moving as a convoy into the interior. He charged it savagely, killed nine men in as many minutes, and drove it back upon its rear. Jarrette closed up at a run and dashed upon the demoralized enemy before they could reform or take position for a further combat. Flying in every direction before his furious assault, and making what haste horse-flesh was capable of, three gunboats anchored in mid-stream saved the remnants of the decimated column. Capturing twenty-seven wagons and killing seventy-two of the convoy, Jarrette received the thanks of Gen. Smith in a special order, and the congratulations of Gen. Shelby upon his brilliant work. Lieut. William Greenwood was wounded in this fight, together with Tom Little, McBurgess and John Poole.

At the little town of Omega, close to the Mississippi, there were stationed two hundred negro soldiers under white officers. Behind the levee breastworks had been built, but upon the higher ground in front of the levee the camp had been established. Dividing his command into two detachments, Jarrette ordered Younger to gain the entrenchments, and hold them at all hazards while he attacked furiously and simultaneously from the front. Just at daylight Younger was in the earthworks shooting the three or four sentinels on duty there and firing from the parapets directly into the scarcely aroused camp in front of him. Jarrette, up to time to the fraction of a minute, caught the lagging negroes on the other side and thus, crouched between two fires, the position was enveloped. One hundred negroes were killed, twenty were taken prisoners, and eighty escaped on foot into some dense swamps that could not be penetrated by horsemen. During the whole of the fight two gunboats shelled the Guerrillas incessantly, but they laughed at their impotence while they loaded into wagons and sent out to the Confederate lines an immense booty.

For two weeks longer, Jarrette, Poole, Morry Boswell, Younger, John Poole, Phil Gatewood and William Greenwood operated up and down the river, commanding each squads of Guerrillas of from ten to twenty-five. They so demoralized the Marine Fleet under Ellet that it landed its marines but rarely. Because of them Federal cavalry scarcely ever ventured to penetrate further from a gunboat than the range of a Parrott shell. Cotton speculation died of a disease similar to paralysis. Cotton speculators sold out contracts at ruinous discounts. Confederate officers, high in authority, took alarm at the terrible doings of these red, iconoclastic hands, and saw profits and margins disappear in the smoke of incessant battle. The quinine patriots, despite the handling of a drug so specific, shook as with the ague. In the operations of three brief weeks twenty-two spies had been hung, seventeen cotton buyers, and five guides known to be in collusion with the enemy. That thing, understood at first as the contraband trade, had become to be a cancer. Jarrette cut it out; Younger hunted for its roots; Poole poured vitriol into the cavity. Patriotic citizens blessed them and rallied to them. Navigation, never entirely safe, became in their vicinity extremely hazardous. The Federal authorities complained through potent yet mysterious sources to Smith; Confederates, neck deep in the plots and counter-plots of rapacious buyers and sellers, worked energetically in the crippling business; a few influential planters—cut off as if by a

wall of fire from all intercourse with the North—played upon
the cupidity of powerful advocates; this interested general
officer pooh-poohed the bloody work of the Guerrillas as bar-
barous, and that general officer denounced it as unchristian;
betwixt them all the howl that went up to Shreveport was
deeply unanimous, and Jarrette was ordered out from the midst
of his operations and back from the field of his successful
labors in the cause of the Confederacy. From the extremities
of the Trans-Mississippi Department—where for some time its
ravages had been remarkable—the dry rot was now about to
reach the heart.

CHAPTER XIV.

JARRETTE, Poole, Younger, Anderson, Todd, Taylor, Yager, Blunt, Clements, the two Jameses, Greenwood, Gregg, Maddox, Shepherd, Little, Flannery, Press Webb, Harrison Trow and Quantrell were destined never to act together again as a compact command, wielded by one intellect and handled in combat at the instance of a single controlling impulse. The old deadly species of fighting and killing was still to continue, but the isolation of it was to be more emphatic and the extent of the territory more considerable. As the war grew older and the license of Guerrilla life more positively unexacting, ambitious rivalries arose. Subordinates sought preferment as was natural, but in relying upon themselves and their resources for the future, they did not sunder a single chord which bound them to the past, nor break away from a single tie of comradeship which had been begotten under the black flag and born in the agony of pitiless battle. Hereafter, indeed, there were to be, instead of one Quantrell, half a dozen.

On the 10th day of March, 1864, Quantrell—still having about him the most of his old men—broke the long inactivity of his winter camp near Sherman, Texas, and started for Missouri. That portion of the Indian Nation extending from Red river to the Arkansas river on the west was comparatively a desert. The Pin Indians—that faction of the Cherokees who belonged to Ross—had burned the property and wasted the substance of the Confederate Cherokees and Choctaws—and the Confederate Cherokees and Choctaws, in retaliation, had burned the property and wasted the substance of the Pins. As a result there was depopulation.

Encountering scarcely a friend or a scout between Boggy Depot and the Arkansas, Quantrell crossed this river fifty miles above Fort Gibson, killing on the further bank five Pin Indians who were in camp there, perfectly oblivious of all danger, and pushed on north to the vicinity of Baxter Springs, Kansas, getting over the Neosho river on the east of the town and at Gilstrap's ferry. West of Neosho, in Missouri, the advance under Col. Vard Cockrell, was ambushed and fired upon, and Col. Cockrell severely wounded in the arm. Richard Kinney, John Coger, Allen Parmer, Andy Walker, Harrison Trow and Frank James charged instantly into the brush from which the fire proceeded, and broke up the ambuscade, killing three militia and capturing seven horses. At the next halting place, which was on Grand river, while Quantrell's men were in the timber cooking and eating, half a regiment of Colorado cavalry were in bivouac two miles away on the prairie doing the same thing. At sunset Quantrell mounted and moved out to within four hundred yards of the house where the Federals were halted, a single soldier advancing from their lines to meet him. William McGuire, dressed in blue, did not tarry for a parley as the Federal demanded, but rode upon him boldly, holding his hands, which were empty, in plain view of his antagonist. Equally as brave, the Federal scorned to halt a single man or threaten him with a weapon, and permitted him thus to ride up fairly by his side. Instantly and without anything of demonstration, McGuire covered him with a revolver drawn unperceived, and bade him go quietly to Quantrell. Lest the act itself should attract attention and reveal prematurely the presence of the Guerrillas in Missouri, McGuire did not disarm his prisoner, nor evince by any hostile movement that the two who were riding so quietly and side by side into Quantrell's ranks were other than old acquaintances. Once there, the deception was still further continued, for many among the Guerrillas rushed from the ranks and shook hands heartily with the captured man. His comrades at the house, watching intently the whole performance, were satisfied with this last indication of friendship and permitted Quantrell, without further investigation, to march away unpursued and unmolested, carrying one of their number with him. This Federal prisoner was a Sergeant Russell, belonging to Baxter Springs, where for some time he had been in command of the post.   War never made a better soldier.   Cool, self-possessed, knowing his duty perfectly, and ready at all times to take whatever extreme fortune sent to him, he yet lacked two important elements of character if in the line of his profession it should become necessary to fight such men as Quantrell trained—enterprise and the power of instantaneous action in peril.   If the first had been his, McGuire's approach would have been forbidden; if the last, he would have staked his life against his captor's and taken the chances of escape from the hands of one man rather than fifty.   Inexperience, however, had made him negligent, and an over-confidence in a prowess which after all consisted in rather the absence of physical fear than real superiority in combat, cost him his life. Quantrell, three miles from the point of capture, ordered John Coger peremptorily to shoot him.   Coger—as brave a man as ever lived, and possessing an innate appreciation of fine courage in others—despised the work apportioned to his hands, but he could not disobey.   Russell, when halted at the spot selected to kill him and informed of his fate, scarcely changed color.   "I die as I have lived," he said to Coger, in a voice calm as the breathing of a healthy sleeper, "and brave to the last.   I have killed no man save in regular combat, and I have waged no war that was not justified by honorable rules.   If you shoot me you do the work of a commander who is both a dog and a coward."   Appealed to by some of his own men Quantrell was inexorable; the old savage mood had come back again.   Russell died, facing his executioner and game to the last.

Leaving the Colorado troops in the rear, Quantrell came full head upon two hundred of the Second Colorado Cavalry in his front, camped in Johnson county, six miles south of Warrensburg. Before he saw their picquets he was within fifty yards of them, but he countermarched without firing and fell back a mile, unpursued.   It had been raining almost continuously since he left Texas, the roads were heavy, and the most of the horses leg-weary or knocked up.   Set upon by a heavy column of cavalry, fresh from a long winter's rest and strong from abundant forage, meant death to his band in detail, and so to avoid it Quantrell formed and executed a heroic manœuvre.   Ordering every Guerrilla who rode an unserviceable or an indifferent

horse to hide temporarily in the brush, he put himself at the
head of the best mounted men and made for the Federals to
follow a trail so broad and bold that it could not possibly be
mistaken. Furthermore, and as if by way of emphasis, he
declared it his intention to strike at the first force he found if it
was as big as a mountain, and draw it after him in pursuit.
Afterwards and when the darkness fell, those left badly mounted
in the rear, might hasten on to the Jackson county rendezvous
in comparative safety.

Those fit to pass muster under Quantrell's critical eyes were
George Todd, Jesse James, Richard Kinney, George Shepherd,
John Barker, James Little, William McGuire, John Jackson,
William Hulse, John Ross, Sim Whitsett, and George Maddox
—a forlorn hope as it were who knew how to die. Skirting
Warrensburg on the west, and pushing ahead in gait and looks
a Federal scout, Quantrell soon saw approaching him a smaller
body of men, hurrying towards Warrensburg. Each detachment halted within speaking distance, and sought to know each
other's banner. Quantrell spoke first and to the point. "We
are Colorado troops going west on special duty. And you?"
"Missouri militia under Lieutenant Nash, *en route* to Warrensburg." There were eight in the party and they came together
at this, all of them, except one militiaman who refused to move
with his comrades and who kept imploring his lieutenant to keep
back and keep away. Quantrell himself shot Nash and one
other militiaman, Jesse James killed one, Hulse one, Maddox
one, Shepherd one, and John Ross the seventh, while the eighth
and last one of the squad—beyond range on a hill—turned his
horse in flight and cried out vociferously, as if crying out to the
dead: "I told you they were bushwhackers! I told you they
were bushwhackers! Oh! men—men—why did you not listen
to me?"

Soon after this episode, so sudden and so bloody, the Colorado troopers were in the saddle and hurrying in pursuit.
Thanks to the mud the pursuit might be rode in a gallop;
thanks to the roads the roads themselves were better than any
country to their right or left. Those Colorado fellows were
slashing fellows, fond of a grapple and fond of a *melee*. They
were grave, quiet, middle-aged men, the most of them, rarely
influenced by sentiment and not at all by any romantic folly.

They volunteered to fight, and they did it as they would follow an Indian trail or develop a silver mine. They could be whipped, and they were whipped; but such fighting as would do for the militia would not do for them. Man to man, the best of the border knew that to drive them required close work and steady work.

Throughout the day, and over broken, washed, and intolerable roads, Quantrell held his little band together and fought the Coloradans from behind every obstruction that could be found along the route, never hurrying in his retreat and never relaxing his grip upon a strong place until he had hurt somebody interfering with his possession of it. Some little while before sunset, however, the toils about the Guerrillas began to be drawn closely. Lying along a hedge-row in front of him, and at the further end of a long lane which had commenced some distance back, Quantrell discovered two companies of infantry crouching down and awaiting his arrival. He could not go forward, because he could neither flank nor get at the infantry, and he could not go back without fighting his way back. He chose to fight his way back, and as he countermarched he charged. Fortunately the Colorado column was not closed up, nor did its commander expect other than a defensive movement from so small a detachment and one which had been driven all day from position to position, try how they would to hold it. Pell mell and back to the mouth of the lane and beyond, Quantrell hurled everything before him, staying for nothing the tide of his savage onset, and caring for nothing that rallied to keep him back. Safe from the ambushment of the infantry, and free to take any course counseled by safety, Quantrell was just on the eve of turning into some timber on the right, when William McGuire was thrown heavily against a tree. He had been riding Sergeant Russell's horse, a high-spirited animal of great speed, and had led the charge down the lane. Of the nine Federals killed, he had shot three, and was rushing upon a fourth when the girth of his saddle burst and hurled him headforemost upon a walnut tree close to the roadside. At first it was thought that a bullet had found some vital spot, but rallying speedily from the blow he essayed to regain his feet, weak and staggering. Vexed at the audacity of a charge so unlooked for and so determined, the Coloradans hurried up from the rear impetuously and sought to get revenge for their temporary disaster. Fighting splendidly in front of McGuire and keeping one hundred troopers at bay until the prostrate rider could mount and ride again, Quantrell held his men as he had never done before in all his long career. But two of the twelve came out unwounded, Quantrell escaping himself and George Todd, and the two at that who were nearest to the enemy.

The country was aroused. Quantrell's coming had been borne on the wings of the wind to all the posts and garrisons throughout the West, and cantonments were at once broken up, isolated detachments hurried in, large bodies of troops put in motion to destroy him, and the word passed from commander to commander that the lion had been heard roaring about his Jackson county lair again. For the Guerrillas, however, the situation was extremely serious. But few leaves were on the trees, the roads were well-nigh impassible, all the streams were swimming and all the bridges were guarded. Listening in the Lake Hills for the report of scouts sent out to try the country, and pondering anxiously over stratagems fit to baffle pursuit until, refitted and remounted, the men were made whole for the warpath, Quantrell awaited information. George Shepherd came to him at midnight on the 22d of March, bringing into camp all who had been left in Johnson county, and bringing also the bad tidings that a column of Federal cavalry, seven hundred strong, would attack him at daylight the next morning. Quantrell moved at once for what was known as the Fire Prairie Bottom, a demi-island as it were, and nearly surrounded by water. For ten miles east and west and for ten miles north and south there was water—water everywhere. It still rained. It rained when he broke camp; it was raining when he reached Fire Prairie Bottom; it rained upon him as he waded, or floundered, or swam, but the trail was lost and the Guerrillas gained breathing time. Gaining the Little Blue toilsomely with water to the saddle-skirts, Quantrell hid his horses in the earliest growth of the season, some five or six acres of luxuriant buckeye, and sent scouting parties out afoot to communicate with reliable citizens and obtain forage and food.

While thus waiting for the leaves, and making scarcely any sign that they were in the country, the main body of the Guerrillas disappeared literally. To some, however, this enforced

idleness was irksome, and Allen Parmer, Ben Morrow, Jesse
James, Frank James, James Noland, Joel Chiles and Ves.
Akers crossed the Missouri river on a raft, waited for nightfall
on the hither bank, and entered Camden, Ray county, three
hours later, hunting that sort of a frolic which mingles blood
with its liquor.   Camden, noted locally for the predatory
nature of the militia who garrisoned it, had remained for some
time undisturbed in the lawlessness of an investiture which
preyed upon the country people and tyrannized over the inhabi-
tants.   It needed to understand a little of the realities of war
and learn from them the philosophy of an equilibrium.

   To all appearances Camden was deserted.   The Guerrillas
rode through the place without seeing a light, and halted
unchallenged before a large stone hotel in which the garrison
was quartered; it was unsentineled.   West of this a square a
saloon was in full blast, and Ben Morrow approached it, dismounted, and looked in.   Eight militiamen were there, card
playing and drinking.   None else in the town seemed to be
astir or awake.   The Guerrillas left their horses in charge of
one of the party and surrounded the saloon.   The conversation
within could be clearly understood without, and as the game
was draw-poker one excited player, carried away evidently by
the formidable nature of his hand, cried out: "Two hundred
dollars better."   Another: "I call your two hundred dollars
and with them these," laying down as he spoke four unmistakable aces.   "Hands off!" shouted Frank James, striding
through the door, a revolver in each hand, "and wait for the
playing out of the game.   Here is a pair that beats four aces."
Astonishment sobered all who were drunk, and silenced all who
were garrulous.   But one Federal retained his self-possession—
the man of the four aces.   He found assurance enough to reply:
"Fairly beat, by g——!   Your pair is good enough, stranger,
and I surrender."   They all surrendered, but somehow the
stone hotel got word of strange men riding about the place and
began to buzz like a hive in June.   Four or five of its inmates
came out upon the balcony and were fired upon.   Others of the
occupants manned its doors and windows and returned the fire,
making the street in a moment lurid with musket flashes.   Held
by sixty soldiers the Guerrillas could not of course capture the
building, but they could imprison its garrison and shoot at

every body that exposed himself. For two hours they did this, helping themselves in the meantime to whatever was needed in the way of horse-flesh and clothing. While skirmishing thus, a Guerrilla, William Gaw, accidentally shot Frank James in the face, inflicting quite a severe wound. This was the only casualty. The Federals lost ten killed and seven wounded.

The leaves began to put out. The saturated soil hardened under the sunbeams. The stir and the strife of the Guerrillas began to be felt. Frank James, that his hurt might heal at his mother's, took with him Allen Parmer, found a convenient log upon the Jackson bank of the Missouri river, put on it their pistols and their clothes, and swam with it to Clay county. In three weeks he was again in the saddle.

William McGuire's time had now come, the intrepid captor of Sergeant Russell. Surprised at the house of a friend, he broke out from his environment, wounded badly, but free. Later on his hiding place in the Sni hills was discovered, together with that of a wounded comrade, Tid Sanders, who was with him. Each fought to the death—two men against eighty. McGuire killed three before he was past praying for, and Sanders two. Five others were wounded. When finished certainly, McGuire, besides two old wounds upon his person, received in his death fight, sixteen new ones; Sanders, to his old one, had added eleven more. Thus the Guerrillas died in that terrible year of 1864—like men, certainly, but *such men!*

Babe Hudspeth, another wounded lion, was lying deep in the brush waiting for convalescence. Tracked to his hiding place, he yet lifted himself up from his blankets and fought as he crawled. For miles he dragged after him his crippled limbs, firing at the nearest as they rushed upon him, and firing with fatal effect. Succored finally by Todd, who happened to be in the neighborhood, and who never heard shooting in his life without going towards it or to it, Hudspeth escaped, leaving as evidences of the borderer's iron that was in him, three dead and three wounded.

Todd, by the first of June, was at the head of forty Guerrillas, splendidly armed and mounted, and mowed with them a swathe through Lafayette county into Saline, capturing the town of Arrow Rock and putting to the sword its garrison of forty-five militia. There Capt. Dick Yager was wounded—a young hero famed for dash and courage. They brought him back to Jackson, hid him as best they could, and left him to nature and a watchful comrade. Discovered, seventy Federals came to his fastness and found him scarcely able to stand. It was the old, old story. His comrade died defending him. Yager—alone, emaciated, face to face with inexorable death— fought as they all fought who had preceded him—McGuire, Sanders, Webster, Haller, Morris, Bledsoe, Hamilton, Williams, and as many more were to fight who were to come after him. Poor Yager! He fell there, propped against a tree that he might face his foes, but as he fell he avenged himself. Three died with him and two were wounded. It might be said of him that he lived literally with his revolver belt buckled. Pure as a child, simple, tranquil, he did everything possible for his country, nothing against her.

Quantrell, suffering somewhat from old wounds, and indisposed generally, took with him into Howard county as a body-guard James Little, John Barker, David Helton, George Shepherd, John Ross, Toler, and ten others—sixteen tried men altogether. His object was not so much to fight as to rest; not so much to seek adventure as to recuperate. He found what he sought for, respite and inactivity.

The Colorado cavalry joined now in the Guerrilla hunt ardently. Capt. Wagner, of the Second Regiment, scattered broadcast the news that at the head of sixty-five picked men me meant to come and go about Jackson county with impunity, fighting everything that came within fighting distance, and riding over every obstacle in preference to riding around it. Todd heard of the boast and sought to verify it. Commanding sixty-four Guerrillas, he followed Wagner here and there for a week, being to-day too far ahead of him, or to-morrow too far behind. The eighth day the two met face to face on the Harrisonville road, seven miles south of Independence. Each formed line of battle. Most of the Colorado troops were old mountaineers, cool, middle-aged and wiry as antelope. Neither were they lacking in that essential quality of a soldier, stead-fastness. Charging simultaneously, the two ranks came together as the jaws of a steel-trap. The *melee* deepened in a moment and became savage and sanguinary. Superior in horsemanship, in pistol practice, and in all the elements of cavalry skirmishing, the Guerrillas made quick work of the combat. Dick Kinney singled out Wagner and bade him fight him man to man. Wagner, brave as the bravest, accepted the challenge and fired at Kinney as they closed. In return, Kinney shot at Wagner and missed; Wagner missed the second time and the third time, and Kinney also, but the fourth shot Kinney was too quick for his antagonist, sending a dragoon revolver ball crashing through his heart. Jesse James, having a trooper on either hand, killed both before but one of them fired; while Todd, raging as he always did like some infuriated animal, shot down three before he turned in the counter-charge. The pistol practice of the Coloradans was simply execrable. Their vollies were steady enough and rapid enough, but they did no execution. The horses of some became unmanageable, and they dismounted to fight on foot. These all perished where they stood. Others, seeing the hopelessness of further resistance, broke away in a furious run toward Independence, followed by a remorseless foe. Twenty-seven of Wagner's picked men were killed, including the captain himself, while among the captures were twenty-four horses, thirty revolvers, and thirty-two Spencer rifles. Todd's entire loss was two men wounded, Si Flannery, shot through the right lung, and Henry Porter through the left leg. Among those who fought splendidly under Todd's immediate eye were the two Flannerys, Si and Ike, Jesse and Frank James, Henry Porter, Dick Kinney, John Coger, John Jackson, Dick Burnes, Andy McGuire, Ben Morrow, Harrison Trow, Bill Basham, William Steward, Babe Hudspeth, William Hulse, George Shepherd, Oll Johnson, Frank Shepherd, and Hence and Life Privin. Kinney, Frank James and Ike Flannery followed the routed enemy in sight of Independence, James killing his fourth man within fifty steps of the picquet post. This fight settled the boastfulness of the Coloradans. Man to man, they had met the much derided Guerrillas and had been cut to pieces. They fought often afterwards, it is true, and long and well, but they always fought as men who had respect for their antagonists and knew by experience the stuff of which they were made.

Todd kept in the saddle almost continuously. With forty men he made a dash into Lafayette county, gathered up Dave and John Poole—just back from Mexico—and raided the German settlement for the third time since the commencement of the war, killing thirty-five militia and burning one fort and several dwelling houses. Poole brought to Todd a reinforcement of thirty additional Guerrillas, making seventy in the aggregate, and with this force he captured Tipton, Moniteau county, putting to the sword its garrison of forty militia, and destroying some valuable government property. From Moniteau county to Cooper county was an easy march, and Todd swooped down by Boonville, killing in every direction and beating up the German neighborhoods with a ferocity unexampled even for him. It was in Cooper county that little Riley Crawford, a boy not seventeen years of age, and the youngest Guerrilla in the brush, was killed. Ambushed and fired on from a fence corner, he fell from his horse dead, lamented by his comrades and mourned for by Poole with an affection rarely exhibited. He had been with Poole in every battle, had followed him to Mexico, and had become to be regarded as something nearer than a member of his company. Boy as he was, none had ever gone further in battle, nor stood to his place longer in extremity. Todd afterwards estimated as the results of his raid: One hundred and fourteen militia killed, eighty horses captured and brought back to Jackson county, fifty recruits gathered up, and half a million of Federal property destroyed.

Anderson, emerging now from the obscurity of a Southern wintering place, was about to begin that ferocious career, that mad, impatient gallop which was only to end with his heroic death, one man, single-handed, closing with and grappling a regiment. Leaving Texas three weeks after Quantrell, some difficulties were encountered which forced him to countermarch even from Boggy Depot back and re-enter Texas. They were characteristic of the man and his surroundings. On the journey up two of his soldiers, Ben Broomfield and Peyton Long, straggled at Sherman and became entangled in a quarrel with some Indians near Colbert's ferry, and killed a Choctaw named Colbert. Pursued, they held their own until Anderson was overtaken at Boggy Depot and made acquainted with the extremity of the Guerrillas. He condemned the shooting, but he stood by the men. An Indian runner, swifter than the Missourians, gained Boggy Depot in advance of them and reported the shooting to the Confederate commander there, having at his back a garrison of three hundred men. As Anderson rode into the town, a Confederate Lieutenant surrounded his little band with sixty soldiers and demanded Long and Broomfield. Anderson refused to deliver them up, but promised to punish them himself. Not satisfied with this, the Lieutenant ordered the soldiers to fire. Scarcely had the command left his lips when Anderson shot him dead, the balance of the Guerrillas receiving and returning a point blank volley. Jim Crow Chiles had his horse killed, and several of Anderson's men were wounded, but he broke through the environment and returned rapidly to Texas, followed by an excited and revengeful posse. Shelby's emphatic influence in the Department, and the immense energy with which he exercised it, saved Anderson from further trouble and enabled him, two weeks later, to start unembarrassed the second time to Missouri.

As he passed up through Arkansas he killed every Federal upon whom he could fasten either by successful ruse or painstaking stratagem. Every man who followed him wore a Federal uniform, and had in addition a Federal bridle and saddle. A diary of the trip, kept by one of the most accurate of the band, enumerates as the summing up of the journey: "Militia killed, eighty-two; regular soldiers, sixteen; mountain Boomers, a species of Federal guerrilla, twenty-eight; Union citizens, active in supplying information to the enemy, forty; and unreliable negroes, ten—total, one hundred and seventy-six."

The long march ended at the hospitable mansion of Chat. Ewing, in Lafayette county, and Anderson—while tarrying a few grateful days for rest and equipment—was attacked by two companies of militia convoying a wagon train from Lexington to Columbus. The militia evidently mistook the nature of the work taken upon themselves to do, for so savage was Anderson's first dash, and so furious the fighting of his men, that he cut the detachment to pieces, killing thirty-nine and burning every one of the twenty-two wagons. He had but one man hurt, Zack Southerland. Peyton Long followed the Lieutenant commanding four miles, shot at him seven times, and finally brought him down with a snap shot and at a distance of seventy-five yards.

While still resting here, Arch Clements, Jesse James, Fletch Taylor, Peyton Long, and James Bisset crossed over into Clay county on a scout, and from Clay went into Platte. There a

Confederate Colonel, Thornton, was operating on a small scale, together with some fifteen or twenty others. Perhaps a dozen of these joined the Guerrillas in an attack upon New Market. *En route* to the town, forty militia were charged and routed, eighteen of whom were killed and the balance scared so terribly that they had made sixty miles from the place of encounter before they stopped running. George and William Fielding, and John Thomas—three new recruits—were in this hot little combat with the Guerrillas, and did fighting worthy of the oldest of the veterans. The next day Ridgely was attacked, held by sixty militia. Repulsed at the first onset and forced back, the Guerrillas tried again and again to get into the town, but ineffectually. Fletch Taylor, who commanded, was a veritable bull-dog in battle and held on with a tenacity never surpassed. He hated to give up the fight. William Fielding, one of the heroes of the previous day's battle, had been killed, together with Capt. Overston, and Polk Bradley badly wounded; but he dashed at them again in a fifth attack, and repulsed as before, abandoned the unequal encounter. Returning through Clay county, Jesse James and Arch Clements caught four militia in an apple orchard getting apples, two up one tree and two up another. As they shot them out they laughed at their awkward tumblings and made sport of the fruit that such apple orchards bore.

In June Anderson crossed the Missouri River into Carroll county below Waverly, but if he had been a Grecian soldier he would have turned back in the presence of the unpropitious augury that greeted him. As he came upon the southern bank of the river he saw upon the northern one a skiff that was indispensable to his crossing. He called for volunteers to swim for it and bring it over, and Jesse Hamlet and Thomas Bell stepped forward. They plunged in and were making headway gallantly when a sharp cry escaped Bell as the cramp seized him, and he sank midway the current never to be seen again. Hamlet, undaunted either on land or water, halted just long enough to know that human aid was powerless, and stretched away, stroke upon stroke, to the thither shore, securing the skiff and returning with it speedily. Bell, poor fellow, had fought gallantly as a Confederate soldier up to and through the siege of Vicksburg, and had, when the surrender became inevitable there, plunged into the Mississippi river on a plank and made

FLETCHER TAYLOR.

CLARK HOCKENSMITH.

ARCH CLEMENTS.

his way out in safety. It was but the old story of the pitcher that went once too often to the well; what one river gave up with a blessing the other devoured.

Four miles out from the crossing-place, Anderson encountered twenty-five Federals, routed them at the first onset, killing eight, two of whom Arch Clements scalped, hanging the ghastly trophies at the head-stall of his bridle. One of the two scalped was a captain and the commander of the squad.

Killing as he marched, Anderson moved from Carroll into Howard, entered Huntsville the last of June with twenty-five men, took from the county treasury $30,000, and disbanded for a few days for purposes of recruiting. The first act of the next foray was an ambuscade into which Anderson fell headlong. Forty militia waylaid him as he rode through a stretch of heavy bottom land, filled his left shoulder full of turkey shot, killed two of his men and wounded three others. Hurt as he was, he charged the brush, killed eighteen of the assailants, captured every horse and followed the flying remnant as far as a single fugitive could be tracked through the tangled undergrowth.

In July Anderson took Arch Clements, John Maupin, Tuck and Woot Hill, Hiram Guess, Jesse Hamlet, William Reynolds, Polk Helms, Cave Wyatt and Ben Broomfield and moved up into Clay county to form a junction with Fletch Taylor. By ones and twos he killed on the march twenty-five militia, and was taking breakfast at a house in Carroll county when thirty-eight Federals fired upon him through doors and windows, the balls knocking dishes on the floor and playing havoc with chinaware and eatables generally. The Guerrillas, used to every phase of desperate warfare, routed their assailants after a crushing volley or two, and held the field, or rather the house. In the *mele*, Anderson accidentally shot a lady in the shoulder, inflicting a painful wound, and John Maupin killed the captain commanding the scout, cut off his head and stuck it upon a gate-post to shrivel and blacken in the sun.

In Ray county, one hundred and fifty Federal cavalry found Anderson's trail, followed it all day, and just at nightfall struck hard at the Guerrillas and viciously. Anderson would not be driven without a fight. He charged their advance guard, killed fourteen out of sixty, and drove it back upon the main body.

Clements, Woot Hill, Hamlet and Hiram Guess had their horses killed and were left afoot in the night to shift for themselves. Walking to the Missouri river, ten miles, and fashioning a rude raft from logs and withes, Hamlet crossed to Jackson county and made his way safely into the camp of Todd. The other three content with almost any kind of a mount, found such horses as they might and followed on, nothing daunted, upon the trail. The James mansion was in the rendezvous, and thither everything tended. In evident anticipation of the gathering together, Mrs. Samuels, as much devoted to the cause as her two heroic boys, had prepared a splendid dinner. Taylor, however, was not with his men, nor would he be with them for sometime to come. Ambushed a few days before in Rush Bottom, in Jackson county, his right arm had literally been shot away at the shoulder, and it was touch and go whether he recovered or not. Frank James commanded the company, and gave it up to Anderson as soon as Anderson arrived within commanding distance, the aggregated column amounting to sixty-five rank and file. The march, begun on the morning of August 12th, 1874, was interrupted the same evening by an attack from seventy-five militia, near Fredericksburg, Ray county, who fought for a few moments as if they meant business, but Anderson's charge, led by such splendid pistol fighters as James Commons, Arch Clements, Tuck and Woot Hill, Bud Pence, Dick West, Frank and Jesse James and Peyton Long, swept the militia column away from the road and scattered it in every direction. Long's horse was killed, Zack Southerland was wounded severely in the leg, and Clements shot the commander of the scouting party, the notorious Captain Colly, whose loss in addition amounted to twenty-two. About noon of the next day, Theo. Castle, Peyton Long and Jesse James captured two couriers carrying a dispatch from Richmond to Chillicothe, narrating the rout and death of Colly, and warning all the posts to beware of impending danger. Pursuers also were gathering upon the trail and strengthening themselves as they followed it. The couriers were killed, and Anderson, understanding something of the position from the captured dispatch, pushed on boldly through Ray and Carroll counties, and halted near Flat Rock Ford, over Grand river, on the evening of the fourteenth. There lived at the house where the forage was obtained, distant from the camp a quarter of a mile, a virulent militiaman who knew the country well, and who watched keenly that the Guerrillas might be taken at an immense disadvantage. Theodore Castle and Hiram Guess were on guard in the rear of the halting place, vigilant and active, but the cunning spy avoided their lookout, gained the main road beyond them, and hurried on towards Richmond until he met a column of three hundred militia and one hundred and fifty Kansas Red Legs, under Col. Catherwood. These, guided by one who knew every inch of ground, dismounted at the foot of a ravine, crept up it to within gun shot, and had the camp, about two hundred yards distant, under the range of their guns before they were discovered. Frank James and Peyton Long shouted first to scare the negligent Guerrillas, and Anderson's voice—rising loud and full and high over the trampling of the horses and the ringing of the musketry—was as steady as the voice of a reaper reaping under a summer sky. "Quick, men! Half of you to bridle up and saddle up, and half of you to hold your own against the devils who won't leave one of you alive to tell the story of the massacre!" A cheer that pealed for miles over the prairie answered the dauntless words of Anderson, and in a second the camp was savage and aflame. To tug at uncertain girths under a biting fire, and bridle and saddle unruly horses when minie balls patter among them as rain drops, are things iron men must needs be a little nervous over; but just as all these things were done and well done, the other half of the Guerrilla force drove the Federals back and covered the balance of their comrades while they mounted and fell into line. Castle and Guess, cut off and isolated, charged home through a lane of fire, and Anderson, recovered perfectly and ready for the dash, rushed furiously upon the foe. The grapple, though momentary, was bloody. Peyton Long and Frank James fell first, each with a horse killed. Anderson next, and then Tuck Hill, the two last slightly wounded. Arch Clements took Anderson up behind him, Oll Shepherd, Frank James, and Broomfield, Long; but Long's revolver was instantly shot from his right hand, and Broomfield's horse, killed at the same time, sank beneath them. Dock Rupe, a gallant boy of seventeen, fell next to Jesse James, who had charged recklessly through the Federals and was charging back again, side by side with Cave Wyatt, McMacane, William Reynolds and William Hulse. Presently Jesse James

16

went down not twenty steps from the Federal ranks, making his third attack upon the line. When first hit he was seen to let his pistol drop and reel in the saddle. Recovering quickly, he drew another pistol and shot till he fell. The heavy ball of a Spencer rifle had struck him fair in the breast, cut through the right lung, and tore its way out at the back a short distance from the spine. Cave Wyatt went next, shot almost in the same place as James and quite as badly. Then McMacane, hurt badly in the left side; then Peyton Long, who had mounted another horse and dashed up to join in the savage *melee;* then William Reynolds fell close to James, his left arm broken; then Frank James, fighting over his brother, was shot again in the face and left leg; and finally Anderson himself received his second wound, a pistol ball in the thigh. When killed, Dock Rupe was leading the charge. Slight almost as a girl, just turned of seventeen, fair-haired and blue-eyed, the blood of some old Viking was surely in his veins, and kinship to that grim Lord of Colonsay who—

> "turn'd him on the ground,
> And laughed in death-pang, that his blade
> The mortal thrust so well repaid."

But the terrible grip of the Guerrillas was never relaxed until the whole Federal line, charged through and cut up, fell back to a stretch of heavy timber and reformed itself, with a loss of seventy-six killed and over one hundred wounded. Woot Hill, under a murderous fire, dismounted and took Rupe's pistols off, receiving the last words he ever spoke—a tender good-bye for his mother. All the wounded were protected by their comrades, Jesse James riding for five miles in great pain, when a wagon was procured, and he was hauled for three miles further. The pursuit, gathering again in the rear, threatening and ominous, warned Anderson that all who were crippled about the column must be hurried to places of safety. Jesse James was sent to the house of Captain John A. Rudd, in Carroll county, under the care of Gooly Robertson, Nat Tigue, Oll Shepherd, and Frank James. The next day they expected to bury him, for it was not supposed that he could live longer than that. Anderson kissed him as he parted from him, and Jesse took a ring from his finger and gave it to Peyton Long, for his sister, Miss Lizzie. Unremittingly nursed by Mrs. Rudd, who was an angel of good deeds in those terrible latter days of the war, and by Mr. and Mrs. S. Neale, he recovered rapidly. Wyatt was sent to Chariton, where he was soon after captured and held a prisoner until the war ended, the enemy never at any time ascertaining that he had been a Guerrilla. The balance of the wounded, hurt much less severely than Jesse James, found hiding places in Howard and Carroll. In Howard also Anderson disbanded until the 2d of September, his brother James—inferior in every fighting respect to William — operating a little along the main thoroughfares and losing an excellent soldier named Jourdan. Others of his squad likewise felt the grip of a bloody hand. Plunk Murray, Joe Holt, Robert Todd, Ed. Phillips, and Dof. Carroll, unsentineled, sat one day at dinner, talking pleasantly of pleasant things and laughingly. Sixty Federals surrounded the dwelling and demanded in the old way an instant surrender. All of the Guerrillas but Holt arose from the table and began to fire as they ran. Todd was killed, a Platte county man; Carroll was killed, a Clay county man; Murray and Phillips escaped, the first shot in the left arm and the second in the right leg, while Holt, a beardless boy, hiding his pistols and his tell-tale shirt, sat steadfast at the table and welcomed the militia as the son of the farmer who was feeding the Guerrillas. Five Federals were killed and three wounded; after being shot down Todd and Carroll had sold out for every life that was possible.

Concentrating rapidly on the 15th of September, Anderson had news brought to him that a Federal captain from Boonville, with seventy-six picked militia, well armed and mounted, was up among his hiding-places hunting for him. In the intervals of his boasting this Boonville officer robbed with an energy worthy of his organization. Sometimes Southern citizens were killed, and now and then an old man who was harmless. Anderson, from the hunted, became to be the hunter. Captain William Stuart, a desperate Guerrilla of much local reputation, was operating with ten men close to Anderson's rendezvous, and he sent James Commons, a swift rider, to Stuart, with orders to report to him. Stuart came speedily, and the Boonville raider was on the eve of annihilation.

Anderson, no less than Quantrell, Todd, Younger, Poole, Jarrette, Gregg, Haller, Yager, Taylor and all the balance of the earlier Guerrillas, had trained his men solely in the art of

horseback fighting. To halt, to wheel, to gallop, to run, to
swing from the saddle, to go at full speed bareback, to turn
as upon a pivot—to do all these things and shoot either with the
right hand or the left while doing them—this was Guerrilla drill
and Guerrilla discipline. Taking the first Federal fire at a splendid rush, they were to stop for nothing. No matter how many
saddles were emptied, the survivors—relying solely upon the
revolver—were to ride over whatever stood against the whirlwind or sought to check it in its terrible career. From the
mighty loins of such tactics as these the Centralia massacre
sprung.

Anderson, above everything else, desired to get the Boonville captain in such a position as to have an uninterrupted
chance at him for four or five hundred yards—such a chance as
would keep him from scattering his men all over an hundred
acre farm or as many acres of prairie land. With such a
purpose in view the Guerrilla chief found a long lane in close
proximity to the enemy, on either side of which was a heavy
rail fence. At the western extremity of this he formed his command in column of fours, sending ahead and through its entire
length twelve well-mounted men to fire upon the Federals
on the east and retreat rapidly back as if in confusion. To
deliver this blow there were chosen Clements, Stuart, Broomfield, Peyton Long, the two Hills, Richard West, James
Commons, the two Maupins—John and Thomas—Zack Southerland and Silas King, who rode forward cheerily upon their
mission, promising to bring back with them more than they
took away. Perhaps they might if they had obeyed orders.
When they found the Federals they converted a sham attack
into a real one, and charged the entire force headlong and
recklessly—twelve against seventy-six. The boaster from
Boonville made scarcely a halt—fired scarcely a single volley.
The race, for it certainly could be called nothing else, lasted
four miles, the Guerrillas killing twenty-three of the fugitives
and capturing forty horses. Anderson, although they returned
from the rout flushed and exultant, gave to Clements, the commander of the twelve, a reprimand that abode with him to the
day of his death.

Three days after this brilliant episode, James Bissett, John
Wilson, Harvey Brown, Thomas Fulton, and Sandy McMacane,

camped together in a stretch of timber, were surrounded by two hundred Federals. Bissett was from Clay county, Fulton and Brown from Platte, Wilson from Jackson, and McMacane from Louisiana. Those who died at Thermopylæ were not braver. The first Federal volley killed all their horses and shot down Bissett and Brown. They crawled each to a tree and fought there until the final rush came which finished them surely. Fulton, a man of powerful voice, cried out every now and then: "Boys, who's killed?" Once or twice he was answered: "No one yet; but the end is here." Presently Wilson did not reply. A carbine ball entered an eye, crashed through the brain, and killed him as he stood, pistol in hand and shooting. After his fifth wound, Fulton shouted for the last time in the fullness of his once magnificent voice: "Good-bye to all of you; I go but a little ways in advance!" Then McMacane, alone with the dead, fell first to his knees and next upon his face; then there was a great silence. The woods no longer offered any resistance save protest such as any corpse might make. Rushing from every quarter, and infuriated at a resistance which had cost them thirteen in killed and twenty-one in wounded, the Federals fired round after round into the already riddled bodies and scalped them afterwards to a man.

Later on Anderson left Ben Broomfield, Laing. Litten, and William Stuart to take care of Plunk Murray, whose right arm had been broken after the fight at Centralia. Forty Federals were after them hot. The splints of Murray's arm having become unloosed, the two ends of the bone jabbed at the flesh and hurt him intolerably as he rode. Broomfield and Stuart, talking together for a few moments in consultation, bade Litten leave the main road with the crippled Guerrilla while they turned about sharp and charged the head of the column in pursuit. It was the last chance and a desperate one. Side by side, and devoting themselves to almost absolute death, these two single-hearted men dashed at the enemy. They simply drove ahead and fought. They killed six of the pursuers and wounded three, but at the further end of the lane through which they charged, Broomfield fell dead from his horse, and Stuart, shot twice and scarcely able to ride, turned off into some timber and made his escape. After the war an Illinois cattle drover shot him for his money while he was asleep.

Ben Broomfield was a splendid specimen of that class of border men who, living on the confines of the great plains, were part citizen and part Comanche. He rode as an arrow might, changed into a *vaquero* and put upon a mustang. The natural bronze of his face having been deepened by wind and weather, Anderson called him his Indian. He had recently married a beautiful young lady of Lexington, a Miss Jordan, and when the enemy came upon him her picture was upon his heart.

Suffering from a wound in the right leg and one through the left shoulder, John Coger had been carried by his comrades to a house close to Big creek, in Cass county, and carried at that when it was night and by no road that was generally travelled. Coger, without a wound of some kind or in some portion of the body, would have appeared as unaccountable to the Guerrillas as a revolver without a mainspring. At the end of every battle some one reckless fighter asked of another: "Of course John Coger can't be killed, but where is he hit this time?" And Coger himself—no matter how often and how badly hurt— scarcely ever waited for an old wound to get well before he was in the front of a fight looking for a new one. He is alive to-day, it is true, but full of lead as a bag of bullets.

The wonderful nerve of the man saved him many times dur- ing the war in open and desperate conflicts, but never where the outlook was so unpromising as it was now and the chances as fifty to one and not in his favor. Despite his two hurts, Coger would dress himself every day and hobble about the house, watching all the roads for Federals. His pistols were kept under the bolster of his bed. One day a scout of sixty militia approached the house so suddenly that Coger had barely time to undress him- self and hurry into bed, dragging in with him his clothes, his boots, his tell-tale overshirt, and his four revolvers. Without the help of the lady of the house he surely would have been lost. To save him she surely—well she did not tell the truth.

The sick man lying there was her husband, weak of a fever. Bottles were about, ostentatiously displayed for the occasion. At intervals Coger groaned and ground his teeth, the brave, true woman standing close at the bedside, wiping his brow every now and then and putting some kind of smelling stuff to his lips. A Federal soldier, perhaps a bit of a doctor, felt Coger's left wrist, held it awhile, shook his head, and murmured seriously: "A bad case, madam, a bad case indeed. Most likely pneumonia." Coger groaned again. "Are you in pain, dear?" the ostensible wife tenderly enquired. "Dreadful!" and a spasm of agony shot over the bushwhacker's sun-burnt face. For nearly an hour the Federal soldiers came and went, and looked upon the sick man moaning in his bed, as deadly a Guerrilla as ever mounted a horse or fired a pistol. Once the would-be doctor skirted the edge of the precipice so closely that if he had stepped a step further he would have pitched headlong into the abyss. He insisted upon making a minute examination of Coger's lungs and laid a hand upon a coverlet to uncover the patient. Coger held his breath hard and felt upward for a revolver. The least inspection would have ruined him. Nothing could explain the ugly wound, suppurating and ragged, in the left shoulder, nothing the older yet not entirely healed wound in the right leg. The iron man, however, did not wince. He neither made protest nor yielded acquiescence. He meant to kill the doctor, kill as many more as he could while life and his pistol balls lasted, and be carried from the room, when he was carried at all, feet foremost and limp as a lock of hair. Happily the woman's wit saved him. She pushed away the doctor's hand from the coverlet and gave as the emphatic order of her family physician that the sick man should not be disturbed until his return. Etiquette saved John Coger, for it was so unprofessional for one physician to interfere with another physician's patient that the Federal left the room and afterwards the house.

Press Webb was a born scout crossed upon a Highlander. He had the eye of an eagle and the endurance of the red deer. He first taught himself coolness, and then he taught it to others. In traveling he did not travel twice the same road. Many more were like him in this—so practicing the same kind of woodscraft and cunning—until the enemy began to say: "That man Quantrell has a thousand eyes."

Press Webb was ordered one day to take with him Sim Whitsett, George Maddox, Harrison Trow and Noah Webster and hide himself anywhere in the vicinity of Kansas City that would give him a good view of the main roads leading east from it, and a reasonably accurate insight into the comings and goings of the Federal troops. The weather was very cold.

Some snow had fallen the week before, had melted, the ground
had frozen again, until everywhere over the country a polished
surface of ice made traveling generally difficult and traveling
over the roads well-nigh impossible. The Guerrillas, however,
prepared themselves well for the expedition, and their horses
better. Other cavalrymen were forced to remain comparatively
inactive, but Quantrell's men were coming and going, and
killing here and there, and daily.

On the march to his field of operations, Webb overtook two
Kansas infantrymen five miles west from Independence and on
the old Independence road. That their foraging expedition had
been successful, the load which each soldier staggered under
gave abundant testimony. One had a goose, two turkeys, a
sack of dried apples, some yarn socks, a basket full of eggs and
the half of a cheese; while the other—more powerful or more
greedy than his companion—toiled slowly homeward, carrying
carefully over the slippery highway a huge bag miscellaneously
filled with butter, sausages, parched and unparched coffee, the
head of a recently killed hog, some wheaten biscuit not remark-
ably well cooked, more cheese, and probably a peck of green
jenniton apples. As Webb and his four men rode up the Kansas
foragers halted and dispossessed themselves of their loads as if
to rest. Piled about them, each load was almost as large as
its owner.

Webb remarked that they were not armed and enquired of
the nearest forager—him of the dried apples—why he ventured
so far from headquarters without his gun. "There is not need
of a gun," was the reply, "because the fighting rebels are all
out of the country, and the stay-at-home ones are all subjugated.
What we want we take, and we generally want a good deal."
"A blind man might see that," Webb rather grimly rejoined,
"but suppose some of Quantrell's cut-throats were to ride up
to you as we have done, stop to talk to you as we have done,
draw out a pistol as I do this minute, cover you thus, and bid
you surrender as I now do, you infernal thief and son of a thief,
what would you say then?" "Say!" and the look of simple
surprise yet cool indifference which came to the Jayhawker's
face was the strongest feature of the tragedy—"what could I
say else but that you are the cut-throat and I am the victim.
Caught fairly, I can understand the balance. Be quick.'

Then the Jayhawker rose up from the midst of his spoils with a sort of quiet dignity, lifted his hat as if to let his brow feel the north wind, and faced without a tremor the pistol which covered him. "I cannot kill you so," Webb faltered, "nor do I know whether I can kill you at all. We must take a vote first." Then to himself: "To shoot an unarmed man, and a brave man at that, is awful."

There amid the sausages and the cheese, the turkeys and the coffee grains, the dried applies and the green, five men sat upon two in judgment. Whitsett held the hat; Webster fashioned the ballots. No argument was had. The five self-appointed jurors were five among Quantrell's best and bravest. In extremity they had always stood forth ready to fight to the death; in the way of killing they had done their share. The two Kansas Jayhawkers came close together as if in the final summing up they might find in the mere act of dying together something of solacement. One by one the Guerrillas put into the hat of Whitsett a little piece of paper written upon. All had voted. Harrison Trow drew forth the ballots silently. As he unfolded the first and read from it deliberately: "*Death!*" the younger Jayhawker blanched to his chin and put a hand on the shoulder of his comrade. The two listened to the count with every human faculty aroused and abnormally impressionable. Not understanding the *animus* of the scene being enacted amid such unromantic surroundings, a passer-by would have halted as he róde and wondered what a bare-headed man was doing there with his hat in his hand, why five were heavily armed and two not armed at all, why lying loosely about were the spoils of hen-roost and larder, why all the faces were sternly set, and all the eyes bent keenly forward to where one grave, calm man was unfolding a dirty slip of crumpled paper and reading therefrom something that was short like a monosyllable and sepulchral like a shroud.

"*Life!*" said the second vote, and "*Life!*" said the third. The fourth was for death and made a tie. Something like the beating of a strong man's heart might have been heard, and something as though a brave man was breathing painfully through his teeth lest a sigh escaped him. Whitsett cried out: "One more ballot yet to be opened. Let it tell the tale, Trow, and make an end of this thing speedily." Trow, with scarcely any more emotion than a surgeon has when he probes a bullet-wound, unfolded the remaining slip of paper and read aloud and mechanically: *"Life!"* The younger Jayhawker fell upon his knees, the elder ejaculated solemnly: "Thank God! How glad my wife will be." Webb breathed as one from whose breast a great load had been lifted, and put back into its scabbard his unerring revolver. The verdict surprised him all the more because it was so totally unexpected, and yet the two men there—Jayhawkers though they were and loaded with the spoils of plundered farm-houses—were as free to go as the north wind that blew or the stream that was running by. As they rode away the Guerrillas did not even suggest to one another the virtue of a parole. At the two extremities of their peculiar warfare there was either life or death. Having chosen deliberately as between the two, no middle ground was known to them. Their richest *largesse* was liberty, and if this were handicapped ever so lightly, or made to limp or halt when its wings should have been as the eagle's, the Guerrilla condemned himself for having done a cowardly thing or permitted himself, according to his creed, to become a party to a mean one.

Press Webb approached to within sight of Kansas City from the old Independence road; made a complete circle about the place, as difficult as the traveling was; entered Westport notwithstanding the presence of a garrison there; heard many things told of the plans and numbers of the Federal forces upon the border; passed down between the Kansas river and what is now known as West Kansas City; killed three foragers and captured two six-mule wagons near to the site of the present gas works; gathered up five head of excellent horses, and concealed himself for two days in the Blue Bottom watching a somewhat notorious bawdy house much frequented by Federal officers and soldiers. These kind of houses during the war, and when located upon dangerous or debatable ground, were man-traps of more or less sinister histories. Eleven women belonged to this bangio proper, but on the night Webb stalked it and struck it, there had come five additional inmates from other quarters equally as disreputable. Altogether, the male attendants numbered twenty, two lieutenants, one sergeant major, a corporal, four citizens, and twelve privates from an Iowa regiment. Webb's attacking column, not much longer than a yard-stick, was composed of the original detail, four besides himself.

The night was dark. The nearest timber to the house was two hundred and fifty yards. There was ice on everything. The trampling of iron-shod feet reverberated as artillery wheels over frozen ground. At the timber line Maddox suggested that one man should be left in charge of the horses, but Webb overruled the point. "No man will stir to-night," he argued, "except he be hunting for either war or women. The horses are safe here. Let us dismount and make them fast."

As they crept to the house in single file a huge dog went at Harrison Trow as if he would not be denied, and barked so furiously, and made so many other extravagant manifestations of rage, that a man and a woman came to the door of the house and bade the dog devour the disturber. Thus encouraged, he leaped full at Trow's throat and Trow shot him dead. In a moment the house emptied itself of its male occupants, who explored the darkness, found the dog with a bullet through his head, searched everywhere for the author of the act, saw no man, however, nor heard any retreating footsteps, and so returned unsatisfied to the house, yet returned, which was a great deal. As for the Guerrillas, as soon as Trow found himself obliged to shoot or be throttled, they rushed back as swiftly as possible and as noiselessly to their horses, mounted them and waited. A pistol shot unless explained is always sinister to soldiers. It is not to be denied. Fighting men never fire at nothing. This is a maxim not indigenous to the brush, nor an outcome from the philosophy of those who made war there. A pistol shot says in so many words: "Something is coming, is creeping, is crawling, is about—look out!" The Federals heard this one—just as pertinent and as intelligible as any that was ever fired—but they failed to interpret aright this significant language of the ambuscade, and they suffered accordingly.

Webb waited an hour in the cold, listening. No voices were heard, no skirmishers approached his position, no scouts from the house hunted further away than the lights in the windows shone, no alarm had been raised, and he dismounted again with his men and again approached the house. By this time it was well on to twelve o'clock. Chickens were crowing in every direction. The north wind had risen high and was blowing as

a winter wind always blows when there are shelterless men
abroad in a winter night. The house, a rickety frame, was two
stories high, with two windows on the north and two on the
south. George Maddox looked in at one of these windows and
counted fourteen men, some well advanced in liquor and some
sober and silent and confidential with the women. None were
vigilant. The six up stairs were neither seen nor counted. At
first it was difficult to agree upon a plan of procedure. All the
Federals were armed, and twenty armed men holding a house
against five are generally apt, whatever else may happen, to get
the best of the fighting. "We cannot fire through the windows," said Webb, "for the women are in the way." "Certainly," replied Whitsett; "we do not war on women." "We
cannot get the drop on them," added Trow, "because we cannot get to them." "True again," replied Maddox, "but I
have an idea which will simplify matters amazingly. On the
south there is a stable half full of plank and provender. It will
burn like pitch-pine. The wind is from the north strong, and it
will blow away all danger from the house. Were it otherwise I
would fight against the torch, for not even a badger should be
turned out of his hole to-night on word of mine, much less a
lot of women. See for yourselves and say if the plan suits you."

They saw, endorsed the proposition, and put a match at once
to the hay and to the bundles of dry fodder. Before the fire
had increased perceptibly the five men warmed their hands at it
and laughed; they were getting the frost out of their fingers to
shoot well, they said. A delicate trigger-touch is necessary to a
dead shot.

"Fire!" All of a sudden there was a great flare of flames, a
shriek from the women, and a shout from the men. The north
wind drove full head upon the stable, and the stable roared as
some great wild beast in pain. The Federals, *en masse*, rushed
to the rescue. Not all caught up their arms as they hurried
out, not all were even dressed. The women looked from the
doors and the windows of the dwelling, and made certain thus
the killing which followed. Beyond the glare of the burning
out-house, and massed behind a fence fifty paces to the right
of the consuming stable, the Guerrillas fired five deadly volleys
into the surprised and terrified mass before—scattered, panic-
stricken and cut to pieces—the remnant frantically regained the

sheltering mansion. Eight were killed where they stood about
the fire; two, mortally wounded, died afterwards; one, wounded
and disabled, quit the service; five, severely or slightly wounded,
recovered; and four, unhurt, reported that night in Kansas
City that Quantrell had attacked them with two hundred men,
and had been driven off, hurt and badly worsted, after three-
quarters of an hour's fight. Press Webb and his four men did
what work was done in less than five minutes.

Sometimes Guerrilla met Guerrilla, yet in no single instance
did the Federal Guerrilla fight as bravely as the regular Federal
soldier. Indeed, the business of the Federal Guerrilla was to
fight just as little as possible. Generally a deserter from one
army or the other, and sometimes from both, he made his home
in the mountains or the broken places where there were frequented roads and preyed upon the passers by. In Arkansas,
this species of predatory soldier was called Boomer and Mountain Boomer. He was at times formidable because he knew the
blind paths, the water courses, the caverns, the inaccessible
retreats, and the invisible hiding places. Commanding a band
of fifty equally alert as himself, and equally at home among the
cliffs and the crags, the Boomer harmed most the lines of communication, and ambuscaded most the couriers and the convoys.
There was a band in 1863 which had a chief named Gordon.
Its operations extended from Van Buren, on the Arkansas
river, to Dardanelle, on the same stream. Couriers were killed,
citizens robbed, supply trains cut off, small squads of Confederates ambushed, marching columns fired upon, and isolated
Southern soldiers betrayed and murdered.

General Holmes ordered General Shelby to do something with
Gordon's band. He had a *carte blanche* to capture it, break it
up, destroy it, decimate it, obliterate it—make the wild places
that had once known it know it no more forever. Shelby had
men who could do anything, who would fight anything, who
needed only a command to attack an ironclad with revolvers.
Shelby himself, if he had not been a general, would have been
a scout or a partisan, seeking adventure as a knight-errant
sought it under Hawkwood or Chandos, and fighting single
combats as Tancred fought them or Ivanhoe. His theory as a
commander was first to make the individual brave, next the
company through the soldier, next the regiment through the

company, and then the brigade through the regiment. First of all, however, he required the individual to be enterprising, more or less handy with a pistol, more or less *en rapport* with his horse, more or less willing to seek for a fight, and *always* ready to stand shoulder to shoulder with the comrade upon his left hand or his right and bide the issue out. Hence for four long years, and whether with a company or a division, this man never knew a rout or a disaster. Beaten back he was, unquestionably; worsted here and there, yes; cut up often and shaken severely, without a doubt; hard bestead many times and enveloped front and rear, certainly—but there lives not any to-day who fought him who truthfully can say that Jo Shelby did not fight as he ran, did not fight always, fight hard, fight fast, fight desperately, and fight just the same upon a victorious field as a stricken one.

Gordon, the Arkansas Boomer, was a young man who had belonged to the Confederate army. On duty east of the Mississippi river, and in command of a company, he sought and was refused a leave of absence to visit his home among the mountains close to Dardenelle. Not long thereafter he deserted, eluded the cavalry sent to capture him, made his way back to his old haunts among the river hills, and defied the authorities. The transition was both easy and natural from a deserter to a robber, and Gordon preyed upon friend and foe alike. Equally with the Confederates the Federals felt the cruelty of his reprisals, but despite the blows dealt them, and the opportunities improved of predatory warfare upon their commissary stores and their supply trains, they constantly furnished Gordon with ammunition. Operating in a country where every natural thing was found to be an enemy, perhaps more friendship than enmity was really conceived for this band of Boomers, who while they killed and plundered every unwary or unlucky Federal, killed also and plundered every unwary or unlucky Confederate.

Gordon was brave, and Shelby, therefore, chose a brave man to exterminate him. William H. Gregg had most of the constituent elements of military genius which nature furnishes to energetic characters—untroubled perspicacity in confusion, firm decision, rapid execution, providence against attack, fertility of resource, and abounding stratagem. When the case was called, two days after Holmes had made known his wishes in the matter, the case stood Gregg versus Gordon.

Colonel John T. C.isp commanded the post at Dardenelle, a town at that time in the midst of what might be truly called a dark and bloody ground. An important crossing place on the Arkansas river, the Confederates held it for the good it might do, and the Federals swarmed about it for the harm it had done. Colonel Crisp was not only a soldier of eminent enterprise and ability, but a most excellent military governor as well for one so young and so inexperienced. His mind—just, comprehensive, and logical in both observation and analysis—sought always for the happy mean which could bring the civil and the military authority face to face without quarreling. He recognized the right of the Revolution to everything the South possessed, but he believed that the right need never be stained by an injustice, nor the exigencies of the civil war changed into a cruel and irresponsible despotism. The last man, the last dollar, the last pound of food and forage he would undoubtedly take to supply the armies in the field; but in taking them he so exalted the virtuous magnanimity of patriotism that a sudden fire came to the breasts of the lukewarm, and a sudden hope to the souls of the timid and the wavering. Faction he remorselessly suppressed, but honest differences of opinion he reasonably combatted or left unnoticed and altogether alone. In battle brilliant, intrepid, and successful; in council firm, emphatic, and swift in conclusion; in administration bold, honest, fair-minded, and thoroughly informed, Shelby called him sometimes his military governor and sometimes his chief-justice. Charged with several delicate and difficult missions, and required twice to exercise authority where grave if not to say serious complications had arisen, so keen was his analysis, so logical were his propositions, so fair and just was his summing up that intractable men admitted his wisdom, and ungovernable and intolerant men the righteousness of his adjudication.

Col. Crisp was on duty at Dardenelle when Capt. Gregg reported to him. Crisp knew all about Gordon. He had fought him and worsted him once; at another time he had chased him and lost him in the mountains; twice he had planned to trap and take him; and finally, whatever could be done to help Gregg forward in the work marked out to do, that thing should be done speedily and well.

Gregg had with him some of Quantrell's old Guerrillas— some of his own in fact—the heroes of fifty desperate combats. Sim Whitsett was there, and George Maddox, Harrison Trow, John Coger, Press Webb, Henry Hockensmith, John Ecket, Fletch Taylor, Andy Blunt, Andy Walker, Dan Vaughn, John Poole, and enough more of the old hands to make twenty-five, and these, together with twenty-five regular Confederates under Arthur McCoy, constituted the entire force. It was not large, fifty-two in all, including the two commanders. McCoy reported to Gregg.

An average Boomer was not generally gregarious. He preferred to do his devilment with as little assistance as possible. Two only frequently hunted together, frequently four, or six, or ten, but very rarely more than twenty. A master spirit among the mountains, however, like Gordon, or Hart, or Parker, or Peter Tolliver, nicknamed Dandelion, preferred a band of fifty. Tolerably accurate information made Gordon's band no smaller, and when asked what number of men he required to make of his expedition a success, Gregg answered promptly and as if a little surprised by the question: "Just fifty, of course. I hear Gordon has only fifty."

All legs, and eagerness, and animal spirit McCoy reported to Gregg as a school-boy might report to his master for a holiday. McCoy laughed a great deal, Gregg scarcely any at all; McCoy sang a song now and then that was next of kin to a bird's song, Gregg was a taciturn, unmusical man; McCoy's face was always mirthful, Gregg's always in repose and as strong as Cromwell's. As steadfast, heroic, and unconquerable fighters, neither could be surpassed.

Col. Crisp entered heartily into the spirit of the expedition, and made haste in every way to ration it and equip it for the unrelenting hunt. For a week Gregg sought Gordon in every direction. Three of his men were encountered and killed, but they were killed so quickly that if they knew they were not accorded time enough to tell aught of their chief. At Van Buren no one knew anything of his whereabouts; on Frog Bayou an old man once lived who had been robbed by him, but the old man had migrated further south; in Ozark he had friends who fled to him with information on the approach of the Confederates, and at Lewisburg the trail grew suddenly cold and finally gave out altogether. Gregg returned, empty-handed and unsuccessful, to Dardenelle.

Meanwhile Crisp—indefatigable and alert—had found a woman who knew Gordon and who had a grievance. Women were made available more frequently during the war than is generally supposed. Shelby used them often as spies, sometimes as scouts, twice or thrice as couriers, and always with satisfaction or success. Most generally revenge was at the bottom of their actions. They loved the South strongly, it is true, but at the same time they hated some one particular person in the ranks of the enemy who had done them grievous wrong or inflicted upon them some mortal injury. The woman—about to become Gregg's guide and Gordon's Nemesis—was young, passably pretty, not strictly prepossessing, yet as relentless in pursuit and as courageous in action as any red Indian bred to the war-path and made stoical by barbarism. Her name—Agnes Masterson—was spoken once about many a camp fire, and the story of her life told in many a cheerless marching night or in many a shelterless bivouac. Her parents were from Tennessee and possessed of a farm close to Dardenelle and north of the river. Before the war her father had died, but her mother—self-reliant, vigorous, and helped by her children—held to the homestead, fought life's battle boldly and energetically, and made headway, year by year. Agnes, at twenty, loved a neighbor's son and was in turn beloved by him. How passionately she loved him she herself did not know until she was bereft of him. The war came, and at a drum beat the lover was changed into a soldier. As he marched away he took her in his arms, kissed her, and said to her: "If I live, wait for me." She did wait—patiently, loyally, womanly. One day the lover returned—bronzed, shot, just able to stretch out his poor crippled arms to his darling and rest himself as he leant upon her breast. Four nights after the return of the wounded Confederate soldier, Gordon attacked the house at which he was being cured, and killed him. The blood was yet upon the floor in great splotches when the girl got to the dead man and covered him with caresses before all the crowd. Then she arose, dry-eyed and disdainful. "Why do you stand gaping here?" she demanded fiercely of the old men present; "why do you mutter among yourselves and shake your empty heads? Can't the
17

oldest among you march, and fight, and shoot as well as a
woman?'' Then she broke down all of. a sudden, wept pitifully
until the corpse was given to the coffin, brooded long at home
in utter seclusion, and mourned truly for her lost love a year and
a day. Had she forgotten? Let the sequel say!

Colonel Crisp had heard this story told in numberless ways
long before Gregg was put upon the track of Gordon, but the
times were unfavorable for the cultivation of either much
romance or sentiment. He heard the tale as it was told to him,
and then it was forgotten. Gregg's quest for Gordon revived
the memory of it, and the girl was sought for and found. No
instrument possible could be more pliant or intelligent. Since
her lover's brutal murder she had never ceased to remember him
or scheme to have his death avenged. Day and night she
brooded over it and dwelt upon a consummation. It mingled
with her dreams while sleeping and with her thoughts while busy
with her household duties. Outwardly she had forgotten the
past to all appearances; inwardly the fever burned without
abatement. .So steadfastly had she pursued her plan of vengeance, and so sure was she that some day God would hear her
pleadings, that she forced her eldest brother to join the Boomers and gain for her all the information that she needed to have of
their fortified points and their hiding places. Twice she had
grown desperate or impatient and had debated within her own
mind whether, if she dressed as a man and became a member
of the band herself, she might not be able to hasten a denouement. If none had known her among the Gordon following, it
is probable she would have tried 'the venture. Exposed as she
would have been, however, and hourly in danger of recognition,
she took counsel with her brother and trusted implicitly to his
courage and discretion.

Miss Masterson and Col. Crisp soon reached an understanding. Her first act was to entice her brother home and to
deliver him up by agreement to Capt. Gregg. Gregg sent him
to Shelby with a full explanation of the entire transaction, and
Shelby, the young man nothing loth, made out of him an excellent Confederate soldier. Then the sister mounted her horse,
put herself at the head of Gregg's column, gathered up the
reins in her left hand as any cavalryman, and spoke quietly to
the commander: "I am ready. It is such a blessing to be

with brave men once more!'' Col. Crisp accompanied the column, which marched rapidly. Modest, uncommunicative, riding always at the side of Gregg, this female guide—strange to the men and the subject of much comment—seemed devoured by an insatiable desire to get forward. Every request she preferred was one for speed. The last to retire and the first to arise, by degrees she communicated her own sleepless activity to the men and they in turn demanded longer marches and greater energy.

Gordon's fastnesses were being approached. Up towards the Boston mountains, and three days' journey north from Ozark, a road turned off to the right from the main road and lost itself in a valley which by degrees lost itself in a series of mountains, one above another. Two miles from the eastern edge of the valley Gordon had built a block-house of unhewn logs. About the block-house were palisades, and all about the palisades, though outside of them, were cabins where the wives of the married men of his band sometimes dwelt or tarried. Miss Masterson turned from the main road at the proper place, picked her intricate way through the valley as if it had been the valley of her nativity, halted at its eastern verge, and bade the column wait for her while she reconnoitered. A house was close to the halting-place, inhabited by a man whom she knew well, she said, and thither she went at a gallop, dismounted, and entered in. In twenty minutes she returned with her face radiant. Gordon, with thirty-eight of his men, had passed through to his hiding-place two days before, since which time the firing of guns and the occasional shout of a soldier had convinced the old man at whose house she had been that the Boomers at their rendezvous were still unsuspicious of any approach and still intact. ''Good!'' said Crisp, ''we will stalk them to-night and attack them in the morning.'' Gregg acquiesced, and McCoy, given ten men, was ordered to advance half a mile up the mountain and wait until midnight for the final advance.

Gordon's late carryings on had been successful and extensive. He had captured several wagons, robbed two stores, burnt four or five houses, killed three straggling soldiers, driven off much stock, and escaped into his mountain with all of the booty. If he had heard of Gregg, or the hunt Gregg was making, he made no sign. He neither quickened his pace nor circumscribed the area of his operations. Burdened with plunder and weary from long marching, he had simply returned to his fastnesses to distribute the spoils and look to the horses.

The Boomers had no picquets out. Guided surely and silently by Agnes Masterson up to the very eaves of the houses where the doomed men, buried in deep sleep, snored and slumbered, the Guerrillas under Gregg and the Confederates under McCoy swept everything before them ere it was yet light enough in the east to distinguish black hair from brown. Some, scarcely awake, died rolled in their blankets. Some, swift to escape if escape were possible, rushed without knowing it upon cool men used to shoot and prone to spare not. A few, snatching such arms as came first to hand, fought as wild beasts fight who are trapped and maimed. The woman would not be denied a place where the firing was hottest. Gregg sought to force her away from the front. McCoy turned her horse's head and bade her go away from the danger line. Crisp reasoned with her and expostulated ; but stay she would and did until the murderous combat was done. Gordon fell among the first, shot by Gregg himself as he rushed from a cabin to escape. Instead of the thirty-eight supposed at first to be with this desperate Boomer, there were sixty-three all told among his followers, seven old men who neither fought nor were harmed, though probably as bad as the worst of the lot, and fifty-six stalwart, strapping young fellows who might have held their own, fortified as they were, against heavy odds if in the first moments of an inexcusable surprise they had not been caught and crushed. Four only of these were taken alive, fifty-two dying where they fought, fighting as best they could to the last. Gregg, with a loss of three killed and eleven wounded, returned to Dardenelle in triumph, after having literally exterminated a band of Confederate and Federal deserters more to be dreaded by the defenceless people whom they preyed upon and plundered than an army of occupation. In further testimony also of the brilliant affair, Colonel Crisp, in a singularly clear and interesting history, made General Shelby acquainted with the details of the somewhat romantic yet thoroughly practical adventure. Gen. Shelby in turn transmitted Crisp's report to Gen. Holmes, and in the end Gregg became a hero and Miss Masterson the talk of the border.

After the combat at the block-house was done, she sought among the slain for Gordon until she found him. He had been sleeping in the cabin nearest the road and had not waited either to put on his upper garments or his boots. Gregg's bullet, entering just below the right eye, had torn through the brain and out through the back of the head. But as ghastly as the face was, this woman gazed upon it long and fixedly and utterly without emotion. Other corpses were about, but these she either avoided or showed pity for. Gordon's attracted her until the men were all mounted and ready to march. As she left it for the last time she spurned it with her foot and her lips moved. Did she curse the disfigured heap lying there unburied for the hogs to eat? Perhaps so! She had loved in a wild, passionate way, and she was human.

There was killed also on the thirteenth of July, of this year, 1863, a young man just turned of twenty-two, whose army life was made up equally of romance and tragedy. Joseph Hart was a Missourian born, tall, sinewy, unusually well educated and more than ordinarily intelligent. His dark gray eyes were frank, yet penetrating. His broad brow, prominent if not to say bulging above the eyes, indicated in need or peril great fertility of resource and much rapidity of execution. Many people, before he had even remarked them himself, spoke often of his small white hands. His mouth was cruel, his chin heavy, his jaws square and covered scantily by a thin red beard, his head fixed firmly upon a massive neck, while his legs had just enough of the curve to make what the Guerrillas called a natural rider. He did not talk a great deal at any time, he boasted never. Seeing everything, he was surprised at nothing. Constantly in practice, no more deadly revolver was known along the border. Quantrell recruited him early in the war, and Shelby took him from Quantrell for a spy. "He has what a spy requires," Shelby sententiously said, as he wrote out himself the order for his transfer, "he has innocence, audacity and common sense." Hart reported to Shelby for duty, but was soon demanded by General Price and given up to him by Shelby just as he had been given up to Shelby by Quantrell. Evidently the young man was in demand. In August, 1862, he was captured in front of Corinth and carried into the presence of Gen. Grant, who interrogated him at length and dismissed him without obtaining the information he sought, but with an order that required his provost marshal to care for him well and guard him carefully. That night Hart escaped. A concealed Derringer pistol, overlooked in the imperfect search of the regular soldiers who were the first to capture him, and who had no skill in the handy ways of the thief-taker or the jailor, was the key which unlocked his prison door. The guard-house, if the term is not a misnomer, was a huge tent, or rather a series of tents. At the door of this a single sentinel stood, while outside of it and far away a *cordon* of other sentinels, near together, alert and vigilant, made a circle that to be avoided had first to be broken through. Sure of the guard at the door, Hart would take the fire of the balance and take his chances in the rush that succeeded it.

At about twelve o'clock he arose from his blanket and crept noiselessly to the door of the tent. A stalwart infantryman was there, his minie musket at a carry. As he walked to and fro, so stately and so calm, Hart's conscience rose upon and mastered him for a moment. "I cannot kill him thus," he said to himself; "I cannot kill him at all if he looks at me." He held his breath and waited a long time, so long that he imagined it must soon be the hour for a change of guards. Then he looked out again for the second time. The night was neither dark nor light. There was no moon, but the stars shone and the sky was azure. From the tent to the timber the distance was probably two hundred yards, the cleared place of the encampment being thick with stumps, logs and brush heaps. Slow-paced and silent, those blue figures meeting and retiring— so voiceless, so mechanical, so grim like phantoms—were trained soldiers doing duty on the guard line. Hart's conscience no longer hurt him. He reasoned now as a desperate man who meant to do a desperate deed, but who meant to do it bravely and face to face. The sentinel paced to and fro, his minie musket still at a carry. For half an hour he had neither quickened his pace nor shifted his gun. The man was both a man and a machine—sentient, yet impassive, harmless, yet full of danger, voiceless, yet lynx-eyed and intrepid.

Hart might have shot him in the back, but he would not. If he killed him at all, he would kill him as he looked into his face. He drew a long breath, marked once well the general direction he had to take, drew the derringer from its hiding place and sprang upon the infantryman at the moment when in pacing his beat he had come the nearest to the door of the guard tent. The sentinel did not speak. There was no time to speak. The glance of a second revealed the situation, and he strove to kill the prisoner as the prisoner rushed upon him. As a panther might leap upon a deer, Hart leaped upon his antagonist, sending, as he grappled with him and threw up his musket with his left hand, a heavy derringer bullet through his neck and spine. The sentinel fell, helpless as a willow wand, and Hart sprang away through the *cordon* of the outer sentinels to the timber. Fifty shots and more were fired at him. As he ran he dodged here behind a stump, there behind a log heap, but halting nowhere. When he reached the timber he was safe. The next day at noon he was at the headquarters of General Price.

Still doing duty as a spy, and still living with his life in his open hand daily, Hart was a private in George Todd's company in 1863. His Captain, in January of that year, sent him to St. Joseph for pistol caps. He fulfilled his mission to the letter, purchasing and sending safely through the lines a noteworthy cargo; but as he came away from the town the utter recklessness of his character—made more thoroughly indifferent by two years of constant peril and hair breadth escapes—caused him to charge a picquet post furiously, cut through it, kill and wound seven of the soldiers, and get safely way for the time. A detachment of cavalry pursued him, however, overtook him, fought him a running fight for eleven miles, and finally killed his horse and captured its rider. Hart was carried back to St. Joseph and placed, heavily ironed, in a dungeon. In the morning after his incarceration of the night before, the manacles put upon his wrists were lying at his feet in the cell. In explanation he was quite frank with his jailor, and showed him his two hands—the smallness and perfect shapeliness of which other people had long before remarked—and argued from them the impossibility of their being fettered. The jailor—a bit of a joker in his way, albeit a cruel one—tapped the handle of his pistol significantly and remarked: "For such people as have hands like you, I keep this. Beware! The first time a reprimand; the last time a revolver bullet." Hart bowed gravely;

"It's good logic, that of your's, and it suits *me*. Will it work both ways?" "How both ways?" "Will you endorse it if our positions are ever reversed, and while I keep the keys you wear the handcuffs?" "I will endorse it." Two days afterward Hart could not be found. The jailor searched his cell. There he saw the manacles of his wrists lying as before upon the floor. The chains with which his ankles had been bound were sawed completely in two. The lock upon the door of the dungeon had been tampered with. None of the guards about the premises knew anything of the escape, but Hart was gone from the jail, gone from the yard of the jail, gone from the town, and this everybody interested understood. An exhaustive search revealed nothing further. Perhaps those charged with his custody have not learned to this day the secret of his escape, but the deputy jailor might have told all about it then, for he was bought for two hundred dollars and furnished the tools Hart needed for his purpose.

In April, 1863, Hart was again in custody. Prowling about Lawrence, Kansas, and making an occasional raid down in the direction of Fort Scott, Jennison laid hands upon him, tried him, and sentenced him to be shot. Arrested on the 4th, dealt with by the court-martial on the 5th, and given a day for prayer and preparation, it was not until the 7th that the fusillade decreed on the 5th was to finish him. Tried at a house eight miles from Olathe, it was thought necessary to send him to the headquarters of the regiment at Kansas City. Evidently none knew Hart; certainly none knew the kind of a man the court-martial had just finished with. A clumsy pair of hand-cuffs, all that could be found, was put about his hands, and with these on Hart was made to mount into a wagon, an armed soldier sitting beside him and keeping him ever under observation. As an escort ten cavalrymen accompanied the wagon. Hart's feet were not even tied, nor his arms, and surely not his tongue. He talked gently, discreetly, and with more or less of interest. Once or twice he noticed the driver take his eyes from the road to listen to him, and once or twice he believed he saw the grim vigilance of his guard relax a little. Night came while the cavalcade was yet some miles distant from Kansas City, and before a heavy stretch of bottom land west from the town had been passed through. The mounted escort behind the wagon had

long before forgotten to keep closed up, the driver was whistling
on his seat, and the taciturn guard—not strongly of the opinion
that his prisoner was either a very bold or a very dangerous
man—had put the pistol which he had been carrying cocked in
his hand back into its scabbard. Hart, without seeming to see
anything saw everything. When half way through the bottom,
and at a place where the surrounding undergrowth was pecu-
liarly thick and heavy, he drew his muscles altogether and suddenly, released his hands from their clumsy shackles, seized with
a motion as quick as the lifting of an eyelid the revolver on the
guard's hip that was nearest to him, and killed him as he sat,
the poor fellow scarcely knowing that he was in danger until his
brains were scattered everywhere. In another second the
driver, likewise a soldier, was shot dead, and Hart was into the
woods and safe from pursuit as the impenetrable brambles and
bushes could make him.

In May, 1863, the following month, he was again and for the
fourth time in the hands of his mortal enemies. Worn down by
almost incessant marching and fighting, he hid himself one day
in some heavy timber close to the Big Blue and fell speedily
into a deep sleep. Fifty of Penick's men scouting through this
timber in every direction, found him thus and awoke him
roughly. There and then it was proposed to put him to death,
but as the Guerrillas had been unusually active of late, and as
the expedition upon which they were thoroughly bent had not
yet been accomplished, they concluded to spare his life until
they at least were out of danger. Hart was disarmed and tied
upon a horse. Up hill and down, over highways and byways,
through cultivated and uncultivated fields, these captors of his
rode steadily, hunting, as they told him, Todd and his Guerrillas. Just before nightfall they found him. Hart was with the
rear files of the column, still bound and disarmed, when there
came from some bushes on the right the terrible yell he knew
so perfectly, a storm of pistol balls, and a great rush. So
sudden and so complete was the surprise that Penick's militia
forgot either to fire a volley or kill their prisoner. The soldier
who held the bridle of Hart's horse let go of the reins in a
moment and dashed away rapidly after his flying comrades. The
danger was now imminent from the direction of his own friends,
and these—breaking into the road from the bushes—followed at a

run the terror-stricken fugitives.   Once a Guerrilla fired at him
as he dashed by, but missed, and once another put a pistol to
his head to kill him, but Hart held up his menacled hands and
shouted: "Don't you see that I am tied?   What should I
be tied for if I belonged to the militia?   Kill me, if nothing
else will do you, but don't, for God's sake, kill me for a Penick
thief."   Instantly Will Gregg rode up who knew Hart well and
hailed him as a brother.   Others gathered about.   One cut the
rope from his wrists, another gave him a pistol, the third
comrade gave him the second pistol, the fourth caps and
cartridges, and by the time it was the turn of the fifth, Hart
was as well mounted and as well armed as the best of the band.

His next adventure was to be his last one.   In July, 1863,
he took with him Henry Coward, Andrew Campbell, William
Gaw and Louis Vandiver, and made a daring and brilliant raid
through Clay, Clinton, Caldwell, and Livingstone counties.
These five men did the work of fifty.   They fired upon marching columns, cut off picquets, charged small squads, killed
thirty-two militia, burned eighteen forage wagons, scared four
counties into attention, and caused to pursue them day and
night for a week a detachment of cavalry which began with a
company and ended with a regiment.   On their return, and
much worn by riding and fighting, they were overtaken asleep
and fired upon.   Hart, probably killed dead before he awoke,
never spoke.   Coward and Campbell, badly wounded, fell into
the hands of their pursuers.   Every horse was also killed, so
near and so fatal was the only volley fired; but Gaw and
Vandiver leaped full armed from their slumbers and fought
their way out untouched, killing two and wounding three of the
enemy.   Considering the manner of his life, his utter fearless-
ness, the risks he ran, the desperate deeds he did, the number
of times he went boldly into the midst of Federal camps and
garrisons, the little thought he bestowed upon his safety, the
number of men he killed, the perfect indifference to consequences that had succeeded to constitutional intrepidity, it was
wonderful how long Joe Hart ran, and rioted, and did his worst,
and was not slain.   And even in the end it was his indifference
at last which caused his destruction.   The extraordinary raid
had already been accomplished.   All that five desperate men
could do in fifteen days of constant marching and fighting had

already been done. A safe return was only a matter of wakefulness and energy. Henry Coward—a brave, cool, untiring Guerrilla—advised against a halt, but denounced in vigorous language the proposition to turn the halt into a bivouac for the night. Hart was immovable. Rest he would and sleep he would, though all the militia of all the four raided counties were at his heels. As he had lived, so he died, a man without emotion and without fear. His brother, Capt. John Hart, had fallen before Joseph, shot dead at the head of his company at Wilson's Creek, and while leading what in other battles would have been called a forlorn hope.

Neither Coward nor Campbell were killed. Taken to St. Joseph and confined in prison there, Henry Coward was tried as a Guerrilla, convicted and sentenced to be shot. His only answer to the death sentence was a laugh—the cool, calm, collected laugh of a man who knew what he intended to do and who had no fear. In the same prison was William Stone, the hero of a dozen desperate escapades. These two men came together by that undefinable law of nature which makes buffalo mass themselves when there is danger, the porcupine show his quills, the beetle feign death. Both were brave, both were under the ban, both understood how on one hand was the devil, on the other the deep sea. On the 16th day of April, furthermore, both were to be shot.

Coward, on the evening of the fourteenth, got a chance to speak a few words to Stone. "We are to be carried from the prison to a guard house across the river," he said. "What for?" "That we may be handy by shooting time." "Indeed!" "Yes, they shoot them all over there—the good, the bad, the indifferent." A sergeant of the guard saw these two young Guerrillas talking together, and he cursed them bitterly and bade them be silent. It was late the next day before Stone and Coward were taken from the military prison under a strong escort and marched down to the ferry boat at the river. By the time they crossed over it was nearly dusk. As they stepped from the lower deck upon the stage plank, Coward touched Stone on the shoulder and whispered much as a ventriloquist might and without moving his lips: "Now or never! To-morrow we die." Stone's face hardened instantly. If the men had been ironed as most desperate prisoners were in those days,

more especially when there was hanging over them a death sentence, the undaunted rush that followed would surely have been
unavailing. Neither was ironed, however. Side by side, and
free with hands and feet, they walked up together from the river
and on towards a guard house several hundred feet away. On
the right was some heavy timber, and on the left an open field,
and beyond the open field a swamp. Fifty feet from the house
where they were to be imprisoned, the two condemned men
broke suddenly from the ranks which environed them and dashed
headlong into the timber on the right. So swift was the rush,
and so totally unexpected, that the guards having the Guerrillas
in charge waited first to fire at them before pursuing. Unless
the aim of some one or two among the marksmen was more
accurate than the aim generally proved to be, that succeeded to
palpable surprise, escape might well be reckoned tolerably
certain. As the Guerrillas calculated so it came about. Not a
bullet touched them, and not a Federal thought of pursuing
them until they were deep among the trees and two hundred
yards at least from the guard house by the river. They did not
turn often to look back. They did not halt long at any point
to get breath. Until the darkness fell all around them, deep
and sheltering, they scarcely spoke to one another. Finally they
felt that they were safe and sat down. There was no sound of
any pursuer in the rear. On the garments of neither of them
was there even the smell of gunpowder. One bold, quick, des
perate rush, and as the wind was free, so were they. Then
they began to walk again. At the first house in the course traveled there was no horse; at the second a colt which could not
be ridden; at the third a blind mule which the two mounted
bare back, with a piece of hickory bark for a bridle. By and
by another horse was picked up, then a bridle here, a saddle
there, a shot gun in one place, and an old squirrel rifle in another, until by the time they reached Todd's headquarters in
safety, they were at least much better mounted than Balaam,
and infinitely better armed than Uriah, put by David in front of
the fight.

Presently Stone began to seek adventure again. Taking with
him Oll Shepherd, and Henry Coward he crossed from Jackson
county into Platte and invaded a German settlement where, as
reports went, some militia were at home on a furlough. Several

were killed, and several caught and paroled who were not killed. For a long spring day these three daring raiders fought, and rode, and rioted. Once they attacked and routed nine militia, once they had been ambushed and fired upon, and at seven separate houses a fight had first to be made and made seriously before any of the inmates in either could be brought to terms. Most generally a German soldier, if he was at home, would fight a regiment. More Guerrillas were killed in this way and unexpectedly than in any other way that was so isolated or detached. Todd lost a valuable man similarly at Heisinger's. Heisinger, of Heisinger's Lake, in Ray county, kept before the war a famous place for hunters. Ducks and geese abounded in season about the waters there. Heisinger was a thrifty, plodding, patient man; but he had the pluck of a grizzly bear and the tenacity. Todd, on a march one day into Howard county, left two men far in the rear as two eyes watching for pursuit. In following on, they stopped at Heisinger's for a meal. Heisinger came upon them suddenly as they sat at the table, killed the youngest of the two, a most formidable Guerrilla, and escaped to the brush. The companion of the murdered man, baffled in his pursuit of Heisinger, galloped up to Todd and reported. Todd turned about, savage with wrath, and burnt every combustible thing about Heisinger's premises.

The day's raid had worn well into its balmy afternoon when the three Guerrillas rode up to a modest house by the roadside and called out at the gate for recognition. Some one fired at them from the dwelling a single shot. To precipitate themselves from their horses, break in through the barred door and make themselves masters of the situation was but the work of a moment. A ladder led from the lower room to a loft, and just as they entered a German was going up this ladder carrying a pitchfork with him. Stone mounted behind him, a revolver in his right hand. By the time the loft was nearly reached, the German had disappeared through the opening, a sort of trap door, and closed it behind him. Through the cracks of the floor Stone saw shining the tines of the pitchfork. "Come down," he called to the German. "Come up," was the savage answer, mocking and gutteral. Stone fired a quick shot and missed. The German thrust his pitchfork suddenly forth, caught Stone's left cheek full upon the two iron prongs, and drove them in and down to the depth of several inches. The Guerrilla stood the iron like an ox. With one hand he grasped the handle of the pitchfork, steadied himself a moment on the rounds of the ladder, waited this time for a sure shot, and fired upward again and into the belly of the savage German. Perhaps he killed him. He must have been dead. When, a little later, the flames were devouring everything, no moan or cry came from the loft where from between the boards blood was oozing. Stone, disfigured for life, survived this terrible wound.

No sooner had the machinations of cotton speculators and the malignant energy of cotton thieves triumphed in the expulsion of Jarrette, Younger and Poole, when another man entered upon the scene. Capt. Joseph C. Lea was a Missourian whose purity of soul and generosity of heart, if nothing else, would have devoted him to a losing cause. In every state of fortune his prudence and firmness were equally conspicuous, no matter whether he marched boldly into the enemy's lines or retreated with a faithful band to secret and difficult places. He strove constantly to moderate the violence without enervating the valor of his men. Everywhere he displayed the courage of a soldier and the conduct of a chief. In grace and growth he was conspicuous among his equals. Tall and straight as a young cypress, of swarthy complexion, his eyes intensely black, modest of speech, attentive and deferential in conversation, a certain taciturnity growing upon him because of his perpetual ambushments and lyings-in-wait, intrepid, sleepless, vigilant, a born partisan and a terrible fighter, Capt. Lea—endorsed and recommended by Gen. Shelby—was sent to the Mississippi river immediately succeeding the recall of Jarrette, Younger and Poole. If at any time it was thought that this new commander would be more lenient with the corruptors of the military, more gracious to the speculators and money-changers, more tolerant of abuses that were shameful, and mal-administrations that cried aloud to the god of the court-martial and the firing party, his first energetic and incisive measures terrified while they undeceived the guilty and caused those who were just and patriotic to rejoice again. The basis upon which his whole military life was erected had this one sententious maxim: The word of a soldier should never be disputed or re-called. This adage made him inexorable, but it also made him honorable. His heart was full of all social virtues. He loved his friends and pardoned his enemies. He never killed save only in the rage and the roar of contending battle. In order to maintain the harmony of authority and obedience he chastised the criminal, protected the weak, rewarded the deserving, secured the citizen, banished skulkers and deserters from his territory, restrained the depredations of his own soldiers, cherished the labor of the planter and encouraged industry in every direction and through every possible channel. At the beginning of his administration anarchy and rapine abounded; at its close a child with a purse of gold in its hand might have carried it untouched from out-post to out-post.

Capt. Lea found this condition of things to exist before a blow had been struck by him or a single squadron set in the field. Federal gunboats were patrolling the Mississippi river ostensibly to prevent communication between the two departments of the Confederate government—really to protect Federal officials who were making immense fortunes from the profits of an illicit intercourse with the enemy. The Marine Fleet—a sort of amphibious flotilla manned half by inferior soldiers and half by highwaymen—landed here and there at undefended points and ravaged everywhere before them as far inland as they dared to go. Shrewd Yankee cotton buyers, possessed of permits from the highest authority known to them —that of Mr. Lincoln himself—ventured upon remote planta-tions and traded, open-handed, with Confederate officers and soldiers. As a result, discipline speedily disappeared. The out-posts were places of traffic and trade. Cotton trains went forward constantly to the river and unmolested. Scouts, combats, skirmishings or battles were either expressly forbidden or permitted to become unpopular of themselves. Those who fought under either flag fraternized. The gunboats had an armistice with the shore, and the predatory marines were guaranteed against ambushments. Spies swarmed in after the speculators and penetrated every secret nook and cranny of the Trans-Mississippi Department. Desertions increased fast, and in the absence of all military discipline, desertion ripened into crime. There had been committed murders, rapes, plunderings, house-burnings, torturings here and there to extract secrets of buried money from suspected misers, wanton destruction of property, numberless outrages perpetrated by refugees from justice and remorseless scoundrels turned banditti when Capt. Joseph C. Lea appeared upon the scene.

Col. John T. Crisp had been sent sometime before into this cancerous scope of country, eating its way rapidly now into the heart of the Trans-Mississippi Department. Gen. Shelby had denounced this traffic in cotton with a persistency and a virulence which attracted the attention of the Shreveport authorities and caused some of its echoes to reach even unto Richmond. He sent Crisp into the robber territory, and Crisp with the coolness, precision, and comprehension for which he was noted, laid bare the whole ulcer to the eyes of Kirby Smith, the commander-in-chief. He diagnosed the malignant disease, traced its every ramification, summed up its every symptom, marked with disinterested accuracy its every ravage, wrote with soldierly brevity an effective prescription, and returned. His report, however, had but one burden—that of the caustic and the knife. There was a man, fit both by nature and inclination to extirpate this ulcer root and branch, and that man was Joseph C. Lea. Shelby had already known Lea and liked his dash and enterprise. Crisp's further and stronger recommendation — based upon an intimate personal knowledge of what the maladministered territory so specially needed to restore it to health and strength— heightened his good opinion of him and hurried up the recommendations he had deemed necessary to forward to Kirby Smith. Lea was chosen and sent immediately into the land of the cotton buyer and the speculator, the spy, the deserter, the Federal turned cattle-lifter, and the Confederate turned thief.

His first word was a blow. At the head of three hundred men he made a forced march upon Wilson's Point, on the Mississippi river, where four hundred Federals were strongly fortified, and furiously attacked. The struggle lasted an hour. At its worst and hottest part, two gunboats joined in the battle, and a portion of the marine fleet landed fifty armed negroes to assist the whites. Ten Confederates, detached by Lea from his main body, drove these into the river despite the succor of the flotilla, while sixty riflemen — especially charged to look after the gunboats—almost completely silenced their fire by the sharpshooters' murderous work upon the port-holes. Finally the fort capitulated. Lea's loss was eight killed and twenty wounded;

the enemy's one hundred and eighty killed and two hundred wounded.

Captain Lea had already established his base of operations at Floyd, Carroll parish, Louisiana, and thither he hurried from Wilson's Point burdened with one hundred wagons, five hundred head of horses and mules, one piece of artillery, many small arms, much ammunition, and over one hundred wounded prisoners. Reinforced by half a regiment of negro cavalry, the marines landed a second time and followed Lea to Bayou Macon, where he turned about suddenly and drove back the pursuing cavalry with heavy loss to the river. The blow struck had been a resounding one. As the swoop of a huge hawk into a barnyard well filled with chickens, so had been the desperate rush of this intrepid soldier who loved his country and who sought only how he best might serve her. Wagons, half loaded with contraband cotton, were abandoned by their guards. The worst among the cattle thieves took to the swamps. The deserters fled the country or joined the most convenient military organization. Between the fleet and the shore the smugglings and the traffickings were few and far between. A superhuman blade had leaped as it were from its scabbard and could be heard hewing away among the bayous and the plantations.

Lea, equally with Van Tromp, might have carried a broom at the head of his column as Van Tromp carried a broom at his foremast. He would sweep away abuses, outrages, wrongs, the tyranny of scoundrels banded together, and the government of thieves in league with authority.

Fighting much during the winter of 1863, and recruiting, drilling, and providing thoroughly for his men, Lea commenced active operations on the 21st of March, 1864, and moved into Tensas parish, on the Mississippi river. Capt. Stevenson, an accomplished young officer of great bravery and intelligence, led the advance and came upon the outposts of the enemy at four o'clock in the morning. Lea had two hundred men and the Federals four hundred. The fight lasted two hours. Having the advantage of position, of numbers, and of long range guns, it was only after some stubborn fighting that he drove the enemy from their first obstructions and finally from their second, which were composed of many negro cabins partially dismantled and great piles of logs thrown promiscuously

18

together. Here they held on tenaciously. Stevenson was sent to the left, Capt. Middleton to the right, while Lea and Captain Lusk charged with the center. Stevenson broke through on the left desperately, swept on into the rear and began to enfilade the sharpshooters holding the log heaps and the abandoned cabins. As they turned to crush him with their whole force, Lea, Lusk and Middleton came on at a run and finished the encounter. One hundred and ten dead Federals were left upon the field, and as many as one hundred wounded were given up to the marines under a flag of truce. Sixty prisoners remained in the hands of the Confederates, the balance of the command saving themselves by a helter skelter flight to the river where the gunboats received them and saved them from destruction.

Close to the scene of this second battle, and within canister range of the guns of the fleet, there had been erected a large building filled from basement to garret with everything fit to sell to a needy people or trade for a pound of cotton. Everything contraband was in this store—powder, lead, percussion caps, new revolvers, whisky, medicines, surgical instruments, clothing, groceries of all kinds, and dress goods of the latest styles and patterns. Lea held on to this house until every valuable thing in it was carried to a place of safety and delivered into the hands of a responsible agent of the Confederate government. For three days and nights he fought a grim, dogged, desperate fight over this building and these goods. Five times shells from the gunboats fired it, and five times he extinguished the flames. Twice large bodies of marines landed from the fleet and sought to retake it by assault, and twice he drove them back with ruinous loss. The bombardment went on and so did the removal of the stores. In the fight seventy-five huge army wagons had been captured with mules and running gear intact, and these were first loaded with supplies and medicines. Then every wagon in the country round about was made to be available. What ordinarily might have been considered freight trains were now come to be called caravansaries. The road to the rear was filled with every sort and kind of vehicle—government wagon, log sled, cotton cart, ox team, and family carriage—Lea held on like a bull-dog and fought every hour until with the building torn and battered about him, with ten of his dead unburied who had fought to save the stores, and thirty of his wounded needing care and succor, he surrendered the shell of a house—wrecked and gutted—to whoever cared to patch it up or inhabit it, and fell back with his immense booty unmolested. Estimated to be worth to the Confederacy $600,000, from all this heap of spoils Captain Lea would not permit to his men the appropriation of a single pound of tobacco or a single bottle of brandy. "If what we have taken," he said in justification, and when remonstrated with for his firmness by some of his officers, "if what we have taken belongs to us we are robbers; if it belongs to the Confederate government and we take so much as the worth of a sixpence we are thieves. Let us by our example deserve the name of neither."

If the first blow struck by this intrepid and indefatigable man had produced consternation, the second was succeeded by rage, mortification, and despair. Unless he was speedily got out of the country, the end of the cotton trade was the one sure thing, however uncertain the balance. Rumors first went to Smith, and then runners, and then protests, misrepresentations, and appeals. It is difficult to understand what charges were brought against Lea, or how any respectable officer found sufficient audacity to honestly ask for his removal; but about the first of June, 1864, Gen. Smith began to manifest signs of displeasure at his subordinate's enterprisinig boldness, and on the twenty-fifth he recalled him to Shreveport. Lea reported instantly and with all of his men. Shelby was there, to stand by his brilliant captain, and Crisp was there to second Shelby. Governor Henry W. Allen, of Louisiana, himself a disabled soldier of conspicuous valor and spotless patriotism, allied with Shelby, Lea and Crisp in every effort made to checkmate the enemies of good administration and military supremacy. In the end the right triumphed. After a thorough examination of the whole situation Gen. Smith became satisfied that Lea was the right man in the right place, and ordered him to return at once and assume command of all the country east of the Ouachita river. Thereafter the sky began to brighten from zenith to horizon.

Several swift, hot skirmishes succeeded to Lea's arrival at Floyd, where—busy with the complicated affairs of a necessary civil and internal administration—he spent several important weeks in giving protection to the planter and peace to the people generally. Banditti no longer lurked in the swamps. Bands of predatory soldiers were broken up. Cotton buyers no longer abounded. Many traps baited for bad men caught spies. Industry revived; women were safe from assault; the roads were no longer dangerous for travelers; the marines lost their amphibious habits; moneyed men with permits found their occupation gone; demoralized Confederates returned to their duty; recruits flocked to the standard of the Missourian, and on every hand and upon every plantation there were signs of abundant thrift and many future possibilities.

On the tenth of September, Capt. Lea took the field again. By the fifteenth he was in front of a Federal force stationed at a point on the Mississippi river known as the Horse Shoe. At the toe of this shoe, which rested upon the river, there was a fortification. Above and below it gunboats kept watch and ward. Lea—with Stevenson leading the advance—struck the left or upper heel of this horseshoe and charged the covering ditches savagely. He was repulsed with loss. He charged again and was again repulsed. Infuriated, he charged for the third time, and for the third time he was driven back. Two gunboats stood on either flank of the fortification and added their deep roar to the sharper and clearer rattle of the musketry. If it was impossible to get the enemy out by a charge, then it was impossible to get him out at all. No other way existed. Lea charged a fourth time and gained a ditch. This he held desperately, despite the fury with which he was counter-charged and the storm of shells bursting upon him from the fleet. A second ditch was next gained, and then a third, until broken and driven away from their last resource, the routed enemy fled to the fleet for immediate shelter. In the last savage combat Stevenson fell at the head of his men, conspicuous for his splendid bearing, as did Rankin Chandler, another young officer of great worth and heroism. Both were buried in the same grave on a bank of the Tensas river. John Barker, an old Quantrell Guerrilla, especially distinguished himself in this fight, as did James Tucker, another Missouri Guerrilla, S. A. Lusk of Louisiana, Charles Moore of New Orleans, and the two Truselow brothers, Pet and Douglass, A. G. Belding, William Dickinson, and Henry Senter. Lusk and Dickinson were especially noted as scouts and guides. If Lusk knew one road across a swamp as he knew his alphabet, Dickinson knew another. The bayous were as books to them for the reading. As they piloted Younger, Jarrette and Poole, so they piloted Lea always to victory. Each had a company which, when the scouting was done, was led always into the thickest of the fight. The country they sought so diligently to free from banditti and birds of prey was a country fair to look upon and fertile as an island in the sea. They loved it with a love that was also a religion. Their patriotism was a holy thing, and their warfare to exemplify and to illustrate it the warfare of Christian men joined to the antique.

In the fight at the Horse Shoe the Federal loss was one hundred and ninety-five killed, seventy-two wounded, and sixty-three captured. Lea lost eighty killed and wounded, and returned across Bayou Mason on the sixteenth of September, with his prisoners and two hundred stands of valuable arms. On the eighteenth he was at the Lum place, situated upon Will Bayou, in Madison Parish. About the Lum place swamps abounded. The road that ran by it ran also through several almost impenetrable stretches of cane and cypress, miry bottoms and extended surfaces of shallow water. At least one hundred and fifty bad whites, skulking deserters, and semi-barbaric negroes infested these swamps, hid themselves in these jungles, splashed about, depraved and half naked among these lagoons, and came often and often to the road on the higher and dryer land at the Lum place and preyed savagely upon the passers by. Many of these had been killed, many robbed, some wounded and left for dead, and not a few taken into the fastnesses and held for ransom under terrible threats of mutilation or torture. It was difficult to get at these outlaws guarded by brake and bramble, morass and stagnant water. Horses could not penetrate to the hiding-places. Footmen could not find them in a two days' tramp. Hounds could not trail them a furlong from the shore. Lea, through a stratagem, surprised and obliterated the band. Dressing Lusk and Dickinson in Federal clothing, and sending them forward with sixty picked men, similarly habilitated, he followed hard upon their rear, not close, it is true, but close enough for succoring distance. The day of the fight saw at the Lum place the most of the banditti. Dickinson and Lusk rode boldly up and asked the leader for news of Confederate cavalry. This leader was a colossal black, with ebony skin, ivory teeth, a skull like a bird, a fist like a trip hammer, a liver like a hog, the form of Goliah of Gath, the strength of a buffalo, and the endurance of an alligator. He was especially delighted to see so many Federals, he said, for since that devil of a Lea had been operating in the country their visits inland had been few and far between. Would they stay long? Rebels were here, there, and everywhere; but just at this time he knew of no particular force in any particular place. The example set by the leader was soon followed by the men, and in a moment or two friends and foes were communicative alike and equally voluble. Presently Lea with the main body was seen approaching. "Who comes there?" the negro leader asked of Lusk, his great white eyes a shining. "More Federals," the Confederate coolly answered him. "More devils!" he yelled, snatching a double-barrelled shot-gun from the hand of a white outlaw and leaping away from the road towards the nearest swamp. "We are betrayed! We are betrayed! Follow me, men, and fight hard and fast as you follow." No braver animal ever got from God a voice that filled all the air for a mile. It was heard loud and clear and high above cries and shots, and furious yells, and the thunder of flying feet. The *melee* was a savage tearing to pieces. Lea reached the combat in time to make the bloody work thorough and instantaneous. From the high land about the Lum place to the nearest swamp it was scarcely a mile, but by the time a dozen fugitives had reached it, the balance of the band had been destroyed. Turned fairly and heroically to bay, James Tucker closed in upon the negro leader and shot him six times without knocking him from his feet. He fired at Tucker three times and hit him once. Another soldier, Carroll, shot him four times, when he ran a dozen yards, fell, struggled to his feet, ran fifty or sixty yards further and fell again. This time he did not get up. The ten pistol balls in his body would have killed an elephant. Of the original organization of one hundred and fifty men, probably not more than twenty survived the reckoning, and these were never heard of again in the country. The roads infested by these desperate marauders became safe again, and the plantations contiguous to their hiding-places as free from imposition as a great fear could make them.

Capt. Lea, indeed, had but little more to do in this portion of the State. He had broken up the contraband cotton trade, driven away deserters, made it unprofitable for speculators to go further inland than a gunboat could throw a canister-shot, caused the cottonwood trees to bear spies, given peace to neighborhoods terrorized over by bad men, protected industry, destroyed a dozen robber bands, fought and worsted several Federal detachments sent to crush him, organized the citizens into home guard companies, armed them with excellent guns taken from the enemy, won the respect of the planters, the adoration of his soldiers, the thanks of the commander-in-chief, and if he would still find employment for his restless energy and his indomitable courage he would have to seek it in Southern Louisiana.

The Achafalaya country had of late been much infested with light armed mosquito boats penetrating the bayous and water courses and trafficking for cotton in every direction. The same demoralization and desertion which attended this traffic on the Mississippi river, in no manner abandoned it when it was transferred to the great lakes and navigable bayous of the South. Lea was ordered there to operate as he had been operating for the past six months, and began the march for his new department on November 28th, 1864. At Black river an immense herd of cattle from Texas was encountered *en route* to the Confederate armies of the East. Here for two weeks he rendered immense and valuable services. Especially charged to keep every hostile thing away from the herd, he fought fourteen fights in fourteen days, holding his ground to the last, though always outnumbered and constantly overmatched.

The Achafalaya country, however, was not reached. Information received at the Shreveport headquarters between the time Lea was ordered to occupy it and return from it—made it necessary for Gen. Smith to send Gen. Buckner into the territory in question with a heavy force of both infantry and cavalry. Lea's orders of recall overtook him a three days' march from his destination, and he turned short about for the mouth of Red river, crossed that stream, halted a day or two there, and then hurried on to the Mississippi river, and struck it at a point opposite Natchez. Camped on Tensas Lake was a regiment of Wisconsin cavalry, veterans all and seasoned to battle. Lea commanded four hundred men and the Wisconsin regiment numbered five hundred. He attacked on three sides simultaneously, Lusk commanding one detachment, Middleton one and Lea the third. It was a bloody combat and a desperate one. Charges and counter-charges followed one another rapidly. The Wisconsin people were finally driven from the field with a loss of seventy-five killed and one hundred and ten wounded, while Lea lost thirty-two in killed and sixty-five in wounded, capturing the camp equipage, the horses, many of the arms, and all of the stores and supplies of the regiment. Those who survived the fight survived it through the succor and the shelter of the river and the gunboats.

It was here that John Barker, a born scout and sleepless Guerrilla, brought word to Lea that a detachment of cavalry, numbering sixty, was convoying seven pieces of heavy artillery from one point to another on the river, from a fort called McPherson to a fort called Halleck. He determined to see about these horsemen and these cannon. He set forth under cover of night with a mounted force sixty strong. For a day he lurked with his band in an immense swamp. In this desolate region there was no lack of guides. On the next night the detachment guarding the guns had halted for the evening at an open and pleasant place four miles from where Lea was crouching. So secure did the officers and men believe themselves that their horses had been turned loose to graze and their sentinels even were asleep. The surprise was complete. Some sprang to their arms and made an attempt to resist, but in vain; about twenty fell; forty were captured. None fled—it appeared as if they did not know how to fly. A huge pile was made of the wagons and pieces of cannon. Every gun was stuffed with powder and fixed with its mouth in the ground. Then great piles of dry cord-wood were brought and piled about them. A torch was put to the whole, and then there came a great explosion and a great destruction. In every way the blow struck had been complete and overwhelming.

At times in Mississippi, at times in Louisiana, and then again in Kentucky, Lea continued to operate with marked ability and success until the end of the war. He was a Guerrilla in the sense and to the extent of fighting in every guise and fashion known to modern warfare. Any weapon fitted his hand that gave promise of success. Ambuscade, stratagem, charge, decoy, feigned retreat, savage fighting — either was easy of employment if profitable, all might be tried in a single battle if without them all the victory were impossible.

When forced to come out from Louisiana and quit operations there, Jarrette and Younger went to Collin county, Texas, where a Confederate officer named George Jackson, was recruiting a battalion for service on the plains. They took service with him, eager for any work, however desperate. Encamped at San Saba, the battalion was quite ready to march, when General Smith ordered Jackson to forego the expedition and report with his men for immediate duty in Texas. The two Guerrillas did not report. Instead, indeed, of going to Shreveport, the headquarters of the Trans-Mississippi Department, they rode rapidly to Presidio del Norte on the Rio Grande, and sought to form a junction with Captain Skillman, operating in that neighborhood. Four days before their arrival, Skillman and thirty of his men had been surrounded by two hundred Lipan Indians, deserters, and highwaymen, but he fought desperately and until the whole detachment were killed. In no manner daunted, Younger and Jarrette, with twenty followers, crossed into Mexico and waited. By and by Colonels Roberts and Kennedy came to their camp, *en route* to California. Commissioned by the Confederate Secretary of War to recruit a regiment of Californians, they requested the Guerrillas to accompany them. Eager for any perilous enterprise, Jarrette, with ten men, broke through the blockade into the State, and Younger, with ten more, marched through Arizona, fought seven desperate fights with Apache Indians, and finally gained the rendezvous at Las Angeles, finding there the balance of the party. A regiment was soon organized, armed, and equipped, and just as it got ready for active operations, Lee surrendered at Appomattox Court House. Where the surrender found Cole Younger, there it left him for a year, trying as best he could to earn a livelihood and live at peace with all the world.

The character of this man to many has been a curious study, but to those who knew him well there is nothing about it of mystery or many sidedness. An awful provocation drove him into the army. He was never a blood-thirsty or a merciless man. He was brave to recklessness, desperate to rashness, remarkable for terrible prowess in battle; but he was never known to kill a prisoner. On the contrary, there are alive to-day fully two hundred Federal soldiers who owe their lives to Cole Younger, a man whose father had been brutally murdered, whose mother had been hounded to her death, whose family had been made to endure the torment of a ferocious persecution, and whose kith and kin even to most remote degrees were plundered and imprisoned. At Lawrence he was known to save a score of lives, in twenty other desperate combats he took prisoners and released them; when the steamer Sam Gaty was captured, he stood there as a protecting presence between the would-be slayers and their victims; at Independence he saved more lives; and in Louisiana probably fifty Federals escaped certain death through Younger's firmness and generosity. His brother James did not go into the war until 1864, and was a brave, dauntless, high-spirited boy who never killed a soldier in his life save in fair and open battle. Cole was a fair-haired, amiable, generous man, devoted in his friendships, and true to his word and to comradeship. In intrepidity he was never surpassed. In battle he never had those to go where he would not follow, aye, where he would not gladly lead. On his body to-day there are the scars of thirty-six wounds. He was a Guerrilla, and a giant among a band of Guerrillas, but he was one among five hundred who only killed in open and honorable battle. As great as had been his provocation, he never murdered; as brutal as had been the treatment of every one near and dear to him, he refused always to take vengeance on those who were innocent of the wrongs, and who had taken no part in the deeds which drove him, a boy, into the ranks of the Guerrillas, but he fought as a soldier who fights for a cause, a creed, an idea, or for glory. He was a hero, and he was merciful.

CHAPTER XV.

SOMETIME in August, 1864, after General Smith had resolved upon the Missouri campaign, and had chosen Gen. Sterling Price to conduct it, this latter commander sent an exceedingly bold and enterprising man, Capt. John Chestnut, into the State with a communication for the Guerrillas. It was directed to Todd, then operating with Quantrell's old company, and it contained an order requiring him to gather together as many Guerrillas as possible and make North Missouri as hot as he could for the militia. Gen. Price reckoned upon keeping the secrets of his expedition tolerably well covered up, and calculated with reasonable certainty upon such a concentration of Federal troops north of the river as would leave the garrisons and the field forces on the south side, if not insignificant, at least not actively aggressive.

Chestnut reached Jackson county the seventh of September, 1864, and found Todd's camp at Judge Gray's, near Bone Hill, on the morning of the eighth. At that time Todd's men were all disbanded but six, those remaining with him being Ben Morrow, Harrison Trow, Jesse and Frank James, Allen Parmer and James Wilkinson. Thanks to the untiring nursing of Mrs. Rudd, and to the indomitable courage of the boy himself, Jesse James had grown better in three weeks of his terrible wound, left the hands of his physician despite her most earnest protests, crossed the Missouri river on a raft, and joined his old commander in Jackson county more like a ghost than a Guerrilla. Todd was a man of prodigious activity. He would do sometimes in an hour what other men would scarcely do in a week. With him the flash and the report were inseparably blended; you saw the lightning and you felt the thunderbolt. "Riding

will do you good," he said to Jesse James, within twenty
minutes after the arrival of Chestnut, "and I desire you and
your brother Frank to hasten fast to Poole in Lafayette—order
him to gather up his men instantly, cross the Missouri river at
or near Hill's Landing, and be somewhere in Howard county by
the twentieth. When you have executed your orders return to
me as fast as you went."

In a day the musterings became active and energetic. Poole
soon had fifty-two men well in hand, and Todd, at the Bone Hill
rendezvous, fifty-six. Lieut. George Shepherd, on the day of
the 12th, was given eleven men and ordered to cross over into
Clay county and begin the work Gen. Price required of the
Guerrillas. He chose for the enterprise: Frank and Jesse
James, Oll Shepherd, Allen Parmer, James Wilkinson, William
Gaw, Richard Johnson, Harrison Trow, James Johnson, and the
two brothers Nolan, but try how he would, not a skiff, not a
make-believe of a boat of any kind, not a raft or a canoe could
be found anywhere at Sibley, the point of crossing, or above or
below it either way for miles and miles. Failing in everything
else, he fell at last upon a horse trough and launched it boldly
upon the stream. Wilkinson and Oll Shepherd were the oars-
men and made a trial trip alone, exploring the further shore
with great minuteness and making by their intelligent examination a sudden ambuscade impossible. Well across afterwards in
an hour, Shepherd pushed rapidly on into the very heart of the
militia country, halting for breakfast at Judge Level's, a mile
from Centreville, now Kearney. It is probable that the nature
of the work performed by the Southern women during the war
will never be understood fully nor to its most important extent.
Without their aid, Guerrilla warfare would have been heavily
handicapped. Born spies, they listened well, saw a great deal,
and reported exactly. Infinite in resource, quick at ruse or
stratagem, and bold as the best of any band that fought for
freedom, they carried information at any hour, and faced any
peril or held their own against any extremity if something practical could be suggested to an enterprising soldier, or something
tangible done to make a blow decisive. Of this class of women
—fearless in danger and intensely Southern in the midst of an
iron occupation—were Mrs. Level and her two daughters,
Louise and Georgie, Mrs. Minerva Fox, and her two daughters,

Georgie and Cassie, Miss Mollie King and Miss Kate Burnes. Couriers or scouts, nurses or physicians, under the ban or free to come and go, they established, in conjunction with other ladies, a tolerably accurate system of signals, and found hiding places and healing for several score of crippled Guerrillas who could neither walk nor ride.

After breakfast Lieutenant Shepherd marched into Centreville, had all of the unshod horses shod, and sent an old citizen of Southern proclivities, into Liberty, fifteen miles distant, with information to the effect that the bushwhackers from Jackson were swarming in Clay. Todd crossed the Missouri on the 13th where Shepherd had on the 12th, and in the same manner, Richard Burnes, one of his soldiers, performing the difficult feat of swimming his horse from bank to bank, sitting himself erect in the saddle, four heavy dragoon revolvers buckled about him, together with the necessary ammunition. On the 14th Todd joined his lieutenant and planned an ambushment for Captain William Garth, who commanded the post at Liberty. Garth, duly informed of Shepherd's appearance in Centreville, picked sixty of his best men and started upon his trail. Todd, meanwhile, had withdrawn to some timber near the residence of Mr. Andrew Means, a sturdy old Southern patriot whom no threats could intimidate nor dangers deter. In front of this timber there was a level meadow three hundred yards across. If Garth once entered upon this meadow and marched over it to the timber where Todd watched, waiting in the saddle, no power this side heaven could save him from destruction. And it seemed at one time as if he might do so. He came within a mile of the ambushment, drove in the Guerrilla picquets, followed them up vigorously as if meaning business, when a professed Southern man named Swinney halted Garth in the midst of his advance, made plain to him the nature of the trap, told what kind of devils Todd led in battle, and then bade him go forward if he felt like it. Garth countermarched instead and hastened back to Liberty.

On the sixteenth, now well advanced into Ray, a citizen informed Todd that a company of forty-five militia were stationed at Shaw's blacksmith shop, in the northeastern portion of the county. Todd, selecting ten men as an advance, put in command of them a new comer named John Thrailkill. He was a Missourian turned Apache. He slept little ; he could trail a column in the starlight; his only home was on horseback, and who had had already mixed with the warp and the woof of his young life the savage agony of tears. Thrailkill, when the war began, was a young painter in Northwest Missouri, as gentle as he was industrious. Loving a beautiful girl, and loved ardently in return, he left her one evening to be absent a week. At its expiration they were to be married. Generally the woman who is loved is safe, but this one was in peril. Her father, an invalid of fifty, was set upon by some militia and slain, and the daughter, bereft of her reason at the sight of gray hairs dabbled in blood, went from paroxysm to paroxysm, until she too was a corpse. The wildest of her ravings were mingled with the name of her lover. It was the last articulate thing her lips lingered over or uttered. He came back as a man in a dream. He kissed the dead reverently. He went to the grave as one walks in his sleep. It was bitter cold, and some one remarked it to him. "Is it?" he said. "I had not felt it." Another friend tried to fashion something of solacement. The savage intensity of the answer shocked him : " Blood for blood ; every hair in her head shall have a sacrifice !" The next day John Thrailkill began to kill. He killed all over Northwest Missouri. Of the twenty militia who were concerned in the murder of his sweetheart's father, and, indirectly in the murder of his sweetheart, he killed eighteen. The remaining two returned to Ohio where they lived originally and lost themselves in the midst of an Eastern army corps. Getting closer and closer to Todd, of course as he was forced to fall back, fighting, he finally took service in his immediate ranks and became as the balance a desperate Guerrilla not afraid to die.

Thrailkill's advance, composed of Dick Kinney, John Jackson, Andy Walker, Dan Vaughn, Andy McGuire, Frank and Jesse James, Sim Whitsett, Oll Shepherd, Ben Morrow, Hence Privin, Harrison Trow and Si Gordon, took the road at a trot. It was to make seven miles an hour, keep one-half mile ahead of the main body, charge everything dressed in blue, and halt within a mile of the blacksmith shop. In two hours fourteen miles had been made ; to the enemy's position it was just a mile further. Camped in a black oak grove, the militia had on one side a large corn field, on the other a meadow. In the midst of them a broad lane ran, fit almost for a column to ride through, company front. As the Guerrillas emerged into the open and entered the lane at a walk, they were mistaken for friends and permitted to advance unchallenged to within two hundred yards of the camp. Then a wild yell was heard, and then came that peculiar rush so terrible in its gathering strength and so resistless. Todd, Walker, Thrailkill, Trow, Jackson and Kinney rode abreast in the front rank; Whitsett, George, Oll and Frank Shepherd, and Ben Morrow in the second; Hudspeth, Coger, and McGuire in the third, and behind them Hendrix, Gregg, Gordon, the Jameses, the Archie brothers, and William Hulse, all striving furiously to be the first in at the death. Ten of the militia were slaughtered helplessly in camp, and the balance scattered to the corn field, some without guns and some without pistols. Instead of a battle there was a *battue*. The Guerrillas hunted them as wild game is hunted, laughing loud when one jumped up from his hiding-place here or there and was shot down. John Jackson, Kinney, and the two Jameses were together when they flushed four from a single covert, killing them, as they imagined, and passing on. One, however, was not only not dead, but he was wicked and unhurt. He rose up in the rear of these four Guerrillas—who in the eagerness of the hunt had not taken time to gather together the arms of the slain—and shot Jackson in the back with a Belgian musket carrying an ounce ball. Almost before he had touched the ground Jesse James avenged him, firing twice into the head of the militiaman as he stood over him with his horse. Thirty-eight of the forty-five Federals were killed, and forty horses were captured, together with considerable camp equipage and commissary stores. Todd lost but one man, Jackson, who was mortally wounded. Tenderly cared for by James Hendrix and John Coger, he was driven for fifteen miles as gently as possible in a buggy and placed in a safe spot on Wakenda river. On the fifteenth he died calmly, and his comrades buried him. One by one the old guard was going. John Jackson, a hero in fifty desperate combats, died as he had lived, one of the bravest men who ever buckled on a pistol.

A little before dawn, on the morning of the 16th, Todd was in front of Keytesville, Chariton county. Eighty militia held the town, occupying the large brick court house there, a really formidable fortification, capable easily of resisting the onset of a thousand men. Todd, unchallenged, surrounded this building and demanded an unconditional surrender. So secure had the garrison felt in the possession of their fort, and so unused had they been to the sudden surprises and rougher realities of war, that no guards were out about the court house, nor any picquets upon the streets. The militia commander parleyed awhile, but to no purpose. Todd promised simply to spare the lives of his men, if a capitulation came in five minutes; if not, then war to the vanquished. Up went the white flag, and out marched eighty militiamen, furious when it was too late at being trapped and taken by scarcely sixty Guerrillas. With the militia there were also taken four hundred muskets, three hundred shot-guns, one hundred army revolvers, two pieces of artillery and forty-four splendid horses. The muskets, shot-guns and the cannon were all piled together in the court house and the court house burnt. The prisoners were paroled—the first and the last time in his career that Todd ever had been known to be merciful. His honor, however, had been pledged, and if any desperate man among his following had spilled even so much as one drop of any militiaman's blood, there, personally, and pistol to pistol, would Todd have exacted of him accountability. Later on, and while doing picquet duty outside of the town, Oll Shepherd caught and killed the sheriff of Chariton, a most obnoxious Radical, but he was not included in the terms of capitulation nor was he connected in any military manner with the garrison. Among the horses appropriated were three elegent race mares, the admiration of the entire command. These, in the distribution, fell to Jesse James, Chat Rennick and Harrison Trow.

On the march out Andy McGuire and Frank James caught and killed two militia who fired on them from a corn-field as they rode by, lagging somewhat in the rear of the column. James Younger, scarcely old enough to do service of any kind, had yet joined Todd as a boy and had already made a name for himself in a command where personal prowess alone brought laurels.

Todd entered Roanoke and occupied it for a short time—just long enough to let all North Missouri know that he was on the war-path—and then cut the telegraph wires for some distance

and tore up the posts. In the extreme eastern part of Howard
on the 17th, Todd halted all the day of the 18th on the Rocheport and Sturgeon road, and rested both men and horses.
About three o'clock, however, fifteen hundred Federals marching down towards Rocheport forced Todd away from the road
four miles and into some heavy timber, where he rested. Oll
Shepherd, Frank Shepherd, Richard Kinney, Dan Vaughn,
Press Webb and Jacob Mead, having been sent out earlier on a
scout, returned to camp in time to be furiously attacked and
furiously followed for several miles, fighting as they ran. The
chase ended, however, as all such chases always ended to the
Federals, in a loss altogether disproportionate to the numbers
engaged. Out of fifty pursuers eight were killed and seven
wounded. Kinney lost his horse, and Oll Shepherd took him
up behind him under a rattling fire and bore him safely away.
This was the only casualty.

Day dawned on the 19th, cold and raw. At intervals an east
wind brought rain in torrents. Nevertheless, it was to be a day
of murder. Todd moved camp only a few miles, when the
muddy roads and the inhospitable weather drove him into it
again. Lieutenant Shepherd, taking with him Kinney, Andy
McGuire, Harrison Trow, Lafe Privin, Jesse and Frank James,
went scouting along the Sturgeon road until one hundred and
fifty Federals were met—seventy-five infantry and seventy-five
cavalry — escorting seventeen wagons. The column was approaching Rocheport, with forty cavalry in advance, the infantry
divided up among the wagons, and in the rear the balance of
the horsemen. It was probable that one of Todd's charges
would make of the march a massacre. He was four miles to the
left of the enemy's line of travel when Jesse James carried to
him swiftly the news of the situation, but by the rapid movement of half an hour he threw himself across the main road and
dashed at the cavalry in front with the old yell and the old
result. Todd killed the first Federal in the fight, a handsome
young captain well ahead of his men and striving to hold them
for a grapple. Then the on-going tide inundated everything.
Those first to the wagons, after breaking through the covering
cavalry as though it had been tissue paper stretched across a
race-course, were Todd, raging like a lion, Thrailkill, the two
Jameses, Gordon, McGuire, Hulse, Oll Shepherd, William and

19

Hugh Archie, Mead, Kinney, Tom Todd, Privin, Glasscock, De Hart, and Vaughn. Death came to men so quickly there that something superhuman seemed to be inflicting it. Corduroyed with corpses, the muddy road in a measure became firm. Inextricably entangled, men and mules fell together. Past the infantry, or rather the remains of it, dashed the two Jameses, De Hart, Kinney, Hulse, Mead, and Vaughn, Jesse James killing as he galloped a Federal lieutenant two hundred yards from the road. This shot was a most remarkable one, and for some time was the talk of the command. The lieutenant was in the act of firing, having just lifted a carbine to his face, when James put a dragoon pistol ball into his head. The rout, if, indeed, it were not better called a butchery, lasted until dark. Ninety-two cavalry and infantry had been killed. All the wagons were burnt, together with fifty-four Ballard rifles, abandoned by the enemy in their frantic efforts to escape. Each of the seventeen wagons had six splendid mules to it, but every mule was killed. In burning the wagons three negro drivers were burned up with them, the Guerrillas not taking the trouble to drag them out from the flames. Driving another wagon was a well known Southern citizen who had been pressed into service and forced to accompany the expedition. Before he could either explain the surroundings or make himself known to the Guerrillas, he was shot dead. The wagons were loaded with ammunition and clothing, and Todd, ordering each of his fifty-three men to help himself to a suit, the line looked as blue after the metamorphosis as any Federal line in Missouri. He had but one man hurt in the fight, Bart Lewis, of Platte county, and he only slightly in the leg. Dick Glasscock had a horse killed. Tom Todd had two men wounded, Jo Davis, of Randolph county, who afterwards died of his wound, and John M. Taylor. The Federals did not fight. After the first volley, a volley fired at long range and with scarcely the semblance of steadiness, everything was flight or panic. Ere the infantry knew the nature of the attack they were overridden. The cavalry in the rear ran away while their comrades in the front were being butchered. The scene after the conflict was sickening. Charred human remains stuck out from the mouldering wagon heaps. Death, in all forms and shapes of agony made itself visible. Limbs were kneaded into the deep mud of the roadway, and faces,

WILL HULSE.

LEE McMURTRY.

T. F. MAUPIN.

under the iron feet of the horses, crushed into shapelessness.

A long night march and a dark one succeeded to the evening of the fight, but by sunrise the next morning Todd had formed a junction with Quantrell, Poole, Anderson, Perkins, and Thomas Todd, these two last being Confederate officers. Aggregated, the force numbered two hundred and seventy-seven rank and file, not a formidable force to do effectively the important work Gen. Price required of it. Poole commanded fifty-two men, George Todd fifty-three, Anderson sixty-seven, Quantrell sixteen, Thomas Todd forty-two, and Perkins forty-seven. All eyes were now turned towards Fayette, the county seat of Howard county, eleven miles north of the rendezvous, where four hundred Federal soldiers did garrison duty, strongly fortified and capable of stout resistance. The command was first offered to Quantrell, but he refused it; next to Anderson, who accepted. Quantrell argued in the counsel against attacking Fayette, and voted against it as a piece of military folly. So did George Todd; but the balance overbore them and decided to make the venture.

On the morning of September 20th, 1864, the March towards Fayette began. Anderson moved first, Poole next, Stuart next, and Quantrell fourth. In the rear were George Todd, Perkins, and Thomas Todd. Fayette had a strong stockade on the north as a defensive work, and in the town itself, both the court house and a female academy were stoutly fortified. Anderson, Poole, and Quantrell were to charge through Fayette and invest the stockade, while the two Todds and Perkins were to look after the buildings inside the corporation. Tom Todd led the advance in the attack on the town, as Fayette was his home.

Fayette was reached about eleven o'clock and attacked furiously. Anderson, Poole, and Quantrell dashed through the square, losing some of their best men, and the two Todds and Perkins faced the two fortified buildings and did what was possible to be done, bare breasts against brick and mortar. Sergeant McMurtry, of George Todd's company, fell first and close to the court house fence. Oll Thompson was mortally wounded; Perkins lost ten men in as many minutes, Tom Todd seven, and Poole eight. Anderson lost in killed, Garrett, Cravens, Agen, Grosvenor, and Newman Wade, and in wounded, Thomas Maupin, Silas King, William Stone and Lawrence Wilcox.

Lieut. Little, one of the oldest of Quantrell's veterans, was badly wounded. Every attack was repulsed, both upon the court house and the stockade, and the Guerrillas retreated finally but unpursued, with a loss of eighteen killed and forty-two wounded. Richard Kinney and Jesse James volunteered to bring McMurtry out from under the guns of the enemy, and they dashed in afoot and succeeded safely amid a shower of balls. Quantrell, infuriated at the loss of so many splendid fellows, fought with a recklessness unusual with him. Leading in person three desperate assaults upon the stockade, and wounded severely in the second assault, he would have commanded a fourth if Poole and Anderson, convinced at last of the uselessness of the sacrifice, had not shown the insanity of the effort and argued him out of his reckless purpose. Many feats of individual and heroic daring were performed. Thomas Todd, his long red beard waving in the wind, and his black plume floating free where the fight was hottest, dashed up once to the main gate of the court house and emptied six chambers of a revolver into a door from which twenty muskets were protruding. Peyton Long, losing his horse early in the fight, rushed desperately into a corral under cover of the stockade, coolly chose the horse which suited him best, mounted him bareback and galloped away unhurt into his own ranks again. Harrison Trow, procuring from a citizen an excellent shotgun, crept to a sheltered place close to the Academy and silenced one window of it by the accuracy and the rapidity of his fire. He was so cool and so calm always in danger that his comrades called him "Iceberg." The night of the retreat Oliver Johnson died. Only twenty-five years of age, he was six feet two in height and large in proportion. Of immense physical strength, in a charge or a close hand to hand fight, he was simply resistless. Wounded six times, the seventh wound killed him. To find one to fill his place who could be braver, more deadly, or more constantly in the saddle was to hunt for gold dust in a straw pile. There were none such. E. P. De Hart took Johnson's place, and was sent to the rear to hold it with John McCorkle, John Barker, Frank Lester, Jack Will, James Clayton, John Rains and Pate Crew, where he did some splendid fighting.

On the twenty-second, Huntsville, in Randolph county, was

surrounded and ordered to capitulate, but its garrison of three hundred militia refused to surrender upon any terms, and Anderson—remembering the sore lesson of Fayette—did not even attempt an assault. On the twenty-third, after the track of the North Missouri Railroad had been torn up for several miles and the telegraph lines interfered with, Quantrell separated himself and his sixteen men from the main body of Guerrillas and returned into Howard. In Audrain county on the twenty-fourth, in Monroe on the twenty-fifth, and back again in Audrain on the twenty-sixth, Anderson, still in command, killed unfortunate militia upon every hand, broke up communication with the various posts, spread terror in every direction, and caused above everything else that concentration of Federal troops so much desired by the Confederate authorities.

From his camp at Singleton's barn, four miles upon the southeast, Anderson moved into Centralia early on the morning of the twenty-seventh. He had with him his own company, Poole, and ten of Poole's men. Todd did not accompany him to the town, nor did John Thrailkill, who had joined him after the Fayette fight with fifty new Guerrillas. These two chieftains, together with Thomas Todd, remained upon their arms, awaiting developments.

The eleven o'clock train from St. Louis would not be due for an hour, and Anderson employed the interval in levying contributions upon the citizens and taking from the stores such things as were needed by his soldiers. By and by a keen whistle was heard, and the dull thunder of advancing cars. The train, halting at the depot, had Federals upon it, some with and some without guns. Some were going up the road on duty, and some to their homes on furlough. When Anderson charged the cars, those who had muskets crowded to the windows and upon the platforms and fired briskly at the Guerrillas. Such resistance, however, was mere child's play. Probably none would have been spared, even though there had been an unconditional surrender, but there was no earthly hope surely after the shooting of a single musket. In all probability the soldiers on the train were frightened beyond discretion. Before the cars had scarcely stopped, one of them put his head from a window and cried out: "Lord! Lord! there is Bill Anderson! Boys, go to praying!" "Pray, hell!" swore a huge Iowa sergeant,

thrusting a musket out and firing as he spoke, "it is the hour
of battle. The devil and all his angels are here!" The fight
should not be called a fight. A few shots from the Guerrillas at
close range cleared the platforms and the windows. White
handkerchiefs were waved in every direction, and a formal surrender had in a very short time. It would have been better for
the Federals to have fought to the death after they had thought
it best to fight at all. All who were on the train were formed in
line, and then the work of winnowing began. Among the citizens was the Hon. James S. Rollins, of Boone county. Sometimes he relates his experience of this terrible event, and if in
some places the narrative is but the story of a bloody tragedy,
in others the humor is quaint and picturesque. Who was he?
Anderson asked. "Oh!" replied Rollins, as mild and as bland
as a wind which had just left the lilacs, "I am Mr. Richard
Robinson"—or whatever the name was that just then came
uppermost in his mind—"and I live only a few miles back.
You must know where I live. It is a house that has a large
grove on the north, and two white chimneys, and some fruit trees
in the front yard, and is a popular place for the boys. They
stop there often," and here the Major looked into the cold, hard
eyes of Anderson and winked. That wink made him a Guerrilla. Certainly Anderson knew the house. But for fear he
might forget it, Rollins took him familiarly by the coat and led
him to where an unobstructed view might be had of the great
stretch of prairie southward from the town. The house was
again pointed out, its surroundings minutely described, and
again the confidential assurance given that it was "a great place
for the boys." The welcome was so hospitable there. Anderson
was satisfied, but by and by the Major felt the need of a superhuman effort. He carried with him everywhere a little hand
valise which might contain one thing or another thing. At any
rate a curious Guerrilla would see for himself. He snatched the
satchel from Rollins' hand and tore it open. There were
clothes there—socks, handkerchiefs, collars, drawers, towels;
but—oh! horror of horrors, there upon all the balance of the
heap was an immaculate white shirt bearing in bold and black
relief the name of *James S. Rollins!* His heart stood still. He
saw first what might soon become to be a death warrant because
he knew it was there, and he laughingly laid a hand upon the

shirt and as laughingly spoke to the Guerrilla: "My friend, I have only one shirt left and I have to return to St. Louis to-night. Of what use is a white shirt to you? It can not be washed. Soldiers on a raid do not wash things. It gets soiled in a day. It does not become you. It is not military." The Guerrilla did not understand what Rollins understood, nor did he know what Rollins knew. As he grasped the shirt he grasped it firmly just over the tell-tale name, now seeming to get blacker and blacker, and to enlarge and grow out from under his extended palm. The Guerrilla hesitated. "Come, come," pleaded the Major, "it's a little thing for you to do me. I've been feeding bushwhackers ever since the war began and I have yet the first cent to take from a single one of them in pay for anything. Give me my shirt." The Guerrilla yielded and the Major crushed the hateful thing back as if it had been a spy and human. Anderson declared afterwards, however, that even if Major Rollins had been identified he should not have been harmed. He had not proscribed Southern people, he had been merciful to women and children, and the Guerrillas respected him not a little.

It was a ghastly line which at last separated the citizens from the soldiers. Twenty-four of the latter and one citizen who wore a soldier's blouse, fell upon that side of the line where death, yet invisible, waited grimly in ambush for its prey. In twenty minutes more all were killed. The train was next set on fire, and the engine, with a full head of steam on, dashed away like the wind towards Sturgeon. Then the depot felt the torch, and finally a gravel train, following close behind the passenger train, was taken possession of and destroyed. After indeed killing everything in and about the town that looked, talked or acted like a Federal soldier, and after destroying completely all those things which he thought might be of the least use to the military authorities of Missouri, Anderson led his men back to Singleton's pasture and reported to Todd the nature of the morning's work. Afterwards, and later on in the day, it was decided to put George Todd in command of the entire force and await further developments. These, bloody beyond all precedent, were not long in coming.

At Paris, in Monroe county, there had been a Federal garrison under the command of a Major Johnson, three hundred

strong. These soldiers, on the watch for Anderson, bad been
busy in scouting expeditions, and had come down as near Centralia as Sturgeon. After Anderson had done all the devilment
his hands could find to do in Centralia, and had retired again to
the Singleton camp, Major Johnson came into the pillaged town,
swearing all kinds of frightful and fearful things. At the head
of his column a black flag was carried. So also was there one
at the head of Todd's column. In Johnson's ranks the stars
and stripes for this day had been forbidden; in the ranks of the
Guerrillas the stars and bars flew fair and free, as if to the desperation of the sable banner there had been an intention to add
the gracefulness and abandon of legitimate war.

The Union citizens of Centralia, knowing only Anderson in
the transaction, besought Johnson to beware of him. He was
no match for Anderson. It was useless to sacrifice both himself
and his men. Anderson had not retreated; he was in ambush
somewhere about the prairie; he would swoop down like an eagle;
he would smite and spare not. Johnson was as brave as the
best of them, but he did not know what he was doing. He had
never in his life fought Guerrillas—such Guerrillas as were now
near unto him. He listened patiently to the warnings that were
well meant and he put away firmly the hands that were lifted to
stay his horse. He pointed gleefully to his black flag, and
boasted that quarter should neither be given nor asked. He
had come to carry back with him the body of Bill Anderson,
and that body he would have, dead or alive. Very well, said
the citizens then, go and get it. Fate, however, had not yet
entirely turned away its face from the Federal officer. As he
rode out from the town at the head of his column, a young
Union girl, described as very fair and beautiful, rushed up to
Major Johnson and halted him. She spoke as one inspired.
She declared that a presentiment had come to her, and that if
he led his men that day against Bill Anderson she knew and
felt that but few of them would return alive. The girl almost
knelt in the dust as she besought the leader. Of no avail.
Johnson's blood was all on fire, and he would march and fight,
no matter whether death waited for him one mile off, or one
hundred. He not only carried a black flag himself, and swore
to give no quarter, but he declared on his return that he would
devastate the country and leave of the habitations of the South-

ern men, not one stone upon another. He was greatly enraged towards the last. He cursed the people as "damned secesh," and swore that they were in league with the murderers and robbers. Extermination, in fact, was what they all needed, and if fortune favored him in the fight, it was extermination that they should all have. It did not favor him.

Johnson rode east of south, probably three miles. The scouts who went to Singleton's barn, where Anderson camped, came back to say that the Guerrillas had been there, had fed there, had rested there, and had gone down into the timber beyond to hide themselves. It was now about four o'clock in the afternoon. Back from the barn, a long, high ridge lifted itself up from the undulations of the more regular country, and broke the vision southward. Beyond this ridge, a wide, smooth prairie stretched itself out, and still beyond this prairie, and further to the south, was the timber in which the scouts said Bill Anderson was hiding himself.

As Johnson rode towards the ridge, still distant from it some mile or more, ten men anticipated him by coming up fair to view, and in skirmishing order. The leader of this little band, Capt. John Thrailkill, had picked for the occasion David and John Poole, Frank and Jesse James, Tuck Hill, Peyton Long, Ben Morrow, James Younger, E. P. DeHart, Ed Greenwood and Harrison Trow. Next to Thrailkill rode Jesse James, and next to Jesse, Frank. Johnson had need to beware of what might be before him in the unknown when such giants as these began to show themselves.

The Guerrillas numbered, all told, exactly two hundred and sixty-two. In Anderson's company there were sixty-one men, in George Todd's forty-eight, in Poole's forty-nine, in Thomas Todd's fifty-four, and in Thrailkill's fifty—two hundred and sixty-two against three hundred.

As Thrailkill went forward to skirmish with the advancing enemy, Todd came out of the timber where he had been hiding, and formed a line of battle in an old field in front of it. Still further to the front a sloping hill, half a mile away, arose between Johnson and the Guerrillas. Todd rode to the crest of this, pushing Thrailkill well forward into the prairie beyond, and took his position there. When he lifted his hat and waved it the whole force was to move rapidly up. Anderson held the right, George Todd joined to Anderson, Poole to George Todd, Thomas Todd to Poole, and Thrailkill to Thomos Todd—and thus were the ranks arrayed.

The ten skirmishers quickly surmounted the hill and disappeared. Todd, as a carved statue, sat his horse upon its summit. Johnson moved right onward. Some shots at long range were fired, and some bullets from the muskets of the Federals reached to and beyond the ridge where Todd watched, Peyton Long by his side. From a column of fours Johnson's men galloped at once into line of battle, right in front, and marched so, pressing up well and calmly. The advanced Guerrillas opened fire briskly at last, and the skirmishing grew suddenly hot. Thrailkill, however, knew his business too well to tarry long at such work, and fell back towards the ridge. As this movement was being executed, Johnson's men raised a shout and dashed forward altogether and in a compact mass, order, formation, ranks all gone. This looked bad. Such sudden exultation over a skirmish wherein none were killed exhibited nervousness—such a spontaneous giving way of a body, that beyond the will of their commander, should have manifested neither surprise nor delight—looked ominous for discipline, and for the defence that needed to be the defence of iron men if it brought any alive out from the unknown.

Thrailkill formed again when he reached Todd's line of battle, and Johnson rearranged his ranks and went towards the slope at a brisk walk. Some upon the right broke into a trot, but he halted them, cursed them, and bade them look better to their line. Up to the hill's crest, however, a column of men suddenly rode into view, halted, dismounted, and seemed to be busy or confused about something. Inexperienced, Johnson is declared to have said to his adjutant: "They will fight on foot—what does that mean?" It meant that the men were tightening their saddle-girths, putting fresh caps on their revolvers, looking well to bridle reins and bridle bits, and preparing for a charge that would have about it the fury of the whirlwind. By and by the Guerrillas were mounted again. From a column they transformed themselves into a line two deep, and with a double interval between all the files. At a slow walk they moved over the crest towards Major Johnson, now advancing at a walk that was brisker.

Perhaps it was now five o'clock. The September sun was low in the west, not red nor angry, but an Indian Summer sun, full yet of generous warmth and grateful beaming. The crisp grass crinkled under foot. From afar the murmur of lapsing streams came softly through the hushed air, and now and then the notes of a bird not musical, but far apart. An interval of five hundred yards separated the two lines. Not a shot had been fired. Todd showed a naked front, bare of skirmishers and stripped for the fight that he knew would be murderous to the Federals. And why should they not stand? The black flag waved alike over each, and from the lips of the leaders of each there had been all the day only threats of extermination and death.

Johnson halted his men and rode along his front speaking a few calm and collected words. They could not be heard in Todd's ranks, but they might have been divined. Most battle speeches are the same. They abound in good advice. They are generally epigrammatic, and full of sentences like these: "Aim low," "keep cool," "fire when you get loaded," "let the wounded lie till the struggle is over." But could it be possible that Johnson meant to receive the charge of the Guerrillas at a halt! What cavalry books had he read? Who had taught him such ruinous and suicidal tactics? And yet monstrous as the resolution was in a military sense, it had actually been taken, and Johnson called out loud enough to be heard from opposing force to opposing force: "Come on, we are ready for the fight!"

The challenge was accepted. The Guerrillas gathered themselves up altogether as if by a sudden impulse, and took the bridle-reins between their teeth. In the hands of each man there was a deadly revolver. There were carbines also, and yet they never had been unslung. The sun was not high, and there was great need to finish quickly whatever had need to be begun. Riding the best and fastest horses in Missouri, George Shepherd, Oll Shepherd, Frank Shepherd, Frank Gregg, Morrow, Trow, McGuire, Allen Parmer, Hence and Lafe Privin, James Younger, Press Webb, Babe Hudspeth, Dick Burnes, Ambrose and Thomas Maxwell, Richard Kinney, Si and Ike Flannery, Jesse and Frank James, David Poole, John Poole, Ed Greenwood, Al Scott, Frank Gray, George Maddox, Dick Maddox, De

Hart, Jeff Emery, Bill Anderson, Tuck Hill, James Cummings, John Rupe, Silas King, Jas. Corum, Moses Huffaker, Ben Broomfield, Peyton Long, Jack Southerland, Wm. Reynolds, Wm. and Chas. Stewart, Bud Pence, Nat Tigue, Gooly Robertson, Hiram Guess, Buster Parr, William Gaw, Chat Rennick, Henry Porter, Arch and Henry Clements, Jesse Hamlet, John Thrailkill, Si Gordon, George Todd, Thomas Todd, William and Hugh Archie, Plunk Murray, Ling Litten, Joshua Esters, Sam Wade, Creth Creek, Theo. Castle, John Chatman, and three score more of other unnamed heroes struck first the Federal ranks as if the rush was a rush of tigers. Jesse James, riding a splendid race mare, led by half a length, then Arch Clements, then Frank James, then Peyton Long, and then Oll Shepherd. There was neither trot nor gallop; the Guerrillas simply dashed from a walk into a full run. The attack was a hurricane. Johnson's command fired one volley and not a gun thereafter. It scarcely stood until the interval of five hundred yards was passed over. Johnson cried out to his men to fight to the death, but they did not wait even to hear him through. Some broke ranks as soon as they had fired, and fled. Others were attempting to reload their muskets when the Guerrillas, firing right and left, hurled themselves upon them. Johnson fell among the first. Mounted as described, Jesse James singled out the leader of the Federals. He did not know him then. No words were spoken between the two. When James had reached to within five feet of Johnson's position, he put out a pistol suddenly and sent a bullet through his brain. Johnson threw out his hands as if trying to reach something above his head and pitched forward heavily, a corpse. There was no quarter. Many begged for mercy on their knees. The Guerrillas heeded the prayer as a wolf might the bleating of a lamb. The wild rout broke away towards Sturgeon, the implacable pursuit, vengeful as hate, thundering in the rear. Death did its work in twos, in threes, in squads — singly. Beyond the first volley not a single Guerrilla was hurt, but in this volley Frank Shepherd, Hank Williams, and young Peyton were killed, and Richard Kinney mortally wounded: Thomas Maxwell and Harrison Carter were also slightly wounded by the same volley, and two horses killed—one under Dave Poole and one under Chat Rennick. Shepherd, a giant in size and as brave as the best in a command where all were brave, had fought the good fight and died in the harness. Hank Williams, only a short time before, had deserted from the Federals and joined Poole, giving rare evidences, in his brief Guerrilla service, of great enterprise and consummate daring. Peyton was but a beardless boy from Howard county, who in his first battle after becoming a Guerrilla was shot dead.

Probably sixty of Johnson's command gained their horses before the fierce wave of the charge broke over them, and these were pursued by five Guerrillas—by Jesse James, Frank James, Peyton Long, Arch Clements and Oll Shepherd—for six miles at the dead run. Of the sixty, fifty-two were killed on the road from Centralia to Sturgeon. Todd drew up his command and watched the chase go on. For three miles nothing obstructed the vision. Side by side over the level prairie the five stretched away like the wind, gaining step by step and bound by bound, upon the rearmost riders. Then little puffs of smoke arose. No sounds could be heard, but dashing ahead from the white spurts terrified steeds ran riderless. Night and Sturgeon ended the killing. Five men had shot down fifty-two. Arch Clements, in the apportionment made afterwards, had credited to him fourteen, Oll Shepherd ten, Peyton Long nine, Frank James eight, and Jesse James, besides killing Major Johnson and others in the charge upon the dismounted troopers, killed in the chase an additional eight. Johnson's loss was two hundred and eighty-two, or out of three hundred only eighteen escaped. History has chosen to call the ferocious killing at Centralia a butchery. In civil war encounters are not called butcheries where the combatants are man to man and where over either rank there waves a black flag. Johnson's overthrow, probably, was a decree of fate. He rushed upon it as if impelled by a power stronger than himself. He did not know how to command, and his men did not know how to fight. He had, by the sheer force of circumstances, been brought face to face with two hundred and sixty-two of the most terrible revolver fighters the American war or any other war ever produced, and he deliberately tied his hands by the act of dismounting, and stood in the shambles until he was shot down. Abject and pitiful cowardice matched itself against reckless and profligate desperation, and the end could only be just what the end was. The Guerrillas did unto the militia just exactly what the militia would have done unto them if fate had reversed its decision and given to Johnson what it permitted to Todd.

Before either Quantrell, Todd, Anderson or Poole began to do bloody work in Howard or any of its contiguous counties, other desperate men had been busy with the enemy. Capt. James Cason, a farmer Guerrilla, had also been operating in Howard county at various times and brilliantly. He was an intrepid man, full of enthusiasm and enterprise. Whenever the enemy came upon him they had to fight him. Unostentatious, clear-headed, vigilant, and thoroughly in earnest, he always got close enough before he fired to hurt somebody. His first encounter was with Major Hunt, of Merrill's Horse, in the Boonslick hills, near Lisbon, on the Missouri river. Hunt was on a horse-pressing expedition of a bright summer day. Cason had with him H. A. Ballew, John A. Cason, John G. Ballew, John M. Taylor, old Tom Childres and his son young Tom Childres, Lt. B. H. Shipp, E. P. De Hart, and Calvin Sartain. These men formed an ambuscade, fired five volleys into Hunt's detachment, killing nine, wounding twenty-two and scattering the balance of the sixty in every direction. De Hart was almost a boy—fair-faced, courageous, and giving great promise even in this his first skirmish of the Guerrilla stuff that was in him.

Capt. Cason's second fight was with eight hundred Federals having two pieces of artillery. This column he ambushed for nearly an entire day, killing thirty-five and wounding fifty-two. He had with him only John A. Cason, Calvin Sartain—who was captured and shot afterwards—Green Wisdom, Tom Childres, Jr., Lt. Ben Shipp, Wat Shiflett, Ab and James Bobett, E. P. De Hart, John and Martin Ballew, Ed and Crat Wilson, John M. Taylor, John Wills, and Harrison Burton. Very soon after this summer day's fight against enormous odds, Capt. Cason went South, taking with him the most of his men.

On the seventeenth of August, 1861, Capt. Cason had word brought to him that two steamboats loaded with troops were coming down the river, en route to St. Louis. An ambuscade was immediately formed on the Howard county side and almost immediately opposite Saline City. Here the current of the river sweeps very near to the shore, which would of necessity bring them within perfect rifle range of the concealed Guerrillas.

Unsuspicious of danger and crowded with a human freight that seemed too confiding to be taken so unawares and so murderously, the boats—the White Cloud and the McDowell—swept swiftly along. A sudden flame leaped out from the bushes as though some hidden fire was there, and then on the crowded decks there were terror, confusion, bleeding men and dead men. For nearly an hour Cason fought the boats thus, making of every embankment an earthwork, and of every tree a fortress. Finally a landing was effected and two pieces of cannon hurried ashore and used for shelling the timber which concealed the Guerrillas. Cason held on. As the infantry advanced, he fell back; as the infantry retired, he advanced. They could not shake loose his grip. Night alone ended the savage duel, the Federal loss being sixty-two killed and nearly a hundred wounded.

Other Guerrillas also had their way in this portion of Missouri before Quantrell, Todd, and Anderson began to operate there—notably the Holtzclaw family. Capt. Clifton Holtzclaw led the first Guerrillas Howard county produced. Capt. William Holtzclaw raised one of the first companies that was raised for Price's army in the State. His brother Clifton was a lieutenant in the company, and his other brothers, James, Benjamin and John were privates. William was killed at Corinth, John and Benjamin at Vicksburg, while James and Clifton survived the war. Here were five brothers who were brave alike, who fought side by side, who were renowned for personal prowess and personal courage, and who sacrificed everything they possessed for the cause and the Confederacy. A tragic circumstance called Capt. Clifton Holtzclaw back to Missouri. His aged father and mother, together with three sisters, had been robbed of everything they possessed, horses, household effects, clothing, even bread. Yet the old patriarch's spirit remained all unsubdued and undaunted. As far advanced as he was in life, and as little fitted for warlike operations, he nevertheless secreted several kegs of powder against a day when they might be worth their weight in gold. Some of this powder becoming damp, old Mr. Holtzclaw attempted to dry it before a fire. There was a terrible explosion, one sister was killed and the two others dreadfully burnt. To care for and protect these, and his two aged parents, Capt. Cliff Holtzclaw hurried home after the

Corinth battle, where a gallant brother had been killed, and sought to be at peace and to rest in quiet. Such things in those savage days were impossible things. Several efforts were made to capture and kill him. Four or five scouting parties went to his house, insulted his parents, abused his sisters, and made all sorts and kinds of terrible threats against his own life. In self-defense he organized speedily a splendid company and fought a desperate Guerrilla fight all through the summer of 1863 and 1864. But did he not have terrible provocation? In the summer of 1863, Lieutenant Jo Strett of Guitar's regiment, a cruel militia officer who tied Southern men to trees and sabred or shot them, went to Capt. Holtzclaw's house, took the aged father from the arms of his aged wife and remorselessly killed him. The son avenged him. He fought thereafter as some savage wild beast. He killed by day and by night. He never took a prisoner. As desperate as Anderson, as unforgiving as Todd, as untiring as Taylor or Jesse James, the timber sent him forth as a scourge and received him back again as though he was a part of its solitude.

In the spring of 1863, Col. S. D. Jackman also came into Howard county from the Confederate army on a recruiting expedition, and rode about as he pleased, and as the bold, cool, dauntless man he was. Indignant, the Federals sent out a detachment under Capt. Samuel Steinmetz, from Glasgow, to look after Jackman. Steinmetz found him near New Franklin, opposite Boonville. With Jackman was Major Rucker, Lieut. Drury Pulliam, Polk Witt, E. P. De Hart and ten other choice spirits. The Guerrillas took up a strong position in a ravine, poured a single deadly fire into Steinmetz's ranks, and scattered them in every direction, no single Federal halting in his race until he reached Fayette. Major Rives Leonard, of Guitar's regiment, aroused at the signal failure of Steinmetz to break up Jackman's recruiting camp, hurried out himself at the head of sixty picked troopers. A bloody combat ensued—brief, savage, exterminating. Jackman and Leonard met face to face and fought a single-handed fight. Leonard was hit once in the head and twice in the side, and Jackman was wounded severely in the leg. When Leonard fell his men shamefully abandoned him and dashed away, as Steinmetz's men had done, without drawing rein, until they too reached Fayette, panic-stricken and exhausted. Leonard and two of his wounded soldiers, fell alive into Jackman's hands, who treated them with marked consideration, releasing them finally, and permitting them to be carried to their homes. Several severe skirmishes followed this bloody little fight, in all of which Jackman was victorious, and for several weeks he was left comparatively undisturbed until July. At this time a very plausible man came to Jackman's camp who sought in every manner to gain his confidence and to ingratiate himself in his good opinions. Frequently he solicited Jackman to ride with him, and once he insisted that Jackman should go to a certain designated spot where he said a lot of recruits were waiting to join him. This last request aroused Jackman's suspicions. He agreed, however, to go, but before setting out sent ahead ten trusty Guerrillas especially charged to develop the ambush if ambush there was. It was soon done. Fifteen ambushed Federals were found completely hidden in the brush and awaiting anxiously the arrival of the intended victim. Eight of these were killed and the balance routed. As the sun set that afternoon its last beams fell upon the pallid face and the destorted features of a man swinging to a huge oak with a rope about his neck. The spy's death had been a dog's death.

Jackman now began to get ready to return again to the South with something like half a regiment of recruits—splendid young Missourians, eager for service and anxious to put on the gray. Before he left, however, he did a daring deed. Gen. Thomas J. Bartholow was a soldier of scars and honors. He had made a name in Mexico first, and latter a name in Missouri. He was a brave, generous, dashing, vigorous man, who fought well, who was humane, enterprising, fond of a battle, and a rough rider on a war-path. He commanded the military district in which Glasgow was located, and had a residence on an outskirt of the town. At night he generally slept there. Duly informed in regard to the General's habits, Jackman resolved to capture him. He chose for the adventure Major Rucker, Drury Pulliam, Polk Witt, E. P. De Hart, Ben Shipp, and four other stalwart Guerrillas, who were cool and who were not afraid to die. Gen. John B. Clark, Jr., now a member of Congress from Missouri, was at home on a leave of absence and accompanied Jackman. One hundred and fifty Federals held Glasgow, picqueting all the
20

roads and exercising generally a vigilant watch. Past midnight —probably between one and two o'clock in the morning—Col. Jackman, avoiding the picquets on the Glasgow and Boonville road, entered the city. Ben Shipp was the guide; he knew every foot of the ground to be travelled over, every rough or dangerous place. He also knew the best way to Gen. Bartholow's house. When this was reached without an accident or an encounter, Jackman secreted his men and sent Major Rucker to the front door, who rang the bell coolly and calmly. Gen. Bartholow answered it in person, a revolver in his hand and a look of questioning on his resolute face. Seeing only a single man there, he bade him enter. Rucker went quietly into the house, and as the two sat face to face, the Confederate slowly stated his business. "I am from Macon City, General," the would-be courier declared, "and I have a dispatch for you." And he had, written by Jackman himself, stating that the Guerrillas were between Roanoke and Huntsville, and that the devil was to pay. Bartholow read it calmly, folded it up, and laid it aside, saying bursquely as he did so, "There is no answer." Rucker rose to go, and Bartholow followed him to the front door to see him depart. As he stepped outside of it he was laid hold of by Rucker, Jackman, Pulliam, and Shipp, who had gained the house unperceived while Rucker was conferring with the General, and completely mastered him. Pistols were against every portion of his body, while in whispers the men bade him keep quiet for his life. Surprised, but in no manner intimidated, Gen. Bartholow's wonderful nerve remained unruffled. He saw the hopeless nature of a struggle, and he submitted without a struggle. Born soldier and educated commander, he saw in the episode only one phase in a war that had a thousand phases, and he faced fortune with the same equanimity that he would have faced a line of battle. Skirting the the town rapidly and regaining the horses unperceived, Jackman furnished an excellent steed for Bartholow to ride and kept by his side himself all through the night, putting by daylight a distance of twenty miles between Glasgow and his halting place in the Boonslick hills. Preceding the capture, Gen. Bartholow had issued certain proclamations containing rewards for Jackman's arrest or death, but these were promised to be withdrawn when brought to his attention by Jackman, and when on the following day Bartholow was released, he scrupulously kept his word. Meanwhile the story of their General's capture had aroused the soldiers of Glasglow as some unlooked for natural convulsion might. A great surprise came at first, and then a great fury. Capt. John Tillman, more of a cut-throat than a soldier, swore he would kill every Southern sympathizer in town if Gen. Bartholow did not return inside of twenty-four hours. Five or six of these kind of people were seized and held ready for the sacrifice. Every point of egress was carefully guarded. Tillman himself, at the head of a strong column, sallied forth to scour the country, but returned late in the day and unsuccessful only to find Gen. Bartholow back at his headquarters, safe, and full of a jolly good humor. Jackman had treated him as one gallant soldier always treats another, and Bartholow on his return after he had narrated the episode fully, and laughed over it until he was tired—restored peace to the distracted city of Glasgow, released the victims marked upon the brow by Tillman, and assured the citizens of every political faith that they should neither be persecuted nor murdered.

Guerrilla fighting began again in good earnest in many directions. Capt. William Jackson, a son of Governor C. F. Jackson, met this same Capt. John Tillman in Richland bottom, opposite Saline City, and whipped him badly. Jackson had five men and Tillman sixteen. When the fight was done, Jackson had four men and Tillman eight. The balance might have been found among the dead.

In 1864, a Kansas Red Leg Captain named Truman, passed through Howard like a scourge, cutting, slashing, hanging and shooting. In Boonslick township he killed Sashel Carson, Oliver Rose, Tazewell Jones, John Stepp, John T. Marshall, and John Cooper, all worthy and peaceful citizens. Others were killed in various parts of the county, and the Guerrillas grew in proportion as the people were preyed upon.

As already stated, Quantrell's object in going to Howard county was not so much to fight as to rest, not so much to hide himself as to be at peace. He was sick, wounded, barely able to ride, and worn from long pain and exposure. He arrived about the 10th of July, 1864, and spent the first few weeks with his old refugee friends from Jackson county, Evan Hall, Reuben Harris, and Samuel Sanders. De Hart and several other Howard county Guerrillas joined him. When Anderson began to operate in the county, Quantrell sent to find him Little, Barker, Thomas Harris, John McCorkle, Logan Tooley, and E. P. De Hart, who, after several severe skirmishes and no little stubborn fighting, found him near Boonesboro, with nineteen men. George Todd was still further away in the Perche hills of Boone county.

Anderson had already been busy with the enemy. Encountering Jackman's old antagonist, Major Leonard, at the head of two hundred and eighty men, he fought him a bushwhacking fight for several hours, killing thirteen of his command and wounding eleven.

Captain William Stuart, with seven men and about the same time, encountered a detachment of the 17th Illinois, near Boonesboro, numbering eighty. Stuart was hunting for Anderson, but he found these Illinois people traveling briskly along from Glasgow towards Boonville. The fight was near Squire Kivett's, the Guerrillas beginning with a charge, continuing with a charge and ending with a charge. The 17th fought badly, and finally ran away without sufficient pressure. Stuart was wounded severely in the left wrist, but Squire Kivett dressed his wound, and he rode forward with his arm in a sling. Of a race that needed to be exterminated to be subdued, what mattered a pin prick more or less, or a bullet or two here and there that reached no vital spot? At Allen, Anderson fought again, and won, killing twenty-two militiamen and wounding as many more. After the fight at Allen, Capt. James Jackson made a dash at Jacksonville, twelve miles below Macon City, on the North Missouri railroad, and charged the depot on horseback and furiously. He killed men on the platform; he killed them in box cars; he killed them on the right hand and the left, but the eighty militia in the depot building proper he could not get out. Among those who distinguished themselves in this desperate little fight with Jackson were Lieutenant Hines, George Heberling, Scott Hackley, Robert Cravens, and William and Charles Landrum. Charles Landrum was shot square through the breast, but he would not die. He rode with his column as it fell back, and rode a dozen and more miles to a safe hiding place before he would dismount or have his wound dressed. Not very long afterwards William Landrum, a splendid soldier, and a cool, desperate fighter, was killed leading a hopeless charge. Robert Cravens was killed at the Fayette fight, superb in the recklessness of a daring which astonished even his daring comrades.

But not all the killing was on one side. One day Anderson lost nine of his best men. At the house of a widow lady named Turner, six were surrounded and shot. They fought to the death, but they died. Six more at the house of Capt. Sebree were also surrounded, three of whom were killed. Three escaped, Hamp. Watts, a fifteen year old boy from Fayette, Anderson Baby and Joe Holt. They cut their way out from the environment, shooting right and left. Leonard's troops did the killing at these two houses.

Little, to get cured of the severe wound received at Fayette, was carried to the Boonslick hills and hidden securely away. Devoted men and women could be found everywhere to succor and shield the wounded or unfortunate Guerrillas. For patriotic devotion and unremitting care, none surpassed Mrs. William Wills, Mrs. Charles Scripture, Mr. Ivin Hall, Reuben Harris, old Billy Grady and old Major James Simms. Two prominent physicians, as brave as they were patriotic, also deserve especial mention—J. W. Hawkins, of Boonesboro, and Thomas Staples, of Saline. These men killed in battle and cured in hospitals. They were soldiers and they were Samaritans. They ennobled their profession twice—once by their heroism and once by their devotion. No danger deterred them, no difficulties baffled them, no proscription caused them to relax their efforts, no adverse circumstances made them negligent—they were noble men and they were Missourians.

Once Anderson entered Glasgow and took Col. B. W. Lewis from his residence, intending no doubt to kill him. Indeed he had sworn some time before to kill him if he ever laid hands upon him. Mrs. James S. Thompson and another lady, both extremely Southern, saved Col. Lewis and rescued him from the grasp of this desperate Guerrilla.

While Quantrell remained in Howard county after the Centralia fight, waiting for Little's wounds to heal, he encountered and killed two Federal soldiers, a Capt. Kimsey and a Robert Montgomery. These two men were out on a little pillaging expedition. They had robbed several citizens of money, and had behaved scandalously at the house of Mr. John L. De Hart. Quantrell, in company with one of his men, Thomas Harris, met these Jayhawkers and ordered them to surrender. They began to draw their pistols, when as instantaneous as the lightning's flash, the skilled Guerrilla shot them both dead from their saddles. The evening of the same day he killed another Federal by the name of John West, àt Lisbon. Not long after he had killed West some Putnam county militia came into Glasgow, stealing, shooting and burning. Lisbon was consumed. Capt. James Cason's house was given to the torch. Quantrell was encountered and driven furiously into his camp, having barely time to take James Little up behind him and fall back behind John Barker and five others of his old men, who ran and fought and held their own for fourteen miles.

CHAPTER XVI.

FROM the battle-field about Centralia, the Guerrillas moved into Callaway county. There Richard Kinney died. Trained first by Shelby and later by Todd, he went about as some mediæval knight, fighting single-handed and against desperate odds. He and Frank James were comrades in arms and inseparable. If one charged the head of a pursuing column, the other was by his side. If one fell in the desperate press of a rush or a *melee*, the other stood over him in rescue or fought against any numbers while he found another horse. Kinney, although one of the bravest of the brave, had the modesty of a women. He never boasted. Indeed, he did not even talk much. After a combat in which his prowess or his intrepidity had been conspicuous, he listened delightedly to others who recited, to others who told of the day. Such was his skill with a revolver that when an exceedingly difficult or an unusually long shot had to be made, the Guerrillas nearest said one to another: "Where is Dick Kinney? Let Dick Kinney try his hand at that d—d blue coat." At his death the notches on a single pistol butt numbered forty-eight, and for each notch a life had been taken. To-day Frank James possesses this pistol —a tragedy thing of wood and iron.

It might be thought that the wild license of Guerrilla life, the freedom from restraint, the constant acting face to face with death, would breed desperate quarrels by the score and make those who in days of concentration preyed upon the enemy, prey upon themselves in hours of disbandment and relaxation. The contrary was the case. But one rencontre can be recorded in all the long four years of terrible fighting and killing. In September, 1864, a difficulty occurred between Joel Chiles and William Ridings. Chiles was a Missourian, and Ridings a young Texan, just seventeen years of age, and the only Texan belonging to the Guerrillas. Chiles shot Ridings dead, and wounded at the same time Fletch Taylor and William Basham. Instantly Basham killed Chiles, and that was the first and the last internal difficulty the Guerrillas ever experienced.

Gathering together hastily with something of a shiver and more of a start, the Federal garrisons throughout Northeast Missouri massed a column of one thousand cavalry, accompanied by a six gun battery, and sent it out hurriedly on the track of the retreating Guerrillas. Its first dash at the rear was rather spirited. Plunk Murray had an arm broken and a minie ball sent into his left side, and Richard Ellington escaped barely with his life, a bullet in one shoulder and one leg. Todd picked thirty men instantly, armed them with Spencer rifles, and put them under Arch Clements to hold the rear. It was a royal rear guard, and it was composed of David and John Poole, Tuck, Tom and Woot Hill, three Guerrilla brothers, Jesse and Frank James, Peyton Long, Ben Broomfield, Zack Southerland, Ben Morrow, Harrison Trow, Richard Burnes, Geo. Maddox, Frank Gregg, the two Noland brothers, Ed Greenwood, George Shepherd, Oll Shepherd, John Thrailkill, John Chestnut, Captain Downing, Ling Litten, Silas King, James Commons, William Hulse, William Stuart, Jeff Emery and Andy McGuire. For twenty-five miles this rear guard fought as only such men could fight. A tree was an ambuscade ; a hill-top was a cover ; hazel-brush hid half a score of riflemen ; at every open there was a charge ; at every creek-crossing a grip that only the artillery could unloose. Thirty-seven Federals were killed in the pursuit and eighty-eight wounded more or less severely. Thrailkill, Greenwood, Maddox and William Hulse were wounded on the part of the Guerrillas, and Clements, Tuck Hill, Poole, and Frank James had their horses killed. Never a single time was this rear guard worsted in a grapple or made to fall back faster than in a walk. After fighting the pursuing militia until dark and providing places of safety for the wounded, Todd disbanded his forces October 5th, 1864. Poole, with twenty-five men, struck a German settlement on his way to Lafayette county, and killed twenty-two home guards, while Todd, taking with him Jesse and Frank James, William and Henry Nolan, Harrison Trow, Ben Morrow, John House and John Hope,

went into Howard to hunt for Quantrell. He could not or did
not find him anywhere within the county, and so sent in his
own name Frank James, the Nolans, Morrow, Trow and
House into Jackson county to arouse the Guerrillas still there
with the news of Price's advance into Missouri, while he, with
Jesse James and John Hope, returned to Anderson, camped yet
in the eastern edge of Howard. After a brief conference,
Anderson and Thomas Todd, commanding between them three
hundred men, moved instantly to meet Price, while Poole and
George Todd crossed to the south side of the Missouri river and
marched up into Cooper county, killing fifteen home guards
eight miles south of Boonville. Syracuse fell next with twenty
militia, who were killed. The depot was burned, the railroad
track torn up, and the telegraph line destroyed into and
up to the railroad bridge across the Lamine river. This
also was destroyed. Peyton Long killed a courier here
disguised as a mule driver. When searched he had, in
addition to his dispatches, two human ears recently cut
from some victim's head. Long scalped this man and
cut off his ears also, nailing them to the first Union man's
gate post he passed on the road. Otterville fell next, its garrison of twenty-two militia being cut to pieces and its depot
burned. From Otterville to Brownsville, in Saline county, Todd
and Poole killed probably a hundred militia, and from Brownsville through Lafayette county to the Missouri river, fifty more.
On the morning of October 9th a raid from their camp at
Blackwater was determined upon. Poole—taking with him as
an advance John Poole, Al Scott, Frank Gregg, Jesse James,
Ed Greenwood, Andy McGuire, James Younger, Lafe Privin,
James Commons and Peyton Long—rode ahead with his ten
men, the front of a Guerrilla column one hundred and sixty-
three strong. The object of the raid was to break up a German
military organization somewhat unfavorably known locally in
Lafayette county. The militia were by no means asleep.
Forewarned of Todd's coming, they attended speedily to the
forearming part. An ambuscade of one hundred men was
formed in some hazel brush close to the road, and fourteen cavalry sent down to meet the head of the Guerrilla column, fire
upon it, and fall back—the old style of stratagem, and yet one
which had never grown old. Two miles from the camp upon

Blackwater, Poole, well ahead of Todd, met the fourteen Federals and charged them with a yell, driving what were not ridden over and killed through the ambuscade and beyond it at a terrific pace. Todd, hearing only the firing in front, followed it at a gallop and came, caring naught for what might be on either hand, full into the jaws of the trap. The close volley that spurted out in the very faces of his men astonished but did not demoralize him. It was as a flea-bite to a bloodhound. Hiram Masterson, Presley Jobson, Thomas Sorrels, William Toothman and Archibald Smoot fell dead from their horses, and Levi Potts and Ves Atchison were wounded; but Todd dashed furiously into the brush and broke up the ambuscade as a whirlwind breaks up an oak tree. Ordinarily such an ambushment would have held well against a column no greater in its superiority than Todd's to the Federal, but instead of a man to combat there was a lion. The scene of silent killing in the tangled undergrowth was sickening. Of the hundred hiding there twenty-two in all escaped, and these because the continued firing in the front admonished Todd of duty pressing otherwheres and urgent.

Meanwhile Poole had killed ten of the fourteen decoy cavalrymen, while hard and fast on the track of the remainder there rushed Jesse James, John Poole, Andy McGuire, and Ed Greenwood. Two of the last four had just fallen, and the other two were well nigh spent and hopeless, when full tilt, pursuers and pursued ran furiously into the advance of a Federal column, two hundred strong. It was touch and go all around. As fast as they had followed a flying foe, so in turn were they followed, shot at and hallooed to at every jump. Finally, Jesse James' splendid race mare, which had carried him so superbly at Centralia, fell, killed, beneath him. John Poole and McGuire had fired their last cartridge. They could neither help themselves nor their comrade. Ed Greenwood turned savagely at bay, however, and fought as though he were fighting for his own life. Presently his horse fell beneath him, and then—side by side and afoot — these two desperate Guerrillas gathered themselves together for the worst. If the Federals had dashed up to them at the first, both inevitably must have perished. Shot in the left arm and side, James fell to his knees, caught himself, and arose again. Greenwood, hit hard in the right leg, stopped firing, sat down calmly in a rain of bullets, and tied above the wound tightly a cravat borrowed from his comrade. Content to fire at long range, the Federals by and by came closer and closer. The end was at hand. James, sheltered behind his dead horse, had already shot down five of the nearest, and Greenwood three, when a yell was heard in the rear and Poole and Todd, just in time, and altogether, dashed furiously up to the rescue. The work that followed was similar to the work done by Todd at the ambuscade. The day's deeds closed with the killing of one hundred and seventeen German militia, and the burning of thirty-five houses throughout their settlement. A citizen also was killed this day by the name of Prigmore, who was mistaken for his brother, and who was a kindly, inoffensive man. Andy McGuire, hung after the war at Richmond, Ray county, or, rather, murdered, killed eleven in the two series of engagements, Peyton Long six, Jesse James, wounded twice, ten, Dick Burnes five, William Hulse eight, Frank Gregg three, Bud Pence three, Poole five, Frank Gray five, Todd ten, John Chestnut four, Si Gordon three, John Poole seven, Al Scott four, Jack Rupe three, George Shepherd ten, John Thrailkill five, Oll Shepherd five, and several others one apiece. After the fight Todd again disbanded to meet on the 22d at Bone Hill, in Jackson county.

Gen. Sterling Price had entered Missouri from the direction of Pocahontas, Arkansas, and had leisurely advanced into the State. He fought at Pilot Knob and was worsted, but his various divisions afterwards were fighting successfully over a large extent of territory and creating as much as possible that diversion so much needed by Joseph E. Johnston, and for which the expedition into the State had been created. He avoided St. Louis, invested Jefferson City, occupied Boonville, captured Glasgow, drove Lane out of Lexington, and was in camp on Fire Prairie, in Lafayette county, when Todd, having gathered together the bulk of his Guerrillas, reported to Gen. Shelby on the morning of the 23d. Shelby's advance had been led valiantly by Capt. Arthur McCoy, and he associated Todd with him and bade them fight together. McCoy had never been a Guerrilla. He had nothing in common with the Guerrillas except their desperation. He was a tinner working in St. Louis when the war commenced. At the first tap of the recruiting

drum, impetuous as a boy and as eager, he espoused the cause
of the South and joined the 1st Missouri Confederate Infantry,
Bowen's immortal yet decimated regiment—that regiment
which Beauregard lifted his hat to as it was marching past—or,
rather, to what was left of it—after Shiloh, and exclaimed: "I
salute the 1st Missouri. I uncover to courage that has never
yet been surpassed."

In the infantry, however, McCoy would have dwindled into a
consumptive—for his chest was weak, and he had that hectic
flush, and that dry, short, rasping cough that were ominous.
He needed the air and the exercise of a Comanche. He had to
breath where there were no canvas houses, no shelter, no
covering save a blanket, and no habitation save the leaves on
the trees.

After Shiloh, the name and fame of Shelby were beginning to
fill the West, and there came to him, attracted by the unexampled enterpise and heroism of the man, quite a large number of
daring spirits who asked only *esprit du corps* and a leader that
would fight every hour in every day for a year and a day.
Among them was Arthur McCoy, one of Bowen's best and
bravest—one whom he trusted and loved—but one whom he
knew had to go the long journey very soon if held in the
poisonous camps of an army, inactive and at rest. A tall,
gaunt man was Arthur McCoy, six feet and over, a little stooped
about the shoulders, very long in the arms, having a stride like
a race-horse, and a nervous energy that was expending itself
even while he slept. All the lower face was massive—the lower
jaw especially square cut and huge. The eyes were of that
cold, glittering, penetrating blue that might be cruel as a ser-
pent's, soft and tender as the eyes of confidence or trust. When
the battle was dubious or desperate, or when the wreck was
darkest and thickest, and the dead lay rank and plentiful, the
eyes seemed to transform themselves and become absolutely
scintillant. About the man's whole nature, too, there was an
element of grotesqueness impossible to analyze. He sang little
snatches of song in battle; he rode out in advance of his own
skirmish line and challenged Federal skirmishers to single
combat; he would get down on his knees under fire the most
pitiless, uncover himself, and pray fervently beside some comrade
mortally wounded; he seemed never to have known w hat the mean-

ing of fear was; he begged incessantly to be sent upon forlorn and desperate service; he was a spy without a peer in either army; he was a scout that seemed to have leagued with the devil and received from his majesty invaluable protection papers; he charged picquets for pastime, and rode yelling and shooting through Federal outposts, at the head of fifty or sixty followers, at all hours and in any weather. Shelby's division gave him the soubriquet of the "Wild Irishman," and yet for cold, calm, penetrating soldier-sense—for acuteness, military logic and undoubted strategy, McCoy had the head of a Vidocq and the nerve of d'Artagnan. *Seven* times during the war—through the Federal lines, and past scouts, patrols, cantonments, and militia and predatory bands—McCoy came into St. Louis with a thousand letters at a time, and departed hence with as many more.

Once, on his many trips into St. Louis, and in company with Captain John Howard, also of the same city, a man in no manner inferior to McCoy in dash and heroism, he visited a house at which there were two Federal officers and several ladies. McCoy had with him an elegant cavalry uniform for a Confederate colonel, and as he was just on the eve of his departure, he concluded to take his farewell in the following manner: He requested one of the ladies to play Dixie, and she politely consented. The Federal officers looked annoyed, but remained quiet. As the tune began to fill the room and the music to expand the blood as it were and put fire into the eyes, McCoy suddenly sprang to his feet, covered the Federal major with his unerring revolver, and bade him get up and dance. The officer refused. McCoy still insisted more sternly, and declared that he should not only dance, but that he should put on a rebel uniform for once in his life, lift his hat at the mention of the name of Jefferson Davis, and dance to the tune of Dixie. Seeing murder in McCoy's cold blue eyes, the Federal major complied with each order strictly, and actually in the full uniform of a Confederate colonel did dance to the music of Dixie, his companion, a lieutenant of the Eighth Missouri Federal infantry, looking on and applauding vociferously.

As McCoy rode out from St. Louis, in the cold gray of the following morning, the devil still seemed to have possession of him. As he passed Benton Barracks a sentinel stood by the roadside with his gun at a right shoulder shift. McCoy rode up to him and halted: "I am a Confederate officer. I represent the Confederate President—if you should present arms to me I should consider that you had presented them to Mr. Jefferson Davis. Present arms!" The sentinel thought the man was evidently mad. It was still early morning. No soldiers were astir anywhere about the barracks. McCoy's revolver was at the soldier's breast before he could take his musket from his shoulder. "You will not present arms to me?" "Not to save your life." "But you see I have the drop on you! Do you want me to kill you?" Still thinking McCoy was one of his own uniform, and being drunk or mischievous, was trying to play a prank on him, the sentinel replied, "shoot and be d—d!"

McCoy's face darkened instantly, and he cocked his pistol. "I will not shoot you so," he said, "nor will I shoot you at all without giving you a chance for your life. Listen, I shall ride back fifty paces, turn my horse, and charge you. As I come by I shall fire at you once. You have but one shot and I who have eighteen will take but one also. Get ready."

The sentinel, as he saw McCoy deliberately countermarch and wheel about to charge, began, at last, to have his suspicions aroused. He took his musket from his shoulder and cocked it and waited. McCoy dashed furiously down upon the sentinel, and the sentinel, when he was within about ten paces of him, fired at point blank range and missed. As McCoy passed him, he put out his pistol suddenly and shot him down where he stood, the garrison turning out in force, and hurriedly saddled, cavalry coming on in rapid pursuit. The sentinel, however, although badly wounded, finally recovered, and McCoy, scarcely quickening his pace, rode on southward unmolested.

Once the Federals had him a prisoner. His escape was, in every way, characteristic of the man. He had been on a scout with eight men towards the Mississippi river. Seventy-three Federals started him in a cane brake and never stopped pursuing him for eleven miles. Finally they killed his horse and literally rode over and crushed him. He was carried to De Val's Bluff previous to being conveyed to St. Louis for trial as a spy and desperado. Shelby was at Clarendon, twelve miles below, on White river, and when the night came—a very dark and gloomy night—McCoy broke suddenly away from his guards and leaped head-foremost into the river. The waves were rough and the wind was blowing. Two hundred shots were fired at him in the darkness, and innumerable yawls put out from the steamers and gunboats in search of the desperate Irishman. He was a fine swimmer, and without using his arms in any manner, he drifted down under the stern of the gunboat Tyler, and hid himself there for over an hour, or until all pursuit was abandoned. Then letting go his hold, the current carried him on past all danger and safe into the lines of his old brigade.

Later, in 1864, a deed was done by McCoy which attracted the attention and won the admiration of two opposing forces. General John B. Clark was attacking Glasgow from one side of the river, in 1864, and General Shelby from the other. Between the two lines drawn about the doomed town were the Federal forts and garrison commanded by General Chester Harding. A large steamboat lay at the wharf and Shelby desired to know if it were serviceable; if it were, he intended to man it and ferry over his command, and to attack from the north side. He did not want to sacrifice over one man in the perilous undertaking, and he did not desire to order any soldier to perform the desperate duty. Volunteers were called for, and while fifty came to the front, McCoy was chosen because he knew more than any of them about steamboats and their machinery, and because he pleaded so hard to be permitted to take the risk. He started in a skiff as slight as a pasteboard. Having to pull himself, his back was necessarily to the town, thus depriving him of whatever advantage he might have attained by watching the operations of the enemy. Glasgow is built upon a hill, and from the foot of the bluff to the river there is probably a stretch of bottom land a dozen paces across. Closely engaged from the south, the Federal skirmishers did not descend from the hill tops, where, half hidden and partially intrenched, they fired closely and vigorously upon McCoy. He kept right onward. As he left the shelter of his own lines, the bullets thickened in the water about him and fairly plowed up the surface of the river with lead. Collins, with two guns of his memorable battery, succored him all that was possible and threw canister rapidly into the skirmishers. Once when the fire was desperately hot, McCoy turned around upon his seat, ceased rowing, and lifted his hat to the Federal sharpshooters. Both sides cheered spontaneously. How he escaped is a matter yet unexplained. Probably two hundred men fired at him, each man firing five shots, or one thousand shots in all. Blood was not drawn once from his body, miraculous to relate. One bullet cut off a lock of his hair, another knocked his cap into the river, which he deliberately stopped to pick up, seven balls struck the skiff in various parts, four more went through his clothes, and one cut almost in two at the oar-lock the left hand oar. In despite of everything, however, McCoy gained the northern bank, landed the boat, obtained what information he desired, and actually returned as he had crossed under a tremendous volley of small arms.

Once he fought a duel—a duel to the death—but not one of his own seeking. In the Western army' there were many Confederate Indians, and in a Choctaw regiment there was a young half-breed captain who had a pony sensible enough to have been a circus pony. It would dance, talk with its head, fire off a pistol, and do other and numerous tricks at the bidding of its master. McCoy owned a savage stallion, a favorite, however, because of its fleetness and strength. The pony and the stallion got together one night, and the next morning the Choctaw had no pony—McCoy's horse having literally devoured him. The Indian was furious. He would have revenge. He would kill the horse that killed his horse. He started to execute his threat. McCoy stood across his path with a drawn sabre in his hand, and said to the Choctaw: "Arm yourself. Shall it be sword or pistol? You want satisfaction and shall have it. My horse's hide is more precious than my own, therefore not one hair upon it shall be ruffled." The Indian chose a sabre also, a ring was formed, seconds appointed, and probably half a brigade gathered to see the desperate work. McCoy fenced warily; the Indian, quick and savage. Both were wounded. McCoy had an ugly cut on his right temple and another on his left hip. The Indian had been slashed twice severely, and once across the sabre arm. Each was getting weak. Finally McCoy made a feint as if he would deliver the right cut, shortened his sword arm, and ran the Indian squarely through the body. Thus ended the fight and the life of the Choctaw as well. He died before midnight.

Curtis' heavy division, retreating before General Price all the way from Lexington to Independence, held the western bank of the Little Blue, and some heavy stone walls and fences beyond. Marmaduke and Shelby broke his hold loose from these, and pressed him rapidly back to and through Independence, the two Colorado regiments covering his rear stubbornly and well. Side by side McCoy and Todd had made several brilliant charges during the morning, and had driven before them with great spirit and dash every Colorado squadron halted to resist the continual marching forward of the Confederate cavalry. Ere the pursuit ended for the day, half of the 2d Colorado regiment drew up on the crest of a bold hill and made a gallant fight. Their Major, Smith, a brave and dashing officer, was killed here, and here Todd fell. Gen. Shelby, as was his wont, was well up with the advance, and leading recklessly the two companies of Todd and McCoy. Next to Shelby's right rode Todd, and upon his left was McCoy. Close to these and near to the front files were Col. Nichols, Thrailkill, Ben Morrow, Ike Flannery and Jesse James. The trot had deepened into a gallop, and all the cloud of skirmishers covering the head of the rushing column were at it, fierce and hot, when the 2d Colorado swept the road with a furious volley, broke away from the strong position held by them, and hurried on through the streets of Independence followed by the untiring McCoy, as lank as a fox-hound and as eager.

That volley killed Todd. A Spencer rifle ball entered his neck in front, passed through and out near the spine, and paralyzed him. Dying as he fell, he was yet tenderly taken up and carried to the house of Mrs. Burns, in Independence. Articulating with great difficulty and leaving now and then almost incoherent messages to favorite comrade or friend, he lingered for two hours insensible to pain, and died at last as a Roman.

George Todd was a Scotchman born, his father holding an honorable position in the British navy. Destined also for the sea, it was the misfortune of the son to become engaged in a personal difficulty in his eighteenth year and kill the man with whom he quarreled. He fled to Canada, and from Canada to the United States. His father soon after resigned and followed him, and when the war began both were railroad contractors in

21

North Missouri, standing well with everybody for business energy, capacity and integrity.

Todd made a name by exceeding desperation. His features presented nothing especial which could attract attention. There was no sign in visible characters of the power that was in him. They were very calm always, and in repose a little stern; but if anything that indicated a "look of destiny" was sought for, it was not to be found about the face of George Todd. His nature was simple and confiding, and a circumspect regard for his word made him a very true but sometimes also a very blunt man. In his eyes the fittest person to command Guerrillas was he who inspired the enemy with the most dread, and he had not been long in the brush before people began to say: "That man George Todd is a tiger. He fights always. He is not happy unless he is fighting. He will either be killed soon or he will do a great amount of killing." It has just been seen that he was not killed until October, 1864—a three years' lease of life that for desperate Guerrilla work never had a counterpart. By and by the Guerrillas themselves felt confidence in such a name, reliance in such an arm, favor for such a face. It was sufficient for Todd to order a march to be implicitly followed, to plan an expedition to have it immediately carried out, to indicate a spot on which to assemble to cause an organization sometimes widely scattered or dispersed to come together as the jaws of a steel-trap. Nature gave him the restlessness of a born cavalryman, and the exterior and the power of voice necessary to a leader of desperate men. Coolness, intrepidity, and immense activity were his main attributes as a commander. Always more ready to strike than to speak, if he talked at all it was only after a combat had been had, and then modestly. His conviction was the part he played, and he sustained with unflinching courage and unflagging consistency that which he had set down for his hands to do. A splendid pistol shot, fearless as a horseman, knowing human nature well enough to choose desperate men and ambitious men, reticent, heroic beyond the conception of most conservative people, and covered with blood as he was to his brow, his fall was yet majestic because it was accompanied by patriotism.

Before the evacuation of Independence, Todd was buried by his men in the cemetery there, and Poole succeeded to the command of his company, leading it splendidly. The night they buried Todd, Ike Flannery, Dick Burnes, Andy McGuire, Ben Morrow, Press Webb, Harrison Trow, Lafe Privin, George Shepherd, George Maddox, Allen Parmer, Dan Vaughn, Jesse and Frank James and John Ross took a solemn oath by the open grave of the dead man to avenge his death, and for the following three days of incessant battle it was remarked how desperately they fought and how long.

Until Gen. Price started Southward from Mine creek in full retreat, the Guerrillas under Poole remained with him, scouting and picqeuting, and fighting with the advance. After Mine creek they returned to Bone Hill, in Jackson county, some going afterwards to Kentucky with Quantrell, and some to Texas with George Shepherd.

Henceforward the history of the Guerrillas of Missouri must be the history of detachments and isolated squads, fighting always but fighting without coherency or other desire than to kill. Anderson had joined Price at Boonville and the meeting was a memorable one. The bridles of the horses the men rode were adorned with scalps. One huge, red-bearded Guerrilla—six feet and over, and girdled about the waist with an armory of revolvers—had dangling from every conceivable angle a profuse array of these ghastly trophies. Gen. Price was shocked at such evidences of a warfare so utterly repugnant to a commander of his known generosity and forbearance, and he ordered sternly that they be thrown away at once. He questioned Anderson long of Missouri; of the forces in the State; of the temper of the people; of the nature of Guerrilla warfare; of its relative advantages and disadvantages, and then when he had heard all he blessed the Guerrillas probably with about as much unction as Balaam blessed Israel. Gen. Price was a merciful man. Equable in every relation of life, conservative by nature and largely tolerant through his earlier political training, thousands living to-day live solely because none of the harsher and crueler indulgencies of the civil war were permitted to the troops commanded by this conscientious officer. Finally, however, he ordered Anderson back into North Missouri, and he crossed at Boonville upon his last career of leave-taking, desperation, and death. Tired of tearing up railroad tracks, cutting down telegraph-poles, destroying miles and miles of wire, burning depots, and picking up and killing isolated militia, terrified at the uprising in favor of Price, Anderson dashed into Danville, Montgomery county, where sixty Federals were stationed in houses and other strong places. He had but fifty-seven men, and the fight was close and hot. Gooly Robinson, one of his best soldiers, was mortally wounded, while exposing himself in a most reckless manner. It was difficult to get the enemy out of the houses. Snatching up torches, and braving the guns of the entrenched Federals, Dick and Ike Berry put fire to one house, Arch Clements and Dick West to another, Theo. Castle, John Maupin, and Mose Huffaker to a third, and Ben Broomfield, Tuck, Tom, and Woot Hill to the fourth. It was a night of terror and agony. As the militia ran out they were shot down by the Guerrillas in the shadow. Some, wounded, burnt to death; and others, stifled by the heat and smoke, rushed, gasping and blackened into the air, to be riddled with bullets. Eight barely of the garrison of sixty escaped the holocaust, and Anderson turned west towards Kansas City, expecting to overtake Gen. Price there. *En route* he killed as he rode. Scarcely an hour of all the long march was barren of a victim. Union men, militia, Federal soldiers, home guards, Germans on general principles—no matter what the class or the organization—if they were pro-United States they were killed.

On the 25th of October, while well advanced in Ray county, he received the first news of the death of Todd and the retreat of Price. By this time, however, he had recruited his own command to several hundred, and had joined it to a detachment of regular Confederates, guiding and guarding to the South a motley aggregation of recruits, old and young. Halting one day to rest, and to prepare for a passage across the Missouri river, Anderson moved on the morning of the 27th towards the spot selected for the crossing—an out of the way place in the bottom above Camden. Barring his passage to it, and having every advantage of position and numbers, Anderson found one thousand Federals—eight hundred infantry and two hundred cavalry. He made haste to attack them. His young Lieutenant, Arch Clements, advised him urgently against a fight, as did Capt. A. E. Asbury, a young and gallant Confederate officer, who was in company with him, commanding fifty recruits. Others of his associates did the same, notably Col. John Holt, a

WOOT HILL.

TUCK HILL.

Confedrate officer, and Col. James H. R. Cundiff. Captain
Asbury was a cool, brave, wary man, who had had large experience in border fighting, and who knew that for a desperate
charge raw recruits could not be depended upon. Anderson
would not be held back. Ordering a charge, he led it himself
furiously, and was fifty feet ahead of every follower when he
was killed. Next to him was William Smith, a veteran Guerrilla of four years' service. Five balls struck him, and three
struck Anderson. Next to Smith was John Maupin, who was
wounded twice, and next to Maupin, Cundiff, who was also hit,
and next to Cundiff, Asbury, who got four bullets through his
clothes. John Holt, Jim Crow Chiles, and Peyton Long had
horses killed. The three Hill brothers, Dick West, and ten
others of Anderson's old company fought their way up to
Anderson's body, and sought to bring it out. Tuck Hill was
shot, his brother Woot, and West. Their wounds were severe
but not mortal. Once they succeeded in placing it upon a
horse ; the horse was killed and fell upon the corpse and held it
to the ground. Still struggling heroically over the body of
their idolized commander, Hank Patterson fell dead, not a foot
from the dead Guerrilla. Next, Simonds was killed, and then
Anson Tolliver, and then Paul Debenhorst, and then Smith
Jobson, and then Luckett, then John McIlvaine, and finally
Jasper Moody and William Tarkington. Nothing could live
before the fire of the concealed infantry and the Spencer carbines of the cavalry. A single blanket might have covered the
terrible heap of dead and wounded who fought to recover all
that remained of that tiger of the jungle. John Pringle, the
red-headed giant of the Boonville scalps, far ahead of his company, was the last man killed, struggling even to the death to
bear back the corpse. He was a captain of a company, and a
veteran of the Mexican war, but he did what he would not
order his men to do, he rushed up to the corpse heap and
fastened about the leg of Anderson a *lariat* that he might drag
the body away. The Federals killed his horse. Shot once, he
tugged at the rope himself, bleeding pitifully. Shot again, he
fell, struggled up to his feet, fired every barrel of three revolvers
into the enemy, and received as a counter-blow two more
bullets. This time he did not rise again, nor stir, nor make
moan. All the wild boar blood in his veins had been poured

out, and the bronzed face from being rigid had become to be august. Joseph and Arch Nicholson, William James, Clell Miller, and John Warren, all young recruits in their first battle, fought savagely in the *melee*, and all were wounded. Miller, among those who strove to rescue the corpse of Anderson, was shot, and Warren, wounded four times, crawled back from the slaughter-pen with difficulty.

William Anderson was a strange man. If the waves of the civil war had not cast him up as the avenger of one sister assassinated and another maimed, he would have lived through it peacefully, the devil that existed within him sleeping on, and the terrible powers latent there remaining unaroused. It is probable that he did not know his own nature. He certainly could not have anticipated the almost miraculous transfiguration that came to him on the eve of his first engagement—that sort of a transfiguration which found him a stripling and left him a giant.

He was a pensive, brooding, silent man. He rarely made manifest any especial individuality in dealing either with the citizens, or with his own soldiers. If he said yes or no, it was as though a pyramid had uttered it—the resolution was unalterable. He went to war to kill, and when this self-declared proposition was once well impressed upon his followers, he referred to the subject no more. Generally those who fought him were worsted; in a majority of instances annihilated. He was a devil incarnate in battle, but had been heard over and over again to say: "If I cared for my life I would have lost it long ago; wanting to lose it, I cannot throw it away." And it would appear from the history of his career up to the time of his death that what in most men might have been regarded as fatalism was but the inspiration of a palpable destiny. Mortal bullets avoided him. At desperate odds, fortune never deserted him. Surrounded, he could not be captured. Outnumbered, he could not be crushed. Surprised, it was impossible to demoralize him. Baffled by adversity, or crippled and wrought upon often by the elements, he wearied no more than a plough that oxen pull, or despaired never so much as the granite mass the storms beat upon and the lightnings strike. Shot dead from his saddle at last in a charge reckless beyond all reason, none triumphed over him a captive before the work was done of the fetters and the rope. His body, however, remained in the hands of the enemy, who dragged it for some distance as two mules might drag a saw log, and finally propped it up in a picture gallery in Richmond and had pictures taken of the wan drawn face of the dead lion and his great mane of a beard that was full of the dead leaves and the dust of the highway.

Lieutenant Arch Clements, just turned of eighteen, succeeded to the command of Anderson's old company, and moved with it after the fight directly to Brunswick, in Chariton county, where he crossed the Missouri river and proceeded to the South. Cool-headed, wary, vigilant, and created especially for a soldier, Clements had long before given ample evidence of the skill and the dash that were pre-eminently a part of his military character. He wore in all the fullness of its old unsparing proportions the mantle of Anderson, and killed just as thoroughly and as remorselessly. South from Brunswick some three days' march, Clements overtook Capt. Grooms, of Shelby's brigade, who was hastening forward with fifty-four recruits. Clements proposed to join forces with Grooms and travel South together, the one command mutually strengthening and giving support to the other. The Confederates refused to have anything to do with the Guerrillas, and as a consequence Grooms and his entire detachment were overwhelmed and cut to pieces. They fought to the last man, but they fought a hopeless battle. Not a soldier of the fifty-four escaped. Clements kept accurately the number of Federals killed on this trip, and an account of the way they were killed. It was a singular and a sanguinary diary, and read about as follows: "Shot, one hundred and fifty-two; throats cut, twenty; hung, seventy-six; shot and scalped, thirty-three; shot and mutilated, eleven. Grand total—two hundred and ninety-two." Every Federal killed, save and alone those killed in open fight, was made acquainted with the reason why he was slain after he had surrendered. Good or bad, the reason was the same; true or untrue, it made none of the victims more content to die. In Anderson's command there were probably fifty men who had formed what was known as the Brotherhood of Death. To become a member of it one had to swear that he would avenge the killing of a brother no matter how killed, or when, or where. Each member had also a companion-in-arms upon whom the pact became especially binding, and who could, because of the direct obligation thus imposed, make the law that much the more certain of enforcement. To avenge the killing of Anderson these two hundred and ninety-wo Federal soldiers were slain in all forms and fashions from the Missouri river to Red river, and it was to give them a good reason for cutting their throats or blowing out their brains that Clements caused to be related to each of them the history of the Brotherhood and the obligations of its organization.

In a personal altercation concerning a hog, while the Guerrillas were in camp on White river, Arkansas, Dick West shot Creth Creek in the mouth, inflicting a severe yet not fatal wound. Creek recovered, and the difficulty would have been renewed, if the collapse of the revolution and the downfall of the Confederacy had not taught the great mass of the Southern combatants that it was no time to think of men, or their personal grievances. In winter quarters at Sherman, Texas, Clements rested from the bloody work of 1864, and waited impatiently for the spring of another year.

Todd's death fell upon the spirits of his men as a sudden bereavement upon the hearts of a happy and devoted family. Those who mourned for him mourned all the more tenderly because they could not weep. Nature, having denied to them the consolation of tears, left them the infinite intercourse, and remembrances of comradeship and soldierly affection. The old bands, however, were breaking up. Lieut. George Shepherd, taking with him Matt Wayman, John Maupin, Theo. Castle, Jack Rupe, Silas King, James and Alfred Corum, Bud Story, Perry Smith, Jack Williams, Jesse James, James and Arthur Devers, Press Webb, John Norfolk and others to the number of twenty-six, started South to Texas on the 13th of November, 1864. With Shepherd also were William Gregg and wife, Richard Maddox and wife, and James Hendrix and wife—these ladies were just as brave, and just as devoted, and just as intrepid in peril or extremity as the men who marched with them to guard them, and, if needs be, to die for them. Jesse James and Frank James separated here, Frank to go to Kentucky with Quantrell, and Jesse to follow the remnant of Todd's still organized veterans into Texas.

Besides killing isolated squads of Federals, and making way with every individual militiaman who supposed that the roads were absolutely safe for travelers because Gen. Price and his army had long been gone, Shepherd's fighting for several days was only fun. On the 22d, however, Capt. Emmet Goss, an old acquaintance of the 15th Kansas Cavalry, Jennison's, was encountered, commanding thirty-two Jayhawkers. Of late Goss had been varying his orgies somewhat. He would drink to excess, and lavish his plunder and money on ill-featured mistresses, who were sometimes Indians, sometimes negresses, and but rarely pure white. Returning northward one day from Cane Hill, in Arkansas, he rode gaily along at the head of thirty-two men rank and file. He was about thirty-five years old, square built, had broad shoulders, a swaggering gait, stood six feet when at himself and erect, had red hair and a bad eye, and a face that meant fight when cornered—and desperate fight at that. November 22d, 1864, was an autumn day, full of sunshine and falling leaves. Riding southward from Missouri Lieut. Shepherd met Capt. Goss riding northward from Cane Hill. Shepherd had twenty-six men rank and file. It was an accidental meeting—one of those sudden, forlorn, isolated, murderous meetings not rare during the war—a meeting of outlying detachments that asked no quarter and gave none. It took place on Cabin Creek, in the Cherokee Nation. Each rank arrayed itself speedily. There were twenty-six men against thirty-two. The odds were not great—indeed they never had been considered at all. There came a charge and a sudden and terrible storm of revolver bullets. Nothing so weak as the Kansas detachment could possibly live before the deadly prowess and pistol practice of the Missourians. Of the thirty-two, twenty-nine were killed. One, riding a magnificent race horse, escaped on the wings of the wind—one, a negro barber, was taken along to wait upon the Guerrillas, and the third, a poor, emaciated skeleton, as good as dead of consumption, was permitted to ride still away northward, bearing the story of the thunderbolt. Among the Missourians four were killed. In the *melee* Jesse James encountered Goss and singled him out from all the press. As James bore down upon him, he found that his horse, an extremely high-spirited and powerful one, had taken the bit in its teeth and was perfectly unmanageable. Besides, his left arm being yet weak from a scarcely healed wound, it was impossible for him to control his horse, or even to guide him. Pistol balls were as plentiful as the leaves that were pattering down. James had, however, to put up his revolver as he rode, and rely upon his right hand to reinforce his left. Before he could turn his horse and break its hold upon the bit, Goss had fired upon him four times. Close upon him at last James shot him through and through. Goss swayed heavily in his saddle, but held on. "Will you surrender?" Jesse asked, recocking his pistol and presenting it again. "Never!" was the stern reply, Goss still reeling in the saddle and bleeding deathfully. When the blue-white smoke curled up again there was a riderless steed among the trees and a guilty spirit somewhere out in the darkness of the unknown. It took two dragoon revolver bullets to finish this one, and yet James was not satisfied with his work. There was a preacher along who also had sat himself steadfast in his saddle, and had fought as the best of them did. James rode straight at him after he had finished Goss. The parson's heart failed him at last, however, and he started to run. James gained upon him at every step. When close enough for a shot, he called out to him: "Turn about like a man, that I may not shoot you in the back." The Jayhawker turned, and his face was white and his tongue was voluble. "Don't shoot me," he pleaded; "I am the chaplain of the Thirteenth Kansas; my name is U. P. Gardner; I have killed no man, but have prayed for many; spare me." James did not answer. Perhaps he turned away his head a little as he threw out his pistol. When the smoke lifted, Gardner was dead upon the crisp, sere grass with a bullet through his brain. Maddox in this fight killed three of Goss' men, Gregg five, Press Webb three, Wayman four, Hendrix three, and others one or two each.

The march through the Indian country was one long stretch of ambushments and skirmishes. Wayman stirred up a hornet's nest late one afternoon, and though stung himself twice quite severely, he killed four Indians in single combat and wounded the fifth who escaped. Press Webb, hunting the same day for a horse, was ambushed by three Pins and wounded slightly in the arm. He charged single-handed into the brush and was shot again before he got out of it, but he killed the three Indians and captured three excellent ponies, a veritable God-send to all. The next day about noon the rear-guard, composed of Jesse

James, Bud Story, Harrison Trow, and Jack Rupe was savagely attacked by seventy-five Federal Cherokees and driven back upon the main body rapidly. Shepherd, one of the quickest and keenest soldiers the war produced, had formed every man of the command in the rear of an open field through which the enemy must advance and over which in return a telling charge could be made. The three heroic women, mounted on excellent horses and given shelter in some timber still further to the rear of the Guerrilla line, bade their husbands as they kissed them fight to the death or conquer. The Indians bore down as if they meant to ride down a regiment. Firing their pistols into their very faces with deadly effect, the rear guard had not succeeded in stopping them a single second; but when in the counter-charge Shepherd dashed at the on-coming line, it melted away as snow in a thaw. Shepherd, Maddox, Gregg, the two Corums, Rupe, Story, James, Hendrix, Webb, Smith, Commons, Castle, Wayman, and King fought like men who wanted to make a clean sweep and a merciless one. John Maupin, not yet well from the two ugly wounds received the day Anderson was killed, insisted on riding in the charge, and was shot the third time by an Indian whom he had put two balls into, and whose horse he rushed up to secure. Jesse James had his horse killed, and a pistol shot from his hand. Several other Guerrillas were wounded, but none killed, and Williams, James Corum, and Maddox lost horses. Of the sixty-five Indians fifty-two were counted, killed, while some, known to be wounded, dragged themselves off into the mountain and escaped.

At Sherman, Texas, which was reached on the second of December, Lieutenant Shepherd disbanded his men, taking a portion of them into Western Texas, while Jesse James, John Maupin, Theo. Castle, Jack Rupe, Bud Story, Silas King, Perry Smith, and James Commons remained to take service with Clements and the remainder of Anderson's Guerrillas. While romping one day in the camp near Sherman, Silas King's pistol was accidentally discharged, killing Perry Smith, a splendid young soldier who had gone through unharmed the crisis of many a stubborn combat. Such deep grief came to King, however, and such had been his love for the young Guerrilla, that a mortal sickness fell upon him, and he died of a fever in two weeks afterwards. King was from Clay county, Missouri, and was buried by Adam Yocum, of Fannin county, Texas.

On the first of March, 1875, Captain Clements—having been reinforced by ten men under the command of Captain David Poole—marched from Sherman to Mt. Pleasant, Titus county; and from Mt. Pleasant, on the fourteenth of April, the march began once more and for the last time into Missouri. The spring of 1865 was known as the spring of the rain storms. Water was everywhere. The lowlands were lakes; the high lands a swamp. In all directions rivers overflowed. Military expeditions, ready for service since the breaking up of winter, could not move because they were not amphibious. Where the Guerrillas could not find dry land, they waded; where they could not find shallow water they swam. At the crossing of the Sulphur river, near Clarksville, Texas, Charles Hammons, from Lexington, Missouri, a brave young soldier, was drowned. At Clarksville a soldier named Jackson, who belonged to Shelby's brigade, and who had been imprisoned for killing a Texas militiaman, was rescued by Poole, Press Webb, and Jesse James, and sent to his command, well mounted and armed. On the sixteenth of April, a reorganization was had. One company of eighty men elected Arch Clements captain, James Anderson—brother of the famous Guerrilla—first lieutenant, and James Sanders, orderly sergeant. The other company, likewise eighty strong, elected David Poole captain, Wm. Greenwood first lieutenant, and Lon Railey orderly sergeant. The first game consisted of three Indians who fired on the advance just after it had emerged from the swimming waters of the Arkansas river, were ridden over by James and Clements and killed. Forming an advance of David Poole, John Poole, John Maupin, Jack Bishop, Theo. Castle, Jesse James and Press Webb, Clements pushed on rapidly, killing five militia in one squad, ten in another, here and there a single one, and now and then as many together as twenty. In Benton county, Missouri, a Federal militiaman was captured named Harkness who had killed a brother of Clements and burnt the house of his mother. James, Maupin, and Castle held Harkness tightly while Clements cut his throat and afterwards scalped him. At Kingsville, in Johnson county, something of a skirmish was had, and ten Federals were killed. A militiaman named Duncan was also captured at the same time who had a bad name locally, and who was described as being a highwayman and a house burner. Fifty-five years of age and gray-headed neither one nor the other saved him. But before the old man surrendered he fought a desperate fight. Knowing instinctively what his fate would be if he fell alive into the hands of any hostile organization, much less a Guerrilla organization, he took a stand behind a plank fence, armed with a Spencer rifle and two revolvers, and faced the enemy, now close upon him. Arch Clements, Jesse James, and Jack Bishop dashed at Duncan. The first shot killed Bishop's horse, and in falling the horse fell upon the rider. At the second fire Clements' horse was also killed, but James stopped neither for the deadly aim of the old man nor for the help of his comrades who were coming up as fast as they could on foot. He shot him three times before he knocked him from his feet to his knees, but the fourth shot—striking him fair in the middle of the forehead—finished the old man and all of his sins together.

On the fourteenth a council was held among the Guerrillas to discuss the *pros* and *cons* of a surrender. Virtually the war was over. Everywhere the regular Confederate armies had surrendered and disbanded, and in no direction could any evidences be discovered of that Guerrilla warfare which many predicted would succeed to the war of the regular army and the general order. All decided to do as the rest of the Southern forces had done, except Clements, Anderson, John and Thomas Maupin, Jack Bishop, Jesse James, Theo. Castle, John Chatman, Capt. Kelly, Joshua Esters, and Samuel Wade. These would go to Mexico with Shelby and espouse either Juarez or Maximilian, but they would never surrender. Anxious, however, to give to those of the command who preferred a contrary course the dignity and the formality of official authority, Captain Clements entered Lexington on the fifteenth with Jesse James, Jesse Hamlet, Jack Rupe, Willis King, and John Vanmeter, and bearing a flag of truce. The provost marshal of Lexington, Major J. B. Rodgers, was a liberal officer of the old *regime*, who understood in its fullest and broadest sense that the war was over, and that however cruel or desperate certain organizations or certain bodies of men had been in the past, all proscription of them ceased with their surrender.

As Clements marched back from Lexington, Jesse James, still riding at the head of the column with the white flag, eight Federal soldiers were met who were drunk, and who, either did not see the truce flag or did not regard it. They fired point blank at the Guerrillas, and were charged in turn and routed with the loss of four killed and two wounded. These eight, however, were but the advance of a larger party of sixty, thirty Johnson county militia, and thirty of the 2d Wisconsin Cavalry. These, in the counter attack, drove back the Guerrillas and followed them fiercely—especially the 2d Wisconsin. Vanmeter's horse was killed, but Jack Rupe stopped under fire for him and carried him out in safety. James and Clements, though riding jaded horses—the same horses, in fact, which had made the long inhospitable trip up from Texas—galloped steadily away in retreat side by side, and fighting as best they could. Mounted on a superb black horse, a single Wisconsin trooper dashed ahead of the balance and closed in swiftly upon James, who halted to court the encounter. At the distance of ten feet both fired simultaneously, and when the smoke cleared away the brave Wisconsin man was dead with a dragoon revolver ball through his heart. Scarcely had this combat closed, however, before another Wisconsin trooper, equally as resolute as his stricken comrade, rushed at James, firing rapidly, and closing in as he fired. James killed his horse, and the Federal in turn sent a pistol ball through James' right lung, the same lung that had before been so severely wounded. Then the rush passed over and beyond him. Another volley killed his horse, and as the Johnson county militia galloped by, five fired at him as he lay bleeding under the prostrate animal. Clements, seeing horse and rider go down together, believed his beloved comrade was killed, and strove thereafter to make good his own escape. Extricating himself with infinite toil and pain, Jesse James left the road for the woods, pursued by five Federals, who fired at him constantly as they followed. At a distance of two hundred yards he killed the foremost Federal and halted long enough under fire to disencumber himself of his heavy cavalry boots, one of which was a quarter full of blood. He fired again and shattered the pistol arm of the second pursuer, the other three closing up and pressing the maimed Guerrilla as ravenous hounds the torn flanks of a crippled stag. James was getting weaker and weaker. The foremost of the three pursuers could be heard distinctly yelling: "Oh! g—d d—n your little soul,

we have you at last! Stop, and be killed like a gentleman!"
James did not reply, but when he attempted to lift his trusty
dragoon pistol to halt the nearest trooper, he found it too heavy
for his hand. But reinforcing his right arm with his left, he
fired finally at the Wisconsin man almost upon him and killed
him in the saddle. Perhaps then and there an end might have
been made to come to the career of the desperate Guerrilla if
the two remaining pursuers had been Wisconsin cavalry instead
of Johnson county militia; but terrified at the prowess of one
who had been so terribly wounded, and who killed even as he
reeled along, the militiamen abandoned the chase, and James,
staggering on four or five hundred yards further, fell upon the
edge of a creek and fainted. From the 15th to the 17th he lay
alongside the water, bathing his wound continually and drinking
vast quantities of it to quench his burning fever. Towards
sunset, on the evening of the 17th, he crawled to a field where
a man was plowing, who proved to be a Southern man and a
friend. That night he rode fifteen miles to the house of a Mr.
Bowman, held upon a horse by his new-found friend, where he
remained, waited upon by Clements and Rupe, until the surrender of Poole, on the 21st, with one hundred and twenty-nine
Guerrillas. Major Rodgers was so well satisfied that James
would die that he thought it unnecessary to parole him, and so
declared. To give him every chance, however, for his life, and
to enable him to reach his mother—then a fugitive in Nebraska
—Rodgers furnished him with transportation, money, and a
pass. While awaiting a steamboat at Lexington, James became
acquainted with the soldier who had shot him—John E. Jones,
Company E., 2d Wisconsin Cavalry. They exchanged photographs, became fast friends, and separated mutually satisfied
with each other's prowess. The end of the war had come for
the wounded Guerrilla, but not the end of his battles or his
besetments. Recovering slowly—so slowly, in fact, that it was
three years before he could back a horse or fire a pistol—he
lives to-day in the full strength of a splendid physical manhood,
an outlaw, yet an innocent and persecuted man, covered with
the scars of twenty-two wounds and as desperate and as undaunted as though there was still war in the land and he a
soldier in the thick of it.

Capt. Arch Clements would not surrender when Poole and his

men did, nor would James Anderson, Joshua Esters, Sam Wade, Samuel Brooks, John and Thomas Maupin, Theo. Castle, Jack Bishop, John Chatman and Capt. Kelley. Many of these preferred to fight to the death, and others to leave the country. Esters, Wade and Brooks crossed over into Clay county, en route to British Columbia, when Esters and Wade were killed, and Brooks wounded and captured. His extreme youth saved his life—being only seventeen, and looking much younger. Esters and Wade fought to the death. Surrounded by sixty militia, they killed six and wounded four.

Clements, pushing boldly in the direction of Howard county from Lafayette, acted just as though the war was still in progress and that it was a part of his military duty to fight and kill as formerly. A heavy rain fell upon the Guerrillas, the roads from being bad had become to be dreadful, and a strong detachment of Federals struck this last of a once terrible organization and killed Thomas Maupin, Theo. Castle, John Chatman and Capt. Kelley. Kelley was a maimed Confederate soldier, whose arm had been shot off at Vicksburg. John Maupin was badly wounded at the same time, but escaped. After this fight, in which two hundred militia were engaged, all the balance of the Guerrillas surrendered except Clements and Anderson. In the fall of 1865 these two went to Texas, but Clements returned to Missouri, and on December 13, 1866, was killed in Lexington.

But before all this disintegration and falling to pieces, much desperate and isolated fighting and killing had been done. Fletch Taylor believed he had a special mission to perform during the war, and he performed it to the letter, despite of wounds, mutilation, the constantly increasing odds he had to encounter and the difficulty of making headway or even holding his own as the strife went on. This mission, practically summed up, was simply to fight. He fought anywhere; he fought always; he fought man to man or one against ten; he fought at all hours and in all weathers; he fought as well with one arm as with two; he fought to kill. Low, square about the jaws, the brow broad, the eyes prominent, the limbs rounded and heavily girt around with muscles, the chest and shoulders massive, tireless in energy, and with immense nervous power, Taylor roamed perpetually at the head of a score of followers equally as intrepid as himself and as enterprising.

After the fight at Ridgely, in Platte county, Capt. Taylor entered Lafayette in company with Anderson and did some hazardous duty for him in the way of picketing the roads while Anderson's men procured horses, moulded bullets, and prepared themselves generally for a savage forward movement. John Hope, Nat. Tigue, Newton Olifant, Gooly Robertson, Press Fugitt, John Fisher and McMacane were the seven men Taylor took with him from Lafayette and re-crossed into Clay. There was to be a season of desperate Guerrilla work, and to do this work who were so well fitted as the old instruments? Where were Jesse and Frank James, and those of their own immediate comrades who came as they came and went as they went? Capt. Taylor would know for himself. Every man of his following was dressed as a Federal. From tasseled hat to spurred cavalry boots, the whole *ensemble* was perfect. But because of their uniform they received at Mrs. Samuels' scant kindness or courtesy. Mrs. Samuels had seen Taylor once in 1863, and briefly; but disguised as he was and as obnoxious as his clothing made him, this unregenerate Southern woman—devoted to the Confederacy with all the passionate attachment of a singularly strong and patriotic nature—bade him find her boys if he wanted to find them with arms in his hands. Taylor laughed and was rejoiced at a manifestation like this of so much defiance, and rode in his quest of the Clay county Guerrillas to the house of Gilbert McElvaine. McElvaine was an old man who feared God much and loved him, and who loved also next to his religion Jefferson Davis and the Southern Confederacy. He fed the Southern soldier, brought news to him, risked fifty times over his old gray head for him, prayed for him as a patriarch of the days of David, and kept thus because of it all a conscience clean and a lamp ready trimmed for the final coming. At Jesse Cole's, Taylor was joined by Jesse James, Oll Shepherd, Frank James, Peyton Long, Theo. Castle, Allen Parmer, Dock Rupe, Silas King and James Commons. Mr. Cole was a Union man, an uncle of the James brothers, but a just and upright citizen. As Captain Moses, of the 2d Colorado, Taylor had established most gratifying social relations with Mr. Cole. In a walk of a morning or a talk in the twilight he

> " had praised the kine,
> The clover's reach and the meadow's fine,
> And so made the 'Squire his friend forever."

22

An exhibition something in the nature of a school exhibition was being held at Mt. Gilead church, in the upper part of Clay county, and Taylor believed something in the way of game worthy of being trapped and slain might be found there or prowling about in the neighborhood. A rapid night march from Cole's left him at daylight within a mile of the church, where he halted in the timber and hid himself. Taking, after a brief rest, seven men with him of his twenty—Frank James, Peyton Long, McMacane, Jesse James, Theo. Castle, Allen Parmer, and John Hope—Captain Taylor surrounded the church in search of an enemy, but found none—not even a straggling militiaman in citizen's dress.

The next day two brothers, Captain and Lieutenant Bigelow, were killed. These men commanded a militia company of sinister local reputation. They lived near the line separating Clinton and Clay counties, and in the northeastern part of Clay. Many bad things had been done by the men they commanded, and some cruel and murderous things. Taylor surrounded their dwelling-house about noon and demanded a surrender on the part of the brothers who were within. Peremptorily refusing this, a fight began instantly. The brothers—unsupported and outnumbered—fought to the death. The house sheltered them much, and they were otherwise cool, dangerous, athletic men. John Hope was wounded and his horse killed, James Commons lost his horse as he stood up in the saddle and sought to shoot through a window. Castle was also wounded slightly, and Jesse James painfully in the left arm. Taylor ordered a charge. Bursting down doors and breaking away all obstructions, the Guerrillas ended the combat with one furious rush. Frank James killed Captain Bigelow at the head of a flight of steps, and Jesse James, wounded as he was, followed the Lieutenant into a lumber room and shot him there, defending himself desperately with a piece of a bedstead.

This savage episode aroused the country from Liberty to St. Joseph, the militia began to swarm, and the regular troops to put themselves in motion. Captain Taylor chose as a camping place a spot somewhat difficult of approach, and some little distance away from the more frequented lines of travel. Here he crouched himself awaiting an opportunity for another spring. Peyton Long, Jesse James, Allen Parmer, Oll Shepherd, Frank

James and Theo. Castle, sent various ways to encounter the enemy and bring tidings of his operations, met by appointment at a church on Clear Fork and attended divine services in a body. Perhaps there was more bravado than piety in this; certainly more curiosity than religion. They talked long to the girls there, renewed some old acquaintances, heard by signs and signals some news it would be of advantage for Taylor to know, and rode away into the brush after lingering late and leaving with reluctance. Busy people and unfriendly as well, made haste to hurry into Liberty where Capt. John Younger commanded, and tell the tale of the terrible Guerrillas. Younger belonged to the county and was a cruel, bold, unscrupulous, unforgiving man. When he had the numbers he fought, and when he had the advantage he killed. The citizens feared him, and the soldiers sought every opportunity to meet him in combat. Man to man, before a Guerrilla attack he would have lasted probably long enough to fire a volley. Younger, at the head of seventy-five men, came rapidly out from Liberty when the news was brought to him, struck the trail of the Guerrillas at the church and followed it up at a gallop. In some timber near the residence of a Mr. Duncan he found them all asleep except Frank James, and charged furiously down upon the helpless camp. Luckily a high fence was between the laggards and the militia, or the surprise must have been murderous. Frank James shot and shouted, and fought as though he bore a charmed life. Peyton Long was wounded in an arm, Frank James in a leg, Jesse James in the face, while the two Jameses had their horses killed, and Shepherd and Parmer theirs captured. If Younger lost a man it was not known among the Guerrillas.

Three days afterward, while scouting well down towards Missouri City, Silas King, Oll Shepherd, Dock Rupe, Nat Tigue, and Press Fugitt were overtaken at the house of a Mr. Anderson by seventy-five Federals and furiously attacked. A running fight of seven miles ended in the killing of Fugitt and six of the pursuing column. It was not permitted at that time to bury dead Guerrillas. Made wild animals by all kinds of proclamations and general orders, if a citizen succored one of them he was himself a cut-throat, and if he gave to one of them who was dying or starving a cup of water or a crust of bread, he was an outlaw who had committed treason. Fugitt lay for some little

time where he had fallen. People passed the corpse by on the
other side. In the land which he had died for there might not
at last be found for him a shallow grave. Then there rose up
an old hero, Mr. Ryland Shackelford, and went forth alone with
mattock and spade and buried the dead man boldly and in the
light of the sun. His neighbors, fearing for his life, besought
him to let the dead Guerrilla be. Passers by who knew him well
and who had known him long, saw him toiling at his work and
bade him beware of the fate the law had decreed for Christian
acts like these or any deeds of charity. He heeded neither
friendly word nor token. He dug the grave both deep and
wide, and he placed therein and reverently the corpse that
neither had shroud nor coffin. Perhaps he said a prayer over
the placid face past all recognition of Pharisee or Samaritan, of
cowardly time-server or Christian man; but be sure if a prayer
were said the good God heard it and gave it heed against the
resurrection day.

The 3d of July, 1864, Captain Taylor was at the hospitable
mansion of Judge Levels, where a hearty welcome was always
in waiting for those who fought for the South. Near the house
of Obadiah Harris, a Union man, the Guerrillas spent the night
of the 3d in the timber, a rainy, barren, tempestuous night, and
returned to Harris' dwelling in the morning for breakfast.
Every carbine was wet, and almost every revolver unserviceable.
While cleaning these and taking them apart thoroughly for
inspection, an old man named Bivens, the father of two gallant
boys who were fighting bravely under Joe Johnston, hurried up
with the information that a body of Federals one hundred and
ten strong was at a Mr. Anderson's only a mile distant, and that
as he passed they were making all haste to get to saddle and
get upon the road. Instantly Spencer rifles were put together,
and dragoon pistols made whole again. The coolest men worked
rapidly, and the most indifferent felt the need of great expedition. It was time! The arms of the Guerrillas had not been
loaded a dozen seconds, nor had they been in line a greater
space themselves before the Federals were upon them, yelling
and shooting. Taylor at a gallop made a trail broad and good
for ten miles or until he reached Fishing river. This stream
was fordable, and turning down where he struck it and marching
down it a few hundred yards, he crossed over where a bluff bank

on the opposite side gave him the basis of an ambuscade. His men were made to dismount and tie their horses, none being permitted to hold them. Frank James was stationed near the stream and especially charged to kill the leader of the pursuing party, as James was recognized as the best and quickest pistol shot in the command. Lining the bluff and ranged wide apart, the balance of the Guerrillas held themselves in readiness to fire when Frank James should have singled out and dispàtched the victim accorded to him.

In tolerable array, considering the long chase and the heavy roads, the Federal column followed right on. It did not halt at the crossing, nor send a single skirmisher forward to penetrate the woods beyond and develop the unknown the forbidding bluff seemed to foreshadow. At sixty feet from the ambush Frank James fired at the man leading the column and killed him. It was Sergeant Kirby, instead of Capt. Kemper, the ranking officer; but he fired again and brought Kemper down with a severe wound. Then the Guerrillas, crouched along the crest of the bluff, poured into the demoralized and affrighted Federal mass half way up from the river and at the crossing of the stream and along the whole width of it, a merciless and unbroken fire. Sixteen were killed and twenty-two more or less severely wounded. Panic succeeded to surprise, and flight to panic. Those mounted the best escaped soonest beyond range. As a great crowd of fleeing fugitives—hatless, without array, heeding no orders if indeed any orders were given—the mass forced its way as best it could back from the stream and then on towards Liberty, *pell mell*, and throwing away arms and accoutrements at every fresh alarm. Taylor pursued scarcely a mile. His horses were of more value to him than the lives of a dozen or so additional militia. It was not at all necessary to catch the enemy in order to inflict punishment upon him, for if all signs did not fail he would only be required to remain a day or two in any given place to have about him as many as he could conveniently accommodate.

Capt. Kemper's intention had been twofold in the commencement of his expedition: first, to extirpate Taylor's audacious band of Guerrillas, and, second, to visit a most hospitable Union man named Gordon and eat a national dinner. The 4th of July came, and a company also; but not the company which was expected, nor Gordon's guest in particular, Captain Kemper. The host, too well-bred to betray surprise when Taylor rode up with his command, marred in no manner the excellence of the feast by stint, or scowl, or niggardly behavior. He served the wine in a generous fashion, listened gravely to the story of the morning's fight, neither said yea nor nay when the tale was finished, and bade his guests goodbye in a stirrup cup that might have warmed again into flowing the blood of some of the dead men down on the Fishing river.

Col. Thornton, recruiting here and there through various counties, was now in Platte, arraying a formidable following. Thither Taylor went, increasing his command from twenty to fifty within a few days. Scarcely any member of his company was older than twenty-one years. Beardless boys they were, veritable devils to fight and to ride, and rapacious as Bedouins for air and exercise. Young soldiers for certain services are superior to old ones. The young soldier excels in deeds of desperation. He stands killing superbly. An intrepid leader can carry him anywhere. He is tireless, energetic, irresistible in attack, impatient of restraint, careless in the presence of danger, often surprised, not always obedient, but in a crisis and brought face to face with absolute death, he fights furiously to the last. He knows nothing of hygiene, while the old soldier, properly trained, looks upon cleanliness as next of kin to godliness. He is not so steady in the face of a pitiless pursuit as his older comrade, he does not rally so quick, he cannot hold himself so still under a fire which, while it distresses him sorely is too remote to be silenced; but for the most of the services the Guerrilla is called upon to perform, the young man of twenty is unsurpassed for dash, cruelty and desperation.

Parkville, Platte county, was garrisoned by twenty-five militia, who bore a good name among the citizens for fair dealing, and merciful conduct. Otherwise they would have been exterminated. Capt. Taylor attacked the place at daylight and was stubbornly resisted. Holding a stone house impervious to pistol balls, the Guerrillas to succeed had need to carry it by assault. Oll Shepherd shot the wife of the captain of the besieged accidentally. She fought at her husband's side during the few hot moments preceding the assault and appeared more than once at a window with a loaded gun which she discharged. The Guerrillas cheered her every time she showed herself and withheld their fire. Finally a man occupied her place, and just as Shepherd, who was nearest to the window, shot at him the woman came again within range and received in her bosom the ball intended for another. Then began the assault led by Taylor with all the furious rush and rapidity of his reckless nature. Six men manned a beam and battered a door down. Others made the windows too hot to be held by the boldest of the besieged. Twenty Guerrillas, massed for the effort, swarmed into the house and swept its lower story bare of defenders by a single volley. Those above capitulated. The Federal dead numbered six and the wounded sixteen. Taylor's loss was eleven wounded. All who fell alive into his hands were honorably treated and generously paroled. Those who fell, fell through the fortunes of open warfare.

While the fight at Parkville was in progress a characteristic tragedy was being enacted in another portion of the county. Five Guerrillas—William Stone, John Thomas, Hines, Morehead and Marshfield—were surrounded by fifty Federals at the house of a man named Bradley, six miles north of Platte City. The five held the house until Hines and Morehead were killed. Three times they were called upon to surrender, and three times the defiant answer was sent back: "Come and take us!" The survivors, their ammunition well nigh exhausted, broke away from the house fighting desperately and striving to cut through the enemy who encompassed them. Thomas and Marshfield were killed in the orchard, riddled by musket balls. Stone, fleet of foot though encumbered by four heavy pistols, gained some timber to the east of the house, followed by three militiamen. He hid behind a tree and killed the nearest. The two others rushed upon him and shot him down. Recovering somewhat from the shock, and crawling barely to his knees, he killed as he crouched thus the surviving pursuers. Then he fell upon his face again, remaining there a long time. The voices of those in search of their comrades aroused him at last and spurred him up for a final effort. A minie ball had gone through his right thigh, and five buckshot into his back and hips. Slowly, however, and with the grim, silent, impurturable endurance of the bull-dog, he dragged his maimed body forward through the brush with his hands and knees. He did not know the course he was going, so only he was going away from where the three dead men lay, whose bodies were being hunted in every direction. He did not care where he went so only it was not back again towards Bradley's. Wounded as he was, and weak as he was, he still held on to his pistols. Twenty rounds yet remained to him, and twenty rounds to a desperate man at best but little better than mortally wounded meant a consolation almost equivalent to a rescue. The voices of men searching carefully gained upon him as he crawled, gained rapidly and on every hand. He reached a fence and essayed to surmount it. Twice he fell back exhausted, his wounds burning as though so many hot pointed things had been thrust therein. Militiamen were in sight, coming straight towards him. He gathered in his front some pieces of rotten wood, dry sticks, and such other debris as might go to make a miserable barricade, laid easily to hand his trusty pistols, maybe said a prayer or two, and then felt himself ready to die. At this instant a furious fire from the direction of Bradley's, a single yell, then a series of yells, then a long, irregular, zigzag volley, halted as if petrified the Federals almost upon Stone, and turned them about and influenced them back at the double-quick. What had happened? As Stone crawled and bled and listened to the firing which became weaker and weaker and finally ceased altogether, his mind kept thinking and repeating: What has happened?

This had happened: George Fielding, a young soldier of Shelby's old Brigade, scarcely turned of nineteen, wounded, and at home on a furlough, knew and loved John Thomas in boyish soldier fashion. Between them had been the fresh confidences and the artless comminglings of youth. They had rode side by side in battle. Together they had shared the same blankets, endured the same cheerless bivouacs, stood the same long picquet watches, were opposites in many things, and yet— one supplying what the other needed—they drew thereby the bond which united them closer and closer, and made what had not been separated in life in death not disunited.

Fielding, in hearing of the guns at Bradley's, mounted his horse at once and rode at a run for the point of combat. He neither knew nor sought to understand the situation. He neither drew rein nor slackened speed until he was upon the enemy and in the midst of them fighting like some madman

intent only upon being killed. He did know that John
Thomas was surrounded, outnumbered, in imminent peril, and
he meant to reach him in time to save him or die by his side.
It is probable that this is all he either comprehended or cared
to comprehend. He had to ride two miles to bring him to the
fray, and these were ridden like a swallow flies. While yet a
quarter of a mile away, John Thomas had received five wounds,
either one of which would have been mortal, but Fielding rushed
right on, a pistol in each hand and the reins of the bridle in
his teeth. As he reached revolver range he fired right and left
and yelled once, a short, sharp, singular, piercing Guerrilla yell,
which was answered by a louder one of mockery and defiance,
and a scattering volley. These were the shots and the shouts
that Stone heard, crouching in his fence corner and waiting
before he began to put up his life at auction the ten or twelve
more forward steps the enemy would undoubtedly have taken,
had not Fielding's hot charge in the rear required a concentration. There could but one thing happen. Fielding seemed
never to have cared to retreat. He rode full tilt upon twenty
Federals ranged along the yard fence, firing as fast as his pistols
would revolve. His horse was killed. Before the animal fell
he was off of his back on the ground, erect, unhurt, and still
firing. He had killed four of the enemy, as strange as the story
may sound, and had wounded two severely, when there was
another cooler, closer, deadlier volley, and a furious rush from
every quarter to where the dead rider lay by his dead steed, but
the work had been done. Shot five times and literally killed
as he stood in the attitude of splendid defiance, George Fielding
was past all pain before his face was upon the ground. Stone
escaped, and lives to-day to tell of that savage combat wherein
six men set upon by fifty fought until five were killed, taking as
a recompense the lives of thirteen Federals.

From Parkville Capt. Taylor moved suddenly into Buchanan
county. At that time there was operating in that portion of
Missouri a Colonel Morrison, whose name and whose fame were
evil together. The citizens were plundered by him indiscrim-
inately. The non-combatant received only hurt at his hands.
Some Confederate soldiers on recruiting service were captured
by him and killed. He burned, proscribed, was unnecessarily
cruel, and thought considerably more of how to avoid an armed

enemy than to meet one in open conflict and crush or kill him there. Capt. Taylor ended speedily that infamous career of Col. Morrison's. Fifty Guerrillas at daylight surrounded his house where sixteen picked soldiers of his regiment not alone formed his body-guard but his garrison. The house, prepared to stand a siege, was as much of a fortress as a dwelling. Heavy fastenings held the doors shut. Plank made the windows impervious to musket balls. Loop-holes at every angle gave to its defenders a perpetual flanking or enfilading fire. In its cellar was a cistern; among its supplies rations enough for any reasonable environment. Taylor made all these advantages worthless in a moment. Volunteers especially called for put torches to this demi-redoubt in five places, losing in the effort three killed and eight wounded. The flames took hold, however; they eat into the woodwork; they climbed up the walls; they clambered along the eaves; they caught in their fierce embrace the whole mass of fortified doors and windows, and then they were in the citadel. As Morrison's men rushed out, some of them afire, blinded with smoke, or tortured to madness with stifling heat and flame, they were shot down as rats are shot when leaving a rat-infested barn. Morrison remained to the last. When finally he broke from his furnace, his beard burnt off and his garments afire, he rushed through the door at which Jesse and Frank James and McMacane were standing guard. Frank James halted him instead of shooting him, and Morrison replied with a pistol ball which cut a black feather from James' hat. Then a dozen Guerrillas fired at the singed and smoking apparition as it ran, and missed it clear. Was it to be over again that wild bull rush of Bertram Risingham?—

> " And where is Bertram ?   Soaring high
>   The general flame ascends the sky;
>   In gathered group the soldiers gaze
>   Upon the broad and roaring blaze,
>   When, like infernal demon sent,
>   Red from his penal element,
>   To plague and to pollute the air—
>   His face all gore, on fire his hair,
>   Forth from the central mass of smoke
>   The giant form of Bertram broke."

Morrison was gaining rapidly upon his pursuers who were afoot and firing defiantly as he ran, when Jesse James—cooler than many there—hurriedly mounted his horse and came riding at a gallop upon the track of the doomed man. Morrison, spent with toil and speed, turned about and stood still. He meant to die in his tracks, and he was dangerous. Jesse James took no note of his attitude, nor did he wait a second for any help or advantage two or three comrades at his back might have given him. He dashed upon Morrison single-handed, fired at him and missed. Morrison returned the fire and shot James' horse in the mouth. James fired again and struck his antagonist just above the right hip. As he reeled and staggered from the blow, his revolver being dischared in the air, James shot again, sending this time a bullet fair into Morrison's forehead. This ended the fight—the garrison had been exterminated.

Colonel Thornton, after having recruited three hundred men— the nucleus of what might have been made a very formidable band—attacked and captured Platte City and its garrison of militia, seventy strong. Then he took up his headquarters there. One of his strange notions entertained at that time was the notion that he commanded an army of occupation. He meant to hold North Missouri and organize a powerful column of Confederates for active service in his new department. Taylor came to him from Buchanan county, preceded by the news of the savage blow dealt Morrison and a portion of Morrison's unregenerate regiment. Thornton proposed to Taylor a division of honors, he retaining command of the infantry, while Taylor took charge of the cavalry. "You have too few men for a regular army, five hundred miles from a base line," was the reply of the cool, keen, common-sense Missourian, "and too many for a band of Guerrillas. Get to the South as soon as possible, Colonel Thornton, or be cut to pieces without hope of escape or succor." Colonel Thornton did not get to the South. He moved from Platte City to Camden Point, where Taylor left him. Two days afterwards he was attacked by four hundred Federals and routed, with a loss of forty killed and sixty-eight wounded. Some of his men also scattered away from their command, while others, choosing commanders for themselves, went to them in a body. John Thrailkill and Joe Macy brought one hundred and twenty-five splendid young fellows to Taylor and asked to be permitted to operate with him in Guerrilla warfare. From the Iowa line to Arkansas, Thrailkill had been running and fighting. He was at home wherever he camped. Wherever he found the enemy he fought him. If he had food, very well—he ate; if he had no food, still very well—he did not eat; if he had blankets he used them, if he had none he did not go to bed; what he understood by sleep was to pull off his spurs and unbuckle his pistol belt; it was night, it was day—no difference to Thrailkill; it was stormy, or frozen, or glorious sunshiny weather—all right, so only whatever the sort of weather was it was good weather for hunting and finding the enemy. He asked only to be allowed to fight, while others were asking for good food, fine horses, showy clothes, ivory-handled pistols, gaudy bridles, McClellan saddles, and city resting places in the winters in the South.

Jo Macy had the ear of an Indian and the horsemanship of a Mexican bull-fighter. Educated on the plains, he preferred a bed even in the snow to a pillow of down. He saw with his eyes and also with his ears. He could listen to the march of a column and tell to the half of a squadron how many ranks were riding by. He fought superbly everywhere. If a charge were needed, Macy was the man to lead it; if a rear pressed to the girth had to be held, who so much like a rock as Macy; if a position was eminently in danger, the watch at night had to be Macy's watch; he rarely ever shot until he knew he could kill; probably in his whole life he was never excited; he did not know what surprise meant; the war found him a patient, truthful, plain-spoken, conscientious man, and it left him just as it found him, with this addition—he was a hero.

Taylor, Thrailkill and Macy entered Ray county from the west and raided it from one end to the other, killing on the trip fifty-seven militia and securing horses sufficient in number for three hundred recruits waiting for a mount before they began their march to the Southern army. On their return into Clay they halted a day or two at the house of Richard King, where ammunition was prepared and cartridges were manufactured for extended operations. There at this camp the services of a young girl were found to be most valuable. The men were almost totally destitute of revolver bullets. Powder in plentiful supplies could be obtained in any direction, but lead was the article that was so necessary and yet so scarce. Miss Mattie King, with the beauty and the bashfulness of one who had lived much with nature, had yet the clear perception and the calm self-reliance of a real heroine. She seems to have anticipated just such a condition of things as had now come about. For months and months before there had been any extraordinary demand for lead among the Guerrillas who were operating generally throughout Clay and the contiguous counties, she had begun to buy it quietly and persistently and to hoard it as though it had been gold. All of her hidden stores were now brought forth, more precious than pearls or rubies. The men blessed her and felt something akin to reverence for the tender maiden as she went about moulding bullets and preparing cartridges for the pistols. As modest as any wood flower blooming alone upon her father's premises, and artless as any wild bird swaying and singing in the trees about her country home, savage Guerrillas softened visibly as she spoke to them as she passed, and boisterous young desperadoes lifted plumed hats to her as to an innocent thing that was to bring them good luck. Lithe, sun-browned, blue-eyed, winning in all frank and ingenuous ways, there are yet left a few of Taylor's Guerrilla band who speak of her to-day as a Queen by the dusk on her hair, and tell in praise of her and as a token of their loyalty to the past that two hundred Federals fell before the bullets moulded by her willing hands.

Captain Taylor rarely rested more than two days in thirty—rarely slept more than four hours in twenty-four. He had a theory of his own touching the struggle which, summed up thoroughly, gave about such a proposition as this: The war cannot last always; the pace is too terrific to continue long; the exertions are too immense to endure. Consequently the more frequently we fight the less those of us who survive the war will have to reproach ourselves with when the end comes. A battle a day is about the average.

Ray county was again invaded. Taylor marched along the Liberty and Richmond road, in the direction of Richmond, leading the advance himself with twenty-four men. Next to Taylor was Thrailkill, and next to Thrailkill, Jo Macy. At the Conrow House, two miles west of Fredericksburg, forty-seven Colorado soldiers were encountered, commanded by Captain Moses.

These, busy at work on the contents of the Conrow House—ripping open mattresses, appropriating whatever was coveted, breaking, destroying, and wantonly trampling under foot—began to form instantly and disencumber themselves of all superfluities as the Guerrillas rode in sight. Without waiting for the detachments under Thrailkill and Macy to close up compactly, Taylor dashed at the Colorado people savagely, unable to restrain his men and unwilling as well. Peyton Long, Jesse James, Fletch Taylor, Frank James, and John Thrailkill were neck and neck in the run. Bud Pence, Dick West, Gooly Robertson, Nat Tigue, McMacane, Dock Rupe, Henry Coward, Silas King, James Commons, Allen Parmer, Jo Nicholson, James Nichols, Garrette Groomer, Joe Macy, Oll Shepherd, William Stone, and a few others strove with desperate emulation the one to surpass the other in speed and prowess. Jesse James, by the time the onset culminated in its crash upon the enemy, was a length ahead of the swiftest riders and killed the first Federal in the midst of his own ranks. Afterward the *melee* passed as a whirlwind. Jesse James was shot severely in the left hand and knocked senseless from his saddle by a powerful blow from the butt of a Colorado soldier's carbine. Another soldier stood over him while he was down and attempted to blow out his brains. Taylor killed him, and in falling he fell across the Guerrilla's body. Captain Moses fought like a frontiersman surrounded by Indians, but of what avail was fighting there? The revolver volleys made it impossible for any Federal force, evenly matched, to live and hold its own beyond a second or two of awful sacrifice. Moses held on until thirty of his men were dead or wounded about him, and then he fled followed by the remnant of his stricken company. Not far away from the point of combat they separated in every direction; Moses and six others keeping boldly to the highway. Jesse James, recovered somewhat from the furious blow dealt him, staggered to his feet, and from his feet to his horse, and then spurred away in the exciting chase. Moses was followed five miles by Peyton Long, Joe Macy, Henry Coward, Frank and Jesse James. Four of his squad of six were killed, while Moses himself—pursued by Jesse James with ferocious intensity—lost his plumed hat, his horse, and his pistols, and only escaped after taking refuge in a dense swamp where it was impossible for horsemen to come after him. The hat—a plumed trophy of no inconsiderable merit in those days—was presented to George Todd afterward by Jesse James. The day he was killed, leading a furious charge upon the rear of this same Second Colorado regiment to which Moses belonged, Todd fell wearing this hat.

The other fruits of the fight besides the dead and the wounded were thirty-three serviceable horses, thirty-three McClellan saddles, twenty-eight dragoon revolvers, and forty Star carbines —one pattern of an innumerable array of breech-loaders the Federal government was then experimenting with, corrupt Congressmen and venal army boards dividing profits equally with the inventor and the manufacturer.

Resuming his march, Taylor passed through Knoxville into Caldwell county, and encountered fifty militia, thirteen of whom were killed, twenty-two wounded, and the balance captured and paroled. At Kingston, Commons, Castle, Tigue and Robertson took from the county treasurer $6,000 in greenbacks and divided it among the Guerrillas *per capita*—a sort of prize money scarcely legitimate and certainly of but little account so generally apportioned.

At Plattsburg, in Clinton county, the court house was held by a Federal garrison numbering eighty militia. Taylor attempted to surprise it but failed. Some citizen spy preceded him with accurate information of his movements and when he charged into the town the court house was defiant and impregnable. Desultory skirmishing followed. The keen, practical, savage Guerrilla had no intention of losing against brick walls and barricaded passage-ways a single man or a single horse. He cooped up the garrison in their citadel a sufficient length of time to obtain all the powder and lead possible and retired afterwards with one man slightly wounded. As the Guerrillas rode out, however, and as Taylor and Thrailkill were moving slowly along together in the rear, they halted upon the last elevation that overlooked the town, and gazed for a moment back upon the fortified building. A man stood in its main door, holding in his right hand a field glass. No firing was going on, for those in the court house imagined that the larger body of the Guerrillas had passed beyond range. Thrailkill spoke to Taylor and said: "I shall try a shot at that Yank with the field glass. Can I hit him?" Always curt, Taylor answered shortly: "Too far." "So it may

be, but some bullets are charmed." "Shoot, then." Thrailkill had a Savage pistol which he generally held in reserve for
skirmishing work—a huge, uncouth, big-bored, unpromising
thing—and this he quickly elevated and fired as a man fires who
expects little from his shot or is indifferent to its effect, whatever it is. With the report the man pitched forward from the
door of the court house upon his face. "If he gets up,"
Thrailkill coolly ejaculated, beginning to load the empty cylinder, "he is hit but not hurt. If he does not get up he is dead."
The two stood there a few brief moments, waiting. He did not
get up. Finally half a dozen soldiers rushed from the court
house, lifted up the prostrate form, and carried it back into the
building with them. It was a limp thing they carried, the back
swagged, the hair trailed, the knees at their joints were helpless
—instead of a man the burden borne away was like a sack filled
with sand. "That will do," Taylor said, as he touched his horse
lightly with a spur, "the man is dead." And he was. Thrailkill, however the thing happened so, had killed the commander
of the garrison, Captain Turner, at a distance of one hundred
and fifty-six measured yards. From that day to this he might
have stood shooting there, as innocent of marksmanship again
so fatal as William Tell was innocent of Colt's revolvers.

Little things sometimes, unnoticed and unimportant, go far
to make up the warp and woof of what men call destiny. An
ambuscade—one of a countless number the war saw and made
to become a part of its tactics—saved Des Moines, Iowa, from
a thunderbolt similar to the thunderbolt which destroyed Lawrence. Some Iowa troops, serving temporarily along the border between Missouri and Kansas, had surpassed the Jayhawkers, if that were possible, in the cruelty of their reprisals and
the completeness of their pillage. They not only burned dwellings, like the Jayhawkers, but put the torch as well to out-
houses, fruit trees, fences, grain in stacks, and forage in the
fields. They not only killed wounded soldiers shot down in
battle, as their omniverous prototypes, but old men fared
roughly at their hands, and non-combatants were put to death.
Taylor fought them wherever he found them, but he meant to
do more. He meant to make them understand what kind
of taste the chalice bore they had so sternly pressed to the lips of
the Missourians. He meant to burn, to pillage, and slay just

as the Iowa troops had burnt, and pillaged, and slain, and he meant to do it speedily. Leaving his company under the command of Frank James, he took with him, after his return from Plattsburg, Thrailkill and Allen Parmer and crossed the Missouri river into Jackson county, for a conference with George Todd. Todd embraced the proposition as though it had been a woman, large-breasted and beautiful. "Iowa!" he exclaimed, when Taylor had told him of his plans, and explained to him how feasible they. were, "I had rather kill ten Iowans to-morrow than fifty Kansas Jayhawkers. Get your men together at once and let us begin to march!"

Taylor, still keeping near him Thrailkill and Parmer, and having been joined in Jackson county by Henry Porter, was making much haste back to his company in Clay. While passing through Rush Bottom, and riding carelessly along, unsuspicious of all danger, a deadly fire from thirty ambushed Federals tore off Taylor's left arm close to the shoulder, hurt Thrailkill badly in the head, put a ball into Porter's right leg, and another into Parmer's right shoulder. Wounded as they were, and as desperately wounded as was Taylor, these four men, bleeding at every step and scarcely able to keep fast to their saddles, fought back their pursuers for eight miles and finally escaped and recovered. With this ambushment ended the Des Moines expedition. Had Fletch Taylor escaped that day the dreadful wound which mutilated him for life, he would have been with Todd the day following with one hundred and fifty of as desperate Guerrillas as Missouri ever furnished, while Todd—still in command of the bulk of Quantrell's original band—would have added fifty additional veteran fighters to the column especially adapted for the work proposed. A single volley, however, saved an Iowa city and many a head and many a habitation round about.

Frank James succeeded to a stormy legacy, the command of a company hunted hourly by a thousand horsemen. At Mrs. Robertson's, where he had taken breakfast, a Federal scout, one hundred and fifty strong, attacked him and drove him into some heavy timber. There—forming an ugly ambuscade—he sent back as a lure from the depths of its obscurity Jesse James and seven picked Guerrillas. The Federals, forming on the edge of the timber and keeping

23

altogether there, would not be moved into the gloom of the overhanging trees and the thicker undergrowth. Jesse James tried to tempt them into pursuit of him by bravado, defiance, annoying volleys at pistol range, insulting cries and motions of contempt, but the wily militia were imperturbable. Then he charged them recklessly. His own horse was shot from under him, James Justis, riding on the right hand, was killed, Fred Breaker was wounded badly, together with Gooly Robinson, Johnson Barbie and Bud Pence, or four wounded and one killed out of the eight skirmishers sent forward as a decoy detachment. The next day Anderson entered Clay county with a hundred followers, Frank James joined him at once, and thereafter, and until his death, the exploits of this noted Guerrilla might be written down equally as the exploits of the Jameses, and the bulk of Taylor's decimated yet desperate organization.

James Justis, not yet eighteen, was a brave boy from Jackson county. Shot dead in the furious charge made by Jesse James, he fell within twenty yards of the enemy. Afoot himself—his disabled horse but a little space behind him—Jesse James halted long enough by Justis, as he ran to the rear, to unbuckle his pistol belt and remove his revolvers. As he did this Dof Carroll stood over him on his horse fighting back a dozen Federals and keeping them back until James had taken away from his boyish comrade, whose wide open blue eyes were tenderly closed, everything which savored of a trophy. All that day the dead body lay where it had fallen. The Guerrillas—too weak to attack the enemy where he stood in position —broke up their ambushment and disappeared. The Federals —content to leave unexplored all that portion of the unknown in front of them—fell back later in the day to Liberty. Neither gave a coffin to the corpse. The young face, very ghastly now and pitiful, still gazed up reproachfully to the sky. At nightfall Mrs. Zerelda Samuel and Miss Bettie Robertson, accompanied by a negro woman of middle age, came to where the dead boy lay. They were going to bury him. The landscape was in unison with the occasion. A summer wind sighed through the great elms, and the slow moving women were as so many phantoms among the trees. Twilight had deepened into darkness. Here and there the noise as of wings told of a night bird flying away to its own. Close by some running water murmured a monotone. The light of the stars needed no moon —it was so soft and quiet. The women dug the grave and bore the boy to it tenderly when it was finished. For shroud there was a white sheet, and about this sheet an army blanket for a coffin. "He has a mother," Mrs. Samuel whispered, "and one day she will bless me for this." As she spoke she stooped and cut from above the bronzed, open brow a long, fair lock of hair, moist with the summer dew. No burial service was read, no audible prayer was spoken. The bare-headed women, alone with the corpse and the darkness, laid the young hero to rest reverently, yet without rite or ritual. Mrs. Samuel's face was calm, earnest, yet fixed and resolute. The fair girl beside her, with her unbound hair about her shoulders, fixed her pure eyes upon the dead. The composure of each was perfect. The negro woman, standing herself at the bottom of the grave, received from the hands of the two above her the shrouded form of the Southern soldier. Over his face, and to keep it fair and boyish to the last, they placed branches with leaves upon them and bunches of sweet smelling grass. Then, toiling there, and speaking briefly to one another there and always in whispers, they filled up the grave, and marked it foot and head, and left it alone for God and the resurrection. But is it any wonder that when the South had such women the South had also such men? The burial of the Guerrilla dead had been forbidden every where along the border. Where one of the accursed class fell there should he remain until the elements wasted him, or the buzzards devoured him, or the hogs ate him up. The citizen who dug a hole to put him in— no matter how shallow or wretched—was an outlaw branded like Cain; and the woman who dared to do what the man was forbidden to do, was a dangerous woman necessary to be caged or ironed. Many women were served thus, Mrs. Samuel among the number; and many old citizens were shot down in cold blood, simply because some Guerrilla corpse upon the highroad had been hidden away or buried.

Frank James, the day when he united his own fortunes to those of Anderson, carried with him into the new organization:

Jesse James,	Dock Rupe,	Silas King
William Grindstaff,	Peyton Long,	James Commons,

William Blackmore,	Joshua Esters,	Samuel Wade,
Richard West,	Jack Rupe,	Dock Corly,
William Stone,	Harvey Brown,	Joe Holt,
David Wade,	Creth Creek,	Bud Pence,
Jeptha Bowles,	Leon Martinez,	Socrates Johnson
Marston Lisle,	Snowy Jenkins,	Parker Talcott,
Richard Ellington,	John Fisher,	Peter Farley,
Newton Oliphant,	Theodore Castle,	John Hope,
Allen Parmer,	Dof Carroll,	Nat Tigue,
William Henaburg,	James Bissett,	Patrick McMacane,
Robert Todd,	Plunk Murray,	George Daily,
Johnson Barbie,	John Wilson,	Thomas Fulton,
Newman Wade,	Abner Creek,	Garrett Groomer,
Gooly Robinson,	Oll Shepherd,	John Chatman,
Ling Litten,	Henry Coward,	Thomas Tuckett,
William Winchester,	Henry Buford,	Rezin Magruder,
Samuel Finnegan,	Oscar Swisby,	Valentine Baker,

Clarence Tomlinson.

Before a year had passed what a harvest death reaped in the ranks of these ardent Guerrillas, young and dauntless. Peyton Long fell among the last of Taylor's heroic band, but many had preceded him and some few had followed him. In unnoted or forgotten graves they sleep from the Ohio river to the Pacific ocean. Not all the killed can be enumerated after the lapse of so many years, but the following are the names of many of the most intrepid ones:

Peyton Long,	Dock Rupe,	Dof Carroll,
Robert Todd,	Garrette Groomer,	Newman Wade,
Theodore Castle,	John Chatman,	Samuel Wade,
Joshua Esters,	James Bissett,	John Wilson,
Patrick McMacane,	Harvey Brown,	Thomas Fulton,
Gooly Bobertson,	Newton Oliphant,	Oll Shepherd,
Joe Holt,	Thomas Tuckett,	Peter Farley,
Marston Lisle,	Snowy Jenkins,	Parker Talcott,
Jeptha Bowles,	Leon Martinez,	Socrates Johnson,
William Winchester,	Henry Buford,	Rezin Magruder,
Samuel Finnegan,	Oscar Swisby,	Valentine Baker,

Clarence Tomlinson.

John Thrailkill. with a bloody rag about his head and that ghastly pallor on his face which betokened much suffering, rejoined his men near Union Mills, in Platte county, after the murderous ambuscade of the Rush Bottom. Many of the recruits desired to go South, and some who had been Guerrillas preferred to become at last regular soldiers. Joe Macy himself was getting ready to lead them into Arkansas, when a desperate battle ensued, one of the most savage and bloody of the altogether too savage border war. A part of Thrailkill's forces were camped in some timber two miles from the road, commanded by Joe Macy, and a part a mile further away, commanded by Thrailkill in person. Altogether the Confederates numbered probably two hundred and fifty. Six hundred militia, made up of detachments from various posts, battalions and regiments, sought to surprise Thrailkill and exterminate him. A forced march of eighteen miles was made with great secrecy and speed. No one was permitted to pass beyond the head of the column. If any traveler upon the highway was overtaken, a guard was set to watch him and to regulate his pace with the pace of the swift moving horsemen. No scout of the enemy had been encountered. Neither picquet, nor sentinel, nor vigilant guard, nor outlying detachment seemed to be abroad anywhere in the darkness. At daylight the energetic leader of the Federal column of attack had reached unobserved to within a mile of Thrailkill's position. If he had pressed on he must unquestionably have ridden into a sleeping camp and broken the slumbers of a too negligent foe with a musket volley. He did not ride on. The night air had given him a keen appetite, and he stopped long enough at a farm house to arouse its inmates and provide for a pot of hot coffee. His host had a daughter— a brave, high-spirited Southern girl—who saw at a glance the situation of affairs and the imminent peril of the Guerrilla camp. She scarcely took time to complete her toilette. She made no effort at obtaining a horse. Half clad, her hair unbound, her feet wet with the night dew, her cheeks aflame, her eyes eager and expectant, she burst into Thrailkill's presence while he was yet wrapped up in his blankets and told him vividly the story of the peril. Many men would have dallied and doubted; this man thanked the brave girl with a look full of reverence and gratitude, and leaped to his feet a living embodiment of skill, courage and determination. A swift runner aroused Macy. A swift whisper encompassed the camp. Som-

nolent things, stupid with sleep, stood armed and clear-eyed
through the clear revealment. Every laggard was alert, every
inert mass was moving. Preparation ran from group to group
as fire from tree to tree in a pine forest. In the gray dawn
gun-barrels glistened. From out the shadows short orders told
of officers. The undergrowth was alive; the morning mist
became inhabited. By this time the Federal commander had
finished his coffee, closed up his column, and burst upon the
Guerrillas. Instead of a surprise, a hurricane of fire awaited
him. Behind each oak, and elm, and cottonwood, and walnut
a covered marksman, border trained and bred, held his tree as
a bull-dog holds its grip. The fight, hot at first and from the
very beginning, grew suddenly desperate. The Federal commander fought splendidly. Once on the left he broke through
a portion of Thrailkill's line and enfiladed mercilessly his whole
position. A charge alone could recover the ground thus furiously
wrested—a hot, swift, unrelenting charge. Thrailkill led it.
He looked like some monstrous nightmare. A bloody rag was
still about his face. His eyes were inflamed because through
much suffering he had not slept. The plaster put upon his
wound had melted and run along his cheeks. His beard was
matted and bristling. One side of his head had been shaved.
He tottered as he walked. The dauntless spirit, however,
burned as the eternal fire of the Persians, and his desperate
hardihood bore him up as though the skeleton was hardest iron.

The charge was as a wave that had no ebb. Twenty Guerrillas fell in as many seconds. Peters was killed, and Johnson,
Love, Marshall, Benedict, Parsons, Sallee, Nuckols, Parker,
Jeter, Samuels, Morgan, Tomlinson, Jeffries, Solomon, Tilton,
Harker, Leftwich, Myers, Snowdon, James, Thoroughman, and
Harrison Norton. Many more were wounded. Thrailkill's
horse was killed. He mounted another—the horse of a dead
comrade—and this was killed. In falling it fell upon him and
broke his left arm. He did not know that it was broken until
the battle was done. A ball carried away his hat and the plaster
about his wound. He had not time to find another covering for
it. Another ball cut through his upper lip and knocked two
teeth away. He spit forth a mouthful of blood and bone, and
shouted loud to his desperate followers: "Hold on, boys! hold
on for your lives! Macy is coming!"

And Macy had come! Delayed somewhat in his efforts to secure the horses, and pestered to a considerable degree by the difficulties of crossing a couple of creeks, he yet arrived at that very moment of time when he was most needed. Thrailkill was whipped undoubtedly. He had lost eighty of his best men killed or wounded. His line was being cut to pieces. His charge, desperate as it had been and as unyielding, had failed. He was afoot and maimed. Some of his soldiers were out of ammunition. Many were falling back. Not a few were running away.

Macy attacked at a run. The Federals—broken considerably themselves, and fighting in squads and detachments—knew nothing of this second force until it was upon them. They rallied fast, however, and faced it manfully. There were some few brief moments of savage combat—another rush, another deadly volley—close, hot, irregular, and decisive—and the whole Federal array broke back from the timber in hopeless disorder and made frantic haste to their horses, followed by Macy with the fury of a whirlwind. A few mounted men at this time might have destroyed the routed militia at a blow, but none were at hand. Every Guerrilla was afoot. Many of their horses had been killed, and those of Macy's were a mile from the battle-field. He had turned a defeat into a victory, however, and by his energy and intrepidity had rescued Thrailkill and saved the remnant of his devoted followers. In the absence of orders he had done simply what every good soldier history deals with had done—as did Desaix at Marengo, Boufflers at Steinkirk, Hancock at Gettysburg, Stonewall Jackson at Antietam—he hastened to where the fire by its intensity told of a terrible fight. If he had tarried a single minute for instructions, if he had waited the bare time a swift horseman might have taken to ride as if riding a race the scant mile between camp and camp, if even when upon the road he had waited to find fords or preserve a soldierly array, the jaws of the fierce Federal attack would have closed upon Thrailkill and crushed him beyond redemption.

But the true victor in the morning's bloody battle was the patriotic young girl, Mary Harrison. Her unerring intuition—almost a sixth sense with a majority of women—had enabled her to understand at a glance the intentions of the Federal com-

mander, and the rapid execution of a courageous purpose had
enabled her thoroughly to prevent their execution. She lives
to-day, a blessed memory in many a faithful heart, a matron
indeed whose husband was once a notorious Guerrilla, and who,
whatever else he may teach his white-haired children, will teach
them that there is—

> "No crime, or curse, or vice
> As bad as that of cowardice."

The death of Andrew Blunt was eminently in keeping with his
stormy and desperate life. Nothing was known of this man's
earlier history. He was one among the first who came to Quantrell. Some said one thing of him, some another. He had been
a private in the 2d United States Cavalry, he had killed a sergeant
and escaped, he had been punished so severely by a lieutenant
in New Mexico that he had shot the lieutenant and made his
way to Missouri, he had some weighty secret always upon his
mind, he had done some terrible deed, he was a brooding and a
mysterious man—these are some of the things told of Blunt
among the Guerrillas, little heeded, however, or accounted of.
Quantrell found him a most excellent orderly sergeant, and
recruited him as such. He wrote an excellent hand. He
certainly had been a soldier at some time in his life. All the
details of a cavalry soldier's duty were as an open book to him.
He rode splendidly. His skill with a pistol was marvelous. He
excelled as a spy. He had as many shapes as Porteus, as
many disguises as a conspirator of the Riye House Plot. No
deed was too desperate for him to attempt, no service too reckless to receive his help. A mingled feeling of devotion and
intrepidity cost him his life.

In December, 1863, Otho Hinton, a comrade in arms of Blunt,
and a Quantrell Guerrilla of great prowess and courage, was shot
badly and captured at the house of Mrs. Neal, of Lafayette
county, situated on the Warrensburg and Lexington road.
Hinton was carried to Lexington, tried as a Guerrilla, found
guilty as a Guerrilla and sentenced to be shot. With something
of a plausible yet bitter irony, those who had condemned him concluded to keep him until his wounds were healed, and it was
while he was in the hands of the surgeon that Blunt with two
men attempted his rescue in January, 1864. Miss Annie Fickel
was taken into his confidence. She was a Southern woman of

action and Patriotism. Cultivated, refined, full of maiden
modesty and timidity, she yet recognized it as her Christian
duty to give aid and encouragement to the Confederate cause,
and to risk much and make use of every resource at her command for the succor or safety of its defenders. She came often
to Lexington from her home in Greenton Valley. She made
herself acquainted with the prison and its surroundings. The
topography of its approaches was impressed thoroughly upon
her mind. Once she obtained an interview with Hinton and
bade him, in the name of Blunt, be of good cheer. The
remarked the points at which guards were stationed, ascertained
accurately the nature of the discipline which prevailed, observed
everything of importance, and finally reported to Blunt, and
with great precision and clearness, the exact conditions of the
case. Blunt's own plan was soon formed. Dressed as Federal
soldiers, he and his two companions were to enter boldly into
Lexington, avoiding the outlying picquets and the grand guards,
and gain unobserved the old Masonic College building where
Hinton, tolerably well cured of his wound, was awaiting execution. There, mingling coolly with the Federals, and asking and
answering questions indifferently, he was gradually to work
his way into the guard room, arm Hinton, kill the sentinel on
duty at the door, and make upon the consummation of the
killing a desperate rush for liberty. The absence of a countersign added probably another chance to whatever the chances
where at any time of success.

Blunt chose the night well upon which the adventure was to
be made. Although it was January a drizzling rain was falling,
and the darkness was of that impenetrable sort which might
indeed have made it almost black to the blind. Accompanied
by two Guerrillas equally desperate with himself, Blunt flanked
the picquets easily, avoided as easily the guards, and entered
the city afoot and unchallenged. Things speedily happened,
however, which alarmed him. Armed men were patroling the
streets. Very few soldiers where to be seen about the saloons.
An unusual air of preparation and expectancy pervaded Lexington. Blunt did not waver. He made his way slowly but
surely to the College and was gliding with his men as three
black spectres into the very building itself when he was discovered and fired at without even being called out to or halted.

He stood perfectly still, hoping that in the darkness he might remain undiscovered until the alarm was over. Such probably might have been the case if none had known of the attempted rescue but himself. It has never been satisfactorily ascertained to this day how the Federal commander at Lexington knew in advance of the intentions of Blunt, but that he did know the extensive preparations made to receive him too well attested. It is probable that an attack in much larger force was expected. Two hundred soldiers at least were under arms about the College. All the guards had been doubled. The patrolling parties about the streets were very strong, and every public way for ingress or egress vigilantly sentineled. Blunt's superb nerve and presence of mind did not save him. Although he neither exhibited by motion nor movement that those who had fired at him had fired at anything more tangible than air, the firing continued viciously, and the Guerrillas were forced to retreat. Then a furious pursuit followed. Blunt lost one of his men, shot dead by his side, as he ran down College street towards Main, and the other over beyond Main barely a square. He was alone now, and beset on every side by a numerous foe. He did not quicken his pace. He was neither nervous, excited, nor alarmed into making haste. He had about his body six heavy revolvers, and he would see. On Franklin street he fired his first shot and killed a Federal who had taken him by the collar. On South street he killed another. His line of retreat was through the cemetery, but so closely was he pressed that at the first fence a musket ball wounded him in the left leg. He stumbled among the graves and fell over tombstones. The fierce hue and cry was at his heels. Every now and then a volley seemed to be trying to search him out in the darkness. At the second or further fence he trusted too much to his wounded leg in climbing, and it gave way beneath him. As he fell he fell upon a pointed paling which inserted itself between his belt and his body and held him tightly there, suspended between heaven and earth. The noise made by his endeavors to free himself attracted two pursuing Federals to the spot, one of whom fired at him, and the other closed upon him. Blunt killed the two almost with as much ease as Bogardus would kill the pigeons from a double rise. He was not yet extricated, however, nor did he wrench himself free from the paling until

twenty or thirty pursuers more had drawn near to him, attracted by the firing, and poured in a telling volley which wounded
him badly in the right side. Here he lost four of his pistols.
As by a mighty effort he bursted the revolver belt which held
him as in a vise, four of his trusty weapons fell upon the side
next to his pursuers, and he was too grievously hurt to venture
an effort to recover them. Finally he cleared the cemetery,
distanced those who followed on his track, reached the road
leading out by the fair ground, and took it at a snail's pace,
faint, bleeding, desperate, dangerous, a pistol in each hand,
and that cruel, hungry look on his face which never yet had
boded good to any enemy. Presently there came the sound of
horses' feet. Blunt drew himself up in the middle of the road
and listened. Those riding through the night and into Lexington were but two, and if they were Federals he would kill them
both. Not until the oncoming horses were near enough to be
taken by their bridles, did he call keenly out, "Halt!" Supposing in the darkness that they had ridden close up to the
advanced outpost of a picquet, the two horsemen halted
instantly and made answer: "We are halted. What will you
have?" Blunt drew a small space nearer, peered up into the
faces of the men on horseback, saw by their dress that one was
a Federal officer and one, perhaps, his orderly, and killed them
both as swiftly and as unerringly as he had killed the two at the
paling fence. Afterwards it was ascertained that one of the two
killed thus was a man named Thomas Mocabee, a Kansas Red
Leg deeply concerned in the murder of Cole Younger's father,
Col. Henry W. Younger. Riding Mocabee's horse and leading
the other, Blunt made what haste it was possible for a badly
wounded man to make to the Sni hills. Resting quietly at a camp
deep in the woods, a woman betrayed him and gave up the
secret of his hiding place to a detachment of Federal soldiers
numbering fifty. Blunt died as a wild boar. So terrible was
the name of the man, and so remarkable was his skill with the
pistol, that he was shot to death with long range guns. Only
two of the fifty ventured to come within revolver range, and
these he killed. Indeed, he rarely ever missed any object at
which he fired. He fought until he was literally shot to pieces,
until eleven bullets had been put into various portions of his
body. Otho Hinton was killed in prison the night of his

attempted rescue, and in a short time afterwards Miss Annie Fickel was arrested for conspiracy against the government and treated with the cold brutality of vindictive cowardice.

In June and July, 1864, there was a reign of terror everywhere along the border. Jesse James and Allen Parmer captured Bradley Bond, a militiaman living near Claytonville, Clay county. Bond was at home on furlough, and though heavily armed, surrendered without a struggle. James wanted him especially. He had, according to James' belief, been the chief of a scouting party who in one day's raiding had killed four Southern citizens, hung his step-father, Dr. Samuel, until life was nearly extinct, insulted his mother, and, with a rope about his own neck, had dragged him from the field where he had been at work, beating him cruelly and without cause. Bond begged hard for his life, but James told him first of his crimes and then killed him.

The next day Frank James, taking with him his brother Jesse and four other Guerrillas, visited the house of Travis Finley, a resident of Clay county, and surprised there and captured a militia soldier named Alvas Dailey. Dailey, though only twenty-two years of age, was regarded by the Guerrillas as an extremely bad man. He had accompanied Bond on the occasion of the Samuel raid, and at several other times and places had been guilty of some grievous crimes. Frank James shot him dead on the highway and left him unburied for the citizens to look after.

Two days after Dailey was killed, Frank and Jesse James visited, dressed in Federal clothing, the house of an old man named Banes, which was situated in the northeastern portion of Clay county. Some Southern citizens had reported more than once to the Jameses that Banes believed in a war of extermination. It was known that he often had dealings with the enemy. Many of his neighbors felt confident that he was a spy. The Guerrillas more than once had been made to suffer severely through the information of their whereabouts conveyed by Banes to the Federal soldiery. It would be a miracle if sooner or later a sudden blow did not destroy him. As soldiers belonging to a Colorado regiment, Jesse and Frank James were cordially received. An excellent supper was served. The aftertalk was both curious and unexpected. It is reported that

Banes was especially anxious to have Mrs. Samuel killed and her property destroyed. The reason of his dislike was asked and boldly given: "She has two devils for sons," he said, "and she is cheek by jowl with all the infernal bushwhackers in the country. In order to break up an immense nest of unclean birds, it would be a righteous thing to burn every shingle on the premises." "Why has it not been done?" her sons asked. "The militia are too cowardly," the old man fiercely replied, "and the regular Federals are too conscientious. Sometimes I feel like trying to do it alone." "Who are these James boys?" was the further enquiry of the ostensible Coloradans. "Two Guerrillas who have killed more Union soldiers and citizens than any other two butchers in Missouri. They are here to-day and gone to-morrow. Their old mother posts them. The Southern citizens feed them. Sometimes they operate together and sometimes with fifty or sixty more. They are veritable wild beasts, I tell you, and they devour everything." "If you will pilot us, Mr. Banes," Jesse James spoke up, "and help us to fight if there is fighting to be done, we will try to-night the virtue of a little fire." The old man's exultation was immense. A saddled horse was soon at the fence for him. From one secret place a Spencer rifle was brought, and from another a brace of navy revolvers. He was impatient to be gone. A mile from his house the trio halted. "Old man," Frank James began in that slow, deliberate, finely modulated voice of his, which was all the more dangerous because it had so often before preceded sudden death, "we had not the heart to kill you nearer home, but if you would pray, pray now. *We are the James boys!*" Instantly, and against each temple a cocked pistol was pressed. Powerless, but not paralyzed, the old man essayed to explain himself. "I believed at the first you were Federals," he said, and that you had come to kill me. What I have said I have said to save myself. These are dreadful times, gentlemen, and sometimes we have to be one thing and sometimes another. Do not kill me, for the love of God." Two pistol shots, deadly and close together, was the only answer to the old man's prayer.

Gen. Bacon Montgomery has been accused by some of the Guerrillas, and unjustly accused, of the murder of Arch Clements. It is true that he was in command of the militia at Lexington at the time he was killed, but he was in no manner responsible for his death, and would have saved him if he could have done so. It was Montgomery's fortune to have to do with a desperate following. The militia commanded by him were bad men, uncontrollable men, ex-Federals and ex-rebels, and totally without honor or civilized impulses. The bulk of them were the dregs of the civil war—the Thenardiers of a struggle that had its Austerlitz as well as its Waterloo. He was a brave, generous, liberal-minded man, individually, and he strove with might and main to protect private property and save human life. That he was not always successful was because almost unsupported in a band which carried into peace times the very worst of the passions of the strife, he could not in every instance enforce obedience or punish the viciousness of his desperadoes. Yet he did what he could energetically and fearlessly. Others in his place would have been monsters. Montgomery saved many a life that even the people among whom he was stationed knew nothing of, and many a house from destruction that the owners to this day do not know were ever threatened. Dave Poole had been into Lexington with his Guerrillas and had gone out soberly and in order, Arch Clements marching with him. Outside of the city he met a comrade, Young Hicklin, who was going in, and Clements turned about and returned with him to the City Hotel. While drinking at the bar they were fired upon, and each made a rush for his horse, fighting as they ran. Probably two hundred shots were fired at them, and Clements was killed, Hicklin making his escape by sheer desperate fighting and running. Montgomery knew nothing even of the cause of this firing until the deadly work had been done. He deplored it, but he neither counselled it nor approved of it. A lot of drunken cut-throats did the work upon two isolated men, cut off from their comrades, which— man to man—they would not have attempted for the county of Lafayette. Montgomery was too brave a man for such devil's doings. He felt that the war was over, and he was anxious that the Guerrillas should come back into peaceful life and become again a part of the peaceful economy of the local administration. In such mood he treated with Poole, and in such mood he would have treated with Clements if it had been permitted for him to have encountered Clements. It was not to be, however, and this young, superb, almost invincible

Guerrilla, died as he had lived, one of the most desperate men the country ever produced.

In the last terrible days of the war, isolated and individual deeds of daring were done everywhere. Coming up from the South, Doc Campbell led a little party from Yellville, Arkansas, composed of Given Horn, Al Scott, George Maddox and James Stewart. Almost every day there was a fight. Campbell was a born scout, who saw in the night and rode fastest when it was darkest. At the crossing of the Osage river, and while they were in the middle of the stream swimming and pushing a sort of a raft ahead of them on which were their clothes, arms and ammunition, twenty Federals gained suddenly the southern bank and fired upon the helpless men. Indifferent to the bullets pattering about them like hailstones, these four desperate men kept evenly on, stroke upon stroke. Presently Horn spoke quick to Campbell: "Doc I am hard hit and I cannot go on. Help me if you can; if you cannot, save yourself." "I will stay with you, Given," was the reply, irreverent it may be, but splendid with devotion, "until hell freezes over." Then he put one arm about Horn, while George Maddox put another, and thus against a strong current and in the face of a furious fire they bore him safely to the shore, standing naked there together with Stewart, and fighting back the twenty militia until Horn tied up his wound, which was in the left arm, dressed himself and got upon his horse. Then they too leisurely performed their own toilettes, stopping every now and then and at the adjustment of every garment, to reply by a rattling volley to the steady fusillade of the persevering enemy. Before the affair was finished, Campbell himself was wounded, but not too badly to ride, nor to continue as the unerring guide of these determined men.

A squad of militia belonging to Capt. John W. Sheets' company surprised at the house of Mrs. Richard Kinney, in Jackson county, a crippled Guerrilla named Charles Saunders. Some little while before Anderson with ten men had had a severe fight near Hopewell Church, in Lafayette county, and Saunders had been badly shot. When he saw that his hiding-place had been discovered he crawled out into the yard in order that none of the family might be hurt. Death was near to him, but a high courtesy and considerateness abode with him to the end. He would face it alone, crippled, surrounded, doomed. He had four loaded pistols with him, and in suggestive Guerrilla vernacular he meant to "sell out." As soon as the militia saw him hobbling to the garden fence they opened their fire. Saunders reached this fence, fell over rather than climbed down upon the other side, and held it for a quarter of an hour. It took that length of time to kill him at long range. Twice they charged him, and twice his accurate and deadly fire drove them back. Seven balls were put into his body before he fell for the last time and never to get up again. Four Federals were killed and five wounded, and a single load remained the last of twenty-four. Too weak to fire this, the hammer of his revolver was at a half-cock in his stiffened fingers when the enemy reached him and found the Guerrilla dead, his eyes wide open, and a look of awful menace on his pinched, yet bronzed and weather-beaten face.

At the house of Richard White, in Jackson county, another savage border tragedy was born. Frank Gregg, Thomas and Ambrose Maxwell, Sam Constable, and Ed Hink were surrounded by fifty-two Federals. Would they surrender? "Never!" shouted Gregg, in a voice that might have been heard a mile, "never while there is a leg to stand on or a bullet to kill. Look out, for we are coming!" As he cried thus, jibing and hilarious, the five savage Guerrillas broke out from the house, shooting. It was about twenty yards to their horses, but they did not make haste towards them. Side by side and steady as men plowing in a fallow field, they marched and fought, taking and returning the fire of the fifty-two. Presently Hink leaped from his feet into the air and fell forward upon his face and as a log might fall from a log-sled to the ground. Gregg stooped and turned him over. A huge round hole where the heart was told the tale without the trouble of a further searching. "Poor Hink!" sighed his comrade, perfectly unconcerned in the pelting bullet rain, "he ran a long time, but he died at last with his boots on." Then Gregg unbuckled the pistol belt and strode forward with the weapons of his dead comrade, a giant. Close to the horses Constable was seen to stagger, fall upon one knee, rise again, and then fall the second time. By this time the Federals had come to within fifty yards, yelling and shooting. Gregg halted by Constable, fired five shots in quick succession at the nearest enemy, knocked two from their saddles, demoralized to a certain extent the balance, and gave place to the Maxwell brothers who kept up the fight desperately. Gregg spoke to Constable, "Where are you hit, Sam? Speak quick, for if this thing lasts much longer, you, and I, and all of us will need as many lives as a cat." "In the right shoulder, Frank, but I can ride if you will put me upon my horse." Frank Gregg was a giant in size and in strength, and he lifted Constable in his arms as though he were lifting a sack of feathers. Just as he straightened up with his burden, a rifle bullet knocked his hat off. "Better the hat than the head," was the dry retort, "but I must have back my hat for all that." He put Constable upon his horse and bade him ride ahead—by and by he would come along after him. Then he lazily walked back to where his hat was, picked it up, brushed from it some specks of dirt, smoothed out its creases and wrinkles, called to the Maxwells to get speedily to horse, took his own time to mount himself, and finally rode away at a walk and in splendid bravado, firing back and with deadly effect wherever he was crowded, or whenever an attempt was made to make his wounded comrade ride faster than he thought it would be good for his hurt. The pursuit was scarcely a pursuit. Evidently the enemy were timid—were afraid of what the brush might contain—of something ahead or in the unknown that savored of stratagem or ambuscade.

Captain John Rudd was one of the coolest scouts, spies, guides, and Guerrilla fighters Shelby ever recruited, trained, or let loose upon the enemy. He entered Missouri five times from the South, bringing and carrying to and fro a multitude of letters. First and last he conducted safely into the Confederate lines a regiment of recruits from Missouri. He knew every road South, every path. trail, direction, water-course, ford, friendly stopping-place, or inaccessible fastness. If he had to fight, he fought savagely. If he could not go round an object, he went over it. If there was no other way to get through, he cut through. When he had to kill he always made a clean job of it. There were five Rudds in Shelby's old brigade, and the five were brothers. Better soldiers never followed, and braver ones never defended a flag. John Rudd had as many disguises as a detective, as many stratagems as an Indian, and as many

24

voices as a mocking-bird. Once he did this manner of a deed: Going South with one hundred and fifty recruits for Shelby's Division, he captured one day seven wagons loaded with Federal clothing. Right then and there he made his men take off one set of garments and put on another. When the dressing was done instead of a speckled or a variegated column, there was a column as blue as a field in the spring sown with blue birds. Seventeen miles from the place of the metamorphosis and close to Yellville, in Arkansas, there was a militia cavalry camp, two hundred strong. Rudd reached it about sunset. In advance with ten men, he rode up to the Federal picquets and made himself known. He was Major William Thatcher, of the 22d Missouri, especially commissioned to inspect all the posts along the border, and to report what was needed in the way of arms, ammunition, and supplies. The officer on duty at this camp was a Lieutenant Jackson, from Fayetteville, Arkansas, who reported promptly to Rudd and awaited his orders. "Lieutenant," said the ostensible Thatcher, "form your command in twenty minutes, without arms, in front of my quarters, that I may first inspect their personal appearance. After that I will look at your guns." Then he went from soldier to soldier in his own ranks and told them of his programme. They were to keep cool, quiet, vigilant, and obey his slightest nod or motion. A line was formed. Two hundred stalwart militiamen dressed up in front of Rudd's quarters, a huge white oak tree, and waited a little curiously to see what the new comer, in the uniform of a major, wanted so far down among the mountains and the outlying militia. They were well informed. Rudd passed slowly along the front of the line, looking once in the face of each soldier there. Then he passed along the rear of the line to about half its distance, and until he had gained the point nearest to his own troops, when he lifted his hat quickly and waved it once. Instantly the Confederates poured out from among their horses, armed, resolute, ready for work. There was some confusion at first among the Federals, but Rudd rushed through their ranks, gained their front, and cried aloud so that all might hear him: "Keep your places if you would keep your scalps. We are Confederate soldiers clothed as Federals, but we will not harm you if there is no resistance. Take but a step towards your guns, and we'll murder you like cattle!"

Not a man stirred. Some of the Confederates seized the muskets, some rushed to where the horses were, and in an hour more Rudd, without the firing of a single shot, was hurrying on into Arkansas with two hundred prisoners, two hundred and eleven horses fit for service, seven wagons loaded with valuable supplies, over two hundred cavalry carbines and revolvers, and five ammunition wagons filled with precious ammunition. He was thanked in general orders for his skill and coolness, and sent back into Missouri with important dispatches to several officers who were recruiting in the State.

Before Gooly Robinson was killed he performed many desperate deeds of bravado and valor, but none that surpased the following in hardihood or abandonment. A desperate Federal scout, whose *soubriquet* was Ben McCoulloch, was known to many upon the border as a bold, bad, cruel, relentless man. He killed, burned, stole, plundered, fought, and was not afraid. If he could have found good backing anywhere in the ranks of the militia, he would have made his mark broad and bloody. Single-handed, he did not give back from any man, Guerrilla or Confederate. He dressed in fringed buck-skin, carried four dragoon revolvers, rode a coal black horse, and hunted at the head of fifty Federals. Quantrell had sought for him once or twice, but failed to find him. Todd sent him a challenge once to meet him on a certain day at the head of fifty men, pledging himself to meet him with twenty-five. If McCoulloch received the message, he never replied to it. Indeed, if he knew Todd as Todd really was, it was no disgrace to him that he did not reply. One day, however, this man of the *soubriquet*—this buck-skin Ben McCoulloch — went a step too far. Gooly Robinson had a widowed aunt living in Johnson county whose house McCoulloch burnt, whose horses he confiscated, whose cattle he drove off, and whose entire substance he wantonly and wickedly wasted. The bereft woman told the story of her ruin truly to her nephew, and the nephew dressed himself as a Federal soldier, mounted a horse as swift as any other Federal's horse, cleaned a double-barrel shot-gun thoroughly, loaded it with buck-shot, buckled on his pistols, and went a man hunting. The second day out he met full in the big road a column of Federal cavalry, and rode boldly up to within twenty yards of it. Ben McCoulloch was at its head, gay with fringes and furbelows. One man against fifty—alone, unsupported, indifferent to consequences, and reckless to a degree exceptional even for him, Robinson fired both barrels of his gun full into the bosom of McCoulloch, literally tearing his heart out, and killing and wounding five of those who were next to and nearest to him. So daring was the deed, so sudden was the fire, so fatal was the aim, that the savage Guerrilla had turned his horse and was dashing away like the wind ere a single volley was fired after him or a single horseman started in pursuit. Of course he was neither harmed nor overtaken, the strangest thing of all, however, being the fact that McCoulloch's splendid black charger sprang away from the Federal column when its rider fell and rushed furiously after Robinson until it overtook and ranged up alongside of his own horse, keeping pace with him and submitting afterwards to capture and control.

Oll Shepherd was a young hero who survived the war, and who was killed in Jackson county, in 1868, by a Vigilance Committee. They went one day to his home near Lea's Summit, to capture him for some alleged offence; but he would not surrender. Shot seven times, he fought to the death. Once he led something almost like a forlorn hope up from Arkansas. It rained on him every day for eight days, and he fought every day for eleven days. Andy Walker was his second in command, one of Quantrell's oldest and best soldiers, and a bosom friend. Probably Walker knew more of Quantrell's secrets than any other Guerrilla along the border. He never talked. He was twice noted, once for his reticence, and once for his deadly skill with the revolver. In battle he neither smiled, shouted, nor spoke. He killed. In camp he neither laughed, sung, nor was boisterous. He watched. On duty he neither sat down nor slept. It might be said of him that he was perpetually in ambush. If one had to fight for a crown with twenty picked men, Walker would have been one of the twenty. *En route* up from the South, Walker in advance, Shepherd came one day to a house in Taney county that was more of a charnel house than a habitation. Eleven militiamen were about the premises. Down stairs the old man was lying in a pool of blood. Some feet from the back door the old man's son-in-law had just died, a great powder-blackened hole above his left eye.

GEORGE SHEPHERD.

OLL SHEPHERD.

The old woman was wild with agony, and some little grand-children, scared speechless, had hidden themselves under the bed. Crazed with grief, a daughter, and the wife ·of the youngest murdered man, had fled to the woods. Shepherd had fifteen men with him, dressed all of them in Federal clothing. As he rode up the militia started to run, but seeing the uniform of the Guerrillas, turned about and came smiling to the fence in front of the house. The Guerrillas dismounted and entered in. They did not need to be told what was meant by the two dead men lying there, the crouching children, the frantic grand-mother, the poor crazed mother shrieking in the woods. As they mingled again with the militia it might have been noticed that eleven Guerrillas stood close to eleven Federals. Shepherd gave the word, and there was a single volley. Not a bullet missed. Eleven men fell as one man. If the earth had opened and swallowed up the victims, the sacrifice could neither have been more crushing nor more instantaneous. As the Guerrillas rode away the dead-house had become to be a sepulchre.

In Clay county and just arrived he had come safely through fire and tempest, when Oll Shepherd was surrounded at the house of Mrs. Fox, and furiously attacked. Captain Rogers and one hundred militia were after him. He broke out, rode through mud knee deep for ten miles, and fought every step of the way, losing two of his best men, and two brothers at that, Alexander and Arthur Dever. Alexander was only eighteen years of age, but a veteran in every soldierly thing. Arthur had served intrepidly under Bragg and Joe Johnston, and was noted among the Guerrillas for a certain stubbornness in battle that nothing could overcome. Both were buried in the same grave, separated neither in life nor in death.

At Dover, in Lafayette county, there was a physician who was also a man without fear. He was under the ban because he penetrated the brush in search of wounded Guerrillas and healed them there. Perhaps he also helped to hide them as well. This man—Dr. S. T. Meng—was a charitable, God-fearing, conscientious man, who prayed now and then, who preached occasionally, who felt to stir within him, as the strife deepened and became more and more savage, something of that fell spirit of Moses when Moses rose up in his wrath and slew the Egyptian. Dr. Meng, however—and notwithstanding the provo-

cations that he had over and over again to take up his gun and
go to the highway—healed instead of killing, saved instead of
taking life. Federal or Guerrilla, Union man or Secessionist,
good man or bad man, if either was in extremity, the calm,
patient face peered at him just the same, and the quick, skilled
hands did what had to be done for him without homily or
upbraiding. One day he was deep in the brush waiting upon a
wounded Guerrilla. There came of a sudden the rattling of
scabbards, the ringing of horses' feet, the noisy clamor
of contending voices, and the peculiar crashing, swishing soun l
of heavy bodies forcing their way through heavy underbrush.
As a turkey-hunter, Dr. Meng had been famous in two States.
From the gliding of a chipmunk, or the pattering of a squirrel,
or the drumming of a pheasant, or the whirring of a partridge,
or the leaping of a buck, he knew all sounds the woods gave
birth to, he could name all approaching things without turning
his head. He was sitting close to the Guerrilla, who was grievously hurt. "They are here," he said to the wounded man,
coolly, "and if we are discovered we are dead. Can you lie
still and be ridden over without crying out?" "I can be roasted
without crying out. Try me!" Rapidly, yet so quietly and so
noiselessly that even the birds in the trees overhead might not
have heard him, Dr. Meng cut a whole armfull of bushes, thick
with leaves, and covered completely the body of the prostrate
man lying at full length upon his blanket and as still as the
silence which follows death. Two feet away from him any eyes
other than a lynx's eyes must surely have failed to discover this
hidden Guerrilla. Then Dr. Meng glided quietly away into
the thick undergrowth and was for a moment lost to sight.
Abreast in a single line, sixty Federals were scouting through
the timber, hunting for some of Poole's men who had been
reported as wounded in Lexington and hidden somewhere in the
river bluffs close to Dover. If they held on as they were they
would surely ride over James Welby, the maimed man lying
there, his left arm shattered almost to the shoulder, and his jaw-
bone fractured. James Welby was one of Poole's men, desperately wounded in a recent combat, and Dr. Meng, with unfaltering devotion, had braved proscription, imprisonment, hourly
danger, and violent death to save him, if human skill could save
him, and restore him cured to his savage leader. The Federals

were within ten paces of Welby and still advancing, when a single voice in their rear, loud and high and penetrating, called out to them to turn about. It was Meng's voice, without a quaver or a tremor. Unobserved, he had watched them ride until in his own mind he had concluded that they would undoubtedly ride over his patient, and then to halt them and divert them from their course he came boldly out from behind his cover and risked everything upon the single chance of a defiant bearing. They did halt and turn about. Meanwhile Meng had mounted his own horse, which had been tied back from where the wounded man was resting, and rode to meet the Federals, a shot-gun crossed before him on the saddle. "What is your business here?" the leader asked, with the air of an educated tyrant crossed upon a born highwayman. "My business," the doctor blandly replied, "is a very simple business indeed. I came out to kill a few squirrels for a squirrel pie. Any orders against that?" "There are orders against carrying guns and dodging about in the bush." "But I am not dodging about. I saw you and I hailed you. I wanted to tell you that if you were looking for rebel Guerrillas you were looking in the wrong part of the country." "How do you know?" "Because I am a physician, and I ride everywhere." "Aha! And so you are a doctor. You wait on all alike, I reckon; you give physic to all alike, don't you? You swear by the rebel and you swear by the Federal, I make so bold as to say; you are indigenous to this soil, you are; you'll do first-rate for a Guerrilla, won't you? Answer quick, lest it is worse for you." Dr. Meng did not even change color. Used to either extreme of fortune and having an abiding faith in the good God, he argued the case. Meanwhile the Federal commander, while he had been talking had also been riding, and before he had finished his tirade he was several hundred yards back from the wounded soldier. Whatever else was to happen, Welby at least was safe. His sturdy old physician had taken the chances of getting himself into trouble that he might make a profitable diversion in favor of his patient. Presently the doctor replied to the officer: "Suppose a gun was to accidentally go off this moment in your column and hurt grievously one of your men. If I did not help him, wait upon him, save him if I could and cure him soundly, would you not make me do it, or at least do my best towards it?" "I would." "If I refused you would shoot me?" "Even so, I would shoot you." "Then as you would do in extremity, so would do the Guerrillas. How—standing as I do between the devil and the deep sea—how, I say, am I to make fish of one and flesh of the other? Answer me this, for so sure as you are here beside me it has been a proposition that has puzzled me sorely." The Federal officer—born robber as he was and cruel —was a logical, practical, sensible fellow, not averse to an argument, and not indisposed to logical things. He pondered for a mile and more over what Meng had said to him, and then when the two, still riding together, reached the main road, the Federal going towards Lexington and the doctor towards Dover, the Federal left instead of a benediction an *ultimatum:* "What you have argued is logical, but not loyal. If in any manner hereafter you give aid and encouragement to the enemy, and if after so doing I ever come to hear of it and to lay hands upon you, I will hang you to the nearest tree, so help me God!" In six days after this savage threat, and while riding at the head of a column on a hunt for Guerrillas south of Wellington, this Lieutenant, Jimison by name, and eight of his troopers were encountered by Todd and slaughtered to a man.

At other times and after other fights, this proscribed yet singularly devoted physician, went here and there and continually, carrying healing to many grievous hurts and comfort to many a crippled soldier. Twice, at the imminent risk of his own life, he faced the fire of a Federal force to do his duty as a Christian man, and twice when none other would go to the wild beast bleeding in his lair, this physician went with splints, and ointments, and food, and raiment and hopeful words from that book which somehow is a blessed book to all when by the bare putting out of the hand waters of the eternal river can be felt cold to the shoulder.

There was one man in the Trans-Mississippi Department who understood the war thoroughly and perfectly. He was the friend and the correspondent of President Davis. He was the confidant and the adviser of Kirby Smith. He was a scholar, a diplomatist, a statesman, and a soldier. The revolution never deceived him, because he never deceived himself. Events and not enthusiasm impressed themselves upon the placid surface of a mind that was singularly clear, penetrating, exacting, and analytical. He looked upon life as too short for little things. He had a motto paraphrased from the French that nothing succeeded like success. Others had their ideals, their hopes, their fears, their superstitions, their whimsical likes or dislikes, their hours of boisterousness or gloom, their playfulness like a kitten, or their sullenness like an owl, but this man—granite in the hour of peril and colossal in the moment of extremity—had that grasp of intellect and that fixedness of purpose which, like Loyola, would have plucked out an eye for the cause, or like Curtius, would have leaped, full statured and panoplied, into any gulf that because of the closing through the sacrifice would have saved the South. This man was Governor Thomas C. Reynolds. The Guerrilla fight was a fight repugnant to every idea of civilized war. He condemned it, deplored it, sought to break it up, stróve to divert its terrible energies into legitimate channels; but when it passed beyond his control and began to assume proportions that were as ferocious as they were unexpected, he saw beneath the black flag an unconquerable spirit of resistance, and in the midst of the fastnesses and the ambuscades a splendid valor that made Thermopylæs, and he calmly weighed these prodigies of Western heroism and as calmly watched the passing of the storm cloud without deploring or condemning its thunderbolts. He stood between the Guerrilla and the native Confederate authorities of the Trans-Mississippi Department. There came times when it was whispered that upon the Guerrilla bands fleeing South for brief shelter and succor, there should be done the work that was done upon the Strelitz, the Jannisaries, and the Mamalukes. Two men stood as two ramparts between the haters and the hated—Reynolds and Shelby; Reynolds because to the inexorable logic of his unobscured mind the Revolution had need to have its excesses, and Shelby because there was a touch of the tiger in his own composition, and because no living thing that struck and bled for the South should have a hair plucked out even though that thing were a dog as lousy as Lazarus.

Instantaneous in action, Governor Reynolds was also as immovable as he was rapid. His processes of thought were so thoroughly perspicuous, and the reach of his analysis so wide and withal so just and penetrating, that what might have come to others as the result of days of mental conflict or discussion,

came to him as intuition comes to genius. He saw at a glance
that the border must of necessity have Guerrillas, and that any
effort made by the Confederate authorities to extripate them
would be an effort little less injurious than the unchecked
revolt of an army corps in an army. He believed conscien-
tiously that this species of warfare was a grievous injury to the
Southern cause; he believed that it encouraged desertion and
called down vengeance upon the innocent and the unprotected;
he believed that isolated fighting, no matter how desperate or
unsparing, was a useless sacrifice of priceless material; he
believed that the destruction which would inevitably come upon
the country made the theatre of savage combats would out-
weigh the damage done to those who invaded it; he believed
that campaigns carried on by regular soldiers were the campaigns which decided all appeals to the sword; he believed that
Quantrell should be in the regular army with his men, and Todd,
Anderson, Taylor, Blunt, Yager, Thrailkill, Poole, and all the
balance of the leaders and demi-leaders; but when they did not
come, and when because of it strange things were whispered
and suggested, this courageous statesman, who was also a soldier and a patriot, said some few words in his low, sententious,
emphatic way which scared the young conspirators about
Shreveport into panic and the older ones into common sense.
Thereafter there was no more talk of fusillades. Missouri's
great war Governor had held out his right hand over the heads
of his people, and though there might not have been seen anywhere about it the iron, those who had reason to know best of
all, knew that it was mailed.

And it was to carry a message from Quantrell to Reynolds that
George Maddox made his memorable trip in 1863. Reynolds,
in order to understand thoroughly the military condition of
Missouri, and to know for special reasons how many militia
were on duty in the State, how many Federal troops, what
posts were fortified, and what the strength of the posts was,
had commissioned Quantrell to ascertain these facts and forward
them to him without delay. Quantrell did what he was ordered
to do, and did it thoroughly. Ten reports were made of this
information, and George Maddox, at the head of nine men, was
entrusted with the hazardous duty of conveying said information to Arkansas. He was to stop for nothing. He was to ride

by night as well as by day. If there were no fords he was to swim; if he could not swim he was to drown. If he had to fight, very well—fight; if he had to run, still very well—run; if he had men wounded, leave them; if. he had men killed, leave them. If he had men crippled leave them. Some one of the ten was to get through as fast as human flesh and horse flesh would hold together and go on. These were Quantrell's iron orders, and he chose an iron man to carry them out. George Maddox was all tenacity and endurance. Tried in the fire of fifty desperate combats, he was a fatalist to the extent of believing in fate's good care of him. He did not speculate; he did not build air castles at night for the mists of the morning to dissipate; if he was an hungered and could not get to eat, he drew his revolver belt a hole or two tighter and forgot that he had an appetite. As he rode he sang, or was glad, or gay. Air and exercise put iron into his blood as wine puts fancies into the brain. When he started southward the night was a summer night, and a waning moon was far and faint in the West—a blindfold moon with a black cloud across its face like any veil.

The country in every direction was swarming with Federals. They were by streams and crossings, at ferries and bridges, in the towns and on the main roads, on scouting expeditions and harrying marches. They were killing everywhere, burning everywhere, destroying everywhere, robbing everywhere, watching everywhere.

Maddox rode fast the first night and fought at daylight the next morning, losing a man killed, William Strother. The dispatch that Strother bore was taken from his person under fire, together with his pistols, and the nine rode on, hard bestead and forced nine times during the day to turn about and give and take whether or no. Just at nightfall John Coger was wounded. The ball knocked him at first from his horse, but he leaped defiantly to his feet and killed the soldier who shot him, mounting again and riding on apparently unhurt with his comrades until the darkness deepened. Then his leg began first to burn and throb, next to grow fiery red, and then to stiffen. Evidently this battered old hero would have to fall out by the wayside and return by easy stages and at his leisure. Where some heavy timber grew in the lower portion of Johnson county, Maddox left Coger, taking first his dispatch, and giving him in place of it Strother's trusty revolvers.

"Watch well behind and before, Coger, old boy," said Maddox cheerily in parting, and the eight rode steadily away to the South.

In Henry county there was another fight, a short, savage, venomous one, wherein the eight Guerrillas charged twenty ambushed Federals and routed them, losing Sam Jessup killed and Newt Majors seriously wounded. Jessup was let remain where he fell, and Majors, carried carefully along to the edge of St. Clair, was deposited at the house of a well known Southern man deep in some timber. Two days afterwards Majors was surrounded and killed, killing, however, even as he died. But neither on the body of Jessup, nor yet on that of Majors, was anything found that told of name, or band, or flag, or mission. These dead men surely told no tales!

In St. Clair, and close to where it abuts upon Cedar, the besetments of a night ambuscade added its terrors to the fatigues of the long day's march, and here before the hidden hornets had done stinging, Sim Whitsett was shot past riding further than to find a place of safety. Whitsett was all nerve, and dash, and rugged endurance, but he was human. He closed his lips tightly, and gripped his horse with his knees, and managed to make five miles painfully before he found a sure asylum; but the five could not tarry. Maddox took his comrade's precious dispatch, blessed him, and bade him goodbye—a parting that might for want of a better simile be likened to the parting of sledge-hammer and anvil.

Cedar county, that Valley of the Shadow of Death for isolated or belated Confederate travelers, was circumvented with a balance left largely to the Guerrilla side. Secure in a security that had scarcely known a stir or a ripple of excitement for a year, Maddox caught nine unwary pillagers and left them past seeing or feeling. The last one to be killed was a preacher who blasphemed beyond all endurance and died cursing God and the devil. As a vengeance, or maybe as a punishment for not mowing a wider swathe through Cedar county, Maddox lost one man, Patrick Nagle, killed in Dade, and another, Silas Woodruff, killed in Lawrence. There were but three left—three guant, grim, silent, desperate men — worn from hard riding, much starving, scant sleep, and continual fighting. In Barry county, Henry Hockensmith—undaunted and unflagging, as he pressed forward with his stern, set face far towards Arkansas, was shot from a roadside hollow and severely wounded. The ball did not even sway him in the saddle. Solid as a young oak, built like a grizzly bear for depth of chest and weight of muscle, cool as a grenadier, schooled by Quantrell, drilled by George Todd, and graduated from a school that knew no peril that would not flee if faced and no bloody ground that would not give up its ogres if penetrated, he rode on for twenty-two miles further with a ball in his shoulder, and into a safe place in Arkansas.

Five days afterwards George Maddox and one other comrade, the indomitable Press Webb, dismounted at Reynolds' tent door—travel-stained, hollow eyed, bronzed brown as Indians, but triumphant. On the exhaustive information thus sent and received, and on similar information similiarly sent in 1864 was the Price Expedition conceived and inaugurated.

CHAPTER XVII.

THE DEATH OF QUANTRELL.

SUFFERING more or less from old wounds, and to a considerable degree from a tenacious sickness, Quantrell's comparative quietude after the Lawrence expedition was simply the quietude of a man who desired above all other things to get well. At times he could scarcely ride. Once or twice he dragged himself with difficulty from one hiding-place to another. But for the devotion of a small body-guard—not at any time larger than twenty picked men—he must have fallen into the hands of the enemy. Those who composed this, however, watched over him day and night, scouted for him while he rested, stood guard for him while he slept, secured for him under every adverse circumstance the most skillful of medical attendance; and finally and as a reward saw the slow fever that was not all a fever broken up and banished—saw the color come back to the cheeks of their Chieftain, the light to his eyes, the elasticity to his figure—and finally and forever saw him mount his horse for the last time in Missouri and ride away from the State forever.

Quantrell believed, after Price had retreated southward from Westport, baffled and broken up, that the end of the regular war was near at hand. His idea at this time was to change his theatre of operations, and transfer from the West to the East that terrible kind of resistance to subjugation which had already made the border a desert inhabited only by graves. He was clearly of the opinion that to the warfare of the regular Confederate government there would succeed the warfare of the Guerrilla. He was anxious to reach Maryland, and to operate from this State into Pennsylvania. As a nucleus for a larger organization after he should have reached his eastern point of hostilities, he deemed it absolutely necessary to secure the services of as many of his old soldiers as possible, and with this view sent John Barker and James Little, on the 20th of November, 1864, to notify the command to meet him at Mrs. Wigginton's on the 4th of the following month.   Mrs. Wigginton lived five miles west of Waverly, Lafayette county, and was a refugee from Jackson, whose husband had been killed, whose property had been destroyed, and whose sons had been fighting the long, merciless fight of the four years' war.

The word for the rendezvous was sped swiftly.   Frank James gathered up Donnie and Bud Pence, Oll Shepherd and George Robinson, and made haste to cross into Jackson.   *En route* to the river, and while at the house of Captain Smith, Frank James found a Federal in Smith's stable.   He ordered him to come out speedily, and the Federal fired at James, the ball cutting through his overcoat, uniform coat, vest, and shirt.   It burnt the skin sharply, but it did not draw blood, and James—putting his pistol through a crack in the stable—killed the soldier before he succeeded in getting in a second bullet.   Occupying the house also was a detachment of militia numbering thirty-two, which opened up a lively fusillade and drove the Guerrillas away from their range after a sharp volley or two.   Captain Smith was badly wounded and his son killed, together with three others of the command.

On the 4th of December forty-seven men were at the Wigginton rendezvous, and Quantrell ranged them in line for a final understanding.   The most of the faces that were turned fair towards him as he stood in front of the line, were familiar faces, and scarred and bronzed.   He saw Peyton Long there, and Will and Henry Noland, John Barker, Chat Renick, Ben Morrow, Rufus and Babe Hudspeth, John Coger, Oll Shepherd, Frank James, William Hulse, and many others of the tried and true. Quantrell's talk to them was brief.   "I have called you together," he said, "that I might say to you what I have not yet said to myself, and ask of you to my proposition the simple answer yes or no.   This side the Mississippi river the war ended with the abandonment of Missouri by General Price.   All the West is overrun with Federal soldiers.   No food, no forage, no horses, no houses, no hiding-places, no traffic any more with the posts—if we operate longer along the Kansas border we operate at a disadvantage altogether disproportionate to our means.

My intention is to cross east of the Mississippi river, pass through Illinois and Ohio as a Federal scout, gain Maryland, and carry into the heart of Pennsylvania the torch and the black flag. If I live I mean that they shall feel in the East what we have felt in the West. How many will follow me to the end?"

As one man those stern, scarred Guerrillas shouted, "*All!*"·

"Many may never come back," continued Quantrell, "and it may be my lot to fall among the first; but those who do not mean to die if the need come ever in the future for them to die, can ride now two paces to the front. They shall lose nothing in name, or fame, or comradeship."

Not a spur stroke fell up a horse's flank, not a left hand lifted a bridle. From right to left the rear rank and front rank were adamant. At noon they marched—the most of them into the unknown.

The ice in the Missouri river ran heavily, too heavily indeed for any patch-work boats launched hurriedly, or any frail craft stumbled upon unawares to live in it. Quantrell, waiting four days at Saline City for either a sudden breaking up of the extreme cold or a solid gorge fit for crossing, saw neither come nor like to come. On the morning of the fifth day he changed his course from east to south, abandoned the intention of marching through Illinois and Ohio, and chose Kentucky as the next best route for a march into Maryland.

Getting well over the Lamine river, he left Union Church upon his left, crossed the Missouri Pacific Railroad eight miles west of Tipton, and marched southeast boldly between Cole Camp and Florence. Each man, clothed perfectly in Federal uniform, met Federals hourly, talked with them, moved with them, mixed with them, ate and slept with them, and every now and then shot numbers of them to death. Of course this killing was done quietly, and in lonesome and sudden places. If any hue and cry were raised over bodies found mysteriously and shot most generally in the head, the echoes thereof did not reach up to Quantrell hurrying on to find a crossing somewhere and put between him speedily and the gathering storm behind him the broad Mississippi.

At a camp twelve miles from Tuscumbia, Miller county, Quantrell had information brought to him that this place was held by a garrison of fifty militia. He asked his men how many

among them thought they could ride boldly into Tuscumbia, as
Federals, talk as Federals, act as Federals, and finally ride out
again just as Federal soldiers would ride out from among their own
comrades. Every Guerrilla imagined himself equal to the task, and
when within a mile of the town Quantrell ordered Frank James
and Peyton Long to ride some fifty paces in advance, continue
directly to the headquarters of the commandant, and notice
whatever seemed to be suspicious, and report it instantly. He
did not know what stories might have preceded him, and most
certainly did he not intend to march blindfold into a trap, and
be dealt with afterwards leisurely and with effectiveness.

The two scouts, however, saw nothing that indicated even a
faint supposition that the assumed Federals were aught but
Federals in reality. The greeting was hearty, the welcome
warm, and the commingling old-fashioned and sincere. As
Quantrell rode up he asked for the ranking officer of the
post, and a Major came to the front door of the house where
his headquarters had been established. The two saluted, and
the Federal asked of the Guerrilla the name of the com-
command to which he belonged. Quantrell promptly responded:
"Company E., Second Colorado Cavalry." "And your name,
Captain?" "Charles W. Moses." "Can I serve you in any
manner?" the Major continued. "Yes," replied Quantrell.
"Some food and forage will be very acceptable indeed. We
have ridden far and fast, and have still great need to make
haste. I have a special mission to perform under special
orders."

The Guerrillas dismounted coolly after this little dialogue,
and went to and fro about the town. At first the novelty of the
adventure and the peril of the situation, kept every man to his
duty. By and by, however, familiarity began to break down
the barriers circumspection had erected. The hands of some of
the more desperate among the band could scarcely be kept from
the throats of the militia. Here and there little quarrels began
to make headway, and ugly though furtive looks were beginning
to be cast at the freest and the most outspoken ones of the garrison. Quantrell formed his resolution instantly. Calling
about him John Ross, John Coger, Frank James, Peyton
Long, Rufus Hudspeth, Babe Hudspeth, Ben Morrow,
and five or six others he bade them inform the balance quietly

25

that it was his intention to disarm the militia. As a torch that passes along a line of ready gaslights, this word went from Guerrilla to Guerrilla almost instantly. Then Quantrell turned sternly to the Major commanding, and ordered him to surrender every musket and pistol belonging to the garrison. Surprised but wholly powerless—for each Guerrilla with a drawn revolver in his hand stood covering a militiaman—the Major yielded with the best grace imaginable and extended his own sword. Quantrell gave it back to him. "I do not want your sword," he said, as he pushed it towards him, "but my duties are imperative. You have permitted your soldiers to steal with impunity, to rob the citizens right and left, to occasionally kill some so-called Southern resident who may have become obnoxious to this or that personal enemy; and because of all these things, and in pursuance of direct and positive orders, I have disarmed you." Not a word in remonstrance did any man or officer put up. Probably a guilty conscience made of each a coward; probably none suspected Quantrell of being other than what he represented himself as being. One of the garrison—a private—broke away from his captors and refused to halt when he was cried out to. Twenty pistols clicked and were covering him in a moment. Quantrell knocked them up. "No shooting here!" he shouted fiercely; "not a single drop of blood. Take him, some of you, but take him alive." Swift as runners, and agile as antelope, John Ross and Dick Burnes separated themselves from the press and dashed after the ungovernable militiaman. Even when overtaken and grappled with, he fought furiously, yielding only after he had been thrown upon the ground, sat upon and choked into submission. For the stubbornness of his resistance he gave stealing as a reason. He had heard the conversation between Quantrell and the commanding officer, and he supposed that for his numerous larcenies, both pettit and grand, the reckoning at last was near at hand. Quantrell broke the guns to pieces, appropriated the pistols, bade the Major commanding report at Rolla under arrest, and marched away South followed by the subdued curses of the disarmed and discomfited militia, but not their suspicions. To all intents and purposes he was still Capt. Charles W. Moses, Company E., 2d Colorado Cavalry.

The *role* of the Federal special scout was renewed again.

Union citizens were to remain unmolested. Union soldiers were not to be killed only in instances where concealment was absolute. Nothing of interference was permitted with individual property. Decorous, in short, and velvet-pawed, these lions of the border were neither to roar nor leave anywhere the marks of claws or jaws. The old lust of conquest, however, so far overcame John Coger one day that he laid violent hands upon a militiaman, who rode a fine horse and carried buckled about him four elegant navies. Quantrell remonstrated sternly with his soldier—and a better one no army ever had—but Coger disarmed his anger by pleadingly proclaiming: "Captain, the temptation was so strong that I weakened. Thar ar the pistols, just bran new, and bully. If a white man had the handling of them, the confidence he mought put into them would neither be denied nor disappointed. As they ar, and left as I found them, and they'll never kill a more dangerous thing, by g—d, than a graybeard or a woman. I sot store by them for the good I thought mought be got out of them; but if it's agin orders, give them back to the skulker who couldn't hit a barn door the length of a hoop-pole." Quantrell did not laugh, neither did he restore to the trooper his revolvers. In fact, and at nightfall, in addition to the pistols, the militiaman lost both his horse and his life. Shot dead and cast into a stream of running water, when found afterwards he could not be recognized because of his disfigurement.

Riding boldly past Rolla, openly and unquestioned, the four thousand Federal cavalry there never even so much as looked towards their horses as the Guerrillas hurried by. At Salem, in Dent county, there was a regiment whose picquets gave and returned the compliments of the day, and at King's Mountain Qauntrell dined with a Federal Colonel named McWilliams, commanding four hundred men. Near Thomasville the Guerrillas crossed into Arkansas, hurried forward to Pocahontas, fraternized with a garrison there of eighty Illinois infantry, and remained in the town several days to refit and recruit. Here Joseph and John Hall were left, the former sick of virulent small-pox, and the later being detailed to wait upon him. Joseph recovered and was killed; John avenged his brother thoroughly and survived the war.

Mr. Charles Morrison lived upon the south bank of the Mississippi river, eighteen miles above Memphis. In the secret service of the Confederate government, and operating with two score or more of scouts with great vigor and perspicacity, was Major Morrison Boswell. At times his headquarters were at Morrison's house, while all the country round about was embraced in the scope of his operations and gave up its military secrets to his untiring quest. Past forty; pulling the beam at two hundred and fifty pounds if pulling it a pound; always laughing; at peace with mankind and ardent to please as a preacher who preaches upon a circuit; the best judge of horse-flesh in the Trans-Mississippi Department; something of a physician, and much of a botanist; patient with children; a little of a priest and a good deal of a confessor; powerful in prayer and unctuous among class leaders; sleepless, omnipresent, brave, unexceptionable as a scout and inexorable at the court-martial, Major Boswell, a Nemesis as it were in a cane-brake, kept watch and ward upon the river, strangling the cotton thieves who to corrupt the soldiery would sometimes venture far inland, and putting to a swift and voiceless death every unmasked and accredited spy who presumed upon the license of the border to penetrate the lines. There was no parade. Ostentation did not belong to this rubicund Colossus, patting a child's curly head while signing a death warrant. Among the weeds there may have been a rustle, and afterwards a volley; but never a noise as of the beseeching of men or the crying out of executioners.

Of course Major Boswell—who had almost everything else—had also a boat. Boats at that time, however, were as precious as a gold mine. What between the ironclads proper and the marine fleet, the regular dry land soldiers and those other fellows who were amphibious, the Confederates had scarcely left to them a flat-boat, skiff, canoe, dug-out, raft, four planks—one upon another—or aught of anything in fact that would float, or swim, or hold safe from wind and water a single courier carrying a single carbine.

Major Boswell's boat was stowed away in a cane-brake. When it was needed it was hauled up out of the mud and carried on men's shoulders a mile to the Mississippi. Quantrell needed it badly, and Major Boswell placed it quickly at his service. Frank James steered, and the horses were forced to swim.

Above, the black smoke of an anchored ironclad floated up from the heavy timber that cut the sky-line and trailed sable garments along the tallest cottonwoods as a presage of discovery. Below, the noise of escaping steam sounded as though a fleet were crouching there. On the thither bank cavalry patrols had passed in numbers but an hour before. Danger was everywhere; the water was in arms against the Guerrillas equally with the land. "Steer boldly!" Quantrell gave no other order. The men buckled tight about them their revolver-belts and manned the boat. In an hour all were over, neither accident nor discovery complicating in any degree an already desperate situation.

When everything was over and well over, and when the line of march was just about to be resumed into the interior, Oll Shepherd, Robert, Rufus, and Babe Hudspeth, and John Coger took leave of Quantrell. They had no need to go further. They had seen him safely reach to within the confines of a territory where at least there might be found comparative succor and shelter. While there was danger, or anything even that suggested danger, they had pressed closer and closer about their Chieftain. Now there was a material lifting of the load of anxiety and doubt, and they stood fully acquit of any further service in the direction of Kentucky. Some wept as these men said good-bye, and Quantrell was sensibly affected. They never met again!

On the first day of January, 1865, the Guerrillas marched northeast from the Mississippi river, and reached Brownsville, Tennessee, after being ambushed and fired upon several times by scouts from Forrest's command, who mistook them for Federal cavalry. From Brownsville to Paris, in Henry county, the journey because of its safety and freedom from restraint was one of real relaxation, but at Paris the Confederate commander of the post required that Quantrell should report to him for duty and sought to detain him. Quantrell remonstrated with the officer without at first disclosing his intentions or revealing his identity. Later on he told him the whole story and urged the necessity of an immediate advance. The Confederate laughed at his assumption of the name of Quantrell, and refused him positively the permission to go forward. Quantrell cut the knot that he could not untie. Causing his men to mount and form instantly, he bade the Lieutenant commanding the post to do the best or the worst that he could, and rode boldly out from the town, crossing the Tennessee river at Birmingham unpursued and unmolested.   At Canton, on the Cumberland, Quantrell—always more or less of a fatalist—had what he called a "premonition of bad luck." "Old Charlie" was the name of his favorite war-horse. He was noted along the border not so much for great speed as for great bottom. He never tired. Under fire no oak tree was steadier. Where the white spots were on his glossy hide, the bullets had scarred him. Trained to either extreme of fortune, he knew how to neigh his exultation in victory or hold his breath hard when the crisis of an ambuscade was about to culminate. Safely through many a forlorn and stubborn fight had he borne his master, and never once in all his inexorable years of service had his proud spirit needed a whip lash or his laboring flanks a spur stroke. Quantrell loved his horse.

Well over the Cumberland river, and seeking to strip the command to the waist as it were for fighting, Quantrell saw at a glance the necessity of having Old Charlie shod. In attempting to do it the horse struggled—an unusual thing for him—and Robert Hall, the blacksmith, accidentally cut the main tendon of his right hind leg with the buttress, ruining him forever. "It is fate," said Quantrell, when the calamity was reported to him, " and now for me the long lane of a successful career is about to have a turn. So be it."

John Ross presented Quantrell instantly with his own horse, a splendid Missouri animal, inured to service and hardened by much exercise and marching, and Quantrell took the road that led to his destiny. He had now assumed the name of Captain James Clark. Capt. Clark was once an officer of the 2d Colorado Cavalry and had been killed by Quantrell in 1863. Dispossessing the dead man of his uniform and preserving it carefully against a time like this when the need for it would be great, he put it on the day the march was resumed from Canton. In height, size, features, and general appearance Clark had been singularly like Quantrell; but as none in Kentucky probably knew Clark, the only advantage his personation possessed was the advantage of a more than usually agreeable fit of coat and pantaloons.

Through Cadiz, in Trigg county, and on towards Hopkinsville, the Guerrillas rode boldly, Federals soldiers in everything —in walk, talk, dress, circumspection, bearing, declaration, and decorous behavior. General Lyon, a Confederate officer of great dash, enterprise and courage had but recently been well up into Kentucky on a raid, and from the pursuit of him and his gallant followers many Federal cavalry detachments were returning. Why not Quantrell among the rest?

Near unto Hopkinsville the Guerrillas struck the trail of thirty Federals and followed it with alacrity. They desired much some fresh horses, and to obtain them they would even risk the breaking up of a disguise which was and had been working in a most satisfactory manner. The Federal cavalry out rode their pursuers, and it was supper time before a portion of them were overtaken at a house and brought to terms. Quantrell attempted to keep up the Federal imposition, but when the countersign was demanded he could not give it. As a result those in the house fired a volley which broke the right thigh of Lieutenant James Little, and caused the balance of the Guerrillas to dismount speedily and surround the dwelling. Those within side held on well, and Quantrell, to save his own men as much as possible, called for volunteers to fire the building. Chat Renick, Peyton Long, William Hulse, Frank James, and Andy McGuire sprang forward to do his bidding, covered by the carbines of their watchful comrades. The flames, however, had not made much headway when there was a surrender, and three cavalrymen crept out through a door, carrying each a Spencer rifle. "Where are the balance?" Quantrell sternly demanded. "There are but three of us," was the reply. "In the stable I have counted twelve horses; that would be four horses for each of you; not thus do cavalrymen ride in the country I came from." "There were nine others with us when you came up—men whom we thought were soldiers, but when they saw you dismount they disappeared afoot. By this time, perhaps, they are safe in Hopkinsville."

It was simple truth, the story they told, and Quantrell admitted that for the first time in his life his command had been brought to bay and held some little time in that defensive attitude by three resolute Kentuckians. He went no further that night, nor did he deem it best to advance upon Hopkinsville and attempt to get horses there from the balance of a detachment whose intrepidity he could well understand and appreciate.

At daylight the next morning he bade James Little goodbye forever. Mortally wounded, the young Guerrilla lingered for a few days at the house where he had been so grievously hurt, and died as he had lived, a soldier who never knew fear. Little was one among the original number who composed Quantrell's first insignificant band. He had participated equally with his chief in the gloom or the glory of every combat. Things changed all about him, and men, and measures. He kept right onward towards where he believed the goal to be. He did not expect to survive the war, and he was not disappointed. None were braver than he, none truer to word or comrade, none more pervious to human mercy or affection, none that fought a nobler fight or died a calmer, happier death. He loved the South as a lover does a mistress, and he gave all that he possessed on earth for her—his life.

Quantrell passed directly through Greenville, in Muhlenburg county, garrisoned heavily by Federals. As Capt. Clark, he succeeded admirably in allaying all suspicion, if, indeed, any suspicion at that time had been aroused. At Hartford, in Ohio county, Quantrell so far varied the monotony of disguise as to eschew the Colorado part of it for the Tennessee counterfeit. To the commander in Hartford he was Capt. Jasper W. Benedict, of A. J. Smith's corps, then stationed at Memphis. His company was a picked company, and had been sent into Kentucky especially to hunt Guerrillas and exterminate them. Did any Federal thereabouts know aught of Guerrilla ways or people? It would give Capt. Benedict great pleasure to have pointed out to him any bands in the neighborhood that needed breaking up. Captain Barnette, a Federal officer at the post there, thought he knew of several cases where a little killing would clear up the military atmosphere amazingly, and so solicited and obtained permission from Capt. Benedict to accompany him upon the hunt. Barnette, between his own men and the men who were eager to volunteer for any service that promised plunder, brought to swell Quantrell's ranks thirty finely armed and mounted Federals, thoroughly equipped and thoroughly demonstrative.

As Quantrell rode out in an easterly direction from Hartford there was on his face the same bad look that many of his men had noticed the morning the Lawrence massacre began. He was polite enough to Capt. Barnette, and listened attentively enough to his garrulous talk of rebel comings and goings; but he did it all with the air of a man who was not thinking of the present, or who was revolving in his mind the *pros* and *cons* of a deed that he had not yet gained the consent of his conscience to commit. Finally he ceased talking altogether to Barnette, and called to his side Frank James, Burnes, Glasscock and William Hulse. Between them there was some earnest colloquy. When they separated Barnette had begun to be communicative again, and to point out with a volubility eminently in keeping with the patriotism of a militiaman, the substance that belonged to the Southern people living along the road that should be wasted, the flocks and herds that should be confiscated, and the houses given over to pillage and the flames. While he was talking, however, and while the march was going on so placidly and so peacefully through the sparkling winter weather, one by one the Guerrillas were devouring the militiamen. Not a gun was fired, not a pistol-shot awoke an echo in the air. At every quarter of a mile there was a corpse, maybe two. Through this pretense or that, and because of a solicitation here or a special pointing out yonder, Federal soldier after Federal soldier dropped back to the rear to lay hold of some rebel's property or beat up the hiding-places about his premises. Not one returned again to the marching column. Four Guerrillas, always by each soldier's side with a rope, hung him in some lonesome place and left him there, stark and stiff, in the freezing weather. The last man to execute thus of the detachment of thirty was a singularly tall and angular man. Something grotesque about his figure, perhaps, awoke the badinage of the Guerrillas detailed to hang him, and they upbraided him savagely for being a bushwhacker. "You came to us ostensibly as a Union soldier," they sneered, "and here you are as full of rebel venom as a Northern Copperhead of the Vallandingham stripe. You can't fool this crowd, however. We know your kind, and we hang them. String him up, boys!" Protesting his innocence to the last the uncouth victim gave in extremity, and as a crowning argument of the faith that was in him, the fact that he had voted for Abraham Lincoln. As Glascock, the executioner, rode away and turned to take a

last look at his victim swinging to and fro in the afternoon's
sun, he said sententiously to William Hulse: "At first I took
his height to be about six feet; now it appears to me to be
eight. Do people grow when they die?"

From the rear of the column that ferocious Nemesis which all
the day had been pursuing its voiceless yet vindictive work,
was about to be transferred to the front. Capt. Barnette was
there, riding knee to knee with Quantrell. Thrice he had said:
"I do not see my men; what has become of my men?" "They
are scouting behind us," was Quantrell's quiet reply, "and if
anything happens you will hear of it. Do not be uneasy."
Later on, and when the sun was about two hours high, Barnette
spoke up again: "I see the most of your men, Capt. Clark,
but I do not see any of mine. Can it be that they have
returned?" "Of course not, Capt. Barnette. Are you not in
command of them?" He had been in command of them, but
the last of the thirty had just been hung twenty minutes before
the end of the dialogue.

Quantrell left the front at this time, and Richard Glasscock
rode up to the left side of Barnette. As Quantrell rode down
the column his quick eyes ran along the ranks quickly of his
own men and saw that not a single Federal soldier marched
with the files of the Guerrillas; then his brow lifted. He even
laughed as he called Frank James to him and whispered briefly
in his ear, and apart from the rest. Frank James spurred at
once to the front.

The sun had set, red and threatening, and in the distance the
night was coming on apace. It was not far to a stream of running water, on the banks of which timber abounded. Barnette's
surname was Frank and James' was the same. The signal
agreed upon was a simple signal. James was to fall in with the
file immediately behind Glasscock and Barnette, and Quantrell
was to take his place two files behind James. At the appointed
time Quantrell, calling out sharply the single word "Frank,"
was to convey thus to his subordinate the order to shoot the
Federal Captain. At the creek the crossing had on either shore
precipitous banks, and when the bed of the stream was reached
the twilight, made more dense by the trees, darkened the space
between the banks perceptibly. A dozen files, reining up to
drink, filled all the space at the crossing, and looked as a huge

wedge driven in there and fastened as if to keep the two banks asunder. For deft hands at killing, and for wary eyes quick at seeing pistol sights, there was still enough light left to give the finishing touches to the last of a detachment of thirty.

"*Frank!*" It was Quantrell's voice that the column heard—questioning, penetrating, emphatic. Barnette, imagining his own name to have been called, turned once fairly in his saddle and looked down along to the rear with an attentive face clearly unsuspecting. As he did so the muzzle of James' huge dragoon pistol almost touched his forehead. He neither had time to speak nor to cry out. A single shot—all the more ringing because so unexpected—stirred the night air just a little, and a cold, suggestive splash in the water summed up for the nearest Guerrillas the meaning of the tragedy. Quantrell scarcely lifted his eyes. Glasscock looked back at James reproachfully and spoke to him as if upbraiding: "As I rode with him it was my right to kill him. You shoot well, comrade, but you shoot out of your turn." "Hush!" answered the executioner; "it was the order of Quantrell." In an hour this episode—one of a thousand such—was as old as the leaves of the summer maples.

The Guerrillas camped that night only a few miles further to the east, and as they returned the next morning past the crossing and on towards Litchfield, in Grayson county, Captain Barnette was lying, face upward, where he had fallen. During the night the freezing water had formed for the wan, drawn features a spotless frame-work of ice. The eyes looked up from this, wide open and appealing, while the frost—as if to banish the ominous splotch from the perfect repose of the rigid picture—had spread above the huge round wound in the centre of the forehead a white veil, fringed and scintillant in the morning sun. As Frank James rode quietly by and looked his last on the evidence of a handiwork he had labored for years to make perfect, he remarked to Hulse: "Whether just or unjust, this thing called war kills all alike in the end. To-day a Federal, to-morrow a Confederate—at any time a Guerrilla. Whose turn will it be next?" "What matters it," replied his comrade, "if the final mustering-out is near at hand for all of us? As for me, I am ready."

The final mustering-out *was* near at hand for many of them!

At Upton's Station, in Hart county, Quantrell crossed the Louisiana and Nashville Railroad, still representing himself and his men as Federal soldiers. Near Marion county he entered the Lebanon and Campbellville turnpike at Rolling Fork and traveled north to New Market, thence east to Bradford, and from Bradford towards Hustonville, camping for the night preceding the entrance into this place at Major Dray's, on Rolling Fork. Thirty Federal soldiers were in garrison at Hustonville, possessed of as many horses in splendid condition, and these Quantrell determined to appropriate. No opposition was made to his entrance into the town. None imagined him to be other than a Union officer on a scout. He dismounted quietly at a hotel in the place and entered at once into a pleasant conversation with the commander of the post. Authorized by their Chieftain, however, to remount themselves as speedily and as thoroughly as possible, the Guerrillas spread quickly over the town in a search for horses, appropriating first what could be found at the public stables and later on those that were still needed to supply the deficiency from the private places.

As Quantrell conversed with the commander, a Federal private made haste to inform him of the kind of work the new comers were doing, and to complain loudly of the unwarranted and outrageous appropriation. Enraged and excited, the commander snatched up a brace of revolvers as he left his headquarters, and buckled them about him as he hurried to the nearest livery-stable where the best among the animals of his men had been kept. Just as he arrived, Allen Parmer was riding out, mounted on a splendid horse. The Federal Major laid hands upon the bridle, and bade Parmer dismount. It was as the grappling of a wave with a rock. No Guerrilla in the service of the South was cooler or deadlier; none less pervious to the influences and emotions of physical fear. He looked at the Federal Major a little curiously when he first barred the passageway of his horse, and even smiled pleasantly as he took the trouble to explain to him the nature of the instructions under which he was operating. "D—n you and d—n your instructions," the Major fiercely shouted. "Dismount!" "Ah!" ejaculated Parmer, "has it really come to this?" and then the two men began to draw. Unquestionably there could be but one result. The right hand of the Federal Major had scarcely reached the flap of his revolver, before Parmer's pistol was against his forehead, and Parmer's bullet had torn half the top of his head off. He fell prone under the horse's feet, with many of his own men gathering about him. A dozen muskets covered Parmer. "Hold hard! Hold for your lives!" shouted Quantrell, rushing down to the rescue, followed by twenty Guerrillas, "for if so be it that one of you fires a gun in anger I swear by the God above us all to murder you in mass!" The terrible look that came from the flashing eyes of this quiet tiger suddenly aroused, the pale face that had absolutely become frightful in its transformation, the avenging attitude of the whole man— standing on the edge of the threatening Federals, a revolver in each hand, made the soldiers nearest to Parmer lower their weapons involuntarily, and those nearest to Quantrell surrender theirs without a blow. In a score of minutes more not a single armed enemy existed in Hustonville, and beyond the dead commander, no other life was taken. The Guerrillas secured horses —fresh, fine unobjectionable horses—but they secured them at the sacrifice of the protecting uniform they wore. Hereafter, Quantrell was Quantrell; he could not, because of the protesting corpse lying there in front of the livery stable, be any longer Capt. Benedict or Capt. Clark. Perhaps Quantrell himself was tired of the *role*. Perhaps he wanted to have over him again the folds of the black flag, to hear the winds spread again the terror of his deeds, to get away from an assumption that was galling to him, to meet death—if he had to meet it—as became one who loved the name that he had done so much to render terrible. In any event, however, the end may not have been kept back or hastened by anything said of human speech or fashioned of human hands.

At Danville, the next place entered after the tragedy at Hustonville, a lady advanced cordially to Quantrell, frankly extended her hand, and addressed him by his proper name. He did not recognize the woman, but he did not deny the truthfulness of her recognition. Flattered because of an acquaintance with a Guerrilla at once so noted and so successful, and anxious to make known as widely as possible the news of his arrival in Kentucky, this woman told everything she knew. Though told of course always as a great secret, it was yet told nevertheless. Finally the story took wings and flew everywhere as

a bird.   Corroborative testimony impressed it upon the readily
impressionable nerves of the Federal authorities.   Dead men
began to be found here and there.   The stark human fruit the
trees bore the wind shook down.   Barnette's face, looking out
from its placid picture-frame, was seen and recognized.   The
Hustonville encounter enraged the regiment to which belonged
the unfortunate Major who in hunting for horses had penetrated
a jungle.   There was mustering and marching, and the State
was in arms.

And in Danville also there was another episode.   About the
town, as about almost every other town or city in Kentucky,
there were a few armed Federals who seemed to pay very little
attention to Quantrell's men one way or the other.   Evidently
they did not believe them to be Guerrillas; certainly they did
not know them to be such.   Quantrell himself took no note of
them.   He came and went as he always did, alone and non-
chalently.   There was one among the Federals, however, a
Lieutenant, who had heard some portions of the woman's conversation earlier in the day, and who—to satisfy himself and to
justify the deed he was about to do—added enough to the
glimpses already obtained from his own imagination to identify
the leader of the newly arrived detachment as the famous
Guerrilla Quantrell.   He cleaned, therefore, a Mississippi rifle
carefully, loaded it as though upon every grain of powder behind
the ball there depended a life, buckled about him four navy revolvers, and commenced at his own time and in his own fashion to
hunt for his man.   Quantrell noticed this officer in uniform, and
wondered what he was doing with the gun of a private.   For an
hour and more as he went from place to place, he saw this Lieutenant, now before him, now behind him, and not unfrequently
close at his side.   He never supposed at any time that he was being
watched, much less was he prepared for what followed.   It was
near the dinner hour; the first bell at the hotel in Danville had
sounded.   Quantrell, still alone and perfectly unsuspicious,
entered a convenient saloon for a drink, and while standing at
the bar and facing it, he saw in the glass before him the Lieutenant fill up the doorway, rifle in hand.   Just as he turned
about he was covered.   The gaping muzzle was scarcely three
feet from his breast, and the eye that ran down the barrel was a
cold, keen eye, full of pluck and purpose.   Quantrell's heavy

overcoat was buttoned to the chin. His pistols were about him, but for the emergency that was upon him, they had just as well have been in California. He did not feel that his heart beat the smallest fraction of a second faster. He felt no blood rush to his face. He leant languidly back against the counter, held up the whisky glass in his hand, as if to let the light filter through it and irradiate it, and then spoke to the Federal in a tone betwixt an enquiry and a caress: "How now, comrade? What are you going to do with that gun?" "Shoot you like a dog if you stir! You are Quantrell. You have played it for a long time, but you have about played the farce out at last. March into that room to the right of you there!"

Quantrell did not stir a finger. He cast his eyes quickly to the right without moving his head, and saw the bar-keeper, evidently in league with the Lieutenant, holding a door open for him to enter. Many things were clear to Quantrell, now—the clearest thing being that he did not mean to obey the Lieutenant. Once well within the confines of this apartment, and guarded in the perfectness and the quietness of its isolation, he might be held there until his men—unable to find him—abandoned the town, or until a heavy body of Federals—already in swift pursuit no doubt—came upon his track and finished his following at a blow. If he had to take the risk of being killed while he hazarded everything upon the chance of getting at a pistol, he meant to take it standing there by the bar and nearer to the daylight. Superb nerve, however, and the coolness for which he was noted, prevented the worst from coming to the worst. Still holding the whisky in his hand, and still leaning back against the counter negligently, he spoke to the Lieutenant and smiled as he spoke: "You take me for Quantrell, but you do wrong. Permit me to call my orderly sergeant, who has all my papers, and a glance at them will convince you in a moment that I am as true to the cause of the Union as you are." The Federal Lieutenant—surprised somewhat at the unruffled bearing of the man, and never from the first perfectly assured of the identity of his prisoner—weakened visibly. Quantrell continued, sure now of a way out from his uncomfortable predicament: "I have heard, perhaps, the same stories you have heard about the whereabouts of the famous Missouri Guerrilla, and if I had not been officially informed to the contrary, equally with yourself I might have believed them. He is not in Kentucky, to my certain knowledge, and you are making a d—d fool of yourself. Put down your gun, pull off your pistols, and as long as we are comrades let us be friends."

Not entirely convinced, and yet more than half way ashamed of the part he was playing, the Lieutenant stepped away from the door several feet and bade Quantrell call his orderly sergeant, keeping him still covered with the gaping muzzle of the Mississippi rifle. Luckily the saloon was but a short distance from the hotel, while about the hotel the bulk of the Guerrillas were grouped waiting for the second ringing of the dinner bell. Standing indifferently in this doorway, with his back to the covering rifle, Quantrell called out quietly: "John Barker!" Several of the men saw him standing there and started down to the saloon. "Go back all of you," he said; "I only want John Barker." John Barker came. As he entered the saloon he saw the leveled gun bearing upon his commander, and his pistol came out from its scabbard so quickly that the Lieutenant, to save his own life, turned the muzzle of the rifle from Quantrell to Barker. "Stop, sergeant," said Quantrell, "you are too fast. Put back your pistol. There need to be no killing here. Our friend, the Lieutenant yonder, has heard much of Quantrell of late, has made up his mind to the fact that I am Quantrell, has armed himself like an arsenal to capture Quantrell, has followed me here and got the drop on me here, and to convince him of his mistake and to show him how absurd and ungenerous he has been, I have called you here as my orderly sergeant to show him our special orders, and to put into his hands the authority of no less a person than the Secretary of War himself, Edwin M. Stanton, per A. J. Smith. Show him these papers, Barker, and then we will go to dinner." Barker stepped forward close to the Lieutenant, felt carefully a moment or two in the breast pocket of his coat, rattled something there audibly that sounded like a package, and then all of a sudden and with the spring of a tiger-cat he threw himself upon the Federal officer, cast aside the Mississippi rifle with his left hand, thrust into his face and close to it the muzzle of a dragoon revolver, and spoke up to him quaintly: "These are the papers, I reckon, you was expectin'. I keep just sich things for people like you. They carry a fellow a long ways, and the oftener you show them the furder they carry you. Say the word, Captain, and I'll put the old mark on him between the eyes." But Quantrell did not say the word. Indeed, he rather seemed to enjoy the episode, and to think more of the Lieutenant for the coolness he had displayed and the hardihood he had made manifest. As for the Lieutenant, he expressed himself as thoroughly satisfied with Barker's papers, stipulating only that a social glass should be taken all around and the episode itself kept a secret from the balance of the soldiers.

After dinner Quantrell marched northwest from Danville towards Washington, and halted the command at sunset eight miles from Harrodsburg. There were present and in line every man who had crossed the Mississippi river except Lieutenant James Little, the following being the role and the roster of the little band:

OFFICERS.

William C. Quantrell, Captain.
James Little, First Lieutenant.
Chatham Renick, Second Lieutenant,
John Barker, Orderly Sergeant.

PRIVATES.

Ves Acres,	Richard Burnes,	William Basham,
John Barnhill,	James Evans,	Richard Glasscock,
Jack Graham,	William Gaugh,	Thomas Harris,
David Helton,	Isaac Hall,	Robert Hall,
Clark Hockensmith,	William Hulse,	Payne Jones,
Frank James,	Foss Ney,	William Noland,
Allen Parmer,	Bud Pence,	John Ross,
Ran Venable,	George Wigginton,	Peyton Long,
James Lilly,	John McCorkle,	Lee McMurtry,
Andy McGuire,	Henry Noland,	Henry Porter,
Donnie Pence,	George Roberson,	James Williams,
	James Younger.	

Little had already been killed, and more were to follow speedily. After the halt, and the inspection of his command, Quantrell ordered John Barker to go with ten men to the house near which the inspection took place and procure rations for the night and ample forage. Accompanied by Lieutenant Renick and the balance of the company, Quantrell marched a mile fur-

26

ther, halted at a hospitable mansion, and made preparations to spend the night. The Guerrillas, however, had scarcely finished the evening meal when a furious volley came back from the direction of the house at which Sergeant Barker had stopped, followed by the fierce counter-fighting of determined men. In a moment Renick was mounted and on the road at a gallop to fathom the meaning of the fusillade. He did not return. Quantrell made his detachment take horse instantly, get into line, and get ready. Then ordering Allen Parmer, Payne Jones, William Hulse and Frank James to go forward rapidly and ascertain the worst or the best, he took an excellent position himself, available for either advance or retreat. The sound of the firing waxed louder and fiercer. The four men rushed away at a pace that had business in it—quick, unmistakable, absolute. Half a mile out on the road Frank James' horse swerved swiftly to one side, and shook him, superb rider as he was, seriously in the saddle. A dead man lay there, where the horse had swerved, face downward and gigantic in the gathering twilight. Over him stood his faithful horse, all but human in his faithfulness and compassion. Taught by kindness to revere his master and trained to go when he went and stop when he stopped, death never severed the tie nor broke down the old habits between them. Living, he loved him—dead, he was at his side.

Hulse dismounted and lifted up a white face to what little was left of the daylight, and cried aloud: "It's our Lieutenant, boys; it's Renick. Through his head there has been put a ball larger than a pistol ball."

Sergeant Barker's detachment, including himself, numbered eleven—Ves Acres, Richard Burnes, Richard Glasscock, George Roberson, James Evans, James Williams, Andy McGuire, William Gaugh, William Noland and Henry Noland. They had unsaddled and fed their horses and were about to begin their own supper when Major Bridgewater, commanding one hundred and eighty Federal cavalry, dashed up to the house, surrounded it on every side, cut off the men from their horses, and opened a furious fire upon the doors and the windows of the dwelling. The Guerrillas, used to either extreme of fortune, accepted the issue as it was made up for them, and fought as they had fought for four years—as wild beasts hunted hard and hemmed at last. In their extremity they were magnanimous; in their furious grapple they were full of chivalry. Gathering together all of the family in the safest room of the mansion—the room least pervious to bullets and least exposed— Ves Acres, as he put into the arms of its mother the youngest child, said consolingly though rather quaintly: "Don't expose yourself for the sake of this little thing, not much bigger than a rabbit. Keep away from the windows; keep close to the floor; do not get excited; do not cry if any of us get killed. What matters a Guerrilla more or less in this world?" And then with a smile on his face and a great resolution in his eyes, this brave, steadfast Missouri hero turned quietly to his duty and fought like a lion until he was shot down.

Eleven men against one hundred and eighty! It was fitting, perhaps, that in those last days of Quantrell such soldiers as he led should fight such odds. It is the revenge courage takes upon history which does not see the immense heroism of the Guerrilla while groping beneath his uniform for his bloody hands and holding them up to the reprobation of mankind.

The fight was the fight of a house against a fence, a tree, a barn, a pile of lumber, an out-building, a covering of any kind large enough to wholly or even partially shelter a trooper. Bridgewater wasted no lives foolishly. He did not assault the mansion; he did not permit his men to expose themselves recklessly; he would not resort to the torch because the house held by the Guerrillas was the house of a Union man, and yet his loss was heavy—thirty-two killed and eighteen wounded. Barker was killed. As he fell he tried to speak, but death caught his speech just on its utterance and strangled it to all eternity. Ves Acres took him up reverently, smoothed out the locks of his long hair, closed tenderly the dauntless eyes wide open to where the dead man may have thought the good God to be, and said as if in sorrow: "Boys, if I knew a prayer I would say it here for John Barker. He was true, he was brave, he never went back on his word, he never left a comrade when it was touch and go and the devil a grabbing for the hindmost, he never faltered because it was dark in the South and the men many days had neither rations nor cartridges; but he's gone. God take care of you, John." If he had been praying instead of fighting for the past four years, Ves Acres could have told to the Infinite no truer or tenderer story.

Henry Noland fell next, killed as he fought at a window. The ammunition of the Guerrillas was becoming exhausted, and a council of war was called. "I have eight rounds," said Dick Glasscock, "and I but four," spoke up Andy McGuire. Others had more or less, the average being five to the man. Ves Acres answered at last for all: "While there is a bullet left there will be a man to shoot it. No surrender if there is a cartridge."

Brief as was this dialogue, before it was finished William Noland was killed standing face to face with Richard Glasscock and talking to him. Brothers they were—these two young Nolands—and in the full vigor of ardent and stalwart manhood. As they lay side by side on the floor of a fort they had died in defending, some wind from without blew over the face of one the hair of the other. Was it a caress? Did the first who had crossed the wonderful river send this as a token to tell the other that all was well? Who knows? The Guerrilla has a God as well as the grenadier.

Ves Acres was down now. There were but two rounds left to the man. He had been shot in the right side and the left shoulder, and was too weak to rise to his place at the window. The rifle balls of the besiegers were coming through the planks of the dwelling-house. No spot was safe. Death was at the windows, at the doors—everywhere. There was no longer any more ammunition. Some dead Federals were close to the house outside, and Glasscock proposed that those who had a round yet left in their revolvers should make a last rush for the road and for Quantrell. "Good!" said Ves Acres, "very good. I will go with you." He tried to drag his crippled body up to his knees, and from his knees to his feet, but he fell over again as a child who had not yet learned how to walk. All his wounds bled afresh. "No use," he said, pleasantly. "I have a couple of chambers left yet. Take my pistol, Glasscock, and use it as you have need. It's a good pistol; it has done a power of shooting in its day; it has two loads left, and two loads sometimes are worth more than two wagon loads of gold."

There was a grand rush now of the survivors—seven in all—who fired once as they leaped the fence, and once more as they struck the line of ambushed Federals beyond it. The answering volley—close, and hot, and full of vengeance—covered them with a cloud of smoke. When the smoke lifted Glasscock was down, Williams was down, McGuire was down, Burnes—shot twice, was unable to continue his rush—while Roberson, Evans, and Gaugh—surrounded on all sides and powerless with empty pistols—surrendered to Major Bridgewater. Then there was a great stillness. The Federals swarmed about the wounded and captured Guerrillas and began to deal with them as each man's generosity or vindictiveness suggested. One smote McGuire in the face, wounded as he was, and another put a pistol to the head of Burnes, threatening to blow out his brains. McGuire snapped his empty revolver at the coward who struck him, and would have been killed instantly in return, if Bridgewater's roaring voice had not driven the Federal aggressor away abashed and threatened instant death to any one who further interfered with a prisoner. At this moment the four men sent back by Quantrell to develop the situation, fired point blank into the Federal mass gathered about the Guerrillas and charged up to the very fence that surrounded the house. Renick had been killed eight hundred yards from Bridgewater's position—shot through the head—and it was only by taking a dangerous fire themselves and charging full tilt down upon the enemy that Frank James and his three companions were enabled to return to Quantrell and report truthfully that all of Barker's detachment were either killed, wounded, or captured.

Hard hit and as much dead as alive, Glasscock—when ordered by Bridgewater to unbuckle his belt and surre nder his pistols—refused to do so. "I have sworn never to give them up voluntarily, and give them I never will. Kill me if it so pleases you, and then unbuckle my belt for yourself. Dead men have no sentiments." A Federal trooper covered him in a twinkling and cursed him bitterly as he spoke to him: "Be quick! Off with them, g—d d—n you. What right has a lousy beggar like you to be a chooser?" "Hush!" commanded Bridgewater, "he is too brave a man to be either shot or insulted. I will disarm him myself," and as he spoke he unbuckled the Guerrilla's belt, containing its six dragoon pistols, and handed it to his orderly. He tried to restrain himself, poor fellow, but in spite of his efforts, large tear-drops forced themselves from his eyes and ran down upon his breast. And of the eleven, how many to-day survive to read this story of the combat literally to the

death. Barker and the two Nolands fell in the house; later
on Glasscock died over Quantrell's crippled body trying to save
it; Andy McGuire was hung by a vigilance committee in Ray
county; Richard Burnes was murdered in Jackson county;
George Roberson was hung soon after in Lexington, charged
falsely with being the soldier who killed the Federal officer in
Hustonville; Acres recovered and is living to-day in Missouri,
while Evans, Gaugh, and Williams—somewhere near the
setting sun—

> " are content and clever
> In tending of cattle and tossing of clover,
> In the grazing of cattle and the growing of grain."

Bridgewater was a brave man, even where the odds were not
in his favor; having the advantage, he pushed the crippled Guer-
Guerrilla band to the wall. All that night and all the next day the
hammering at Quantrell's rear went on—the Missourians fighting
as they had fought two hundred times before. Ambuscades were
tried with good effect. Bridgewater did not know apparently
what possibilities there were connected with an ambuscade. He
believed he could ride through, or ride down, or ride over everything. Quantrell undeceived him speedily. During the night
pursuit succeeding his successful attack upon the little squad
under Barker, he lost eleven of his boldest riders. By daylight
he was desperate but not convinced; more wary, perhaps, but
scarcely any more cautious. Another sudden snare was necessary to make the furious hunter appreciate at its ultimate
worth the game that had been long afoot and for a night and
a day in the front of him.

The traveled road towards ten o'clock crossed a bold stream
abruptly. On the further bank where it came up from the
water it ran for fifty feet or more between perpendicular banks,
rocky but wooded. On either side six Guerrillas were posted,
in the road in front and back some distance from the crossing
nine more under Quantrell in person were massed to charge
the pursuers when they should have received the fire of those
commanding the cut, while the remaining four—consisting of
John Barnhill, John Ross, John McCorkle and John Graham,
were sent back half a mile to skirmish with Bridgewater and
lure him forward. The four Johns were four giants. Not in
size—because they were young and beardless—but in dash,
enterprise and intrepidity. Barnhill was a sleepless, vigilant,

gay-hearted, laughing Guerrilla, who would fight all day and frolic all night. Sometimes between his scouts and his slumbers there was a lapse of fifty hours. John Ross was a boy turned Paladin. Ordered to charge, he would have ridden over a precipice. Looking at his face, one would have said: There is an amiable youth; at his attitude in battle: there is an oak tree. McCorkle and Graham were of that old iron breed who had seen death so often and in so many sudden and curious ways that he had become to be regarded as an old acquaintance. The four had begun by making the sign of the cross when he approached; they would end by saying: "How now, comrade?"

Barnhill—by a sort of intrepid assurance—took command of the four and posted them wisely—two on one side of the road and two on the other. "Most likely," he argued, "the first volley of these fellows following us will go between the two flanks."

Bridgewater came on at a swinging trot. Barnhill leaped recklessly into the middle of the highway, fired thrice at the foremost files, followed by the balance of the Guerrillas in a deadly volley, and then retreated, seemingly without understanding or firmness of purpose. Bridgewater's men yelled once fiercely and broke from a trot into a furious gallop. Over the creek at a dead run, and up through the narrow way beyond the pursuers and pursued came as a thunder cloud, the revolver vollies the electric explosions. Then the trees as it were joined in the *melee*. The Guerrillas behind them — safe to a large extent from any fire directed from below—shot coolly and with a deadly precision into the compact mass, filling the ambushed gorge. Then Quantrell charged just in the first wild moment of the Federal agony—that supreme moment when the bravest who were ever chosen for battle must have time to think a second and get just a second's breath if they would not fall away panic stricken or run as those run who are not pursued. No combat of the war excelled this for prowess and execution. Frank James surpassed himself; Allen Parmer multiplied his capabilities as a fighter; Payne Jones—a pistol shot never surpassed among the Guerillas—improved, if that were possible, upon his markmanship; James Younger—riding a fleet, powerful horse, led the pursuit and refrained from killing a handsome young Federal whose own steed was crippled, and who could

not escape with his comrades.   Younger captured him, secured
for him a fresh horse, paroled him, and bade him go free.
Clark Hockensmith, close by Quantrell's side, saw a Federal
aiming at his Chief from behind a tree, and spurred his horse
instantly between the sharp-shooter and the sharp-shooter's
mark.   The bullet intended for Quantrell killed Hockensmith's
horse, but in a second George Wigginton had killed the sharp-
shooter.   What was done in that fight had need to be done
quickly.   William Hulse, carried away by a battle ardor that he
very rarely ever cared to curb, fought his way into the midst of
the struggling and stricken Federal rear only to be surrounded
in turn and put in desperate jeopardy.   John Barnhill, John
Ross, John McCorkle, John Graham, fighting altogether, cut
him out, helped by Lee McMurtry, William Basham, Bud Pence
and Donnie Pence.   Thomas Harris, Isaac Hall, David Helton,
and Robert Hall were wounded slightly but fought all the harder,
killing two men each and capturing five valuable horses.   Henry
Porter won the admiration of the whole command by an exhibition of superb coolness and dash.   He was cut off from Quantrell and fired at by six Federal cavalrymen who closed in upon
him and would have killed him but for his own rapid fighting and
the help of a few comrades.   Ran Venable, nearest to him, rushed
to his assistance, followed by Frank James, Peyton Long, and
James Lilly.   These, together with Porter, killed the six who
were about him, and four others who rushed up to succor the
six.   The gorge was now cleared of all save the dead and the
wounded.   Bridgewater—in a *melee* that had not lasted longer
than twenty minutes—had lost in killed fifty-two of his bravest
followers, and in wounded seven.   He withdrew the remnant of
his shattered advance speedily from the gorge, reformed his
ranks on the open ground beyond, and çame on slowly in
pursuit and after the lapse of some time, but always thereafter
in skirmishing order.   The lesson taught him was a bitter one,
but it may have been useful as well.   It saved Quantrell also.
Eight of his men were wounded—none of them, however, very
seriously — but whenever he formed in the future and faced
about as if to fight, those who were following him did him at
least the honor of forming too and coming towards him slowly
and in cautious array.

Snow lay upon the ground to the depth of at least four inches,

and a cold north wind cut like a knife. The pursuit of the
night had to light it a splendid winter moon ; of the day a great
garment of white that filled all the woods and the ways. But
the Guerrillas, inured to every hardship and proof against every
extreme, starved and fought, and fought and froze for a stretch
of fifty-two hours, losing sight of Bridgewater and his constantly increasing column of pursurers in Washington county.

After food, rest and forage Quantrell rode on into Chaplain,
in Nelson county, where he arrived early in the afternoon.
Just as he had passed well to the centre of the city, Captain
Edward Terrell, at the head of sixty Federal Guerrillas, reached
the outskirts of Chaplain, hard upon his track. Terrell was a
soldier as thoroughly desperate as Quantrell in some respects,
but his men were not equal to Quantrell's men. Terrell understood well the value of dash, of rush, of quick fighting, of a
blow that carried with it the power of its own perpetuation. That
is to say, he knew how—when he once got thoroughly warmed up
to his work—to keep at it until something yielded or somebody
got badly hurt. As soon as he saw Quantrell he dashed at him
as a greyhound at a hare. Quantrell had just escaped a
formidable antagonist after a bloody grapple. Substract from
his original thirty-seven men the five who had been killed, the
eight who had been wounded and captured, and the eight who
had been wounded and not captured, and Quantrell was
scarcely in a condition to fight Terrell's sixty fresh Guerrillas
effectively. He did fight them, however, those who were wounded holding the rear in turn equally with those who were not
wounded. The fight lasted for five miles along the Bloomfield
turnpike. William Hulse, John Barnhill, Frank James, John
Ross, John Graham, John McCorkle, Payne Jones, Allen
Parmer, Foss Ney, Clark Hockensmith, Peyton Long and James
Younger doing two hours battle work so splendid and so superb
that Terrell himself spoke of them afterwards as devils and not
men. Try how he would, the Federal commander could never
break up Quantrell's rear. In every rush he got the worst of
the *melee*. His men could not shoot like Quantrell's men,
neither could they ride so surely. There was a fierce conflict
at the point where Quantrell left the turnpike and took a road
leading to Taylorsville, in Spencer county, and once thereafter
on the Taylorsville road proper ; but Terrell was worsted so

badly in the first encounter, and cut up so seriously in the second that he abandoned the pursuit and returned with his wounded and his dead to Chaplain.

Resting a day and a night at the hospitable house of a well-to-do farmer living near Taylorsville, who loved the South, Quantrell threw off all Federal disguise and boldly declared his name, his principles, and his intentions. He sought to find Sue Mundy, a Kentucky Guerrilla of Confederate proclivities, who had already done much valuable spy work and delivered many swift and telling blows. Mundy was away at the time on an extended scout, but a comrade of his—Captain Marion—in no way inferior as a fighter or less enterprising as a partisan, met Quantrell at an interview arranged by the host of the hospitable mansion, part Guerrilla himself and part non-combatant. The meeting took place in Taylorsville. Naturally distrustful, and made extremely cautious because of the imminence of the danger that daily confronted him—Marion talked at first with his eyes rather than with his lips, and listened with his right hand upon his revolver. He neither denied nor affirmed that Quantrell was Quantrell. Man for man he was not of course afraid to meet him in a friendly way, discuss events with him, plan with him expeditions, compare with him notes, and lay schemes with him to entrap and inveigle a common enemy; but when it came about that he had to march side by side with these scarred, bronzed Missourians, who might be Missourians and who might not, Captain Marion's yes sounded mightily like an unmistakable no.

Finally, however, Marion agreed to this: Commanding forty Guerrillas of his own, if Quantrell would put at his disposal all the serviceable Missourians who were willing for work, he would inaugurate a raid at once and march immediately towards its accomplishment. But as an absolute guarantee of good faith it would be necessary for Captain Quantrell to report temporarily to Captain Marion. Quantrell felt annoyed at the suspicions of his Kentucky comrade, and vexed that he should be required to separate himself even temporarily from his constantly decreasing band, but the surroundings of the situation required something of a sacrifice. He was hunted everywhere by his enemies, and suspected everywhere by those who, if they had known all, would have been his steadfast friends. In order to place himself as speedily as possible *en rapport* with the Confederate Guerrillas of Kentucky, and be enabled to utilize at once the valuable services of their spies, guides, couriers, hiding-places, and horse purveyors, he had to convince Marion of his own identity and put himself also in his power as a kind of hostage for the good behavior of his men. Quantrell chose to do deliberately what he was required to do, and Marion moved with the Missourians for Georgetown. Quantrell remained behind, after first explaining to his men the necessity of the separation, and the need of faithfulness on their part and the exercise of the old bravery as well.

Marion caused a strong guard to be stationed about the Missourians the first night, and one not so strong the second night. By the fifth night he had become so thoroughly convinced of their principles that he put them on watch over the Kentuckians, while early in the morning of the sixth day out—after having charged, routed, and killed to a man a Federal scout of eleven cavalry—Marion opened his heart to his suspected allieis and praised them loudly for their fidelity and courage.

The crossing of the Kentucky river at Worthville was not without its episode. A portion of Marion's men were well over, a portion in mid-stream, and a portion still upon the nearer shore when an alarm was given and a volley fired. Marion had crossed, and the bulk of the Kentuckians, but the attack came from the rear and its full brunt had to be borne by the Missourians. Frank James sprang first to his horse and charged back upon the enemy. Hulse followed him, then Ross, Barnhill, Ney, McMurtry, Venable, the two Halls, Porter, Long, Younger, Wigginton, Graham, McCorkle, Parmer, Bud and Donnie Pence, Jones, Lilly, Hockensmith, Basham, Harris, Helton, and several Kentucky Guerrillas as brave as the best of them. Outnumbered, the Guerrillas yet fought a fight that could not be resisted. The enemy was driven a mile and more at a headlong pace, his dead dotting the road in ghastly spots where when living they had gallantly formed and gallantly stood to keep the Guerrillas back. It was in this combat that Frank James killed a Federal with the butt of his heavy dragoon revolver. So relentless had been the race and so fierce the fighting that every barrel of his six pistols had been discharged. Ahead of him was a stalwart rider whose revolver was also empty. James called upon him to halt and surrender himself. The Federal turned sideways in his saddle, looked back once as if in superlative derision, and shouted: "Shoot, and be d—d to you!" James could not shoot, but he sent his horse ahead furiously by a spur stroke, lifted himself up sheer in the stirrups, grasped his heaviest dragoon revolver by the barrel and struck once and struck hard as he ranged alongside the galloping enemy. The skull crashed as a hazel-nut. A sound came from the blow like the sound of wood upon wood—dull, yielding, deadened—and all of a heap and prone under his horse's feet, the stricken Federal pitched forward, a writhing and contorting figure in the middle of the road. Hulse seized and appropriated his horse, a most serviceable animal, and the pursuit ended with this ferocious episode.

Well over the Kentucky river and well beyond and unmolested, Marion pushed boldly and rapidly on towards Georgetown. The enemy had gained the town ahead of him, however, and were in full possession of the place when the Guerrillas reached to within an hour's march. Marion—possessed of considerable enterprise and no small amount of stubborn courage—refused to fall back without a fight. It might be feasible to assume a Federal *role* and take under the guise of comradeship an immense advantage of the garrison. Once well among them and secure from attack for the first few moments of entrance, Marion believed that he could either kill or capture the entire command. As the Missourians alone wore the United States uniform, he sent these ahead to reconnoitre the position and ascertain if the *ruse* proposed to be practiced was practicable. Peyton Long carried a Federal flag in the front file, having Frank James on his left. Behind these two came Hulse, Basham, Barnhill, Graham, Helton, the two Halls, Hockensmith, Jones, Ney, Lilly, and McCorkle. Behind these—and as blue in their great cavalry overcoats as a bar of indigo—there rode as a reserve, McMurtry, Parmer, Porter, the brothers Pence, Ross, Venable, Harris, Wigginton, and Younger. Long boldly approached the picquets with his flag and was not even halted. The others rode up and rode through these covering cavalrymen unchallenged. So far the scheme advised by Marion was working admirably. It might be possible to win with it along the entire line. In any event the next twenty minutes were big with the fate of the whole adventure.

Eighteen miles from Georgetown, Marion had halted the night before with his Guerrillas and occupied the house of a Union citizen. The Missourians—quartered to themselves in the barn—were quiet, taciturn and discreet. They did not talk of military men or things. They looked like Federals, they acted like Federals, they neither denied nor affirmed that they were Federals: were they Federals? Their host said that they were, but their host had a pretty daughter who peered with all the eyes she had and listened with all the ears she had for further information *pro* or *con*. Not so circumspect as Quantrell's old men, nor so watchful of little things, Marion had a soldier of his own at the supper table to disclose the secret of the expedition with a sentence. Desultory conversation had been generally indulged in. The Guerrilla Captain desired nothing but agreeable things to be left in his rear, and so had made himself especially communicative to the host, and especially agreeable to his hostess and her charming daughter. His men also had been firmly admonished to keep upon their good behavior. Matters were moving smoothly along, and an assuring social footing had just been reached, when supper was announced. During the meal, one of Marion's Kentucky followers spoke quietly but significantly to another: "How we will fool them to-morrow if we find them in Georgetown." In a second he had caught himself and was striving to recover what he had lost by changing the conversation. Too late! Neither the man nor the woman of the house looked up or gave by any sign heed to the talk of the babbler; but the daughter heard the words of exultation, divined their meaning with all a woman's swift intuition and flushed scarlet to her hair. Marion frowned, bit his lips and tried to annihilate with his eyes the garrulous offender. That night, when all the soldiers slept, and when the frost and the north wind were abroad in the midnight together, the young girl crept from her bed to the stable, saddled a swift horse for herself, and rode as only country girls know how to ride full tilt into Georgetown. The mistake the imprudent Guerrilla made, even though his words had been taken at their real meaning, might easily have been provided against if Marion's caution had in any manner approximated his audacity. Four guards advantageously posted would have made impossible the Union girl's night ride, and a watchful sentinel about the house might even have prevented the attempt. As it was, she carried to the Federals stationed near to Georgetown the news of Marion's approach and the probable nature of the stratagem he would attempt to play. The Federals early the next morning occupied the place in force, posted their picquets with orders to admit the Guerrilla column without question, and then prepared themselves thoroughly, by fortification and ambushment, to destroy it.

It was well for Marion and well for his men that the Missourians rode that day in front of the column. As the leading files advanced half through the town and were nearing the larger and heavier buildings about the public square, Peyton Long, the standard bearer, stopped. Marion, some few paces in advance of Frank James, turned to know the reason. "It does not become me, aptain," James spoke up, "to either advise with you or suggest to you unless I am so requested, but I must tell you respectfully that we do not like the looks of things. There are no soldiers upon the streets; the picquets did not halt us; Georgetown is as quiet as a graveyard; there is treachery somewhere; if we go further without developing the situation, we shall be surrounded and savagely attacked. Ten skirmishers thrown well forward now may save thirty lives further on. Evidently we are expected, but not as friends are expected. Look yonder, Captain!"

Four men, running in a stooping position with their guns in their hands, were seen making much haste from one house to another. Marion saw them and understood in a moment the whole situation. In five minutes more the skirmishers had developed the enemy and there was a terrible fire going on from the doors and the windows of the buildings upon the Guerrillas in the street. Frank James' horse was killed, and Hulse, Bud Pence, James Younger and John Ross were slightly wounded. Nothing remained but a countermarch. Increased by accessions here and there on the trip, Marion's command numbered probably seventy, the Federals one hundred and eighty-two. As many as one hundred and eighty-two in addition should be counted for the houses. Indeed, to fight at all with Marion would have been madness. There was still time to get away from the trap whose jaws in springing had grazed with their teeth the bulk of the column, but the need was to make haste. Larger bodies of the enemy were hastening up from two directions, and the country now must certainly be aroused. Frank James' watchfulness had stood all in good stead so far, but superior watchfulness could not always avail against superior numbers. Marion retreated rapidly, first gathering up the picquets who had deliberately sacrificed themselves for the success of the ambushment inspired by a woman. From these he learned of the young girl's mission, and the motive, other than patriotism, which inspired her. Beloved by a young Lieutenant stationed near to Georgetown, and betrothed to him, she had more than once carried to his Colonel information of military movements hostile or suspicious. Suspecting Marion from the first, and more than usually curious and vigilant, she had divined at last the true character of the Guerrillas and the true intention of their mission.

Frank James, afoot, would not leave Georgetown without a horse. Under the point blank range of the guns of one of the largest houses in the place there was a livery stable filled with splendid cavalry animals. For this he made a rush, a revolver in each hand, killed two guards by the door who disputed his passage, mounted the finest horse feeding there—a magnificent gray, pure blooded as Lexington—and dashed back to his comrades, leading four others in no way inferior to his own valuable capture. The Federals fired at him furiously without effect, and then they ceased firing and chased him heartily as long as he was in sight.

Marion made haste through Owen county, after his repulse at Georgetown, and into Woodford county, where he swooped down upon the famous stock farm of Colonel R. A. Alexander. Alexander was an importer and breeder known to the country. The blood in the veins of his horses was royal blood. King Lexington had by almost immortal speed established a dynasty and begotten a long line of imperial racers. Federals and Confederates alike had spared him, but the Guerrillas were inexorable and took from his stables thoroughbred horses to the number of nineteen, and valued in the aggregate at $100,000. Alexander offered $10,000 for the release of a favorite stallion, Bald Chief, but Marion refused the offer and marched away with the property.

Re-crossing the Kentucky river near Lawrenceburg, and halting beyond a few miles for breakfast, Frank James suddenly leaped from his seat upon the table, and from the table to the door, shouting: "Yonder they come! To the stable, quick! to the stable, boys, for your horses and your lives!"

There was a rush and a volley. All the road was blue with overcoats. James led, behind him came Hulse, behind Hulse, Donnie Pence, and behind Pence, Clark Hockensmith. Marion formed the balance of the company behind fences and out-buildings. The first four, James, Hulse, Pence and Hocken-smith, tarried not a moment until they reached the stable, fifty yards from the dwelling. A few of the enemy were already there and shot through the cracks at the Guerrillas as they bridled and saddled their horses. They fired back, even while busy with buckle and strap, and killed three of the boldest forcing the fighting from the outside. All about it was touch and go. Of the eight horses feeding in the stable, the four Guerrillas got safely out with only the four they rode. Bald Chief was killed in the *melee*, and two others of Alexander's most valuable thoroughbreds disabled permanently by wounds. Marion extricated himself finally from the heavy force which threatened him, and rode away, fighting fiercely for several miles. Eight of his men were wounded, seven of whom were brought off by their more fortunate comrades, leaving the eighth man, Thomas Henry, too hard hit to ride. Henry was a Ken-tuckian, young, dauntless, and utterly fearless in combat. He had helped hold the rear against desperate odds for two long miles, fighting foot by foot and hand to hand. Many remarked his prowess. Frank James especially complimented him and spoke to him banteringly: "You ought to be a Missourian—you fight like a Jackson county man." Finally Henry fell, shot sheer through the right breast, and the Federal wave swept over and beyond him. As it returned from a pursuit which for their numbers had been singularly barren and unprofitable, a savage trooper dashed up to the wounded hero still lying there, bleed-ing and helpless, and shot him twice full in the face. So close each time was the muzzle of the pistol that powder was blown into the skin, and the eye-lashes and eye-brows burned completely off. The first ball entered his mouth and passed out on the left side of his neck, while the second—entering the right cheek an inch below the eye—made its exit near to and below the base of the right ear. Finished apparently, and bloody, disfigured, and still, the soldier who shot him rifled his pockets, disposed of his boots, and rode away boasting that there was "one d—d bushwhacker less in the world." But in spite of his three desperate wounds, Henry lived on. When he awoke to consciousness he crawled, half frozen, through the bitter February weather to the house of a Southern man, three miles away. There he found food, succor, shelter, a nurse, a doctor, and a courier who went for Marion. Marion was a man who never feared an enemy or forgot a friend. As none in battle were braver or more reckless, so none in its lapse or lull were more faithful to the hurt or gentle with the crippled. Twenty times over had he risked his own life to save what little life yet remained to some grievously wounded yet gallant follower. He turned about at once as soon as word was brought to him of Henry's condition, and watched over him day and night until he could be carried to a place of safety. He survived the war, and makes in peace an upright, stalwart citizen, without fear and without reproach. His scars are his decorations, and for fewer many major-generals have been made.

Captain Marion, without further adventure or serious combat, delivered again into Quantrell's keeping that portion of Quantrell's command which had followed him so far and followed him so well. He thanked him briefly for their services, and summed up briefly the praise all felt was but a portion of what was due to them: "Braver men," he said, "I never saw in battle, truer men never fired a gun since the war began."

Marion and Quantrell parted for awhile now, but temporarily. Before the separation, however, he prevailed upon Marion to restore to Alexander the remaining sixteen blooded horses still in his possession. Marion readily consenting, delivered the horses over to Quantrell, and Quantrell in turn delivered them over to their owner. As an appreciation of this disinterested act, and as a real token of gratitude to the two men who were the most instrumental in this transfer, Alexander presented Quantrell with a magnificent thoroughbred, and Frank James with another, known everywhere by his name of Edwin Forrest, and noted everywhere for his speed and for the prowess of his rider.

The Missouri Guerrillas needed rest. They had ridden and fought, with scarcely a day of real quiet, from Jackson county,

27

Missouri, to Nelson county, Kentucky—through Arkansas, Tennessee, and Kentucky—and it was time for a little re- laxation. The February weather, even in the latitude in which they were, was bitter cold, and the State in every di- rection was overrun with Federal regiments. Quantrell, there- fore, resorted once more to his old tactics of Missouri and dis- banded his Guerrilla following until further orders. Some went to one portion of Nelson county and some to another. Among the mountains in the west, and at the truly hospitable mansions of the Thomases, Russells, and McClaskeys, about Bloomfield, the battle-scarred and war-worn Guerrillas found a hearty wel- come. One detachment, consisting of Lee McMurtry, Bud Pence, Frank James, Donnie Pence, Payne Jones, William Hulse and John Ross, made homes with Mrs. Samuels and Mrs. Finetta E. Sayers. These families were especially kind to the Missouri Guerrillas. Food, shelter, information, skillful medical attendance, fresh horses—everything in fact was furnished to them ungrudgingly when they were either sick, hard pressed, wounded, ahungered, or afoot. Mrs. Samuels was truly a South- ern mother in Israel. Mrs. Sayers feared nothing—neither pro- scription, arrest, military punishment, the confiscation of prop- erty, nor the imprisonment of her people. Another famous rendezvous, their few brief resting days knew, was at the house of Dock Hoskins—Old Dock as the Guerrillas called him. He lived in a prominent and comfortable dwelling on the top of a hill. For many miles round about this mansion might have been remarked. Cedar woods surrounded it. A shout of warn- ing, a cry, a galloping horse, a single pistol shot, and no matter what the number of the attacking force, ten steps in a retreat hid the Guerrillas and as effectually protected them from pursuit as a ship in a harbor is protected from a storm. Once only during the war did an enemy beat up these commodious quar- ters. Bud Pence and Henry Turner, scouting well up in the direction of Samuels' Depot, were attacked by Lieut. Hancock, commanding a detachment of the 47th Kentucky, and driven rapidly towards Dock Hoskins' house. Pence fought them step by step. Turner was shot through the right shoulder, and Pence in the right arm, but they escaped among the cedars and Hancock halted awhile at Hoskins'.

Thus Mrs. Samuels, Mrs. Sayers, Dock Hoskins, the Russells,

and the McClaskeys ministered to the Missourians. What hurts there were among them were speedily healed. Those who needed clothing were bountifully supplied. Bad horses had been traded away for good ones. Small supplies of ammunition were increased to large ones. Carbines were looked to, pistols cleaned, the men grew restless, and the signs visibly increased of stormy movements, to be stormily made. It was March now, and something of the Spring was felt in the air, seen on the trees, heard in the streams, and made known by the springing grasses. The nights, less cheerless and full of frost, were getting fit again for bivouacs. In the maple trees some sap was rising, and from the South a soft wind was beginning to blow.

Those who at the fight in Jessamine county had been wounded and captured — Ves Acres, Dick Glasscock, McGuire, Burnes, Gaugh, Evans, Roberson, and Williams—had been carried to Louisville and imprisoned there. Helped from the outside, and finding numerous friends throughout the city, these desperate Guerrillas sawed asunder the iron bars of their dungeons, dug and burrowed as veritable badgers, crawled through holes a ferret could scarcely have found feasible, and reached daylight and liberty both at once, wounded as some of them were and emaciated. Further safety required immediate separation. Acres escaped in one direction, Williams in another, Burnes and McGuire in a third, Gaugh in a fourth, Evans and Roberson in a fifth, Glasscock alone of all the fugitives reached Quantrell in safety and Roberson alone of all of them was recaptured. Taken at Lexington and transferred again to Louisville, he was tried by a drum-head court-martial and sentenced to be hung. The charge upon which he was convicted was a charge shamefully false. Infuriated at the escape of men so notoriously desperate as were these Guerrillas of Quantrell, the Federal authorities at Louisville needed a victim. George Roberson was found. Any evidence was sufficient for conviction. No evidence at all would have answered just as well. He was accused of having killed the Federal officer in Hustonville who attempted at the livery stable to prevent the appropriation of the horses of his men. Allen Parmer killed that officer, as all the command knew. Parmer and Roberson had no single feature alike. In nothing did they resemble each other—neither in eyes, hair, form, gait, speech, or general appearance. Mistaken identity was a plea too preposterous to be put up. Those who swore away his life were simply murderers after another fashion. Instead of cutting his throat while asleep, or shooting him unawares, or crushing his skull with a blow from behind, they hung him with a lie. Even the wolf's courage was wanting to them; it was the weasel which they assimilated. Few friends were about the scaffold when the young Missourian—intrepid as though it was a battle-day—was brought forth to die. These friends dared not speak to him, much less to bid him be cool and brave. He had asked permission to be shot as a soldier, but murders for revenge have no appreciation of chivalry, and this being a precious boon to him was of course denied. Bound as he was, he walked like La Tour de Auvergne at the head of his Grenadiers. The drums beat, there was the tread of marching men—cavalry and infantry—and the rabble called to one another and laughed as the procession wound its way slowly along from the prison to the scaffold. Brave men in the ranks of the cordon about him spoke soldierly words afterwards of his quiet grace and dauntlessness. He was but a wild beast, many said and no doubt honestly believed — for the name Guerrilla was synonymous then with extermination—but the wild beast died like a demigod. He looked once at the houses, the people, the white clouds far to the west, the sea of faces upturned and all about him, and then to the bright sun shining over all. Yes,

> " He walked out from the prison wall,
>   Dressed like a prince for a parade,
>   And made no note of man or maid,
>   But gazed out calmly over all;
>   Then look'd afar, half paused, and **then**
>   Above the mottled sea of men
>   He kiss'd his thin hand to the sun;
>   Then smiled so proudly none had **known**
>   But he was stepping to a throne."

A few friends begged the body from the hangman and buried it away beyond the reach of the resurrectionist. None the less had he died for his country in dying upon the scaffold. The principle for which the hero dies, and not the mode of dying, makes the consecration. If patriotism has anywhere beyond the river an abode where the spirits of the dead who died for the right are gathered together and re-endowed with form and substance, be sure the angel keeping watch and ward by the golden gates will never know anything of difference between the scar the rope made and the scar of the bullet in open battle.

Dr. McClaskey gave to the Guerrillas a re-union feast. Magruder, a Kentuckian somewhat of the fashion of George Todd, came to it. He was a bold, cool, untiring, venturesome man, used to hard knocks and difficult to kill. When he fought he fought to exterminate. Those who followed him had also to follow a black flag. His frame, gigantic as it was, sat upon a horse as a rider might who was riding for a crown. If he got four hours of sleep he got enough. The Federals called him a butcher; his own men Rough and Ready. Sue Mundy came to it, a quiet, gentle, soft-spoken dandy, with his hair in love-knots six inches long, a hand like a school-girl, and a waist like a woman. Sometimes he dressed also as a woman, hence the *soubriquet* of Sue. As a spy he came and went as a wind that blew. So many were his shapes and disguises, so perfectly under control were his speech and bearing, that in some quarters his identity was denied, in others his sex was a matter of doubt, in all, those who did not fear him had an improbable idea both of the man's prowess and personal appearance. Mundy was a cool, brave, taciturn, experienced soldier, well acquainted with the country where he operated and utterly fearless. In addition, he was also a thorough fatalist. His smooth, open, rosy-cheeked face made almost any disguise easy of encompassment. His iron nerve carried him easily through many self-imposed difficulties that without it extrication could not have come through a regiment of cavalry. When he fought he fought savagely. Beneath an exterior as effeminate as a woman of fashion he carried the muscles of an athlete and the energy of a racer. His long hair in battle blew about as the mane of a horse. The dandy in a *melee* became a Cossack; in desperate emergencies a giant. Mundy, Marion and Magruder were a Kentucky trio famous as fighters and fit to be relied upon equally with the best of any Guerrilla band, Quantrell's not excepted.

To this feast also came Quantrell, a deeper light in his clear blue eyes, and a graver cast on his grave, cold features. The few who were left to him of all his desperate following and who remarked their chief at this last reunion this side eternity, remarked as they had never done before, how tall and straight he was, how fair if not to say florid his complexion was, how much darker his hair had become, how broad his shoulders were, and how if anything his nose had become longer and more aquiline. All who had ever studied him knew from the first that his application was indefatigable, his temper cool, his understanding vigorous and decisive, and that in his practice he preserved that rare and salutary moderation in the government of intractable men which pursued his own ideas at an equal distance from the opposing ideas of those who were the most ambitious among his band, and invariably enforced them without seeming to control. He had come now again and for the last time to propose a raid.

There was mirth at Dr. McClaskey's, and music, and feasting, and dancing, and many tender words spoken at parting—for Southern girls had gathered in from all the country round about—but good-byes were said at last and the Guerrillas rode away. The road they took ran towards Lebanon. At sunset a bivouac was had, still a little crisp and chilly in the night air, and a rousing fire made. In the morning an advance was formed, Magruder, Bud Pence, John Ross, William Hulse and Frank James comprising it. Quantrell and Mundy marched with the reserve. Entered well upon the turnpike leading from Lebanon to Campbellsville, Hulse and James discovered a wagon train making its way up from Lebanon, convoyed by a detachment of Federal soldiers, four of whom were in front of it. Magruder first sent Hulse back to notify Quantrell of the near proximity of the enemy, and then moved boldly forward. For awhile the Federal advance guard looked upon Quantrell's advance guard as friends, as their uniform was like their own, and permitted them to approach within a few feet unchallenged. At the order to surrender, the Federals attempted to draw their pistols, when three of them were shot down instantly, the fourth one turning to run, followed by Frank James at a furious pace to within half a mile of the fort at Lebanon. Almost safe and nearly within reach of shelter and succor, Frank James shot him running fifty yards away, putting a bullet in the back of his head. The train, composed of twenty wagons, was burnt, and its escort—numbering thirty-eight cavalrymen—was totally destroyed, twenty-seven being killed, ten wounded, and one taken alive and unhurt.

At a toll-gate two miles west from Bradfordsville, Quantrell's rear was heavily attacked. Sue Mundy held it and turned

upon the head of the pursuing column with an energy so sudden
and savage that he staggered it until it reeled, when rushing
down at the charge and clearing everything down before him as
of old in his murderous onset, Quantrell checked the pursuit
for the day, after killing and wounding seventy-six of the
enemy. In the first moments of this fight, however, and before
Quantrell had quite reached to the rescue of his Kentucky
comrade holding the rear, Mundy was down under his dead
horse, held as though a log were upon his body. Fifty Federals
were hacking at him with swords and firing at him with
revolvers. His own men nearest to him and available for
immediate help were Magruder, William Hulse, George Wigginton, John Barnhill, Frank James, John Ross, Parmer, Porter,
Venable and James Younger. These charged *en masse* upon
Mundy's assailants, fought off those immediately bent upon
killing him as he lay prostrate there, and held them off until
Quantrell finished the combat by a pistol fight remarkable for
its rapidity and execution. The next day Capt. Fidler was
encountered commanding sixty men, each man leading an
excellent cavalry horse. Fidler did not fight, and perhaps it
was no part of his programme to fight. He sacrificed forty-
five of his best horses, seven of his men, and escaped with the
balance.

Quantrell's old antagonist, Colonel Bridgewater, lived on
Rolling Fork, in Marion county, and he would beat up his quarters and pounce upon him if possible. Reaching Bridgewater's
house about ten o'clock at night, Quantrell surrounded it at
once, but soon satisfied himself that the Colonel was not at home.
He then marched to the neighborhood of Hustonville and was
attacked twelve miles from this place by an entire regiment of
cavalry. Here Foss Ney was killed, one of his old men, as brave
as any of the band, and Jo Lisbon. Fighting superbly in the
rear, James Younger was badly wounded and captured, together
with William Merriman, who rushed up in the face of two hundred Federals to rescue his comrade and bring him out.
Younger, when his horse was killed and his comrades had been
driven back far beyond his ability to reach them on foot, stood
up in front of the whole Federal line which had been firing at
long range and fired every barrel of his six revolvers. Probably
five hundred Federals fired at him specially. Shot in the right

shoulder, he used his pistols with his left hand, and when he fell
the enemy were within a dozen yards of him, and he had been
again shot badly in the right breast. While closing in upon
him, many in the advancing line cried out to him to surrender.
He answered neither yes nor no, but he continued to shoot.
When Merriman reached him, he was too badly hurt to mount
up behind, even though Merriman's horse in that fire could have
lived a moment. A second later, Merriman's own horse was
killed, and shot twice and badly hurt, Merriman himself was
lying a few feet from James Younger, incapable of resistance.
The Federals were particularly kind to these two prisoners,
Guerrillas though they were, and extended to them many
friendly acts and favors because of a bravery never surpassed.

Quantrell extricated himself from the desperate pursuit with
difficulty. He formed and fought, and fought and formed, but
outnumbered as he was nearly ten to one, he scarcely made an
impression upon the bold horsemen who constantly came on.
Payne Jones was afoot, Allen Parmer was afoot, James Lilly
was afoot, Lee McMurtry was afoot, Frank James was afoot,
John Barnhill's horse was standing up barely under his wounds,
Ike Hall was wounded, Venable was wounded, Clark Hockensmith was wounded, and others of his men had been more or
less severely handled. Quantrell passed the word hurriedly
along his own ranks to the effect that with the men not yet disabled he would charge once more furiously, but that during the
charge those who were dismounted must leave the road, as
whether successful or unsuccessful, he would order a disbandment. The charge was made furiously, and it swept away the
head of the Federal column as a strong stream sweeps away a
mass of driftwood. There was a halt, a lull in the storm of the
pursuit, a sudden change of the combat from a column of rough-
riding cavalrymen into a line of cautious skirmishers, and in the
interval of time thus gained by one audacious counter-move-
ment, the dismounted men escaped and the wounded men were
carried off by their comrades.

As of old the second rendezvous was in Nelson county. Lee
had surrendered. Everywhere the Confederate armies were
falling to pieces. Neither the Southern soldiers nor civilians
knew anything of the intentions of the Confederate authorities.
Even in the air there were evidences of gloom and disaster.

Discipline was gone. The masses were not in favor of making a Guerrilla war succeed to that of the war of a regular government. Kentucky, like Missouri, had furnished more soldiers to the Northern than to the Southern armies, and was willing to make peace almost before there had been a commencement of hostilities. While Lee stood everything stood—erect, hopeful, defiant. When Lee fell, the fabric which four years of heroic fighting had erected and the blood of half a million of men had been poured out to make its foundations immutable, fell with him and with a great crash. African Slavery was buried at Appomattox court house, and—let us take care that American Liberty was not buried there as well.

The last week in April, 1865, Quantrell, having with him only John Ross, Payne Jones, William Hulse and Frank James, started to Winchester, in Clark county, but before he reached it the town was occupied by the enemy. Every day for a week there was a fight. In single combat with a Federal cavalryman, Quantrell killed his man nearly a hundred yards. At the head of his squad he encountered late one afternoon a superior body of the enemy and advanced alone to inspect them further. A single Federal rode out to encounter him, and halted at the distance of fifty yards. Quantrell called to him to come closer, but he refused, and Quantrell fired and missed him. The Federal returned the fire with his carbine and missed, and then followed it up with three additional shots from his revolver. The range evidently being too great for his skill, he turned quickly and was galloping back to his comrades when Quantrell fired his second shot and put a bullet in the Federal's neck just at the base of the skull. Something of the desperation of those combats in Missouri when it was darkest along the border, came now to the winnowed and battered few who still rallied about their beloved leader and obeyed him with a touching devotion abnormal in that time of falling away and abandonment. John Ross and Frank James, sent to a house to procure horses for three dismounted comrades, were fired upon from the stable and slightly wounded. They burnt the stable and killed the three soldiers who had ambushed them.

Glasscock, Ike Hall and Venable were ordered to bring provisions from a citizen's house to Quantrell's camp in the woods. Hall, the spokesman, was refused everything. A fair talking,

amiable, upright man, he pleaded his own positive orders and
the peculiar exigencies of the situation. No use! There were
five Federal militia at the house, and no three Missourians in
arms anywhere could take from five Kentuckians a pound of
meat or a baking of flour. Short work and very sharp! When
the smoke lifted, four of the militia were dead, and the fifth so
badly wounded that he begged to be killed, a request Venable
was in more than half a humor to gratify.

Later on Clark Hockensmith, John Barnhill, David Helton,
and Thomas Harris were surrounded by thirty cavalrymen while
at dinner. As Helton lifted a cup of coffee to his lips he happened to look through the window of the dining room and saw
the head of the Federal column almost jutted up against the
house. An alarm and a volley, and the Guerrillas fought their
way desperately to their horses and escaped, after killing and
wounding five of the pursuers, Harris receiving a severe wound
in the face.

Quantrell returned at last to Nelson county, much worn by a
week's incessant fighting, and more badly cut up and crippled
than he had ever yet been in men and horses since his entrance
into Kentucky. While one of the Missourians lived, however,
he might surely count upon a following. Man by man they
would march at his bidding and die at a word.

Mundy, Marion, and Magruder, within a few days after
Quantrell's arrival in Nelson county, passed through on a raid.
Of the Missouri Guerrillas but one—Peyton Long—joined them.
Fighting successfully about Owensboro, in Owen county, and
holding their own pretty well in several hot fights in Breckin-
ridge county. Marion was sent with twelve men into Bewley-
ville, Meade county. Thirty Federal cavalry attacked him
there and Marion charged them fiercely. Peyton Long led this
charge. He was ahead of the foremost rider, shooting with the
terrible effect of his old Missouri training. Four of the enemy
had already fallen, shot dead from their saddles. He was close
upon the fifth when an ambushed body of Federals variously estimated at from two hundred to two hundred and fifty rose suddenly up from behind fences and trees and poured one deadly
volley into the ranks of Marion's little band. A heavy carbine
ball cut Peyton Long's pistol belt between the U. and the S. and
wounded him mortally in the bowels. Five others of the Guer-

rillas were killed or wounded. Even under that fire Marion halted long enough to lend a hand to Long and steady him in the saddle. For eight miles—such was his wonderful nerve and endurance—he held to his horse, riding upright as a soldier on duty. Far in the rear Marion, with that devotion to his wounded which made him conspicuous among the Guerrillas, fought back the pursuit and held it back until the sun set. Then he halted long enough for Peyton Long to die. A comrade holding his head in his lap, suggested that to mitigate somewhat the pain his belt be taken off. "No," said the suffering man, gently, "I will die so. Tell my comrades that while life was left my belt was buckled about me." Once he lifted himself up and looked fair at the west where the sky still shone with the darkening glories of the sun. His lips moved but he did not pray. Perhaps some name, sweeter then than any name life had ever made soft for him, came back just once again for the fashioning. Perhaps he saw a face somewhere in the gathering twilight, just a little pale but surely not reproachful. No matter: when the twilight came and the night deepened somewhere out in the infinite and the unknown a spirit wandered, made pure before God and beautiful because of an intrepidity no man has ever yet surpassed, fight how he might for king, or cause, or creed, or country.

Peyton Long was a soldier before Fort Sumpter fell. He left Liberty, Clay county, Missouri, in May, 1861, a private in Capt. Tom McCarty's company, of John T. Hughes' regiment. McCarty was a Missouri lawyer who should have been a Crusader or a mediæval knight. He abhorred a lie, believed female purity a thing fit to be worshiped, scarcely understood the meaning of the word fear, was simple, child-like, confiding, a lion in combat, and a patriarch in his camp and among the soldiers of his company. McCarty enlisted Peyton Long—took him, indeed, a boy and left upon him the impress of a hero. In every battle fought west of the Mississippi river Long participated—Carthage, Oak Hills, Dry Wood, Lexington, Elk Horn —and when General Price crossed east of the river after Shiloh, Long crossed with him, fighting a brave man's fight at Iuka and Corinth. In the summer of 1863 he became a Guerrilla. Quantrell was not more cool, Todd was not more desperate, Haller was not more dashing, Anderson was not more reckless,

Taylor was not more deadly, none of them were more persistent and eternally in the saddle than this Missouri infantryman, turned bushwhacker. At Lawrence his intrepidity was conspicuous; at Centralia he was one of four who followed up the remnant of Johnson's exterminated command to within a hundred yards of the block-house at Sturgeon; everywhere he was face to face with danger, noted alike for coolness, prowess, horsemanship, and desperation. A people whose cause after having been appealed to the sword perishes by the sword, feel satisfied perhaps with here and there a monument. This man, this Confederate, Guerrilla, bushwhacker, border fighter, black flag follower, this hero, whatever else he may be called—deserves one. It need not be costly. A plain stone, barely large enough for an inscription, is all the patriotic fitness of the act requires—a stone whereon this might be written: *"Death smote him in the harness and he fell where it was an honor to die."*

On the 11th day of June, 1865, Quantrell started from Bedford Russell's, in Nelson county, with John Ross, William Hulse, Payne Jones, Clark Hockensmith, Isaac Hall, Richard Glasscock, Robert Hall, Bud Pence, Allen Parmer, Dave Helton and Lee McMurtry. His destination was Salt river. At Newel McClaskey's the turnpike was gained and traveled several miles, when a singularly severe and penetrating rain storm began. Quantrell, to escape this, turned from the road on the left and into a woods pasture near a post-office called Smiley. Through this pasture and for half a mile further he rode until he reached the residence of a Mr. Wakefield, in whose barn the Guerrillas took shelter. Unsuspicious of danger, and of the belief that the nearest enemy was at least twenty miles away, the men dismounted, unbridled their horses, and fed them at the racks ranged about the shed embracing two sides of the barn. While the horses were eating the Guerrillas amused themselves with a sham battle, choosing sides and using cobs as ammunition. In the midst of much hilarity and boisterousness, Glasscock's keen eyes saw through the blinding rain a column of Federal cavalry, one hundred and twenty strong, approaching the barn at a trot. He cried out instantly, and loud enough to be heard at Wakefield's house, sixty yards away: "Here they are! Here they are!" Instantly all the men were in motion and rushing for their horses.

Capt. Edward Terrell, known well to Quantrell and fought
stubbornly once before, had been traveling the turnpike from the
direction of Taylorsville, as completely ignorant of Quantrell's
proximity as Quantrell had been ignorant of Terrell's, and would
have passed on undoubtedly without a combat if the trail left
by the Guerrillas in passing from the road to the pasture had
not attracted his attention. This he followed to within sight of
the barn, understood in a moment the character of the men
sheltered there, and closed upon it rapidly, firing as he came
on. Before a single Guerrilla had put a bridle upon a horse,
Terrell was at the main gate of the lot, distant some fifty feet
from the barn, and pouring such a storm of carbine bullets
among them that their horses ran furiously about the lot, difficult
to approach and impossible to restrain. Fighting desperately
and deliberately, and driving away from the main gate a dozen
or more Federals stationed there, John Ross, William Hulse,
Allen Parmer, Lee McMurtry and Bud Pence cut their way
through, mounted and defiant. The entire combat did not last
ten minutes. It was a fight in which every man had to do for
himself and do what was done speedily. Once above the
rattling of musketry, the neighing of horses and the shouting of
combatants Quantrell's voice rang out loud and high: "Cut
through, boys; cut through, somehow. Don't surrender while
there is a chance to get out!" The fire upon the Guerrillas was
furious. Quantrell's horse—a thoroughbred animal of great
spirit and speed, could not be caught. His master, anxious to
secure him, followed him composedly about the lot for several
minutes, trying under a shower of balls to get hands upon his
favorite. At this moment Clark Hockensmith, who was mounted
and free to go away at a run, saw the peril of his chief and
galloped to his rescue. Quantrell, touched by this act of devotion, recognized it by a smile and held out his hand to his
comrade without speaking. Hockensmith dismounted until
Quantrell took his own place in the saddle, and then sprang up
behind him. Another furious volley from Terrell's men lining
all the fence about the great gate, killed Hockensmith and
killed the horse Hockensmith and Quantrell were upon. The
second hero now gave his life for Quantrell. Richard Glasscock had also secured his own horse as Hockensmith had done,
and was as free to ride away in safety as he had been. Opposite

to the main entrance of the barn lot there was an exit uncovered by the enemy, and beyond this exit a stretch of heavy timber. Those who gained this timber were safe. Hockensmith knew it when he faced about and deliberately laid down his life for his chief, and Glasscock knew it when he also turned about and hurried up to the two men struggling there—Quantrell to drag himself out from under the body of the horse, and Hockensmith in the agonies of death. The second volley from the gate mortally wounded Quantrell and killed Glasscock's horse. Then a charge of fifty shouting and shooting men swept over the barn lot. Robert Hall, Payne Jones, David Helton and Isaac Hall had gone out some time before on foot. J. B. Tooley, A. B. Southworth and C. H. Southworth, wounded badly, escaped, fighting. Only the dead man lying by his wounded chief, and the dauntless Glasscock—erect, splendid and fighting to the last—remained as trophies of the desperate combat. Two balls had struck Quantrell. The first, the heavy ball of a Spencer carbine—entered close to the right collar bone, ranged down along the spine, injuring it severely, and hid itself somewhere in the body. The second ball cut off the finger next to the little finger of the left hand, tearing it from its socket and lacerating the hand itself painfully. The shoulder wound did its work, however, for it was the mortal wound. All the lower portion of Quantrell's body was paralyzed, and as he was lifted and carried to Wakefield's house his legs were limp and his extremities cold and totally without sensation. At no time did he either complain or make moan. His wonderful fortitude and endurance remained unimpaired to the end. His mind, always clearest in danger, seemed to recognize that his last battle had been fought and his last encounter finished. He talked very little. Terrell came to him and asked if there was any good service he might do that would be acceptable. "Yes," said Quantrell, quietly, "have Clark Hockensmith buried like a soldier." After he had been carried to the house of Wakefield and deposited upon a pallet, he spoke once more to Terrell: "While I live let me stay here. It is useless to haul a dying man about in a wagon, jolting out what little life is left in him." Terrell pledged his word that he should not be removed, and rode away in pursuit of those who had escaped.

Meanwhile a tragedy was being enacted which was a fitting

sequel to the war work of the great Missouri Guerrilla. Richard Glasscock had seen Quantrell trying in vain to catch his own
horse, had seen Hockensmith spur to his help, had seen the two
mount together and essay to escape, had seen them go down
under a fearful volley all of a heap, had seen Quantrell struggle
up from the wreck unhurt, and he, too—free to dash away in
safety as Hockensmith had been—rushed like Hockensmith to
Quantrell's assistance. It was then the second volley was fired
which struck Quantrell to the earth and killed Glasscock's horse.
Even then, untouched as he was, he might have still escaped.
He did not even try. He stood over his wounded chief and
emptied the remaining barrels of the last revolver left loaded,
killing two of Terrell's men almost upon him and wounding three.
Fifty infuriated Federals fired then full upon Glasscock. He
alone of all the band stood erect and defiant. His life appeared
to be charmed. Not a bullet drew blood. One cut his shirt,
another his hat, two his pantaloons, the fifth a heavy lock of
hair, but the skin nowhere was broken. He was stooping to
take a pistol from Quantrell's belt, which still contained a few
loads, when a furious Federal charge rushed over him and beat
him down. When he arose he had been stamped upon, beaten
about the head and shoulders with the butts of pistols, and disarmed. No, not disarmed! Desperate Guerrilla as he was and
had been, a singular superstition clung to him tenaciously
through all his war life. He had believed that at some one time
in his career he would be a prisoner and that maybe to run out
from his environment or cut out, he would be compelled to surrender himself and take the chances afterward of escape. So
firmly had this idea become fixed in his mind that he bought a
Derringer pistol at the earliest opportunity and kept it constantly concealed about his person. This he inspected frequently and knew from such inspection that it was fit to stake
his life upon. Those who beat him down and disarmed him,
took only his revolvers, six huge dragoons that had done for
four terrible years ceaseless and unsparing work. Perhaps it was
thought unnecessary to search him for any other weapon, and
he was not searched. Guarded by a single cavalryman and permitted to ride at the rear of the Federal column unconfined, he
waited calmly until as tretch of heavy timber was reached, and
until the column upon its march had widened the distance

between the files perceptibly. Of a sudden then and with a movement as certain and swift as long and sure practice could make it, Glasscock drew from his bosom the cocked Derringer and snapped it full in the face of the Federal trooper. The keen bursting of the cap alone awoke the echoes and revealed to the guard the imminence of the danger averted by a hair's breadth. Wetted by the morning's soaking rain and false in the only moment possible for execution, the Derringer, with a dauntless life staked upon it, did not win. The whole theory of the Guerrilla's four years' hoarding and inspecting disappeared in the explosion of a pistol cap. He cursed his luck with a savage curse, short and gutteral, stood upright a second in his stirrups and struck the guard by his side a terrible blow over the head with the useless weapon. Stalwart and huge, it did not even knock him from his saddle. Now began the grapple of the tiger with the elephant. The Federal shortened his carbine and sought to shoot Glasscock as he sat. Glasscock seized the muzzle of the gun and hurled it aside just as it was discharged. Both men leaped upon the ground and grappled one another almost under the feet of their horses. Glasscock was doomed. An old wound in the left shoulder, not yet entirely healed, and an old wound in the right leg, still discharging pieces of bone and clothing, made him a child in the grasp of a giant. His antagonist—six feet in height and powerful in proportion—clasped him in an embrace that was crushing like a bear's and sinewy like an anaconda's. The crippled Guerrilla, however—all the old Berserkyr blood in his veins on fire—fought until they killed him. The strange combat in the rear had caused the bulk of the column to turn back. Twenty cavalrymen, with carbines cocked, gathered about the desperate wrestlers waiting to shoot the Guerrilla the moment he stood clear and free from the body of their comrade. Meanwhile Glasscock had managed to get from his pocket and unclasp a small knife, scant two inches being the length of its longest blade. With this he made battle until he died. So deadly was the hug of the Federal, however, and so tense was the vise-like grip of his arms, that Glasscock could use his last weapon only partially. Once he thrust the point of the knife blade a quarter of an inch in his back, once he cut him across the chin, several times he slashed him slightly about the body, but he was too weak to break loose from the iron arms of the Federal and too close to him to kill him. Suddenly a quick-eyed soldier put a carbine to Glass-cock's hips and shot him through. So close was the muzzle of the gun that the powder set his shirt on fire. As he fell, or rather as he settled down at the feet of the Federal who was grappling with him, and who felt a limp, yielding body slipping from his hold, Glasscock laughed a savage laugh and strove in dying to drive the steel home to his heart. Too weak even to cut through the clothing, he kept fast hold upon the knife and held it fast under the bullets of at least twenty soldiers who fired into the body long after it was stiff and cold.

These two men who died for Quantrell were, with the lights before them, Guerrilla Bayards. Either was free to go—neither went. Each was commanded by Quantrell to leave him—neither obeyed. It is probable both believed that they could not save him, yet steadfast in the equanimity of accepted death, they both died striving to serve their chief. Clark Hockensmith, even in his boyhood, had been singularly devoted in his friend-ships and unfaltering in the discharge of what he considered his duty. At school, if those he loved had to be punished, he shared such punishment with them. If trouble came to any companion—magnified by boyish fears and aggravated by boy-ish fancies — he stood undismayed by his side. It there was danger, the youth became a man—so cool he was, so steadfast, and so calm. As he grew up he grew braver and gentler. All who knew him loved him. Patient, generous, frank, guileless, accommodating—with those of his own age he was popular and trusted, and with those who were older and more sedate, he was the ideal of manly courtesy and ingenuous deference. When the war came he joined the Guerrillas. The desperate nature of their warfare awoke in his nature an emotion that responded quickly to every phase of their fighting. Noted among cool men for coolness, among daring men for superlative daring, among devoted men for pre-eminent devotion, among unsparing men for winning sweetness of disposition and patience of behavior, he never killed a foe save in open battle or shot at an enemy except the enemy were shooting at him. In one of Poole's fights close to Wellington, in which Poole was worsted, a gallant Guerrilla defending the rear was wounded and left afoot. The pursuit was merciless, the murder of the wounded

28

man absolute. Who would go back to save him? Clark Hockensmith of course. He did go back, but the venture was well
nigh hopeless. Entrenched behind his dead horse, the crippled
Guerrilla had made his peace with God and was ready to get
for his life the best price the Federals might be willing to pay
for it. Fifty of them were close to him, firing and advancing.
In the face of these, and in spite of a fire that would have
beaten back and demoralized a less intrepid soldier, Hockensmith helped his hurt comrade up upon his own horse and brought
him to a place of safety with such a gentle resolution that it
seemed simple because it was so perfectly undemonstrative.
And as he did at Wellington, so did he do twice afterwards.
The fourth time was his last time. As he rode up to rescue
him, Quantrell bade him go back. Hockensmith did not reply
save to dismount under a fire that was hotter and more concentrated than any he had ever endured before, as many as he had
faced, and helped his chief into his own saddle. Quantrell
needed help. Two days before his horse had kicked him on the
left knee and injured the joint seriously. It gave him great
pain to hobble even over a perfectly level surface, but to use
the leg in mounting and dismounting without assistance was
agony of the intensest sort. The volley that killed Hockensmith would certainly have killed Quantrell also, but the faithful
comrade, considerate even in death, had mounted *behind* his
chief and built up thus with his own body a barricade that only
failed to furnish shelter when it neither knew nor felt any more
the world's human heroism and devotion.

Richard Glasscock, though coming by a road different from
the one traveled by Hockensmith, reached the same goal. He
was devoted through sheer excess of physical courage. If he
cared well enough for any one to fight at all for him, he cared
well enough to die at his back. He had stood over wounded
comrades as often as Hockensmith, and had as often in the
supremest fury of a combat torn from the hands of the victorious foe some crippled Guerrilla, too hard hit to fly afoot, and
too far in the rear to overtake his routed friends. Noted also
for dash and intrepidity, Glasscock—while wanting the higher
emotion of devoted friendship in his attempted rescue of Quantrell—had in lieu of it that which would carry him just as far—
the reckless ambition to save the coolest and fiercest fighter

known to border warfare. He cared nothing for his life, because he had never taken a moment's thought of it. He cared nothing for the danger to be dared, because he probably did not know the meaning of the word. Hockensmith died through the excess of devotion; Glasscock through the excess of personal courage. Hockensmith for his faith would have been burnt at the stake; Glasscock for his faith would have died as Harold died, sword in hand and heroic, on the battle-field of Hastings.

John Ross, Allen Parmer, William Hulse, Lee McMurtry and Bud Pence escaped, pursued fiercely, but turned at intervals and fought the Federals back so savagely that it was not long before they were permitted to continue their retreat unmolested. All of these men would have died with Quantrell if Quantrell's own order had not been of the *suave qui peut* armament. "Take care of yourselves, everbody!" he had shouted several times to the Guerrillas fighting in groups and squads about the barn lot, and as these men supposed that everybody naturally would endeavor to save himself, Quantrell equally with the balance, they fought out together and escaped.

Robert Hall had his horse killed, as did Isaac Hall, Payne Jones, and David Helton. Afoot and followed, they turned once beyond the exit gate and made a desperate rally, driving back the pursuers and gaining some brief breathing time. A separation next followed, Payne Jones going in one direction, Robert Hall in another, while Isaac Hall and David Helton kept together. These two, both wounded, took refuge in a pond four hundred yards from Wakefield's house. Gathering together sticks and bunches of grass they made of them a sort of screen for their heads which, from the nose up, was all that remained above the water. Hunted everywhere, they crouched for an hour thus, chilled to the marrow but undiscovered. Leaving the pond and hurrying as fast as possible to a wheat field, they were again seen, fired at, and followed. In the midst of the growing grain they concealed themselves for the second time, pulling up great quantities of wheat and covering their bodies with it completely. After nightfall they emerged once more from their hiding-place and escaped before morning entirely out of the neighborhood.

Some of the fugitive Guerrillas soon reached the well known rendezvous at the house of Alexander Sayers, twenty-three miles from Wakefield's, with tidings of the fight. Frank James heard all the story through with a set face, strangely white and sorrowful, and then he arose and cried out: "Volunteers to go back! Who will follow me to see our chief, living or dead?" "I will go back," said Allen Parmer," "and I," said John Ross, "and I," said William Hulse. "Let us ride, then," rejoined James, and in twenty minutes more—John Ross having exchanged his jaded horse for a fresh one—these four devoted men were galloping away to Wakefield's. At two o'clock in the morning they were there. Frank James dismounted and knocked low upon the door. There was the trailing of a woman's garment, the circumspect tread of a watching woman's feet, the noiseless work of a woman's hand upon the latch, and Mrs. Wakefield—cool and courtly—bade the strange, armed men upon the threshhold enter. Just across on the other side of the room from the door a man lay on a trundle-bed, watchful but very quiet. James stood over the bed, but could not speak. If one had cared to look into his eyes they might have been seen full of tears. Quantrell, by the dim light of a single candle, recognized James, smiled, held out his hand, and said to him very gently, though a little reproachfully: "Why did you come back? The enemy are thick about here; they are passing every hour." "To see if you were alive or dead, Captain. If the first, to save you; if the last to put you in a grave." "I thank you very much, Frank, but why try to take me away? I am cold below the hips. I can neither walk, ride, nor crawl. I am dead and yet I am alive." Frank James went to the door and called in Parmer, Ross, and Hulse. Quantrell recognized them all in his old, calm, quiet fashion, and bade them wipe away their tears, for they were crying visibly. Then Frank James—joined in his entreaties by the entreaties of his comrades, pleaded with Quantrell for permission to carry him to the mountains of Nelson county by slow and easy stages, each swearing to guard him hour by hour until he recovered or die over his body, defending it to the last. He knew that every pledge made by them would be kept to the death. He felt that every word spoken was a golden word, and meant absolute devotion. His faith in their affection was as steadfast and abiding as of old. He listened till they had done, with the old staid courtesy of victorious Guerrilla days, and then he silenced them with an answer which from its resoluteness they knew to be unalterable. "I cannot live. I have run a long time; I have come out unhurt from many desperate places; I have fought to kill and I have killed; I regret nothing. The end is close at hand. I am resting easy here, and will die so. You do not know how your devotion has touched my heart, nor can you ever understand how grateful I am for the love you have shown for me. Try to get back to your homes, and avoid if you can the perils which beset you."

Until 10 o'clock the next day these men remained with Quantrell. He talked to them very freely of the past, but never of his earlier life in Kansas. Many messages were sent to absent friends, and much good advice was given touching the surrender of the remnant of the band. Again and again he returned to the subject of their earlier struggles in Missouri and dwelt long over the recollections and the reminiscences of the two first years of Guerrilla warfare. Finally the parting came, and those who looked the last on Quantrell's face that morning as they stooped to tell him goodbye, looked their last on it forever.

Terrell had promised Quantrell positively that he should not be removed from Wakefield's house, but in three days he had either broken or forgotton this pledge. He informed Gen. Palmer, commanding the department of Kentucky, of the fact of the fight, and of the desperate character of the wounded officer left paralyzed behind him, suggesting at the same time the advisability of having him removed to a place of safety. Gen. Palmer sent an ambulance under a heavy escort to Wakefield's, and Quantrell—suffering greatly and scarcely more alive than dead—was hauled to the military hospital in Louisville and deposited there. Until the question of recovery had been absolutely decided against him, but few friends were admitted into his presence. If any one conversed with him at all, the conversation of necessity was required to be carried on in the presence of an official. Mrs. Ross visited him thus—a Christian woman, devoted to the South, and of active and practical patriotism—and took some dying messages to loved ones and true ones in Missouri. Mrs. Ross left him at one o'clock in the afternoon, and at four o'clock the next afternoon the great Guerrilla died. His passing away—after a life so singularly fitful and tempest-

uous—was as the passing of a summer cloud. He had been
asleep, and as he awoke he called for water. A Sister of Charity
at the bedside put a glass to his lips, but he did not drink. She
heard him murmur once audibly—"Boys, get ready!"—then a
long pause—then one word more—"Steady!"—and then when
she drew back from bending over the murmuring man she fell
upon her knees and prayed. Quantrell was dead!

Before his death he had become a Catholic and had been
visited daily by two devoted priests. To one of these he made
confession, and such a confession! He told everything. He
was too serious and earnest a man to do less. He kept nothing
back, not even the least justifiable of his many homicides. As
the good priest listened and listened, and as year after year of
the wild war work was made to give up its secrets, what manner
of a man must the priest have imagined lay dying there—cool,
precise, picturesque, an Apache warrior, and a Guerrilla Chief!
Did he get absolution where there is only one priest, one propitiation, one God—the Father, Son and Holy Ghost? Did
Marco Bozzaris? Did Leonidas? Did Charlotte Corday? Did
William Tell? Did Arnold Winkelreid?

Let history be just. On that hospital bed, watched by the
calm, colorless face of a Sister of Charity, a dead man lay who,
when living, had filled with his deeds four years of terrible war
history. A singularly placid look had come with the great
change. Alike was praise or censure, reward or punishment.
Fate had done its worst, and the future stood revealed to the
spirit made omniscient by its journey through the Valley of the
Shadow of Death. He had done with summer's heat and winter's cold, with spectral ambuscades and midnight vigils.
There would never be any war in the land of the hereafter.
The swoop of cavalry—the ringing of revolvers—the rapture of
the charge—the roar of combat—the agony of defeat—white
faces trampled by the iron feet of horses—the march—the
bivouac—the battle; what remained of these when the transfiguration was done and when the river called Jordan rolled
between the shores of the finite and the infinite? Nothing!
And yet by these, standing or falling, must the great Guerrilla
be judged.

Quantrell differed in some degree from every Guerrilla who
was either his comrade or his contemporary. Not superior to

Todd in courage or in enterprise, nor to Haller, Poole, Jarrette, Younger, Taylor, Anderson, Frank James, Thrailkill, Gregg, Lea, Maddox, DanVaughn, Blunt, or Yager, he yet had one particular quality which none of these save Gregg, Frank James, Lea and Younger possessed to the same pre-eminent degree—extraordinary resource or cunning. All the Guerrillas fought. Indeed, at certain times and under certain circumstances fighting might justly have been considered the least of their accomplishments. A successful leader required coolness, intrepidity, robust health, fine horsemanship, expert pistol practice, quick perception in peril, great rapidity of movement, immense activity, and ine orable fixedness of purpose. Those menticned excelled in these qualities, but at times they were too eager to fight, took too many desperate chances, or rushed too recklessly into combats where they could not win. Quantrell counted the cost of everything; watched every way lest an advantage should be taken of him; sought to shield and save his men; strove by much strategy to have the odds with rather than against him; traveled a multitude of long roads rather than one short road once too often; took upon himself many disguises to prevent an embarrassing familiarity; retreated often rather than fight and be worsted; kept scouts everywhere; had the faculty of divination to an almost occult degree; believed in young men; relied a little upon mystification; paid attention to small things; listened to every man's advice and then took his own; stood by his soldiers; obeyed strictly the law of retaliation; preferred the old dispensation to the new— that is to say the code of Moses to the code of Jesus Christ; inculcated by precept and example the self-abnegation and devotion of comradeship; fought desperately; carried a black flag; killed everything; made the idea of surrender ridiculous; snapped his finger at death; was something of a fatalist; rarely drank; trusted few women, but these with his life; played high at cards; believed in religion; respected its ordinances; went at intervals to church; understood human nature thoroughly; never quarreled; was generally taciturn, and one of the coolest and deadliest men in a personal combat known to the border. He rode like he was carved from the horse beneath him. In an organization where skill with a pistol was a passport to leadership, he shot with a revolver as Leatherstocking shot with a rifle. The strength of his blow was in its fury. No force not greatly superior to his own ever stood before his onset. He drilled his men to fight equally with either hand. Ambidextered, they fought finally with both. Fairly matched, God help the column that came in contact with him!

As to the kind of warfare Quantrell waged, that is another matter. History must deal with him as it finds him. Like the war of La Vendee, the Guerrilla war was one rather of hatred than of opinion. The regular Confederates were fighting for a cause and a nationality, the Guerrillas for vengeance. Mementoes of murdered kinsmen mingled with their weapons, vows consecrated the act of enlistment, and the cry for blood was heard from homestead to homestead. Quantrell became a Guerrilla because he had been most savagely dealt with, and he became a chief because he had prudence, firmness, courage, audacity, and common-sense. In personal intrepidity he was inferior to no man. His features were pleasing without being handsome. His eyes were blue and penetrating. He had a Roman nose. In height he was five feet eleven inches, and his form was well-knit, graceful, and sinewy. His constitution was vigorous, and his physical endurance equal to an Indian's. In vigilance, diligence, and perseverance he was pre-eminent. His greatest qualities were developed by great emergencies. His glance was rapid and unerring. His judgment was clearest and surest when the responsibility was heaviest, and when difficulties gathered thickest around him. Based upon skill, energy, perspicacity, and unusual presence of mind, his fame as a Guerrilla will endure for generations.

Quantrell died a Catholic and was buried in the Catholic cemetery at Louisville. Since 1865 many impostors have appeared in various portions of the country, claiming to be none other than the noted Missouri Guerrilla. A somewhat peculiar case of this kind occurred in the Spring of 1866. General Shelby, in company with probably half a dozen settlers of the Carlotta Colony of Cordova, were in Vera Cruz waiting for the American steamer to come in. They had been long upon the mole and were returning, impatient, to their hotel. At that moment a boat from the steamer landed some passengers on the quay, one of whom recognized Shelby and called out to him to tarry awhile longer. Quantrell was aboard the ship and would soon be on shore. "Quantrell?" repeated Shelby, in surprise, "what Quantrell?" "The Guerrilla Quantrell," was the reply of the new comer. "Impossible," rejoined the General. "The man of whom you speak was killed in Kentucky and buried there." While they were talking the reputed Quantrell made his appearance in their midst. He seemed to be anxious and nervous. He had been told that at Cordova there were some of Quantrell's old men, and that at Paso del Macho he would meet John Thrailkill, a famous companion in arms. When introduced to Shelby he changed color visibly. Shelby looked once at him, looked once through and through him, and then summing him up said curtly: "You are not Quantrell." "I know it, General. nor have I ever claimed to be. When I took passage at New York for Vera Cruz a Confederate aboard the ship greeted me as Quantrell, and introduced me as Quantrell to all the passengers. Against my will I was lionized. Necessity bade me keep my peace, however, and my passage was paid, money was subscribed for me, the captain was very kind, the ladies were very gracious; but at no single time and in no single unguarded moment did I claim to be the famous border fighter of the West. I am not Quantrell, as none know better than yourself, nor have I ever in my life seen Quantrell." The man spoke the simple truth. His imposition had been one rather of omission than commission. He had found it profitable to be considered the celebrated Guerrilla in question, and he made no explanation as long as it paid him to acquiesce in the identity.

Once again in British Honduras, thirteen of those who had participated in Shelby's romantic expedition into Mexico, were wrecked and cast away upon the coast. Further inland where the mahogany cutters were at work a man was hiding who called himself Quantrell. He was a smart, suspicious, taciturn fellow, armed like an arsenal and lazy as a hedge-hog. With the thirteen castaways there were two Guerrillas who had really good cause to hide and were hiding, but when brought face to face with the mysterious impostor they found to their infinite disgust a yellow-bellied Indian from Costa Rica, scraping his sores in the ashes like Job and alive with vermin as any beggar.

Once again on the Rio Grande, in 1868, the famous Guerrilla revealed himself. A man had been murdered for his money, twenty head of cattle driven successfully into Mexico, a ranche plundered, and a band of specious cut-throats organized for extensive devil's work. Its leader declared himself to be Quantrell. He issued a proclamation and signed it Quantrell. He forewarned obnoxious cattle-men and threatened with death unpliant store-keepers over the signature of Quantrell. Four of Shelby's old Brigade, and two of Todd's original company, banded themselves together to destroy the bogus Quantrell. Ten Texans joined them, and altogether they broke into a chaparral where the robbers were, killed the whole band save seven, and brought the seven, wounded, back, the so-called Quantrell among the number. On the heels of the capture came the confession. The leader of these bandits, instead of being the terrible Missourian, was a Tennessee man who in 1858 had killed his brother and fled to Texas. There—giving full play to his ferocious passions—he became speedily a murderer and a thief. For a cold blooded killing in Navarro county he had been sent to the penitentiary for ten years, had escaped by a desperate rush, had fled to the unknown along the Rio Grande, had made himself an evil name and fame in its inaccessible hiding-places, and had at last been wounded and brought bound to the judgment-seat. After his story had been fully told, there was a brief trial and a sudden punishment. The man-slayer and the cattle-stealer hung for weeks and weeks on a tree by a traveled highway, a terror to evil-doers and a ghastly warning.

Once again a bogus Quantrell appeared in Arkansas, in 1870. The worst this one did was to borrow money from credulous sympathizers, and successfully elude pursuit after having appropriated two valuable trotting horses.

The last scoundrel to appropriate the name and the fame of the great Guerrilla made his appearance in Colorado, close to the New Mexican line. He only confessed his identity to a few confidential friends. He was a rancheman and ostensibly Mr. William Harrison. He bought cattle, sheep, mules, dry goods, and groceries on credit. He imposed upon ex-Guerrillas in various ways, but always through the agency of those who had not known Quantrell, and finally fled the country, a fugitive from justice and a swindler to the extent of four thousand dollars. It was reported afterwards that a vigilance committee hung him in Utah.

Quantrell, a little while before he died, suggested that Henry Porter should collect together the remnant of the Guerrillas and surrender them in a body. He understood Porter's capacity, and had unbounded confidence in his cool courage and practical sense. Porter fully deserved every encomium passed upon him by his chief. Circumspect, prompt to avail himself of favorable surroundings, of deliberate judgment, intrepid, devoted to his comrades in arms, bold in the expression of opinion, and unyielding in his demands for the same treatment accorded to the regular Confederate soldier, he ·conferred promptly with Gen. Palmer and was as promptly granted an interview. Gen. Palmer was in every sense of the word an upright soldier. While the war raged, he believed in making war mean war; when the end came he believed in making peace mean peace. He was eminently a just man. He despised those cruel hangers-on of the Union cause who lived in bomb-proofs. The Cossacks of his command he court-martialed. In the field he was bold, enterprising and full of fight. He knew how to follow up a blow, to extract from a victory its least possible advantage, to advance far, to get much, to remain where he had halted, and to retain what he had captured. Palmer's terms to Porter were most liberal. Each Guerrilla was permitted to retain two revolvers, what horses he owned, and what amunition was left to him. If he was destitute, he was to receive transportation to any portion of the country he might desire to go to. No matter about his past—it was not enquired into; no matter how evil his reputation had been—the war was over. His oath wiped out his outrages—his parole was to be looked upon as his pardon.

In the meanwhile a horrible outrage had been committed. A most respectable woman, a Mrs. Clark, had been outraged under circumstances of peculiar atrocity. Riding an unfrequented road to a neighboring town in quest of medicine or medical attendance for an ailing neighbor, she was overpowered by two ruffians and monstrously abused. Some who both feared and hated the remnant of Quantrell's little band accused them of the atrocious act. Gen. Palmer—in a moment of unreasoning indignation unusual for him, joined in the outcry without investigation and declared bitterly that until the savages who did the deed were brought to him, living or dead, the Missouri Guerrillas should take their chances as outlaws and be hunted accordingly. Equally with the indignation of the Federal General, was the indignation of the Missourians. Frank James especially was furious. Before Palmer even knew of the outrage, James had taken William Hulse with him and had struck and followed rapidly the trail of the scoundrels. On the Chaplin river, above Chaplin town, and after a sleepless hunt of two days and nights, the Guerrillas came upon their prey. One was a Kentuckian named Brothers, and the other a nondescript called Texas. His true name was probably Jonathan Billingboy. These two desperadoes had been joined by a third, who, while he was in no manner connected with the outrage, would probably in a fight make common cause with his companions. "There are three," said Hulse, when the trail had ended at a house, and when a further reconnoisance revealed the fact that none of them had left it. "Yes," replied James, "there are three. If there were six it would not matter." They dismounted and tied their horses in some timber back from the dwelling and then gained it unobserved. Those whom they sought were at dinner, armed but indifferent. Throwing back the door of the dining room unceremoniously, the two Guerrillas strode in, wrathful and accusing. Frank James, always one among the coolest and and deadliest fighters known to the border, called out in a singularly placid yet penetrating voice: "Keep your seats, all of you; keep your hands up; keep your eyes to the front." Two sat stone still, scarcely breathing, hardly lifting or letting fall an eyelid. Brothers, desperate even in extremity such as this, snatched swiftly for his pistol. Frank James blew his brains out across the table. The other two did not move. Hulse covered both, but did not fire. He did not know Texas, and he would not kill an innocent man. Texas, however, was not one of the party, nor had he been with Brothers since the outrage. When this was ascertained, Frank James spoke to Hulse: "Our work is but half done; let us go and finish it." It was twenty miles to Alexander Sayer's house, and these two men rode the distance rapidly. They desired to find as soon as might be the trail of the second scoundrel, no matter how cold or indistinct. Others of his comrades had been ahead of him, as swiftly as he had ridden, and Texas had shared the fate of Brothers. Captured by John Ross, Henry Porter and Allen Parmer, he had so vociferously defended himself, and so eloquently pleaded his own innocence, that these three intrepid men—unable, through the very excess of those soldierly qualities which had made them desperately brave, to understand how it was possible to commit such a crime—listened rather favorably to his protestations and permitted him to retain his pistols and ride leisurely along with them towards the house of Benedict Pashe. Mr. Pashe would establish his innocence beyond all controversy. Mr. Pashe knew of his immediate whereabouts the day Brothers did his devil's work, and Mr. Pashe would make his alibi impervious to assault. Mr. Pashe never had an opportunity to say to the plausible story yea or nay. While yet distant from his house a mile and more, Texas broke away from his accommodating captors and fled like an Arab. Better mounted than either Ross or Porter, Texas soon outstripped them, untouched by the bullets sent after him, and would have escaped altogether if the speed of the start had been joined to the bottom of Parmer's horse. A gallop of a mile, however, told the story of the chase. Texas was a thorough cavalryman, though a born robber. He knew by the laboring breath of his steed, the reeling stride, the foam of an unnatural perspiration, the uncertain way the feet took hold of the ringing turnpike, the almost human agony the faithful animal manifested over its own failing powers, that the end was nigh at hand. He looked back once as he crowned the crest of a sudden hill and saw Parmer, fixed as fate in the saddle and as immovable, gaining upon him hand over hand. There was one resource left—common alike to the ant or the elephant—he could fight. He halted his blown horse and turned about. Parmer came right on, a pistol in his right hand and the reins well gathered up in his left. At fifty paces he fired at Texas and missed him. Texas stood fast, his face wearing a hunted look and his eyes wolfish. At thirty paces the two fired simultaneously, Parmer missing again, but Texas wounding his horse severely if not fatally. Parmer lessened the distance by a spur stroke and fired the third time at Texas barely ten feet away. This time he did not miss. Game to the last, Texas, even as he reeled in the saddle, gripped his own horse with his knees, steadied himself for a moment or two, and fired twice at Parmer before he fell. He had been hurt too badly, however, to be accurate. Another bullet in the breast finished him. As he had lived, so had he died—a bad, stoical, unrepentant man. The bodies of both Texas and Brothers were carried by the Federals into Bardstown and identified by Mrs. Clark as the bodies of her assailants. Justice was satisfied, and Palmer was appeased. The Guerrillas had washed out the stain cast upon them in blood, and public opinion—from being their slanderers and detractors—commenced suddenly to flatter and to speak many gracious words in praise of them. Coolly circumspect and quick to recognize the turn of a tide that had risen to flood in their favor, Henry Porter gathered hurriedly together the remnant of Quantrell's torn, scarred and decimated Guerrilla band, just eighteen in all, and surrendered them at Samuels Depot, Nelson county, July 25th, 1865. Captain Younger, of the 47th Kentucky, assisted by Lieutenant Campbell, of the same regiment, received and paroled the Guerrillas. These two gallant officers were especially generous and obliging. Soldiers themselves who had seen real service, they respected brave men and recognized intrepidity even in an enemy. Capt. Younger, as delicately as possible, administered the oath, and Lieut. Campbell, with equal good-breeding, required of the Guerrillas their promise simply that they would not retain more pistols than were permitted by the terms of surrender. This little band—scarcely a fragment of that terrible organization known so well to the border—was the last of the Guerrilla race. They went their separate ways quietly and in order. It had been a cruel, desperate, remorseless race. It was the offspring of the fury and the agony of invasion. It did as it was done by; it killed and it was killed. As the Missouri Guerrilla excelled in certain military characteristics, so also did his reputation have over it the glare of a more sinister light. Personal prowess always attracts, no matter how utterly abused or misapplied. In the West especially is this the case. Individual daring, more perfect the nearer the man approaches the pastoral life, is a peculiar feature of Western civilization. It existed in a latent yet easily aroused condition before the war, now and then breaking forth into deeds of sudden yet antique heroism, and since the war—uickened by all the tremendous energies of the strife, and given a new phase because of a society that in losing its homogenity lost its power to entirely control an element so liable to excess—it has become a part of the character of the people themselves. With such, and for the next two or three generations, the Guerrilla will be an object of study, admiration, or respect. The Missouri Guerrilla—eminently pastoral, desperate in extremity, unsparing in combat, and savage to the last, will remain the typical Guerrilla of the war. As he lived, and fought, and died, this narrative shows, if it shows anything. As he was beat upon by the fierce blasts of the civil strife and driven hither and thither, sometimes a fugitive and sometimes a wild beast at bay, it has likewise been the mission of this history to set forth. He is interesting because he was Anglo-Saxon. If through similar convulsions the race — of which he was the best living exponent — should again make its appearance, those who choose to understand something of his nature, and something of his mode of warfare, may not conclude that this book has been altogether written in vain.

CHAPTER XVIII.

TO THE great mass of the Guerrillas the end of the war also brought an end to their armed resistance. As an organization, they never fought again. The most of them kept their weapons; a few had great need to keep them. Some were killed because of the terrible renown won in the four years' war; some were forced to hide themselves in the unknown of the outlying territories; and some were mercilessly persecuted and driven into desperate defiance and resistance because they were human and intrepid. To this latter class the Jameses and Youngers belonged. No men ever strove harder to put the past behind them. No men ever submitted more sincerely to the result of a war that had as many excesses on one side as on the other. No men ever went to work with a heartier good will to keep good faith with society and make themselves amenable to the law. No men ever sacrificed more for peace, and for the bare privilege of doing just as hundreds like them had done— the privilege of going back again into the obscurity of civil life and becoming again a part of the enterprising economy of the commonwealth. They were not permitted so to do, try how they would, and as hard, and as patiently.

After the death of Quantrell and the surrender of the remnant of his Guerrillas, Frank James was not permitted, at first, to return to Missouri at all, much less to his home in Clay county. He lingered in Kentucky as long as possible, very circumspect in his actions and very conservative in his behavior. Tempted one day by his beardless face and innocent walk and talk to bear upon him roughly, four Federal soldiers set upon Frank James in Brandenburg and made haste to force an issue. For a moment the old fire of his earlier and stormier days flared up all of a sudden from the ashes of the past and consumed as with a single

hot blast of passion prudence, accountability, caution and discretion. He fought as he had fought at Centralia. Two of the
Federals were killed instantly, the third was desperately
wounded, while the fourth shot Frank badly in the point of
the left hip, inflicting a grievous hurt and one which caused him
afterwards a great deal of trouble and pain. Staunch friends
hid him while the hue and cry were heaviest, and careful surgical
attention brought him back to life when he lay so close to
death's door that by the lifting of a hand he might also have
lifted its latch. This fight, however, was not one of his own
seeking, nor one which he could have avoided without the exhibition of a quality he never had known anything about and
never could know anything about—physical cowardice.

Jesse James—emaciated, tottering as he walked, fighting what
seemed to every one a hopeless battle of "the skeleton boy against
skeleton death"—joined his mother in Nebraska and returned
with her to their home near Kearney, in Clay county. His
wound would not heal, and more ominous still, every now and
then there was a hemorrhage. In the spring of 1866 he was
just barely able to mount a horse and ride a little. And he did
ride, but he rode armed, watchful, vigilant, haunted. He might
be killed, waylaid, ambuscaded, assassinated; but he would be
killed with his eyes open and his pistols about him. The hunt
for this maimed and emaciated Guerrilla culminated on the
night of February 18th, 1867. On this night an effort was made
to kill him. Five militiamen, well armed and mounted, came to
his mother's house and demanded admittance. The weather was
bitterly cold, and Jesse James, parched with a fever, was tossing
wearily in bed. His pistols were under his head. His step-father,
Dr. Samuel, heard the militiamen as they walked upon the front
porch, and demanded to know what they wanted. They told him
to open the door. He came up to Jesse's room and asked him
what he should do. "Help me to the window," was the low,
calm reply, "that I may look out." He did so. There was
snow on the ground and the moon was shining. He saw that
all the horses hitched to the fence had on cavalry saddles, and
then he knew that the men were soldiers. He had but one of
two things to do—drive them away or die. He had never surrendered and he never would. Incensed at his step-father's
silence, they were hammering at the door with the butts of their
29

muskets and calling out to Jesse to come down, swearing that they knew he was in the house, and that they would have him out, dead or alive. He went down stairs softly, having first dressed himself, crept up close to the front door and listened until from the talk of the men he thought he was able to get a fatally accurate pistol range. Then he put a heavy dragoon revolver to within three inches of the upper panel of the door and fired. A man cried out and fell. Before the surprise was off he threw the door wide open, and with a pistol in each hand began a rapid fusillade. A second man was killed as he ran, two men were wounded severely, and surrendered, while the fifth marauder, terrified, yet unhurt, rushed swiftly to his horse and escaped in the darkness.

What else could Jesse James have done? In those evil days bad men in bands were doing bad things continually in the name of law, order and vigilance committees. He had been a desperate Guerrilla; he had fought under a black flag; he had made a name for terrible prowess along the border; he had survived dreadful wounds; it was known that he would fight at any hour or in any way; he could not be frightened out from his native county; he could be neither intimidated nor robbed, and hence the wanton war waged upon Jesse and Frank James, and hence the reasons why to-day they are outlaws, and hence the reasons also that—outlaws as they are and proscribed in county, or State, or territory—they have more friends than the officers who hunt them, and more defenders than the armed men who seek to secure their bodies, dead or alive.

Since 1865 it has been pretty much one eternal ambush for these two men—one unbroken and eternal hunt *twelve years long.* They have been followed, trailed, surrounded, shot at, wounded, ambushed, surprised, watched, betrayed, proscribed, outlawed, driven from State to State, made the objective points of infallible detectives, and they have triumphed. By some intelligent people they are regarded as myths; by others as in league with the devil. They are neither, but they are uncommon men. Neither touches whisky. Neither travels twice' the same road. Neither tells the direction from which he came nor the direction in which he means to go. They are rarely together, but yet they are never far apart. There is a design in this—the calm, cool, deadly design of men who recognize the perils which beset them and who are not afraid to die. They travel this way because if any so-called friend—tempted by the large rewards offered for the life of either—should seek to take it and succeed, the other, safe from the snare and free to do his worst, is pledged to avenge the brother slain through treachery, and avenge him surely. That he will do it none doubt who know the men. In addition, the Jameses trust very few people— two probably out of every ten thousand. They come and go as silently as the leaves fall. They never boast. They have many names and many disguises. They speak low, are polite, deferential and accommodating. They do not kill save in stubborn self-defence. They have nothing in common with a murderer. They hate the highwayman and the coward. They are outlaws, but they are not criminals, no matter what prejudiced public opinion may declare, or malignant partisan dislike make noisy with reiteration. The war made them desperate Guerrillas, and the harpies of the war—the robbers who came in the wake of it and the cut-throats who came to the surface as the honorble combatants settled back again into civilized life—proscribed them and drove them into resistance. They were men who could not be bullied—who were too intrepid to be tyrannized over—who would fight a regiment just as quickly as they would fight a single individual—who owned property and meant to keep it—who were born in Clay county and did not mean to be driven out of Clay county—and who had surrendered in good faith, but who because of it did not intend any the less to have their rights and receive the treatment the balance of the Southern soldiers received. This is the summing up of the whole history of these two men since the war. They were hunted, and they were human. They replied to proscription by defiance, ambushment by ambushment, musket shot by pistol shot, night attack by counter attack, charge by counter-charge, and so will they do, desperately and with splendid heroism, until the end.

Jesse James, to-day however, owes his life to Dr. A. P. Lankford. After the night attack on his mother's house, and after his escape from the toils which beset him so closely there, much exposure in pitiless weather made his wound open and bleed afresh. He could neither walk, ride, nor be hauled about in a wagon. He had to be left at a house deep in some heavy

timber, and to run twice the risk of death—once from the wound
which would not heal, and once from blood-thirsty enemies up
and after him in every direction.   Lankford even then was both
surgeon and Samaritan.   He had a theory that he never knew a
man until he handled his wrist, and he had also two mistresses,
science and great good humor.   An excellent appetite gave him
always a hearty laugh, and this to a certain extent was infec-
tious.   It had this principle of magnetism, it was always genial.
In the capacity of a man of all hours he came to surprise the
secrets of this wounded Guerrilla.   Maybe he was a little super-
stitious; what physicians are not?   He had also his favorites.
He believed in calomel, pulled off his hat to quinine, flattered
carbolic acid high up in the pharmacopœia, caressed chloroform,
gazed at opium through his half shut eyes, laid a hand warily
upon hydrate of chloral, and kept his knifes and his needles,
his cutting things and his thrusting things as the young Lochin-
var kept the steed that he was to ride out of the West.   He
called nature the good God of the cleanly man.   He loved to
meet death face to face, to grapple with him, to overthrow him.
Death is a coward, he said.   Half the time he will run if he is
crowded.   One day a heavy wagon ran over a man's leg and
crushed the bones horribly.   A crowd collected.   Sympathy
was given, but the man wanted air—he had fainted.   Dr. Lankford charged the crowd, awed, cowed, dispersed it, and seized
the leg as he would a thief by the throat.   "It must come off,"
said a young physician standing by, with a fine experimental
frenzy rolling in his scared, uncertain eyes and the monotonous
sing-song of the mechanical graduate in his hesitating voice.
"Eh?   What!   Come off?   So must a man's hat when the king
passes; but suppose the king does not pass, what then?   The
hat stays on.   Water, water, water—is all you want.   Water
enough to swallow up the knife, and drown the surgeon, and
rust away the teeth of the saw.   It is the mission of the surgeon
not to mutilate.   The steel—yes; the steel is good like fire, or
strychnine, or prussic acid, or the dead man brought to the dis-
secting room dead of a plague; but back of the whole business
there must be common sense.   Lift him up, some of you, and
carry him home.   In twenty minutes after he is laid upon his
wife's bed I'll make that mangled leg of his as good as new."
It was this manner of a man who went deep into the brush in

quest of the crippled Guerrilla, and found him where on one hand was a swamp, on the other a river bottom, and everywhere malaria. He stripped him and summed him up. Those blue and red spots about his body were bullet wounds. Across his head was a long white scar. The breech of a gun in the sinewy hands of a powerful Federal had made this. The great open ulcer from right breast to back was the ulcer of the ounce ball the carbine of a Wisconsin cavalryman fired. At intervals the skeleton was hot or cold, at intervals it shook or was on fire. The malaria had taken hold. "Will I die, Doctor?" a mighty weak voice asked of Lankford. "How brave are you?" "Brave enough to know the worst." "Then you will not die. But you must get away from here—get on the sea—get where the air is pure—get where you can feel the sunshine as a man feels wine—get far from this river mist which is perpetually in ambush, far from this tawny exhalation that is even now creeping about the matted undergrowth and the stagnant water." For a month Lankford waited on James, put him once more on his feet, enabled him once more to encompass praying ground and pleading terms, added a little color to his cheeks one day and a little iron to his blood the next, forced him to ride and to walk, built up the fortifications in one direction that fever and suppuration had thrown down in another, and finally cured his patient for good, and all by getting him aboard a ship at New York and ordering him to stay aboard until he got to San Francisco.

The future of the Youngers after the war closed was similar in many respects to that of the Jameses. Cole was in California when the surrender came, and he immediately accepted the situation. He returned to Missouri, determined to forget the past, and fixed in his purpose to re-unite the scattered members of his once prosperous and happy family, and prepare and make comfortable a home for his stricken and suffering mother. Despite everything that has been said and written of this man, he was during all the terrible border war a generous and a merciful man. Others killed, and killed at that in any form, or guise, or fashion—he alone in open and honorable battle. His heart was always kind, and his sympathies always easily aroused. He not only took prisoners himself, but he treated them afterwards as prisoners, and released them to rejoin commands that spared nothing alive of Guerrilla associations that fell into their hands. He was the oldest son, and all the family looked up to him. His mother had been driven out of Cass county into Jackson, out of Jackson into Lafayette, and out of Lafayette into Jackson again. Not content with butchering the father in cold blood, the ravenous cut-throats and thieves followed the mother with a malignity unparalleled. Every house she owned or inhabited was burnt, every out-building, every rail, every straw stack, every corn pen, every pound of food and every store of forage. Her stock was stolen. Her household goods were even appropriated. She had no place to lay her head that could be called her own, and but for the kindness and Christianity of her devoted neighbors, she must have suffered grievously. At this time Coleman and James returned to Missouri and went hopefully and bravely to work. Their father's land remained to them. That at least had neither been set fire to, hauled off in wagons, appropriated, confiscated, nor driven over into Kansas. Western Missouri was then full of disbanded Federal soldiers, organized squads of predatory Red Legs and Jayhawkers, horse thieves disguised as vigilance committees, and highway robbers known as law and order men. In addition, Drake's constitution disfranchised every property owner along the border. An honest man could not hold office; a civilized man could not officially stand between the helpless of his community and the imported lazzaroni who preyed upon them; a decent man's voice could not be heard above the clamor of the beggars quarrelling over stolen plunder; and a just man's expostulation penetrated never into the councils of the chief scoundrels who planned the murders and the robberies.

Coleman Younger's work was like the work of a pioneer in the wilderness, but he did it as became the hardy descendant of a stalwart race of pioneers. He cut logs and built a comfortable log house for his mother. He made rails and fenced in his land. In lieu of horses or mules, he plowed with oxen. He staid steadfastly at home. He heard rumors of threats being made against his life, but he paid no attention to them. He took part in no political meetings. He tried to hide himself and be forgotten. The blood-hounds were on his track, however, and swore to either kill him or drive him from the country. A vigilance committee composed of skulking murderers and red-

handed Kansas robbers went one night to surprise the two
brothers and end the hunt with a massacre. Forewarned,
James and Coleman fled. The family was wantonly insulted,
and a younger brother, John, a mere boy, was brutally beaten
and then hung until life was nearly extinct. This was done to
force him to tell of the whereabouts of James and Coleman. Mrs.
Younger never entirely recovered from the shock of this night's
work, lingering along hopelessly yet patiently for several months
and finally dying in the full assurance of the Christian's blessed
hereafter.

The death of this persecuted woman, however, did not end
the persecution. Cole Younger was repeatedly waylaid and
fired at. His stock was killed through mere deviltry, or driven
off to swell the gains of insatiable wolves. His life was in
hourly jeopardy, as was the life of his brother James. They
plowed in the fields as men who saw suspended over them a
naked sword-blade. They permitted no lights to be lit in the
house at night. They traveled the public highways warily.
They were hunted men and proscribed men in the midst of their
own people. They were chased away from their premises by
armed men. Once Cole was badly wounded by the bullet of an
assassin. Once, half-dressed, he had to flee for his life. If he
made a crop, he was not permitted to gather it, and when something of success might have come to him after the expenditure
of so much toil, energy, long-suffering and forbearance, he was
not let alone in peace long enough to utilize his returns and
make out of his resources their legitimate gains.

Of course there could be but one ending to all this long and
unbroken series of malignant persecutions, lyings-in-wait, midnight surprises, perpetual robbings, and most villainous assaults
and attempted murders—Coleman and James Younger left home
and left Jackson county. They buckled on their pistols and
rode away to Texas, resolved from that time on to protect themselves, to fight when they were attacked, and to make it so hot
for the assassins and the detectives who were eternally on their
track that by and by the contract taken to murder them would
be a contract not particularly conducive to steady investments.
They were hounded to it. They endured every species of insult
and attack, and would have still continued to endure it in silence
and almost unresisting, if such forbearance had mitigated in any

manner the virulence of their enemies, or brought any nearer to
its appeasement the merciless fate which seemed to be eternally
at their heels.   What they did in self-defense any Anglo-Saxon
would have done who did not have in his veins the blood of a
slave.   The peaceful pursuits of life were denied to them.   The
law which should have protected them was over-ridden.   Indeed
there was no law.   The courts were instruments of plunder.
The civil officers were cut-throats.   Instead of a legal process,
there was a vigilance committee.   Men were hung because of a
very natural desire to keep hold of their own property.   To the
cruel vigor of actual war, there had succeeded the irresponsible
despotism of greedy highwaymen buttressed upon assassination.
The border counties were overrun with bands of predatory plunderers.   Some Confederate soldiers dared not return home, and
many Guerrillas fled the country.   It was dark everywhere, and
the bravest held their breath, not knowing how much longer they
would be permitted to remain peacefully at home, or suffered to
enjoy the fruits of their labors.   Fortunately for all, however,
the well nigh extinct embers of a merciless border war were not
blown upon long enough and persistently enough to kindle
another conflagration.

But neither the Jameses nor the Youngers have been permitted to rest long at any one time since the surrender of the
Confederate armies.   Some dastardly deeds have been done
against them, too, in the name of the law.   Take for example
Pinkerton's midnight raid upon the house of Mrs. Zerelda
Samuel, the mother of the James boys.   The family were
wrapped in profound sleep.   Only women and children were
about the premises, and an old man long past his prime.   The
cowards—how many is not accurately known, probably a
dozen—crept close to this house through the midnight, surrounded it, found its inmates asleep, and threw into the kitchen
where an old negro woman was in bed with her children, a lighted
hand-grenade, wrapped about with flannel saturated with tur-
pentine.   The lurid light from this inflammable fluid awakened
the negro woman, and she in turn awakened the sleeping whites.
They rushed to subdue the flames and save their property.
Children were gathered together in the kitchen, little things,
helpless and terrified.   All of a sudden there was a terrible
explosion.   Mrs. Samuel's right arm was blown off above the

elbow, a bright little boy, eight years of age, had his bowels torn out, Dr. Samuel was seriously cut and hurt, the old negro woman was maimed, and several of the other children more or less injured. The hand-grenade had done its work, and there had been a tragedy performed by men calling themselves civilized, in the midst of a peaceful community and upon a helpless family of women and children that would have disgraced Nero or made some of the monstrous murders of Diocletian as white is to black. Yet Pinkerton's paid assassins did this because his paid assassins knew better how to kill women and children than armed men in open combat.

Take for example another act of Pinkerton's paid assassins. The first party of men sent down into St. Clair county, Missouri, looking for the Youngers, was encountered by Cole Younger, having with him his three brothers, James, Robert and John. There were fifteen of the hunters, heavily armed and prolific in promises of speedy overthrow. Cole came upon them suddenly, covered the whole detachment with a double-barreled shot-gun, and demanded a surrender. It was instantly accorded, and Cole then calmly and kindly reasoned with them against the injustice of their course. They were hunting him and his brothers, he said, without cause, and as wild beasts were hunted. He told them that he wanted to live at peace with the law and his neighbors. God knew that he had had strife enough. He had never in all his life harmed a man wantonly, or killed a man wantonly, or imposed upon a man wantonly. He had never committed a robbery in his life, no matter what the reports were, and he asked only to be put upon the same footing exactly that other law-abiding citizens occupied, and to be treated as a human being instead of an outlaw. Then he restored their arms to the posse and dismissed them without a scratch. These were citizens of the county, however, and were satisfied with the treatment they had received and with Cole's explanation. Not so with Pinkerton and his paid assassins. This great Chicago bugaboo had been worsted in every encounter with those of the border whom it was his especial and self-imposed mission to slay or entrap, and he grew morbidly desirous of striking a blow that had vengeance in it. As an instrument he selected a detective named Lull, said to be cool, skillful, vigilant, and desperate. He had need to be! He came down into St. Clair, with another detective, and recruited at Osceola the deputy sheriff of the county, a young man named Daniels. These three began to hunt the Youngers, just as any lot of trappers might begin to hunt a pack of wolves. It is not believed that they had any warrant for the arrest of either of the brothers. Only vague rumor or sensational journalism had connected them in any manner with bank or railroad robberies. The people among whom they lived believed in their innocence and had borne testimony to it several times in such a manner as to carry with their defence the convincing evidence of its truth. Nevertheless, according to the theory of Pinkerton and Pinkerton's paid assassins, they were to be shot down as so many horses with the glanders or so many dogs with the hydrophobia. Lull began his hunt with a bravado and ended it with a bullet. He found John and James Younger, or, rather, John and James Younger found him. As Cole had done with the first party of hunters, so would James and John do with the second. They covered Lull's party with their shot-guns and called out to them to surrender. The desperate Lull, picked man as he was and chosen pre-eminently above a host of men, did surrender to all intents and purposes. He threw his own revolver upon the ground. He caused Daniels also to throw down a pair. He made the other detective give up his, and then when he had succeeded perfectly in disarming his companions, and when because of such disarmament John Younger lowered his own gun and permitted himself for the first and the last time in his history to be taken unawares—he drew a smaller pistol, which up to this time had been concealed, and shot the unsuspecting man through the neck, cutting the jugular vein, yet not knocking him from the saddle. With the hand of death already clutching savagely at his own throat, and with the blood spurting out in great jets at every heart beat, John Younger yet steadied himself by a superhuman effort, mortally wounded Lull, killed Daniels, and dashed at the third detective, who turned about, born coward that he was, and fled, as the wind flies, into Osceola. When James Younger reached John the tragedy was over and the dauntless boy was dead. No more infamous murder was ever committed in Missouri than this killing of John Younger. He had not even been accused of doing criminal things. His name had never even been connected with the name of any railroad or bank robbery. He was a peaceful man, living in the midst of a peaceful community, respected by his neighbors, trusted by men of business, honest, energetic and enterprising. He was hunted to his death because his name was Younger, and because all the guns in the world and all the enemies in the world could neither scare him nor drive him away from his own. In the full flower of his early manhood, his lonely and premature grave to-day in his native State, cries out for vengeance on the head of a civilization which permits an irresponsible and an accursed system of legalized assassination to prey upon innocent people equally with the guilty, and defy and rise above the law while professing to obey its mandates and keep clearly within the limits of its just provisions.

Other Guerrillas did some desperate things after the war, and escaped. One of Quantrell's best scouts, Jack Bishop—a cool, desperate, dauntless, iron man, fell under the ban of the Kansas people and was driven about from pillar to post until he got tired. His brother, another daring Guerrilla, was waylaid at a creek-crossing south of Westport by some disbanded Kansas militia, and killed. Jack determined to avenge him. With this object in view he rode boldly into Kansas City where Major Ransom, an ex-Federal officer, was doing the duties of a civil office, and opened fire upon him as coolly as if he were saddling and bridling a horse. Ransom was a Kansas man, well known to the border, and Bishop would have killed him surely if Ransom, running for his life, had not taken refuge in a strong building. As it was he wounded him badly and rode slowly out of town and away into the unknown of the Western territories.

The most of the survivors of the border war are scattered far and wide. Oll Shepherd, as has already been stated, was killed by a Jackson county vigilance committee, fighting to the death. George Shepherd is ranching somewhere in the West. Andy McGuire was hung by a mob at Richmond, Ray county, Missouri, charged but charged unjustly with having been engaged in the robbery of the bank there and the killing of three of the citizens of the town. Payne Jones survived Quantrell's desperate raid into Kentucky, and returned to Missouri to be killed by Jim Crow Chiles. Later on Jim Crow Chiles himself was killed by a citizen of Independence. Dick Burnes, another of Quantrell's most desperate men, went to sleep one might in an orchard where there was some straw, and when found the next morning he was found with his head cleft in twain as though while he slept some powerful assassin had cloven it with an axe. John Jarrette has a sheep ranche somewhere in the wilds of Arizona. Jesse and Frank James are outlaws and trading in cattle along the lower Rio Grande river, sometimes in Texas and sometimes as far in-land in old Mexico as Monterey. Fletch Taylor is a most worthy citizen, rich, popular, and universally respected. James Anderson, William Anderson's brother, was cut to pieces in Texas in a bowie-knife fight. Dave Poole is in New Mexico. William Greenwood is a prosperous farmer in northeastern Missouri. Dick Maddox was killed by a Cherokee Indian just after the close of the war. George Maddox was arrested arbitrarily after the surrender for his participation in the Lawrence Raid, and was confined a long time in jail. He escaped, however, to go back into peaceful life, and made as good a citizen as he made a soldier. Arch Clements was murdered in Lexington. Frank Gregg, charged with the killing of a citizen of Lafayette county while the war was going on, was arrested in Independence and carried to Lexington for trial. Gen. Shelby interposed in his behalf, and Frank Gregg was acquitted. Tom Little was hung by a vigilance committee in Warrensburg, Johnson county, one of the most virulent and blood-thirsty committees ever known to the criminal annals of Western Missouri. Tom Maupin tends his flocks and herds far down in Texas— many a long days' ride southward from Sherman. Some went to Mexico with Shelby in that famous Expedition of his which aspired to an empire and ended with an exodus—notably Crockett, one of Anderson's original desperadoes, Joe Macey, John Thrailkill, Erasmus Woods, William Yowell, and the noted Berry brothers, Richard and Isaac. There is but space to record briefly some of the deeds these Guerrillas did in Mexico. Shelby had just crossed the Rio Grande at Piedras Negras, opposite Eagle Pass, in Texas, and had, after selling his surplus arms, ammunition and cannon to Governor Biesca, of the State of Coahuila, dismissed his men in the afternoon for a little rest and relaxation.

The day had been almost a tropical one. No air blew about the streets, and a white glare had come over the sands and settled as a cloud upon the houses and upon the water. The men scattered in every direction, careless of consequences, and indifferent as to results. The *cafes* were full. Wine and women abounded. Beside the bronzed faces of the soldiers were the tawny faces of the *senoritas*. In the passage of the drinking horns the men kissed the women. Great American oaths came out from the *tiendas*, harsh at times, and resonant at times. Even in their wickedness they were national.

A tragedy was making head, however, in spite of the white glare of the sun, and the fervid kisses under the rose. The three men, soldiers of Lee's army ostensibly—men who had been fed and sheltered—were tempting providence beyond the prudent point. They had joined the expedition some distance back, and were lavishly provided for because it was supposed they had once belonged to the army of Northern Virginia. Having the heart each of a sheep, they were dealing with lions. To their treachery they were about to add bravado—to the magazine they were about to apply the torch. There is a universal Mexican law which makes a brand a bible. From its truth there is no appeal. Every horse in the country is branded, and every brand is entered of record, just as a deed or legal conveyance. Some of these brands are intricate, some unique, some a single letter of the alphabet, but all legal and lawful brands just the same, and good to pass muster anywhere, so only there are alcaldes and sandaled soldiers about. Their logic is extremely simple too. You prove the brand and you take the horse, no matter who rides him, nor how great the need for whip or spur. In Shelby's command there were a dozen magnificent horses, fit for a king's race, who wore a brand of an unusual fashion—many-lined and intricate as a column of Arabesque. They had been obtained somewhere above San Antonio, and had been dealt with as only cavalry soldiers know how to deal with their horses. These the three men wanted—these three men ostensibly from Lee's army. With their knowledge of Spanish they had gone among the Mexican soldiers, poisoning their minds with tales of American rapine and slaughter, depicting, with not a little of attractive rhetoric, the long and weary march they had made with these marauders, that their beloved steeds might not be taken entirely away from them.

The Mexicans listened, not from generosity, but from greed,

and swore a great oath by the Virgin that the *gringos* should
deliver up every branded horse across the Rio Grande. Ike
and Dick Berry rode each a branded horse, and so did John
Rudd, Yowell and two other Guerrillas equally fearless, and
equally ignorant of any other law besides the law of possession.
The afternoon drill was over. The hot glare was still upon the
earth and the sky. If anything the noise from the *cafes* came
louder and merrier. Where the musical voices were the sweet-
est, were the places where the women abounded with disheveled
hair, and eyes of tropical dusk.

Ike Berry had ridden one of these branded horses into the
street running by regimental headquarters, and sat with one
leg crossed upon the saddle, lazily smoking. He was a low,
squat Hercules, free of speech and frank of nature. In battle
he always laughed; only when eating was he serious. What
reverence he had came from the appetite. The crumbs that fell
from his long, yellow beard were his bendiction.

Other branded horses were hitched about, easy of access and
unnoted of owner. The three men came into the street, behind
them a young Mexican Captain, handsome as Adonis. This
Captain led thirty-five soldiers with eyes to the front and guns
at a trail. Jim Wood lounged to the door of a. *cafe* and
remarked them as they filed by. As he returned, he spoke to
Martin Kritzer, toying with an Indian girl, beaded and beautiful: "They are in skirmishing order. Old Joe has delivered
the arms; it may be that we shall take them back again."

One of the men went straight up to Ike Berry as he sat cross-
legged upon his horse, and laid his hand upon the horse's bridle.

Ike knew him and spoke to him cheerily:

"How now, comrade!"

Short answer, and curt:

"This is my horse; he wears my brand; I have followed him
to Mexico. Dismount!"

A long white wreath of smoke curled up from Ike's meer-
schaum in surprise. Even the pipe entered a protest. The old
battle smile came back to his face, and those who were nearest
and knew him best, knew that a dead man would soon lay upon
the street. He knocked the ashes from his pipe musingly; he
put the disengaged foot back gently in the stirrup; he rose up
all of a sudden the very incarnation of murder; there was a

white gleam in the air; a heavy sabre that lifted itself up and circled, and when it fell a stalwart arm was shredded away, as a girl might sever a silken chain cr the tendrils of a vine. The ghastly stump, not over four inches from the shoulder, spouted blood at every throb. The man fell as one paralyzed. A shout arose. The Mexicans spread out like a fan, and when the fan closed it had surrounded Berry and his comrades. Yowell alone broke through the cordon and rushed to Shelby.

Shelby was sitting in a saloon discussing cognac and catalan with an Englishman. A glance convinced Shelby that Yowell was in trouble.

"What is it?" he asked.

"They are after the horses."

"What horses?"

"The branded horses; those obtained from the Rosser ranche."

"Ah! and after we have delivered the arms, too. Mexican-like, Mexican-like!"

He arose as he spoke and looked out on the street. Some revolvers were being fired. These, in the white heat of the afternoon, sounded as the tapping of wood-peckers. Afterwards a steady roar of rifles told how the battle went.

"The rally! the rally!—sound the rally!" Shelby cried to his bugler, as he dashed down to where the Mexicans were swarming about Berry and the few men nearest to him. "We have eaten of their salt, and they have betrayed us; we have come to them as friends, and they would strip us like barbarians. It is war again—war to the knife!"

At this moment the wild, piercing notes of an American bugle were heard, clear, penetrating, defiant—notes that told of sore stress among comrades, and pressing need of succor.

The laughter died in the *cafes* as a night wind when the morning comes. The bugle sobered all who were drunk with drink or dalliance. Its voice told of danger near and imminent—of a field-meeting of harvesters who were not afraid to die.

The men swarmed out of every doorway—poured from under every portal—flushed, furious, ravenous for blood.

They saw the Mexicans in the square, the peril of Berry and those nearest to him, and they asked no further questions. A sudden crash of revolvers came first, close and deadly; a yell, a shout, and then a fierce, hot charge. Ras Woods, another Guerrilla, with a short Enfield rifle in his hand, stood fair in the street looking up at the young Mexican Captain with his cold gray eyes that had in them never a light of pity. As the press gathered about him, the rifle crept straight to the front and rested there a moment, fixed as fate. It looked as if he was aiming at a flower—the dark olive beauty of the Spaniard was so superb.

"Spare him!" shouted a dozen reckless soldiers in a breath, "he is too young and too handsome to die." In vain! A sharp, sudden ring was the response; the Captain tossed his arms high in the air, leaped up suddenly as if to catch something above his head, and fell forward upon his face, a corpse. A wail of women arose upon the sultry evening —such as may have been heard in David's household when back from the tangled brushwood they brought the beautiful Absalom,

> " The life upon his yellow hair,
> But not within his eyes."

The work that followed was quick enough and deadly enough to appal the stoutest. Seventeen Mexicans were killed, including the Captain, together with the two Americans who had caused the encounter. The third, strange to say, recovered from his ghastly wound, and can tell to this day, if he still lives, of the terrible prowess of that American soldier who shredded his arm away as a scythe blade might a handful of summer wheat.

There were Guerrillas also in Mexico, native Mexican Guerrillas, who fought the French, robbed the rich, preyed upon the passers by, and hovered about Shelby's column as it marched on boldly into the South. He forbade his men to fight with them. He could not take the time, he said, to brush away gad-flies and have to do every day with mosquitoes. He would guard his camp against them at night, and carefully shelter his stock from their stealthy approaches, but for some several day's march this was all. These Guerrillas, however, became emboldened in the face of such tactics. On the trail of a timid or wounded thing they were veritable wolves. This long gallop could never tire. In the night they were superb. Upon the flanks, in the front or rear, it was one eternal ambush—one incessant rattle of musketry which harmed nothing, but which yet annoyed, like the singing of misquitoes. At last they brought about a swift reckoning—one of those sudden things which leave little behind save a trail of blood and a moment of savage killing.

The column had reached to within two days' journey of Lampasas. Some spurs of the mountain ran down to the road, and some clusters of palm trees grouped themselves at intervals by the wayside. The palm is a pensive tree, having a voice in the wind that is sadder than the pine—a sober, solemn voice, like the sound of ruffled cerements when the corpse is given to the coffin. Even in the sunlight they are dark; even in the tropics no vine clings to them, no blosom is born to them, no bird is housed by them, and no flutter of wings makes music for them. Strange and shapely, and coldly chaste, they seem like human and desolate things, standing all alone in the midst of luxurious nature, unblessed of the soil, and unloved of the dew and the sunshine.

In a grove of these the column halted for the night. Beyond them was a pass guarded by crosses. In that treacherous land these are a growth indigenous to the soil. They flourish nowhere else in such abundance. Wherever a deed of violence is done, a cross is planted; wherever a traveler is left upon his face in a pool of blood, a cross is reared; wherever a grave is made wherein lies the murdered one, there is seen a cross. No matter who does the deed—whether Indian, or Don, or Commandante, a cross must mark the spot, and as the pious wayfarer journeys by he lays on all reverently a stone at the feet of the sacred symbol, breathing a pious prayer and telling a bead or two for the soul's salvation.

On the left a wooded bluff ran down abruptly to a stream. Beyond the stream and near the palms, a grassy bottom spread itself out, soft and grateful. Here the blankets were spread, and here the horses grazed their fill. A young moon, clear and white, hung low in the West, neither sullen nor red, but a tender moon, full of the beams that lovers seek, and full of the voiceless imagery which gives passion to the song of the night, and pathos to deserted and dejected swains. As the moon set the horses were gathered together and tethered in amid the palms. Then a deep silence fell upon the camp, for the sentinels were beyond its confines, and all

30

withinside slept the sleep of the tired and the healthy. It may have been midnight; it certainly was cold and dark. The fires had gone out, and there was a white mist like a shroud creeping up the stream and settling upon the faces of the sleepers. On the far right a single pistol shot arose, clear and resonant. Shelby, who slumbered like a night bird, lifted himself up from his blankets and spoke in an undertone to Thrailkill:

"Who has the post at the mouth of the pass?"

"Joe Macey."

"Then something is stirring. Macy never fired at a shadow in his life."

The two men listened. One a grim Guerrilla himself with the physique of a Cossack and the hearing of a Comanche. The other having in his hands the lives of all the silent and inert sleepers lying still and grotesque under the white shroud of the mountain mist. Nothing was heard for an hour. The two men went to sleep again, but not to dream. Of a sudden and unseen the mist was lifted, and in its place a sheet of flame so near to the faces of the men that it might have scorched them. Two hundred Mexicans had crept down the mountain, and to the edge of the stream, and had fired point-blank into the camp. It seemed a miracle, but not a man was touched. Lying flat upon the ground and wrapped up in their blankets, the whole volley, meant to be murderous, had swept over them.

Shelby was the first upon his feet. His voice rang out clear and faultless, and without a tremor:

"Give them the revolver—Charge!"

Men awakened from deep sleep grapple with spectres slowly. These Mexicans were spectres. Beyond the stream and in amid the sombre shadows of the palms, they were invisible. Only the powder-pall was on the water where the mist had been.

Unclad, barefooted, heavy with sleep, the men went straight for the mountain, a revolver in each hand, Shelby leading. From spectres the Mexicans had become to be bandits. No quarter was given or asked. The rush lasted until the game was flushed, the pursuit until the top of the mountain was gained. Over ragged rocks and cactus and dagger trees the hurricane poured. The roar of the revolvers was deafening. Men died and made no moan, and the wounded were recognized only by their voices. When it was over the Americans had lost in killed eleven and in wounded seventeen, most of the latter slightly, thanks to the darkness and the impetuosity of the attack. In crawling upon the camp, the Mexicans had tethered their horses upon the further side of the mountain. The most of these fell into Shelby's hands, together with the bodies of the two leaders, Juan Anselmo, a renegade priest, and Antonio Flores, a young Cuban who had sold his sister to a wealthy *haciendaro* and turned robber, and sixty-nine of their followers.

It was noon the next day before the march was resumed— noon with the sun shining upon the fresh graves of eleven dauntless Americans sleeping their last sleep, amid the palms and the crosses, until the resurrection day.

There was a grand *fandango* at Lampasas when the column reached the city. The bronzed, foreign faces of the strangers attracted much of curiosity and more of comment; but no notes in the music jarred, no halt in the flying feet of the dancers could be discovered.

Shelby camped just beyond the suburbs, unwilling to trust his men to the blandishments of so much beauty, and to the perils of so much nakedness.

Stern camp guards soon sentineled the soldiers, but as the night deepened their devices increased, until a good company had escaped all vigilance and made a refuge sure with the sweet and swarthy *senoritas*, singing:

> O ven ama!
> Eres alma,
> Say corazon.

There were three men who stole out together in mere wantonness and exuberance of life—obedient soldierymen—who were to bring back with them a tragedy without a counterpart in all their history. None saw Boswell, Walker, and Crockett, three of Quantrell's and Anderson's old Guerrillas, depart—the whole command saw them return again, Boswell slashed from chin to waist, Walker almost dumb from a bullet through cheeks and tongue, and Crockett, sober and unhurt, yet having over him the sombre light of as wild a deed as any that stands out from all the lawless past of that lawless band.

These men, when reaching Lampasas, floated into the floodtide of the fandango, and danced until the red lights shone with unnatural brilliancy—until the fiery *catalon* consumed what little of discretion the dancing had left. They sallied out late at night, flushed with drink, and having over them the glamour of enchanting women. They walked on apace in the direction of the camp, singing snatches of Bacchanal songs, and laughing boisterously under the moonlight which flooded all the streets with gold. In the doorway of a house a young Mexican girl stood, her dark face looking out coquettishly from its fringe of dark hair. The men spoke to her, and she, in her simple fashion, spoke to the men. In Mexico this meant nothing. They halted, however, and Crockett advanced from the rest and laid his hand on the girl's shoulder. Around her head and shoulders she wore a *sebosa*. This garment answers at the same time for bonnet and bodice. When removed the head is uncovered and the bosom is exposed. Crockett meant no real harm, although he asked her for a kiss. Before she had replied to him, he attempted to take it. The hot Southern blood flared up all of a sudden at this, and her dark eyes grew furious in a moment. As she drew back from him in proud scorn, the *sebosa* came off, leaving all her bosom bare, the long, luxurious hair falling down upon and over it as a cloud that would hide its purity and innocence.

Then she uttered a low, feminine cry as a signal, followed instantly by a rush of men who drew knives and pistols as they came on. The Americans had no weapons.

Not dreaming of danger, and being within sight almost of camp, they had left their revolvers behind. Boswell was stabbed three times, though not seriously, for he was a powerful man, and fought his assailants off. Walker was shot through his tongue and both cheeks, and Crockett, the cause of the whole *melee*, escaped unhurt. No pursuit was attempted after the first swift work was over. Wary of reprisals, the Mexicans hid themselves as suddenly as they had sallied out. There was a young man, however, who walked close to Crockett—a young Mexican who spoke no word, and who yet kept pace with the American, step by step. At first he was not noticed. Before the camp guards were reached, Crockett, now completely sobered, turned upon him and asked:

"Why do you follow me?"

"That you may lead me to your General."

"What do you want with my General?"

"Satisfaction."

At the firing in the city a patrol guard had been thrown out who arrested the whole party and carried it straight to Shelby. He was encamped upon a wide margin of bottom land, having a river upon one side, and some low mountain ridges upon the other. The ground where the blankets were spread was velvety with grass. There was a bright moon; the air, blowing from the grape gardens and the apricot orchards of Lampasas, was fragrant and delicious, and the soldiers were not sleeping. Under the solace of such surroundings Shelby had relaxed a little of that grim severity he always manifested toward those guilty of unsoldierly conduct, and spoke not harshly to the three men. When made acquainted with their hurts he dismissed them instantly to the care of Dr. Tisdale. Crockett and the Mexican still lingered, and a crowd of some fifty or sixty had gathered around. The first told his story of the *melee*, and told it truthfully. The man was too brave to lie. As an Indian listening to the approaching footsteps of one whom he intends to scalp, the young Mexican listened as a granite pillar vitalized to the whole recital. When it was finished he went up close to Shelby and said to him, pointing his finger at Crockett: "That man has outraged my sister. I could have killed him, but I did not. You Americans are brave, I know; will you be generous as well, and give me satisfaction?"

Shelby looked at Crockett, whose bronzed face, made sterner in the moonlight, had upon it a look of curiosity. He at least did not understand what was coming. "Does the Mexican speak the truth, Crockett?" was the question asked by the commander of his soldier.

"Partly; but I meant no harm to the woman. I am incapable of that. Drunk, I know I was, and reckless, but not willfully guilty, General."

Shelby regarded him coldly. His voice was so stern when he spoke again that the brave soldier hung his head:

"What business had you to lay your hands upon her at all? How often must I repeat to you that the man who does these things is no follower of mine? Will you give her brother satisfaction?"

He drew his revolver almost joyfully and stood proudly up,

facing his accuser. "No! no! not the pistol!" cried the Mexican; "I do not understand the pistol. The knife, Senor General; is the American afraid of the knife?"

He displayed as he spoke a keen, glittering knife, and held it up in the moonlight. It was white, and lithe, and shone in contrast with the dusky hand which grasped it.

Not a muscle of Crockett's face moved. He spoke almost gently as he turned to his General:

"The knife, oh! well, so be it. Will some of you give me a knife?"

A knife was handed to him and a ring was made. About four hundred soldiers formed the outside circle of this ring. These, bearing torches in their hands, cast a red glare of light upon the arena, already flooded with the softer beaming of the moon. The ground under foot was as velvet. The moon not yet full, and the sky without a cloud, rose over all, calm and peaceful in the summer night. A hush as of expectancy fell upon the camp. Those who were asleep slept on; those who were awake seemed as under the influence of an intangible dream. Shelby did not forbid the fight. He knew it was a duel to the death, and some of the desperate spirit of the combatants passed into his own. He merely spoke to an aide:

"Go for Tisdale. When the steel has finished, the surgeon may begin."

Both men stepped fearlessly into the arena. A third form was there, unseen, invisible, and even in *his* presence the traits of the two nations were uppermost. The Mexican made the sign of the cross, the American tightened his sabre belt. Both may have prayed, neither, however, audibly.

They had no seconds—perhaps none were needed. The Mexican took his stand about midway of the arena, and waited. Crockett grasped his knife firmly and advanced upon him. Of the two, he was taller by a head and physically the strongest. Constant familiarity with danger for four years had given him a confidence the Mexican may not have felt. He had been wounded three times, one of which wounds was scarcely healed. This took none of his manhood from him, however.

Neither spoke. The torches flared a little in the night wind, now beginning to rise, and the long grass rustled curtly under foot. Afterwards its green had become crimson.

Between them some twelve inches of space now intervened. The men had fallen back upon the right and the left for their commander to see, and he stood looking fixedly at the two as he would upon a line of battle. Never before had he gazed upon so strange a sight. That great circle of bronzed faces, eager and fierce in the flare of torches, had something monstrous yet grotesque about it. The civilization of the century had been rolled back, and they were in a Roman circus, looking down upon the arena, crowded with gladiators and jubilant with that strangest of war-cries: *Moritusite salutant!*

The attack was as the lightning's flash. The Mexican lowered his head, set his teeth hard, and struck fairly at Crockett's breast. The American made a half-face to the right, threw his left arm forward as a shield, gathered the deadly steel in his shoulder to the hilt and struck home. How pitiful! A great stream of blood spurted in his face. The tense form of the Mexican bent as a willow wand in the wind, swayed helplessly, and fell backward lifeless, the knife rising up as a terrible protest above the corpse. The man's heart was found.

Cover him up from sight! No need of Dr. Tisdale here. There was a wail of women on the still night air, a shudder of regret among the soldiers, a dead man on the grass, a sister broken-hearted and alone forevermore, and a freed spirit somewhere out in eternity with the unknown and the infinite.

Crockett was afterwards killed in a desperate night attack upon a *hacienda*, but before this attack was made it was John Thrailkill's turn to come upon the scene in the strangest guise, perhaps, ever yet known to Guerrilla.

Maybe Fate rests its head upon its two hands at times, and thinks of what little things it shall employ to make or mar the character—save or lose a life—banish beyond the light or enter into and possess forevermore a Paradise.

The march was running by meadow and by river, and the swelling of billowy wheat, and great groves of orange trees wherein the sunshine hid itself at noon with the breeze and the mocking birds. It was far into the evening that John Thrailkill sat by the fire of his mess, smoking and telling brave stories of the brave days that were dead. Others were grouped about in dreaming indolence or silent fancy—thinking, it may be, of the northern land with its pines and firs—of great rolling waves of prairie and plain, of forests where cabins were and white-haired children all at play.

Thrailkill was a Guerrilla who never slept—that is to say, who never knew the length or breadth of a bed from Sumpter to Appomattox. Some women in Platte county had made him a little black flag, under which he fought. This, worked into the crown of his hat, satisfied him with his loyalty to his lady-love. In addition to all this, he was one among the best pistol shots in a command where all were excellent.

Perhaps neither before nor since the c ircumstance here related, has anything so quaint in recklessness or bravado been recorded this side the Crusades. Thrailkill talked much, but then he had fought much, and fighting men love to talk now and then. Some border story of broil or battle, wherein, at desperate odds, he had done a desperate deed, came uppermost as the night deepened, and the quaint and scarred Guerrilla was over-generous in the share he took of the killing and the plunder.

A comrade by his side—Anthony West—doubted the story and ridiculed its narration. Thrailkill was not swift to anger for one so thoroughly reckless, but on this night he arose, every hair on his bushy beard bristling.

"You disbelieve me, it seems," he said, bending over the other until he could look into his eyes, "and for the skeptic there is only the logic of a blow. Is this real, and this?" and Thrailkill smote West twice in the face with his open hand, once on either cheek. No insult could be more studied, open and unpardonable.

Comrades interfered instantly, or there would have been bloodshed in the heart of the camp and by the flames of the bivouac fire. Each was very cool—each knew what the morning would bring forth, without a miracle.

The camp was within easy reach of a town that was more of a village than a town. It had a church and a priest, and a regular Don of an Alcalde who owned leagues of arable land, and two hundred game cocks besides. For Shelby's especial amusement a huge main was organized, and a general invitation given to all who desired to attend.

The contest was to begin at noon. Before the sun had risen, Capt. James H. Gillette came to Thrailkill, who was wrapped up in his blankets, and said to him:

"I have a message for you."

"It is not long, I hope."

"Not very long, but very plain."

"Yes, yes, they are all alike, I have seen such before. Wait for me a few minutes."

Thrailkill found Isaac Berry, and Berry in turn soon found Gillette.

The note was a challenge, brief and peremptory. Some conference followed, and the terms were agreed upon. These were savage enough for an Indian. Colt's pistols, dragoon size, were the weapons, but only one of them was to be loaded. The other, empty in every chamber, was to be placed alongside the loaded one. Then a blanket was to cover both, leaving the butt of each exposed. He who won the toss was to make the first selection, and Thrailkill won. The loaded and the unloaded pistol lay hidden beneath a blanket, the two handles so nearly alike that there was no appreciable difference. Thrailkill walked up to the tent, whistling a tune. West stood behind him, watching with a face that was set as flint. The first drew, cast his eyes along the cylinder, saw that it was loaded, and smiled. The last drew—every chamber was empty! Death was his portion as absolutely and as certainly as if death already stood by his side. Yet he made no sign other than to look up to the sky. Was it to be his last look?

The terms were ferocious, yet neither second had protested against them. It seemed as if one man was to murder another because one had been lucky in the toss of a silver dollar. As the case stood, Thrailkill had the right to fire *six shots* at West before West had the right to grasp even so much as a loaded pistol—and Thrailkill was known for his deadly skill throughout the ranks of the whole Expedition.

The two were to meet just at sunset, and the great cock main was at noon. To this each principal went, and each second, and before the main was over the life of a man stood as absolutely upon the prowess of a bird as the Spring and its leaves upon the rain and the sunshine.

And thus it came about: In Mexico, cock-fighting is a national recreation—perhaps is a national blessing as well. Men engage in it when they would be robbing else, and waylaying convoys bearing specie, and haunting the mountain gorges until the heavy trains of merchandise entered slowly in to be swallowed up.

The priests fight then, and the fatter the *padre* the finer his chicken. From the prayer-book to the pit is an easy transition, and no matter the *aves* so only the odds are in favor of the church. It is upon the Sundays that all the pitched battles begin. After the matin bells, the matches. When it is vespers, for some there has been a stricken and for some a victorious field. No matter again—for all there is absolution.

The Alcalde of the town of Linares was a jolly, good-conditioned Mexican, who knew a bit of English, picked up in California, and who liked the Americans for but two things—their hard drinking and their hard swearing. Finding any ignorant of these accomplishments, there flowed never any more for them a stream of friendship from the Alcalde's fountain. It became dry as suddenly as a spring in the desert. Shelby won his heart by sending him a case of elegant cognac—a present from General Douay—and therefore was the main improvised which was to begin at noon.

The pit was a great circle in the midst of a series of seats that arose the one above the other. Over the entrance—which was a gateway opening like the lids of a book—was a chair of state, an official seat occupied by the Alcalde. Beside him sat a bugler in uniform. At the beginning and the end of a battle this bugler, watching the gestures of the Alcalde, blew triumphant or penitential strains accordingly as the Alcalde's favorite lost or won. As the main progressed the notes of gladness outnumbered those of sorrow.

A born cavalryman is always suspicious. He looks askance at the woods, the fences, the ponds, the morning fogs, the road that forks and crosses, and the road that runs into the rear of a halted column, or into either flank at rest in bivouac. It tries one's nerves so to fumble at uncertain girths in the darkness, a rain of bullets pouring down at the outposts and no shelter anywhere for a long week's marching.

And never at any time did Shelby put aught of faith in Mexican friendship, or aught of trust in Mexican welcome and politeness. His guard was perpetual, and his intercourse, like his marching, was always in skirmishing order. Hence one-half the forces of the Expedition were required to remain in camp under arms, prepared for any emergency, while the other half, free of restraint, could accept the Alcalde's invitation or not as they saw fit. The most of them attended. With the crowd went Thrailkill and West, Gillette and Berry. All the village was there; the pit had no caste.

Benevolent priests mingled with their congregations and bet their *pesos* on their favorites. Lords of many herds and acres, and mighty men of the country round about, the Dons of the *haciendas*, pulled off their hats to the peons and staked their gold against the greasy silver, palm to palm. Fair *senoritas* shot furtive glances along the ranks of the soldiers—glances that lingered long upon the Saxon outline of their faces and retreated only when to the light of curiosity there had been added that of unmistakable admiration.

The bugle sounded and the betting began. The sport was new to many of the spectators—to a few it was as a sealed book. Twenty-five cocks were matched—all magnificent birds, not so large as those fought in America, but as pure in game and as rich in plumage. There, too, the fighting is more deadly; that is to say, it is more rapid and fatal. The heels used have been almost thrown aside here. In the North and West absolutely—in New Orleans very nearly so. These heels, wrought of the most perfect steel and curved like a scimeter, have an edge almost exquisite in its keenness. They cut asunder like a sword-blade. Failing in instant death they inflict mortal wounds. Before there is mutilation there is murder.

To the savage reality of combat there was added the atoning insincerities of music. These diverted the drama of its premeditation, and gave to it an air of surprise that, in the light of an accommodating conscience, passed unchallenged for innocence. In Mexico the natives rarely ask questions—the strangers never. Shelby seated himself by the side of the Alcalde; the first five or six notes of a charge were sounded and the battle began. Thereafter with varying fortune it ebbed and flowed through all the long afternoon. Aroused into instant championship, the Americans espoused the side of this or that bird, and lost or won as the fates decreed. There was but scant gold among them, all counted, but twenty dollars or twenty thousand, it would have been the same. A nation of born gamblers, it needed but a cock fight to bring all the old national traits upper-

most.   A dozen or more were on the eve of wagering their carbines and revolvers, when a sign from Shelby checked the unsoldierly impulse and brought them back inst antly to a realization
of duty.

Thrailkill had lost heavily—that is to say every dollar he
owned on earth.   West had won without cessation—won in
spite of his judgment, which was often adverse to the wagers
laid.   In this, maybe, Fate was but flattering him.   Of what
use would all his winnings be after the sunset?

It was the eighteenth battle, and a magnificent cock was
brought forth who had the crest of an eagle and the eye of a
basilisk.   More sonorous than the bugle, his voice had blended
war and melody in it.   The glossy ebony of his plumage needed
only the sunlight to make it a mirror where courage might have
arrayed itself.   In an instant he was everybody's favorite—in
his favor all the odds were laid.   Some few cluster ed about his
antagonist—among them a sturdy old priest who did what he
could to stem the tide rising in favor of the bird of the beautiful
plumage.

Infatuated like the rest, Thrailkill would have staked a crown
upon the combat; he did not have even so much as one *real*.
The man was miserable.   Once he walked to the door and
looked out.   If at that time he had gone forth, the life of West
would have gone with him, but he did not go.   As he returned
he met Gillette, who spoke to him:

"You do not bet, and the battle is about to begin."

"I do not bet because I have not won.   The pitcher that goes
eternally to a well is certain to be broken at last."

"And yet you are fortunate."

Thrailkill shrugged his shoulders and looked at his watch.
It wanted an hour yet of the sunset.   The tempter still
tempted him.

"You have no money, then.   Would you like to borrow?"

"No."

Gillette mused awhile.   They were tying on the last blades,
and the old priest cried out:

"A doubloon to a doubloon against the black cock!"

Thrailkill's eyes glistened.   Gillette took him by the arm.
He spoke rapidly, but so low and distinct that every word was a
thrust

"You do not want to kill West. The terms are murderous—
you have been soldiers together—you can take the priest's bet
—here is the money. But," and he looked him fair in the
face, "if you win you pay me; if you lose I have absolute
disposal of your fire."

"Ah!" and the Guerrilla straightened himself up all of a
sudden, "what would you do with my fire?"

"Keep your hands clean from innocent blood, John Thrailkill. Is not that enough?"

The money was accepted, the wager with the priest was laid,
and the battle began. When it was over the. black cock lay
dead on the sands of the arena, slain by the sweep of one
terrific blow, while over him, in pitiless defiance, his antagonist, dun in plumage and ragged in crest and feather, stood a
victor, conscious of his triumph and his prowess. The sun was
setting, and two men stood face to face in the glow of the
crimsoning sky. On either flank of them a second took his
place, a look of sorrow on the bold bronzed face of Berry, the
light of anticipation in the watchful eyes of the calm Gillette.
Well kept, indeed, had been the secret of the tragedy. The
group who stood alone on the golden edge of the evening were
all who knew the ways and the means of the work before them.
West took his place as a man who had shaken hands with life
and knew how to die. Thrailkill had never been merciful, and
this day of all days were the chances dead against a moment of
pity or forgiveness. The ground was a little patch of grass
beside a stream, having trees in the rear of it, and trees over
beyond the reach of the waters running musically to the sea. In
the distance there were houses from which peaceful smoke
ascended. Through the haze of the gathering twilight the
sound of bells came from the homeward plodding herds, and
from the fields the happy voices of the reapers. West stood
full front to his adversary—certain of death. He expected
nothing beyond a quick and a speedy bullet—one which would
kill without inflicting needless pain.

The word was given. Thrailkill threw his pistol out, covered
his antagonist once fairly, looked once into his eyes and saw
that they did not quail, and then, with a motion as instantaneous
as it was unexpected, lifted it up overhead and fired in the air.

Gillette had won the wager!

The fight in which Crockett was killed was also a fight of Thrailkill's contriving. It was a fight based upon a romance, a night attack that grew from a goatherd's story into a savage scene of shooting and killing.

As Shelby's Expedition won well its way into Mexico, many places old in local song and story, arose, as it were, from the past, and stood out, clear-cut and crimson, against the background of a history filled to the brim with rapine, and lust, and slaughter. No other land under the sun had an awakening so storm-begirt, a christening so bloody and remorseless. First the Spaniards under Cortez—swart, fierce, long of broadsword and limb; and next the Revolution, wherein no man died peacefully or under the shade of a roof. There was Hidalgo, the ferocious priest—shot. Morales, with these words in his mouth —shot: "Lord, if I have done well, Thou knowest it; if ill, to Thy infinite mercy I commend my soul." Leonardo Bravo, scorning to fly—shot. Nicholas Bravo, his son, who had offered a thousand captives for his father's life—shot. Matamoras— shot. Mina—shot. Guerrera—shot. Then came the Republic—bloodier, bitterer, crueler. Victoria, its first President— shot. Mexia — shot. Pedraza — shot. Santmanet — shot by General Ampudia, who cut off his head, boiled it in oil, and stuck it up on a pole to blacken in the sun. Herrera—shot. Paredes—shot. All of them shot, these Mexican Presidents, except Santa Anna, who lost a leg by the French and a country by the Americans. Among his game-cocks and his mistresses, he lived many a day in Havana, seeing only when his aged eyes had lost their lustre the white brow of Orizava from the Southern Sea, and resting only again under the orange and the banana trees about Cordova, a tottering frame that had felt to their fullest the heat and the cold of Mexican revolution. It was a land old in the world's history that these men rode into, and a land stained in the world's crimes—a land filled full of the sun and the tropics. What wonder, then, that a deed was done on the fifth day's marching that had about it the splendid dash and bravado of mediæval chivalry.

Keeping outtermost guard, one balmy evening, far beyond the silent camp of the dreaming soldiers, John Thrailkill and James Wood did vigilant duty in front of the reserve. The fire had gone out when the cooking was done, and the earth smelt sweet with grasses and the dew on the grasses. A low pulse of song broke on the bearded faces of the cacti, and sobbed in fading cadence as the waves that came in from the salt sea, seeking the south wind. This was the vesper strain of the katydid, sad, solacing, rhythmical.

Before the wary eyes of the sentinels a figure rose up, waving his blanket as a truce-flag. Encouraged, he came into the lines, not full assured of his bearings—frightened a little and prone to be communicative by way of propitiation. Had the Americans heard of Encarnacion. No, they had not heard of Encarnacion. What was Encarnacion?

The Mexican, born robber and devout Catholic, crossed himself. Not to have heard of Encarnacion was next in infamy to having slaughtered a priest. Horror made him garrulous. Fear, if it does not paralyze, has been known to make the dumb speak. Encarnacion was a *hacienda*, and a *hacienda*, literally translated, is a plantation with royal stables, and acres of corral, and abounding water, and long rows of male and female slave cabins, and a Don of an owner, who has music, and singing-maidens, and pillars of silver dollars, and a passionate, brief life, wherein wine and women rise upon it at last and cut it short. Even if no ill-luck intervenes, the pace to the devil is a terrible one, and superb riders though they are, the best seat in the saddle sways heavily at last, and the truest hand on the rein relaxes ere manhood reaches its noon and the shadows of the west.

Luis Enrico Rodriguez owned Encarnacion, a Spaniard born, and a patron saint of all the robbers who lived in the neighboring mountains, and of all the *senoritas* who plaited their hair by the banks of his *arroyos* and hid but charily their dusky bodies in the limpid waves. The hands of the French had been laid upon him lightly. For forage and foray Dupin, that terrible Contre-Guerrilla, had never penetrated the mountain line which shut in his guarded dominions from the world beyond. When strangers came he gave them greeting; when soldiers came, he gave them of his flocks and herds, his wines and treasures.

There was one pearl, however, a pearl of great price, whom no stranger eyes had ever seen, to whom no stranger tongue had ever spoken a fair good morning. The slaves called it a spirit, the confessor a sorceress, the lazy gossips a *gringo* witch, the man who knew best of all called it wife, and yet no sprinkling of water or blessing of church had made the name a holy one.

Rodriguez owned Encarnacion, and Encarnacion owned a skeleton. This much James Wood and John Thrailkill knew when the half goat-herder and robber had told but half his story. When he finished his other half this much remained of it:

Years before, in Sonora, a California hunter of gold had found his way to some streams where a beautiful Indian woman lived with her tribe. They were married, and a daughter was born to them, having her father's Saxon hair and her mother's eyes of tropical dusk. From youth to womanhood this daughter had been educated in San Francisco. When she returned she was an American, having nothing of her Indian ancestry but its color. Even her mother's language was unknown to her. One day in Guaymas Rodriquez looked upon her as a vision. He was a Spaniard and a millionaire, and he believed all things possible. The wooing was long, but the web, like the web of Penelope's, was never woven. He failed in his eloquence, in his money, in his passionate entreaties, in his stratagems, in his lyings-in-wait—in everything, indeed, that savored of pleading or purchase. Some men come often to their last dollar—never to the end of their audacity. If fate should choose to back a lover against the world, fate would give long odds on a Spaniard.

At last, when everything else had been tried, Rodriguez determined upon abduction. This was a common Mexican custom, dangerous only in its failure. No matter what the risk, no matter how monstrous the circumstances, no matter how many corpses lay in the pathway looking up from plotting to fulfilment, so only in the end the lust of the man triumphed over the virtue of the woman. Gathering together hastily a band of bravos, whose devotion was in exact proportion to the dollars paid, Rodriguez seized upon the maiden returning late one night from the opera, and bore her away with all speed towards Encarnacion. The Californian, born of a tiger race that invariably dies hard, mounted such few men as loved him and followed on furiously in pursuit. Bereft of his young, he had but one thing to do—*kill*.

Fixed as fate and as relentless, the race went on. Turning

once fairly at bay, pursuers and pursued met in a death grapple. The Californian died in the thick of the fight, leaving stern and stark traces behind of his terrible prowess. What cared Rodriguez, however, for a bravo more or less? The woman was safe, and on his own garments nowhere did the strife leave aught of crimson or dust. Once well in her chamber, a mistress, perhaps—a prisoner certainly, she beat her wings in vain against the strong bars of her palace, for all that gold could give or passion suggest had been poured out at the feet of Inez Walker. Servants came and went at her bidding. The priest blessed and beamed upon her. The captor was fierce by turns, and in the dust at her feet by turns; but amid it all the face of a murdered father rose up in her memory, and prayers for vengeance upon her father's murderers broke ever from her unrelenting lips. At times fearful cries came out from the woman's chamber. The domestics heard these and crossed themselves. Once in a terrible storm she fled from her thraldom and wandered frantically about until she sank down insensible. She was found alone with her beauty and her agony. Rodriguez lifted her in his arms and bore her back to her chamber. A fever followed, scorching her young face until it was pitiful, and shredding away her Saxon hair until all its gloss was gone and all its silken rippling stranded. She lived on, however, and under the light of a Southern sky, and by the fitful embers of a soldier's bivouac, a robber goatherd was telling the story of an American's daughter to an American's son.

" Was it far to Encarnacion ?"

Jim Wood asked this question in his broken Spanish way, looking out to the front, musing.

" By to-morrow night, Senor," the goatherd made answer, "you will be there."

" Have you told the straight truth, Mexican?"

"As the Virgin is true, Senor."

"So be it. You shall sleep this night at the outpost. To-morrow we will see."

The Mexican smoked a cigarito and went to bed. Whether he slept or not he made no sign. Full confidence rarely lays hold of an Indian's heart. Replenishing the fire, Wood and Thrailkill sat an hour together in silence. Beyond the sweeping, untiring glances of their eyes, the men were as statues.

31

Finally Thrailkill spoke to Wood:

"Of what are you thinking?"

"Encarnacion. And you?"

"Inez Walker. It is the same."

The Mexican turned in his blanket, muttering. Wood's revolver covered him:

"Lie still," he said, "and muffle up your ears. You may not understand English, but you understand this," and he waved the pistol menacingly before his eyes. "One never does know when these yellow snakes are asleep."

"No matter," replied Thrailkill, sententiously, "they never sleep."

It was daylight again, and although the two men had not unfolded their blankets, they were as fresh as the dew on the grasses—fresh enough to have planned an enterprise as daring and as desperate as anything ever dreamed of in romance or set forth in fable.

The to-morrow night of the Mexican had come, and there lay Encarnacion in plain view under the starlight. Rodriguez had kept aloof from the American encampment. Through the last hours of the afternoon wide-hatted *rancheros* had ridden up to the corral in unusual numbers, had dismounted, and had entered in. Shelby, who took note of everything, took note of this also.

"They do not come out," he said. "There are some signs of preparation about, and some fears manifested against a night attack. Save for our grass and our goats, I know of no reason why our foraging should be heavier now than formerly."

Twice Wood and Thrailkill had been on the eve of telling him the whole story, and twice their hearts had failed them. Shelby had been getting sterner and sterner of late, and the reins had become to be drawn tighter and tighter. Perhaps it was necessary. Certainly since the last furious attack by the Mexican guerrillas those who had looked upon discipline as an ill-favored mistress had ended by embracing her.

As the picquets were being told off for duty, Wood came close to Thrailkill and whispered:

"The men will be ready by twelve. They are volunteers and splendid fellows. How many of them will be shot?"

"*Quien sabe?* Those who take the sword shall perish by the sword.'

With all his gold, and his leagues upon leagues of cattle and land, Rodriguez had only for eagle's nest an adobe eyrie. Hither his dove had been carried. On the right of this long rows of cabins constituted the quarters of his peons. Near to the great gate were acres of corral. Within this saddled steeds in state were lazily feeding. A Mexican loves his horse, but this is no reason why he does not starve him. This night, however, Rodriguez was bountiful. For fight and flight both men and animals must not go hungry. On the top of the main building a kind of tower lifted itself up. It was roomy and spacious, and flanked by steps that clung to it tenaciously. In this tower a light shone, while all below and about it was hushed and impenetrable. High adobe walls encircled the mansion, the cabins, the corral, the acacia trees, the fountain that splashed plaintively, and the massive portal which had mystery written all over its rugged outlines.

The nearest picquet was over beyond Encarnacion, and the camp guards were only for sentinel duty. Free to come and go, the men had no watchword for the night. None was needed. Suddenly, and if one had looked up from his blankets he might have seen a long, dark line standing out against the sky. This line did not move.

It may have been twelve o'clock. There was no moon, yet the stars gave light enough for the men to see each other's faces, and to recognize one another. It was a quarter of a mile from the camp to the *hacienda*, and almost the same distance to the picquet post from where the Americans had fórmed. In the ranks one might have seen such veteran campaigners—stern and rugged, and scant of speech in danger—as McDougall, Tom Boswell, Armstead, Winship, Ras Woods, Joe Macey, Vines, James Kirtley, Blackwell, Rudd, Crockett, Collins, Jack Williams, Owens, Timberlake, Darnell, Johnson, the two Berrys— Richard and Isaac—and a dozen others of like courage and material. Wood and Thrailkill stood forward by right as leaders. All knew that they would carry them far enough, some may have thought, perhaps, that they would carry them too far. The line, hushed now and ominous, stood still as a wall. From front to rear Thrailkill walked along its whole length, speaking some low and cheering words.

"Boys," he commenced, "none of us know what is waiting

inside the corral. Mexicans fight well in the dark, it is said, and see better than wolves; but we must have that American woman safe out of their hands or we must burn the buildings. If the hazard is too great for any of you, step out of the ranks. What we are about to do must needs be done quickly. Shelby sleeps little of late, and may be even at this moment searching through the camp for some of us. Let him find even so much as one blanket empty, and from the heroes of a night attack we shall become its criminals.''

Sweeney, a one-armed soldier who had served under Walker in Nicaragua, and who was in the front always in hours of enterprise or peril, replied to Thrailkill:

''Since time is valuable, lead on.''

The line put itself in motion. Two men sent forward to try the great gate, returned rapidly. Thrailkill met them.

''Well?'' he said.

''It is dark all about there, and the gate itself is as strong as a mountain.''

''We shall batter it down.''

A beam was brought—a huge piece of timber wrenched from the upright fastenings of a large irrigating basin. Twenty men manned this and advanced upon the gate. In an instant thereafter there were tremendous and resounding blows, shouts, cries, oaths and musket shots. Before this gigantic battering-ram adobe walls and iron fastenings gave way. The bars of the barrier were broken as reeds, the locks were crushed, the hinges were beaten in, while with a fierce yell and rush the Americans swarmed to the attack of the main building. The light in the tower guided them. A legion of devils seemed to have broken loose. The stabled steeds of the Mexicans reared and plunged in the infernal din of the fight, and dashed hither and thither, masterless and riderless. The camp where Shelby rested was instantly alarmed. The shrill notes of the bugle were heard over all the tumult, and with them the encouraging voices of Wood and Thrailkill crying out: ''Make haste, men, make haste! In twenty minutes more we will be between two fires.''

Crouching in the stables and pouring forth a murderous fire from their ambuscades in the darkness, some twenty *rancheros* made sudden and desperate battle. Joe Macey and Ike Berry charged through the gloom upon the unknown, guided only by the lurid and fitful flashes of the muskets. When the work was over the corral no longer vomited its flame; silence reigned there, that fearful and ominous silence fit only for the dead who die suddenly.

The camp, no longer in sleep, had become menacing. Short words of command came out of it, and the tread of trained men forming rapidly for battle. Some skirmishers, even in the very first moments of the combat, had been thrown forward quite to the *hacienda*. They were almost nude, and stood out under the starlight as white spectres, threatening yet undefined. They had guns at least and pistols, and in so much were mortal. These spectres had reason also and discretion. Close upon the fragments of the great gate and looking in upon the waves of the fight as they rose and fell, they yet did not fire. They believed at least that some of their kindred and comrades were there.

For a brief ten minutes more the combat raged evenly. Cheered by the voice of Rodriguez and stimulated by his example, his retainers clung bitterly to the fight. The doors were as redoubts. The windows were as miniature casements. Once on the steps of the tower, Rodriguez showed himself for an instant. A dozen of the best shots in the attacking party fired at him. No answer save an oath of defiance so savage and harsh that it sounded unnatural even in the roar of the furious hurricane.

There was a lull. Every Mexican outside the main building had been either killed or wounded. Against the massive walls of the adobes the rifle bullets made no headway. It was murder longer to oppose flesh to masonry. Vickers was killed, young and dauntless; Crockett, the Guerrilla hero of the desperate Lampasas duel, was dead; Rogers was dead; the boy Provines was dead; Matterhorn, a stark giant of a German, shot four times, was breathing his last, while the wounded were on all sides, some hard hit, and some bleeding yet fighting on.

"Once more to the beam!" shouted Thrailkill.

Again the great battering ram crashed against the great door leading into the main hall, and again there was a rending away of iron, and wood, and mortar. Through splintered timber, and over crumbling and jagged masonry, the besiegers poured.

The building was gained. Once well withinside, the storm of revolver balls was terrible. There personal prowess told, and there the killing was quick and desperate. At the head of his hunted following, Rodriguez fought like the Spaniard he was, stubbornly and to the last. No lamps lit the savage *melee*. While the Mexicans stood up to be shot at they were shot where they stood. The most of them died there. Some few broke away towards the last and escaped, for no pursuit was attempted, and no man cared how many fled or how fast. It was the woman the Americans wanted. Gold and silver ornaments were everywhere, and precious tapestry work, and many rare and quaint and woven things, but the powder-blackened and blood-stained hands of the assailants touched not one of these. It was too dark to tell who killed Rodriguez. To the last his voice could be heard cheering on his men and calling down God's vengeance on the *gringos*. Those who fired at him specially fired at his voice, for the smoke was stifling, and the sulphurous fumes of the gunpowder almost unbearable.

When the *hacienda* was won, Shelby had arrived with the rest of the command. He had mistaken the cause of the attack, and his mood was of that kind which but seldom came to him, but which when it did come, had several times before made some of his most hardened and unruly followers tremble and turn pale. He had caused the *hacienda* to be surrounded closely, and he had come alone to the doorway, a look of wrathful menace on his usually placid face. "Who among you have done this thing?" he asked, in tones that were calm, yet full and vibrating.

No answer. The men put up their weapons.

"Speak, some of you. Let me not find cowards instead of plunderers, lest I finish the work upon you all that the Mexicans did so poorly upon a few." Thrailkill and Wood came forward to the front then. Covered with blood and powder stains, they seemed in sorry plight to make much headway in defence of the night's doings, yet they told the tale as straight as the goat-herd had told it to them, and in such simple soldier fashion, taking all the sin upon their own heads and hands, that even the stern features of their commander relaxed a little, and he fell to musing. It may have been that the desperate nature of the enterprise appealed more strongly to his own feelings than he was willing that his men should know, or it may have been that his set purpose softened a little when he saw so many of his bravest and best soldiers come out from the darkness and stand in silence about their leaders, Wood and Thrailkill, some of them sorely wounded, and all of them covered with the signs of the desperate fight, but certain it is that when he spoke again his voice was more relenting and assuring.

"And where is the woman?"

Through all the terrible moments of the combat the light in the tower had burned as a beacon. Perhaps in those few seconds when Rodriguez stood alone upon the steps leading up to the dove's-nest, in a tempest of fire and smoke, the old love might have been busy at his heart, and the old yearning strong within him to make at last some peace with her for whom he had so deeply sinned, and for whose sake he was soon to so dreadfully suffer. Death makes many a sad atonement, and though late in coming at times to the evil and the good alike, it may be that when the records of the heart are writ beyond the wonderful river, much that was dark on earth will be bright in eternity, and much that was cruel and fierce in finite judgment will be made fair and beautiful when it is known how *love* gathered up the threads of destiny, and how all the warp was blood-stained and all the woof that had bitterness and tears upon it, could be traced to a woman's hand.

Grief-stricken, prematurely old, yet beautiful even amid the loneliness of her situation, Inez Walker came into the presence of Shelby, a queen. Some strands of gray were in her glossy, golden hair. The liquid light of her large dark eyes had long ago been quenched in tears. The form that had once been so full and perfect, was now bent and fragile; but there was such a look of mournful tenderness in her eager, questioning face that the men drew back from her presence instinctively and left her alone with their General. He received her commands as if she were bestowing a favor upon him, listening as a brother might until all her wishes were made known. These he promised to carry out to the letter, and how well he did so none know better than those who followed him to Mexico.

John Thrailkill still remains where Shelby left him in 1868, a soldier of fortune, who to-day is hidden by a shadow, and to-morrow made joyous with the sunshine. He fought for Juarez against Maximilian, and commanded at Queretaro a battalion of American scouts famed throughout the Republic for extraordinary daring and enterprise.   Later, he was a revolutionist under Porfirio Diaz, and later still, he joined with Diaz in the overthrow of both Lerdo and Iglesias.   Others of his Guerrilla comrades who accompanied him to Mexico scattered in every direction, as many of those did who remained in the United States.   Some joined the French and returned with the Zouaves to Algeria.   Some took service on the sea, some went to China, some to the Sandwich Islands, and some remained half brigands and half *haciendaros*, to live by the sword and, sooner or later, to perish by it.

THE END.

Books Published by Morningside Bookshop

ALLAN, WILLIAM 1837-1889, — HOTCHKISS, JEDEDIAH, 1827-1899; History of the Campaign of Thomas J. Jackson in the Shenandoah Valley of Virginia Nov. 1861-June 1862. Maps. The best study of Jackson's Valley operations by his chief ordnance officer of the Confederate 2nd Corps. Dayton, 1974.   Price $15.00

ANDERSON, EPHRAIM McDOWELL, Memoirs: Historical and Personal; Including the CAMPAIGNS OF THE FIRST MISSOURI CONFEDERATE BRIGADE edited by Edwin C. Bearss, Index by Margie Riddle Bearss, with Map by Barbara Long, 616 pp. Dayton, 1972.   Price $15.00
One of the better Confederate narratives written by an upper class Southerner and strongly revealing for social conditions in the Confederacy — Civil War Books, L.S.U. Press.

CALDWELL, J. F. J.; The History of a Brigade of South Carolinians, known first as "Gregg's" and subsequently as "McGowan's Brigade" 249 pp. Dayton, 1974.   Paperback $7.50, Cloth Price $12.50
The best unit history from the Palmetto State. The author describes all the brigades many engagements and adds enough personal material to make the account both personal and human in scope. — Civil War Books, L.S.U. Press.

CASLER, JOHN O., of Co. A, 33rd Virginia Infantry, A.N.V., Four Years in the Stonewall Brigade. 362 pp. Edited by Dr. James I. Robertson. Dayton, 1971.   Price $10.00
There can be no true portrayal of the private soldier of that army (ANV) unless Casler is consulted. — D. S. Freeman.

CHAMBERLAIN, JOSHUA L., The Passing of the Armies, an account of the final Campaign of the Army of the Potomac. 392 pp. Maps. Dayton, 1974. A very moving description of the surrender at Appomattox.   Price $17.50
. . . "The Passing of the Armies" is one of the finest Civil War books I have ever read. — Thanks for reprinting it! — Noted Scholar, Brooks Davis.

Confederate Ordnance Manual: Crandall 1382, Charleston. Evans and Cogswell, 1863. The Ordnance Manual for the use of the officers of the Confederate States Army. Prepared under the direction of Col. J. Gorgas, Chief of Ordnance. C.S.A. introduction by Sydney C. Kerksis.   Price $25.00
Contains much information not found elsewhere.

Confederate Veteran Magazine Index, 1893-1932. An exact reprint of the indices as issued 1893-1932, 296 pp. Dayton, 1972.   Price $25.00

DACUS, DR. ROBERT H., Reminiscences of Company "H", First Arkansas Mounted Rifles, 47 pp. Dayton, 1972.
                    Paperback $5.00, Cloth $7.00

DICKERT, D. AUGUSTUS, History of the Kershaw Brigade. New introduction by Dr. Wm. Stanley Hoole, 583 pp. Index, errata, photos, roster and biographical sketches. $20.00
"This account of a famous Brigade of McLaw's Division, First Corps, expands many incidents scarcely mentioned in reports." — D. S. Freeman.
. . . Makes Kershaw's Brigade a great book, a human book, and one that is an absolute must for any historian, amateur or professional, who wished to taste the true flavor of the Civil War. — Warren Ripley in Charleston Evening Post.

DINKINS, JAMES, 1861-1865, by an Old Johnnie. Personal recollections and experiences in the Confederate Army. 280 pp. Service with Barksdale's Mississippi Brigade, and as a staff officer on Chalmers'

Books Published by Morningside Bookshop

Staff, of Forrest Cavalry. Reprint of 1897 edition.   Price $15.00

Dinkins . . . an interesting book to read, a good reference and a must for all Civil War "Buffs" . . . Yanks or Rebs — Chedwato Book Review Service, December 1975.

EDWARDS, JOHN NEWMAN, 1839-1889, Noted Guerrillas, or Warfare of the Border, being a history of the lives and adventures of Quantrell, Anderson, Todd, and numerous other well known guerrillas of the West. Reprint of 1877 edition with introduction by Dr. Albert Castel, West Michigan University, 488 pp. Maps, Illustrations.   Price $20.00

FOX, WILLIAM F., Regimental Losses, 1861-1865, 595 pp. A must for every C. W. or Confederate library. Dayton, 1974.   Price $35.00

GRAINGER, GERVIS D., Co. I, 6th Kentucky Infantry, Four Years with the Boys in Gray, 45 pp. Dayton, 1972. Grainger's experiences as an escaped prisoner.   Paperback $5.00, Cloth $7.00

HAY, THOMAS ROBSON: Hood's Tennessee Campaign, a Neale Classic reprint, 272 pp. Maps, introduction by Dr. Robert J. Womack of Middle Tennessee State University.   Price $17.50

HOTCHKISS, JEDEDIAH, 1827-1899. Confederate Military History, Virginia Expanded Volume, 1295 pp. Photos, maps. Hundreds of personal sketches of lesser known Virginia soldiers.   Price $32.50

Contains over 600 more pages than the regular Virginia Volume of C.M.H.

HOWARD, JAMES McHENRY, 1839-1916. Recollections of a Maryland Confederate Soldier and Staff Officer under Johnston, Jackson and Lee. Edited by Dr. James I. Robertson, Jr., 483 pp. Photographs, map. A very readable book by Francis Scott Key's grandson.   Price $20.00

JACKSON, MARY ANNA (Morrison), 1831-1915, Memoirs of T. J. (Stonewall) Jackson by his widow, Mary Anna Jackson with introduction by Lieut. Gen. J. B. Gordon and Rev. Henry M. Fields, and sketches by Gens. Fitzhugh Lee, S. G. French, and Col. G. F. R. Henderson. Reprint of the 1875 Louisville edition. 647 pp. Photos, maps, with Morningside edition introduction by Lowell Reidenbaugh.   Price $25.00

This volume is one of the most difficult to locate in the original. Contains many intimate letters not found elsewhere.

JONES, BENJAMIN WASHINGTON: Under Stars and Bars, a history of the Surry Light Artillery, edited by Lee A. Wallace, Jr., Photos, map, frequent observations of Richmond in wartime. Reprint of 1909 Edition with notes, index.   Price $20.00

One of the best sellers of the Morningside reprints. . . . one of the best of Virginia Unit Histories — The Virginia Magazine.

JONES, JOHN WILLIAM 1836-1909, Army of Northern Virginia Memorial Volume. Compiled by the Rev. John William Jones . . . at request of the Virginia division of the Army of Northern Virginia Association. Reprint of 1880 edition. 347 pp, with introduction to Morningside edition by Dr. James I. Robertson, Jr. This is a series of useful addresses made at annual reunions of Confederate veterans; all of the material treats of battles and other, purely military matters.   Price $17.50

Books Published by Morningside Bookshop

JORDAN & PRYOR'S, The Campaigns of Lt. Gen. Forrest and of Forrest's Cavalry. No other book written about him or his exploits carries the General's imprimatur, for every word of which he assumed responsibility. It is the most cited of all sources in biographies of Forrest. 704 pp. This was the best selling book published by Press of Morningside and if orders warrant it, it will be re-issued.
Out-of-Print

LOEHR, CHARLES T., War History of the Old First Virginia Infantry Regt. Reprint of 1884 edition. Introduction by Lee A. Wallace, Jr.
Out-of-Print

MINOR, KATE PLEASANTS, An Author and Subject Index to the Southern Historical Society Papers. Introduction by Ray O. Hummel, Jr., Dayton, 1970. Reprint of 1913 Edition.
Paperback $10.00, Cloth $12.50

OATES, W. C., War Between Union and Confederacy and History of 15th Alabama, edited by Robert Krick, of Fredericksburg Battlefield. 808 pp. A NEALE CLASSIC reprint, Dayton, 1974.   Price $20.00

OPIE, JOHN N., 6th Virginia Cavalry, A Rebel Cavalryman with Lee, Stuart and Jackson, 336 pp. Reprint of the 1899 Edition. Dayton, 1972. With introduction to Morningside Edition by Author's son Gen. E. Walton Opie.   Price $12.50

REID, JESSE WALTON, History of the Fourth Regiment of South Carolina Volunteers. 143 pp, cloth. $12.50

SMITH, GUSTAVUS WOODSON, 1822-1846, The Battle of Seven Pines, 202 pp. Maps, Dayton, 1974. This book is the only book on this important battle by the officer who temporarily was in command of Confederates.   Price $15.00

STEVENS, CAPT. C. A., Berdan's United States Sharpshooters in the Army of the Potomac, 1861-1865, illustrated, 554 pp.   Price $15.00

TAYLOR, WALTER H., General Lee, his Campaigns in Virginia, 1861-1865, with personal reminiscences, nine colored folding maps, 314 pp. The most reliable of books on Campaigns of Lee by his adjutant of four years, reprint of 1906 edition. If you do not own the Official Records Atlas this is the 2nd best book to have. The most important maps from the O.R. Atlas are reproduced from the study of Lee's Campaigns.   Price $22.50

THOMPSON, ED. PORTER. History of the Orphan Brigade, new introduction by Wm. C. Davis, 1264 pp. Photos, biographical sketches, rosters, index.   Price $32.50

TUCKER, GLENN, Chickamauga, Bloody Battle in the West, maps by Dorothy Thomas Tucker. The ablest study of the Greatest Battle in the West; highly documented and based solely on printed sources. 448 pp.   Price $9.00

TUCKER, GLENN, High Tide at Gettysburg, New 1974 revised edition, 462 pp. Dayton, 1974. A competently documented story of the Campaign.   Price $9.00

Books Published by Morningside Bookshop

TUNNARD, WILLIAM H., and BEARSS, EDWIN C., 3rd Louisiana Infantry, 581 pp, index by Margie Riddle Bearss; notes, roster and introduction by Edwin C. Bearss, reprint of rare 1866 Edition. An excellent composite of personal accounts of army and battle life in the Arkansas, Missouri, Vicksburg area. Price $15.00

WYETH, JOHN ALLAN, M.D., The Life of General Nathan Bedford Forrest. Reprint of 1899 edition, with original photographs. 656 pp. Written by a Confederate veteran whose regiment served under Forrest, this detailed and uncritical study is concerned almost entirely with military operations. Price $20.00

YOUNG, JESSE BOWMAN, 1844-1914, The Battle of Gettysburg, a comprehensive narrative, reprint of 1913 edition, endsheet maps. One of the ablest and clearest studies of this pivotal campaign; includes valuable biographical sketches of all officers above regimental command. 462 pp. Introduction to Morningside edition by Jacob Sheads retired teacher at Gettysburg. Price $17.50

YOUNG, JOHN PRESTON, The Seventh Tennessee Cavalry (Confederate) reprint of the 1890 Edition. (Jackson's-Stock's-Duckworth's Regiment) Regiment formed April 1, 1862, paroled Gainsville, Alabama May 1865. This regiment served most of its time under Bedford Forrest and was one of his dependable regiments. Introduction to Morningside Edition by Herbert L. Harper of Tennessee Historical Commission. 227 pp. Reprint of this book continues the Morningside policy of reprinting basic regimental source books. Price $17.50

Our thanks to L.S.U. Press to allow us to quote from their Bibliography — Civil War Books by Nevins, Robertson and Wiley.

IN PREPARATION:

To be issued in one volume — War Dept: Marcus Wright's List of Field Officers, Regiments and Battalions in the Conf. States Army. — List of Staff Officers of the Conf. States Army 1861-65. We are reprinting from Marcus Wright's corrected copy — Being edited and corrected by Lee A. Wallace, Jr. Price not set.

TUCKER, GLENN, The Battle of Brice's Cross Roads, Mississippi. This book should be ready in early 1977 and will be published by the Press of Morningside. Price and size not set.

EVANS, C. A., Confederate Military History, The South Carolina Expanded Volume. Index, and introduction by the author's (Ellison Capers) grandchild. Due out fall 1976.

Morningside Bookshop

Publishers and Booksellers
Post Office Box 336, Forest Park Station
Dayton, Ohio 45405

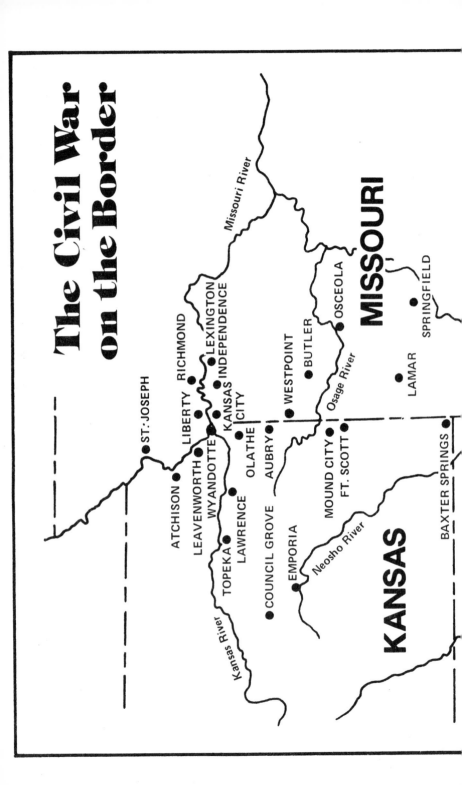

The Civil War on the Border

ST. JOSEPH

RICHMOND

LIBERTY

LEXINGTON

INDEPENDENCE

KANSAS CITY

ATCHISON

LEAVENWORTH

WYANDOTTE

OLATHE

AUBRY

WESTPOINT

BUTLER

OSCEOLA

MISSOURI

SPRINGFIELD

LAMAR

Missouri River

Osage River

TOPEKA

LAWRENCE

COUNCIL GROVE

EMPORIA

MOUND CITY

FT. SCOTT

Neosho River

Kansas River

KANSAS

BAXTER SPRINGS